British Playwrights, 1880–1956

British Playwrights, 1880–1956

A RESEARCH AND PRODUCTION SOURCEBOOK

Edited by WILLIAM W. DEMASTES
and KATHERINE E. KELLY

GREENWOOD PRESS
Westport, Connecticut • London

Library of Congress Cataloging-in-Publication Data

British playwrights, 1880–1956 : a research and production sourcebook
  / edited by William W. Demastes and Katherine E. Kelly.
     p. cm.
  Includes bibliographical references and index.
  ISBN 0–313–28758–9 (alk. paper)
    1. English drama—20th century—Dictionaries. 2. English
drama—20th century—Bio-bibliography—Dictionaries. 3. English
drama—19th century—Bio-bibliography—Dictionaries. 4. Dramatists,
English—20th century—Biography—Dictionaries. 5. Dramatists,
English—19th century—Biography—Dictionaries. 6. English
drama—19th century—Dictionaries. I. Demastes, William W.
II. Kelly, Katherine E.
PR736.B7   1996
822'.809'03—dc20   95–53105

British Library Cataloguing in Publication Data is available.

Library of Congress Catalog Card Number: 95–53105
ISBN: 0–313–28758–9

First published in 1996

Greenwood Press, 88 Post Road West, Westport, CT 06881
An imprint of Greenwood Publishing Group, Inc.

Printed in the United States of America

The paper used in this book complies with the
Permanent Paper Standard issued by the National
Information Standards Organization (Z39.48–1984).

10 9 8 7 6 5 4 3 2 1

Contents

Preface

The British playwrights featured in this volume initiated, developed, or in some way resisted the appearance of English dramatic modernism. The date 1880 marks the onset of the "new" or "modern" drama in small, coterie theaters; 1956 marks a surge of postwar dramatic energy afforded, in part, by state patronage. From subscription-funded to state-subsidized theaters, from a centralized system of London-based production to a decentralized regional theater, from publishers' small press runs to the mass printing of play texts, from script-based stage drama to the proliferation of dramatic media (radio, television, and film), the two ends of this period contain between them two world wars and a vast amount of cultural change both forming and formed by a changing set of theatrical practices. At both ends of this chronological continuum, as well as at most points along it, British playwrights wrote predominately "realist" drama, some of it commenting directly on offstage social relations. A smaller number of playwrights chose to write in nonrealist modes, using the conventions of poetic, symbolist, and allegorical drama, to render the workings of mythic or individual consciousness. The playwrights included in this volume document the variety in twentieth-century British theater, a variety underscored by recent efforts to open the canon to once valued but since overlooked female playwrights and writers from the provinces.

Defined at its origins by historians and commentators like William Archer and Allardyce Nicoll, the canon of modern British drama has favored written (as opposed to musical or performance-oriented) genres marked by the skillful use of literary devices and the circulation of philosophical themes. Certain comedies found favor with the "new drama" coterie, most notably the "high" comedies of G. B. Shaw rather than, for example, the popular operettas of Gilbert and Sullivan. But with rare exceptions, the origins of British modern drama lay in serious treatments of social, sexual, and philosophical themes. The onset of dramatic modernism is usually placed somewhere between the late 1860s and the 1890s, but all agree that the appearance of Ibsen in translation galvanized a select, influential group of English playwrights, translators, actors, and spectators who became the promoters of the ''new'' or ''modern'' drama. Ibsen's plays, successfully promoted by actress/playwright Elizabeth Robins and recontextualized by G. B. Shaw's *The Quintessence of Ibsenism,* signaled a new intellectual seriousness and coincided with a growing preference for ''realism'' among actors, directors, and scenographers. Detailed stage business, illusionistic settings, and the careful integrating of character and material motives like heredity and environment became the norm for serious dramas by Arthur Wing Pinero, Harley Granville-Barker, John Galsworthy, Somerset Maugham, and others.

At the outbreak of the First World War, the London theater scene was vital and diverse, with spoken dramas played at the major, commercial theaters, and musicals, spectacles, variety, and—increasingly—cinema played in other venues. The repertory had been established in London through the efforts of J. T. Grein's Independent Theatre and its successor, the Stage Company, and of the Court Theatre. Annie Horniman, one of the founders of Dublin's Abbey Theatre, helped to establish the first English repertory company, the Gaiety in Manchester. The repertory idea spread to Glasgow, Liverpool, and Birmingham, where it fostered new playwrights, actors, and audiences.

The war changed the face and the structure of theater. In the 1920s higher production costs influenced repertory selection, which, in turn, influenced canon formation. The plays of Noël Coward, Somerset Maugham, Frederick Lonsdale, and others found an outlet in the commercial West End, but the self-styled artistic theater associated with the origins of dramatic modernism remained dormant until the mid- to late 1920s and the 1930s. Both the Oxford Repertory Company and the experimental Cambridge Festival Theatre began offering provincial audiences innovative theater on a seasonal basis in 1923. In the West End brief but often extraordinary productions at the Lyric Theatre, the Gate Theatre Studio, and the Barnes Theatre, for example, pushed the limits of spoken drama with experimental productions of Continental classics.

J. B. Priestley's conventional treatments of spiritual and metaphysical themes dominated the legitimate drama of the 1930s and 1940s, which also saw the founding of small, experimental, and typically left-wing theaters, such as Rupert Doone, W. H. Auden, and Robert Medley's Group Theatre, Joan Littlewood's Theatre of Action (later known as the Theatre Union) and her Unity Theatre, and Ashley Dukes's Mercury Theatre. The 1930s and 1940s also saw the appearance of nonrealist poetic dramatists with ambitious plans for renovating dramatic language and action. The Second World War again eclipsed dramatic innovation but prompted state patronage for theater through the 1939 formation of the Council for the Encouragement of Music and the Arts (CEMA). CEMA brought Shakespeare to the troops, paving the way for a provincial repertory movement and later a National Theatre. CEMA was incorporated under royal charter in 1946 as the Arts Council of Great Britain, which derived its budget directly from the Treasury. The state and the British Broadcasting Corporation (BBC) also played a role during the Second World War in promoting radio as a mass medium. Radio plays reached thousands of listeners simultaneously and provided playwrights with more ready access to a mass audience than they were likely to find through the stage. As an aural medium, radio encouraged literary writing by playwrights who often later went on to write for the stage.

Shaw died in 1950, at the beginning of a decade in which British drama was transformed from its depleted postwar condition to a state of electrified brilliance. During the next six years the National Theatre foundation stone was laid; Samuel Beckett's *Waiting for Godot* received its English premiere (1955); the Berliner Ensemble gave its first London performance of Brecht's work (1956); George Devine founded the English Stage Company (1956); and John Osborne's *Look Back in Anger,* produced at the now Royal Court Theatre, was heralded as part of a new generation of plays by gifted young writers. The new wave of postwar playwrights gathered momentum and, in spite of severe losses of state support, has continued through the present day.

Each entry in this reference book consists of the following components, designed to allow the flexibility necessary to accommodate the range of artists included while providing a unified structure that will permit the reader easiest access to the materials presented:

1. *Biographical Overview:* A thumbnail sketch of significant events in the playwright's life, intended to introduce him or her to the reader. ''Selected Biographical Sources,'' appearing at the end of the overview, lists references that will provide further biographical information.

2. *Major Plays, Premieres, and Significant Revivals: Theatrical Reception:* A selective list with dates (usually for first production) and runs of significant productions, including important revivals (many of which occurred after 1956). Summaries of the published critical receptions of these productions (generally from newspaper and magazine reviews) follow.

3. *Additional Plays, Adaptations, and Productions:* Includes theatrical events that were less significant in the playwright's career.

4. *Assessment of the Playwright's Career:* Includes general assessments from the entries' authors, which also incorporate summary references to published evaluations from critics/scholars writing in magazines, journals, dissertations, and books.

5. *Archival Sources:* A listing of locations housing unpublished materials.

6. *Primary Bibliography:* A selective list of the playwright's published plays and of essays and articles by the playwright relevant to the theater and/or his or her playwriting career.

7. *Secondary Bibliography:* A selected list of materials relevant to the playwright's life and career, including materials referenced in the preceding sections. Secondary materials referred to within the entry by authors of multiple works in the Secondary Bibliography will be distinguished by [1], [2], and so on.

8. *Bibliographies:* If available, bibliographies concentrating on the playwright are listed for further referral to material not included in the Secondary Bibliography.

The contributors to this volume have selected materials they judged most significant to future scholarship on their respective playwrights, but few if any of the entries should be viewed as exhaustive in their bibliographic references. The selected bibliography at the end of this volume lists significant general books on British drama and theater during the period 1880–1956. For further sources of material, especially for those playwrights who have not yet received individualized bibliographic attention beyond this reference volume, readers should consult the following works:

Carpenter, Charles A. *Modern British Drama.* Goldentree Bibliographies in Language and Literature. Arlington Heights, IL: AHM Publishing Corporation, 1979.
Salem, James M. *A Guide to Critical Reviews.* Pt. 3. *British and Continental Drama from Ibsen to Pinter.* Metuchen, NJ: Scarecrow Press, 1968.

For a current, annual bibliography of scholarly materials, refer to issue 2 (June) of each annual volume of the journal *Modern Drama.* Additional current scholarly journals carrying articles on late nineteenth- and early twentieth-century theater are *Drama,* published quarterly by the British Drama League (1946–89), *New Theatre Quarterly, Nineteenth Century Theatre, Theatre History Studies, Theatre Journal, Theatre Notebook, Theatre Research International,* and *Victorian Studies.*

Many newspapers are difficult to locate in libraries. The *Stage Year Book,* 38 volumes (London, 1908–69), contains cast lists of all London productions, as well as other articles on theater and drama, including obituaries. In addition to *The [London] Times* and the *Observer,* the following periodicals, several of them available in microfilm, carry play reviews and articles of general interest on theater and drama: *Theatre* (1877–97); *Era* (1868–1919); *Playgoer* (1901–4); *Playgoer and Society Illustrated* (1909–13); *Play Pictorial* (1902–39) (an excellent source for production and studio photographs); *Theatre World* (1925–65); and *Plays and Players* (1953–   ). *Theatre 54 to 55* and *Theatre 55 to 56* (London, 1956 and 1957) are comprehensive annuals carrying criticism, checklists of London first nights, and other articles, as well as announcements of honors, awards, and obituaries.

Katherine E. Kelly

British Playwrights, 1880–1956

William Archer
(1856–1924)

VINCENT F. PETRONELLA

George Bernard Shaw's preface to *Three Plays by William Archer* informs us that his friend and colleague of forty years was not simply a stereotyped "dour Scot" but a complex individual whose persona blended both fable and reality. By analyzing the Archer mask, Shaw not only demystified the supposedly detached, overly reserved Archer but also humanized him as one who was quite capable of profound emotional response: one who knew how to laugh. Attesting to his friend's warm, jovial side, Shaw indicated that Archer considered him the incarnation of a joke. As the author of *Masks or Faces?* (1888), Archer projected a public persona not as elaborate and as far-reaching as that of Shaw, but a mask nonetheless. Although not a stage actor, Archer was an exponent of what he himself called the dual-consciousness paradox (*Masks or Faces?*, 150).

Photographs of Archer capture the "dour Scot" very well: the tall, dignified appearance, the dark suit and high collar, the commanding, well-formed Celtic features set off by carefully groomed dark hair and moustache. This is the man who at a gathering of friends called upon Shaw to finish a reading of his own translation of Ibsen's *Little Eyolf* because he himself had become too moved by the content. A mask of reserve, then, concealed Archer's actual sensitivities. That he was not to be stereotyped impressed Shaw and others quite favorably.

The son of Thomas Archer and Grace Morison, William Archer was born in Perth, Scotland, on 23 September 1856, just two months after his friend and nearly exact contemporary, Bernard Shaw, was born in Dublin. Archer's father came from a Nonconformist family of Walkerites, separatists who broke from the Episcopal Church of Ireland and whose doctrines resembled those of the Glasites founded in 1730 by the Scots minister John Glas. His mother was the daughter of James Morison, a celebrated Glasite. Archer's family was steeped in Bible worship and a divine, otherworldly Jesus, but he himself became skeptical of any kind of supernaturalism and hence gradually moved toward a rationalist frame of mind. His views of the occult would undergo a forced change, however, when his life began to resemble that of Sir Arthur Conan Doyle, who, like Archer, was shocked by the death of a son in World War I. Both freethinking men turned to spiritualism and parapsychology in a desperate attempt to communicate with the dead. But Archer's own death was imminent. Shortly after undergoing surgery for the removal of a tumor, he died on 27 December 1924. Shaw, who was in Spain at the time, responded to this news angrily. He personally believed that his old friend had been killed by blundering doctors, those very dunderheads raked over the coals in *The Doctor's Dilemma,* the play written in response to Archer's 1906 challenge asking Shaw to address dramatically the issue of death. Now, eighteen years later, Archer had died as a result, so thought Shaw, of botched surgery. Mrs. Archer, finding it difficult to follow her husband's burial instructions, which derived much of their content from Shakespeare, arranged a traditional service. So even in death William Archer was adorned with a mask: the staunch secularist was draped in Christian ceremony. Also covered in the cloth of respectability and hence not mentioned at this somber time was the matter of Archer's romantic liaison, which had started in 1891, with the captivating American actress Elizabeth Robins (see Whitebrook, 133–35; John, 4, 8, 75–85).

Contributing to Archer's multifaceted constitution was his close connection with Norway. The oldest of nine children, he enjoyed thoroughly the visits to Tolderodden, affectionately called "Odden." The family alternated between residences in Scotland and Norway before deciding to settle in Scotland, and as a child Archer spoke Norwegian. He became bilingual in English and Norwegian and gradually multilingual after acquiring several other languages: Danish, German, Italian, and French. Linguistically it is the translations of Ibsen's dramas that placed Archer in the center of dramatic history in the 1890s and early 1900s. As a literary and intellectual force, Henrik Ibsen entered Archer's life in 1873, and by 1878 Archer completed his first translation of *The Pillars of Society* (called *The Supports of Society*), which was staged as *Quicksands; or The Pillars of Society* at the Gaiety Theatre on 15 December 1880. Although presented at a single matinee only, this performance was the first ever of an Ibsen play in England.

Just a year earlier, Archer suffered an emotional crisis brought on not so much by the demands of his work as a journalist and theater critic as by his family's settling in London after returning from an eight-year stay in Australia. Family proximity created tensions growing out of differences regarding matters of religion and career. His parents' unwillingness to accept the idea of the theater as a proper endeavor intensified Archer's depression. Travel abroad was suggested, and although his family proposed Germany, Archer himself chose Italy, especially since Henrik Ibsen was at that time living in Rome. By December 1881 Archer was in Italy and specifically at Rome's Scandinavian Club, where he formally met the playwright whose *Pillars of Society* he had already translated and seen staged the previous year. Archer and Ibsen then met regularly to take an afternoon glass of vermouth at a Roman café. Archer's two-part essay on Ibsen in the *St. James Magazine* had recently appeared; he was pleased during this time to present a copy to the great Norwegian. At one of their meetings, Ibsen spoke about a recent publication of his own: the literary bomb-shell that would be translated as *Ghosts*. Postlewait, who dealt thoroughly with the Archer-Ibsen connection, argued for Archer's centrality in energizing and directing approaches to Ibsen's drama and took issue with those scholars who single out Henry James and James Joyce as vanguards for the Ibsen era in England. If anything, it was Archer together with Shaw who showed Joyce and James the way regarding Ibsen. Archer may have disagreed with the principal contentions in Shaw's *Quintessence of Ibsenism* (1891), but both nonetheless provided the main force in England behind the growing interest in Ibsen during the 1890s, thanks especially to Archer's initial interest and, of course, to his ability to write translations that worked well on the stage (see Postlewait and Wisenthal).

The Italian journey meant meeting and communicating with Ibsen; but even more, Italy brought Archer the very emotional restorative he needed. In the United States three years earlier, he had visited Boston's Beacon Street, Cambridge's Longfellow House and Harvard College, Philadelphia's Walnut Street Theatre, and many sites in New York City—locales associated with American writers he greatly admired: Emerson, Cooper, Lowell, Holmes, Poe, Twain, and Hawthorne. Like most of these writers, Archer found intellectual and emotional enrichment in Italy. Caught up in the imagination of Hawthorne, for example, he used with pleasure *The Marble Faun* as a guide to Rome and parts of Tuscany. This heightened the excitement of his romantic adventure, which was topped off by his falling in love with Frances Elizabeth Trickett, an English girl traveling with her family through Europe. To Archer she was the intelligent, pretty girl with the face of a Della Robbia sculpture; he first saw her in Rome and would see her again in Florence, Venice, and at Lake Como. By the end of the Italian idyll they were virtually engaged. Looking ahead to an official engagement and marriage, Archer set out to increase and stabilize his financial resources. Helpful in this regard were two timely publications, both calling for change in the theater: *English Dramatists of To-day* (1882) and *Henry Irving, Actor and Manager* (1883), the latter a moderate follow-up to the scathing critique of Henry Irving in *The Fashionable Tragedian* (1877), which Archer published together with Robert Lowe and illustrator/caricaturist George R. Halkett. The anti-Irving views, the involvement with Ibsen, the call for a new English drama, and a far-reaching interest in a national theater, which he formalized when he coauthored *A National Theatre: Scheme and Estimates* (1907) with Harley Granville-Barker: all of these made the friendship between Archer and Bernard Shaw a logical, almost inevitable, event. Even before they met, their thoughts were moving in similar channels.

The Archer-Shaw meeting was actually Archer's "discovery" of the future

G.B.S. In 1883 Archer went to the Reading Room of the British Museum, sat near a young, red-haired, red-bearded man in a wool Jaeger suit, and was struck by what the man was studying: a French translation of Karl Marx's *Das Kapital* and the orchestral score of Wagner's *Tristan und Isolde.* Once introduced, Archer and Shaw quickly realized that they had many common interests and hence became fast friends. They did disagree about what mutually interested them, but they still maintained a lifelong friendship that only temporarily grew lukewarm just prior to Archer's death in 1924. Archer secured for Shaw various journalistic posts: with the *Magazine of Music* (1884), the *Pall Mall Gazette* (May 1885–December 1888), the *Dramatic Review* (starting in 1885), and the *World* (1886–89). These would turn out to be extremely important in the development of Shaw, who left the *World* to become music reviewer for the *Star* using the persona of "Corno di Bassetto." The era of "Bassetto" ended when in May 1890 Archer persuaded the *World* to rehire Shaw, whose contributions were now, thanks to Archer, published through a new persona: "G.B.S." All that was needed was an involvement with Shaw's early playwriting career, and this occurred with the *Rhinegold* collaboration.

In the summer of 1884 Archer and Shaw mapped out a play based upon Émile Augier's cup-and-saucer comedy *Ceinture dorée.* Archer derived the plot line from Augier and presented it to Shaw, who then created witty dialogue. The play assumed various titles: *The Way to a Woman's Heart, Rheingold,* and finally *Rhinegold.* Shaw, hoping to develop socialist views in the play, quickly exhausted the plot material; and trying to incorporate details from his own novel, *An Unsocial Socialist,* from Dickens's *Little Dorrit,* and from Fabian essays did not help. *Rhinegold* was shelved. For Archer, successful playwriting had to wait, but as a writer generally he was prolific. As he proceeded to publish many books and essays on a variety of subjects, what had started as *Rhinegold* eventually became Shaw's *Widowers' Houses.* Premiering on 9 December 1892 at London's Royalty Theatre, with Archer and Elizabeth Robins in the audience (Whitebrook, 142), Shaw's play would at least echo the unfinished collaboration: the opening scene is set at a hotel overlooking the Rhine. Oscar Wilde enthusiastically ranked the play with his own work (*Lady Windermere's Fan,* in particular) and thanked Shaw for writing "Op. 2 of the great Celtic School" (Evans, 59). Revival productions of *Widowers' Houses,* like the one performed at Boston's Lyric Stage in late 1992, marked the play's centennial. Archer, who was discussed in the introductory remarks for the Lyric Stage playbill, was cited as having judged the play faulty and yet ten times better than what he called the contemptible *Rhinegold*—the collaborative play that might have turned out to be his first significant success as a dramatist.

Selected Biographical Sources: Charles Archer; Evans; Postlewait; Whitebrook.

MAJOR PLAYS, PREMIERES, AND SIGNIFICANT
REVIVALS: THEATRICAL RECEPTION

War Is War; or, The Germans in Belgium: A Drama of 1914. 1919. Never performed.

Archer's first play of note, an indignant drama about German war atrocities in Belgium. "It failed of production when peace was declared" (Matlaw). Shaw's review of the play was anticipated in a letter to Archer from Ayot St. Lawrence (29 April 1919): "It is quite a good play and suggests that you may, like Lady Gregory, begin a career as dramatist at an age when most dramatists are retiring. . . . The war has at last made you feel strongly enough to compel you to genuine dramatic utterance. . . . I always told you, on the strength of your youthful *Clive* [Archer's early one-act play], that you had the faculty. But you never really wanted to use it. . . . Why didnt *you* write *Widowers' Houses?*" (Laurence [2], 599–600; italics added). Archer wrote *War Is War* after closely and extensively studying relevant documents, and the play was important both in itself and for its indirect influence on his later years; his knowledge of the facts exposed the absurdity of the arguments being used to excuse Germany's involvement in the alleged Belgian atrocities (Charles Archer, 347–48). Finished in 1918, the play never reached the stage. The large cast (including many supernumeraries) was one problem. The other "problems" were the 1918 Armistice and the public fatigue regarding serious war plays. Archer's "Postscript: The Evidence in the Case" is an account of the documents concerning the events depicted in *War Is War*. The drama is an original three-part historical play depicting the military occupation of a typical Belgian village (Quinn [1], 8). Archer himself spoke of his attempt to dramatize the catastrophic descent from unapprehensive serenity to devastation, decimation, and ruin. That the play bears a superficial resemblance to Maurice Maeterlinck's *Burgomaster of Stilemonde* is to be expected if we remember that Archer earlier translated three of Maeterlinck's plays (Quinn [1], 8). Sending a copy of *War Is War* to Shaw, Archer hoped for a faithful evaluation. Since Lieutenant Kessler in the play commits suicide rather than order the execution of innocent Belgian civilians, Archer was not at all certain of Shaw's response, especially given the glaring contrast between Kessler and Shaw's practical-minded hero in *Arms and the Man,* Captain Bluntschli, who loads his cartridge belt with chocolate creams rather than with deadly bullets (Quinn [2], 102). Whitebrook wrote that Kessler "represents cultured Germany infected by the malignant spirit of militarism, a fair-minded man who no longer has either the conviction or the courage to defy the extremists" (326).

The Green Goddess. 1920. Opened 27 December 1920 at the Walnut Street Theatre (Philadelphia); reopened 18 January 1921 at the Booth Theatre (New York) for 440 performances; then on to Boston, Chicago, and throughout the northeastern states. With the exception of a brief recess during the summer of

1922, it was performed in America for nearly two and a half years, closing 5 May 1923; opened again 6 September 1923 at St. James's Theatre (London) for 416 performances.

Originally called *The Raja of Rukh,* the play, which Archer literally dreamed, was proposed as another collaboration with Shaw (Laurence [2], 639). The joint effort, Archer believed, would be the play of the century, but at Shaw's urging, Archer wrote *The Green Goddess* himself. The play makes reference to Shaw by name and includes details reminiscent of at least two of Shaw's plays: *Misalliance* and *Man and Superman.* So Archer, the prophet of realism for forty years, made his fortune at sixty-five as the author of a romantic thriller (Woodbridge, 218). That *The Green Goddess* was a successful melodrama is no contradiction, for although Archer was generally thought of as the apostle of higher theatrical things, he never looked down on the kind of drama that *The Green Goddess* is (Gebauer, 187). Critics liked saying that the play was a far cry from the work of Ibsen, but Archer was not trying to imitate Ibsen. He wrote a "thumping melodrama" that became "tremendously popular" (Matlaw, 35). All his life Archer tried writing plays, but success was elusive; then just before he died, he dreamed the plot of *The Green Goddess,* dramatized it with sufficient skill, and experienced a financial windfall (Lucas, 149–50). In the preface to Archer's *Three Plays* Shaw reacted to the story of Archer's dream: "The result proved that the complexes which inhibited him from writing effective plays when he was awake, did not operate when he was asleep" (Shaw, reprinted in Russell, 973).

Three Plays (*Martha Washington, Beatriz Juana,* and *Lidia*). 1927. Published posthumously with a preface by George Bernard Shaw.

Martha Washington. Eight-scene history play. No record of performance.

The three plays published after Archer's death are all costume pieces, and all of them focus attention on a central female character. *Martha Washington,* in particular, is a series of casually linked scenes with minimal dramatic value, but it may be that Archer, good liberal that he was, wished to pay dramatic tribute to Washington (Woodbridge, 218–19). The play sprawls episodically as it spans forty years and uses many different locations as settings. It is a dramatic classicist's nightmare. In two letters to Harley Granville-Barker (30 January and 12 April 1923) Archer lamented the lukewarm reception the play received when Winthrop Ames was asked to consider it for production and said that "America regards *Martha Washington* with chilling aloofness" (Charles Archer, 385–86).

Beatriz Juana. Four-act blank-verse drama based on Thomas Middleton and William Rowley's Jacobean tragedy *The Changeling* of 1622. No record of performance.

In the preface to his adaptations of two Jacobean verse dramas, Archer stated that after rereading many Elizabethan-Jacobean plays in preparation for a series of lectures at King's College in 1920, he was "struck by the fact that several of the themes treated by the minor Elizabethans and Jacobeans contained elements of enduring vitality that were overlaid and obscured by the technical and spiritual crudities of a semi-barbarous age" (*Three Plays,* 93). Woodbridge, slightly misquoting the same preface by omitting the qualifying prefix and hence leaving us with a description of the Jacobean era as a "barbarous age," saw Archer attempting to free the two older plays from "technical and spiritual crudities" after having become fascinated by the subjects of those plays (218). *Beatriz Juana* is a markedly better-constructed play than the Middleton-Rowley original (Woodbridge, 218–19). Quinn [1] indicated that Archer transformed Middleton's changeling into his own Beatriz Juana, a nonchangeling, a triumphant Lady Macbeth, a demon-woman who cuts through all obstacles that would thwart her desires (10). Shakespeare was also on Archer's mind when in a letter to Granville-Barker (30 January 1923) he teasingly left undisclosed the identity of an actress who was suggested to play Beatriz Juana. He flatly declined to offer the role to this unnamed actress "just as my eminent colleague Shakespeare would decline . . . if [that same actress] had been proposed for Lady Macbeth" (Charles Archer, 385–86).

Lidia. Four-act blank-verse comedy based on Philip Massinger's *The Great Duke of Florence.* No record of performance.

Comic love intrigue is central here. Archer's experiment results in a thoroughly charming, clearly artificial comedy (Woodbridge, 218). Archer disliked the way Massinger clumsily had Lidia informed of Giovanni's summons to the palace and had Petronella, her maid, impersonate Lidia to discourage the Duke's affections. Attempting to "correct" Massinger, Archer created more an academic exercise than a far-reaching contribution to neo-Jacobean drama (see Quinn [1], 10). Archer knew a great deal more of stagecraft than Middleton, Rowley, Massinger, or their contemporaries; but he has been described as knowing less of poetry and the making of poetry (*"Beatriz Juana* and *The Changeling,"* reprinted in Temple and Tucker, 15). Writing about Robert Louis Stevenson, Archer indicated his own sensitivity to blank-verse technique: "[Stevenson's] blank verse, if it lacked freedom and variety of accent, attained a singular dignity, as of exquisite carving in alabaster" ("In Memoriam," 95).

ADDITIONAL PLAYS, ADAPTATIONS, AND PRODUCTIONS

The Jeweller's Daughter; or, The Assassins of Paris (1876) was a four-act drama ("melodrama," by Archer's own admission [Charles Archer, 49]) based on a Hoffmann story, and is unpublished and nonextant. *Our Special Correspondent* (1878) was a one-act farce coauthored by Robert Lowe, unpublished and nonextant. *Rosalind* (1878) a two-act comedy, received a single performance 1 March 1878 with Robert Lowe portraying Mr. Moncrieff, an actor-manager resembling Sir Henry Irving. It is unpublished and nonextant. *Clive* (no date), a one-act play, dealt with a failed attempt at suicide. It is unpublished and nonextant. Shaw referred to this play in his preface to *Three Plays* (Shaw, reprinted in Russell, 972). Shaw also mentioned "another play" but gave no title or details. *Rhinegold* (also *The Way to a Woman's Heart*) (1884) was the basic plot of the play that would become Shaw's *Widowers' Houses* (1892). *The Samurai* (1923), a one-act play, received at least one performance at the Hippodrome Theatre (Bristol) on 4 December and was perhaps performed more than once (see Quinn [1], 3, 10). It is unpublished and nonextant. *The Joy Ride* (1925) was performed 18 May at the Prince's Theatre (London) and 8 February 1926 at the Q Theatre (London) (see Quinn [1], 10). It is unpublished and nonextant. For other unpublished plays by Archer, see Whitebrook (421–22).

Three film adaptations of *The Green Goddess* have been made. A silent version came out in 1923 starring the Anglo-American stage and screen actor George Arliss as the Rajah. Arliss, who became a friend of Archer, had performed the same part on the stage from 1920 through 1923. A "talkie" version appeared in 1924, again with George Arliss as the Rajah (Nash and Ross, 1110). Arliss was very much disappointed to find that many of his favorite scenes had been cut from Archer's text for the screenplay. He learned the hard lesson that in Hollywood action and thrills are of more vital importance than dialogue (Arliss [1], 38). In 1943 appeared the third film adaptation, an inferior, low-budget Warner Brothers undertaking called *Adventures in Iraq*. This starred Ruth Ford as Tess Torrence and Paul Cavanagh (now best remembered for his roles in several of the Basil Rathbone–Nigel Bruce Sherlock Holmes films) as Sheik Ahmid Bel Nor (i.e., the Rajah character of Archer's play).

During the 1923–24 run of *The Green Goddess* in London, a different kind of "theatrical" production was mounted to commemorate the stage presentation: Selfridge's department store devoted an entire window to the characters, setting, and props for Archer's popular play (Arliss [2], 305). This is typical of Selfridge's, which on another occasion—the Royal Jubilee Year of 1977—decorated several of its windows with scenes and characters from the plays of Shakespeare.

ASSESSMENT OF ARCHER'S CAREER

One of the few to assess Archer's achievement in the drama is George Arliss, who, as a stage and screen actor, knew him as a practicing playwright. He spoke highly of Archer as one whose influence on the theater should not go unrecognized (Arliss [1], 302). Like many others, Arliss was quite aware of Archer as the translator of Ibsen and especially as the dramatic critic possessing exemplary integrity, that glittering feature inevitably singled out whenever his criticism is discussed. Even the brief entry on Archer in the Italian encyclopedia of world drama necessarily devoted space to his stature as critic: "I suoi numerosi scritti di critica teatrale mostrano l'intransigente rigore, l'orrore per compromessi, ciò che H. G. Wells chiamò 'un integrità senza scrupoli' " (his numerous critical writings on the theater reveal the intransigent rigor, the aversion to compromises that H. G. Wells called "an unscrupulous integrity") (Guerrieri, 787). This comment epitomizes Archer as critic and reviewer; but what Arliss makes us particularly aware of is Archer's ability as a playwright, a craftsman who provides not only a workable text for a stage production but also language that achieves literary power.

Structurally *The Green Goddess* combines the well-made play with romantic melodrama. In its story line it anticipates James Hilton's *Lost Horizon* (1932) and what Hollywood then would do with materials like the Hilton novel and a host of adventure screenplays culminating in the *Indiana Jones* films. Archer, at the same time, offers us, as he does in *War Is War,* dramatic prose that succeeds in propelling the narrative in uncluttered fashion. His ability to pace the action and maintain a verbal forthrightness enables his play to give equal due to event and character. The melodrama is there, but so also is complexity of character, especially in the case of the embittered British-educated Rajah who slowly entraps the marooned Westerners as he gradually reveals, with sadistic irony, his distaste for them and their culture. The cinematic possibilities of *The Green Goddess* quickly become evident, and one is not at all surprised to learn that three film adaptations of the play were produced. Unlike Shaw, Archer was not given to the long speech or to dramatic philosophizing. He proceeded in a different stylistic direction.

By contrast, *Martha Washington* is devoid of the dramatic impact of *The Green Goddess.* Using a well-known historical figure as the central character immediately poses a problem of dramatic effect. Will the playwright present the biographical personage convincingly and avoid the creation of a two-dimensional pasteboard character unsatisfactorily animated by stilted, predictable language? Place, in fact, takes on more significance than fully drawn people. The play derives most of its dramatic energy through the several changes of geographical locales over the course of eight scenes: from Virginia (the York River area and Mount Vernon) to Massachusetts (at Washington's Cambridge headquarters [now the Longfellow House Museum] where events in Lexington and Boston are monitored), to Valley Forge, and to Virginia again (Eltham and finally Mount Vernon). Despite spanning forty years of time and many hundreds of square miles of space, *Martha Washington* is more a domesticated chronicle play than a dramatic epic. The forthright prose, however, does manage to capture the clearheadedness, if not the depths, of many of the characters who inhabit the Enlightenment world that Archer creates. This is not Broadway material, but it is worthy of at least a short run (at Ford's Theatre or the Kennedy Center for the Performing Arts in Washington, D.C.) during a national-holiday period.

Martha Washington has received little or no critical attention. The same is true for the two "Jacobean" plays: *Beatriz Juana* and *Lidia.* Not wanting simply to reproduce *The Changeling* and *The Great Duke of Florence* photographically, Archer effectively rewrote the plays by altering the plots, reconceptualizing characters, liberalizing the blank verse, and toning down the richness of poetic imagery. Although the full baroque quality of both the Middleton-Rowley and Massinger plays was sacrificed, Archer managed to maintain the "Jacobean" aura as he added elements from the nineteenth-century romantic theater and created an immediately accessible blank-verse technique that anticipated what T. S. Eliot would do in his verse plays. Both *Beatriz Juana* and *Lidia* are worthy of production by repertory companies or by university theater-arts workshops.

Like *The Green Goddess*, these are playable dramas revealing that Archer, who was so prolific as a critic of society and dramatic art, had only started, in his later years, to develop as a playwright. His dramatic work, had he lived some five or six years longer, might have matched at least that of Galsworthy and Granville-Barker, if not that of George Bernard Shaw.

ARCHIVAL SOURCES

Archer's papers are found in various repositories: The British Library, the Enthoven Collection at the Victoria and Albert Museum, the British Theatre Association of London, the National Library of Scotland, the Sarolea Collection at Edinburgh University, the Berg Collection at the New York Public Library, the Folger Shakespeare Library (Washington, D.C.), and the Mitchell Library (Sydney, Australia).

PRIMARY BIBLIOGRAPHY

Plays

The Green Goddess. New York: Alfred A. Knopf, 1921.
Three Plays by William Archer. (Includes *Beatriz Juana, Lidia,* and *Martha Washington.*) Foreword by George Bernard Shaw. London: Constable, 1927.
War Is War; or, The Germans in Belgium: A Drama of 1914. London: Duckworth, 1919.

Translations of Plays

The Collected Works of Henrik Ibsen. 12 vols. London: Heinemann, 1906–12.
Maurice Maeterlinck: Three Plays. Trans. Archer and Alfred Sutro. London and Glasgow: Gowans & Gray, 1911.

Essays and Articles on Drama and Theater

"Ibsen As I Knew Him." *Monthly Review* 69 (June 1906): 1–19.
"In Memoriam" [for Robert Louis Stevenson]. *New Review* 12 (1895): 94–95.
"Mr. Oscar Wilde's New Play." *Black and White* 5 (11 May 1893): 89–97.
"The Psychology of G.B.S." *Bookman* 67 (Dec. 1924): 139–41.
The Theatrical "World" of 1893–1897. 5 vols. London: Walter Scott, 1894–98. Reprint. New York: Benjamin Blom, [1969].
"To Henrik Ibsen." *Daily Chronicle* (21 Mar. 1898): 3.

Books on Drama and Theater

About the Theatre: Essays and Studies. London: Unwin, 1886.
English Dramatists of To-day. London: Sampson Low, 1882.
Henry Irving, Actor and Manager: A Critical Study. London: Field & Tuer, 1883.
Masks or Faces? A Study in the Psychology of Acting. London: Longmans, 1888.
A National Theatre: Scheme and Estimates. Archer and Harley Granville-Barker. London:
    Duckworth, 1907.
Play-making: A Manual of Craftsmanship. London: Chapman & Hall, 1912. Reprint.
    New York: Dover, 1960.
William Charles Macready. London: Kegan Paul, 1890.

SECONDARY BIBLIOGRAPHY

Archer, Charles. *William Archer: Life, Work, and Friendships.* New Haven, CT: Yale
    University Press, 1931.
Arliss, George. [1]. *My Ten Years in the Studios.* Boston: Little, Brown, 1940.
———. [2]. *Up the Years from Bloomsbury.* New York: Blue Ribbon, 1927.
"Beatriz Juana and *The Changeling.'' The New Age* (4 June 1927): 310. *A Library of
    Literary Criticism: Modern British Literature,* ed. Ruth Temple and Martin
    Tucker, 15. New York: Ungar, 1966.
Evans, T. F., ed. *Shaw: The Critical Heritage.* London: Routledge & Kegan Paul, 1976.
Gassner, John. *Dramatic Soundings.* New York: Crown, 1968.
Gebauer, Emanuel L. "The Theatrical Criticism of William Archer." *Quarterly Journal
    of Speech* 24 (Apr. 1938): 183–92.
Guerrieri, Gerardo. "William Archer." In *Enciclopedia dello spettacolo,* vol. 1, 788–89.
    Rome: Casa Editrice Le Maschere, 1954.
Holroyd, Michael. *Bernard Shaw.* 4 vols. New York: Random House, 1988–92.
John, Angela V. *Elizabeth Robins: Staging a Life, 1862–1952.* London and New York:
    Routledge, 1995.
Laurence, Dan H., ed. [1]. *Bernard Shaw: Collected Letters, 1898–1910.* New York:
    Dodd, Mead, 1972.
———. [2]. *Bernard Shaw: Collected Letters, 1911–1925.* New York: Viking, 1985.
Lucas, E. V. *Reading, Writing, and Remembering.* New York: Harper, 1932.
Matlaw, Myron. *Modern World Drama: An Encyclopedia.* New York: Dutton, 1972.
Nash, Jay Robert, and Stanley Ralph Ross. *The Motion Picture Guide.* Chicago: Cine-
    books, 1986.
Postlewait, Thomas. *Prophet of the New Drama: William Archer and the Ibsen Cam-
    paign.* Westport, CT: Greenwood Press, 1986.
Quinn, Martin. [1]. "William Archer." In *Dictionary of Literary Biography,* vol. 10,
    Modern British Dramatists, 1900–1945, ed. Stanley Weintraub, pt. 1, 3–11. De-
    troit: Gale Research, 1982.
———. [2]. "William Archer and *The Doctor's Dilemma.'' Shaw* 4 (1984): 87–106.
Shaw, George Bernard. "How William Archer Impressed Bernard Shaw." Preface to
    Three Plays by William Archer (1927). Reprinted in *Bernard Shaw: Selected
    Prose,* ed. Diarmuid Russell, 949–80. New York: Dodd, Mead, 1952.
Whitebrook, Peter. *William Archer: A Biography.* London: Methuen, 1993.
Whitworth, Geoffrey. *The Making of a National Theatre.* London: Faber & Faber, 1951.

Wisenthal, J. L., ed. *Shaw and Ibsen: Bernard Shaw's "The Quintessence of Ibsenism" and Related Writings.* Toronto: University of Toronto Press, 1979.

Woodbridge, Homer. "William Archer: Prophet of Modern Drama." *Sewanee Review* 44 (1936): 207–21.

W. H. Auden
(1907–1973)

JANE SEAY HASPEL

W. H. Auden is best known for the poetry that influenced a generation of poets, but for a period of about ten years, he experimented with drama in an attempt to find a form that would appeal to a wider audience than poetry. Had he concentrated his talents more closely on drama, he might very well have been able to realize this vision.

Born on 21 February 1907 in York, England, to Constance Rosalie Bicknell and George Augustus Auden, Wystan Hugh Auden was the youngest of three boys. Auden went away to school for the first time when he was eight years old and flourished there. At St. Edmund's he first met Christopher Isherwood, who became his lifelong friend and occasional literary collaborator. Auden began writing poetry in 1922 while in public school at Gresham's, and by the end of the year he had published his first poem in the school magazine.

In 1925 Auden entered Christ Church, Oxford, and in his last year at Oxford, 1928, he wrote his first play, *Paid on Both Sides,* a charade he hoped would be performed during a country visit at the home of friends. Although it was not performed at that time, a revised version was published by T. S. Eliot in the *Criterion* in 1930.

While Auden spent the next several years teaching, he was also busy writing both poetry and drama. Auden's next play was *The Dance of Death,* written for the Group Theatre (no relation to the Group Theatre in New York), a new theatrical cooperative founded by Rupert Doone and Robert Medley in February 1932. Soon Auden was doing much of the Group's writing, not only contributing his own plays, but recommending plays to be performed and writing program notes, subscription requests, and Group manifestos.

Although Auden was a homosexual, in 1935 he married Erika Mann, daughter of Thomas Mann, so she could obtain a British passport and leave Germany.

From September 1935 to February 1936 Auden worked with John Grierson's GPO (General Post Office) Film Unit. Here he met and collaborated with director Alberto Cavalcanti, artist William Coldstream, and composer Benjamin Britten, producing verse narration for several documentaries. Most notable of these is *Night Mail,* a film documenting the London-to-Glasgow mail train that included narration by Auden and music by Britten. Unfortunately, the unit had few projects that would exercise Auden's talent, and he became concerned that the unit's dependence on government financing would jeopardize the integrity of their work.

Auden's next three plays were written in collaboration with Christopher Isherwood, although according to Isherwood they typically worked independently on their respective parts, then put them together. *The Dog beneath the Skin* (1936), *The Ascent of F6* (1937), and *On the Frontier* (1938) were all produced by the Group Theatre. None made Auden's reputation as a playwright, and his interest in playwriting seems to have evolved into an enthusiasm for writing opera librettos.

In 1937 Auden went to Spain, intending to drive an ambulance in support of the government in the Spanish civil war, but instead he broadcast propaganda to a mostly Spanish—and Loyalist—audience. After a little over a month, Auden returned to England disillusioned with communism in general.

Auden claimed that while writing *The Ascent of F6,* he realized that he had to leave England in order to pursue his art in a less confining atmosphere. So in January 1939 he abandoned playwriting and politics and, along with Isherwood, left for America, where each would pursue his own work.

Auden's time in America was spent writing poetry, teaching, lecturing, and, for a time, living a rather bohemian life in New York in a three-story house inhabited by an eclectic group of artists and writers. In New York Auden met Chester Kallman, the man fourteen years his junior who would become Auden's lover early in their relationship and companion for most of Auden's life. Kallman was responsible for deepening Auden's appreciation for opera, and they collaborated on most of Auden's operatic ventures.

Auden was castigated by the British literary establishment for leaving England on the brink of World War II, but he did apparently offer his services toward the war effort to the British embassy. In late April 1945 he went to Germany as a member of the U.S. Strategic Bombing Survey, and in 1946 Auden became an American citizen.

Beyond his poetry, Auden's work turned to adaptations, translations, and librettos. He and Kallman collaborated on several operas, most notably *The Rake's Progress* (1951) with Igor Stravinsky.

From 1948 to 1956 Auden lived each summer in Europe. He continued to return to America to earn his living primarily by editing, writing reviews, and lecturing from fall to early spring. Auden was elected professor of poetry at Oxford in 1956, and in 1957 he bought a house in Kirchstetten, Austria. In 1972 he retired to Christ Church, Oxford, and spent his summers in Kirchstetten. On

29 September 1973 Auden died of a heart attack in his hotel room in Vienna after giving a poetry reading at the Austrian Society of Literature.

Selected Biographical Sources: Carpenter; Mendelson [1]; Osborne; Sidnell [1].

MAJOR PLAYS, PREMIERES, AND SIGNIFICANT REVIVALS: THEATRICAL RECEPTION

Paid on Both Sides: A Charade. 1931. Opened at Briarcliff College (New York) in March; produced by Hallie Flanagan and Margaret Ellen Clifford. Opened at the Festival Theatre, (Cambridge, England) 12–17 February 1934; conducted as part of a program of "Experiments" by Joseph Gordon MacLeod.

Written for his friends to perform during a visit to their country home, this charade was ostensibly about a blood feud between two families in which war becomes a never-ending cycle, but was full of private jokes and allusions. At the time of its publication, T. S. Eliot wrote E. McKnight Kauffer asking him if he would be interested in producing it, calling it "a brilliant piece of work," and twenty years later still hailed the play as the "forerunner of contemporary poetic drama" (Haffenden, 77). Many readers, however, found it obscure, including poet and critic William Empson, who also noted that the inclusion of modernist ways of thinking, specifically its use of surrealism and psychoanalysis, gave the play "the completeness that makes a work seem to define the attitude of a generation."

The Dance of Death. 1934. (one act). Opened at the Westminster Theatre (London) for 2 performances for Group Theatre subscribers on 25 February and 4 March (double-billed with *The Deluge*). Reopened 1 October 1935 at the Westminster (London) for 15 performances (double-billed with T. S. Eliot's *Sweeney Agonistes*). Both productions by the Group Theatre (London). Directed by Rupert Doone. Music by Herbert Murrill. Set and costumes by Robert Medley. First American performance by the Experimental Theater at Vassar College, Poughkeepsie, New York (as *Come Out into the Sun*), 2–3 August 1935. Opened at the Adelphi Theatre (New York) May 1936. Produced by the Federal Theatre Project. Supervised by Alfred Kreymborg. Music by Clair Leonard.

This experimental work—part ballet, part charade, part agitprop, part mummers' play—is, according to the Announcer, a "picture of the decline of a class." Auden's leftist, didactic, and often-obscure approach to enlightening his audience to the ills of society may have put off many viewers and critics alike. But even though much has been made of the negative reviews, the response was mixed. The *New Statesman and Nation* ("Plays and Pictures") said that the play was too unfocused and "unpolished," and Verschoyle [1] agreed, calling the satire propaganda, "for the most part crude and jaded."

However, many critics found Auden's satire brilliant in spite of its flaws. The critic for *The Times* ("Westminster Theatre: 'The Dance of Death' "), while commenting that Auden developed his political theme with "desperate single-mindedness," also applauded Auden's use of music and dance to enhance his ideas, noting that the play "gives a hint of how poetry, by basing itself upon contemporary speech-rhythms, may regain its old place in the theatre." Hawkins considered the play a learning experience for Auden. He praised it for its energy and poetry and saw in it some hope for renewal of the "decrepit Drama" of the time. Sayers was ecstatic in his praise of this new direction for the theater: "Here is theatre springing from the rhythms and idiom of your own life . . . with its slang and jazz heightened into poetry, your own fevers and languors made tragic, pathetic, comic, so that the action seems familiar, and at the same time disturbing." Dukes found it "a blend of some inspiration and much nonsense" and called Auden "raw and not too level-headed" but still "a writer for a future poet's theatre."

The Dog beneath the Skin; or, Where Is Francis? A Play in Three Acts. (with Christopher Isherwood). 1936. Opened at the Westminster Theatre (London) 30 January for 52 performances. Produced by the Group Theatre. Directed by Rupert Doone. Designed by Robert Medley. Music by Herbert Murrill. Revival: Cherry Lane Theatre (New York) 22 July 1947, for 27 performances.

This satire on European decadence by way of a young man's search for the heir to his ancestral home accompanied by a dog who is really the lost nobleman in disguise was considered by most critics to be an improvement over *The Dance of Death*—less heavy-handed and, as Morgan [1] in the *New York Times* suggested, "at some pains to make its meaning clear," certainly a charge not usually leveled at Auden. In fact, many reviewers, including Verschoyle [2], commented on their pleasant surprise that Auden had lightened up on the political rhetoric that had annoyed so many in *The Dance of Death*. *The Times* critic ("Westminster Theatre: 'The Dog beneath the Skin' ") wrote that even though propaganda was expected of two such earnest playwrights, they "are often genuinely eloquent and seldom wilfully freakish."

The Ascent of F6: A Tragedy in Two Acts. (with Christopher Isherwood). 1937. Opened at the Mercury Theatre (London) 26 February for 50 performances. Moved to the Arts Theatre (Cambridge) on 22 April for 4 performances. Moved to the Little Theatre 30 April for 42 performances. Presented by Ashley Dukes in association with the Group Theatre. Directed by Rupert Doone. Designed by Robert Medley. Music by Benjamin Britten. Revival: Old Vic Theatre, 27 June 1939, for 15 performances. Produced by the Group Theatre, with Alec Guinness as Ransom.

Many critics again saw improvement in Auden's and Isherwood's dramatic work, but as usual the reception was mixed. The plot of this complex play concerns a protagonist modeled on T. E. Lawrence who is challenged to scale a mountain, and the moral, political, and psychological implications this challenge represents for each character. Spender, writing in the *Left Review* about the text, was disappointed that the dramatists failed to realize the implications of the protagonist's character, "that Ransom was a prig, a fact, after all, even more significant than that he was in love with his mother." Morgan [2] found the play improved over the dramatists' previous play, especially for its "introspective passages." *The Times* ("Old Vic") found the Old Vic production better than previous ones and even exciting, but thought that the writers had "started a dozen hares and seem to be themselves uncertain which to pursue." Stonier grew tired of the complaints and, like most, found the ending unsatisfactory, but still proclaimed that the play "succeeds brilliantly."

On the Frontier: A Melodrama in Three Acts. (with Christopher Isherwood). 1938. Opened 14 November at the Arts Theatre (Cambridge) for 6 performances. Moved to the Globe Theatre (London) 12 February 1939 for 1 performance. Produced by the Group Theatre. Directed by Rupert Doone. Scenery and costumes by Robert Medley. Music by Benjamin Britten.

On the Frontier was a return for Auden and Isherwood to the themes of war and capitalism. It was not successful, either popularly or with the critics, with a few exceptions. The *New Statesman* called it "precisely topical," and *The Times* ("Group Theatre") also reviewed it favorably, saying that even though it was propaganda, it "can be watched with continuous interest even by those who do not come to a theatre in the same spirit in which they attend a political meeting." Barnes, however, reviewing the published text, said that Auden and Isherwood "continue to follow their principle of putting Marxist pap into bourgeois bottles." Even MacNeice, a longtime friend of both writers, offered only faint praise. He noted the important theme, but said that when the play was compared with *The Ascent of F6,* there was "less sparkle, less poetry, less thought and even more embarrassment." But he also noted that even with its flaws, it was "a great deal more worth while [*sic*] than an alpha-plus domestic triangle among the sherry glasses."

ADDITIONAL PLAYS, ADAPTATIONS, AND PRODUCTIONS

Several of Auden's early plays remain unproduced, their parts having been cannibalized for later plays. Subplots and poems in *The Enemies of a Bishop* (1929), a collaboration with Isherwood, and *The Fronny* (1930), of which only a fragment exists, eventually appeared in *The Chase* (1934), which turned into *The Dog beneath the Skin.*

By the mid-1930s Auden was eager to branch out from drama and poetry. He contributed the narrative for several documentary films: *Coal Face* (1935); *Night Mail* (1935); *Negroes* (1935), which was completed in 1938 and renamed *God's Chillun,* but appears never to have been exhibited (Mendelson [3], 669); *Beside the Seaside* (1935); *The Way to the Sea* (1936); and *The Londoners* (1939).

He was also becoming increasingly interested in music. He collaborated with Benjamin Britten on the narrative to the song cycle *Our Hunting Fathers* (1936) and wrote the libretto for the badly received *Paul Bunyan* (1941).

He was more successful after he began collaborating with Chester Kallman. With Stravinsky, Auden and Kallman wrote the libretto for *The Rake's Progress* (1951), which became Auden's most successful operatic work and one of the few modern operas to enter the opera canon (Carpenter, 371). With Hans Werner Henze, the two wrote *Elegy for Young Lovers* (1961); *The Bassarids* (1966), considered one of Henze's greatest accomplishments; and *Moralities* (1969). With Nicolas Nabokov they collaborated on an adaptation of Shakespeare's *Love's Labour's Lost* (1973). During the same period Auden translated or adapted a number of works for the dramatic and operatic stage, including John Webster's *The Duchess of Malfi* (1946) and Bertolt Brecht's *The Seven Deadly Sins of the Middle Class* (1959). See Mendelson [2,3] and Beach for texts and notes on the librettos and other dramatic writings.

ASSESSMENT OF AUDEN'S CAREER

Hobson's comment in a review of *The Dance of Death* probably applies to Auden's whole career: "Mr. Auden belongs more to the pioneers than to the masters of drama. His achievement consists rather in pointing out a fresh road than in traveling down it very far himself." Sidnell [2] noted that although Auden and Isherwood were innovators in the use of song, dance, poetry, and prose to convey serious themes, they were not sufficiently committed to the theater to achieve the success they might have. While Auden revitalized the verse drama in English, he was less influential on verse drama than Brecht, whose epic theater with its similar goals and techniques remains the standard by which such plays are judged.

In his 1934 *Listener* review of Priscilla Thouless's *Modern Poetic Drama,* Auden set down the tenets by which he would write poetic drama. He would embrace all popular forms of entertainment, including the variety show, the pantomime, the musical comedy, the revue, the thriller, even the ballet. The playwright, he said, should use stock characters, characters a proletarian audience would be familiar with. Only then would poetic drama succeed. In the program notes to *The Dance of Death,* Auden noted that since drama "began as an act of the whole community," the audience should be an integral part of the performance and that "the subject of drama . . . is the Commonly Known, the universally familiar stories of the society or generation in which it is written."

Auden proved better at theorizing than he did at putting his ideas into action. Verschoyle [1] skewered each of Auden's principles, saying, "The characters are 'simplified' only because they are poorly observed and feebly drawn, and the subject-matter is made up of the 'familiar stories of the society or generation in which it is written,' only in the sense that it is identical with the contents of most undergraduate communist magazines and similar repositories of popular myth."

More than one critic pointed out that it often seemed as if Auden and Isherwood had failed to take the time necessary to properly hone a scene. Benét called Auden "a careless sort of writer" who "depends too much on flashes of brilliance." John Maynard Keynes, who backed *The Ascent of F6,* considered it generally a fine play but complained, "I remain exceedingly angry that being so good it should not be better, for the gifts in it seemed to be from God and the errors avoidable" (Haffenden, 21). Even Spender chided them for their lackadaisical approach, for throwing "fragments of good stuff into a loosely constructed play."

Auden seemed unable to devote enough time and energy to the theater to evolve as a playwright. Williams pointed out that many of the thematic elements in his plays are imposed rather than allowed to develop through dramatic means, resulting in the loss of dramatic integrity (252, 256). It may be that had Auden been associated with a more experienced theater group, he would have learned more about the requirements of good drama. Clearly, he was more than willing to make revisions in response to criticism and the demands of the production (Carpenter, passim). He was constantly rewriting the endings to his plays, yet perhaps because of his lack of experience in the theater, even with Isherwood's help, his endings were never quite right.

Auden gradually came to doubt the power drama could actually exert on its audience. Auden's own political convictions—if they were ever convictions—were fading, especially after his trip to Spain in 1937. Mendelson [1] noted that *The Ascent of F6* may be autobiographical, with Ransom representing the private poet who tried to become a public one, only to discover that there is no place in this world for a redeemer (285–86).

What little commitment Auden had to the theater faded along with his political agenda. If the theater could not make a political statement that would move men to act, then Auden's dream of bringing poetry to the masses was no longer so inspired, and the public poet found himself powerless to effect change. MacNeice, although commenting specifically on Auden and Isherwood's last play, seemed to sum up Auden's theatrical career, saying that "it does not hit us like a wedge but like a number of escaped posters and photographs blown by the wind in one's face." Auden's dramatic work was innovative and refreshing during a stagnant period of English theater, but he never quite focused enough on it to be fully effective as a playwright or as well known for his drama as he is for his poetry.

ARCHIVAL SOURCES

The most extensive collection of Auden's published and unpublished writing is in the Berg Collection of the New York Public Library. The Harry F. Ransom Humanities Research Center at the University of Texas at Austin also holds a significant collection of Auden manuscripts.

PRIMARY BIBLIOGRAPHY

Plays

The Ascent of F6: A Tragedy in Two Acts. With Christopher Isherwood. London: Faber,
    1936; New York: Random House, 1937. Also in *W. H. Auden and Christopher
    Isherwood: Plays and Other Dramatic Writings by W. H. Auden, 1928–1938,* ed.
    Edward Mendelson, 293–355. Vol. 1 of *The Complete Works of W. H. Auden.*
    Princeton, NJ: Princeton University Press, 1988. (Hereafter cited as Mendelson,
    W. H. Auden and Christopher Isherwood.)
The Chase: A Play in Three Acts. In Mendelson, *W. H. Auden and Christopher Isher-
    wood,* 109–187.
The Dance of Death. London: Faber, 1933. Also in Mendelson, *W. H. Auden and Chris-
    topher Isherwood,* 81–107.
The Dog beneath the Skin; or, Where Is Francis? A Play in Three Acts. With Christopher
    Isherwood. London: Faber, 1935; New York: Random House, 1935. Also in Men-
    delson, *W. H. Auden and Christopher Isherwood,* 189–292.
The Enemies of a Bishop; or, Die When I Say When: A Morality in Four Acts. In
    Mendelson, *W. H. Auden and Christopher Isherwood,* 35–79.
The Fronny [fragment]. "The Fronny: Fragments of a Lost Play." In Mendelson, *W. H.
    Auden and Christopher Isherwood,* 464–489.
On the Frontier: A Melodrama in Three Acts. With Christopher Isherwood. London:
    Faber, 1938. Also in Mendelson, *W. H. Auden and Christopher Isherwood,* 357–
    418.
Paid on Both Sides: A Charade. In Mendelson, *W. H. Auden and Christopher Isherwood,*
    3–34.
*W. H. Auden and Christopher Isherwood: Plays and Other Dramatic Writings by W. H.
    Auden, 1928–1938.* Ed. Edward Mendelson. Vol. 1 of *The Complete Works of
    W. H. Auden.* Princeton, NJ: Princeton University Press, 1988.

Essays and Articles on Drama and Theater

"Are You Dissatisfied with This Performance?" Program note to Group Theatre Pro-
    duction of *Agamemnon.* Reprinted in "Auden and the Group Theatre." Sidnell
    [1], 499–500.
The Dyer's Hand and Other Essays. New York: Random House, 1962.
Review of *Modern Poetic Drama,* by Priscilla Thouless. *Listener* (9 May 1934): 808.
"A Modern Use of Masks." *Group Theatre Paper* 5 (Nov. 1936). Reprinted in "Auden
    and the Group Theatre." Sidnell [1], 500–502.
"The Outlook for 'Poetic Drama.' " *France-Grande Bretagne* (July–Aug. 1939): 230.
    Reprinted as "The Future of English Poetic Drama" in "Two Reported Lec-
    tures." In Mendelson, *W. H. Auden and Christopher Isherwood,* 513–522.
"Preliminary Statement." With Christopher Isherwood. In Mendelson, *W. H. Auden and
    Christopher Isherwood,* 459–462.
Program notes to *The Dance of Death* (1 Oct. 1935). Reprinted in "Auden and the Group
    Theatre." Sidnell [1], 497–98.

"Selling of the Group Theatre." *Group Theatre Paper* 1 (June 1936). Reprinted in "Auden and the Group Theatre." Sidnell [1], 498–99.

SECONDARY BIBLIOGRAPHY

Barnes, T. R. "Auden and Isherwood." *Scrutiny* 7.3 (Dec. 1938): 361–63.

Beach, Joseph W. *The Making of the Auden Canon.* Minneapolis: University of Minnesota Press, 1957.

Benét, William Rose. "The Phoenix Nest: Contemporary Poetry." *Saturday Review* 14.6 (6 June 1936): 18.

Carpenter, Humphrey. *W. H. Auden: A Biography.* Boston: Houghton Mifflin, 1981.

Dukes, Ashley. "The English Scene." *Theatre Arts Monthly* 19 (Dec. 1935): 906–8. Reprinted in Haffenden, 156–59.

Empson, William. Review of *Paid on Both Sides. Experiment* 7 (Spring 1931): 61. Reprinted in Haffenden, 78–80.

"Group Theatre: 'On the Frontier.' " *The Times* (13 Feb. 1939): 10.

Haffenden, John, ed. *W. H. Auden: The Critical Heritage.* Boston: Routledge & Kegan Paul, 1983.

Hawkins, A. Desmond. "Recent Verse." *New English Weekly* 4 (12 Apr. 1934): 617. Reprinted in Haffenden, 150–51.

Hobson, Harold. Review of *The Dance of Death. Christian Science Monitor* (22 Oct. 1935): 12A. Reprinted. in Haffenden, 154–156.

MacNeice, Louis. "The Theatre: *On the Frontier.*" *Spectator* (18 Nov. 1938): 858.

Mendelson, Edward. [1]. *Early Auden.* New York: Viking, 1981.

———, ed. [2]. *W. H. Auden and Chester Kallman: Libretti and Other Dramatic Writings by W. H. Auden.* Princeton, NJ: Princeton University Press, 1993.

———, ed. [3]. *W. H. Auden and Christopher Isherwood: Plays and Other Dramatic Writings by W. H. Auden, 1928–1938.* Vol. 1 of *The Complete Works of W. H. Auden.* Princeton, NJ: Princeton University Press, 1988.

Morgan, Charles. [1]. Review of *The Dog beneath the Skin. New York Times* (23 Feb. 1936): 1:3.

———. [2]. "Two New Plays." *New York Times* (28 Mar. 1937): 11:2.

"Old Vic: 'The Ascent of F6.' " *The Times* (28 June 1939): 12.

Osborne, Charles. *W. H. Auden: The Life of a Poet.* New York: Harcourt Brace, 1979.

Paine, Tom [Kingsley Martin]. "On the Frontier." *New Statesman and Nation* (19 Nov. 1938): 826.

"Plays and Pictures: 'Dance of Death' and 'Sweeney Agonistes' at the Westminster." *New Statesman and Nation* (5 Oct. 1935): 446–47.

Sayers, Michael. "Theatre at Last!" *New English Weekly* 7 (10 Oct. 1935): 435. Reprinted in Haffenden, 151–52.

Sidnell, M. J. [1]. "Auden and the Group Theatre." In Mendelson, *W. H. Auden and Christopher Isherwood,* 490–502.

———. [2]. "W. H. Auden." In *Dictionary of Literary Biography,* vol. 10, *Modern British Dramatists, 1900–1945,* ed. Stanley Weintraub, pt. 1, 13–24. Detroit: Gale Research, 1982.

Spender, Stephen. "The Poetic Dramas of W. H. Auden and Christopher Isherwood." *Left Review* 2 (Nov. 1936): 779–82.

Stonier, G. W. "The Ascent of F6." *New Statesman and Nation* (1 July 1939): 13.
Verschoyle, Derek. [1]. "The Theatre." *Spectator* (11 Oct. 1935): 547.
———. [2]. "The Theatre." *Spectator* (7 Feb. 1936): 211.
"Westminster Theatre: 'The Dance of Death.' " *The Times* (2 Oct. 1935): 12.
"Westminster Theatre: 'The Dog beneath the Skin.' " *The Times* (31 Jan. 1936): 12.
Williams, Raymond. *Drama from Ibsen to Eliot.* London: Chatto & Windus, 1952.

BIBLIOGRAPHY

Bloomfield, B. C., and Edward Mendelson. *W. H. Auden: A Bibliography, 1924–1969.*
    2nd. ed. Charlottesville: University Press of Virginia, 1972.

Sir James Matthew Barrie
(1860–1937)

VALERIE C. RUDOLPH

Sir James Matthew Barrie "could make a good play out of a doorknob and two spools" ("Barrie's Little Mary"). Best known for *Peter Pan,* sometimes remembered for *Dear Brutus, The Admirable Crichton,* and *The Little Minister,* and often forgotten for the remainder of his more than forty plays and theatrical pieces, Barrie intriguingly masked the technical and aesthetic depth of his work under surface simplicity and sentimentality. To look anew at his dramatic achievements, therefore, is, in Barrie's own words, to embark on "an awfully big adventure."

James Matthew Barrie, third son and youngest child of David and Margaret Ogilvy Barrie, was born in Kirriemuir, Forfarshire, Scotland, on 9 May 1860. Kirriemuir later became Thrums, the fictional setting for many of Barrie's novels. Barrie was devoted to his mother, who belonged to an austere religious group known as the Auld Licht sect. Both his mother and the group gave rise to prose works—Barrie's *Auld Licht Idylls* (1888) and *Margaret Ogilvy* (1896). Always devoted to his mother, Barrie spent many years after the accidental death of his older brother David trying to console her by replacing her absent son. Indeed, mother-child relationships and "lost" children appear often in Barrie's plays.

Barrie's dramatic career began in childhood when he presented various entertainments in the washhouse in his own backyard. His first play, *Bandolero the Bandit* (1877), was presented at Dumfries Academy, which he attended from 1873 to 1878. From 1878 to 1882 he studied at Edinburgh University, earning a master of arts degree. Upon graduation he worked briefly for the *Nottingham Journal* before moving to London in 1885. There Barrie the journalist developed the Kirriemuir/Thrums sketches that led to Barrie the novelist and eventually to Barrie the dramatist.

Barrie's first plays were slight pieces—*Richard Savage* (1891), a collaboration with H. B. Marriott Watson that painted a saintly portrait of an eighteenth-century sinner, and *Ibsen's Ghost; or, Toole Up-to-Date* (1891), a burlesque of Ibsenism. His next play, *Walker, London* (1892), was more substantial and more successful, running for 511 performances. Cast in this play was Barrie's future wife, Mary Ansell, whom he married in 1894 and divorced in 1907. She subsequently wed critic Gilbert Cannan, but when that marriage disintegrated also, Ansell tried unsuccessfully to reconcile with Barrie. By that time Barrie's new friend and confidante was his secretary, Lady Cynthia Asquith, whose close association with the writer continued for the remainder of his life.

Walker, London was followed by Barrie's lone comic opera, *Jane Annie; or, The Good Conduct Prize* (1893) and also by *Becky Sharp (1893),* his adaptation of the conclusion of Thackeray's *Vanity Fair.* His next play, *The Professor's Love Story* (1893), enjoyed successful runs in both New York and London. This play showcases Barrie's knowledge of Scottish village life as well as his ability to use Scottish dialect effectively.

In 1894 the Barries settled near Kensington Gardens, where Barrie loved to walk his St. Bernard, Porthos, and where he met George Davies, the eldest of five sons of Arthur Llewelyn and Sylvia DuMaurier Davies. Barrie's adventures with the boys—George, Jack, Peter, Michael, and Nicholas—inspired many of the characters and adventures in *Peter Pan* (1904). Eventually, Barrie became the children's guardian. Tragically, however, George died in World War I; Michael and Peter committed suicide; and Jack eventually estranged himself from Barrie.

The year 1897 saw the New York opening of *The Little Minister,* an immensely successful play, adapted from Barrie's novel of the same title. Barrie himself hated the play, refusing even to include it in his *Complete Plays.* Three years later (1900) Barrie laid aside his burlesque of Ibsenism to try his hand at the real thing in *The Wedding Guest,* a dark play about characters with destructive "pasts." A decade later (1910) he would return to burlesque in *A Slice of Life: An Advanced Drama,* in which the main characters' shocking secret is that neither of them has a "past."

Two of Barrie's most popular plays, *Quality Street* (1901) and *The Admirable Crichton* (1902), as well as the less successful *Little Mary* (1903), preceded *Peter Pan; or, The Boy Who Wouldn't Grow Up* (1904). Not only Barrie's contemporaries, but also succeeding audiences, have shared his fantasy of Peter, Wendy, the "lost boys," Tinker Belle, Tiger Lily, and, of course, Captain Hook. Actresses from Nina Boucicault to Maude Adams, Mary Martin, and beyond have coveted the role of Peter, while technicians have marveled at the complexity of the play's staging. In 1908, to honor impresario Charles Frohman, who wanted to know what happened to the characters in later years, Barrie wrote a brief dramatic sequel, *When Wendy Grew Up: An Afterthought.* It was performed only once and not published until 1957.

Barrie's subsequent dramatic output can be divided into full-length plays, "half-hours" and other playlets, and various sketches, revues, and entertainments. His full-length plays include *Alice-Sit-by-the-Fire* (1905), *What Every Woman Knows* (1908), *The Adored One* (1913), *A Kiss for Cinderella* (1916), *Dear Brutus* (1917), *Mary Rose* (1920), and *The Boy David* (1936). Barrie's short plays include his commedia dell'arte pantomime *Pantaloon* (1905), *The Twelve-Pound Look* (1910), *Old Friends* (1910), *Rosalind* (1912), *The Will* (1913), *Half an Hour* (1913), *Seven Women* (a revision of the first act of *The Adored One;* 1917), and five playlets about World War I: *Der Tag; or, The Tragic Man* (1914), *The New Word* (1915), *The Old Lady Shows Her Medals* (1917), *A Well-remembered Voice* (1918), and *Barbara's Wedding,* also written in 1918 but not performed until 1927. The last four plays were published together as *Echoes of the War* (1918). Barrie's miscellaneous pieces include *Josephine* (1906), *Punch: A Toy Tragedy* (1906), *The Dramatists Get What They Want* (1912), *Rosy Rapture, the Pride of the Beauty Chorus* (1915), *The Fatal Typist* (1915), *The Real Thing at Last* (1916), *Shakespeare's Legacy* (1916), *Reconstructing the Crime* (1917), *La Politesse* (1918), *The Truth about the Russian Dancers* (1920), and the unfinished murder mystery *Shall We Join the Ladies?* (1921).

Barrie's work brought him many honors. In 1913 King George V made him a baronet. In 1919 Barrie was made rector of St. Andrew's University in Scotland. In 1922 he received the Order of Merit. Oxford granted him an honorary D.Litt. in 1926, and Cambridge followed suit with an honorary LL.D. in 1930, the same year that Barrie was installed as chancellor of Edinburgh University.

Barrie died at age seventy-seven on 19 June 1937. He is buried in Kirriemuir beside his mother and his brother David.

Selected Biographical Sources: Birkin; Dunbar; Geduld; Mackail; Markgraf.

MAJOR PLAYS, PREMIERES, AND SIGNIFICANT REVIVALS: THEATRICAL RECEPTION

Walker, London. 1892. Opened 25 February at Toole's Theatre (London) for 497 performances; moved to the Parkhurst Theatre (London) in June 1893; returned to Toole's Theatre on 26 December for 34 performances; opened at the Park Theatre (New York) on 26 February 1894; returned to Toole's Theatre on 16 June for 4 performances and on 26 December for 36 performances. Revival: Royalty Theatre (Glasgow), January–April 1914, directed by Lewis Casson. Musical version: Birmingham Repertory Theatre (England), opened 29 May 1962. Lyrics by John Harrison and music by Christopher Whelen.

Originally titled *The Houseboat,* this play examined social roles and personal relationships in the idyllic setting of a houseboat moored on the Thames. "Walker, London" was a euphemism for lying, and the play deals lightheartedly with deception—self- and otherwise. McCarthy and Scott both found "realism" in the play's depiction of contemporary English life. Morton praised the apparent ease that belied the play's complex construction. Walbrook categorized it as yet another "well-made play." It was the play that successfully launched Barrie's career as a dramatist.

The Little Minister. 1897. Copyright performance on 13 July at the Haymarket Theatre (London); opened 13 September for one week at the LaFayette Opera House (Washington, D.C.); moved on 27 September to the Empire Theater (New York) for 300 performances, including some at the Garrick Theatre (New York); opened at the Theatre Royal, Haymarket (London) on 6 November 1897 and again on 3 September 1898 for a total of 330 performances. There have been numerous revivals, the last being at the Birmingham Repertory Theatre (England) on 12 January 1943. Movie versions: 1915, 1922, and 1934. German adaptation: Imperial Burgtheater (Vienna) on 9 March 1908. Musical (*Wild Grows the Heather*): Hippodrome Theatre (London), 3–26 May 1956, and 9 May 1960 in Kirriemuir, Scotland.

In this play the decorous English Lady Barbara stoops to conquer the stuffy minister, Scottish Gavin Dishart, by disguising herself as Babbie, a gypsy. Beerbohm [2] found Barrie's characters charming and praised the playwright's skill in adapting his novel to the stage. Sampson criticized Barrie's use of Scottish dialect as detracting from the play's focus. To Morton, however, the play was "full of [delightful] surprises," which Barrie exploited entertainingly and effectively.

Quality Street. 1901. First performance on 14 October 1901 in Toledo, Ohio; moved to the Knickerbocker Theatre (New York) on 11 November 1901 for 549 performances; opened at the Vaudeville Theatre (London) on 17 September 1902 for 437 performances. Revivals: numerous, the latest being 27 May–2 June 1946 at the Northampton Repertory Theatre (England). Movies: 1927 and 1937. Musicals: *Phoebe of Quality Street,* 1921, and *Dear Miss Phoebe,* 1950.

Archer [3] and Beerbohm [3] noted the Jane Austen–like qualities of this play, in which a staid spinster pretends to be her own fluffy-headed niece in order to captivate the man she loves. Chambers pointed out the "psychological subtlety" of the main character's "rivalry with her other self," but criticized the play's tendency to slip from humor to burlesque as well as its unsatisfactory plot resolution, claiming that the entire last act "add[ed] nothing." Jack [1] later disagreed with this assessment, finding "grave social implications" underlying the play's conventional resolution.

The Admirable Crichton. 1902. Opened on 4 November at the Duke of York's Theatre (London) for 326 performances; opened at the Lyceum Theatre (New York) on 17 November 1903 for 144 performances; opened a second time at the Duke of York's Theatre on 2 March 1908 for 117 performances. Revivals: numerous, the latest being in 1983 at the Pitlochry Festival (Scotland). Movies: *Male and Female,* 1919, and *Paradise Lagoon,* 1958. Television: NBC "Hallmark Hall of Fame," 2 May 1968. Musical: *Our Man Crichton,* 1965.

This play about the "naturalness" of social class structures divided critics into those like Fyfe [1] and Hartung, who saw the work as fantasy and escapism, and those like Hammerton and Moult, who understood it as a problem play with a touch of "Nietzschenism." Sampson represented a middle position and considered Barrie a "fabulist," pointing a moral.

Peter Pan; or, The Boy Who Wouldn't Grow Up. 1904. Opened on 27 December at the Duke of York's Theatre (London) for 150 performances; opened on 17 October 1905 at the National Theatre (Washington, D.C.), then moved to the Empire Theatre (New York) for 237 performances. Revivals: numerous; the work is still frequently played. Movies: 1924 and 1953 (Disney, animated). Recording: HMV, 1940. Radio: BBC, 1941. Television: NBC, 1956; BBC-1, 1965; ATV (England), 1976. Musicals: Bernstein, 1950, and Leigh and Charlap, 1954, with revivals in 1979, 1981, and 1984.

Critics such as Beerbohm [1] and Shore praised the dreamlike beauty of Barrie's fantasy about a boy who chooses perpetual childhood. Herbert Beerbohm Tree, on the other hand, thought that Barrie had exceeded the bounds of sanity and rejected the play for his theater (quoted in Pearson, 163). Billington heard a note of melancholy, surprisingly not for leaving childhood, but for perpetually remaining there as Peter chooses to do. Jack ([2], 162) called the play an "artificial, perspectivist, creation myth," focusing on the notion of authorship. Negative criticism centers mainly around accretions of unnecessary or unworkable stage business.

What Every Woman Knows. 1908. Opened at the Duke of York's Theatre (London) on 3 September for 384 performances (some at Hick's Theatre); opened in October at Atlantic City before moving to the Empire Theatre (New York) for 198 performances. Revivals: numerous, the latest being at the Brunton Theatre (Musselburgh, Scotland) in 1983. Movie: MGM, 1934. Television: "Dupont Show of the Month," 1959; BBC, 1961; and BBC-1, 1978. Musical: *Maggie* (Hugh Thomas and William Roy), 1953, and Michael Wild, 1977.

"What every woman knows" is that "every man who is high up loves to think that he has done it all himself." John Shand, an ambitious politician, is forced to tacit acknowledgment of this observation when he realizes that leaving his wife Maggie for an empty-headed, flirtatious socialite will irretrievably diminish the brilliance of his career, since it is Maggie who suggests the witty touches that characterize his speeches and catapult him into the political limelight. Fyfe [2] saw Maggie as a "grown-up Wendy." Archer [2] praised the "ingenuity" and "charm" of a play that could be "manifestly unreal" yet still convey "a great deal of truth," whereas Barnes criticized the play as "the celebration of a cliche not the investigation of a life."

Rosalind. 1912. Opened at the Duke of York's Theatre (London) on 13 October; transferred to the Haymarket Theatre (London) on 14 December for a total of 138 performances; opened at the Lyceum Theatre (New York) on 6 September

1915 for 48 performances. Revivals: Open Space Theatre (London), 1975. Movie: *Forever Female,* Paramount, 1953.

In this one-act play an aging actress laments the lack of dramatic roles for older women, forcing her to play younger women, including Shakespeare's Rosalind. She reveals to a stagestruck young man that the middle-aged actress he encounters is really the much younger one he seeks. As she prepares to play Rosalind once more, Mrs. Page reminds her suitor that in the theater "everything is real except middle age." Despite criticism of the play's sentimentality, it was considered one of Barrie's most successful one-act plays—"a sparkling little masterpiece," according to the reviewer for the *Graphic* ("A Radiant Rosalind").

A Kiss for Cinderella. 1916. Opened at Wyndham's Theatre (London) on 16 March for 158 performances; tryout at the Academy Theatre (Baltimore) on 18 December; moved to the Empire Theatre (New York) on 25 December for 152 performances. Revivals: several, the most recent being at the Q Theatre (London), December 1948. Musical: *The Penny Friend* (William Roy) at Stage 73 Theatre (New York), December 1966, for 32 performances. Movie: 1925.

Set against the background of World War I, the fantasy of Miss Jane Thing, "a slavey," that she is really Cinderella, whose invitation to a ball is imminent, is realized briefly in a dream scene wherein the policeman who comes to investigate her sheltering of a German orphan is transformed into Prince Charming. Chilled from waiting outside for her royal invitation, Jane dies shortly thereafter, but not before her policeman/prince proposes and seals the offer with a kiss. Baughan suggested that the "kind[ness] . . . sentiment and fantasy" of this work was just what a wartime audience needed, while Atkinson [1] called the dream scene at the royal ball "one of the finest improvisations in dramatic literature." Gilder, however, cautioned against overlooking the "chocolate-coated," "acid bite" of the play's satiric elements.

Dear Brutus. 1917. Opened at Wyndham's Theatre (London) on 17 October for 365 performances; opened at the Empire Theatre (New York) on 23 December 1918 for 184 performances. Revivals: numerous, the most recent being at the Quaigh Theatre (New York), 5 December 1983. Radio: BBC, 10 May 1937. Television: BBC-1 27 January 1981.

This *Midsummer Night's Dream*–like play is about wished-for "second" chances that ultimately prove as unsatisfactory as the "first" chances that the characters have longed to escape. Jelliffe and Brink found psychoanalytic elements in the dream scene as well as evidence of "mother-fixation" in the character of Margaret. Despite Barrie's reputation for sentimentality, MacCarthy (109) expected the play to be "unpleasant to sentimentalists" because the characters do not use their second chances to improve their lives. For Archer [1], however, *Dear Brutus* wore "a spell as potent as Puck's," while Reilly applauded Barrie's ability "to make the unreal real and the impossible possible."

Mary Rose. 1920. Opened at the Haymarket Theatre (London) on 22 April for 400 performances; opened at the Empire Theatre (New York) on 22 December for 127 performances. Revivals: chiefly at repertory theaters and small festivals, the most recent being at the Greenwich Theatre (London) and also at Watford Palace Theatre (London) in 1987.

Mackail (546) asserted that even Barrie himself did not understand this enigmatic play. Mary Rose suddenly disappears for twenty-five years on the mysterious "Island That Likes to be Visited." Later ghostly mother and full-grown son, searching for each other, have a momentary but unsuccessful reunion before she follows the call of celestial music into the empyrean. Atkinson [2] criticized the play as too "personal"; Delavenay noted its coupling of "Calvinist pessimism" and "astonishing vitality." Goitein called *Mary Rose* "a religious drama" played out between "Heaven and Earth," whereas Ormond saw the title character as Wendy-like and her exit as a flight to the Neverland. The difficulty of interpreting *Mary Rose* continues to pique critical interest, making this play, like the island central to it, a place that "likes to be visited."

The Boy David. 1936. Opened at the King's Theatre (Edinburgh) on 21 November 1936; opened at His Majesty's Theatre (London) on 14 December for 55 performances; opened at the Pasadena Playhouse (California) on 20 December 1938. Revivals: Studio Theatre (New York) in 1941 and Pitlochry Festival (Scotland) in 1954.

Barrie's last play develops a countryside dialogue between Israel's King Saul and a youthful David. Saul's fondness for David is sinisterly overshadowed by his growing realization that David is the prophesied rival for his throne whom Saul will eventually have to kill. Andrews dismissed the work as "pure 'Peter Pan,' " while the reviewer for the *New Statesman and the Nation* (Review of *The Boy David*) saw it as little more than "a clockwork mouse for the nursery." Barrie was accused of having run out of either steam or imagination in tacking on the final act wherein a visionary David is shown the future deaths of both Saul and Saul's son Jonathan, who will by then have become David's closest friend. Despite these problems, Mackail (709) asserted that *The Boy David* played in Edinburgh "to sixty thousand people in seven weeks"—hardly a box-office failure.

ADDITIONAL PLAYS, ADAPTATIONS, AND PRODUCTIONS

Additional plays by Barrie include the following: *Caught Napping* (1883), called a "comedietta" by *The Times* (in Mackail, 85); a "duologue," *A Platonic Friendship* (1898); *Frank Tinney's Revue* (1914), a wartime benefit show, which contained the following Barrie sketches: *The Bulldog Breed, One Night, Taming a Tiger, When the Kye Came Home, Why?,* and *A Conundrum,* in addition to an adaptation of *The Adored One; Irene Vanbrugh's Pantomime* (1916); a ballet scenario, *The Origin of Harlequin* (1917); a one-act play, *The*

Happy New Year (1922); a children's play, *Where Was Simon?* (1926); and a play for a private family performance, *The Wheel* (1927).

ASSESSMENT OF BARRIE'S CAREER

Assessing Barrie's career is often akin to assessing the meaning of a Rorschach inkblot. Mention Barrie in psychoanalytic circles, and whispers of "mother-fixation" and "pedophilia" soon arise. Mention Barrie north of the English border, and the cry goes up that "Barrie betrayed Scotland." Mention Barrie in England, and "sentimentality" and "commercialism" are almost simultaneously voiced. Mention Barrie anywhere, and "whimsy" and "fantasy" are sure to accompany his name. "Deep meaning" and "technical brilliance," however, are heard far less frequently than they ought to be.

Freudians are fond of reading Barrie's plays as highly personal intimations of troubled childhood and adult sexuality. Rose said that this is to misread Freud; that the plays are really about the process of establishing identity begun in childhood but remaining incomplete and problematical into adulthood.

Scots critics resent that Barrie's success came chiefly in England and in commercial theaters rather than in the festival theaters favored in Scotland. They also accuse Barrie of being insufficiently Scottish and of ridiculing his brother Scots. Jack ([2], 18) refuted these accusations, arguing that the limited number of theaters in Barrie's Scotland virtually required him to go to England, that "commercial" and "inartistic" are not necessarily synonymous, and that Barrie made fun of the English and the Irish as well as the Scots.

English critics who also complain of Barrie's commercial successes fail to examine why these plays drew such large, sustained, and appreciative audiences. Beneath the attractions of whimsy, fantasy, and sentimentality lies a core reality that touches more than one responsive chord. Beneath the dramatist lies the theater technician who knows what will play because he knows what will stage. Indeed, Barrie meticulously supervised the rehearsals of many of his plays, often stretching the physical limits of various theaters, as in the flights of Peter Pan, Wendy, and the boys.

Growing into roles, growing out of roles, and remaining in roles are preoccupations common to many of Barrie's plays. Children, such as Wendy and the boys, grow up; single women, such as Miss Phoebe of *Quality Street,* grow into wives and sometimes mothers; couples grow out of marriage and into actual or virtual singlehood, as in *The Twelve-Pound Look* and in *The Will;* whereas circumstances compel some, like Mrs. Page in *Rosalind,* to remain in roles that they would prefer to relinquish. Others remain in those same roles even when given second chances, as in *Dear Brutus.*

Jack ([2], 155) argued that Barrie's plays are complex, and that "critical attention" must therefore move from "the psychological to the metafictional." Barrie generates multiple perspectives within many of his plays by, in Jack's ([2], 164) words, "alterations of mode or genres." *Peter Pan,* he asserted, is a veritable "meeting place of modes," including ballet, acrobatics, and so on. Myth, fairy tale, fantasy, domestic drama, and other elements extend the play's action from the Darling's home to a wider Cosmos, with the resulting ambivalences not totally resolved by the play's end. The same could be said of many other Barrie plays, especially *Mary Rose,* where son and mother find each other but ironically in that finding also lose each other. The meeting between Saul and David in *The Boy David* ends similarly. Somehow Barrie's wit, charm, and comic dexterity never quite seem to overcome the sadder realities of human existence, making them at best poignantly tolerable.

Barrie critics would do well to imitate Barrie's own complexity and subordinate single-perspective analyses of his plays to more multifaceted approaches. If the speaker of Yeats's poem "Among School Children" could not separate the dancer from the dance, neither can we separate the whole of Barrie from the whole of his works. He is not just psyche; he is not just Scots; he is not just an adult "Peter Pan." He is one who recognizes the illusions of reality as well as the reality of illusions and has both the courage and the creativity successfully to dramatize the resulting paradox. Critics must not be too quick to walk away from what Barrie's audiences stayed to see.

ARCHIVAL SOURCES

Yale's Beinecke Library houses the greatest collection of Barrie materials. The Lilly Library at the University of Indiana has the original draft of *Peter Pan.* The New York Public Library and the Scottish National Trust are repositories for many other materials.

PRIMARY BIBLIOGRAPHY

Plays

The Admirable Crichton. London, New York, and Toronto: Hodder & Stoughton, 1914.
Alice Sit-by-the-Fire. London, New York, and Toronto: Hodder & Stoughton, 1919.
The Boy David. London: Peter Davies, 1938; New York: Charles Scribner's Sons, 1938.
Dear Brutus. London: Hodder & Stoughton, 1922; New York: Charles Scribner's Sons, 1922.
Ibsen's Ghost; or, Toole Up-to-Date. London: Cecil Woolf, 1975.
A Kiss for Cinderella. London, New York, and Toronto: Hodder & Stoughton, 1920.
Mary Rose. London, New York, and Toronto: Hodder & Stoughton, 1918.
Peter Pan. [Play in book form.] London: Hodder & Stoughton, 1928.
Quality Street. London: Hodder & Stoughton, 1913; New York: Charles Scribner's Sons, 1918.
Richard Savage. London: privately printed, 1891.
Shakespeare's Legacy. London: Clement & Shorter, 1916.
Shall We Join the Ladies? London: Hutchinson, 1927.

"Der Tag"; or, The Tragic Man. London, New York, and Toronto: Hodder & Stoughton, 1914; New York: Charles Scribner's Sons, 1914.
Walker, London. London and New York: Samuel French, 1907.
The Wedding Guest. Copyright ed. London: Chapman & Hall, 1900; New York: Charles Scribner's Sons, 1900.
What Every Woman Knows. London: Hodder & Stoughton, 1918; New York: Charles Scribner's Sons, 1918.
When Wendy Grew Up: An Afterthought. New York: Dutton, 1957.

Anthologies

Echoes of the War. (*The New Word, The Old Lady Shows Her Medals, A Well-remembered Voice, Barbara's Wedding.*) London: Hodder & Stoughton, 1918; New York, Charles Scribner's Sons, 1918.
Half Hours. (*Pantaloon, The Twelve-Pound Look, Rosalind, The Will.*) London, New York, and Toronto: Hodder & Stoughton, 1914; (with addition of *Der Tag*) New York: Charles Scribner's Sons, 1914.
The Plays of J. M. Barrie. (*Alice Sit-by-the-Fire, What Every Woman Knows, Old Friends, Seven Women, Half an Hour, The New Word, A Kiss for Cinderella, Dear Brutus, Mary Rose, Peter Pan, Quality Street, The Admirable Crichton, Pantaloon, Rosalind, The Will, The Twelve-Pound Look, A Well-remembered Voice, Barbara's Wedding, The Old Lady Shows Her Medals, Shall We Join the Ladies?*) New York: Charles Scribner's Sons, 1930.
The Plays of J. M. Barrie in One Volume: The Definitive Edition. Ed. A. E. Wilson. (*Walker, London, The Professor's Love Story, The Little Minister, The Wedding Guest, Quality Street, The Admirable Crichton, Little Mary, Peter Pan, Pantaloon, Alice Sit-by-the-Fire, What Every Woman Knows, Old Friends, The Twelve-Pound Look, Rosalind, The Will, Half an Hour, The New Word, A Kiss for Cinderella, Seven Women, The Old Lady Shows Her Medals, Dear Brutus, A Well-remembered Voice, Mary Rose, Shall We Join the Ladies?, Barbara's Wedding, The Boy David.*) London: Hodder & Stoughton, 1928; rev. ed., 1942.
Representative Plays. (*Quality Street, The Admirable Crichton, What Every Woman Knows, Dear Brutus, The Twelve-Pound Look, The Old Lady Shows Her Medals.*) New York, Chicago, and Boston: Charles Scribner's Sons, 1926.
The Works of J. M. Barrie. 16 vols. New York: Charles Scribner's Sons, 1929–1940.

Letters and Speeches on Drama and Theater

The Ladies Shakespeare (speech). Privately printed. London: Eyre & Spottiswoode, 1925.
The Letters of J. M. Barrie. Ed. Viola Meynell. London: Davies, 1942; New York: Charles Scribner's Sons, 1947.
M'Connachie and J. M. B. (collection of speeches). London: Davies, 1938; New York: Charles Scribner's Sons, 1939.

SECONDARY BIBLIOGRAPHY

Andrews, D. B., Jr. "New Barrie Play Opens in Scotland." *New York Times* (22 Nov. 1936): 6:7.

Archer, William. [1]. "The Drama in London." *Nation* 105 (29 Nov. 1917): 601–3.

———. [2]. *The Old Drama and the New.* Boston: Small, Maynard, 1923.

———. [3]. Review of *Quality Street World* (London) (24 Sept. 1902): 502–3.

Atkinson, Brooks. [1]. "A Kiss for Cinderella." *New York Times* (11 Mar. 1942): 22.

———. [2]. "Mary Rose." *New York Times* (5 Mar. 1951): 25.

Barnes, Clive. "Stage: 'What Every Woman Knows.' " *New York Times* (3 June 1975): 27:1.

"Barrie's Little Mary." *Bookman* 18 (1904): 593, 596, 598.

Baughan, E. A. "Drama of the Year." In *"The Stage" Year Book 1917,* ed. Lionel Carson, 1–7. London: "The Stage," 1917 [for 1916].

Beerbohm, Max. [1]. "The Child Barrie," *Saturday Review* (7 Jan. 1905): 13–14.

———. [2]. "A Load of Weeds from the Kailyard." *Saturday Review* (30 Dec. 1905): 838.

———. [3]. "A Pretty Play Spoilt." *Saturday Review* (20 Sept. 1902): 361–62.

Billington, Michael. "Midwinter's Night Dream." *Guardian* (17 Dec. 1982): 15.

Birkin, Andrew. *J. M. Barrie and the Lost Boys: The Love Story That Gave Birth to Peter Pan.* New York: Potter, 1979.

Review of *The Boy David. New Statesman and Nation* 12 (19 Dec. 1936): 1028.

Chambers, E. K. "Phoebe of the Ringlets." *Academy* 63 (27 Sept. 1902): 312.

Delavenay, Emile. " 'Mary Rose' et le problème de la personnalité chez Barrie." *Revue Anglo-Americaine* (Paris) 6 (Apr. 1929): 327–43.

Dunbar, Janet. *J. M. Barrie: The Man behind the Image.* Boston: Houghton Mifflin, 1970.

Fyfe, H. Hamilton. [1]. "The Admirable Crichton." *World* (11 Mar. 1908): 421.

———. [2]. "The Theatre." *World* (9 Sept. 1908): 454–55.

Geduld, Harry M. *Sir James Barrie.* New York: Twayne, 1971.

Gilder, Rosamond. *Theatre Arts* 26 (May 1942): 289–90.

Goitein, P. Lionel. "A New Approach to an Analysis of *Mary Rose.*" *British Journal of Medical Psychology* 6 (1926): 178–208.

Hammerton, J. A. *Barrie: The Story of a Genius.* New York: Dodd, Mead, 1929; London: Sampson, Low, 1929.

Hartung, Philip. *Commonweal* 67 (31 Jan. 1958): 458.

Jack, R.D.S. [1]. "From Novel to Drama: J. M. Barrie's *Quality Street.*" *Scottish Literary Journal* 14 (1987): 48–61.

———. [2]. *The Road to the Never Land: A Reassessment of J. M. Barrie's Dramatic Art.* Aberdeen: Aberdeen University Press, 1991.

Jelliffe, Smith E., and Louise Brink. "*Dear Brutus:* The Dramatist's Use of the Dream." *New York Medical Journal* 109 (1919): 577–83.

MacCarthy, Desmond. *Drama.* New York: Benjamin Blom, 1970.

Mackail, Dennis. *Barrie: The Story of J.M.B.* 1941. Reprint. Freeport, NY: Books for Libraries Press, 1972.

McCarthy, Justin Huntley. "Pages on Plays: *Walker, London.*" *Gentleman's Magazine* 272 (Jan.–June 1892): 421–22.

Morton, Edward. "Mr. J. M. Barrie as a Dramatist." *Bookman* 13 (Jan. 1898): 117–20.

Moult, Thomas. *Barrie.* New York: Charles Scribner's Sons, 1928.

Ormond, Leonee. "J. M. Barrie's *Mary Rose.*" *Yale University Library Gazette* 58 (1983): 59–63.

Pearson, Hesketh. *Beerbohm Tree: His Life and Laughter.* New York: Harper & Bros., 1956.

"A Radiant Rosalind." *Graphic* 86 (19 Oct. 1912): 584.

Reilly, Joseph J. "J. M. Barrie." *Catholic World* 146 (Oct. 1937): 47–49.

Rose, Jacqueline. *The Case of Peter Pan; or, The Impossibility of Children's Fiction.* London: Macmillan, 1984.

Sampson, George. "J. M. Barrie as Dramatist." *Bookman* 55 (Dec. 1918): 104.

Scott, Clement. "The Playhouses." *Illustrated London News* (30 July 1892): 156.

Shore, W. Teignmouth. "Peter Pan." *Academy* 68 (7 Jan. 1905): 19.

Walbrook, H. M. *J. M. Barrie and the Theatre.* 1922. Reprint. Port Washington, NY: Kennikat Press, 1969.

BIBLIOGRAPHIES

Beinecke, W., Jr. "Barrie in the Parrish Collection." *Princeton University Library Chronicle* 17.2 (Winter 1956): 96–98.

Cutler, B. D. *Sir James M. Barrie: A Bibliography.* New York: Greenberg, 1931.

Garland, Herbert. *A Bibliography of the Writings of Sir James Matthew Barrie, Bart., O. M.* London: Bookman's Journal, 1928.

Markgraf, Carl. *J. M. Barrie: An Annotated Secondary Bibliography.* Greensboro, NC: ELT Press, 1989.

Mott, H. S. "The Walter Beinecke, Jr., J. M. Barrie Collection." *Yale University Library Gazette* 39 (1965): 163–67.

Nicoll, Allardyce. [1]. *A History of Late Nineteenth-Century Drama, 1850–1900.* Cambridge: Cambridge University Press, 1946, 2 vols. Cambridge: Cambridge University Press, 1959.

———. [2]. "Hand-List of Plays, 1900–1930." In *English Drama, 1900–1930: The Beginnings of the Modern Period,* 496–97. Cambridge: Cambridge University Press, 1973.

Sir Max Beerbohm
(1872–1956)

COLETTE LINDROTH

When Henry Maximilian Beerbohm was born, on 24 August 1872 in London, the British Empire was at the height of its size and power, the Victorian era was in full bloom, and the peace and prosperity of a bustling industrial age seemed indestructible. When he died, on 20 May 1956, England had been scarred by two world wars, the Empire was in tatters, and even the industrial era would shortly bow to the microchip. It seems appropriate that Beerbohm should have been born into one world and died in another, for throughout his life he proved himself adept at thriving in several environments. He was familiar with the world of Aubrey Beardsley and Oscar Wilde, of decadence and dandyism; with the world of George Bernard Shaw and Henrik Ibsen, theatrical revolutionaries; with the world of dramatist and that of drama critic; with the world of satire and that of serious comment; with the world of Victorianism and that of modernism. In each of these worlds Beerbohm left his mark.

His youth was one of comfort, order, and even privilege. Max was the youngest child of Julius Ewald Beerbohm and his second wife, Eliza Draper Beerbohm. Max had four sisters and, from his father's first marriage to Constantia Draper (Julius married her sister after Constantia died in 1858), three half brothers and one half sister. This large combined family lived in prosperous homes in London, where Julius was a grain merchant in the City.

From the first, however, Max (as he was always called) gravitated from industry and toward the arts. In this he had ample help from his eldest half brother, Herbert (later Sir Herbert) Beerbohm Tree, a highly successful actor and theatrical producer from 1878 until his death in 1917. Although he was twenty years younger than Herbert, Max was very close to him, and he never forgot the thrill of his boyhood excursions into London's West End, where he met actors and watched his brother's plays. He always considered this early exposure to the theater a major part of his education.

Max's formal schooling, however, took place at Charterhouse (William Makepeace Thackeray's old school), where he studied from 1885 until 1890, and at Merton College, Oxford, which he entered in October 1890. He was not particularly happy at Charterhouse, which he remembered as a place of hard work, little privacy, and great discomfort in the gently satirical essay "Going Back to School" and elsewhere. He was successful enough, however, enjoying his Latin studies, writing poetry and essays, and drawing the first of the caricatures that were to be a lifelong passion and amusement for him. He was more at home at Oxford. Here he contributed to the *Strand* magazine, exhibited his caricatures, became involved in the Oxford Union Dramatic Society, and made friends with Reggie Turner (a writer) and William Rothenstein (a painter), men who were to be close friends for the rest of his life. He also became better acquainted with Oscar Wilde, whom he had originally met with his brother Herbert. In short, though he left Oxford without taking a degree, he made the most of his time there to make good friends, develop his taste in a variety of arts, and significantly expand his theatrical experience. In fact, his first publication, with the wittily overstated title *The Works of Max Beerbohm, with a Bibliography by John Lane* (1896), consisted mainly of works written while he was an undergraduate.

When Beerbohm left Oxford in June 1894, he returned to London to live with his family, enjoying a life of theatergoing, attending art galleries, drawing, and writing. He contributed to Beardsley's *The Yellow Book* and to the *Strand* and drew caricatures for *Sketch, Pall Mall,* and other popular magazines. In 1895 he accompanied Herbert on a theatrical tour of America, serving as his secretary for part of the journey.

In 1898 Beerbohm was suddenly thrust into a new level of theatrical prominence when George Bernard Shaw retired as drama critic for the *Saturday Review,* recommending as his successor a member of the "younger generation knocking at the door . . . the incomparable Max." With characteristic modesty and understated wit, Beerbohm entitled his first official article, on 28 May 1898, "Why I Ought Not to Have Become a Dramatic Critic," but he was the only one who felt that way. He held the post with great distinction until 1910, writing at least fifty articles a year for that publication alone.

Despite his modesty about his own abilities, Beerbohm was a significant drama critic. As was always the case with his writing, his reviews were marked by a graceful, deceptively easy, conversational style. Despite their apparent simplicity, however, these pieces are remarkable for perceptiveness and for their reliance on individual judgment, independent of "schools" of criticism or theory. It was his stated purpose to present his own responses to plays and to suggest, as clearly as possible, the reasons for these responses. In doing so he made his reviews a model of thoughtful, unprejudiced clarity.

He also had strong ideas about the state of the theater in early twentieth-century England, finding it much closer to mere entertainment than to the serious art that it had been in former times. In an effort to correct this situation, he featured the most significant and challenging dramatists of his time, notably Shaw, Henry Arthur Jones, Arthur Wing Pinero, and Somerset Maugham. Even with these towering figures, however, he was always judicious, pointing out their shortcomings as well as their strong points and being less willing than most of his colleagues to hail anyone a "genius." He embraced realism, but not blindly, noting that many dramatists who called themselves realists were in fact often unconvincing. Throughout his career as a reviewer he called for more credibility in dialogue, situation, and motivation and less reliance on audience-pleasing tricks of melodrama or farce.

Along with the realists, Beerbohm also supported the dramatists of fantasy and poetic effects, especially William Butler Yeats, J. M. Barrie, and Maurice Maeterlinck. As always, he found faults as well as strengths in poetic drama, but he was one of the strongest early supporters of these experimental movements.

In March 1910, to the surprise of many of his friends, Beerbohm retired from full involvement in the London literary and dramatic scene. On 4 May of that year he married Florence Kahn, an American actress to whom he had been engaged for some time. They settled in Rapallo, Italy, where they lived for the rest of their lives with the exception of the years during World War I and World War II, when they returned to London. This did not mean that Beerbohm retired from his creative interests, however. For the rest of his life he was involved in his drawings and caricatures, which he exhibited regularly, in publishing collections of his essays and reviews, and in producing full-length works like *Zuleika Dobson* (1911) and *Rossetti and His Circle* (1922). He also became very much involved in radio broadcasts, which he delivered with great success for many years and which were also collected and published. In 1939 he was knighted. He also received an honorary doctorate from the University of Edinburgh (1930) and an honorary fellowship at Merton College (1945) as well as many other honors, including the formation of the Maximilian Society in 1942 to honor his seventieth birthday.

In 1951 his wife, Florence, died, and Elisabeth Jungmann, Beerbohm's nurse, became his companion. In 1956 he married her only a month before his own death. His ashes are interred at St. Paul's Cathedral.

Selected Biographical Sources: Behrman; Cecil; McElderry; Riewald [1], [2].

MAJOR PLAYS, PREMIERES, AND SIGNIFICANT REVIVALS: THEATRICAL RECEPTION

The Happy Hypocrite. 1900. A one-act play performed as a curtain raiser for Frank Harris's *Mr. and Mrs. Daventry.* Opened 11 December at the Royalty Theatre (London) for 52 performances. Produced by Mrs. Patrick Campbell. A three-act version by Clemence Dane (pseudonym of Winifred Ashton), with music by Richard Addinsell, based on Beerbohm's original, opened at His Majesty's Theatre (London) 8 April 1936 for 68 performances. Ivor Novello produced and starred. A radio adaptation was broadcast on 13 January 1941 starring Deborah Kerr, produced by Douglas Cleverdon. The three-act version was revived in September 1968 at the Bouwerie Lane Theatre (New York). Also done as a one-act radio opera, *Ipocrita felice,* by Giorgio Federico Ghedini in 1952.

Beerbohm's most famous theatrical production, *The Happy Hypocrite* is best known in its short-story form first printed in *The Yellow Book* in 1896 and often reprinted thereafter. In both short-story and dramatic form it is a morality–fairy tale dealing with Lord George Hell, a Regency rake who reforms when overcome by love for Jenny Mere, an innocent young girl. The plot is reminiscent of *The Picture of Dorian Gray,* since Hell dons a wax mask to hide his dissolute persona from Jenny's innocent gaze. When he is finally unmasked, unlike Dorian Gray, however, his angelic exterior has shaped his interior. Both his appearance and his behavior have changed, and he is redeemed.

Critics were generally kind to *The Happy Hypocrite,* although reviews suggested that the content was rather slight. Walkley, however, in two considerations in *The Times* [1, 2], defended Beerbohm's ideas in the play as making a real contribution to "the scanty theatrical stock" of the current scene. He praised the "delicate sentiment" and "airy fantasy" of the tale, concluding that the play, though "a trifle," was "new and strange and audacious, something which must give every playgoer with the slightest tincture of letters a distinct thrill."

Dane's version was also well received, with praise both for what she had done with the material and for the original from which it was taken. The reviewer for *The Times* ("Entertainments") was especially pleased by the light, delicate touch with which Beerbohm's idea was treated. The radio version was also praised, with Kerr's performance singled out as especially skilled given her youth (she was fifteen at the time).

The play did not age well, however. Oliver, in considering the 1968 version, called it "a disaster," although a "pleasant one." Despite a fine effort on the part of producers and actors, she said, the play was simply not relevant to the modern world, and no amount of trying could make it so.

The relationship between *The Happy Hypocrite* and Oscar Wilde's *The Picture of Dorian Gray* caused considerable controversy and has been widely debated. Although many critics see extended similarities and read a negative commentary on Wilde in Beerbohm's story, Beerbohm himself said that the idea was entirely his and, while influenced by Wilde, was not in any way intended as a parody of his work.

Caesar's Wife. 1902. An anonymous adaptation of Paul Hervieu's *L'Enigme,* written in collaboration with Frank Harris. Opened at Wyndham's Theatre (London) 1 March for 36 performances. Produced by Charles Wyndham and directed by Herbert Beerbohm Tree.

Unusually for Beerbohm, who most often dealt with light comedy and satire, *Caesar's Wife* deals with adultery, revenge, and suicide. It tells the story of two men, Raymond and Gérard, their wives, Léonore and Giselle, and of Vivarce, who is the lover of one of the women—which one, however, remains a secret until the play is nearly over. The play explores questions of sexual relationships, the possibility of equality between the sexes, love, fidelity, and honor. The end is intensely emotional, with Vivarce committing suicide rather than destroy a woman's good name.

The play was reviewed seriously, if not entirely favorably, with several critics seizing the opportunity to discuss the differences between what was permitted on the French stage and the English. *The Times* reviewer (''Wyndham's Theatre'') especially developed this theme, complaining that what he saw as the bowdlerization of the play undercut its effectiveness, making its emotional heights less persuasive than they should be. He did, however, praise the development of intellectual themes and the dramatic tension achieved.

Because the play was presented anonymously, it allowed for a curious situation: Beerbohm himself reviewed it for the *Saturday Review* (''A Triple Bill'') without revealing that he had in fact collaborated in its writing. He was not especially kind to himself. His review contrasted English stage traditions with those of France, praising the French tendency to write excellent short plays on serious subjects in contrast to the English fondness for lightweight ''curtain raisers.'' This willingness to write seriously in a small form justified *Caesar's Wife*, he averred, despite many weaknesses in the play. He did, however, praise the acting and the tension and suspense of the play.

The Fly on the Wheel. 1902. One-act play written with S. Murray Carson. Opened at the Coronet Theatre, Notting Hill Gate (London), 4 December, for 1 performance, a benefit matinee.

The Fly on the Wheel deals lightheartedly with rather serious themes as it follows several characters in search of treasure. As they pursue their elusive goal, they permit the play to make witty comments on the British Empire, on love both serious and frivolous, and on the possibilities of flirtation. Finally, most of the characters discover that love, not silver or gold, is the real treasure they have found—all but the Acting Commissioner of Pootanah, a Colonel Blimp type who doggedly wields his pickaxe after the rest of the cast has happily given up money for romance.

Although Beerbohm's lighthearted wit was praised, *The Fly on the Wheel* was not favorably received. *The Times* review (''Coronet Theatre'') found it ''nimble'' and ''impish,'' but finally determined that it ''had no chance'' as a drama but was instead only ''a delicious tit-bit.'' While the dialogue and the acting were praised, the play was ultimately found to be too slight for real consideration.

A Social Success. 1914. This one-act play, which was a curtain raiser for Alfred Sutro's *The Two Virtues,* opened at St. James's Theatre (London) 18 March for 53 performances. First performed (1 performance) at the Palace Theatre (London) 27 January 1913. Produced by Sir George Alexander. Revived for 1 performance at the Drury Lane Theatre (London) 4 December 1914, and again at His Majesty's Theatre (London) 9 February 1915. Produced by Sir Herbert Beerbohm Tree.

A Social Success is a witty social satire presenting Tommy Dixon, a man too popular for his own good. As the play opens, he has just committed the unimaginable scandal of being caught cheating at cards. His noble friends, grieving but horrified, flee his company as they would an outbreak of plague, one woman wishing that she could be carried out so that her clothing would not touch anything sullied by Dixon's touch. Dixon himself, however, seems unruffled. As he finally manages to make clear to his saddened friend, Robbins, cheating was the only way he could find to end his burdensome popularity. Dixon, it seems, is bored by all his social obligations but is too amiable to say no to pressing invitations, and he has contrived to disgrace himself so that his friends will stop importuning him for his company. Ironically, however, the reverse happens; although his friends all fled in horror at his misbehavior, they creep back, one by one, willing to forgive him and even more eager for his companionship. The play ends with Dixon haplessly resigning himself to being "a social success" no matter what he does.

A Social Success was a dramatic success both for its author and for Sir George Alexander, who appeared as Dixon. Alexander was praised for having chosen this vehicle to appear in; *The Times* ("St. James's Theatre") called the play "bright, smart," and flickering with Beerbohm's "characteristic flashes of wit and happy ideas." The deftness of the social satire was also praised.

Savonarola. 1930. One-act play first performed in a benefit matinee at the Haymarket Theatre (London) 26 February for 1 performance. Produced by Nigel Playfair. Also performed by the Merton Floats, Merton College, Oxford, 3 March 1936.

Savonarola is in the nature of an extended joke, and the joke is on almost everyone. Although billed as a tragedy in five acts, it is in fact very brief and very funny. Although written by Beerbohm, it is credited to "Ladbroke Brown," the fictional author created for the essay " 'Savonarola' Brown," which appeared in Beerbohm's *Seven Men and Two Others*. The plot is a send-up of everything from Elizabethan tragedy to Browning's poems. It pits the monk Savonarola against Lucrezia Borgia, both of them against the Pope, and the entire play against a too-reverent attitude toward the drama. Along the way it presents hilarious deadpan satire of tragic devices, melodrama, romanticism, and, above all, the contemporary reviewers' inability to tell good drama when they saw it.

Savonarola was reviewed as much for its relationship to Oxford and the Oxford Preservation Trust as for its merits as a play. Brown found it the best part of a very mixed program, the "very bright spot" in an otherwise "feeble" evening's entertainment. He especially praised the play's style, commending Beerbohm for his ability to sound like "an overworked Shakespeare . . . turning the stuff out to time by using every trick in his work-basket." He pronounced

Savonarola "a great success." *The Times* ("Oxford Preservation Trust") agreed, finding the play a "masterly piece of burlesque that never loses its own balance though all the decasyllabic world tumble in bathos around it."

ADDITIONAL PLAYS, ADAPTATIONS, AND PRODUCTIONS

Some of Beerbohm's stories, including *Zuleika Dobson,* were dramatized for radio broadcast by Douglas Cleverdon during the 1930s and 1940s. In 1951 Wolcott Gibbs wrote a musical comedy based on *Zuleika Dobson.*

ASSESSMENT OF BEERBOHM'S CAREER

About the significance of Beerbohm's career in its entirety there can be no question. Despite his own insistence that his was only "a small talent," he has been almost universally admired since he began publishing his work. As a stylist, caricaturist, essayist, reviewer, and satirist he has been numbered among the most popular figures of the twentieth century, and the critical commentary on his work is as voluminous as the work itself.

As a dramatist, however, he has received very little criticism. This is not surprising, for his dramatic output was not large: five one-act plays that were produced in connection with other works, and none of which enjoyed long runs. Much can be said about these plays, however. There is, for example, his assertion, in his review of his anonymously done *Caesar's Wife* ("A Triple Bill"), that the short play, in the hands of the French, could accomplish as much as a longer work. His choice of the one-act play as a genre would make for revealing study. The effectiveness of his style has also been lengthily studied in his other works, but remains little investigated in his plays. This is particularly true in *Savonarola,* whose richness of satiric targets belies its brevity. The connection between his own plays and his ideas about other playwrights, especially in the light of his satire, is also yet to be investigated. Much remains to be done in the serious study of Beerbohm the dramatist.

ARCHIVAL SOURCES

Beerbohm's papers are so numerous and so widely dispersed that reference to the bibliographies by Gallatin, Gallatin and Oliver, and Riewald [2], as well as the *Catalogue* published by Sotheby's, is recommended. Especially significant holdings are in Charterhouse School; Merton College and the Ashmolean Museum, Oxford; Trinity College, Cambridge; the British Library; the National Library of Scotland in Edinburgh; the Glasgow University Library; the Houghton Library at Harvard University; the Berg Collection of the New York Public Library; the Fales Collection of New York University; the library of the University of Southern California in Los Angeles; and the Yale University Library.

PRIMARY BIBLIOGRAPHY

And Even Now. London: Heinemann, 1920.

Around Theatres. 2 vols. New York: Alfred A. Knopf, 1930.

Herbert Beerbohm Tree: Some Memories of Him and His Art. London: Hutchinson, 1920.

Last Theatres, 1904–1910. New York: Taplinger, 1970.

Letters of Max Beerbohm, 1892–1956. Ed. Rupert Hart-Davis. London: John Murray, 1988.

Letters to Reggie Turner. Ed. Rupert Hart-Davis. London: Rupert Hart-Davis, 1964.

Mainly on the Air. London: Heinemann, 1946.

Max and Will: Max Beerbohm and William Rothenstein, Their Friendship and Letters, 1893–1945. Ed. Mary M. Lago and Karl Beckson. London: John Murray, 1975.

More Theatres, 1898–1903. London: Rupert Hart-Davis, 1969.

"Savonarola, an 'Elizabethan' Play." *Living Age,* 8th ser. (Apr.–June 1919): 98–112.

Seven Men and Two Others. London: Heinemann, 1950.

"A Triple Bill." *Saturday Review* (8 Mar. 1902): 295–96.

A Variety of Things. London: Heinemann, 1928.

The Works of Max Beerbohm. 10 vols. London: Heinemann, 1922–28.

The Works of Max Beerbohm, with a Bibliography by John Lane. London: John Lane, 1896.

SECONDARY BIBLIOGRAPHY

Behrman, S. N. *Portrait of Max: An Intimate Memoir of Sir Max Beerbohm.* New York: Random House, 1960.

Brown, Ivor. "The Theatre: Better Than Shakespeare?" *Saturday Review* (1 Mar. 1930): 263–64.

"Caesar's Wife." *Athenaeum* (21 Mar. 1914): 420.

Catalogue of the Library and Literary Manuscripts of the Late Sir Max Beerbohm. London: Sotheby, 1960.

Cecil, David. *Max: A Biography.* London: Constable, 1964.

Cookman, A. V. Review of the three-act version of *The Happy Hypocrite. London Mercury and Bookman* (May 1936): 53–54.

"Coronet Theatre." *The Times* (5 Dec. 1902): 11.

Danson, Lawrence. *Max Beerbohm and the Act of Writing.* New York: Oxford University Press, 1991.

"Entertainments: His Majesty's Theatre: 'The Happy Hypocrite.' " *The Times* (9 Apr. 1936): 12.

Lynd, Robert. "Mr. Beerbohm." In *Essays on Life and Literature,* 147–55. London: J. M. Dent, 1951.

McElderry, Bruce R. *Max Beerbohm.* New York: Twayne, 1972.

Morgan, Charles. "The Happy Hypocrite." *New York Times* (10 May 1936): 10:1.

Oliver, Edith. "The Theatre." *New Yorker* (14 Sept. 1968): 129–30.

"Oxford Preservation Trust: 'Savonarola.' " *The Times* (26 Feb. 1930): 12.

"The Palace Theatre: The Appearance of Sir George Alexander." *The Times* (28 Jan. 1913): 9.

Riewald, J. G. [1]. *Remembering Max Beerbohm: Correspondence, Conversations, Criticisms.* Assen, The Netherlands: Van Gorcum, 1991.

————. [2]. *Sir Max Beerbohm, Man and Writer: A Critical Analysis with a Brief Life and a Bibliography.* The Hague: Nijhoff, 1953.

————, ed. [3]. *The Surprise of Excellence: Modern Essays on Max Beerbohm.* Hamden, CT: Archon Books, 1974.

"St. James's Theatre: 'A Social Success.' " *The Times* (19 Mar. 1914): 10.

Walkley, A. B. [1]. "The Drama: 'The Happy Hypocrite.' " *Literature. The Times* (22 Dec. 1900): 503.

————. [2]. "Royalty Theatre." *The Times* (17 Dec. 1900): 11.

Ward, A. C. *Twentieth-Century English Literature, 1901–1960.* (14th ed.) London: Methuen, 1966.

"Wyndham's Theatre." *The Times* (3 Mar. 1902): 8.

BIBLIOGRAPHIES

Gallatin, A. E. *Sir Max Beerbohm: Bibliographical Notes.* Cambridge, MA: Harvard University Press, 1944.

Gallatin, A. E., and L. M. Oliver. *A Bibliography of the Works of Max Beerbohm.* Cambridge, MA: Harvard University Press, 1952.

Gordon Bottomley

(1874–1948)

RONALD E. SHIELDS

During the early years of this century Gordon Bottomley, a promising Georgian poet, turned his attention to verse drama in the manner of William Butler Yeats. He wrote at least thirty plays of notable literary style and questionable theatrical viability. Most of his later plays were written as short lyrical scenes to meet the needs of his amateur casts and as experiments in creating mood and image through the spoken word. Two of Bottomley's longer plays, written before 1923 and inspired by Shakespearean characters, contributed to the brief revival of verse drama on the professional stage early in this century: *King Lear's Wife,* which premiered on 25 September 1915 at the Birmingham Repertory Theatre under the direction of John Drinkwater; and *Gruach,* which opened 30 March 1923 at the Athenaeum Theatre in Glasgow, a production sponsored by the Scottish National Theatre. The latter drama was awarded the Femina–Vie Heureuse Prize in 1923. Bottomley received the Arthur Benson Medal of the Royal Society of Literature in 1925 and was installed as a fellow in that group the following year. He was awarded three honorary degrees from the universities of Aberdeen, Durham, and Leeds.

Gordon Bottomley was born to Alfred and Maria Gordon Bottomley on 20 February 1874 in Keighley, Yorkshire. It was there that he was educated in the local grammar school. While working as a bank clerk, Gordon Bottomley, at the age of nineteen, first showed signs of persistent and severe hemorrhages, a debilitating ailment that would progressively limit his physical activity throughout his life. In 1905 he married Emily Burton, and together they moved to Silverdale, a small village in northern Lancashire near Carnforth.

At first glance there is little to record concerning the private life of Gordon Bottomley. No detailed biography exists. Nonetheless, the personality of the man and the range of his poetical and theatrical sensibilities can be gleaned by reading his unpublished letters to friends and associates, many of whom were leading poets, community drama leaders, performers, teachers, and artists, such as John Drinkwater, Lascelles Abercrombie, and Paul Nash, among others. Bottomley was a tireless correspondent, and these letters written throughout his years at the Shieling, Silverdale, speak to the ebb and flow of his health and his un-yielding artistic proclivities and causes—particularly the importance of com-munity drama and the need for a revival in verse drama and verse speaking. His words reflect his sensitivity to balance and correctness in language, his tenacity and wit, and, most of all, his tastes as a man of the earth as well as art. His letters reveal a stoic faith without formal religion, an artistic sensibility without sentimentality, and a learned concern for language and dialect, literature, and history beyond the limits of antiquarianism. His letters tell all we can ever know about his homelife at Silverdale, the place where he wrote most of his plays. A future biographer, if so critically inclined, may ponder the contrast between the commonplace domestic details of his life and the frequent violence and longings found within many of his plays.

Bottomley's early playwriting career produced several promising plays for the professional theater, specifically, the two plays on Shakespearean subjects men-tioned earlier and *Britain's Daughter,* which opened at the Old Vic in London on 11 November 1922. All had brief runs and were rarely revived. For a time during the 1920s his plays were championed by the fledgling Scottish National Players in Glasgow, a group fashioned after and inspired by Yeats and his work at the Abbey Theatre. Founded by David Glen MacKemmie, Tyrone Guthrie, and others, the Scottish National Players became the most influential and im-portant group in Scottish theater during the 1920s and defined Scottish theater for almost two decades. It was while working with this group that Bottomley discovered the teaching and verse-speaking talents of Marjorie Gullan of Glas-gow. After the failure of *Gruach* in Birmingham and London, he abandoned the professional stage and began his quest for a new style of verse speaking for the stage, including theatrical experiments in choric drama and shorter forms of verse drama written for amateur troupes.

When his health permitted, he joined with others in support of pioneering work in the areas of verse speaking, verse drama, choral speaking, and com-munity drama. During the late 1920s and 1930s he assumed leadership positions in the Speech Fellowship, the British Drama League, the Scottish Community Drama Association, and the Village Drama Society. Members within these or-ganizations produced the bulk of his verse dramas. Beginning with the arts festivals in Scotland immediately following the First World War, Bottomley often served as an adjudicator for verse-speaking festivals, such as John Mase-field's Oxford Recitations during the 1920s and Marjorie Gullan's London Speech Festival during the 1930s.

As part of John Masefield's Oxford Recitations in 1928, Bottomley was in-vited to compose plays written for two speakers, what Bottomley called "duo-logues." The short dramas were performed with very little movement, in daylight, with limited properties and set. The playwriting experiment was met with praise from the invited public, performers, and poets alike. These small-scale verse dramas opened the way for more ambitious experiments: the following year Bottomley presented two plays, *The Singing Sands* and *Ardvorlich's Wife*. Bottomley later declared that Masefield's 1929 festival was the birthplace for a new theater, a "theatre unborn." Whereas his earlier plays had been written for the professional stage, a "theatre outworn," the plays presented in the Music Room, Masefield's private theater at his home in Boar's Hill outside Oxford, epitomized Bottomley's concept of a "theatre unborn" dependent upon exquisite speech, expressive movement, and stylized setting and costumes. These plays, produced using choruses composed of previous Oxford contestants impersonating forces of nature, demonstrated the importance of musicality in verse speaking and the theatrical viability of choric verse drama.

During the early 1930s Bottomley established formal artistic ties with two teachers and a talented director—Duncan Clark, Marjorie Gullan, and E. Martin Browne. Clark directed former students from Falkirk High School, Falkirk, Scotland, and presented Bottomley's *Singing Sands* in 1930; Gullan's London Verse Speaking Choir premiered Bottomley's *Culbin Sands* in 1931. In 1934 E. Martin Browne staged Bottomley's *The Acts of Saint Peter* in London at St. Margaret's, Westminster, a production featuring Gullan's London Verse Speaking Choir. Bottomley renewed his association with Browne when the Pilgrim Players presented Bottomley's comedy, *Kate Kennedy,* during their spring 1944 tour.

Shortly before his death at the age of seventy-four, Bottomley published *A Stage for Poetry,* a lengthy work describing his purpose, practice, and vision for his plays: a "theatre unborn" replacing the "theatre outworn." In his introduction to this book he acknowledged his debt to the collaborative efforts of others who staged his plays for the theater unborn, specifically his contact with two gifted teachers and their student performers—references to Marjorie Gullan and Duncan Clark. He died at Oare, near Marlborough, England, in 1948.

Selected Biographical Sources: Abbott and Bertram; Browne; Browne and Browne; Moir; Nelson; Shields [1, 2, 3]; Stone.

MAJOR PLAYS, PREMIERES, AND SIGNIFICANT REVIVALS: THEATRICAL RECEPTION

King Lear's Wife. 1915. Opened 25 September at the Birmingham Repertory Theatre under the direction of John Drinkwater. The London premiere was on 19 May 1916 at His Majesty's Theatre on a triple bill with *Hoops* by Wilfred Wilson Gibson and *Lithuania* by Robert Brooke. Given a single performance, the triple bill was organized by Viola Tree. The cast of *King Lear's Wife* included Lady Tree as the Queen, Viola Tree as Goneril, and Murray Carrington as Lear.

Bottomley published several poems and *King Lear's Wife* in a series of volumes introducing the "Georgian" poetical movement. Edited by his friend and supporter Edward Marsh, the anti-Victorian contents of the first volume received extensive critical notice (see Rogers, 19–41; Ross, 3–26). Squire singled out *King Lear's Wife,* published in the second volume, as inferior, in particular the play's closing corpse-washing scene, a potentially comic rather than boldly tragic scene. Mixed critical responses followed the play into the theater as well.

Critics following the Birmingham premiere dismissed the play as a gifted mistake (see Nelson, 64). After the London performance, a critic for *The Times* (Review of *King Lear's Wife*) wryly mocked certain details of the plot: King Lear pursued a young handmaiden while his Queen slowly expired. Although this was neither a complete nor a sympathetic plot summary, such critical reduction did point to the larger question of stageworthiness. Calling the play halting in action and lampooning the playwright's ability to create convincing nobility of character and diction, the critic concluded that the drama appeared intelligent rather than inspired.

The contrast between the theatrical reception and literary assessments of *King Lear's Wife* is striking (see Rogers, 163). Muir [1] described the action of the play as Lear's past as remembered and retold by Goneril: an ambitious but flawed exercise in Shakespearean criticism (143). Reading Bottomley's Goneril as a Diana-like character, Muir [1] considered Bottomley's Goneril as implausible when connected to the unscrupulous Goneril of Shakespeare's play (142–43). Cramer declared *King Lear's Wife* a vivid companion piece to Shakespeare's tragedy: one of the most beautiful poetic dramas of modern times, the harbinger of modern verse drama (158).

Gruach. 1923. Opened at the Athenaeum Theatre, a hall rented by the Scottish National Theatre, in Glasgow on 30 March. Opened in London on 20 January 1924 for a single performance at St. Martin's Theatre, double-billed with *Phoenix* by Lascelles Abercrombie. *Gruach,* the story of young Macbeth and his future bride, was performed by members of the Reandean Company and featured Sybil Thorndike and Esmé Beringer in the leads and Hermione Baddeley in the supporting cast. A further revival occurred at John Masefield's private Boar's Hill Theatre in November 1926.

Following the pattern established after the premiere of *King Lear's Wife,* Bottomley's *Gruach* met with strong literary praise and mostly indifference from the theater critics. Farmer called the work an inspired effort and appreciated the depth of characterization in the work, the soaring poetry, and the overall Shakespearean quality of the work. In recent times Nelson considered the play Bottomley's dramatic masterpiece: a triumph of careful narrative development and detailed characterization, primarily in the dominating presence of the title role.

However, the critic for the *London Mercury,* reviewing the London staging, declared the play a shambles: the entire play appeared disjointed and drawn out, some speeches were verbose, some of the verse sounded too stilted to be convincingly voiced, and the final-curtain scene was "one of the most ineffective curtains ever seen on any stage" (quoted in Muir [1], 144). Given that there were only six rehearsals before the London opening, such harshness may have been unwarranted. Bottomley dismissed such criticisms (and critics) as indicative of a professional theater unable to cope with the staging demands of verse drama (Abbott and Bertram, 167–172).

Culbin Sands. 1931. First performed at the London Regent Street Polytechnic Institute, Portland Hall, by Marjorie Gullan and her pupils (members of the London Verse Speaking Choir) on 1 May as part of a double bill with *Exodus* by J. Redwood Anderson; a matinee was presented on 2 May. In February of the following year, *Culbin Sands* was revived (with the same cast) for a meeting of the English Verse Speaking Association at the Parry Theatre, Royal College of Music.

Stone recalled that the production at the Polytechnic was a low-budget affair: costumes for some characters were garments reworked from old dresses worn by Gullan's Scottish verse-speaking choir (called the Glasgow Nightingales). Gullan prepared the production, and Bottomley attended the final rehearsals and opening night; neither performance received professional reviews. The first American staging was a student production at the Yale University Theatre, 22 March 1935. The announcement for the American premiere of *Culbin Sands* in the *New York Times* (Review of *Culbin Sands*) emphasized the novelty of choric speech and the experimental nature of the student production. Photographs from the Yale staging reprinted in *Theatre Arts Monthly* testify to the influence of E. G. Craig and A. Appia on the student designers from Yale (''Choric Speech and the Stage''). Following the publication of *Culbin Sands* in 1932, literary critics praised Bottomley's use of a chorus to impersonate forces in nature (see Thouless; Shields [1]).

The Acts of Saint Peter. 1933. Opened on 27 June in celebration of the octocentenary of Exeter Cathedral; directed by Arnold Reilly. A revival, sponsored by the Religious Drama Society, was staged by E. Martin Browne at St. Margaret's Cathedral, Westminster, in London on 20 March 1934, with four additional performances given over the next three days.

Beryl Moir, a cast member in the St. Margaret's production of *The Acts of Saint Peter,* recalled that neither production met with great acclaim, although both producer and poet seemed obviously pleased with each and each other. Although the acoustics in St. Margaret's were ideal, the church's architecture was not as compatible to the staging as that of Exeter Cathedral. Bottomley (*A Stage for Poetry,* 62–64) recalled that Browne designed ramps and platforms to solve the problems and provide effective stage pictures. Describing the London Verse Speaking Choir's performance, Kerby later noted that the chorus had formed a living curtain, moving back and forth across the stage when each scene finished in order to punctuate and guide the divisions of time and place during the performance. Geoghegan concluded that the cumulative effect of the choral speaking was cathartic, ''gathering up the threads of all the grief, fear, joy, and suffering of the various acts'' (40).

ADDITIONAL PLAYS, ADAPTATIONS, AND PRODUCTIONS

The Crier by Night (1916) was first staged by the Portmanteau Theatre in Wyoming (a touring production company), with a brief appearance at the Princess Theatre in New York on 18 December. *Britain's Daughter* (1922) opened 11 November 1916 at the Old Vic. Duncan Clark's Scottish players produced several of Bottomley's plays as winning competitive entries in the Scottish Community Drama Festival and the British Community Drama Festival: *Singing Sands* (1930), *The Bower of Wendal* (1931), *Ardvorlich's Wife* (1931), and *Ealasaid* (1939). The most stylized of Bottomley's Noh-influenced plays, *Suilven and the Eagle* (1932), was first given at the Norwich Training College for Teachers (see *Lyric Plays*).

ASSESSMENT OF BOTTOMLEY'S CAREER

The major difficulty for Bottomley scholarship today involves the application of contemporary critical concerns to plays lacking a clear place in theatrical history or understandable performance style. The subjects and style of Bottomley's plays reveal the essence of the short-lived Georgian period as a transitional era, a time when poets replaced the verbal flights of Victorian poetry with a more modern sensibility, voiced on stage (in tone and subject) in the misty idealism of an earlier time, either mythical or historical. As argued by Mahony (261) and Simon (52–53), the subjects and style of Gordon Bottomley's poetry and plays seem, paradoxically, at times both Georgian and Pre-Raphaelite; in addition, many of his plays in subject matter and tone continue the Celtic twilight tradition popular during the closing decades of the nineteenth century. As the amount of literal action decreased in his plays (as it did in the choric verse dramas), the dramatic emphasis shifted to the haze and motion of beautiful words (Muir [2]).

Spanos (55) noted that Bottomley failed to reach modern audiences in *Gruach,* even though the play possesses vivid psychological reality. According to Spanos (56), Bottomley failed to reach his audiences in *Gruach* as well as in *The Acts of Saint Peter* because the characters unconvincingly voice the spiritual doubt of the modern age through the language, images, and subjects of the past. Using the stage conventions of realistic time and place in *Gruach,* Bottomley created a sense of the past primarily through elevated diction; to do so without the inclusion of symbolist elements or allusions to contemporary themes, according to Spanos (63), distances the action from the audience through unrelenting remoteness. Bottomley's religious play remains fundamentally secular, a historical pageant devoid of a sense of sacramental time and redemptive force: in short, the story of a world-weary saint who appears to seek death as a means to avoid his spiritual calling. In both plays Bottomley failed to create a sense of sacramental time and relevance through his use of dramatic structure and poetic diction.

Comparing the theatrical viability of T. S. Eliot's religious verse dramas with Bottomley's *Acts of Saint Peter,* E. Martin Browne (the director of both *The Acts of Saint Peter* and *Murder in the Cathedral*) credited Bottomley with making the chorus a modern dramatic technique, flexible and theatrical. However, Browne also relegated the poetic diction of Bottomley's religious drama to an earlier age and praised the choruses in Eliot's *The Rock* and *Murder in the Cathedral* as poetry that "ushers in the new one" (Browne, 20). Reinforcing the image of Bottomley as a transitional figure, Spanos (54) explicated how the vestiges of modern Christian theology assumed theatrical form in modern religious drama in the years between the two world wars. In *Murder in the Cathedral* T. S. Eliot shaped a drama of moral profundity and contemporary relevance through moments of action, both literal and sacramental, played out by characters and chorus preoccupied with point of view: theatrical elements that destroy a sustained sense of literal time through the complex structural juxtaposition of the historical within and against the contemporary.

Bottomley's shorter verse dramas written after 1923 have been ignored by professional theater critics and producers. However, when these shorter works and his one religious drama did appear on stage, Bottomley and his supporters found them satisfying and considered them theatrical exemplars of a new theatrical tradition (*A Stage for Poetry*, 3; Moir). Bottomley called these works "plays for a theatre unborn" and wrote them for those who embraced his artistic vision: supporters of community drama and those lovers of the spoken word— primarily educators, performers, and poets—interested in the revival of verse speaking as a means of literary study, popular entertainment, and cultural renewal. Analysis of these experimental plays as performance texts rather than printed texts is yet to be done, specifically in the area of textual musicality and performance style. These plays were designed for a refined acoustical aesthetic. Can this aesthetic be re-created for modern audiences in a theatrical and meaningful way?

Bottomley's relevance as a significant figure in cultural history is untried. Almost all of Bottomley's plays possess vivid female characters; many of these women resist or negotiate their place in their fictional worlds. Consequently, Bottomley's female characters, if studied from a contemporary feminist perspective, could be placed alongside Shaw's female characters. Such contemporary critical revisitings have yet to occur. In addition, Shields [3] argued the connections between Gullan's festival activities and her innovations in performance pedagogy as an effective means of developing constituencies for educational and social change. Bottomley's festival adjudications and plays supported these innovations in the teaching of literature in the schools and the development of community drama as a middle-class leisure activity. Recent scholarship in the area of Scottish theater history from a cultural perspective (Marshalsay, Scullion) have focused on the connections between the production of various art forms (community drama, a national theater) and the personal and political attitudes toward regional identity and dialect. During the early decades of this century these social and cultural issues became social and cultural tensions when the Scottish BBC was formed, thereby prompting public debate concerning what voice and what programming should be featured. Members of the Scottish National Theatre presented dramas on the Scottish BBC and organized regular tours throughout Scotland in order to encourage the establishment of a unique regional theatrical presence. Theater scholars, by focusing on professional productions rather than academic or amateur theatricals, neglect Bottomley's contributions in these areas. Bottomley's reputation as a minor voice in the theater may be revised if future scholars move beyond the history of the professional stage and focus their critical lens on cultural and aesthetic issues surrounding the production and reception of his plays.

ARCHIVAL SOURCES

The two major collections of Bottomley's unpublished professional and private correspondence are housed at the following: the Harry Ransom Humanities Research Center, the University of Texas, Austin; and the Theatre Collection, University of Glasgow, Scotland.

PRIMARY BIBLIOGRAPHY

Plays

The Acts of Saint Peter: A Cathedral Festival Play. London: Constable, 1933.
The Crier by Night. London: Unicorn, 1902.
Deir dire. Inverness: Northern Chronicle Office, 1944.
Kate Kennedy: A Comedy in Three Acts. London: Constable, 1945.
Laodice and Danae. Boston: Four Seas, 1916.
Maids of Athens. Dublin: Dublin Magazine, 1945.
Midsummer Eve. Harting, Petersfield, Hampshire: Pear Tree Press, 1905.
The Riding to Lithend. Flansham: Pear Tree Press, 1909; Portland: Thomas B. Mosher, 1910.

Anthologies

Choric Plays and a Comedy. London: Constable, 1939.
Gruach and Britain's Daughter: Two Plays. Boston: Small, Maynard, 1921.
King Lear's Wife and Other Plays. Boston: Small, Maynard, 1913.
Lyric Plays. New York: Macmillan, 1932; London: Constable, 1932.
A Parting and The Return. New York: Macmillan, 1928.
Scenes and Plays. New York: Macmillan, 1929; London: Constable, 1929.

Selected Essays and Articles on Drama and Theater

"Choric Speech and the Stage." *Theatre Arts Monthly* 7 (July 1935): 531–34.
"Poetry Seeks a New Home." *Theatre Arts Monthly* 12 (Dec. 1929): 926–29.
A Stage for Poetry. Kendal, England: Titus Wilson & Son, 1948.

SECONDARY BIBLIOGRAPHY

Abbott, Claude Colleer, and Anthony Bertram, eds. *Poet and Painter: Being the Correspondence between Gordon Bottomley and Paul Nash, 1910–1946.* London: Oxford University Press, 1955.
Browne, E. Martin. *The Making of T. S. Eliot's Plays.* London: Cambridge University Press, 1969.
Browne, Henzie. With a chapter on the organization by E. Martin Browne. *Pilgrim Story: The Pilgrim Players, 1939–1943.* London: F. Muller, 1945.
Cramer, Carl. "Gordon Bottomley and Poetic Drama." *Theatre Arts Monthly* 14 (1930): 157–63.
Review of *Culbin Sands. New York Times* (23 Mar. 1935): 10.
Farmer, A. J. "Gordon Bottomley." *Etudes Anglaises* 4 (Oct.–Dec. 1956): 325–27.
Geoghegan, Teresa. Review of *The Acts of Saint Peter. Good Speech* 4 (July–Sept. 1934): 40.
Review of *Gruach. The Times* (21 Jan. 1924): 8.
Kerby, Gertrude. "The Development of Choral Speaking in Great Britain." *Good Speech* 5 (April–June 1935): 5–8.
Review of *King Lear's Wife. The Times* (20 May 1916): 9.
Mahony, Christina Hunt. "Gordon Bottomley." In *Critical Survey of Drama,* 253–61. Englewood Cliffs, NJ: Salem Press, 1985.
Marshalsay, Karen Anne. " 'The Quest for a Truly Representative Scottish Native Drama': The Scottish National Players." *Theatre Research International* 17 (Nov. 1991): 109–16.
Moir, Beryl. Letter to author, 9 Mar. 1982.
Muir, Kenneth [1]. "The Plays of Gordon Bottomley." In *Essays and Studies 1980,* 139–52. Atlantic Highlands, NJ: Humanities Press, 1980.
———. [2]. "Verse and Prose." In *Contemporary Theatre: Stratford-upon-Avon Studies* 4, 97–116. London: Edward Arnold Publishers, 1962.
Nelson, Raymond S. "Gordon Bottomley." In *Dictionary of Literary Biography,* vol. 10, *Modern British Dramatists, 1900–1945,* ed. Stanley Weintraub, pt. 1, 61–66. Detroit: Gale Research, 1982.
Rogers, Timothy, ed. *Georgian Poetry, 1911–1922: The Critical Heritage.* London: Routledge & Kegan Paul, 1977.
Ross, Robert H. *The Georgian Revolt, 1910–1922.* Carbondale: Southern Illinois University Press, 1965.
Scullion, Adrienne. "Scottish Theatre and the Impact of Radio." *Theatre Research International* 17 (Nov. 1991): 117–31.
Shields, Ronald E. [1]. "Like a Choir of Nightingales: The Oxford Recitations, 1923–1930." *Literature in Performance* 3 (Nov. 1982): 15–26.
———. [2]. "Noble Poetry, Nobly Spoken: Marjorie Gullan and the Glasgow Nightingales." *Literature in Performance* 7 (Apr. 1987): 34–45.

————. [3]. "Nurturing a Festival Spirit: The London Speech Festival, 1928–1939." *Text and Performance Quarterly* 14 (1994): 321–29.

Simon, Myron. *The Georgian Poetic.* Berkeley: University of California Press, 1975.

Spanos, William V. *The Christian Tradition in Modern British Verse Drama: The Poetics of Sacramental Time.* New Brunswick, NJ: Rutgers University Press, 1967.

Squire, J. C. "Books in General." *New Statesman* (25 Dec. 1915): 281.

Stone, Kathleen. Letter to author, 26 May 1982.

Thouless, Priscilla. *Modern Poetic Drama.* Oxford: Basil Blackwell, 1934.

James Bridie (Osborne Henry Mavor)
(1888–1951)

COLETTE LINDROTH

James Bridie, the man who was to become a leading figure in twentieth-century Scottish cultural history, grew up in circumstances that seemed entirely unrelated to that artistic destiny. Born Osborne Henry Mavor on 3 January 1888 in Glasgow to Henry A. and Janet Osborne Mavor, he lived the ordinary middle-class childhood of a boy born to hardworking, ambitious parents. From the beginning, however, he experienced a sense of a mixed destiny. As a boy he was dominated by his strong-minded father, who, while reading to him from Carlyle, Emerson, Shakespeare, Ruskin, and other creative, individualistic writers, was also directing him strongly toward medicine, the field to which he himself had aspired but that he could not afford to pursue.

Young Osborne attended schools in Glasgow and in 1904 went to Glasgow University to study medicine. He qualified as a doctor in 1913, at which point he joined the staff of the Glasgow Royal Infirmary. With the beginning of the Great War he joined the Royal Army Medical Corps. He served in France, Mesopotamia, Persia, India, and Turkey, and in 1919, when the war was over, he bought a medical practice in Glasgow and joined the staff of Victoria Infirmary. Here he married Rona Locke Bremmer in 1923, and together they raised a family in Glasgow.

This bare recital of biographical details cannot suggest the real quality of Bridie's life, however. Despite the tranquil surface of his successful medical career and family life, there were clearly other impulses at work. It is evident that from the beginning he was more inclined to the arts than to science; in school he was much better known as the lively, creative illustrator of a student publication than as a scholar. This interest in the arts continued at the university, where he first wrote for and then became editor of the university magazine. He was also busy writing plays for student productions, turning out works with fanciful and suggestive titles like *The Son Who Was Considerate of His Father's Prejudices.* These activities were at least partly responsible for the fact that he took eight rather than the usual four years to complete his medical studies.

Even during the war years he maintained his creative interests, working as a cartoonist and writer for service publications. When he returned to civilian life and his medical duties, he also returned to his stage work, and by 1922 he was well launched in his dramatic career with the production of *The Switchback* by the Birmingham Repertory Theatre.

These conflicts between art and science, between the domestic and the creative life, are reflected in the variety of pseudonyms under which he wrote. His first major effort, *The Sunlight Sonata,* appeared under the name of Mary Henderson, a character in that play. For a time he also wrote under the name of Archibald Kellock, a character he created in *Colonel Wotherspoon.* It was not until Mavor was fifty years old that the two halves of his identity were merged in the form of ''James Bridie,'' the name under which he wrote successfully for the rest of his life. While the pseudonym was obviously a mask behind which part of his creative identity hid, it is also a tribute to his family, since the two names are taken from his maternal and paternal grandfathers. From this point on, the two halves of his divided personality merged into one, that of the dramatist, and he devoted the rest of his life to the stage.

His contribution to the stage was of great significance, not least because he remained insistently loyal to Scotland, Scottish drama, and Scottish intellectual traditions. While his dramas were staged in London and the United States, they all originated in Scotland, and he lived his entire life in Glasgow, where he founded and remained closely connected to the Glasgow Citizens' Theatre. Through this and other organizations Bridie consistently encouraged the development of new talent. His name was also connected to other distinguished Scottish dramatic figures, notably Tyrone Guthrie, who acted in some of his early productions and directed several others, and Alastair Sim, who not only appeared in many of Bridie's plays but was a lifelong friend. Bridie's name is in fact synonymous with Scottish drama in the twentieth century.

His contributions were recognized by many awards, including a C.B.E. in 1946. He died in 1951 at the Edinburgh Royal Infirmary, of a heart condition.

Selected Biographical Sources: Bannister; Cameron; Luyben [3]; Ronald Mavor [2]; Tobin.

MAJOR PLAYS, PREMIERES, AND SIGNIFICANT REVIVALS: THEATRICAL RECEPTION

A Sleeping Clergyman. 1933. First performed at the Malvern Festival 29 June. Opened at the Piccadilly Theatre (London) 19 September 1933. Produced by H. K. Ayliff; 230 performances.

With a plot so complex that Bridie himself joked about it, *A Sleeping Clergyman* is one of his most ambitious plays. Attacking pseudoscience generally and eugenics particularly, the play ranges through several generations of brilliant nonconformists, dealing with alcoholism, illegitimacy, seduction, laws of inheritance, and the difficulty of real scientific discovery as opposed to fads whose popularity eclipses the real. Despite the confusion of theme and action, the play's intensity carries it along, with good winning out in the end: irresponsible people have responsible grandchildren, credit for scientific discoveries is finally given where it is due, and immature people manage to grow up. In the nature-nurture controversy that is the play's focal point, well-intentioned efforts at nurture finally win the day.

Although the play was a popular success, its scattered structure (nine scenes spanning nearly seventy years, with numerous interrelated characters) puzzled some critics and annoyed others. Krutch liked its ideas and its intensity, but found that its diffuse structure destroyed the singleness of effect that was essential to good drama. Most critics, however, found that the play's strong characters and effective theme outweighed its faults.

Storm in a Teacup. (an adaptation of Bruno Frank's *Stürm im Wasserglas,* 1930). 1936. First performed at the Lyceum Theatre (Edinburgh) 20 January. Opened at the Royalty Theatre (London) 5 February 1936. Transferred to the Haymarket Theatre (London) 17 February, and to the Garrick Theatre (London) 25 March 1936. Produced by W. G. Fay; 432 performances.

Another of the plays in which Bridie uses fantastic effects in order to make his characters stand for more than just themselves, *Storm in a Teacup* was one of his most popular efforts. Using the story of a working woman's lost dog (the pet has been taken away from her because she cannot afford a license) as his starting point, he satirizes small-town provincialism, political attitudes both liberal and conservative, sentimentality, and a host of contemporary clichés. The plot is so slight as to be ridiculous, dealing only with the riotous effects of the woman's attempts to get her pet back, but through his manipulation of character Bridie reveals how important apparently foolish situations can be. As one character says, "Oppression is never a very small thing."

One of Bridie's biggest popular successes (it was also made into a film), *Storm in a Teacup* received mixed reviews. The strength of the acting, the liveliness and robust energy of the comedy, and the pointed social satire all won praise, but some critics found the overall effect somewhat confusing and wondered if it was not after all more "storm in a teacup" than substantial theater.

Daphne Laureola. 1949. Opened at Wyndham's Theatre (London) 23 March. Produced by Sir Bronson Albery, presented by Laurence Olivier; 369 performances.

One of the many plays in which Bridie examines male-female relationships and especially the institution of marriage, *Daphne Laureola* is a study of individual characters, of English attitudes, and of the social and moral structure of post–World War II Europe. The play begins and ends in a Soho restaurant with a carefully selected cross-section of characters present: careless young people, shady characters, bored waiters, and Lady Katherine Pitts, a representative of both the aristocracy and an older world. A middle-aged woman, she is looking for something new, and she seems to find it in Ernest, an intensely romantic and idealistic Polish refugee who professes his love for her.

The scene moves to the garden of Sir Joseph, Lady Pitts's elderly husband, and the debate there sets old, safe ways against new, dangerous ones. Sir Joseph, who seems to notice nothing, in fact realizes that his wife wants more than he can give her. He sees that she has planted a laurel tree, the "daphne laureola" of the title, but doubts that it will grow since it was planted so late in the season. This brings to the fore the myth of Daphne, who, in an effort to escape Apollo's amorous advances, was turned into a laurel tree. Both the pain and the possible glory of transformation are suggested in this symbol, with many possible implications both to the individuals and to the social themes of the play.

In the last act much has changed. Sir Joseph has died, but instead of marrying the ardent, poetic Ernest, Lady Pitts has married Vincent, her former servant and a man of very limited vision. Ernest accuses Katherine of callous materialism, but she refuses to be criticized. Instead she accuses Ernest of typically male behavior, of casting her in the image he desires for her rather than seeing what she is really like.

Daphne Laureola was a resounding success, with high praise for the play itself as well as for the outstanding performances of Dame Edith Evans as Katherine Pitts and Peter Finch as Ernest. Critics praised Bridie's poetic style, his symbolic development of ideas, and his ability to create characters who were both recognizably individual and suggestive of the situation of postwar England. As was often the case with Bridie's plays, however, there was also some complaint that the play had failed to resolve some of the intriguing questions it had asked. American critics especially, notably Nathan in the *Nation,* found the play too extravagant in its use of dream and symbol and ultimately silly and annoying.

The Baikie Charivari. 1952. Opened at the Royal Princess's Theatre (Glasgow) 6 October. Produced by Peter Potter; 14 performances.

One of Bridie's most complex, symbolic, and challenging plays, *The Baikie Charivari* is a rich blend of myth, legend, figures from Judeo-Christian history, realistic modern Scotsmen, and Punch-and-Judy extravagance. The ominous figure of The De'il broods over the imaginary Scottish town of Baikie, watching as characters including Sir James MacArthur Pounce-Pellott (whose name is used to recall both Pontius Pilate and Punch), his family, and a collection of locals including a constable, a social scientist, and other symbolically suggestive characters try to decide how to arrange their lives. Their symbolic relevance is clear; Pounce-Pellott, for example, is an administrator who returned from India when that country gained its independence. Clearly the play means to be taken not just as a presentation of individuals, but as a reflection on the state of the British Empire after World War II.

Characters blend into one another; prophets both ancient and modern proclaim their message; several characters attack each other with Punch-and-Judy violence as the question of individual responsibility in the modern world is thrashed out. The ending is fairly happy: The De'il has been balked at least for the moment, Pounce-Pellott has slain The De'il's Seven Prophets, and order has to some extent been restored. Questions remain, however, especially since Pontius Pilate, who only jested with Truth, is an ambiguous model for Bridie's lead character. Even if he has been victorious, one must wonder how long the victory will last, both for the individual and for England.

While *The Baikie Charivari* has been called Bridie's best play by later scholars, its initial critical and popular response was lukewarm. Reviewers seemed puzzled and annoyed by the play's complexity and bewildering shifts of time and place, and its varied symbolism seemed to many to defeat its purpose. Most critics praised the lively realism of the play, however, especially Bridie's ability to move from modern English to Scots dialect and from prose to poetry and song with such speed and effectiveness. Elliot was one of the first critics to praise the play wholeheartedly in his preface to the published version. He found it one of Bridie's finest accomplishments, a profound investigation of humanity and its relationship to good and evil that is "a standing challenge to the stage," the "Peer Gynt of Scotland."

ADDITIONAL PLAYS, ADAPTATIONS, AND PRODUCTIONS

The Anatomist was first performed at the Lyceum Theatre (Edinburgh) 6 July 1930. It opened at the Westminster Theatre (London) 7 October 1931 and was produced by Tyrone Guthrie; 127 performances. Based on the sensational nineteenth-century murder/grave-robbing duo of Burke and Hare, *The Anatomist* is an investigation of an egocentric character, Dr. Knox, who can make others, especially his young assistant, Walter Anderson, do his bidding. Knox is a character type Bridie was to explore throughout his career, part demon, part prophet. Knox's needs begin innocently enough—a dedicated doctor, he needs cadavers to work on—but they progress to the corruption of others who first rob graves and then commit murder to supply his demands. While the material of the play is exaggerated and melodramatic, including the use of a rhinoceros as a symbol of egotism, the play is also a serious study in good and evil and especially the question of whether good can sometimes come from evil. Body snatching is obviously evil, yet Knox uses this practice to further scientific knowledge to help humanity. Is he justified? Bridie poses the question to the audience without giving a clear cut answer.

As was often the case, the critical response to the play was mixed. It was a popular success and was generally favorably reviewed, but critics were puzzled at the ambiguity of the ending, the lack of definitive answers about the nature of good and evil. Many critics debated the question of whether it was right to pose such moral problems without answering on the side of right, but all were intrigued by Bridie's investigation and by his vivid presentation, which held the audience's interest to the end.

Tobias and the Angel was first performed at the Cambridge Festival 20 November 1930. It opened at the Westminster Theatre (London) 9 March 1932. It was produced by Evan Johnson; 86 performances; and is frequently revived. One of several plays Bridie based on biblical material, *Tobias and the Angel* is based on the Book of Tobit in the Apocrypha. Bridie develops the material considerably beyond his original, however, turning it into a complex, often-hilarious tale of suffering and redemption with obvious relevance to audiences painfully aware of the economic depression of the 1930s. Tobit and his family suffer blindness, illness, hunger, and poverty as they strive to accept their fates, often handed to them by mysterious beings who are in fact angels. Bridie's talent for comic overstatement and uproarious situations is developed to the fullest as the humans and angels interact with comic misunderstandings and mistaken identity. The play ends happily: the poor are made rich, the blind see, and human beings manage to understand their relationship with the divine more clearly than they had done before.

One of Bridie's most popular and often-revived plays, *Tobias and the Angel* won both popular success and critical praise when it opened. The performance of Tyrone Guthrie as the angel Raphael was especially singled out, as were the wit and liveliness of the play. Bridie's ability to make Old Testament characters speak lively, colloquial language was especially praised, along with the effectiveness of his characterization of both human beings and angels.

Dr. Angelus was first performed at the Lyceum Theatre (Edinburgh) 23 June 1947. It opened at the Phoenix Theatre (London) 30 July 1947 and was produced by Hendrik Baker; 195 performances. Based on a real murder case in nineteenth-century Glasgow, *Dr. Angelus* deals with questions of loyalty, idealism, and the allure of the charismatic leader, ideas that intrigued Bridie throughout his creative life. The title character, a strong-minded, unconventional man, manages to inveigle his idealistic young assistant, Dr. Johnson, into signing highly questionable death certificates for the deaths of Dr. Angelus's wife and mother-in-law. Johnson, high-minded but weak, cannot resist Angelus's brilliant rhetoric even as he becomes convinced that Angelus has in fact killed both women and has gotten a hapless servant girl pregnant.

In a complex blending of dream and realism, the resolution is reached: Angelus will be arrested, and justice is seen to be done, but it is almost an accident. The questions of good or evil, angelic or devilish behavior, remain tantalizingly unanswered.

The play received favorable reviews and an enthusiastic popular response, winning praise for its portrayal of Scottish eccentricities, its farcical extravagance, and its ability to be both chilling and amusing in its investigation of moral and legal issues. Stokes mentioned the play's ambiguity, pointing out that it was difficult to decide what to make of Bridie's villain, but added that this was presumably Bridie's intention. While some critics complained that the ending left too many moral questions unresolved (a charge several of Bridie's plays received), the general reception was strongly favorable, especially for the blend of realistic and symbolic elements.

ASSESSMENT OF BRIDIE'S CAREER

Throughout his life Bridie was a controversial figure, gaining both extravagant praise and stinging criticism, often for the same dramas. As several of his most perceptive critics have pointed out, his mixed reception was to some extent the result of the face (or faces) he presented to the world. As his fondness for pseudonyms suggests, Bridie's ideas were often hidden behind a series of disguises, and sometimes these disguises fooled the public and the reviewers. Part of the image Bridie projected was that of the jokester or dilettante, the part-time playwright, full-time doctor who tossed plays off in a single draft. His gift for caricature and buffoonery helped support this image, as did his own tendency to speak slightingly of work that he in fact took seriously. An example of this is his description of comedy as "part and parcel of a binge" and farce as "an hour or two filled with anything that comes into the heads of the author or the actors," as he wrote in *Tedious and Brief.* This pose of clownlike lack of seriousness was bolstered by his gift for delightful comic dialogue. When The De'il speaks in broad Scots dialect and Old Testament characters sound like City insurance salesmen or financiers, it is easy to think that uncomplicated laughter is the playwright's main intention.

Added to this is Bridie's consistent refusal to make final choices for his viewers, to come to final conclusions. This refusal often made his plays look, on first or superficial glance, muddled or inconclusive, shying away from answers to questions that the plays themselves raised. Nothing could be farther from the complex nature of Bridie's thought, however, as critics who have penetrated beyond his disguises have discovered.

Part of the reason Bridie was often misunderstood was a failure to appreciate the techniques with which he unified theme and structure. He was most severely attacked on the grounds of craftsmanship. Nathan articulated this point of view in his scathing review of *Daphne Laureola:* "There is about most of his work an unmeditated air and slapdash preparation that give it the sense of a first draft. . . . Shreds of the fantastic and whimsical mix awkwardly with patches of conventional polite comedy and the pseudo-philosophical." This was an attitude often expressed by his reviewers. Other critics, however, realized that this mixture of unresolved opposites is, along with his refusal to come to conclusions, what makes Bridie's dramatic work so distinctive. As Luyben [3] points out, "Inconclusiveness, or ambiguity, is inherent in [his work] because the plays are arguments in which the balance of thesis and antithesis is maintained. . . . They are arguments about, or searches for, truth, and about truth there is no finality" (17).

Other critics, notably Tobin, have expanded on this idea, pointing out that the Scottish intellectual tradition is especially fond of this kind of intellectual activity in which the process itself, rather than any kind of oversimplified conclusion, is the point of the activity. Bridie, far from being timid or inconclusive, is simply being true to his Scottish inheritance in this respect. Under his comic disguises he is a serious writer of modern morality plays that investigate questions of good and evil, order and chaos in the modern world. The questions he raises are unresolved in his plays because they are unresolvable in human existence.

If his structural peculiarities and his ability to dramatize his ideas were strongly debated, however, other talents were praised from the start. Above all he has been praised for his comic abilities and especially for the overwhelmingly eloquent language through which he made his comic points. His lively, fast-moving, convincing dialogue placed him in the forefront of twentieth-century English drama. Many critics have compared him favorably with Henrik Ibsen, J. M. Barrie, and George Bernard Shaw. Lumley, for example, credited Bridie with rescuing "English theatre when there was no one left after Shaw who could write the polished and witty conversation pieces which English audiences had grown to admire and demand" (10).

Also much mentioned is his use of symbol. While most critics praised his ability to make characters in *Daphne Laureola* and *The Baikie Charivari,* for example, function successfully as symbols of postwar English society, other plays fared less well. The fact that the title figure in *A Sleeping Clergyman* was meant to symbolize an inattentive God seems to have been missed by most of the play's reviewers, and others found the symbol in *Mr. Bolfry* or *Jonah and the Whale* to be heavy-handed. For the most part, however, Bridie's use of symbol has been admired and praised.

The value of his contributions to Scottish drama has never been questioned. As dramatist and founder of the Glasgow Citizens' Theatre, and as a man who spent his life working to promote distinctively Scottish theater, his significance is unparalleled in the twentieth century. For this if for nothing else Bridie is assured a major position in modern dramatic history.

For the most part Bridie's name was, during his lifetime, linked with thoughtful, witty, entertaining plays that managed to be both profound and comic at once, and that featured some of the most famous actors of his era. Recently his reputation has dwindled, however, so much so that Dibb entitled a 1970 article on him "Some Neglected Dramatists." Dibb argued cogently that Bridie is due for revival and rediscovery. Citing Bridie's challenging intellectual debate and his provocative and incisive dialogue "written in shapely, colourful and often poetic English," Dibb challenged the British dramatic community to realize what an undiscovered gem it had in Bridie's work. It is a challenge that still stands.

ARCHIVAL SOURCES

Bridie's papers and manuscripts can be found in the Mitchell Library of Glasgow; the University of Glasgow Library; the National Library of Scotland in Edinburgh; and the Newberry Library in Chicago. Some typescripts and promptbooks can be found in the Theatre Collection of the New York Public Library.

PRIMARY BIBLIOGRAPHY

Plays and Anthologies

The Amazed Evangelist. London: Constable, 1931.
The Anatomist. London: Constable, 1932.
The Anatomist and Other Plays. (*The Anatomist, Tobias and the Angel,* and *The Amazed Evangelist.*) London: Constable, 1931.
Babes in the Wood: A Quiet Farce. London: Constable, 1938.
The Baikie Charivari, or, The Seven Prophets: A Miracle Play. London: Constable, 1953.
The Black Eye: A Comedy. London: Constable, 1935.
Colonel Wotherspoon and Other Plays. (*Colonel Wotherspoon, What It Is to Be Young, The Dancing Bear,* and *The Girl Who Did Not Want to Go to Kuala Lumpur.*) London: Constable, 1934.
Daphne Laureola. London: Constable, 1949.
Dr. Angelus. London: Constable, 1950.
It Depends What You Mean: An Improvisation for the Glockenspiel. London: Constable, 1948.
John Knox and Other Plays. (*John Knox, It Depends What You Mean, Dr. Angelus,* and *The Forrigan Reel.*) London: Constable, 1949.
Jonah and the Whale. London: Constable, 1932.
The King of Nowhere and Other Plays. (*The King of Nowhere, Babes in the Wood,* and *The Last Trump.*) London: Constable, 1938.
The Last Trump. London: Constable, 1938.
Marriage Is No Joke: A Melodrama. London: Constable, 1934.
Mary Read. Written with Claud Gurney. London: Constable, 1935.
Meeting at Night. Introduction by J. B. Priestley. London: Constable, 1956.
Moral Plays. (*Marriage Is No Joke, Mary Read,* and *The Black Eye.*) London: Constable, 1936.
Mr. Gillie. London: Constable, 1950.
Mr. Waterbury's Millennium. London: Samuel French, 1935.
One Way of Living. London: Constable, 1939.
Paradise Enow. In *One-Act Plays for the Amateur Theatre,* ed. M. H. Fuller. London: George Harrap, 1949.
Plays for Plain People. (*Mr. Bolfry, Lancelot, Holy Isle, Jonah 3, The Sign of the Prophet Jonah,* and *The Dragon and the Dove.*) London: Constable, 1944.
The Queen's Comedy: A Homeric Fragment. London: Constable, 1950.
Roger—Not So Jolly. With Ronald Mavor. London: Samuel French, 1937.

A Sleeping Clergyman. London: Constable, 1933.
A Sleeping Clergyman and Other Plays. (*A Sleeping Clergyman, The Anatomist, Tobias and the Angel, The Amazed Evangelist,* and *Jonah and the Whale.*) London: Constable, 1934.
Some Talk of Alexander. London: Methuen, 1926.
Storm in a Teacup: An Anglo-Scottish Version. London: Constable, 1936.
Susannah and the Elders and Other Plays. (*What Say They, Susannah and the Elders, The Golden Legend of Shults,* and *The Kitchen Comedy.*) London: Constable, 1940.
The Switchback. London: Constable, 1931.
The Switchback, The Pardoner's Tale, The Sunlight Sonata. London: Constable, 1930.
Tobias and the Angel. London: Constable, 1931.
The Tragic Muse. In *Scottish One-Act Plays,* ed. John MacNair Reid. Edinburgh: Porpoise Press, 1935.
What Say They? London: Constable, 1939.

Essays and Articles on Drama and Theater

"The Actor and the Cinema." *London Mercury* (Apr. 1936): 619–20.
The British Drama. British Way Pamphlet Series, no. 12. Glasgow: Craig & Wilson, 1945.
"Dramaturgy in Scotland." *Proceedings of the Royal Philosophical Society of Glasgow* 74 (1949).
"Equilibrium." *London Mercury* (Apr. 1939): 585–89.
"Foreword." In *Alfred Wareing: A Biography.* Winifred Isaac. London: Green Bank Press, 1951.
"Foreword." In *North Light: Ten New One-Act Plays from the North.* Ed. Winifred Bannister. Glasgow: William MacLellan, 1947.
"Foreword." In *The Story of Glasgow Citizens' Theatre 1943–48,* ed. Jack Gourlay and R. C. Saunders. Glasgow: Stage & Screen Press, 1948.
Mr. Bridie's Alphabet for Little Glasgow Highbrows. London: Constable, 1934.
"Plays of Ideas." *New Statesman and Nation* (11 Mar. 1950): 270.
"Preface." In *Classic Crimes: A Selection from the Works of William Roughead.* London: Cassell, 1951.
"Shaw as Playwright." *New Statesman and Nation* (11 Nov. 1950): 422.
A Small Stir: Letters on the English. With Moray McLaren. London: Hollis & Carter, 1949.
Tedious and Brief. London: Constable, 1944.
"Three Score and Ten." *Spectator* (1 Dec. 1944).

SECONDARY BIBLIOGRAPHY

Bannister, Winifred. *James Bridie and His Theatre.* London: Rockliff, 1955.
Bentley, Eric. *In Search of Theater,* 42–43. New York: Alfred A. Knopf, 1953.
Brown, Ivor. [1]. "Biblical (*Tobias and the Angel*)." In *Specimens of English Dramatic Criticism, XVII–XX Centuries,* ed. A. C. Ward. London: Oxford University Press, 1945.

————. [2]. "Bridie: Review of His Five Plays." *New Statesman and Nation* (5 May 1934): 674.

Cameron, Alasdair. "Bridie: The Scottish Playwright." *Chapman* (Spring 1989): 124–32.

Crawford, Iain. "Auld Nick and Mr. Bridie." *Theatre Arts* (July 1950): 25.

Dibb, Frank W. "Some Neglected Dramatists." *Amateur Stage* (July 1970): 13–15.

Elliot, Walter. "Bridie's Last Play." In *The Baikie Charivari; or, The Seven Prophets: A Miracle Play,* by James Bridie. London: Constable, 1953.

Gerber, Ursula. *James Bridies Dramen.* Bern: Francke Verlag, 1961.

Greene, Anne. "Bridie's Concept of the Master Experimenter." *Studies in Scottish Literature* (Oct. 1964): 96–110.

Kerr, Walter. "The Theater." *Commonweal* (6 Oct. 1950): 630.

Krutch, Joseph Wood. "A Fig from Thistles." *Nation* (24 Oct. 1934): 486–87.

Linklater, Eric. *The Art of Adventure,* 25–43. London: Macmillan, 1948.

Low, John Thomas. *Doctors, Devils, Saints, and Sinners: A Critical Study of the Major Plays of James Bridie.* Edinburgh: Ramsay Head Press, 1980.

Lumley, Frederick. "The State of the Drama." In *Trends in 20th Century Drama: A Survey since Ibsen and Shaw.* London: Rockliff, 1956.

Luyben, Helen. [1]. "Bridie's Last Play." *Modern Drama* (Feb. 1963): 400–14.

————. [2]. "James Bridie and the Prodigal Son Story." *Modern Drama* (May 1964): 35–45.

————. [3]. *James Bridie, Clown and Philosopher.* Philadelphia: University of Pennsylvania Press, 1965.

Mardon, Ernest G. *The Conflict between the Individual and Society in the Plays of James Bridie.* Glasgow: William MacLellan, 1972.

Marshall, Margaret. "Drama." *Nation* (30 Sept. 1950): 295.

Mavor, Ronald. [1]. "Bridie Revisited." *Chapman* (Spring 1989): 146–51.

————. [2]. *Dr. Mavor and Mr. Bridie: Memories of James Bridie.* Edinburgh: Canongate and the National Library of Scotland, 1988.

Michie, James A. "Educating the Prophets." *Modern Drama* (Feb. 1969): 429–31.

Nathan, George Jean. Review of *Daphne Laureola.* In *The Theatre Book of the Year, 1950–1951,* 31–32. New York: Alfred A. Knopf, 1951.

Paterson, Tony. "James Bridie: Playwright as Impresario?" *Chapman* (Spring 1989): 139–45.

Stokes, Sewell. "The English Spotlight." *Theatre Arts* (Nov. 1947): 47.

Tobin, Terence. *James Bridie (Osborne Henry Mavor).* Boston: Twayne, 1980.

Walter, Marie. "The Grateful Dead: An Old Tale Newly Told." *Southern Folklore Quarterly* (Dec. 1959): 190–95.

Weales, Gerald. *Religion in Modern English Drama,* 51–90. Philadelphia: University of Pennsylvania Press, 1961.

Williamson, Audrey. "The Thistle and the Leek." In *Theatre of Two Decades.* London: Rockliff, 1951.

Wittig, Kurt. "Scottish Drama." In *The Scottish Tradition in Literature,* 318–22. Edinburgh: Oliver & Boyd, 1958.

Wright, Allen. "Kelvinside, Kirriemuir, and the Kailyard." *Chapman* (Spring 1989): 134–37.

Harold Brighouse
(1882–1958)

LIBBY SMIGEL

Harold Brighouse achieved international notice as a dramatist in 1915 with his play *Hobson's Choice,* which has overshadowed the other work of his long and successful career. He was born 26 July 1882 in Eccles, Lancashire, to John Southworth Brighouse, a cotton spinner, and his second wife (née Harrison). A scholarship permitted him to attend the Manchester Grammar School, but at age seventeen he quit school to become an assistant buyer in a mercantile firm. In 1902 he moved to London with the firm's buyer when a small office was opened there. When the firm failed, Brighouse returned to Lancashire, married his local fiancée, and lived at Withington, Cheshire.

Brighouse's first dramatic effort was rejected by Johnston Forbes-Robertson, who advised him to start with one-act pieces and to write what he knew. Thus in 1908 he wrote *Lonesome-like,* a one-act play about a Lancashire woman whose poverty and age demand that she move to a workhouse. Offered to a number of London theater managers first, it premiered in Glasgow in 1911.

Brighouse abandoned the cotton business in 1909 when Annie Horniman's newly organized Manchester theater company at the Gaiety Theatre (with producer Ben Iden Payne) encouraged fledgling local playwrights to submit their work. Of the three one-act plays he offered for the opening season, *The Doorway* was selected. The following year his first full-length play, *Dealing in Futures,* successfully opened the 1910 Gaiety season.

When the Liverpool Repertory Theatre established itself in the Liverpool Playhouse in 1910, Brighouse became its most produced playwright. This early association was revitalized in 1922, when William Armstrong replaced Nigel Playfair as producer and solicited new plays from Brighouse, notably *Mary's John* (1924), *What's Bred in the Bone* (1927), *It's a Gamble* (1928), and *British Passport* (1939).

To honor his friend and colleague, Stanley Houghton, who died in 1913, Brighouse assembled a three-volume edition of selected works by Houghton for which he wrote a biographical introduction. Their collaborative play, *The Hillarys,* was produced in London in 1915. Brighouse continued to write plays during World War I while serving in London on the intelligence staff of the Royal Air Force. For the 1914 theater season he provided the Gaiety Theatre (Manchester) with *Garside's Career,* acclaimed by some critics as his best play. During this period he also wrote *Hobson's Choice,* which would become known as his masterpiece. But with the English theater scene scuttled by the war, Brighouse offered the play to his old friend from the early Gaiety years, Iden Payne, who was employed in theater in the United States. Payne arranged financing by the Shubert consortium and directed the play at the Princess Theatre in New York City in 1915, after trial runs in Poughkeepsie, New York, and Atlantic City, New Jersey. The play received its London premiere the following year.

After the war Brighouse settled in London, though he traveled to North America in 1925, 1929, and 1936. His visits abroad yielded many friends as well as the opportunity of contributing a column on London theater to the New York *Drama Magazine* in the early 1930s. In addition to his contributions to the *Manchester Guardian,* Brighouse wrote several novels, short stories, and full-length dramas. But he turned his attention primarily to crafting one-act plays for a number of purposes and venues. He experimented with open-air dramas, which he published in two collections, and, with John Walton, authored one-act plays and a volume of four "costume plays" under the pseudonym of Olive Conway. Many of his plays appealed to the amateur drama societies that flourished during this period. Brighouse continued to contribute articles to the *Manchester Guardian* until 1949. He died suddenly in London on 25 July 1958.

Selected Biographical Sources: Brighouse, *What I Have Had;* Pogson; Tyson.

MAJOR PLAYS, PREMIERES, AND SIGNIFICANT REVIVALS: THEATRICAL RECEPTION

The Doorway. 1909. (one act). Opened 10 April at the Gaiety Theatre (Manchester). Produced by B. Iden Payne for Miss Horniman's Theatre Company. Revivals: Horniman Company, Coronet Theatre (London), for 2 performances, June 1909; Horniman Company, Gaiety (Manchester), for 1 benefit performance for Hebrew Bread, Meat & Coal Fund, 6 December 1909; Horniman Company, Gaiety (Manchester), for 1 performance, 22 May 1911.

Brighouse's first professionally produced play concerned two tramps sharing a doorway on a cold night.

Dealing in Futures. 1909. Opened 7 October at the Glasgow Repertory Theatre (Scotland). Revival: Miss Horniman's Company, the Gaiety Theatre (Manchester), on a double bill with Basil Dean's *Effie,* August 1910, and on a double bill with Stanley Houghton's *Master of the House,* November 1910; Liverpool Repertory Theatre, 1911–12 season. Television adaptation titled *Vitriol* by Gerald Savory for Granada TV, 1960.

The critical response to this industrial comedy characterized the two reactions that Brighouse's drama regularly generated: that his skillful writing was sincere, but the effect was didactic more than dramatic (Pogson, 92–93). The play has been compared to Galsworthy's *Strife* (Rowell and Jackson, 44), but Manchester colleague Stanley Houghton described *Strife* as concentrating on the social problem, while *Dealing in Futures* focused on the people (Brighouse, *What I Have Had*).

The Price of Coal. 1909. (one act). Opened 15 November at the Royalty Theatre (Glasgow). Produced by the Glasgow Repertory Theatre. Directed by Alfred Wareing. Revivals: Playhouse (London), 1 matinee performance, 28 November 1911; Court Theatre (London), performed by the Arts League of Service Travelling Theatrical Dramatic Company, June 1923.

A Glasgow journalist assisted Brighouse in translating the Lancashire dialect of his original script into Lanarkshire for the Scottish premiere. In London Cyril Maude paired it with J. J. Bell's full-length play *Oh! Christina,* but the *Illustrated London News* ("A Scottish Programme at the Playhouse") said that the curtain raiser was of "higher artistic quality." *The Times* critic ("The Playhouse") called it "a clever and convincing little picture of life in a mining town." For an ensuing tour, Maude paired Brighouse's piece with the popular *Bunty Pulls the Strings.* Rowell and Jackson (44), characterized the play as a study in Lancashire stoicism.

The Polygon. 1911. Opened 5 February at the Court Theatre (London), performed by the Play Actors. Revivals: Miss Horniman's Company, Gaiety Theatre (Manchester), September 1911; Court Theatre (London), 1 performance, 2 May 1911. License from Lord Chamberlain for Lyceum Theatre (London) performance, 30 October 1911, as *Graft;* no evidence that this performance took place. Television adaptation titled *Fiddlers Four* by Gerald Savory for Granada TV, 1960.

The critics agreed that didacticism dominated drama in this play about housing problems (see Pogson, 136).

Lonesome-like. 1911. (one act). Opened 6 February at the Royalty Theatre (Glasgow). Revivals: Miss Horniman's Company at the Coronet Theatre (London), May 1911, and at the Gaiety Theatre (Manchester), August 1911 (Summer Company) and September 1911; Liverpool Repertory Theatre, 1912–13, 1922–23, and 1926–27 seasons. U.S. film with Mary Merrall as Sarah Omerod.

This one-act is regarded as a small gem by critics and producers alike: it stayed active among repertory and amateur groups, so that its peak year was recorded as 1947. Rowell and Jackson (44) characterized the play as a study in Lancashire sentiment.

Spring in Bloomsbury. 1911. (one act). Opened 3 April at the Gaiety Theatre (Manchester). Produced by B. Iden Payne.

Brighouse (*What I Have Had,* 53) admitted that audience and actors disliked the play, but the company producer gave it another performance, nonetheless.

The Oak Settle. 1911. (one act). Opened 7 April at the Theatre Royal (Dalston). Revivals: Liverpool Repertory Theatre, Playhouse, January 1912.

This tightly constructed comedy of a rural couple who pass off old furniture as antiques to unsuspecting tourists was widely imitated in other English and American plays (*What I Have Had,* 97).

The Odd Man Out. 1912. Opened 16 April at the Royalty Theatre (London) for 6 matinee performances through May 3. Directed by Frank Vernon. Revivals: Boston and South Africa during World War I. A professional London evening production was in rehearsal during World War I, but never opened.

Dennis Eadie's comic rendering of the runaway husband received accolades from the *Illustrated London News* ('' 'The Odd Man Out,' at the Royalty''), although the first and third acts were labeled as structurally weak. *The Times* (''Royalty Theatre'') thought that the comedy degenerated for a few moments into clumsy farce in a ''shapeless third act.'' Where *The Times* reveled in the trouncing of the sanctimonious husband, Palmer criticized the dramatic practice of setting up foolish characters as Christians just for the sport of knocking them down.

Garside's Career. 1914. Opened 2 February at the Gaiety Theatre (Manchester). Performed by Miss Horniman's Company. Revivals: Miss Horniman's Company, Gaiety (Manchester), April 1914, and the Coronet Theatre (London) for 1 week, May 1914.

The plot of a wife's intervention when upper-class living tempts a working-class Parliamentarian was inspired by the political career of Victor Grayson (Brighouse, *What I Have Had,* 57). Rowell and Jackson (44) considered the play inferior to J. M. Barrie's *What Every Woman Knows,* though Pogson (169–70) believed that it was Brighouse's best effort to date because of better character development.

The Northerners. 1914. Opened 27 August at the Gaiety Theatre (Manchester). Produced by B. Iden Payne. Revival: Octagon Theatre (Bolton), 1979.

Brighouse's dramatization of the 1820 riots of the cotton laborers has been compared favorably to Hauptmann's *The Weavers* (Pogson, 183). Brighouse attributed the indifferent audience response to its correspondence to the retreat from Mons. However, in the revival, Shorter [2] found the man-versus-machine plot of the play to be tractish and melodramatic, though he said that the theme had contemporary parallels.

The Road to Raebury. 1915. Opened 12 April at the Prince's Theatre (Manchester). Revival: Criterion Theatre (London) for 11 performances (with afterpiece *The Devil among the Skins*), June 1915. Produced by Milton Rosmer.

The London production received contradictory reviews. The *Illustrated London News* ('' 'The Road to Raebury,' at the Criterion'') lauded the "bright talk and ingenious turns" that Brighouse used to transform an otherwise "hackneyed formula" into a diverting comedy. *The Times* reviewer ('' 'The Road to Raebury' '') said that the cast's fine performance "only makes the unreality of their actions and speeches the more incongruous."

Hobson's Choice. 1915. Opened 16 October in Poughkeepsie, (New York), then moved to the Princess Theatre (New York) on 23 November 1915. Transferred to Boston and Chicago. Simultaneous tours in North America. Revivals: Opened at the Apollo Theatre (London), 22 June 1916, with Horniman company actress Edyth Goodall as Maggie, Joe Nightingale (a pantomimist) as Mossop, and Norman McKinnel as Hobson. Produced by McKinnel. C. V. France replaced McKinnel during the run. Transferred to the Prince of Wales's Theatre, November 1916. Played daily matinees and Wednesday and Saturday nights for 246 wartime performances. Other revivals: Liverpool Repertory Theatre for a seven-week run, produced by William Armstrong, 1922, and also 1923–24 and 1925–26, with Herbert Lomas (for whom the role was originally written) as Mossop and James Harcourt as Hobson. Birmingham Repertory Company, 1950 and 1960. Blackpool Repertory, for fifteen weeks, 1951. Arts Theatre (London), June 1952. Yvonne Arnaud Theatre (Guildford), 1975.

The rebellion of a daughter against her domineering father reflected aspects of Arnold Bennett's and Stanley Houghton's work, yet showed an original version of the "rawness" of northern middle-class life with "legitimate comedy," according to the *Illustrated London News* ('' 'Hobson's Choice,' at the Apollo''). *The Times* ('' 'Hobson's Choice' '') compared the assertive Maggie to Bunty of *Bunty Pulls the Strings*. Shorter [1] criticized the 1975 Guildford revival in which Leslie Sands as Hobson failed to maintain a "natural dignity, to avoid becoming a mere ass."

The Clock Goes Round. 1916. Opened 25 September at Devonshire Park, Eastbourne. Revivals: Globe Theatre (London) for 13 performances, October 1916.

The *Illustrated London News* ('' 'The Clock Goes Round,' at the Globe'') charged Brighouse with abandoning artistic responsibility by rushing this play into production to capitalize on the success of *Hobson's Choice* (although the play had been written two years earlier). The reviewer added that the juxtaposition of realism and fantasy frequently struck a false note.

Zack. 1916. Opened 30 October, in Syracuse Theatre (New York). Revivals: Comedy Theatre (London), for 1 performance by the Repertory Players, April 1922, produced by Tristan Rawson and Harold Brighouse. Liverpool Playhouse,

1923–24, produced by William Armstrong. BBC version, 1950. Royal Exchange Company (Manchester), 1977.

The *Times* ("'Zack'") found Zack too passive a character to elicit sympathy and make this comedy of northern manners a success. Shorter [3] noted that the play's criticism of class distinctions was evoked through a subtle combination of sadness and laughter in the 1977 revival. Mayer, however, felt that Brighouse's plot line of bliss achieved by exchanging one tyrant for another was "questionable psychology."

Other Times. 1920. Opened 6 April at the Little Theatre (London) for 14 performances. Silent film titled *Children of Jazz,* directed by Jesse L. Lasky, 1923.

The *Times* ("'Other Times'") criticized the inaccurate allusions to period costumes and dialogue, though it noted that the play was a hit. The *Illustrated London News* ("'Other Times,' at the Little") objected to the pillorying of modern English youth by such a "graceless and offensive" portrayal.

ADDITIONAL PLAYS, ADAPTATIONS, AND PRODUCTIONS

The Scaring Off of Teddy Dawson (one act) opened 7 April 1911 at the Theatre Royal (Dalston). *Little Red Shoes* (one act) opened 20 May 1912 at the Prince of Wales's Theatre (London) for 88 performances. *The Game* opened 19 November 1913 at the Liverpool Repertory Theatre, Playhouse. It was revived at the King's Theatre (Hammersmith) in August 1921 and was made into a silent film titled *The Winning Goal* directed by George B. Samuelson, 1920. *Followers* (one act) opened 19 April 1915 at the Prince's Theatre (Manchester). It was revived at the Criterion Theatre (London), on a double bill with Houghton and Brighouse's *The Hillarys,* for 18 performances, June 1915, produced by Milton Rosmer. *The Hillarys* (with Stanley Houghton) opened 30 April 1915 at Kelly's Theatre (Liverpool). It was revived at the Criterion Theatre (London) for 18 performances, June 1915, produced by Milton Rosmer. *Converts* (one act) opened 23 August 1915 at the Gaiety Theatre (Manchester). It was revived by Miss Horniman's Company at the Duke of York's Theatre (London), on a double bill with *Hindle Wakes,* for 33 performances, September 1915.

The Maid of France (one act) opened 16 July 1917 at the Metropolitan Theatre (New York). It was revived at the Coliseum (London), 1918, produced by Normah Page and designed by Charles Ricketts, and at the Greenwich Theatre (New York), April 1918. It toured U.S. vaudeville through 1919. *Jack o'Lantern* opened 16 October 1917 at the Globe Theatre (New York). *The Bantam V.C.* opened 16 July 1919 at the St. Martin's Theatre (London) for 11 performances. *Once a Hero* opened 26 June 1922 at Ambassadors Theatre (Southend) and was revived at the Playhouse (Liverpool) in 1923. *A Marrying Man* (one act) opened 28 January 1924 at the Liverpool Playhouse, produced by William Armstrong. *Mary's John* opened 30 September 1924 at the Liverpool Playhouse, produced by William Armstrong, and was revived at the Royal Academy of Dramatic Arts

(London), October 1927. *The Happy Hangman* (one act) opened 15 June 1925 at the Court Theatre (London) for 1 matinee performance. Nicoll (530) recorded a Lord Chamberlain's license for Cripplegate Institute for 1 November 1922, but there seems to be no record of this performance.

What's Bred in the Bone opened 4 April 1927 at the Liverpool Playhouse, produced by William Armstrong. This comedy of north-country manners was a commercial success for the Liverpool company (Goldie, 154). *It's a Gamble* opened 27 November 1928 at the Liverpool Playhouse, produced by William Armstrong, and it was revived at the Northampton Repertory Theatre, March 1930. It was directed by Herbert Prentice and designed by Osborne Robinson. *Safe amongst the Pigs* opened 27 April 1929 at the Birmingham Repertory Theatre. This comedy played on hatred of airplanes, and though it was not one of Brighouse's best pieces, it was a "stageworthy essay in character drawing" whose humor appealed to the theatergoing public (Kemp, 27). *British Passport*, opened 1939 at the Liverpool Playhouse, produced by William Armstrong.

Four plays (*The Man about the Place, Maypole Morning, The Paris Doctor,* and *The Prince Who Was a Piper*) were granted licenses from the Lord Chamberlain for performances at Cripplegate Institute on 1 November 1922 (Nicoll, 530), but it is not known whether these took place. Other plays, many published for use by the amateur acting clubs and societies, have no record of professional production: *The Apple Tree; or, Why Misery Never Dies,* published in 1923; *How the Weather Is Made,* 1926; *The Little Liberty, The Night of "Mr. H.,"* and *Fossie for Short* (adapted from Brighouse's 1917 novel), 1927; *Behind the Throne, The Sort-of-a-Prince,* and *Coincidence,* 1929; *The Stoker,* 1930; *A Bit of War, Smoke-screens, The Wish-Shop,* and *The Witch's Daughter,* 1932; *The Romany Road,* 1933; *Exhibit C,* 1934; *Back to Adam, The Boy: What Will He Become?,* and *The Friendly King,* 1935; *Below Ground,* 1936; *New Leisure* and *Passport to Romance,* 1937; *Albert Gates, The Funk-Hole,* and *Under the Pylon,* 1938; *Air-Raid Refugees,* 1939; *The Man Who Ignored the War,* 1940; *The Golden Ray* and *London Front,* 1941; *Sporting Rights,* 1943; *Hallowed Ground, The Inner Man,* and *Let's Live in England,* 1945; *Alison's Island,* 1948; *The Dye-Hard,* 1950; *Above Rubies,* 1953; and *Disclosure Day,* 1955. *When Did They Meet Again?* was licensed for the Grecian Theatre (Lancaster) for 7 October 1926, but there is no record of performance. Brighouse's translation of Ferenc Molnar's *Valaki,* titled *Mr. Somebody,* opened 4 August 1936 at the Colorado Springs Fine Arts Center.

ASSESSMENT OF BRIGHOUSE'S CAREER

Brighouse's self-deprecating evaluation of himself as a "one-play playwright" (*What I Have Had,* 179) has perhaps dissuaded scholars and dramaturges from investigating his career and awarding him more serious consideration. The success of *Hobson's Choice* abroad and its subsequent acclaim in England has focused attention primarily on this one play, with little curiosity for the others.

Hobson's Choice is typical of the plays written by provincial playwrights that were met with positive critical reception in London. As long as their social comedies concerned regional lifestyles and characters, the London critics could accept them. *Lonesome-like* and *Zack,* along with *Hobson's Choice,* show a characteristic blend of ironic wit and sensitivity in their depiction of regional foibles. The charm of the dialects, however, often tempted productions toward caricature rather than letting the humor arise unforced from the dialogue and situation. It is not surprising, then, that in describing different productions of these three plays, Brighouse tactfully identified the original Horniman Company actors of the Gaiety Theatre, Manchester, as his preferred interpreters of lead roles (*What I Have Had,* 64, 68, 95). The regional actor would not have had to "affect" dialect or mannerisms. Despite London's critical indifference, the Liverpool Repertory Theatre, one of the few provincial theaters to continue after the First World War, relied on *Hobson's Choice* and several newly commissioned plays from Brighouse to keep the theater financially afloat through the 1920s.

The local specificity of many of Brighouse's early plays may work against their being reexamined or revived. Shorter ([2], 63) has remarked how topical many of the plays remain, sixty years later, in their treatment of ongoing concerns. Mainstream scholars divert interest from these works through labeling them as "unimportant" or "falsely melodramatic" (Nicoll 273, 280) or by describing his full-length plays as "confusing turns of plot and psychology" (Tyson 79). Perhaps a more fair appraisal would indicate that Brighouse refrained from oversimplifying or from setting up straw men in depicting the conflicts between adversarial approaches or entities.

Through his early experiments with the one-act play, Brighouse developed an admirable concision in character drawing and plot structure. The most successful of these efforts (such as *Lonesome-like* and *The Price of Coal*) used dialect, regional setting, and local topicality that had a specific appeal for the emerging provincial repertory theaters. The intervention of World War I diverted theater audiences from an interest in problem plays on domestic themes and also constricted the theater scene itself, as evening performances were limited in many theaters. Correctly assessing the postwar theatrical market, Brighouse abandoned his role of social critic and redirected his abilities to new theatrical ventures. Excising his one-acts of regional allusions or dialects, he applied his craftsmanship to more general concerns: for example, corporate responsibility (*The Boy: What Will He Become?*), bureaucracy (*The Bureaucrats*), status seeking (*Albert Gates*), unemployment (*New Leisure*), or generation gaps (*Smoke-screens*). While his later one-acts still showed a complexity in construction and character that could be developed by experienced performers, the linear structure and wry dialogue for small casts made them accessible and serious vehicles for the amateur and juvenile dramatic societies that he sought to nurture. Although proficiency in the one-act play and involvement with amateur societies did not carry the kind of prestige that Brighouse was beginning to achieve at the outbreak of World War I, the economic rewards permitted him to support himself as a playwright by these endeavors until his death.

ARCHIVAL SOURCES

Brighouse's manuscripts and papers, including a bound typescript of *The Hillarys,* which he wrote with Stanley Houghton, are held by the Harold Brighouse Collection in the Eccles Public Library, Greater Manchester. Seventeen volumes of press clippings of the Gaiety Theatre (Manchester) productions, collected by Annie Horniman, are available at the library of John Rylands University of Manchester (Deansgate). The papers of his colleague, Stanley Houghton, are located at the University of Salford Library. Henry Jewitt's typescript prompt-book for the Shubert production of *Hobson's Choice* is held by the Folger Shakespeare Library.

PRIMARY BIBLIOGRAPHY

Plays

Above Rubies. In *The Best One-Act Plays of 1952–53,* ed. Hugh Miller. London: Harrap, 1953.

Air-Raid Refugees. London: Samuel French, 1939.

Albert Gates. London: Samuel French, 1945. Also in *The Best One-Act Plays of 1937.* London: Harrap, 1938.

Alison's Island. In *The Best One-Act Plays of 1946–47,* ed. J[ames] W[illiam] Marriott. London: Harrap, 1948.

The Apple Tree; or, Why Misery Never Dies. London: Gowans & Gray, 1923; Boston: LeRoy Phillips, 1923.

Back to Adam. London: Samuel French, 1935; Baker, 1937. Also in *The Best One-Act Plays of 1935.* London: Harrap, 1936.

The Bantam V.C. Boston: Baker International Play Bureau, 1925.

Behind the Throne. Evanston, IL: Row, Peterson, 1929.

Below Ground. In *8 New One-Act Plays of 1936,* ed. William Armstrong. London: L. Dickson, 1936; Toronto: Macmillan, 1936.

A Bit of War. London: Samuel French, 1932.

The Boy: What Will He Become? In *The Best One-Act Plays of 1934,* ed. J[ames] W[illiam] Marriott. London: Harrap, 1935.

British Passport. London: Samuel French, 1939.

The Bureaucrats (under the pseudonym Olive Conway, with John Walton). In *The Best One-Act Plays of 1934,* ed. J[ames] W[illiam] Marriott. London: Harrap, 1935.

Coincidence. New York: Samuel French, 1929.

Converts. London: Gowans & Gray, 1920; Boston: LeRoy Phillips, 1920.

Dealing in Futures. London: Samuel French, 1913.

Disclosure Day. In *The Best One-Act Plays of 1954–55,* ed. Hugh Miller. London: Harrap, 1955.

The Doorway. London: Samuel French, 1913; J. Williams, 1913.

Dux (under the pseudonym Olive Conway, with John Walton). In *The Best One-Act Plays of 1936,* ed. J[ames] W[illiam] Marriott. London: Harrap, 1937.

The Dye-Hard. In *One-Act Plays of To-day,* 6th series, ed. J[ames] W[illiam] Marriott. London: Harrap, 1934.

Exhibit C. In *The Best One-Act Plays of 1933,* ed. J[ames] W[illiam] Marriott. London: Harrap, 1934.

Followers. London: Gowans & Gray, 1922; Boston: LeRoy Phillips, 1922. Also in *One-Act Plays for Secondary Schools.* Boston: Houghton Mifflin, 1923; *One-Act Plays of To-day,* 1st series. London: Harrap, 1924.

Fossie for Short. London: French, 1927.

The Friendly King. London: National Association of Boys' Clubs, 1935.

The Funk-Hole. London: Samuel French, 1938.

The Game. London: Samuel French, 1920.

Garside's Career. London: Constable, 1914; New York: Samuel French, 1914; Chicago: McClurg, 1915.

The Golden Ray. London: Samuel French, 1941.

Graft [The Polygon]. London: Samuel French, 1913.

Hallowed Ground. In *The Best One-Act Plays of 1944–45,* ed. J[ames] W[illiam] Marriott. London: Harrap, 1945.

The Happy Hangman. London: Gowans & Gray, 1922; Boston: LeRoy Phillips, 1922.

Hobson's Choice. New York: Doubleday, Page, 1916; Constable, 1916; Samuel French, 1924. Also in *Modern American and British Plays.* New York and London: Harper, 1931.

How the Weather Is Made. In *One-Act Plays of To-day,* 3rd series, ed. J[ames] W[illiam] Marriott. London: Harrap, 1926.

The Inner Man. London: Samuel French, 1945.

Let's Live in England. In *The Best One-Act Plays of 1944–45,* ed. J[ames] W[illiam] Marriott. London: Harrap, 1945.

The Little Liberty. London: Samuel French, 1927.

Little Red Shoes. Boston: Baker International Play Bureau, 1925. Also in *Baker's Anthology of One-Act Plays.* Boston: Baker International Play Bureau, 1925.

London Front. London: Samuel French, 1941.

Lonesome-Like. London: Gowans & Gray, 1914. Also in *One-Act Plays of To-day,* 2nd series. London: Harrap, 1926; *The Atlantic Book of Modern Plays.* Boston: Little, Brown, 1934.

The Maid of France. London: Gowans & Gray, 1917; Boston: LeRoy Phillips, 1917. Also in *One-Act Plays by Modern Authors.* New York: Harcourt, Brace, 1921.

The Man Who Ignored the War. New York: Samuel French, 1940.

A Marrying Man. London: Samuel French, 1924.

Mary's John. London: Samuel French, 1925.

Mimi (under the pseudonym Olive Conway, with John Walton). In *One-Act Plays of To-day,* 3rd series, ed. J[ames] W[illiam] Marriott. London: Harrap, 1926.

New Leisure. In *The Best One-Act Plays of 1936,* ed. J[ames] W[illiam] Marriott. London: Harrap, 1937.

The Night of "Mr. H." London: Samuel French, 1927. Also in *More One-Act Plays by Modern Authors.* New York: Harcourt, Brace, 1927.

The Northerners. London: Samuel French, 1920.

The Oak Settle. London: Samuel French, 1911.

The Odd Man Out. London: Samuel French, 1912.

Once a Hero. London: Gowans & Gray, 1922; Boston: LeRoy Phillips, 1922.

Passport to Romance. London: Samuel French, 1937; Baker, 1938.

The Price of Coal. London: Gowans & Gray, 1911. Also in *Nine Modern Plays.* London: Nelson, 1927.

The Prince Who Was a Piper. In *One-Act Plays of To-day,* 4th series, ed. J[ames] W[illiam] Marriott. London: Harrap, 1952.

The Road to Raebury. London: Samuel French, 1921.

The Romany Road. In *The Best One-Act Plays of 1932,* ed. J[ames] W[illiam] Marriott. London: Harrap, 1933.

Safe amongst the Pigs. London: Samuel French, 1930.

The Scaring Off of Teddy Dawson. London: Samuel French, 1911.

Smoke-screens. London: Samuel French, 1933. Also in *The Best One-Act Plays of 1931.* London: Harrap, 1932.

The Sort-of-a-Prince. London: Samuel French, 1929.

Sporting Rights. London: Samuel French, 1943.

Spring in Bloomsbury. Manchester Playgoer (May 1912): 174–90; London: Joseph Williams, 1912; New York: Samuel French, 1913.

The Starlight Window (under the pseudonym Olive Conway, with John Walton). New York: Samuel French, 1929.

The Stoker. London: Samuel French, 1930. Also in *One-Act Plays for Stage and Study,* 5th series. London: Harrap, 1929 and *One-Act Plays of To-day,* 5th series. London: Harrap, 1951.

Under the Pylon. In *One-Act Plays for Stage and Study,* 9th series. New York: Samuel French, 1938.

What's Bred in the Bone. London: Samuel French, 1927.

When Did They Meet Again? London: Samuel French, 1927.

The Wish-Shop. In *New Plays for Women and Girls,* ed. John Hampden. London: Samuel French, 1932.

The Witch's Daughter. In *One-Act Plays for Stage and Study,* 4th series. New York: Samuel French, 1928.

Women Do Things Like That (under the pseudonym Olive Conway, with John Walton). In *The Best One-Act Plays of 1931,* ed. J[ames] W[illiam] Marriott. London: Harrap, 1932.

Zack. London: Samuel French, 1920.

Anthologies

Costume Plays (under the pseudonym Olive Conway, with John Walton). (*Becky Sharp, Mimi, Prudence Corner, The King's Waistcoat.*) London: Samuel French, 1926.

Four Fantasies. (*Cupid and Psyche, The Exiled Princess, The Ghost in the Garden, The Romany Road.*) London: Samuel French, 1931.

Modern Plays in One Act (under the pseudonym Olive Conway, with John Walton). (*The*

Bureaucrats, The Desperationist, Dux, One of Those Letters, When the Bells Rang, Women Do Things Like That.) London: Samuel French, 1937.

Open Air Plays: Five One-Act Comedies. (*How the Weather Is Made, The Laughing Mind, Maypole Morning, The Prince Who Was a Piper, The Rational Princess.*) New York: Samuel French, 1926.

Plays for the Meadow and Plays for the Lawn. (*The Man about the Place, Maypole Morning, The Paris Doctor, The Prince Who Was a Piper.*) London: Samuel French, 1921.

Six Fantasies. (*Cupid and Psyche, The Exiled Princess, The Ghost in the Garden, The Ghost of Windsor Park, The Oracles of Apollo, The Romany Road.*) London: Samuel French, 1931.

Three Lancashire Plays. (*The Game, The Northerners, Zack.*) London: Samuel French, 1920.

Essays and Articles on Drama and Theater

"American Drama As a Londoner Sees It." *Theatre Arts Monthly* (May 1924): 311–16.

"Foreword." In *The One-Act Plays of Percival Wilde,* 1st series, ed. J. W. Marriott. London: Harrap, 1933.

"Introduction." In *The Works of Stanley Houghton,* vol. 1. London: Constable, 1914.

"The Manchester Drama." *Manchester Quarterly* (Apr. 1917): 75–90.

"News of the European Theatre, England." *Drama Magazine* (Oct. 1930–June 1931): 20–21.

"Other People and the Artist." *Manchester Guardian* (10 Aug. 1922).

What I Have Had: Chapters in Autobiography. London: Harrap, 1953.

SECONDARY BIBLIOGRAPHY

"Arts Theatre: 'Hobson's Choice.' " *The Times* (5 June 1952): 4.

Review of *The Bantam V.C. Athenaeum* (25 July 1919): 662.

" 'The Bantam V.C.,' at the St. Martin's." *Illustrated London News* (26 July 1919): 162.

" 'The Bantam V.C.': New Farce at St. Martin's Theatre." *The Times* (17 July 1919): 10.

Clark, Barrett H. *A Study of the Modern Drama,* 301. New York and London: Appleton, 1925.

" 'The Clock Goes Round,' at the Globe." *Illustrated London News* (14 Oct. 1916): 460.

" 'The Clock Goes Round': New Play at the Globe." *The Times* (5 Oct. 1916): 9.

"Dramatic Gossip." *Athenaeum* (26 June 1915): 578.

"Fiddlers Four Revived on Television." *The Times* (27 Feb. 1960): 9.

Goldie, Grace Wyndham. *The Liverpool Repertory Theatre, 1911–1934.* Liverpool: University Press of Liverpool, 1935.

Gooddie, Sheila. *Annie Horniman: A Pioneer in the Theatre.* London: Methuen, 1990.

" 'The Hillarys,' at the Criterion." *Illustrated London News* (12 June 1915): 748.

" 'Hindle Wakes' and 'Converts' at the Duke of York's." *Illustrated London News* (11 Sept. 1915): 348.

Review of *Hobson's Choice. Athenaeum* (July 1916): 352.

Review of *Hobson's Choice. Nation* (11 Nov. 1915).

" 'Hobson's Choice.' " *The Times* (21 Nov. 1916): 11.

" 'Hobson's Choice,' at the Apollo." *Illustrated London News* (1 July 1916): 28.

" 'Hobson's Choice': Lancashire Comedy at the Apollo." *The Times* (23 June 1916): 11.

Hudson, Lynton. *The English Stage, 1850–1950.* London: Harrap, 1951.

Keatley, Charlotte. Review of *Zack. Plays and Players* (Nov. 1986): 29.

Kemp, Thomas C. *Birmingham Repertory Theatre: The Playhouse and the Man.* 2d ed., rev. Birmingham: Cornish Brothers, 1948.

Longaker, Mark, and Edwin C. Bolles. *Contemporary English Literature,* 413–14. New York: Appleton-Century-Crofts, 1953.

Mayer, David. "Lights of Lancashire." *Plays and Players* (Jan. 1977): 29.

Millett, Fred B. *Contemporary British Literature: A Critical Survey and 232 Author Bibliographies.* New York: Harcourt, Brace, 1935.

Müller-Zannoth, Ingrid. "Lektüre und Kommunikation im Englischunterricht der Sekundarstufe II: Harold Brighouse: *Hobson's Choice." Neueren Sprachen* 84:1 (Feb. 1985): 27–41.

Nicoll, Allardyce. *English Drama, 1900–1930: The Beginnings of the Modern Period.* Cambridge: Cambridge University Press, 1973.

" 'The Odd Man Out,' at the Royalty." *Illustrated London News* (20 Apr. 1912): 570.

" 'Other Times,' at the Little." *Illustrated London News* (17 Apr. 1920): 680.

" 'Other Times': New Play at the Little Theatre." *The Times* (8 Apr. 1920): 8.

Palmer, John. "The Comedy of Ninepins." *Saturday Review* (27 Apr. 1912): 517–18.

"The Playhouse." *The Times* (29 Nov. 1911): 10.

Pogson, Rex. *Miss Horniman and the Gaiety Theatre, Manchester.* London: Rockliff, 1952.

Review of *Repertory Plays: No. 3, The Price of Coal. Athenaeum* (25 Nov. 1911): 671.

" 'The Road to Raebury,' at the Criterion." *Illustrated London News* (26 June 1915): 814.

" 'The Road to Raebury': Mr. Brighouse's Comedy at the Criterion." *The Times* (19 June 1915): 11.

Rowell, George, and Anthony Jackson. *The Repertory Movement: A History of Regional Theatre in Britain.* Cambridge: Cambridge University Press, 1984.

"Royalty Theatre: 'The Odd Man Out.' " *The Times* (17 Apr. 1912): 6.

Savory, Gerald, ed. *Granada's Manchester Plays: Television Adaptations of Six Plays Recalling the Horniman Period at the Gaiety Theatre, Manchester.* Manchester: Manchester University Press, 1962.

"A Scottish Programme at the Playhouse." *Athenaeum* (2 Dec. 1911): 707.

"A Scottish Programme at the Playhouse." *Illustrated London News* (2 Dec. 1911): 956.

Shorter, Eric. [1]. Review of *Hobson's Choice. Drama: The Quarterly Theatre Review* (Winter 1975): 71–72.

———. [2]. Review of *The Northerners. Drama: The Quarterly Theatre Review* (Summer 1979): 63.

———. [3]. Review of *Zack. Drama: The Quarterly Theatre Review* (Spring 1977): 52–53.

Review of *Three Lancashire Plays. The Times Literary Supplement* (19 Feb. 1920).

Trewin, J[ohn] C[ourtenay]. ''Speaking Their Minds.'' *Illustrated London News* (21 June 1952): 1056.

Tyson, B. F. ''Harold Brighouse.'' In *Dictionary of Literary Biography,* vol. 10, *Modern British Dramatists, 1900–1945,* ed. Stanley Weintraub, pt. 1, 75–80. Detroit: Gale Research, 1982.

'' 'Zack': Repertory Players at Comedy Theatre.'' *The Times* (25 Apr. 1922): 10.

Noël Coward
(1899–1973)

SARAH DUERDEN

Few writers have invested as much care into the personal image they publicly project as did Noël Coward. As a result, within popular culture the name ''Coward'' has become synonymous with a certain English style: the elegant silk dressing gown, the cigarette holder, charm, wit, clipped phrases, upper-class accents, and sex appeal. His plays reinforced this image, and Coward was not averse to audiences confusing him with his leading male heterosexual characters.

Coward's homosexuality is now well understood, as is the fact that his public persona was a careful construction designed to hide his homosexuality from the general public. He was, for example, unimpressed with Oscar Wilde, calling him ''a silly, conceited, inadequate creature . . . a dreadful self-deceiver'' (*The Noël Coward Diaries,* 135). Although by the 1960s Coward was writing openly about the Homosexual Bill in Parliament in both his diaries and his play *Shadows of the Evening,* he failed to realize that his whole mannerism—the silk dressing gown, the cigarette holder, the raised eyebrow—was deeply artificial and camp. In addition to the creation of an immensely enjoyable persona, Coward's homosexuality may have also led him to the acidly witty exposure of society characteristic of so many of his plays and the comedy of manners (Lahr). He well understood society's double standards and knew exactly how they might best be exposed through language. However, his success lay not with the epigrammatic phrase, but rather with the timing so that ordinary phrases become witty, hilarious, hysterical, or loaded with desperation.

The recent revival of Coward in London, labeled by some critics as Coward for the nineties, attests to Coward's enduring qualities. To a certain extent he ignored modernism and sweeping changes in the theater, preferring instead to perfect the comedy of manners. Yet his sparse but witty dialogue that relies on situation and moment, his consciousness of language as a weapon that can damage, and the gap between the grace of the language and what people actually do to one another ensure that Coward is more than merely an entertaining period comedy writer

Even Coward's birth date of 16 December 1899 seems suspiciously auspicious, falling at the end of an old century, and early on Coward appeared determined to embody the new century. He was born into a middle-class suburb in Teddington, Middlesex, and not into the world of cocktails and dressing gowns that his plays were to celebrate. His devoted mother Violet had married a piano salesman, Arthur, from a musical family, and she adored the theater and certainly passed that on to her son. With her encouragement, Noël took acting lessons at the age of ten in Miss Janet Thomas's Dancing Academy, and in September, 1911 he auditioned for his first part in *The Goldfish*. The year 1911 saw the beginning of his relationship with Charles Hawtrey, one of the great Edwardian actor-managers, when Noël first appeared in Hawtrey's *The Great Name*. Hawtrey cast him in a series of plays: *The Great Name, Where the Rainbow Ends, A Little Fowl Play,* and *The Saving Grace*. Between 1911 and 1917 Coward appeared in a number of plays and quickly learned to appreciate the pleasure of an audience, which, he claimed, launched him on his writing career. He was finally drafted into the army in 1918, but his tubercular tendency and neurasthenia ended his army career after a few short months. Between 1918 and 1920 Coward survived by acting in a few small roles and writing stories for magazines and song lyrics.

Early success came with *I'll Leave It to You,* a vehicle he wrote for himself and Esmé Wynne-Tyson staged in Manchester and London. Critics agreed that a new talent had emerged. At the age of twenty-four, Coward confirmed this with *The Vortex.* Coward was hailed as a sensational talent. He shocked audiences with the subject matter of the play, but those who got beyond shock appreciated Coward's talent for writing. He seemed to epitomize the age's need to live life at a fast rate. His early success was confirmed with *Hay Fever,* produced in 1925, and *Easy Virtue.*

Coward's finest play, *Private Lives,* written, like so many others, at high speed and as a vehicle for his dear friend Gertrude Lawrence, opened the 1930s. During this decade Coward wrote his finest work. In 1931 he wrote *Cavalcade,* in 1932, *Design for Living,* in 1935, ten one-act plays in *Tonight at 8:30,* and in 1939, *This Happy Breed.* During this decade he also acted as a somewhat unsuccessful spy and more successful patriot. In 1940 he toured Australia for the armed forces and in 1941 toured New Zealand. In that same year *Blithe Spirit* was produced, and he wrote the screenplay for *In Which We Serve.*

During the early 1940s Coward enjoyed success with films. In 1943 he produced *This Happy Breed;* in 1944 he produced *Blithe Spirit;* also in 1944 he wrote the screenplay for *Brief Encounter,* based on *Still Life,* a play from the ten in *Tonight at 8:30,* and the film was produced in 1945.

With the end of the war Coward's popularity declined. His musical *Pacific 1860* was not successful and was followed by the equally unsuccessful *Peace in Our Time,* written in 1946 and produced in 1947. These failures continued through the 1950s with the musical *Ace of Clubs* in 1950 and the plays *Relative Values* in 1951 and *Quadrille* in 1952. In 1953 his career took a new shift when he performed as a cabaret entertainer at Cafe de Paris. In 1954 he wrote *Nude with Violin* and moved first to Bermuda and then in 1959 to Switzerland.

During the late 1950s and 1960s Coward once more enjoyed success with a production of *Waiting in the Wings* in 1959, the musical *Sail Away,* and an attack on the new drama written by Coward himself in 1961 for *The Sunday Times.* In 1964 *Hay Fever* was revived and directed by Coward at the National Theatre. His last appearance on the West End stage came in 1966 with *Suite in Three Keys.* In 1970 Coward was knighted, and there followed in 1972 a revue in London named *Cowardy Custard* and *Oh! Coward* in Toronto, which reached Broadway in 1973. Coward died of a heart attack in 1973 at his retreat in Jamaica.

Selected Biographical Sources: Fisher; Lesley; Morley.

MAJOR PLAYS, PREMIERES, AND SIGNIFICANT REVIVALS: THEATRICAL RECEPTION

The Vortex. 1924. Opened at the Everyman Theatre (Hampstead) on 25 November; moved after 12 performances to the Royalty Theatre on 16 December 1924, where it ran for 224 performances; moved to the Comedy Theatre (London) on 9 March 1925; moved to the Little Theatre (London) 4 May 1925. Opened at the National Theatre (Washington, D.C.) on 7 September 1925 and made its debut on Broadway at the Henry Miller Theatre (New York) on 16 September 1925, where it ran for 157 performances. Revived in 1932 at the Malvern Festival Theatre by a repertory company devoted to the plays of Coward under the supervision of Noël Coward. Revived by the Lyric Theatre of London 4 March 1952 following a tryout at the Theatre Royal (Brighton) on 18 February 1952 and at Cambridge on 25 February; moved to the Criterion Theatre (London) 9 April 1952. Produced by Tennent Productions and directed by Michael Macowan. Revived again at the Garrick Theatre (London) 26 January 1989, following a tryout at the Citizen's Theatre (Glasgow) in January 1988.

This play, dealing with a mother's affair with a young man the same age as her son, and a son addicted to drugs, launched Coward's career. Both characters long to be adored, and both promise to change at the end of the play and give up their respective vices. Although the Lord Chamberlain almost refused the play a license, Coward managed to obtain one by persuading the Lord Chamberlain that the play was really a moral tract. Agate noted that Coward lifted the play from disagreeable to "philosophic comment," but complained that "the third act is too long" (quoted in Mander and Mitchenson, 69). Hastings commented firmly that this was a "dustbin of a play" (quoted in Morley, 83). Nevertheless, most critics praised the play, especially those in America such as the reviewers for the *New York World,* the *New York Post,* and the *New York Tribune,* who called it "the season's best new play" (quoted in Cole, 47). Later critics such as Lahr (18–26) and Gray (34–41) still praised the play for the literary leap Coward exhibited. The 1952 revival was set in the 1920s and received mixed praise: the *London Daily Mail* complained about its "frantic piano-playing at every crisis" but noted that "the wit still sparkles and that final hysterical scene between the son and the mother with a lover of just his own age has lost little of its old dramatic sting" (quoted in Mander and Mitchenson).

Fallen Angels. 1923. Produced by Anthony Princep and directed by Stanley Bell at the Globe Theatre (London) on 21 April for 158 performances. Revived at the Festival Theatre (Malvern) in 1932 by a repertory company devoted to the works of Coward; revived in 1949 at the Ambassadors Theatre (London) on 29 November; revived in New York at the Playhouse on 17 January 1956; revived by the Vaudeville Theatre (London) on 4 April 1967, directed by Philip Wiseman; revived in New York by Roundabout Stage Two Theatre on 22 April 1980, produced by the Roundabout Theatre and directed by Stephen Hollis, running for 104 performances.

A comedy of manners involving husbands and wives and a lover, the play was not generally well received. Although *Punch* praised the play for its writing that "relieved" the play of "all offensiveness," the *London Sketch* called the play "still nothing more than a clever play," and most other critics found the play disgusting (quoted in Cole, 47). Nevertheless, upon reading these vituperative reviews, Coward rebutted such criticism with his usual wit: "The realization that I am hopelessly depraved, vicious, and decadent has for two days ruined my morning beaker of opium" (quoted in Lahr, 31).

Easy Virtue. 1925. Tried out at the Broad Theatre (Newark) on 23 November 1925; moved to the Empire Theatre (New York) on 7 December, running for 147 performances. Produced by Charles Frohman Inc., directed by Basil Dean. In 1926 the play moved to Duke's Theatre following a tryout as *A New Play in Three Acts* at the Opera House (Manchester) on 31 May 1926. The play ran for 124 performances in London with largely the same cast. This production was directed and produced by Basil Dean. Revived at the Garrick Theatre (London) on 21 April 1988, directed by Tim Luscombe.

In this play Coward explored the issue of charm once more, but this time tried to align charm with courage. In New York the play received some praise. However, it was called "*The Second Mrs Tanqueray* brought down to date" by the *New York Times,* which suggested its somewhat hackneyed nature (quoted in Mander and Mitchenson). The *Daily Express* echoed what had become a cliché: it was a "[p]lay from an author not yet grown up" (quoted in Cole, 155). Later critics found the play somewhat troublesome in its debt to Pinero and its old-fashioned nature.

The 1988 revival of *Easy Virtue* received lavish praise. The *London Daily*

Mail called it a "triumph," noting that the play "is astonishing" for its "radical assault on all the deep seated prejudices and smug moral certainties with which the middle class have defended themselves against anything they fail to understand" (quoted in Cole, 155). *Punch* agreed, praising Coward for going "directly to the jugular of the moralistic but fundamentally hypocritical society of the 1920s" (quoted in Cole).

Hay Fever. 1925. Opened at the Ambassadors Theatre on 8 June; moved to the Criterion Theatre on 7 September, running for 337 performances, directed by Noël Coward and produced by Alban B. Limpus. Revived by the Avon Theatre (New York) on 29 December 1931, directed by Constance Collier, running for 95 performances; revived in England in 1932 by a repertory company devoted to Coward's work at the Festival Theatre (Malvern); on 27 October 1964 in London by the National Theatre at the Old Vic, directed by Coward; at the Duke of York's Theatre in London on 14 February 1968; revived on 26 November 1992 by the Theatre of Comedy at the Albery Theatre (London), produced by the Theatre of Comedy Company and directed by Alan Strachan.

Hay Fever is the closest Coward came to writing high farce. The members of a literary family are led by laissez-faire so that each member invites a weekend guest without notifying other family members. The play received favorable reviews and is considered by many critics to be his best comedy. *The Times,* in a 9 June 1925 review (quoted in Cole, 46), praised it for Coward's wit. Later critics such as Lahr regarded the play as "the first and finest of his major plays" (57). The Broadway version premiered on 5 October 1925 at Maxine Elliott's Theatre, directed by Noël Coward and Laura Hope Crews and produced by Messrs. Shubert. The *New York Times*'s 6 October review complained that while the play was enjoyable, "it has many colorless moments" (quoted in Cole, 66).

The 1931 revival received a more favorable review from the *New York Times* calling the play "infernally delicate and accomplished. It is dry subtle, mettlesome comedy, and it's enormously entertaining" (quoted in Cole, 48). The *Sunday London Telegraph* complained of the 1964 revival that Coward was "in danger of being mistaken for Pinter. There is barely one witty epigram in the entire dialogue" (quoted in Cole, 127). The 1968 revival received more praise. Although this production was less lavish in terms of costuming and period, the *London Observer* claimed that the play "belongs with 'Twelfth Night,' 'Love for Love' and 'The Importance of Being Earnest.' It is Coward's profoundest play" (quoted in Cole). The *London Daily Mail* argued of the 1992 revival that the play was much more than "high camp and high jinks. Something much deeper and enduring must bind it to our collective consciousness. Alan Strachan's wildly inventive revival succeeds brilliantly on both levels" (quoted in Cole, 162). Similar praise came from the *London Daily Telegraph,* which reiterated an old Tynan comment: "As you listen to the deadly precision of the dialogue, you realize with a shock what a large debt Harold Pinter owes to

Coward'' (quoted in Cole, 162). Similarly, *The Sunday Times* added, ''Noël Coward was the Harold Pinter of the Jazz Age. *Hay Fever* is a comedy of menace'' (quoted in Cole, 162).

The Queen Was in the Parlour. 1926. Produced at St. Martin's Theatre (London) on 8 August; transferred to the Duke of York's Theatre on 4 October, produced and directed by Basil Dean, running for 136 performances.

The play, labeled ''Ruritanian,'' was regarded with some suspicion by critics, a problem Coward was to encounter several times in his career. The *London Daily Mail* questioned whether ''Mr Coward wrote the play with his tongue in his cheek'' (quoted in Cole, 50).

Private Lives. 1929. Tried out on 18 August 1930 at the King's Theatre (Edinburgh), the play opened at the Phoenix Theatre (London) on 24 September 1930 and ran for 101 performances. Produced by Charles B. Cochran; cast starred Coward as Elyot Chase, Gertrude Lawrence as Amanda Prynne, and Laurence Olivier as Victor Prynne. The New York production at the Times Square Theatre in New York opened on 27 January 1931, running for 256 performances. Revived first by the repertory theater company devoted to Coward in 1932 at the Festival Theatre (Malvern); on 8 November 1932 at the Apollo Theatre (London), directed by John Clements, running for 716 performances. Revived on 4 October 1948 in New York at the Plymouth Theatre, directed by Martin Maulis, running for 248 performances. Revived in 1963 by the Hampstead Theatre Club (London) on 24 April and transferred to the Duke of York's Theatre (London) on 3 July, running for 216 performances; at the Billy Rose Theatre (New York) on 4 December 1969, directed by Stephen Porter, running for 204 performances before moving to the Broadhurst Theatre (New York) on 27 April 1970; at the Queens and Globe theatres in London on 21 September 1972, produced by H. M. Tennent Ltd. and directed by John Gielgud, running for 517 performances and starring Maggie Smith as Amanda; transferred to the Forty-sixth Street Theatre (New York) on 6 February 1975; on 16 April 1980 at the Duchess Theatre until 10 January 1981, when it was transferred to the Greenwich Theatre, directed by Alan Strachan and produced by John Gale; at the Lunt-Fontanne Theatre on 8 May 1983, produced by the Elizabeth Theatre Group and directed by Milton Katselas; on 19 September 1990 at the Aldwych Theatre (London), produced by Michael Codron and directed by Tim Luscombe; on 20 February 1992 at the Broadhurst Theatre (New York).

While *Private Lives* is still regarded as Coward's most perfect play, the plot is slight, and early reviewers homed in on this. At the London opening *The Times* praised the timing and acting, but added, ''Mr Coward can pad as no one else can pad; he has made of dramatic upholstery an art'' (quoted in Cole, 62). Similarly, the *London Weekend Review* commented on Coward's brilliance and yet complained of the ''flimsy'' nature of this ''trifle'' (quoted in Cole, 62). The New York opening received a very positive response. Nevertheless, like most contemporary reviews, the *New York World*'s review described the play as essentially "an admirable piece of fluff" brilliantly acted (quoted in Cole, 63).

In the 1969 New York version Tammy Grimes, who played Amanda, won a Tony Award for her performance. The *New York Times* commented on the 1983 revival that the play "is a wise and painful statement about both the necessity and the impossibility of love" (quoted in Cole, 130). However, in the cast Elizabeth Taylor and Richard Burton attracted so much attention that this disastrous revival was labeled by the *New York Daily News* as "It's Liz and Dick Together Again" (quoted in Cole, 147). In the 1990 revival Joan Collins played Amanda, and Sarah Prynne, who played Sybil, won the Olivier Award for Best Supporting Actress. Joan Collins resumed the role in the 1992 American revival, which first toured eleven cities in sixteen weeks. This version did much worse once it reached New York. Collins was praised for not falling on her face. The Associated Press complained that "Joan Collins and company nearly batter the life, and humour, out of Coward's best-known work" (quoted in Cole, 160).

Cavalcade. 1931. Opened at the Theatre Royal, Drury Lane (London) on 13 October, directed by Coward and produced by Charles B. Cochran, running for 405 performances. Revived at the Chichester Festival Theatre, 1 May 1985, directed by David Gilmore.

This historical overview received much contemporary praise. Beginning Sunday, 31 December 1899, to the present, 1930, the play traces the life of an upper-class family and its servants through such national events as the Boer War, the death of Queen Victoria, and the sinking of the *Titanic*. The *Daily Mail*'s review was particularly pleasing for Coward, praising not only the play, but also the directorship, adding, "Our national theatre has a theme worthy of itself" (quoted in Mander and Mitchenson). The film version would later win the Academy Award for Best Picture. However, the *London Observer* called the 1985 revival "meretricious crap," whereas the *Daily Mail* called it "a wonderful night of theatre" (quoted in Cole).

Design for Living. 1933. Tried out at the Hanna Theatre (Cleveland) on 2 January; moved to the Ethel Barrymore Theatre (New York) on 24 January, where it ran for 135 performances. Opened in London at the Haymarket on 25 January 1939, where it ran for 203 performances. Moved to the Savoy Theatre (London) on 13 June 1939, but the run was interrupted by the outbreak of the Second World War. Resumed at the Savoy on 23 December and continued for 33 performances. Revived 21 November 1973 by the Phoenix Theatre (London), directed by Michael Blakemore; on 4 August 1983 at the Globe Theater, directed by Alan Strachan; and on 22 February 1995 at the Gielgud, directed by Sean Mathias.

Written for Coward's friends, the Lunts, the play was a vehicle for Lynn Fontanne and Alfred Lunt. The London opening received unenthusiastic reviews: *The Times* complained that the "theme is not faced; the subject is not worked out. For these reasons, the play is disappointing'' (quoted in Mander and Mitchenson, 179).

The 1973 Blakemore revival included such stars as Vanessa Redgrave, Peter Bayliss, Jeremy Brett, and Connie Booth and was generally well received. Revived again in 1983, the play received high praise from *Punch* for the production at the Greenwich Theatre before it transferred to the Globe (London): ''The triumph of Alan Strachan's new production is the awareness that it's also about the history of the 1930's.'' *The Times* praised it for its dealing with ''liberations in matters other than sexual'' (quoted in Cole, 148). The 1995 revival received very mixed reviews for its blatant sexuality. Kingwill complained of the production's crudity and, at times, buffoonish acting, and *The Sunday Times* reviewer (''Design for Living'') called the play ''ostentatiously erotic and as camp as an air vice-marshall in a tutu,'' whereas Coward is not. Kellaway, in contrast, praised Mathias for the overt sexuality and declared that this play is ''pure Coward, just right.''

Tonight at 8:30. 1936. Tried out on 15 October 1935 at the Opera House (Manchester); moved to the Phoenix Theatre (London) on 9 January 1936 and ran for 157 performances. After its London run, the play toured major cities in Britain. Directed by Coward.

The members of this group of ten one-act plays were combined in various orders to make a three-evening sequence of plays in which three plays were performed each night. *Star Chamber* was performed only once, on 29 March 1936. The sequence includes *We Were Dancing, The Astonished Heart, ''Red Peppers,'' Hands across the Sea, Fumed Oak, Shadow Play, Family Album, Ways and Means, Still Life,* and *Star Chamber.* Coward was generally praised for attempting such diversity, but his less successful pieces were not overlooked. Nevertheless, the *London Observer*'s review praised Coward: ''The variety of the programme is a tribute to Mr Coward's interest in experiment'' (quoted in Cole, 77). Reviving the one-act play, Coward and his partner Gertrude Lawrence proved how exciting they could be on stage.

Blithe Spirit. 1941. Tried out at the Opera House (Manchester) on 16 June; moved to the Piccadilly Theatre (London) on 2 July 1941; moved to St. James's Theatre on 23 March 1942; moved to the Duchess Theatre (London) on 6 October 1942 and ran for 1,997 performances; directed by Coward. Premiered on Broadway at the Morosco Theatre (New York) on 4 November 1941, where it ran for 657 performances. Revivals: on 23 July 1970 at the Globe Theatre, where it ran for 204 performances; in 1976 by the National Theatre, Lyttleton Theatre (London), on 24 June, directed by Harold Pinter; on 30 January 1986 at the Vaudeville Theatre (London), directed by Peter Farago; on 31 March 1987 at the Neil Simon Theatre (New York), directed by Brian Murray; at the Lyric Theatre, 12 June 1989, directed by John David.

Subtitled *An Improbable Farce,* this ghost story dealing with adultery attempts to recapture the wit of Coward's earlier plays. The London premiere received generally positive reviews; the *London Daily Mail* called it "riotously witty stuff," and the *New York Daily News* agreed (quoted in Cole, 153). The play went on to win the Drama Critics Circle Award as best play for 1941–42 and toured extensively in both Britain and America. The 1986 revival garnered positive praise from the *London Daily Mail,* which called the play a "minor masterpiece, a triumph of style, technique, and theatrical daring" (quoted in Cole). The 1987 production was less successful, criticized primarily for the acting.

Present Laughter. 1943. Opened 29 April at the Haymarket Theatre (London) following a twenty-five-week tour of Britain of *Play Parade* consisting of *Present Laughter* alternating with *This Happy Breed* and *Blithe Spirit,* directed by Coward. Premiered on Broadway at the Plymouth Theatre (New York) on 29 October 1946 following a tryout at the Playhouse in Wilmington on 26 September 1946, directed by John C. Wilson. Revivals: on 16 April 1947 at the Haymarket Theatre (London), running for 528 performances; in New York on 31 January 1958 alternating with *Nude with Violin,* directed by Noël Coward; on 21 April 1965 at the Queen's Theatre (London), running for 364 performances, directed by Nigel Patrick; on 29 March 1975 at the Kennedy Center in Washington, D.C., and then on to the Forest Theatre (Philadelphia) in September 1975, directed by Stephen Porter; in November 1978 at the Kennedy Center, directed by Roderick Cook; on 17 March 1981 at the Vaudeville Theatre (London) following a tryout at the Greenwich Theatre on 29 January 1981, directed by Alan Strachan; on 15 July 1982 at Circle in the Square (New York), where it ran for 175 performances, directed by George C. Scott.

Although this vehicle for Coward created a charm-and-manners triumph in England, the New York production was criticized by the critics and by Coward himself. The *New York Sun* review called it "second best Noël Coward" (quoted in Cole, 90). Though the play is not generally believed to be Coward's strongest effort, the 1981 revival garnered positive critical comment from the *London Financial Times,* which called the play "the best of Noel Coward's plays" (quoted in Cole, 141).

This Happy Breed. 1943. Opened 20 April at the Haymarket Theatre (London), directed by Noël Coward and produced by H. M. Tennent Ltd. and John C. Wilson.

A middle-class family's drama spanning time from 1919 to 1939, the play acts as a tribute to Coward's middle-class roots. Despite a positive review from the *Daily Telegraph* (see Cole), others complained that Coward patronized his salt-of-the-earth subjects.

ADDITIONAL PLAYS, ADAPTATIONS, AND PRODUCTIONS

The Marquise (1927) opened at the Criterion Theatre (London) on 16 February and ran for 129 performances. *Sirocco* (1927) opened on 24 November at Daly's Theatre in London, directed by Basil Dean, running for only 28 performances. *Point Valaine* (1934) tried out at the Colonial Theatre, Boston, on December 25; moved to the Ethel Barrymore Theatre on 16 January 1935 and ran for 55 performances, directed by Coward.

Peace in Our Time (1947) opened at the Lyric Theatre in London on 22 July, where it ran for 167 performances following its tryout at the Theatre Royal, Brighton, on 15 July 1947. The play moved to the Aldwych Theatre (London) on 29 September 1947. It was directed by Alan Webb under the supervision of Noël Coward. It is an intriguing play set in England under Nazi occupation; despite a positive review from the *London Daily Telegraph* (see Cole), the play was perhaps too close to recent history to be successful.

Relative Values (1951) opened at the Savoy Theatre, London, on 29 October, where it ran for a very successful 477 performances. It was directed by Noël Coward. This stylish comedy's satire is directed at the loss of class distinctions, and although by 1951 this was a condition long past, the play enjoyed considerable success. The 6 September 1973 revival at the Westminster Theatre, London, directed by Charles Hickman, revealed the dated nature of the play, even when it was written, said the *Sunday Times* review (see Cole).

Quadrille (1952) opened at the Phoenix Theatre, London, on 12 September, where it ran for 329 performances following a tryout at the Opera House, Manchester, on 15 July 1952, directed by Noël Coward. Regarded by some as an inferior *Private Lives* in a Victorian setting, the play was recognized as a vehicle for Coward's friends, the Lunts. *South Sea Bubble* (1956) opened on 25 April at the Lyric Theatre, London, where it ran for 276 performances following a tryout on 19 March 1956 at the Opera House, Manchester. The play was a revision of *Island Fling* (itself a revision of *Home and Colonial*) and received a surprisingly positive review from *The Sunday Times,* which stated that it "is the best play Mr. Coward has written for a long time" (quoted in Cole, 108). Nevertheless, the play is not memorable. *Nude with Violin* (1956) opened at the Globe Theatre, London, on 7 November, directed by John Gielgud and Noël Coward. It premiered on Broadway at the Belasco Theatre, New York, on 14 November 1957. It is a Coward comedy that attempts to explore the notion that avant-garde art is merely a joke, and it garnered rather poor reviews.

Waiting in the Wings (1960) opened on 7 September at the Duke of York's Theatre, London, directed by Margaret Webster. Set in a home for aged actresses, the play is well constructed, but it was a critical and commercial failure. Levin commented that it was "the most paralyzingly tedious play I have ever seen" (quoted in Fisher, 230). *Suite in Three Keys* (1966) opened at the Queen's Theatre, London, on 14 April. Set in a hotel suite in Switzerland, this suite consists of three plays: *Shadows of the Evening, Come into the Garden Maud,* and *A Song at Twilight.* A somewhat successful return to the theatre, *A Song at Twilight* is perhaps the most interesting because the play deals openly with homosexuality.

ASSESSMENT OF COWARD'S CAREER

Ironically, Coward's immense popularity and the diversity and sheer number of his works may account for the difficulty academic scholars have today. During the 1920s and 1930s Coward was immensely successful; challenging the establishment with his wit and humor, Coward embodied the bright young things. During the 1940s his patriotism matched the times, and although his plays were less witty and somewhat more trite, he was still successful. In the 1950s his career began to wane, and Coward turned his attention to being a successful cabaret star. His sometimes acid-tongued attacks on the new playwrights of the 1960s paralleled Coward's decline as a writer, but his earlier plays were revived and enjoyed considerable success. Coward wrote fifty plays and revues, forty-two of which were produced, three films, and numerous songs. Furthermore, he enjoyed considerable success. *Blithe Spirit* ran for over 1,900 performances. Such popularity casts doubt on the worth of his work, and indeed his work is uneven. Some plays, such as *Point Valaine,* are superficial and boring. Others, such as *This Happy Breed,* seem condescending. Nevertheless, Coward was a successful playwright, and his longevity deserves some critical attention.

One of the earliest critics to give Coward serious attention was Swinnerton. Swinnerton argued that Coward belonged to the postwar pessimists who reacted to the horror of the First World War. He found that Coward mirrored a part of contemporary life. Coward's other early critics, Agate, Ervine, and Furnas, praised his early work and panned his work after *Cavalcade.* However, Coward's reputation really suffered with the emergence of the new writers like John Osborne, and even though Osborne's reputation was to rise as Coward's declined, and Osborne claimed that his feelings toward Coward changed, he could not help but add, in a recent book review, that "the Master did irreparable damage to my profession and all those in it. No one has yet managed to dispel the aura with which he surrounded the word 'theater,' an abiding synonym for superficiality and deception."

This accusation best condenses the problem critics have with Coward: they are unable to separate the myth of the man, the dressing gown, the cigarette holder, and cocktails from the works that he produced. Fortunately, there have been some recent studies that attempt to measure the worth of Coward. The best to date remains Lahr's study, *Coward the Playwright.* Lahr argued that Coward constructed an elaborate persona to mask his homosexuality from a public that would never accept it. Living under the cloud of Oscar Wilde, Coward, suggested Lahr, took great trouble to keep his private life private, and through his plays, Coward's mask was charm, designed to hide his homosexuality and his middle-class roots.

More recently Kiernan and Gray have analyzed Coward's work. Kiernan examined Coward's plays in terms of comedies of manners, light comedies, and melodramas, and he found that for Coward "frivolity was even a kind of aesthetic" (158). Gray explored the notion of Coward's mask and found that in his major plays "he achieved an eroticism that was strangely androgynous.... Gender becomes irrelevant. Laughter replaces lengthy displays of lovemaking ... [and] this androgyny plays merry hell with sexual stereotypes." He created, argued Gray, "in a handful of plays, a vein of erotic comedy that was both original and truthful" (15–16). Furthermore, she argued, the "consciousness of language and its potential for word play is one of Coward's lasting legacies to such writers as Pinter, Orton and Ann Jellicoe" (197–98).

Therefore, Coward's brilliance as a playwright stems not from plot, not from his depiction of or inquiry into a burning social question of the day, but from his use of language. In the best Coward plays language becomes a weapon, and the greater the contrast between the graceful, artificial, crisp lines and what the characters actually do to one another, the finer Coward's language and the play become. His best work remains his comedies. He distinguished between his plays with the labels "A Light Comedy" and "A Comedy." Levin suggested that "those called 'light' are high farces, and those labeled simply 'comedies' are in the tradition of the comedy of manners" (60). As Lahr pointed out, Coward had an "immense reputation for wit" (7), but his best lines result from their context. For example, the line "Very flat, Norfolk" is not immensely witty. But when the line is delivered on stage, its deflationary effect is humorous. Similarly, although Tynan tried to claim that Coward originated the language Pinter employs, Lahr pointed out that unlike Pinter's characters, Coward's characters mean what they say (8).

With his early successful play, *The Vortex,* Coward became at once the symbol of the bright young things: selfish, depraved, disturbing, and frighteningly attractive. The son, a cocaine addict, and the mother, an aging woman who has affairs with young men, share their need, adoration from others. The play suggested the emergence of a playwright who would shock the theatrical world. Coward provided his audience with an image of his generation: nervous, hysterical, self-centered, and possessing a sad awareness of age. Nicky explains to Bunty: "It's funny how mother's generation always longed to be old when they were young, and we strain every nerve to keep young." But at heart, there is a traditional moral center that was to appear most noticeably in Coward's plays of the 1940s. In the play Nicky does resolve to give up cocaine, and his mother resolves to give up young men.

Coward's finest work came during the late 1920s and early 1930s. In a series of comedies Coward established his reputation as a writer who can unmask those around him. In *Hay Fever* (1925) the members of the Bliss family labor under the illusion that their bohemianism liberates them from societal constraints; they are self-indulgent, self-obsessed, and finally without good manners. Their guests, whom they have systematically ignored, belittled, and insulted, creep away, leading David Bliss to exclaim, "People really do behave in the most extraordinary manner these days.'' The Blisses expect to behave as they wish, but they expect the rest of society to behave conventionally.

Coward's finest play, *Private Lives,* claims no political message, and each element is fully resolved in this beautifully symmetrical play. Amanda and Elyot have each remarried and meet on their honeymoons with their exceedingly dull spouses. Elyot and Amanda appear in turn on their Riviera balconies, each having a similar conversation with their new spouses. The play begins by contrasting balanced scenes in which Amanda and Elyot discover that the only way to communicate with their new spouses is through language, but they are unable to do so. Thus, when Elyot attempts to probe Sibyl's mind and discover her future plans, she responds: ''I haven't the faintest idea what you're talking about.'' She functions on the simplest level of language as talk, of words having a precise and limited meaning. Similarly, Amanda finds Victor equally limited. When she articulates her belief that communication depends on ''a combination of circumstances'' and takes place ''if all the various cosmic thingummys fuse at the same moment, and the right spark is struck,'' Victor can only reply that she is not nearly as complex as she thinks she is.

For Elyot and Amanda, language communicates all too well on a literal level, but their feelings do not align with the words or with each other's words. They use the language of the commonplace as a weapon. In one of their most memorable scenes, they display their sophisticated barbs when Amanda asks, ''Whose yacht is that?'' and Elyot replies ''The Duke of Westminster's, I expect. It always is.'' Amanda, opening herself for the next retort, exclaims, ''I wish I were on it,'' to which Elyot replies, ''I wish you were too.'' None of these lines is especially witty alone, but given their context and the timing, they are funny and sad. This couple cannot live apart, and yet as act 2 reveals, neither can they live together. Indeed, in the second act language becomes too effective a weapon, so that periodically Amanda and Elyot must resort to a technique to literally stop communicating. When language threatens to communicate their old jealousies and recriminations too starkly, they resort to using the word ''sollocks''; the device fails and language refuses to submit to such control.

When Amanda and Elyot refrain from relying on language, they can communicate. Thus, if they divert themselves with word games such as deciding whether it is a ''covey of Bisons, or even a school of Bisons,'' or perhaps ''the Royal London school of Bisons,'' they succeed. But when they try to discuss something meaningful, such as their five years apart and the question of other lovers, they find language powerful and disturbing. Amanda says that she would not expect Elyot to have been more or less celibate than she was in their five years apart, but he cannot separate the words from the meaning they imply. He cannot bear the thought that she was not celibate, and in the ensuing argument he concludes, ''We should have said sollocks ages ago.'' They should have ceased conversation because language is too destructive.

What makes Coward very much a twentieth-century writer is his refusal to restore harmony to this chaos. We must accept that Amanda and Elyot cannot live together without fighting and there will be no happy ending because their attempts to control language are futile. Moreover, this futility infects Victor and Sibyl so that their previous united front disintegrates, and as they echo the arguments of Amanda and Elyot, Amanda and Elyot sneak out to fight another day. Coward's couples find that language communicates only too well so that they can neither live together nor apart, and in this, Coward embodies the awful dilemma of the human condition. Contemporary scholarship should continue to explore Coward to dispel the notion that he is just a period writer.

PRIMARY BIBLIOGRAPHY

Coward's plays were published at first as individual titles, then in collections of two or three, then in multiple volumes. The following selected bibliography contains those editions of the plays that are most readily available.

Plays

Collected Sketches and Lyrics. London: Hutchinson, 1931; Garden City, NY: Doubleday, 1932.
Plays. 5 vols. Introductions by Raymond Mander and Joe Mitchenson. The Master Playwrights Series. London: Methuen, 1979–83.
    Volume 1: *Hay Fever, The Vortex, Fallen Angels, Easy Virtue.* London: Methuen, 1979.
    Volume 2: *Private Lives, Bitter Sweet, The Marquise, Post Mortem.* London: Methuen, 1979.
    Volume 3: *Design for Living, Cavalcade, Conversation Piece, Tonight at 8:30 (1) [Hands across the Sea, Still Life, Fumed Oak].* London: Methuen, 1979.
    Volume 4: *Blithe Spirit, Present Laughter, This Happy Breed, Tonight at 8:30 (2) [Ways and Means, The Astonished Heart, "Red Peppers"].* London: Methuen, 1979.
    Volume 5. *Relative Values, Look after Lulu!, Waiting in the Wings, Suite in Three Keys [A Song at Twilight, Shadows of the Evening, Come into the Garden Maud].* London: Methuen, 1983.
Play Parade. 6 vols. London: Heinemann, 1934–62.
    Volume 1: *Design for Living, Cavalcade, Private Lives, Bitter Sweet, Post-Mortem, The Vortex, Hay Fever.* London: Heinemann, 1934.
    Volume 2: *This Year of Grace!, Words and Music, Operette, Conversation Piece, Fallen Angels, Easy Virtue.* London: Heinemann, 1939.
    Volume 3: *The Queen Was in the Parlour, "I'll Leave It to You," The Young Idea, Sirocco, The Rat Trap, "This Was a Man," Home Chat, The Marquise.* London: Heinemann, 1950.
    Volume 4: *Tonight at 8:30 (We Were Dancing, The Astonished Heart, "Red Peppers," Hands across the Sea, Fumed Oak, Shadow Play, Ways and Means, Still Life, Family Album), Present Laughter, This Happy Breed.* London: Heinemann, 1954.

Volume 5: *Pacific 1860, "Peace in Our Time," Relative Values, Quadrille, Blithe Spirit.* London: Heinemann, 1958.
Volume 6: *Point Valaine, South Sea Bubble, Ace of Clubs, Nude with Violin, Waiting in the Wings.* London: Heinemann, 1962.

Autobiography

Australia Visited. London: Heinemann, 1941.
Future Indefinite. London: Heinemann; Garden City, NY: Doubleday, 1954.
Middle East Diary. London: Heinemann; Garden City, NY: Doubleday, 1944.
The Noël Coward Diaries. Ed. Graham Payn and Sheridan Morley. Boston: Little, Brown, 1982.

Novel

Pomp and Circumstance. London: Heinemann; Garden City, NY: Doubleday, 1960.

Satires

Chelsea Buns. London: Hutchinson, 1925.
Spangled Unicorn. London: Hutchinson, 1932.
A Withered Nosegay. London: Christophers, 1922.

Short-Story Collections

Bon Voyage. London: Heinemann, 1967.
The Collected Stories of Noel Coward. New York: Dutton, 1983.
Pretty Polly Barlow and Other Stories. London: Heinemann, 1964.
Star Quality. London: Heinemann, 1951.
To Step Aside. London: Heinemann, 1939.

Verse Collections

The Collected Verse of Noël Coward. Ed. Graham Payn and Martin Tickner. New York: Methuen, 1985.
The Lyrics of Noël Coward. London: Heinemann, 1965.
The Noël Coward Song Book. London: Michael Joseph, 1953.
Not Yet the Dodo. London: Heinemann, 1967.

SECONDARY BIBLIOGRAPHY

Agate, James. "The Ingenium of Noël Coward." In *My Theatre Talks,* 185–92. London: A. Barker, 1935, 1947. New York: Benjamin Blom, 1971.
Braybrooke, Patrick. *The Amazing Mr. Noël Coward.* London: Archer, 1933.
Briers, Richard. *Coward and Company.* London: Robson Books, 1987.

Cole, Stephen. *Noël Coward: A Bio-Bibliography.* Westport, CT: Greenwood Press, 1993.

"Design for Living." *The Sunday Times* (26 Feb. 1995): 10:52.

Dunn, Douglas. "Pity the Poor Philosopher: Coward's Comic Genius." *Encounter* (Oct. 1980): 49–51.

Ervine, St. John. "The Plays of Mr. Noël Coward." *Queen's Quarterly* 43 (Spring 1935): 1–21.

Fisher, Clive. *Noël Coward.* London: Weidenfeld & Nicolson, 1992.

Furnas, J. C. "The Art of Noël Coward." *Fortnightly Review* 134 (Dec. 1933): 709–16.

Gray, Frances. *Noël Coward.* Basingstoke, Hampshire: Macmillan, 1987.

Review of *Hay Fever. The Times* (9 June 1925).

Kellaway, Kate. "Life Gets Ardour and Ardour." *Observer Review* (26 Feb. 1995): 10.

Kiernan, Robert F. *Noël Coward.* New York: Ungar, 1986.

Kingwill, Marilyn. "Coward Models Lingerie." *The Times* (22 Feb. 1995): 2:39.

Lahr, John. *Coward the Playwright.* London: Methuen, 1982.

Lesley, Cole. *Remembered Laughter.* New York: Alfred A. Knopf, 1976.

Lesley, Cole, Graham Payn, and Sheridan Morley. *Noël Coward and His Friends.* New York: William Morrow, 1979.

Levin, Milton. *Noël Coward.* Updated ed. Boston: Twayne, 1989.

Mander, Raymond, and Joe Mitchenson. *Theatrical Companion to Coward.* London: Rockliff, 1957.

Marchant, William. *The Privilege of His Company.* Indianapolis: Bobbs-Merrill, 1975.

Morley, Sheridan. *A Talent to Amuse: A Biography of Noël Coward.* Boston: Little, Brown, 1985.

O'Casey, Sean. "Coward Codology." In *The Green Crow,* 87–115. New York: Braziller, 1956.

Osborne, John. "Final Victory to the Silk Dressing Gown." *Spectator* (2 May 1992): 31.

Swinnerton, Frank. "Post-War Pessimism." In *The Georgian Scene,* 433–59. New York: Farrar & Rinehart, 1934.

Trewin, J. C. "Tap-Tap: Noël Coward." In *Dramatists of Today,* 151–161. London: Staples Press, 1953.

Tynan, Kenneth. [1]. "In Memory of Mr. Coward." In *The Sound of Two Hands Clapping,* 58–63. London: Cape, 1975.

———. [2]. "A Tribute to Mr. Coward." In *A View of the English Stage, 1944–1963,* 135–37. London: Davis-Poynter, 1975.

BIBLIOGRAPHY

Cole, Stephen. *Noël Coward: A Bio-Bibliography.* Westport, CT: Greenwood Press, 1993.

Clemence Dane (Winifred Ashton)
(1887–1965)

JANICE OLIVER

Remembered today as the author of over thirty plays and fourteen novels, Winifred Ashton adopted the pen name Clemence Dane from the London church on the Strand, St. Clement's Dane, reflecting her lifelong love of the city. Dane had a richly varied career as an author, writing, in addition to her novels and plays, screenplays and radio drama, along with works of nonfiction such as her memoir and history of Covent Garden, *London Has a Garden*. Of her thirty plays, most written in the 1920s and 1930s, many stand today as representative popular drama of the period. More importantly, Dane's success as a woman playwright can be profitably examined, since few women attempted at this time to write for an English stage that was not receptive to their efforts.

Before turning finally to writing, Clemence Dane first tried her hand at teaching school, painting portraits, and acting on the stage. Born in 1887 in Blackheath, London, Dane was raised in a typically late-Victorian household and was educated in private schools. She went to Switzerland for a year to become a French tutor in 1903; she would later teach overseas again, this time in Ireland (1907–13). In the meantime she studied art for three years at the Slade School in London and for another year in Dresden took a keen interest in portrait painting, and began a promising career painting theatrical posters: her portrait of playwright Ivor Novello hangs today at the Theatre Royal in Drury Lane. In 1913 Dane began acting in London and on tour under the stage name Diana Portis, but she abandoned that career with the coming of World War I. Dane suffered a decline in her health during the war, but took up writing as a career when her health returned afterward, publishing a successful novel in 1917 called *Regiment of Women* about her experience of teaching at a girls' boarding school. Because of its dramatic situation, her third novel, *Legend* (1919), directly influenced her decision to begin writing for the stage: on the night of her death, the plot reveals, a charismatic novelist's life and career are thoroughly analyzed by a group of her literary friends.

Soon after *Legend,* Dane wrote *A Bill of Divorcement* (1921), her first and most successful play. Undoubtedly due to her experience as an actress and an artist in the theater, Dane seemed to understand from the beginning what constituted a commercially viable play, but her drama is also remarkable for its variety and artfulness, as well as for the willingness to experiment that it displays. Dane's canon ranges from light West End fare like *Granite* (1926) and *Eighty in the Shade* (1959) to more experimental pieces like *Will Shakespeare* (1921) and *Come of Age* (1934) with stops in between for adaptations like Rostand's *L'Aiglon* (1934), as well as musicals like *Adam's Opera* (1928). In addition, Dane contributed scripts for film and radio, the most famous of which was that for the film *Anna Karenina* (1935), written with Salka Viertel and starring Greta Garbo. Other screenplays include the classic *Fire over England* (1936), written with Sergei Nolbandov, and *Perfect Strangers* (1945), with Anthony Pelissier. For radio, Dane most notably wrote the seven-play religious cycle *The Saviours: Seven Plays on One Theme* (1940–41).

In 1941 Dane was elected president of the Society of Women Journalists, and in 1953 she was made a Commander of the Order of the British Empire. She died on 28 March 1965.

Selected Biographical Sources: Adcock; Dane, *London Has a Garden.*

MAJOR PLAYS, PREMIERES, AND SIGNIFICANT REVIVALS: THEATRICAL RECEPTION

A Bill of Divorcement. 1921. Opened 14 March at St. Martin's Theatre (London) for 402 performances. Produced by Basil Dean. Opened 10 October 1921 at Times Square Theater (New York) for 173 performances.

This play poses the social question, should the spouse of a person declared insane be given the right to have the marriage annulled? Most British reviewers admired Dane's play about unfair divorce law and a sacrifice for the sake of loved ones. Ervine [1] remarked that although the play started off sounding like propaganda, the splendid acting by several female principals lifted it to the level of fine theater. American critic Lovett observed that this problem play offered philosophical and ethical challenges, as well as an apt solution in the daughter's sacrifice. Reviewers for both productions particularly cited Meggie Albanesi (English) and Katharine Cornell (American) for outstanding performances as the daughter Sydney. Later critics would qualify their praise. Young [2] noted that this trim piece of work lacked the mystery of human spirit because of its relentless fictional quality. Nicoll (433) called the play well constructed, but one that looked back to the worn-out play of ideas. Lewisohn faulted Dane for writing a play whose crisis came from artificial and improbable external sources.

Will Shakespeare. 1921. Opened 17 November at the Shaftesbury Theatre (London) for 62 performances. Produced and directed by Basil Dean. Opened 1 January 1923 at the National Theatre (New York) for 80 performances.

Called an invention, this highly imaginative version of the Bard's life has him leaving Anne Hathaway, enticed by London and the Dark Lady, Mary Fitton, who in turn would become the cause of his accidentally murdering his competitor for her affections, Kit Marlow. Most reviewers had difficulty accepting the premise. Ervine [3] criticized this Shakespeare's humorlessness ad Dane's supposed inability to write sympathetic male characters. Young ([1], 21) thought the situations forced, but since the American production had been effectively cut, the *New York times* (Review of *Will Shakespeare*) found it a more satisfying play that was actually about the three women in Shakespeare's life. Nathan (704) and the *Spectator* (Review of *Will Shakespeare*) dissented, the former calling it excessively pretentious, the latter the worst play so far from an essentially "good" author. Special acclaim from most went to Haidee Wright as Queen Elizabeth, whose last scene Young [1] called one of the finest inventions in modern drama.

The Way Things Happen. 1924. Opened 2 February at the Ambassadors Theatre (London) for 65 performances.

The Way Things Happen is a melodrama about a young woman's sacrificing herself to a villainous man in order to save the man she loves from going to prison for embezzlement. The play's depictions of men preoccupied reviewers, who called attention to Dane's inability or unwillingness to write convincingly realistic male characters. Griffith pointed to the play's "definite anti-man tendency," while *The Times* (Review of *The Way Things Happen*) described the three male "bounders" as unbelievable stereotypes. The *Illustrated London News* (Review of *The Way Things Happen*) said that these same three were "mere melodramatic types." *The Times* reviewer's bias, in particular, surfaced when he referred to Dane as a "spinster-dramatist" whose guilelessness compelled her to offer impossibly romanticized male characters. Only the *Spectator* (Review of *The Way Things Happen*) examined the possible psychological premise underlying the play, when the main character was rendered "helpless" by the subtly manipulative, overbearing love of a selfless-seeming mother and sacrificing girlfriend. Most remarked that the lascivious villain and insufferably arrogant thief limited the credibility of the piece, but several thought that these were credible human beings. All did agree, however, on the remarkably effective performance, and death scene, by Haidee Wright (who also played Queen Elizabeth in *Will Shakespeare*) as the mother.

Granite. 1926. Opened 15 June at the Ambassadors Theatre (London) for 62 performances. Produced by Lewis T. Casson.

Set off the wild English coastline on the Isle of Lundy, this otherworldly drama tells the story of a desperate, spiritually stultified women who desires her insensitive husband's half brother. A shipwrecked convict makes possible her wish, but a problem arises for the woman when the convict brings the same consequence—death—to her second husband, the half brother, as he did to her first. Most reviewers faulted what they saw as Dane's equivocating about the character of the shipwrecked convict: is he the devil incarnate or simply an avaricious con man who finds a willing victim in the heroine, Judith Morris? *The Times* (Review of *Granite*) criticized Dane for placing the character in a fantastic mode one moment and then rationally "explaining [the fantasy] away" in the next. The *Spectator* (Review of *Granite*), however, noted that although this character directs the action by "laws outside its possibilities," the play was nevertheless "cleverly constructed." Agate [1] cited Dane's inability to pull off this version of the Faust myth, saying that the play was too lengthy to sustain intensity and lacked "philosophical substance." Ervine [2], however, praised Dane's success in creating believable male characters, the lack of which she had been faulted for in her earlier plays and novels. One problematic element running through all commentaries is the motivation of Judith: is she a woman trapped by her own sexual desires, or one frustrated by the stony island terrain— the granite of the title—which mirrors her husband's cold nature?

ADDITIONAL PLAYS, ADAPTATIONS, AND PRODUCTIONS

Wild Decembers opened on 26 May 1933 at the Apollo Theatre (London) for 50 performances. A depiction of the Brontë story, this attempt was faulted for having too many episodic scenes, especially those of Charlotte's life in Brussels. Additionally, the problematic casting of the beautiful Diana Wynyard as mousy Charlotte hampered its effectiveness.

Come of Age opened on 12 January 1934 in New York at Maxine Elliott's Theatre for 35 performances. A fantasy musical written with Richard Addinsell about the rebirth and death of the poet Thomas Chatterton, this experiment in verse starring Judith Anderson was admired by a few for its magnitude (see Benét), but criticized by most for its artificiality, Nathan calling it "pretentious fiddle faddle." *Eighty in the Shade* opened at the Globe Theatre on 8 January 1959, running for 179 performances. The play was written by Dane for her longtime friend Sybil Thorndike. The critics faulted it for its sentimentality, but audiences were enthusiastic because of affection for Thorndike and her skillful performance.

Dane adapted for the stage Edmond Rostand's *L'Aiglon* (1934), Sir Max Beerbohm's *The Happy Hypocrite* (1936), and Friedrich Hebbel's *Herod and Mariamne* (1938). Collaboration figuring prominently in her career, Dane worked with Addinsell on the musicals *Adam's Opera* (1928) and *Alice's Adventures in Wonderland and Through the Looking Glass* (1948). She also wrote children's plays, *Shivering Shocks* (1923) and *Mr. Fox* (1927) among them. Finally, Dane created, either individually or with others, over twenty scripts for radio, television, and film.

ASSESSMENT OF DANE'S CAREER

As is the case with many dramatists, Dane was hindered by the early, phenomenal success of *A Bill of Divorcement,* having to overcome the spectre, as Ervine [4] termed it, of being a "oncer," one whose career might outlive her limited abilities. In addition, Dane's success as a novelist, ability as a painter, and experience as an actress may have advanced the fallacy that diversity lessens power. Early critics like Mais (264–65) and Young ([1], 21–22) commended Dane's stagecraft, but faulted her for her failure to flesh out her characters, especially the male ones. Later critics disagreed on Dane's reputation as a dramatist of note. Nicoll relegated her to the theater of the past, notably for her attempts at writing a play of ideas (*A Bill of Divorcement*), a verse drama (*Will Shakespeare*), and regional theater (*Granite*) (433–34). Ervine [4] called Dane "the most distinguished woman dramatist in the history of the theatre," faint praise, however, in the context of his patriarchal attitude about women in the theater. It seems that Dane was either treated with genteel civility (Adcock, 37; Lawrence, 365) or, as by Ervine, dismissively. Trewin most accurately estimated Dane's worth when he said that the "representative woman dramatist" (128) in England at the time (1953) would not be disregarded by posterity.

In the 1920s, at the ascendance of Dane's productivity as a playwright, early postwar idealism had melted in the face of difficult economic times, the mood shifting to disillusionment and escapist fare. Now, as plays were written not so much for their literary merit as for their theatricality, critics perhaps more than audiences admired her more intellectual, experimentally daring work, like *Will Shakespeare,* which expanded on poetic drama through use of symbolism. Audiences used to melodrama, the problem play, and the drawing-room drama responded well to plays like *A Bill of Divorcement* and *The Way Things Happen,* plays that tended to enhance traditional forms through keen observation of human behavior expressed in wit-filled language. Later, when some playwrights were experimenting with ideas for the theater based upon a more imaginative realism/naturalism, Dane responded with *Granite,* which tested the boundaries of realism as well as women's sexuality, and *Wild Decembers,* a well-made play, but with less plot and more finely drawn characters. At a time when English drama remained relatively untouched by the explosion of dramatic forms in Europe, Dane experimented with the limited types available to her, especially in the way she persistently tested the limits of language to expand dramatic possibilities. Certainly, a fruitful study could be made of her experiments, even the failed ones, and their contribution to the evolution of drama in England at the time.

Foremost, Dane was a female theater practitioner working in so thoroughly entrenched a man's world that she, along with other women playwrights like "Gordon Daviot" (Elizabeth Mackintosh), adopted a male pseudonym, one can assume because of a male author's easier access to public acceptance. In an era when the tyrannical reign of the male actor-manager had just waned, and when actresses like Ellen Terry had just come into their own power, female play-wrights had as yet no footing; consequently, Dane could look to no one as a gauge for success or influence. Additionally, she worked in a theater dominated by personalities like St. John Ervine [4], author and critic, whose virulent male bias prompted him to say that a "womanized theatre" dominated by females, by definition "less apt than men," would devitalize the robust male theater where great male playwrights find production in safe masculine hands. Because of voices like these that subjugated women, the complex of strong-willed egos in the theater, and interior constraints that cultivated only nurturing roles, it is incredible that Dane gained as much critical and commercial success as she did. A study of how this particular woman's career evolved in a society that routinely marginalized women's creative efforts would contribute greatly to our under-standing of women's social history.

Fortunately for Dane, from the beginning some of the finest actors were cast in her plays. Strongly written female characters attracted Haidee Wright (*Will Shakespeare, The Way Things Happen*), Judith Anderson (*Come of Age*), Sybil Thorndike (*Granite, Eighty in the Shade*), and Katharine Cornell (*A Bill of Divorcement*). Despite the fact that Dane was faulted for creating less believable male characters, the casting of talented actors like Lewis Casson (*Granite, Eighty in the Shade*), Emlyn Williams (*Wild Decembers*), and Ralph Richardson (*Wild Decembers*) would suggest that this was not the case. Actors routinely gave critically superlative performances in Dane's drama, even when the plays them-selves were found wanting. Carrying her collaborative spirit into codirecting the thoroughly experimental *Come of Age* with Judith Anderson, Dane would say that this was the only time she found fulfillment in a play. This collaborative relationship between an actress turned playwright and those artists drawn to her work should be examined to see how each affected the other in terms of aes-thetics and stage presentation.

In a presidential address to the English Association, Dane in her mid-seventies surveyed twentieth-century drama, decades in time but millennia in form and attitude. Seeing few answers in society to the question of what we should do with evil in the world, this traditional humanist looked to drama for an answer to this question. Dane described theater in the 1920s and 1930s as speaking against the atrocities of war but also easing the pain of interwar anxiety, while contemporary drama of the 1960s, she went on to say, revolted against all of society. Mentioning Wesker, Behan, and Osborne, Dane singled out Pinter's *The Caretaker* as a singular example of imagination and skill that transforms ex-perience. Showing a remarkable grasp of the theatrical as well as the philo-sophical and psychological history of the English, Dane never did span the ages she discussed with her art, but neither did any other writer of her time. She does, however, deserve scholarly attention as the only female of the first half of the twentieth century to produce so prolific and varied a canon of drama.

ARCHIVAL SOURCES

The Harry Ransom Humanities Research Center at the University of Texas, Austin, holds some of Dane's manuscripts.

PRIMARY BIBLIOGRAPHY

Plays

A Bill of Divorcement. London: Heinemann, 1921; New York: Macmillan, 1921.
Call Home the Heart. London: Heinemann, 1947.
Come of Age. Garden City, NY: Doubleday, Doran, 1934; London: Heinemann, 1938.
Cousin Muriel. London: Heinemann, 1940.
Eighty in the Shade. London: Samuel French, 1959.
England's Darling. London: Heinemann, 1940.
Granite: A Tragedy. New York: Macmillan, 1926; London: Heinemann, 1926.
Herod and Mariamme. Garden City, NY: Doubleday, Doran, 1938.
Mariners. London: Heinemann, 1927; New York: Macmillan, 1927.
Moonlight Is Silver. London: Heinemann, 1934.
Naboth's Vineyard. London: Heinemann, 1925.
A Traveller Returns. London and New York: Samuel French, 1927.
The Way Things Happen: A Story in Three Acts. London: Heinemann, 1923; New York: Macmillan, 1924.
Wild Decembers. London: Heinemann, 1932; Garden City, NY: Doubleday, Doran, 1933.
Will Shakespeare: An Invention in Four Acts. London: Heinemann, 1921; New York: Macmillan, 1922.

Anthology

The Collected Plays of Clemence Dane. London: Heinemann, 1961.

Essays and Articles on Drama and Theater

Approaches to Drama: Presidential Address to the English Association. London: Amen House, 1961.
London Has a Garden. New York: Norton, 1964.
The Women's Side. London: Herbert Jenkins, 1926.

SECONDARY BIBLIOGRAPHY

Adcock, A(rthur) St. John. *The Glory That Was Grub Street: Impressions of Contemporary Authors.* London: S. Low, Marston, 1928; New York: F. A. Stokes, 1928.
Agate, James. [1]. Review of *Granite. The Sunday Times* (20 June 1926): 6.

———. [2]. Review of *The Way Things Happen. The Sunday Times* (3 Feb. 1924): 12.

Benét, William Rose. "A Play like Poetry." *Saturday Review* (10 Feb. 1934): 476.

Carroll, Sydney W. [1]. Review of *A Bill of Divorcement. The Sunday Times* (20 Mar. 1921): 4.

———. [2]. Review of *Will Shakespeare. The Sunday Times* (20 Nov. 1921): 4.

Ervine, St. John. [1]. Review of *A Bill of Divorcement.* In *Specimens of English Dramatic Criticism,* ed. A. C. Ward. London: Oxford University Press, 1945.

———. [2]. Review of *Granite. The Observer* (20 June 1926): 13.

———. [3]. "On Clemence Dane's *Will Shakespeare." The Observer* (20 Nov. 1921): 11.

———. [4]. *The Theatre in My Time.* London: Rich & Cowan, 1933.

Review of *Granite. The Spectator* (26 June 1926): 1076–77.

Review of *Granite. The Times* (16 June 1926): 14.

Griffith, Hubert. Review of *The Way Things Happen. The Observer* (3 Feb. 1924): 14.

Krutch, Joseph Wood. "On Make Believe and Acting." *Nation* (30 Mar. 1927): 350.

Lawrence, Margaret. *The School of Femininity.* New York: Frederick A. Stokes Co., 1936.

Lewisohn, Ludwig. "Pity and Terror—II." *Nation* (9 Nov. 1921): 545.

Lovett, Robert Morss. "After the Play." *New Republic* (28 Dec. 1921): 130.

Mais, S.P.B. *Some Modern Authors.* London: Grant Richards, 1923.

Nathan, George Jean. *The Theatre in the Fifties.* New York: Alfred A. Knopf, 1953.

Nicoll, Allardyce. *English Drama, 1900–1930: The Beginnings of the Modern Period.* Cambridge: Cambridge University Press, 1973.

Sutton, Graham. *Some Contemporary Dramatists.* London: L. Parsons, 1924.

Trewin, J. C. *Dramatists of Today.* London: Staples Press, 1953.

Review of *The Way Things Happen. Illustrated London News* (9 Feb. 1924): 246.

Review of *The Way Things Happen. Spectator* (8 Mar. 1924): 362–63.

Review of *The Way Things Happen. The Times* (4 Feb. 1924): 10.

Review of *Will Shakespeare. New York Times* (2 Jan. 1923): 14.

Review of *Will Shakespeare. Spectator* (26 Nov. 1921): 704.

Young, Stark. [1]. *Immortal Shadows: A Book of Dramatic Criticism.* New York: Charles Scribner's Sons, 1948.

———. [2]. "More Than Clear." *New Republic* (13 July 1921): 198.

T. S. Eliot
(1888–1965)

RANDY MALAMUD

Renowned for poetry that virtually defined modernism during and after World War I ("The Love Song of J. Alfred Prufrock," *The Waste Land,* "The Hollow Men") and during World War II (*Four Quartets*), Eliot actually spent as much time and energy during the second half of his literary career as a dramatist as he had during his younger days as a poet. Yet Eliot's drama has received considerably less critical attention than his poetry: his plays lacked the avant-garde panache that marked his poetry and made him the pioneer and hero of a generation of writers. His verse drama never exerted as much influence as his drastically new poetic breakthroughs. (A revival of verse drama in the 1930s and 1940s faltered in the 1950s in the face of more vital drama emanating from such playwrights as Pinter, Beckett, and Osborne.) In the views of many critics, his plays simply were not as good as his poetry: they were judged tame, conventional, and derivative.

Born in St. Louis, Missouri, on 26 September 1888, Eliot left behind the American heartland that he saw as staid and banal, adopting an East Coast elitism during an undergraduate and graduate career at Harvard (1906–14). As a student of philosophy, Eliot's accomplishments were auspicious, and the contacts he made at Harvard and the Sorbonne (including George Santayana, Bertrand Russell, and Henri Bergson) were impressive. But Eliot abandoned Harvard and philosophy as he had earlier abandoned St. Louis, relocating in London in 1914 and ensconcing himself in English and European culture.

His early poetic triumphs, along with voluminous well-respected literary essays, won him the favorable attention of London's burgeoning literary avant-garde. The publication of *The Waste Land* in 1922, still considered by many as the catalyst of literary modernism, earned him acclaim as the keenest of the voices of postwar Europe.

In the 1920s Eliot's credentials as modern poet and literary critic were impeccably established. He was accumulating influence at Faber and Faber, England's foremost publisher of serious contemporary literature, where he would work the rest of his life; as poetry editor, Eliot was a key "gatekeeper" for two generations of English poets. During this period Eliot extended his oeuvre beyond poetry. Attracted by what he considered the primitive ritualistic power inherent in drama, dating back to its classical roots, Eliot experimented with theater in his jazzy fragment *Sweeney Agonistes* (published 1926–27, first performed 1933). Marked by much of the harsh cynicism that filled his poetry, the play caught the eye of fringe theatrical circles and Eliot's usual audience, especially during 1934–35 productions by Rupert Doone's Group Theatre troupe.

But Eliot's next theatrical production, *The Rock* (1934), marked a significant departure from what *Sweeney Agonistes* seemed to have foretold. In 1928 Eliot announced his conversion to Anglo-Catholicism, and this pageant play—a benefit for a London church-building drive presented largely by amateur actors—featured an aggressively Christian campaign that seemed remote from his writing of the 1910s and 1920s. In later years the play's choruses (preserved, apart from the rest of the play's text, in Eliot's *Collected Poems*) found some favor with critics; otherwise the play has lapsed into obscurity.

The Christian focus, however, remained in all Eliot's subsequent plays—explicitly in *Murder in the Cathedral* (1935), more subtly in the others. The story of Thomas Becket's twelfth-century martyrdom was commissioned for the Canterbury Festival and performed close to where the assassination had taken place. The dramatic verse, often evocative of "Burnt Norton" (on which Eliot was working as he composed the play), was widely judged successful and compelling. The play is perhaps Eliot's best-known and is still often performed, generally by amateur troupes at colleges and churches.

Eliot's last plays were popular drawing-room comedies; all grew out of classical analogues. *The Family Reunion* (1939) is the darkest of these: a reconsideration of the *Oresteia,* it concerns the attempts of Harry, Lord Monchensey, to escape from the ghosts that have been tormenting him since his wife's death many years earlier—a death in which he was somehow complicit. *The Cocktail Party* (1949), which garnered three Tony Awards for its Broadway run, is a loose reworking of the *Alcestis* of Euripides. Lighter and more comedic than *The Family Reunion,* this play established Eliot's reputation as a popularized intellectual, entertaining mass audiences with drama that packed some deeper punch, though some of Eliot's oldest admirers found his message somewhat trite.

The Cocktail Party premiered at the Edinburgh Festival, as did Eliot's two subsequent plays, *The Confidential Clerk* (1953) and *The Elder Statesman* (1958). The first of these spins webs of intrigue and confusion in the mode of its classical analogue, the *Ion* of Euripides, about the parentage of a young man, Colby Simpkins, trying to discover his true identity and calling. Eliot's last play, indebted to Sophocles' final play, *Oedipus at Colonus,* examines the remorse and spiritual regeneration of Lord Claverton, a statesman who accumulated numerous skeletons during his rise to prominence. Eliot died in London on 4 January 1965; an urn with his ashes was placed in East Coker, the English village from which an ancestor had sailed to New England in the seventeenth century.

Selected Biographical Sources: Ackroyd; Browne; Bush; Gordon [1, 2].

MAJOR PLAYS, PREMIERES, AND SIGNIFICANT REVIVALS: THEATRICAL RECEPTION

Sweeney Agonistes. 1933. First performed on 6 May at the Vassar Experimental Theatre, Vassar College, Poughkeepsie, New York, directed by Hallie Flanagan. London premiere by the Group Theatre at the Group Theatre Rooms for sporadic performances starting on 11 November 1934, directed by Rupert Doone; moved on 1 October 1935 to the Westminster Theatre for 15 performances (double-billed with Auden's *The Dance of Death*). Revivals: Living Theater Company (New York), March 1952; Globe Theatre (London), June 1965; Cocteau Repertory (New York), August 1972; Birkenhead Exchange (London), August 1988.

Most reviewers appreciated the play's jazzy, avant-garde tenor: Coghill applauded an exquisite blend of violence and restraint, while MacCarthy [2] saw in the play Eliot's negative impulse, his lurid (and fashionable) fascination with the sordid. Bishop, though, called the play pretentious and pointless. The work, though revived fairly infrequently, has aged well: Worth (58) called the 1965 production exhilaratingly open, while Edwards complimented its urbane brittleness and stylish nightmare quality in 1988. Spanos (9–10) saw the play as a vintage example of theater of the absurd. Evans (146) discussed the play's hypnotic focus on rhythm and the nature of language; like many critics, he noted Eliot's keen ear for contemporary idiom.

The Rock. 1934. Opened 28 May at Sadler's Wells Theatre (London) for 13 performances. Directed by E. Martin Browne.

Literally "preaching to the converted" in this play about the continuity of Christian tradition (which some saw as glib propaganda), Eliot had his first exposure to large audiences with this production. Sewell lauded the pageant play as lucid, brilliant poetry, and Isaacs (152–53) called the production the first popular example of contemporary poetic drama. Sayers, though, called the dialogue tedious and spiritless, while Moore, like other reviewers, called the play unworthy of the author of *The Waste Land*. Verschoyle found the content unconvincing, writing that Eliot's case for the importance of the church was based upon invocation rather than definition, devoid of logical justification. Grover Smith's response (171) is emblematic of the general sensibility of Eliot scholars: he called Eliot's effort so unfortunate that nobody would have imagined that Eliot had a future in drama. Ward (186) called the work a failed combination of crude expressionism and flaccid choruses. Olshin, however, defended the play's integrity in terms of the Christian discourse to which it aspires.

Murder in the Cathedral. 1935. Opened 15 June at the Canterbury Cathedral Chapter House. Directed by E. Martin Browne. Moved to the Mercury Theatre (London) on 1 November for 180 performances, and to the Duchess Theatre (London) on 30 October 1936 for 113 performances. The New York premiere opened 20 March 1936 at the Manhattan Theatre, by the Popular Price Theatre of the Work Projects Administration's Federal Theatre Project, produced by Hallie Flanagan and directed by Halsted Welles. Revivals: Ritz Theatre (New York), opened on 16 February 1938 for 21 performances; Gateway Theatre (Edinburgh), 1947; Old Vic Theatre (London), 1953; American Shakespeare Festival Theatre (Stratford, Connecticut), June 1966; Canterbury Cathedral, 1970; Aldwych Theatre (London), August 1972.

Aiken, citing its living and natural poetry, called the Canterbury premiere of this saint's play a turning point in English drama. When the play moved to the West End's Duchess Theatre, Brown [2] complained that the production suffered for the relocation; the cathedral setting, he felt, was essential. The New York premiere, though sometimes obscure and dull, was also dignified and beautiful, wrote Watts. Gabriel called the production the bravest and most artistic play staged to date by the Federal Theatre Project. The 1953 revival was clarified and more magnificently theatrical than in the play's first incarnation, wrote Atkinson. Spender appreciated the way in which Eliot depicted a hero's discovery of religious vocation, while Carol H. Smith (110) called the play Eliot's most successful implementation of his dramatic theories. Donoghue (83), though, complained that the play evaded, rather than solved, the problems of dramatic verse. Several critics, like Ayers, found that the play's unity lies in its debt to the ceremony of the Mass; Billman, similarly, saw a metaphysical structure as a force of dramatic coherence.

The Family Reunion. 1939. Opened on 21 March at the Westminster Theatre (London) for 38 performances. Directed by E. Martin Browne. The New York premiere opened in November 1947 at the Cherry Lane Theatre, directed by Frank Corsaro. Revivals: Mercury Theatre (London) in October 1946; Gateway Theatre (Edinburgh) in 1947; Phoenix Theatre (London) in June 1956; Phoenix Theatre (New York) in October 1958; Vaudeville Theatre (London) by the Royal Exchange Theatre Company in June 1979.

In this play Eliot began to write in a style he would maintain for the rest of his career: drawing-room comedy-dramas, suited for broad popular West End and Broadway audiences. Eliot's verse aspires to the condition of prose, wrote Morgan; it captures the rhythms of everyday conversation while maintaining a poetic texture. MacCarthy [1], like others, found an absence of dramatic motivation, judging the play's blend of realism and symbolism a failure. Aston called the 1958 revival labored and rambling. Roberts (185–86) viewed the play as a transition between the religious tragedy of *Murder in the Cathedral* and the serious comedy of the later plays. Brooks found the tenor close to that of Eliot's poetry, a recapitulation of his poetic symbolism.

The Cocktail Party. 1949. Opened on 22 August at the Royal Lyceum Theatre (Edinburgh) as part of the Edinburgh International Festival, directed by E. Martin Browne, produced by Gilbert Miller and Henry Sherek; moved to Henry Miller's Theatre (New York) on 21 January 1950; that show ran for 409 performances. The London opening was on 3 May 1950 at the New Theatre; that show ran for 325 performances. Revivals: Lyceum Theatre (New York) in October 1968; Wyndham's Theatre (London) in November 1968; Phoenix Theatre (London) in July 1986.

Acclaimed as Eliot's most popularly successful verse comedy, *The Cocktail Party* garnered *The Sunday Times* literary prize and three Tony Awards for its Broadway run. Yet critics, especially those comfortable with Eliot's vintage complexities, found fault with a play that was perhaps too glib. Brown [1] found the play pretentiously mystifying, and Shawe-Taylor called the play chilly, wanting a human naturalness; Barnes, while lauding Eliot's prosody and symbolism, found a lack of emotional substance and no catharsis. Clurman called the play morally dishonest and Eliot's philosophizing banal. Winter analyzed the play as a depiction of the archetypal condition of "Prufrockism," in the mode of Eliot's poetry. Peter and Barber (passim) explored ways in which it both meets and fails to meet the generic expectations of theatrical comedy. Gardner (43) found the work unabashedly comic, consciously marking the final phase in Eliot's career.

The Confidential Clerk. 1953. Opened at the Royal Lyceum Theatre (Edinburgh) on 25 August as part of the Edinburgh International Festival, directed by E. Martin Browne and produced by Henry Sherek; moved to the Lyric Theatre (London) on 16 September for 259 performances. The New York opening was at the Morosco Theatre on 11 February 1954; that show ran for 117 performances. Revival: London Academy of Music and Dramatic Art in November 1976.

Darlington [2] spoke for many reviewers, calling the play pleasant, light, and well contrived, though not deep or important. Weightman called the content dubious and clumsy, while Donald found the play exceedingly contrived and accused Eliot of raising expectations and then failing to fulfill them. Hawkins wrote that the play was more accessible and less pretentious than Eliot's previous play. McElroy (44–45) saw the drama as Eliot's most mature confrontation of existentialism, specifically the problem of establishing the self. Davies wrote that the play reflected Eliot's coming to terms with his audience, no longer trying to dazzle or mystify them.

The Elder Statesman. 1958. Opened at the Royal Lyceum Theatre (Edinburgh) on 24 August as part of the Edinburgh International Festival, directed by E. Martin Browne, produced by Henry Sherek; moved to the Cambridge Theatre

(London) on 25 September for 92 performances. American premiere at the Fred Miller Theatre (Milwaukee) on 27 February 1963. Revival: Malvern Festival in June 1979.

Darlington [1] appreciated the play more than Eliot's previous two because he found it less austere. Hobson praised its spirit of love, hope, and forgiveness. Hope-Wallace, though, found the play tedious, lacking the edge of novelty found in Eliot's earlier work. Brien called the drama a zombie play for the living dead—pallid, snobbish, melodramatic, and vulgar. Abbott (101) saw the play as a formal completion to the cycle begun in *Murder in the Cathedral,* presenting a world of everymen rather than saints. Weales found a warmth previously absent from Eliot's drama. Grover Smith (233) analyzed the play's "ghosts" as prototypical recurrences from all Eliot's earlier poetry and plays.

ADDITIONAL PLAYS, ADAPTATIONS, AND PRODUCTIONS

Cats, with lyrics adapted from Eliot's 1939 collection *Old Possum's Book of Practical Cats* and a score composed by Andrew Lloyd Webber, opened at the West End's New London Theatre on 11 May 1981, and in New York at the Winter Garden on 7 October 1982. The Broadway musical won seven Tony Awards in 1983: Eliot was posthumously awarded the Tony for musical book and shared with Lloyd Webber the Award for score. Several of Eliot's other poetic works have been set to music, including Igor Stravinsky's *Anthem: The Dove Descending Breaks the Air* and Benjamin Britten's *Canticle IV: Journey of the Magi* and *Canticle V: The Death of Saint Narcissus. Murder in the Cathedral* was filmed by George Hoellering (with Eliot's collaboration) in 1951 and was performed as an opera (*Assassinio nella Catedrale*) by Ildebrando Pizzetti at La Scala in Milan in 1958.

ASSESSMENT OF ELIOT'S CAREER

During the time when Eliot's plays were being produced, they held the rapt attention of the literary and academic establishments. Typifying the response of this period, Donoghue (passim) argued that each of Eliot's plays improves on the previous one; and Kline (472) lavished boundless adulation, writing that the plays bring a depth more profound than anything previously realized in successful drama—a solution to the human dilemma.

In 1972 Bergonzi (189) offered a verdict that runs to the other extreme, calling the plays irredeemably trivial and asserting that Eliot's promising dramatic stirrings in the 1920s and 1930s proved to have taken a mistaken turn thereafter. The fashionable critical slant on the plays most recently has been to regard them largely as the watery attempts of a poet past his prime, who had said all he had to say by the time he finished *Four Quartets* but determined to stay in the spotlight and found the theater a vehicle for this. The plays may be found of minor interest only to the extent that they resonate with affinities to the poetry.

The kinds of dramatic intricacies and complexities that Carol H. Smith detailed in her 1963 study—a dualism of levels reflecting Eliot's auspicious agenda of secular and metaphysical explorations of morality—are largely absent from current scholarship, but Gordon's excellent biographical attention to Eliot has resurrected interest in the phase of his life during which the plays were written and has provided provocative leaping-off points for further study of the plays. Aspects of Eliot's life and career that were previously glossed over have come into sharper focus and have proven to indicate that his later dramatic career deserves attention, both on its own merits and in terms of the way issues from his more prominent youth and middle age linger in the dramatic literature of his more mature period.

In addition, future scholarship of Eliot's plays will probably expand as academics become increasingly skeptical of monolithic, established canons. Eliot was among the most successful writers of his age in propounding a fixed and sacrosanct canon, a prescribed aesthetic orientation, in which his own poetry is central. Now that such a sensibility has been challenged and Eliot's critical postures are subject to drastic revisionism, scholars may start to look beyond what we had been instructed were the greatest masterpieces of the greatest modernist poet. The plays, then, may benefit from a renewal of interest as readers scurry away from *The Waste Land.*

Eliot's plays offer, first, a sense of atonement for the solipsistic hostility of his poetry: an attempt to provide alternative visions of the possibility of thinking, speaking, and enduring life in the modern world. The plays do not reject or contradict the stance of Eliot's youth; rather, they augment this vision. The facts of modern waste lands, muteness and alienation, are not absent from his plays; but they are a starting point from which Eliot set himself the task of working to find a realm of community, of human understanding and interaction. These communities are neither arcadian nor utopian and often seem mitigated, or compromised, or understated. In terms of the constitution and sustenance of the dramatic communities he envisions, Eliot was a pragmatist and realized that the track record of contemporary Western society does not justify glorious idealism. He was satisfied, though, to light a single candle—which was a drastic reversal indeed for the poet who made his name brilliantly cursing the darkness.

A master wordsmith throughout his career, Eliot revised his focus in the genre of drama. Rather than retreating into a sanctuary/prison of refined, intellectually elite language, as he had done in his dazzlingly obscure poetry, he set his sights on trying to find, through the communal medium of drama, a sensibility "where the words are valid" (a phrase he used at the end of act 2 of *The Cocktail Party*). His language is less elevated (though it retains, for those who attend carefully, a subtle delicacy and nobility), but ultimately more meaningful—by definition, since meaning is predicated upon shared understanding of a community of speakers, which is what Eliot's plays offer resplendently.

ARCHIVAL SOURCES

Harvard University's Houghton Library holds the manuscript of *Murder in the Cathedral* and typescript scenarios and notes for *The Family Reunion*. The John Hayward Collection at Cambridge University's King's College Modern Archives contains drafts and manuscripts of *The Family Reunion, The Cocktail Party, The Confidential Clerk,* and *The Elder Statesman,* as well as a draft of *The Superior Landlord,* a version of *Sweeney Agonistes.* Oxford University's Bodleian Library contains scenarios, notes, and typescript drafts of *The Rock.* The Eliot Collection at the University of Texas, Austin, holds a typescript of *The Cocktail Party,* manuscript excerpts from *The Confidential Clerk,* and a typescript of *The Elder Statesman.* The Performing Arts Research Center of the New York Public Library holds an archival collection of programs, reviews, production details, and photographs of the plays.

PRIMARY BIBLIOGRAPHY

Plays

The Cocktail Party. New York: Harcourt, Brace, 1950.
The Confidential Clerk. New York: Harcourt, Brace, 1954.
The Elder Statesman. New York: Farrar, 1959; Noonday, 1964.
The Family Reunion. New York: Harcourt, Brace, 1939.
Murder in the Cathedral. New York: Harcourt, Brace, 1935.
The Rock. New York: Harcourt, Brace, 1934.
Sweeney Agonistes. In *Collected Poems, 1909–1962,* 111–24. New York: Harcourt Brace
    Jovanovich, 1970.

Monographs, Essays, and Articles on Drama and Theater

Many of these essays are reprinted in one or more of the following anthologies of Eliot's essays: *On Poetry and Poets* (New York: Noonday, 1957); *The Sacred Wood* (London: Methuen, 1920); and *Selected Essays* (New York: Harcourt, Brace, 1950).

"Audiences, Producers, Plays, Poets." *New Verse* 18 (Dec. 1935): 3–4.
"The Beating of a Drum." *The Nation and Athenaeum* 34.1 (6 Oct. 1923): 11–12.
"Ben Johnson." *Times Literary Supplement* (13 Nov. 1919): 637–38. Reprinted in *The
    Sacred Wood,* 104–22, and *Selected Essays,* 127–39.
"Cyril Tourneur." *Times Literary Supplement* (13 Nov. 1920): 925–26. Reprinted in
    Selected Essays, 159–69.
"A Dialogue on Poetic Drama." Preface to *Of Dramatick Poesie: An Essay, 1688,* by

John Dryden. London: Frederick Etchells & Hugh Macdonald, 1928. Reprinted as "A Dialogue on Dramatic Poetry" in *Selected Essays,* 31–45.

"Dramatis Personae." *Criterion* 1.3 (Apr. 1923): 303–6.

"Euripides and Gilbert Murray: A Performance at the Holborn Empire." *Art and Letters* 3.2 (Spring 1920): 36–43. Reprinted as "Euripides and Professor Murray" in *The Sacred Wood,* 71–77, and *Selected Essays,* 46–50.

"Five Points on Dramatic Writing." *Townsman* 1.3 (July 1938): 10.

"Four Elizabethan Dramatists." *Criterion* 2.6 (Feb. 1924): 115–23. Reprinted in *Selected Essays,* 91–99.

"The Future of Poetic Drama." *Drama (Journal of the British Drama League, London)* 17 (Oct. 1938): 3–5.

"Hamlet and His Problems." *Athenaeum* (19 Sept. 1919): 940–41. Reprinted in *The Sacred Wood,* 95–103, and *Selected Essays,* 121–26.

"Introduction." In *Seneca His Tenne Tragedies,* ed. Thomas Newton. London: Constable, 1927, i.v–liv. Reprinted as "Seneca in Elizabethan Translation" in *Selected Essays,* 51–88.

"John Ford." *Times Literary Supplement* (5 May 1932): 317–18. Reprinted in *Selected Essays,* 170–80.

"The Need for Poetic Drama." *Listener* (25 Nov. 1936): 994–95.

"Philip Massinger." *Times Literary Supplement* (27 May 1920): 325–26; continuation, "The Old Comedy." *Athenaeum* (11 June 1920): 760–61. Reprinted in *The Sacred Wood,* 123–43 and *Selected Essays,* 181–95.

"The Poetic Drama." *Athenaeum* (14 May 1920): 635–36.

Poetry and Drama. Cambridge, MA: Harvard University Press, 1951. Reprinted in *On Poetry and Poets,* 75–95.

"The Possibility of a Poetic Drama." *Dial* (New York) 69.5 (Nov. 1920): 441–47. Reprinted in *The Sacred Wood,* 60–70.

"Preface." In *The Film of Murder in the Cathedral,* with George Hoellering. New York: Harcourt, Brace, 1952.

Religious Drama: Mediaeval and Modern. New York: House of Books, 1954.

Shakespeare and the Stoicism of Seneca. London: Published for the Shakespeare Association by H. Milford, Oxford University Press, 1927 and London: De la More Press, [1960]. Reprinted in *Selected Essays,* 107–20.

"Some Notes on the Blank Verse of Christopher Marlowe." *Art and Letters* 2.4 (Autumn 1919): 194–99. Reprinted in *The Sacred Wood,* 86–94, and as "Christopher Marlowe" in *Selected Essays,* 100–106.

"Thomas Heywood." *Times Literary Supplement* (30 July 1931): 589–90. Reprinted in *Selected Essays,* 149–58.

"Thomas Middleton." *Times Literary Supplement* (30 June 1927): 445–46. Reprinted in *Selected Essays,* 140–48.

The Three Voices of Poetry. Cambridge: Cambridge University Press, 1953. Reprinted in *On Poetry and Poets,* 96–112.

"Whether Rostand Had Something about Him." *Athenaeum* (25 July 1919): 665–66. Reprinted as " 'Rhetoric' and Poetic Drama" in *The Sacred Wood,* 78–85, and *Selected Essays,* 25–30.

SECONDARY BIBLIOGRAPHY

Abbott, Anthony S. *The Vital Lie: Reality and Illusion in Modern Drama.* Tuscaloosa: University of Alabama Press, 1989.

Ackroyd, Peter. *T. S. Eliot: A Life.* New York: Simon & Schuster, 1984.

Aiken, Conrad [under the pseudonym of Samuel Jeake, Jr.]. "London Letter." *New Yorker* (13 July 1935): 61–63.

Aston, Frank. "T. S. Eliot Play a Ghostly Tale." *New York World-Telegram* (21 Oct. 1958).

Atkinson, Brooks. "Triumph at Old Vic." *New York Times* (26 Apr. 1953).

Ayers, Robert W. "*Murder in the Cathedral:* A 'Liturgy Less Divine.' " *Texas Studies in Literature and Language* 20.4 (Winter 1978): 579–98.

Barber, C. L. "The Power of Development . . . In a Different World." In *The Achievement of T. S. Eliot,* by F. O. Matthiessen, 198–243. 3d. ed. New York: Oxford University Press, 1958.

Barnes, Howard. "Modern Morality Play." *New York Herald Tribune* (23 Jan. 1950): 12.

Bergonzi, Bernard. *T. S. Eliot.* New York: Macmillan, 1972.

Billman, Carol. "History versus Mystery: The Test of Time in *Murder in the Cathedral.*" *Clio* 10.1 (Fall 1980): 47–56.

Bishop, George. "Plays by Modern Poets." *London Daily Telegraph* (2 Oct. 1935).

Brien, Alan. Review of *The Elder Statesman. Spectator* (5 Sept. 1958): 305–6.

Brooks, Cleanth. "Sin and Expiation." *Partisan Review* 6 (Summer 1939): 114–16.

Brown, Ivor. [1]. Review of *The Cocktail Party. Observer* (28 Aug. 1949).

———. [2]. "Murder in the Cathedral." *Observer* (13 Nov. 1936):

Browne, E. Martin. *The Making of T. S. Eliot's Plays.* London: Cambridge University Press, 1969.

Bush, Ronald. *T. S. Eliot: A Study in Character and Style.* New York: Oxford University Press, 1983.

Clurman, Harold. "Theatre: Cocktail Party." *New Republic* (13 Feb. 1950): 30–31.

Coghill, Nevill. "*Sweeney Agonistes* (An Anecdote or Two)." In *T. S. Eliot: A Symposium,* ed. Richard March and Tambimuttu, 82–87. Freeport, NY: Books for Libraries Press, 1968.

Darlington, W. A. [1]. "By T. S. Eliot." *New York Times* (31 Aug. 1958): 2:3.

———. [2]. Review of *The Confidential Clerk. New York Times* (30 Aug. 1953).

Davies, R. T. "Mr. T. S. Eliot's 'The Confidential Clerk.' " *Theology* (Oct. 1953): 411–14.

Donald, Henry. "Edinburgh Festival." *Spectator* (4 Sept. 1953): 238.

Donoghue, Denis. *The Third Voice: Modern British and American Verse Drama.* Princeton, NJ: Princeton University Press, 1959.

Edwards, Christopher. Review of *Sweeney Agonistes. London Theatre Record* 8.16 (29 July–11 Aug. 1988): 1042.

Evans, Gareth Lloyd. *The Language of Modern Drama.* London: Dent, 1977; Totowa, NJ: Rowman and Littlefield, 1977.

Gabriel, Gilbert W. "Murder in the Cathedral." *New York American* (21 Mar. 1936): 11.

Gardner, Helen. "The Comedies of T. S. Eliot." *Sewanee Review* 74.1 (1966): 153–75.

Gordon, Lyndall. [1]. *Eliot's Early Years.* New York: Oxford University Press, 1977.

———. [2]. *Eliot's New Life.* New York: Farrar Straus Giroux, 1988.

Hawkins, William. "Comedy, Pathos Mix in 'Confidential Clerk.'" *New York World-Telegram and Sun* (12 Feb. 1954).

Hobson, Harold. "T. S. Eliot's 'The Elder Statesman.'" *Christian Science Monitor* (6 Sept. 1958): 4.

Hope-Wallace, Philip. "T. S. Eliot's New Play: 'The Elder Statesman.'" *Manchester Guardian* (27 Aug. 1958).

Isaacs, J. *An Assessment of Twentieth-Century Literature.* London: Secker & Warburg, 1951.

Jones, David. *The Plays of T. S. Eliot.* Toronto: University of Toronto Press, 1960.

Kline, Peter. "The Spiritual Center in Eliot's Plays." *Kenyon Review* 21.3 (Summer 1959): 457–72.

MacCarthy, Desmond. [1]. "Some Notes on Mr. Eliot's New Play." *New Statesman* (25 Mar. 1939): 455–56.

———. [2]. "Sweeney Agonistes." *Listener* (9 Jan. 1935): 80–81.

McElroy, Davis D. *Existentialism and Modern Literature.* New York: Philosophical Library, 1963.

Moore, Harry T. Review of *The Rock. Adelphi* 9.3 (Dec. 1934): 188–89.

Morgan, Charles. "The Family Reunion." *The Times* (22 Mar. 1939): 12.

Olshin, Toby. "A Consideration of *The Rock.*" *University of Toronto Quarterly* 39.4 (July 1970): 310–23.

Peter, John. "Sin and Soda." *Scrutiny* 17.1 (Spring 1950): 61–66.

Roberts, Patrick. *The Psychology of Tragic Drama.* London: Routledge & Kegan Paul, 1975.

Sayers, Michael. "Mr. T. S. Eliot's 'The Rock.'" *New English Weekly* 5 (21 June 1934): 230–31.

Sewell, J. E. "Satire in Church Pageant-Play." *London Daily Telegraph* (29 May 1934): 4.

Shawe-Taylor, Desmond. Review of *The Cocktail Party. New Statesman* (3 Sept. 1949): 243.

Smith, Carol H. *T. S. Eliot's Dramatic Theory and Practice.* Princeton, NJ: Princeton University Press, 1963.

Smith, Grover. *T. S. Eliot's Poetry and Plays: A Study in Sources and Meaning.* Chicago: University of Chicago Press, 1960.

Spanos, William V. " 'Wanna Go Home, Baby?': *Sweeney Agonistes* as Drama of the Absurd." *PMLA* 85.1 (Oct. 1970): 8–20.

Spender, Stephen. "Martyrdom and Motive." In *T. S. Eliot: Plays,* ed. Arnold Hinchliffe, 96–101. Basingstoke, Hampshire: Macmillan, 1985.

Verschoyle, Derek. "The Theatre." *Spectator* (1 June 1934): 851.

Ward, David. *T. S. Eliot between Two Worlds.* London: Routledge & Kegan Paul. 1973.

Watts, Richard, Jr. "Bringing the Middle Ages to Broadway." *New York Herald Tribune* (29 March 1936): 5:1, 5.

Weales, Gerald. "The Latest Eliot." *Kenyon Review* 21.3 (Summer 1959): 473–78.

Weightman, J. G. "Edinburgh, Elsinore, and Chelsea." *Twentieth Century* (Oct. 1953): 302–10.

Winter, Jack. " 'Prufrockism' in *The Cocktail Party.*" *Modern Language Quarterly* 22.2 (June 1961): 135–48.

Worth, Katharine. *Revolutions in Modern English Drama.* London: Bell, 1973.

BIBLIOGRAPHIES

Brooker, Jewel Spears. "Materials" and "Works Cited" in *Approaches to Teaching Eliot's Poetry and Plays*. New York: Modern Language Association, 1988.

Carpenter, Charles A. "T. S. Eliot as Dramatist: Critical Studies in English, 1933–1975." *Bulletin of Bibliography and Magazine Notes* 33.1 (Jan. 1976): 1–12.

Gallup, Donald Clifford. *T. S. Eliot: A Bibliography*. New York: Harcourt Brace and World 1969.

Malamud, Randy. *T. S. Eliot's Drama: A Research and Production Sourcebook*. Westport, CT: Greenwood Press, 1992.

Martin, Mildred. *A Half-Century of Eliot Criticism: An Annotated Bibliography of Books and Articles in English, 1916–1965*. Lewisburg, PA: Bucknell University Press, 1972.

Ricks, Beatrice. *T. S. Eliot: A Bibliography of Secondary Works*. Metuchen, NJ: Scarecrow Press, 1980.

Christopher Fry
(1907–   )

JACKIE TUCKER

Born on 18 December 1907, Christopher Fry, né Arthur Hammond Harris, has spent most of the twentieth century as a participant in and an observer of the stage and film scenes. Although his fame is based primarily on the verse dramas he penned between 1939 and 1970, he has also achieved considerable reputation as a translator and a film scriptwriter.

Fry is the younger son of Charles John Harris and Emma Marguerite Hammond. His father, originally an architect and builder, became a lay minister for the Church of England in Bristol, where Fry was born. The work apparently caused his health to deteriorate, for he died when Fry was three. Fry was then raised by his mother and an aunt, Ada Louise Hammond. The family's early years were needy, but Mrs. Harris took in boarders so that Fry could attend the Bedford Modern School. In his late teens Fry assumed the name "Christopher Fry" because he liked the sound and because Fry was the name of his maternal grandmother's family, with whom he felt more intimate at the time (Roy, 8). For many years he believed that his family was connected to the Quaker Frys, of whom the prison reformer Elizabeth Fry was one of the more famous members. In his autobiography *Can You Find Me,* he discussed his error (17). Because of this misunderstanding by the dramatist himself and because of the passive nature of his ideas, some sources have mistakenly labeled Fry a Quaker. In fact, he has always been a member of the Church of England. Wiersma clarified this situation in his discussion of Fry (23–24).

Apparently Fry's theatrical interests began early in his youth. Roy reported that at the age of five, Fry was composing on the piano and appearing in a civic pageant and, furthermore, that he went on to write a farce at age eleven, a poem at age twelve, and a verse drama at age fourteen (7, 8). By 1924 Fry had written the first of his verse plays to eventually be produced. The play, *Youth and the*

Peregrines, was performed on 1 May 1934 in the Pump Room at Tunbridge Wells as the curtain raiser for the premiere of Shaw's *Village Wooing* (in which Fry also acted).

Fry spent the years following his formal education at a variety of jobs. For a time he taught at the Bedford Froebel Kindergarten (1926–27), served as an actor in the Bath Repertory Company (1927), became the schoolmaster of Hazelwood Preparatory School in Limpsfield, Surrey (1928–31), and was secretary to H. Rodney Bennet (1931–32). Fry was feeling rather discouraged at this time, as he attested in his dedication to *A Sleep of Prisoners,* published almost twenty years later. The dedication to Robert Gittings recalled the summer of 1932 when they spent two months at Thorn St. Margaret while Fry attempted to write a play entitled *Seige* (which remains unpublished and unperformed). He had ''written almost nothing for five or six years'' and would write ''almost nothing again for five years following,'' but he came out of the summer holiday with a ''hope that one day the words would come'' (*Selected Plays,* 201).

His apprenticeship in the theater continued in 1932 when Fry became a director of the Tunbridge Wells Repertory Players. In 1934 he collaborated with Monte Crick and F. Eyton on a musical revue, *She Shall Have Music,* which was produced in London at the Saville Theatre (London). In the same year he was employed by Dr. Bernardo's Homes. During this time he was commissioned to write a drama on the life of Thomas John Bernardo, the founder of these homes for children. Fry toured with the play, *Open Door,* for two years. In 1936 he met and married Phyllis Marjorie Hart, a journalist. The relationship was to last for some fifty years, until Mrs. Fry's death in 1987. The couple had one son, Tam, in 1937.

Fry began working on *The Boy with a Cart* in 1937, at the request of Lilford Causton, vicar of the church at Coleman's Hatch. The play was to commemorate the fiftieth anniversary of the founding of the church at Steyning, another Sussex village. It was performed in Coleman's Hatch in 1938 and again in 1939 in Bishop George Bell's garden at Chichester. Fry wrote two other pageants at this time: *Thursday's Child,* commissioned by the Girls' Friendly Society, and *The Tower,* written to celebrate the repair of the Abbey tower at Tewkesbury.

The next year Fry joined the Oxford Playhouse, but he soon enlisted for military service. As a conscientious objector, Fry was assigned to the Pioneer Corps, where he spent four years helping with noncombatant chores. Fry's health seems to have suffered from the stresses he encountered; he wound up in a military hospital in 1944 and was discharged the same year.

About this time Fry renewed his acquaintanceship with E. Martin Browne. The two had met some years before the war when Browne produced *The Tower* and *Thursday's Child.* During the war years Browne had established the Pilgrim Players, a touring group that performed religious plays. He recalled that he invited Fry to join the group, but the playwright chose instead to enter the Pioneer Corps (154). After the war Browne moved his group into the Mercury Theatre in London. Fry's *A Phoenix Too Frequent* was on the program in 1946.

This one-act play, one of the most frequently performed of all Fry's works, initiated the dramatist's greatest sustained creative period. In addition, it seems to have marked Fry's deliberate decision to concentrate on verse as his preferred form. His subsequent dramas are almost entirely written in irregular blank verse.

In the fall of 1946 *Phoenix* moved to the Arts Theatre Club in London. Fry subsequently became the resident dramatist of the Arts Theatre, but he continued to accept commissions for festival plays. In 1948 he wrote *Thor, with Angels* for the Canterbury Festival and completed the revision of *The Firstborn* for the Edinburgh Festival. Three years later, for the Festival of Britain, he wrote *A Sleep of Prisoners* (1951), which toured various churches throughout the country. However, the Arts Theatre (London) was the site for the premiere of Fry's most commercially successful play, *The Lady's Not for Burning* (1948). In 1949 the play was produced at the Globe Theatre, London, where it became a tremendous success, winning the Shaw Prize Fund Award for 1948 and, subsequently, the New York Drama Critics Circle Award for 1951.

With *The Lady's Not for Burning,* Fry began a series of what he called "seasonal" comedies in which he attempted to create a mood by merging the season with the characters and the scene. *The Lady's Not for Burning,* representing the spring season, was followed by *Venus Observed* (1950) representing autumn and *The Dark Is Light Enough* (1954) representing winter. Over fifteen years later the cycle was completed with *A Yard of Sun* (1970) representing summer. Although Fry wrote two other original plays during this creative period, *A Sleep of Prisoners* (1951) and *Curtmantle* (1961), he also turned to other outlets for his creativity. He was acclaimed for a number of translations as well as for film and television scripts.

In 1986, at the age of seventy-nine, Fry returned to his creative origins by accepting a commission to write another festival play, *One Thing More; or, Caedmon Construed.* Today Fry resides at the Toft, East Dean, near Chichester, in West Sussex.

Selected Biographical Sources: Can You Find Me; "Christopher Fry"; Leeming; Prescott; Roy; Wiersma.

MAJOR PLAYS, PREMIERES, AND SIGNIFICANT REVIVALS: THEATRICAL RECEPTION

The Boy with a Cart. 1938. (one act). First produced at the church in Coleman's Hatch, Sussex, England. Revived at the Lyric Theatre (Hammersmith), 16 January 1950, with John Gielgud directing and Richard Burton as Cuthman. Revived at Regent's Park Open Air Theatre (London) 29 July 1952 (double-billed with *Comus*) for 25 performances. Presented in the United States by the Chapel Players at the Broadway Tabernacle Church for 9 performances beginning 4 April 1954.

One of Fry's early religious dramas, *The Boy with a Cart* concerns the founding of an English village by St. Cuthman. Although not one of Fry's great successes, it reveals his early leaning toward religious topics and verse format. When it was performed at the Lyric Theatre, Trewin [3] thought that it came "rather dully to the stage" and that it was "not really strong enough for professional performance." Later critics were hardly enthusiastic, but they were generally more positive. *The Times* reviewer (" 'Comus' ") called the 1952 production a "charming story" that "mingles piety with the pastoral." Of the U.S. production, Shanley reported that there was nothing "unintelligible" about the play (a charge leveled against some of Fry's later works) and that it appeared to have been "written with devoted care."

A Phoenix Too Frequent. 1946. (one act). Opened at the Mercury Theatre in London on 25 April for 64 performances (double-billed with Yeats's *The Resurrection*). Directed by E. Martin Browne for the Pilgrim Players. Moved to the Arts Theatre (London) 20 November 1946, for 39 performances. Directed by Noël Willman. Produced in the United States at Broadway's Fulton Theatre (New York), 26 April 1950. Closed after 5 performances. Double-billed with *Thor, with Angels* at the Lyric Theatre (Hammersmith), beginning 27 September 1951, running for 36 performances. Directed by Michael Macowan. Revived at Houston's Alley Theatre, 10 March 1958, on a triple bill including Sean O'Casey's *Bedtime Story* and Noël Coward's *Still Life.*

Set in a tomb in ancient Ephesus, this early comedy was praised by *The Times* (Review of *A Phoenix Too Frequent*) and the *New Statesman* (" 'A Phoenix Too Frequent' ") for its wit, poetry, and imagination. The *New Statesman,* however, criticized the "undisciplined emotion" and the lack of philosophical content. Trewin [2] compared Fry to Christopher Marlowe. In his review of the 1950 New York production, Atkinson [9] liked the "web of irreverent verse" but thought that Fry deserved "a more highly lacquered performance," the lack of which, he suggested, might have caused the quick closing. Eight years later when Atkinson [10] reviewed the Houston production, he praised both the wit and the literary quality of the writing.

The Firstborn. 1946. Amateur performance by the Sunderland Drama Club, 19 March 1947. First produced professionally at the Gateway Theatre (Edinburgh) for the Edinburgh Festival, 6 September 1948. Directed by E. Martin Browne. Presented at London's Winter Garden Theatre, 29 January 1952, for 46 performances. Directed by John Fernald. A concert reading, 6 January 1957, at Kaufman Concert Hall (New York) was presented by the Young Men's and Young Women's Hebrew Association. Directed by E. Martin Browne. Revived 30 April 1958 at the Coronet Theatre, New York, by the America-Israel Cultural Foundation; songs by Leonard Bernstein.

The story of Moses, Pharaoh Seti, and Prince Ramases, *The Firstborn* was revised several times after its Edinburgh performance. Critics hailed the London production as Fry's best work to date. Hamilton, Darlington [1], and Raymond praised the power and imagination revealed in the play. Both Raymond and *The Times* (Review of *The Firstborn*) criticized Fry's failure to sufficiently account for Moses' final strong feeling for Ramases. When Funke reviewed the 1957 concert reading, he found that it still succeeded in "bounding into life." However, when Atkinson [2, 6] reviewed the 1958 production, he described it as too "mannered" and "circuitous."

The Lady's Not for Burning. 1948. First produced at the Arts Theatre (London), 10 March, for 22 performances. Directed by Jack Hawkins. Moved to the Globe Theatre (London) in the West End, 11 May 1949, for 293 performances. John Gielgud directed (with Esmé Percy) and played Thomas Mendip. The production at Broadway's Royale Theatre began 8 November 1950, running for almost 300 performances. Revivals include productions in New York at Carnegie Hall, 21 February 1957; in the Bronx and Queens by the Equity Community Theatre, 4 performances beginning 30 January 1959; and in Chichester, England, at the Theatre Festival, May–September 1972.

The first of Fry's seasonal series, this spring comedy follows the hero as he questions whether life is worth living. Both the English and American productions were immensely successful. The reviews set the tone for later critiques as well. Invariably critics praised the language and poetry, the wit and charm, but faulted the plot. Darlington [2] concluded that the play had "nearly all the qualities anybody could ask" but lacked a story; Atkinson [7] remarked on Fry's "witchery with words" and even compared Fry to early Shakespeare, but found the story "rambling and inconsequential"; even *Time* (Review of *The Lady's Not for Burning*) admitted that "the play is not to be dredged for large meanings . . . its forte is fireworks, not illumination." Worsley [3] also praised Fry's poetry but found the story weak; on the other hand, he concentrated on the poor characterization, finding Mendip and Jourdemayne "never credible," a situation that robbed the poetry of any "dramatic significance." Nevertheless, Worsley [4] rated it one of the best plays in London during the 1949 season. When the play was revived in 1957 and 1972, the critics were not so kind. While Calta [2] still paid homage to its rich language, he labeled it only "interesting." Barnes remarked on the diminished standing of the play and of Fry's reputation after twenty years.

Thor, with Angels. 1948. (one act). First performed in June for the Canterbury Festival. Revived in 1951 at the Lyric Theatre (Hammersmith) on a double bill with *A Phoenix Too Frequent*. First New York presentation by the Broadway Chapel Players, December 1956, at the Broadway Congregational Church.

Another of Fry's explicitly religious dramas, *Thor* is concerned with the reintroduction of Christianity into Britain about 596 A.D. *The Times* ("Plays") praised the "gorgeous verbiage," while Trewin [2] thought that the language was "superb." The *New Statesman* (" 'A Phoenix Too Frequent' ") called it "one of the most interesting of Fry's plays." On the critical side, Trewin [2] found it "static," and Gelb considered it Fry "at his most arcane and symbolic."

Venus Observed. 1950. Opened at St. James's Theatre (London) on 18 January for 229 performances. Laurence Olivier staged the production and played the duke. First American performance at the Century Theatre (New York), 13 February 1952, again directed by Olivier and presented by the Theatre Guild, with Rex Harrison as the duke.

This autumn play in Fry's seasonal series is loosely based on the myth of the judgment of Paris. Audience reception was generally positive, but critics were cool. Atkinson [8, 12], Fleming [2], Trewin [3], and Worsley [1] praised the witty, exuberant language, but recognized Fry's lack of plot and characterization. Trewin [3] maintained that Fry's remarkable dialogue did not necessarily imply a rich theatrical experience, a judgment confirmed by Fleming [2] and *Time* (''Muse''). Atkinson [12] actually found the play ''frequently tedious.''

A Sleep of Prisoners. 1951. (one act). Commissioned by the Religious Drama Society in England for the Festival of Britain. Performed at the University Church (Oxford), 23 April. Moved to St. Thomas's Church (London), 15 May. Directed by Michael Macowan for the Pilgrim Players. Played at St. James's Church (New York), 16 October. Revived in Paris at the Marigny Theatre, 13 January 1955, by Jean-Louis Barrault and Madeleine Renaud.

Fry's most allegorical play, *Sleep* was universally criticized for its obscurity. Set in a church turned prison, the play revolves around the dream sequences of each of the prisoners. In their dreams they relive Old Testament stories that pit good against evil. Atkinson [1, 11] found the dream sequences difficult to understand, although he thought that the last scene had some of Fry's best verse. *The Times* (''Mr. Fry's New Play''), agreeing on the difficulties, criticized Fry for leaving too much work to the audience that he should have done himself, a judgment shared by the *New York Times* (Review of *A Sleep of Prisoners*). The *Time* reviewer (Review of *A Sleep of Prisoners*) labeled it an ''allegorical wasteland'' and a ''confusing kaleidoscope.'' *Life* (''A Play for Churches'') called it ''a good play for the church.'' The stormiest reception came in Paris, where the performance was greeted by boos and a near riot ('' 'A Sleep of Prisoners' Arouses Paris Audience'').

The Dark Is Light Enough. 1954. First produced at the Lyceum Theatre (Edinburgh) on 22 February. Moved to Aldwych Theatre (London), 30 April, for 243 performances, with Edith Evans as the countess. Opened in New York at the ANTA Theatre, 23 February 1955, with Katharine Cornell and Tyrone Power in the leads. Produced by Cornell and Roger Stevens; directed by Guthrie McClintic.

Fry's winter comedy is set during the 1848 Hungarian revolution. Critics were generally divided in their estimation of the play. Hartley and Atkinson [4] were among the most critical, condemning primarily the lack of theme and structure. Atkinson agreed with the *Time* reviewer (Review of *The Dark Is Light Enough*) who criticized the characterization. Trewin [5] and Dobrée were quite positive, both considering the play good theater. Worsley's [6] judgment was in between:

some parts were interesting and brilliant, but the overall performance was seriously lacking. He praised the first act, but thought that the second act made less sense. In a follow-up review Worsley [5] was more complimentary, finding the play stronger than he had first surmised. *The Times* (Review of *The Dark Is Light Enough*) best summarizes the general reaction: "Not perhaps a major play but an immensely interesting one."

Curtmantle. 1961. First performed in Dutch at the Stadsschouwburg Theatre (Tilburg, Netherlands) on 1 March. Presented by the Ensemble Company; directed by Karl Guttmann. Premiered in English at the Lyceum Theatre (Edinburgh), 4 September 1962. Presented in London at the Aldwych Theatre, 6 October 1962. Directed by Stuart Burge.

This story of Henry II was Fry's first play in almost eight years, and the critics were not kind. Worsley [2], Gelbert, and *The Times* reviewer ("A Royal Progression") agreed that the language was much sparer, Fry having stripped away all ostentation. Worsley [2] felt that this directness increased the power of the language but did not compensate for the lack of dramatic impact. Gelbert found it simply an "intellectual pageant" in which "nothing resounds," while *The Times* reviewer called it confusing and lacking in expressiveness, with "no sign of fire under the surface." Worsley [2] summarized the critics' opinions when he said that the play would not "restore, much less add to, Mr. Fry's reputation."

A Yard of Sun. 1970. Opened at the Nottingham Playhouse (Nottingham, England) on 11 July. Produced at the Old Vic Theatre (London), 10 August 1970.

This summer comedy completed Fry's series of seasonal plays. Set in Siena in 1946, it explores how one neighborhood deals with the complexities of life after the war. In 1970 critics were still commenting on Fry's colorful language (Nightingale [1] and Billington), but no longer finding it a vital contribution to the work. Nightingale [1] judged the play "shallow" and "inconsequential." Interestingly enough, he wrote a follow-up review [2] in which he mentioned that letters from his readers showed that they had responded to the play far more positively than he.

ADDITIONAL PLAYS, ADAPTATIONS, AND PRODUCTIONS

Two of Fry's early pageants were performed in 1939: *Thursday's Child* at Albert Hall in London, 1 July; and *The Tower* at the Tewkesbury Festival, 18 July. Fry's translations/adaptations include Jean Anouilh's *Ring round the Moon* (1950) and *The Lark* (1955); Jean Giraudoux's *Tiger at the Gates* (1956), for which Fry received the New York Drama Critics Circle Award, *Duel of Angels* (1958), and *Judith* (1962); Henrik Ibsen's *Peer Gynt* (1970); and Edmond Rostand's *Cyrano de Bergerac* (1975). Film credits include screenplays for Gay's *The Beggar's Opera* (1953), Wallace's *Ben Hur* (1958), *Barabbas* (1961), and *The Bible: In the Beginning* (1966). Television contributions include an adaptation of Anne Brontë's *The Tenant of Wildfell Hall* (1968) and original scripts for *The Brontës of Haworth* (1973), *The Best of Enemies* (1976), *Sister Dora* (1977), and *Star over Bethlehem* (1981). *One Thing More, or Caedmon Construed* was produced at Chelmsford Cathedral on 4 November 1986, broadcast on BBC Radio on 16 November of the same year, and televised on BBC-TV in the winter of 1987.

ASSESSMENT OF FRY'S CAREER

Christopher Fry rose to prominence in the years following World War II. His plays were primarily comedies, though he wrote one tragedy (*The Firstborn*) and one historical drama (*Curtmantle*). The plots are either explicitly or implicitly religious in nature. Although he is certainly conscious of the evil that exists in the world, Fry celebrates the joy of living and the essential goodness of life. One reason for his popularity was that his plays seemed to fit the mood of audiences in the postwar era. In addition, however, both the verse-drama movement and the religious-drama revival were under way, with dramatists such as Eliot, Anderson, and Williams leading the way. Walsh suggested a further explanation for Fry's success in the yearning that assails many devotees of drama, namely, that drama, poetry, and religion be reunited as they were in the theaters of ancient Greece and Elizabethan England. For a time, when Fry was able to achieve this integration, audiences and critics responded enthusiastically. Quite soon, of course, dramatic fashions turned to a more realistic type of play, and Fry's popularity waned.

Although Fry had previously written several plays, his fame actually began with the first production of *The Lady's Not for Burning*. For the next fifteen years he was one of the most commercially successful dramatists around. One indication of Fry's popularity is found in the 1950–51 Broadway season, when Fry had four plays in production. Effusive praise was rather typical of Fry's critical reception during these first successful years. When *Venus Observed* was produced in London, *Time* ("Muse") called Fry "a meteoric new playwright" whose name was "marquee magic." Another indication of the extravagant response with which Fry was greeted can be seen in the comparisons of Fry to other playwrights. In November 1950, when Fry made the cover of *Time,* the reviewer noted reflections of Eliot, Keats, and Shakespeare in Fry's work ("Enter Poet"). Trewin [3] thought that Fry wrote "dialogue more remarkable than that of any dramatist but Sean O'Casey" and that Fry and O'Casey were the dramatists "nearest to the Elizabethans." In a later review Trewin [2] compared Fry's sense of words to that of Marlowe "without the bombast"; Atkinson [5] suggested that Fry was closest to Congreve and Wilde but compared Fry's verse to early Shakespeare in its "sunny gusto" and "light-footed humor"; and Worsley [3] called Fry "a poet, the most brilliant and fertile . . . that has appeared since Auden."

The attribute that critics invariably praised in Fry's plays was his language.

Worsley's [3] comment in 1948 is indicative: the audience was "launched into a sea of dazzling verbal invention which never for a moment flags." Atkinson [7] concurred when he stated that Fry had "restored the art of literature to the stage by writing a sparkling verse that also is shot with wit and humor." A *Time* book review of *The Lady's Not for Burning* ("Another Language") agreed that its real triumph "lies in its speech." Some years later when Calta [2] reviewed a revival of *The Lady's Not for Burning,* he, too, praised the "richness of Mr. Fry's language." Dobrée concluded that Fry relied "for his effect on the sheer joy of words and proliferating imagery."

Paradoxically, the language was also seen as one of the major flaws in Fry's plays. While critics enjoyed his exuberant verse, they often deemed it little more than ornamentation. Atkinson [7] said that Fry's "passion for words runs away with him," and Fleming [1] complained that the writing slipped into "whimsy." Barnes was one of the harsher critics: Fry had "a gift for the gab," he confessed, but he did not write poetry. In his later plays Fry used language more sparingly and more powerfully, but even in 1970 Billington was calling the poetry "more often decorative than practical." Fry reacted to this view of his language in an oft-quoted speech to the Critics' Circle at the Arts Theatre (London). He disclaimed the picture of himself "reeling intoxicated with words" that the critics had drawn and suggested instead that the writing task "feels more like a slow death by ground glass" (*An Experience of Critics,* 23–24). The criticism of the language centered on its tendency to hide with excessive verbiage a lack of plot or theme and shallow, unmotivated characters (see Atkinson [5, 7], Worsley [3], Nightingale [1, 2], Hartley).

Scholarly reception of Fry's plays has generally echoed that of the contemporary reviewers. Some scholars have been even harsher in proclaiming that the language is mere embellishment, and others have found Fry's works without timeless, universal value. Donoghue, for example, expressed a rather virulent opinion of Fry's dramatic reputation. He believed that Fry had "little to say and therefore little to take seriously" (183). He even found Fry's popularity "disquieting" (180). On the other hand, some writers have displayed a more positive outlook when interpreting Fry. Spears considered him "a genuine poet" (28) but was not afraid to take Fry to task for what he considered the autonomy of the poetry. Arrowsmith is one among the few scholars who see in Fry's works a "marriage of language to theme" (211). Weales agreed that the verse "is an expression of his [Fry's] view of the world" and that it thus becomes an integral part of the plays' themes (223).

Scholarly studies of Fry's works have been rather meager. Most often Fry has been discussed in connection with the verse-drama movement or the religious-drama revival (see Innes, Nicoll, Spanos, Weales, and Williams). A few comprehensive studies, such as those of Roy and, most recently, Wiersma and Leeming, have attempted to interpret Fry's entire canon from a particular perspective. Roy's study concentrated on the way Fry develops characters and confronts contemporary issues. Wiersma argued that the waning of interest in Fry derived from the antitheological bias that developed among literary scholars during the 1960s. His purpose was to reawaken interest in Fry by considering the relationship between the theology and the literary form in each play. Leeming's interest centered around the connections between text and theatrical production.

In an article on the occasion of Fry's eightieth birthday, Trewin [1] praised the playwright as one of the "undeniably great dramatists" of this century. Such an appellation is somewhat exaggerated and probably a comment on our mortal admiration for productivity and longevity rather than an objective judgment of the literary merits of Fry's dramas. The final assessment of Fry's canon is not yet in; nevertheless, it is appropriate to say that Fry is a significant dramatist in the twentieth-century theater and that avenues for future research on his canon are abundant. In-depth analyses of Fry's poetry, studies of the relationship between form and theme, and up-to-date considerations of his contributions to the verse-drama movement as well as the religious-drama revival should help to unfold the depth of Fry's ideas, the strength of his poetry, and his overall legacy to the theater.

ARCHIVAL SOURCES

Harvard University's Theatre Collection includes a manuscript collection of Fry's plays.

PRIMARY BIBLIOGRAPHY

Plays

The Boy with a Cart. London: Oxford University Press, 1939.
Curtmantle. London: Oxford University Press, 1961.
The Dark Is Light Enough. London: Oxford University Press, 1954.
The Firstborn. 3rd ed. London: Oxford University Press, 1958.
The Lady's Not for Burning. Rev. ed. London: Oxford University Press, 1973.
One Thing More; or, Caedmon Construed. London: Oxford University Press, 1985.
A Phoenix Too Frequent. London: Hollis & Carter, 1946.
A Sleep of Prisoners. 2nd ed. London: Oxford University Press, 1965.
Thor, with Angels. London: Oxford University Press, 1949.
Venus Observed. London: Oxford University Press, 1950.
A Yard of Sun. London: Oxford University Press, 1970.

Anthologies

Plays. (*The Boy with a Cart, The Firstborn, Venus Observed.*) London: Oxford University Press, 1970.

Plays. (*A Sleep of Prisoners, The Dark Is Light Enough, Curtmantle.*) London: Oxford University Press, 1971.

Plays. (*Thor, with Angels, The Lady's Not for Burning.*) London: Oxford University Press, 1969.

Selected Plays. (*The Boy with a Cart, A Phoenix Too Frequent, The Lady's Not for Burning, A Sleep of Prisoners.*) Oxford: Oxford University Press, 1985.

Three Plays. (*The Firstborn, Thor, with Angels, A Sleep of Prisoners.*) London: Oxford University Press, 1960.

Essays and Articles on Drama and Theater

Can You Find Me. Oxford: Oxford University Press, 1978.
"Comedy." *Tulane Drama Review* 4.3 (1960): 77–79.
An Experience of Critics. London: Perpetua, 1952.
"How Lost, How Amazed, How Miraculous We Art." *Theatre Arts* 36 (1952): 27.
"Recollections of T. S. Eliot." *Southern Review* 21 (1985): 967–73.

SECONDARY BIBLIOGRAPHY

"Another Language." *Time* (24 Apr. 1950): 112.

Arrowsmith, Martin. "Notes on English Verse Drama: Christopher Fry." *Hudson Review* 3 (1950): 203–16.

Atkinson, Brooks. [1]. "Church Drama." *New York Times* (28 Oct. 1951): 2:1.

———. [2]. "Cornell Is Starred in Fry's 'The Firstborn.' " *New York Times* (11 May 1958): 2:1.

———. [3]. "Cornell's Drama." *New York Times* (6 Mar. 1955): 2:1.

———. [4]. Review of *The Dark Is Light Enough. New York Times* (24 Feb. 1955): 20.

———. [5]. "Don't Burn the Lady." *New York Times* (26 Nov. 1950): 2:1.

———. [6]. Review of *The Firstborn. New York Times* (1 May 1958): 35.

———. [7]. Review of *The Lady's Not for Burning. New York Times* (9 Nov. 1950): 42.

———. [8]. "Literary Comedy." *New York Times* (24 Feb. 1952): 2:1.

———. [9]. Review of *A Phoenix Too Frequent. New York Times* (27 Apr. 1950): 36.

———. [10]. " 'A Phoenix Too Frequent.' " *New York Times* (11 Mar. 1958): 33.

———. [11]. Review of *A Sleep of Prisoners. New York Times* (17 Oct. 1951): 36.

———. [12]. Review of *Venus Observed. New York Times* (14 Feb. 1952): 24.

Barnes, Clive. Review of *The Lady's Not for Burning. New York Times* (22 Aug. 1972): 51.

Bewley, Marius. "The Verse of Christopher Fry." *Scrutiny* 18 (June 1951): 78–84.

Billington, Michael. "Summer Comedy." *The Times* (11 Aug. 1970): 7.

Browne, E. Martin. *Two in One.* Cambridge: Cambridge University Press, 1981.

Calta, Louis. [1]. Review of *The Lady's Not for Burning. New York Times* (31 Jan. 1959): 13.

———. [2]. " 'The Lady's Not for Burning' Staged." *New York Times* (22 Feb. 1957): 26

"Christopher Fry." *Writers Directory, 1992–94,* 341. Chicago and London: St. James, 1991.

" 'Comus' and 'The Boy with a Cart' at Regent's Park Open Air Theatre." *The Times* (30 July 1952): 9.

Review of *The Dark Is Light Enough. Time* (7 Mar. 1955): 92.

Review of *The Dark Is Light Enough. The Times* (1 May 1954): 3.

Darlington, W. A. [1]. Review of *The Firstborn. New York Times* (10 Feb. 1952): 2:2.

———. [2]. Review of *The Lady's Not for Burning. New York Times* (12 June 1949): 2:3.

Dobrée, Bonamy. "Some London Plays." *Sewanee Review* 68 (1955): 270–80.

Donoghue, Denis. *The Third Voice: Modern British and American Verse Drama.* Princeton, NJ: Princeton University Press, 1959.

"Enter Poet, Laughing." *Time* (20 Nov. 1950): 58–64.

Review of *The Firstborn. The Times* (30 Jan. 1952): 8.

Fleming, Peter. [1]. Review of *The Lady's Not for Burning. Spectator* (20 May 1949): 678.

———. [2]. Review of *Venus Observed. Spectator* (27 Jan. 1950): 106.

Funke, Lewis B. "Drama by Fry Has Concert Reading." *New York Times* (7 Jan. 1957): 29.

Gelb, Arthur. " 'Thor, with Angels' Is Offered at Church." *New York Times* (15 Oct. 1956): 29.

Gelbert, Roger. "Cold Fry." *New Statesman* (14 Sept. 1962): 333–34.

Hamilton, Ian. Review of *The Firstborn. Spectator* (8 Feb. 1952): 173.

Hartley, Anthony. Review of *The Dark Is Light Enough. Spectator* (7 May 1954): 541.

Innes, Christopher. *Modern British Drama, 1890–1990.* Cambridge: Cambridge University Press, 1992.

Kerr, Walter. "Christopher Fry." In *Essays in the Modern Drama,* ed. Morris Freedman, 294–99. Boston: Heath, 1964.

Review of *The Lady's Not for Burning. Time* (20 Nov. 1950): 58.

Review of *The Lady's Not for Burning. The Times* (11 Mar. 1948): 2.

Review of *The Lady's Not for Burning. The Times* (12 May 1949): 7.

Lecky, Eleazer. "Mystery in the Plays of Christopher Fry." *Tulane Drama Review* 4.3 (1960): 80–87.

Leeming, Glenda. *Christopher Fry.* Boston: Twayne, 1990.

"Miracle Play for Moderns." *Time* (28 May 1951): 70–71.

"Mr. Fry's New Play." *The Times* (16 May 1951): 6.

"Muse at the Box Office." *Time* (3 Apr. 1950): 50–51.

"New Play by Fry Opens in London." *New York Times* (1 May 1954): 12.

Nicoll, Allardyce. *English Drama: A Modern Viewpoint.* New York: Barnes, 1968.

Nightingale, Benedict. [1]. "In Search of a Style." *New Statesman* (24 July 1970): 97.

———. [2]. "Man of Promise." *New Statesman* (14 Aug. 1970): 87.

Review of *A Phoenix Too Frequent. The Times* (21 Nov. 1946): 6.

" 'A Phoenix Too Frequent' and 'Thor, with Angels,' at the Lyric, Hammersmith." *New Statesman and Nation* (6 Oct. 1951): 366.

Pickering, Kenneth. *Drama in the Cathedral: The Canterbury Festival Plays, 1928–1948.* Worthing, West Sussex: Churchman, 1985.

"A Play for Churches." *Life* (12 Nov. 1951): 73–77.

"Plays by Mr. Christopher Fry." *The Times* (28 Sept. 1951): 8.

Prescott, Jani. "Christopher Fry." In *Contemporary Authors: New Revision Series,* ed. James G. Lesniak, vol. 30. Detroit: Gale Research, 1990.

"Prose Play by Fry Wins London Critics." *New York Times* (27 Jan. 1950): 29.

Raymond, John. "A Biblical Story." *New Statesman and Nation* (9 Feb. 1952): 152–53.

Roy, Emil. *Christopher Fry.* Carbondale: Southern Illinois University Press, 1968.

"A Royal Progression without Fire." *The Times* (10 Oct. 1962): 16.

Shanley, Jack P. Review of "Boy with a Cart." *New York Times* (5 Apr. 1954): 19.

Review of *A Sleep of Prisoners. New York Times* (16 May 1951): 46.

Review of *A Sleep of Prisoners. Time* (29 Oct. 1951): 38.

" 'A Sleep of Prisoners' Arouses Paris Audience." *New York Times* (15 Jan. 1955): 10.

Spanos, William V. *The Christian Tradition in Modern British Verse Drama: The Poetics of Sacramental Time.* New Brunswick, NJ: Rutgers University Press, 1967.

Spears, Monroe K. "Christopher Fry and the Redemption of Joy." *Poetry* 78 (1951): 28–43.

Trewin, J. C. [1]. "Christopher Fry at Eighty." *Drama* 1.167 (1988): 19–20.

———. [2]. " 'High Astounding Terms.' " *Illustrated London News* (13 Oct. 1951): 594.

———. [3]. "Make Believe." *Illustrated London News* (11 Feb. 1950): 228.

———. [4]. "The Plays of Christopher Fry." *Adelphi* 27 (Nov. 1950): 40–45.

———. [5]. "Tune and Words." *Illustrated London News* (15 May 1954): 806.

Trewin, Wendy, and J. C. Trewin. *The Arts Theatre, London, 1927–1981.* London: Society for Theatre Research, 1986.

"Two Plays by Poets." *The Times* (26 Apr. 1946): 6.

Review of *Venus Observed. The Times* (19 Jan. 1950): 4.

Vos, Nelvin. *The Drama of Comedy: Victim and Victor.* Richmond: John Knox Press, 1966.

Walsh, Chad. Preface. In *More Than the Ear Discovers,* by Stanley M. Wiersma, 11–14. Chicago: Loyola University Press, 1983.

Weales, Gerald. *Religion in Modern English Drama.* Philadelphia: University of Pennsylvania Press, 1961.

Wearing, J. P. [1]. *The London Stage, 1940–1949: A Calendar of Plays and Players.* Vol. 1. Metuchen, NJ, and London: Scarecrow Press, 1991.

———. [2]. *The London Stage, 1950–59: A Calendar of Plays and Players.* Vol. 1. Metuchen, NJ, and London: Scarecrow Press, 1991.

Wiersma, Stanley M. *More Than the Ear Discovers: God in the Plays of Christopher Fry.* Chicago: Loyola University Press, 1983.

Williams, Raymond. *Drama from Ibsen to Eliot.* London: Chatto & Windus, 1952.

Worsley, T. C. [1]. "Conjuring Tricks." *New Statesman and Nation* (28 Jan. 1950): 96–97.

———. [2]. " 'Curtmantle' Examines the Tragedy of Henry II." *New York Times* (5 Sept. 1962): 44.

———. [3]. " 'The Lady's Not for Burning,' at the Arts." *New Statesman and Nation* (20 Mar. 1948): 233.

———. [4]. "Mr. Fry's Verse Comedy." *New Statesman and Nation* (21 May 1949): 527.

———. [5]. "Saving a Lost Game." *New Statesman and Nation* (4 Sept. 1954): 262–63.
———. [6]. "A Winter Comedy." *New Statesman and Nation* (8 May 1954): 596.

BIBLIOGRAPHY

Schear, Bernice, and Eugene Prater. "A Bibliography on Christopher Fry." *Tulane Drama Review* 4.3 (1960): 88–98.

John Galsworthy
(1867–1933)

LUE MORGAN DOUTHIT

One of the many interesting aspects about John Galsworthy's playwriting career is how easily it seemed to have been started. While it took him over nine years to be accepted as a novelist (a reputation by which most know him), his first play, *The Silver Box,* was an instant hit. Another interesting fact to note is that both writings—novels and plays—gained popularity around the same time (1906). Galsworthy was deemed a man of letters, and it is that reputation that has somewhat obscured considering his plays stageworthy today.

Galsworthy was born on 14 August 1867 at Kingston Hill, Surrey, England, into the silver-spooned lifestyle that he used later for the settings of his plays and novels. His father was a solicitor, and he had two sisters and a brother. His education was quite classic—prep school at Bournemouth, Harrow, and then New College at Oxford. He received his law degree from Oxford in 1889 and was called to the bar in 1890.

In 1891 he went on a hunting trip to Canada, which was the first of many trips abroad. On his return to England, he met Ada Pearson Cooper Galsworthy (who would become his future wife) at a family party to celebrate her wedding to Major Arthur Galsworthy, John's cousin. In 1892–93 he traveled to Australia, the South Seas, and New Zealand, where he met Joseph Conrad on aboard the S.S. *Torrens* (Conrad was first mate). They became lifelong friends.

Back in England, Galsworthy and Ada were becoming closer friends. By September 1895 they would become lovers. Ada is credited with giving John the impetus to write. Knowing how unhappy he was with law as a profession, she reputedly remarked to him: "Why don't you write? You're just the person." From 1897 to 1901 he published two novels and two collections of short stories under the pseudonym of John Sinjohn. In 1902 he sent a draft of his novel *The Island Pharisees* to his friend the critic Edward Garnett for his comments. This practice of soliciting advice from colleagues became the standard for Galsworthy's submission and editing process. The novel was published in 1904.

After the death of his father in 1904, John and Ada decided to give grounds for divorce and traveled to Austria and Italy throughout the period of the proceedings. They were married on 23 September 1905 and lived in Galsworthy's house in London. Ada became John's secretary and typist as well as advisor for the rest of his writing life.

In 1906 his novel *The Man of Property* was published and received excellent reviews. Its reception established Galsworthy as a writer. Later that year, in September, his first play, *The Silver Box,* was produced by the Barker-Vedrenne management at the Royal Court Theatre (London). Galsworthy was very involved with many aspects of the production, from casting to rehearsals. He would be this involved in the majority of his plays' productions.

In 1908 *A Commentary,* a collection of articles on different subjects, including censorship in the theater and solitary confinement, was published. It clearly demonstrated Galsworthy's stance on many of the leading social issues of the day. His play *Justice,* which would be produced in 1910, was a direct commentary on the horrors of prison life, especially solitary confinement.

On 9 March 1909 *Strife* was produced at the Duke of York's Theatre (London). It was an instant success. As the *Evening Standard* summed up: ''It is the English play for which we have been waiting'' (quoted in Nightingale). In 1911, during the Manchester production of *The Little Dream,* an allegorical play with music and dance, John fell in love with nineteen-year-old actress Margaret Morris. In 1912, realizing how hurtful his relationship with Morris had been to his wife, he and Ada traveled extensively to France and America. Two more plays were produced before England's entry into World War I: *The Eldest Son* in 1912 and *The Fugitive* in 1913. Both were commercial failures.

While Galsworthy wanted to volunteer in the war effort, he felt that he could not leave Ada and instead worked hard at raising relief funds. In 1916 he donated a house in London to the Red Cross as a Wounded Soldiers' Club, and both he and Ada went to France to work at a convalescent home for wounded soldiers. In 1918 Galsworthy was offered a knighthood but declined. With the war finally over, he could get back to writing full-time.

In 1920 *The Skin Game* was produced at the St. Martin's Theatre (London), and *Loyalties* followed two years later at the same theatre. In 1921 Galsworthy was elected the first president of the Founding Centre of the International PEN Club, an office that he held until his death. In 1922 he became honorary professor of dramatic literature of the Royal Society of Literature. In 1926 his play *Escape* ran successfully for a year at the Ambassadors Theatre.

In 1929 Galsworthy was awarded the Order of Merit, and an anthology of his plays was published by Duckworth. In 1931 he suffered his first attack of loss of speech. He continued to force himself to write as his illness (undiagnosed at the time) became more debilitating. In December 1932 he was awarded the

Nobel Prize for Literature but was too ill to travel to Stockholm. He gave the prize money of nine thousand pounds in trust to the PEN Club.

On 31 January 1933 Galsworthy died at Grove Lodge, Hampstead, and was cremated. A memorial service was held at Westminster Abbey, and his ashes were scattered at the top of Bury Hill in West Sussex on 28 March by his nephew, as he had requested.

Selected Biographical Sources: Gillett [1]; Gindin [2]; Nightingale; Sternlicht.

MAJOR PLAYS, PREMIERES, AND SIGNIFICANT REVIVALS: THEATRICAL RECEPTION

The Silver Box. 1906. Opened 25 September at the Court Theatre (London) and ran for 29 performances.

Galsworthy's friend Edward Garnett suggested that he write a play for the Barker-Vedrenne management at the Royal Court Theatre, which was looking for contemporary plays. Galsworthy wrote *The Silver Box* (originally titled *The Cigarette Box*) in about six weeks (January to mid-March) and by April had revised it. This version was sent to the theater on a Saturday, read by Shaw and Barker on a Sunday, and accepted for production on Monday.

The main theme of the play deals with the discrepancy of how the law is applied as it affects rich and poor. While drunk, the good-for-nothing son of a member of Parliament lifts a purse from a prostitute. As part of his adventure, he invites home the indigent husband of the household's charwoman, who promptly takes a silver cigarette case as payment for helping Jack get home. While both are guilty of a crime, Jack gets off scot-free and Jones is sent to prison with a month's hard labor.

Although the play did not gain wide popularity with audiences, it was a big success with critics. Archer (passim) connected Galsworthy along with Shaw and Barker to the "new drama." Naturalism was the new style, and with his first play, Galsworthy was inextricably linked to it (Scrimgeour).

Strife. 1909. Opened 9 March at the Duke of York's Theatre (London) and later transferred to the Haymarket and Adelphi theaters. It initially ran for 21 performances.

Written roughly between February and April 1907, *Strife* was turned down by several managers before being accepted by Charles Frohman. It was scheduled for six matinees at the Duke of York's Theatre but garnered such interest that it ran in the evenings at the Haymarket and the Adelphi. The run ended because the cast had previous engagements. At its original performance in America (at the New Theatre in New York in 1909), *Strife* changed its locale to Ohio.

In a Welsh tin works a strike is on, and both leaders—from the workers and the chairman of the works—are equally obstinate about compromising. As a result, both sides suffer greatly. In the end, the leaders are overthrown by their followers, and the terms adopted to end the strike are the ones suggested from the beginning.

Galsworthy later claimed that the play was not about capital and labor, but rather about extremism or fanaticism. Reviews were generally enthusiastic. *The Times* [London] excerpt is a typical example: "When an artist of Mr. Galsworthy's high endeavour, mental equipment and technical skill writes a play like *Strife,* he has done much more than write a play; he has rendered a public service" (quoted in Nightingale, x).

Justice. 1910. Opened 21 February at the Duke of York's Theatre (London) and ran for 26 performances. Produced by Charles Frohman.

The play is ostensibly an indictment of the penal system in Edwardian England. Galsworthy first visited Dartmoor Prison in 1907 and later went to the gaols at Lewes and Chelmsford for further research on solitary confinement. It took a public controversy chronicled in the newspapers regarding the management of the Sing Sing Prison before *Justice* was given its first professional production (1916) in America. It had been rejected by seven managers before being accepted by John D. Williams.

A young law clerk, Falder, changes one of his employer's checks from nine pounds to ninety pounds and pockets the difference. He plans on starting a new life in South America with a young married woman whose husband abuses her. After surviving the prison sentence (the stage action contains one of the most famous scenes in Galsworthy's oeuvre, depicting the effects of solitary confinement on Falder's psyche), he tries to deal with the world. When he is arrested for failing to report to his parole office, he commits suicide.

Justice is the only play of Galsworthy to directly effect social change. Even before the play was produced, after Galsworthy has visited conditions at Dartmoor Prison, he wrote then Home Secretary Sir Herbert Gladstone about the harm of solitary confinement on the prisoners. Later, after seeing the production, Winston Churchill, the new home secretary, went even further with the reforms, reducing the time one spent in solitary as well as allowing its use as punishment for fewer circumstances.

The Fugitive. 1913. Opened on 16 September at the Court Theatre (London) and later transferred to the Prince of Wales's Theatre. It ran for 27 performances.

Clare Dedmond is unhappy with her well-born husband. She has no legal grounds for divorce—he is neither violent toward her nor unfaithful. To her, his crime is that he is dull and uninterested in her. Despite his pleas, she leaves and takes refuge at the bohemian artist Malise's place. While she is there, her husband and family come to claim her, assuming that Clare and Malise are lovers (they are not at this point). Clare leaves Malise and tries her hand as a working girl, selling gloves. Three months later she offers herself to Malise as his mistress. Soon she sees that he is losing jobs because of the scandal. Unable to live one way or the other, Clare commits suicide, one year after leaving her husband.

Ervine (passim) compared the play to Ibsen's *A Doll's House.* It resembles

Justice in that both plays deal with protagonists hounded by society and their own sensitivities, and to whom death comes as a relief. Aside from Pinero's *The Second Mrs. Tanqueray,* Galsworthy's Clare "is one of the finest tragic women in all of modern English drama" (Sternlicht, 108).

The Skin Game. 1920. Opened 21 April at the St. Martin's Theatre (London) and ran for 349 performances. Produced by Basil Dean. Galsworthy's first commercial success, the play ran for nearly a year.

The Skin Games chronicles the clash between the aristocrats and the nouveau riche. The aristocratic Hillcrists have been selling off family land a bit at a time to make ends meet; the parvenu Hornblowers, who acquired vast wealth in the trade business, want to build a factory on the Hillcrist land they have purchased. When the land is sold at an auction, the Hornblowers acquire it through a "skin game." But the Hillcrists counter with a skin game of their own. They threaten to expose the scandal of the Hornblowers' daughter-in-law in exchange for the land.

Several New York reviewers interpreted the play as an allegory of World War I, which Galsworthy denied (see Gindin [2]). Lewisohn claimed that it illustrated the tragic process itself. "For the staggering truth concerning all human conflict, whether between groups of men or individuals, is that each contestant is both right and wrong; that each has the subjective conviction of being wholly right; that as the conflict grows in length and bitterness each is guilty of deeds that blur his original rightness and bring him closer to the wrongness against which he fights; that hence to be victorious to your own and to be defeated is to gain the only chance of saving your soul" (172).

Loyalties. 1922. Opened on 8 March at the St. Martin's Theatre (London) and ran for 407 performances. Produced and directed by Basil Dean.

Loyalties, written in the summer of 1921, was an even greater success than *The Skin Game.* Galsworthy said of it, "No manager will refuse this" (Gillett [2], xii).

A rich Jew, De Levis, has one thousand pounds stolen from him while staying at the house of upper-class gentile friends. At first everyone sympathizes with him, but when he accuses one of the guests of the theft, they demonstrate their loyalty to class as they rally around the accused.

De Levis, as claimed by Gillett [2] was "one of the finest acting parts ever created by Galsworthy" (xiv). The *Daily Sketch* felt that the play was better than *Justice.* A play structured with conflict and action rather than just ideas, it demonstrated that "the author's power lies in his scrupulous impartiality," and while it was "psychologically a fine play," it also worked on the "lower plane of a crime drama" (quoted in Nightingale, xviii).

Escape. 1926. Opened on 12 August at the Ambassadors Theatre (London) and ran for 243 performances.

Galsworthy's third postwar success, *Escape* was produced by Leon M. Lion and ran for about a year. The story is told in a prologue and nine episodes.

Matt Denant has been sentenced to Dartmoor Prison for killing a police officer. He escapes from the prison and, in order to avoid recapture, disguises himself and meets up with various people on the moors who either help or hinder him. When a clergyman is about to lie to the authorities that Denant is not in the church, Denant surrenders himself to save the cleric's honor.

As Sternlicht put it, "The play's title is ironic: no one escapes from life, the law, and most significantly for the play—himself" (111). Gillett [2] noted its "vivid contrast" (xv), illustrated by its very black-and-white approach to the situation. It was later made into a film. Sternlicht likened it to a morality play, with Denant as Everyman, "who makes mistakes, sins, and repents. He ends with a good deed, a sacrificial act that saves a fellow human. In that process he saves himself" (111).

ADDITIONAL PLAYS, ADAPTATIONS, AND PRODUCTIONS

Galsworthy's second full-length play to be produced was *Joy,* which opened 24 September 1907 at the Savoy Theatre (London). It ran for 24 performances. The play dealt more with personal problems than social ones.

The Pigeon, a play about philanthropy, opened on 30 January 1912 at the Royalty Theatre in London. Henderson thought that the play would "eventually rank as Galsworthy's finest achievement in drama" (475). *The Eldest Son* opened later that year on 23 November at the Kingsway Theatre in London.

While Galsworthy claimed that *Escape* would be his last play, two more plays were produced before his death. (As Gillett [2] speculated, Galsworthy may have wished that he had kept to his decision not to write any more plays after *Escape* [xv].) Both *Exiled* and *The Roof* were produced in 1929; neither was successful. Galsworthy was at work on a play titled *Similes* when he died. A little more than half of it was completed.

ASSESSMENT OF GALSWORTHY'S CAREER

With the republication of five Galsworthy plays by Methuen in 1984 and several revivals in the 1970s and 1980s, one might have expected a cavalcade of praise and productions to follow the rediscovery of Galsworthy's dramatic works. But that has not been the case. Instead, the occasional essay surfaces in *Modern Drama* and interest is piqued for the moment. In retrospect, many critics dismiss Galsworthy as a major dramatist mainly because of both his form (a simplified well-made play) (see Borreca; Taylor) and content (topical issues in Edwardian England) (see Scrimgeour). While these are certainly issues with which one must grapple when approaching Galsworthy's plays, the truth of the matter is that he was the second most popular English playwright (after Shaw) in the first two decades of the century and was a part of a movement that put

English playwriting back on the Continental map. His play *Justice* is the only play in the twentieth-century English dramatic canon that directly effected social change. That fact at least gets him mentioned. Examining his dramatic theory within a historical context makes him a much more interesting fellow than the lawyer-turned-novelist who impulsively tried his hand at writing plays.

The Barker-Vedrenne management, begun in 1905 at the Royal Court Theatre, had put out the word that it was looking for new English plays by new English playwrights. Its seasons at the Court were the beginnings of a National Theatre. Galsworthy balked at the initial suggestion from his friend Edward Garnett to write a play and send it to the Court management but eventually changed his mind and wrote *The Silver Box,* which was accepted immediately for production. Few critics mention how extraordinary it was (and is) for a novelist to write a successful play (and vice versa). Galsworthy apparently had no trouble telling stories in either medium.

What the Barker-Vedrenne team brought to England was realism and naturalism. In an attempt to break from the entertaining melodramas and well-made plays of the nineteenth century, Barker and company embraced the tenets of realism. As a contemporary, Galsworthy was caught up in the movement as well. He staunchly approached his artistry from a realistic point of view. "My own method was the outcome of the trained habit (which I was already employing in my novels) of naturalistic dialogue guided, informed, and selected by a controlling idea, together with an intense visualisation of types and scenes. I just wrote down the result of these two, having always in my mind's eye not the stage, but the room or space where in real life the action would pass" (quoted in Scrimgeour, 66). Many critics (both his contemporaries and later) have had difficulty reconciling the arbitrariness of the well-made-play form with the impartial, observant qualities of naturalism as they analyze Galsworthy's plays (see Scrimgeour; Henderson). This is an interesting argument that misses the point: while Galsworthy employed naturalistic techniques (such as realistic dialogue and allowing each character his or her own point of view with no intervention from him), plays are still arbitrary constructions based on a playwright's conscious selection and combination of events and characters.

Galsworthy saw that in writing plays there were "three courses open to the serious dramatist" ("Some Platitudes Concerning Drama," 45). The first is to write what the public wants to see and believes; the second is for playwrights to write their codes and beliefs; and the third is to "set before the public no cut-and-dried codes, but the phenomena of life and character, selected and combined, but not distorted, by the dramatist's outlook.... This third method requires a certain detachment; ... it requires a far view for no immediately practical result" ("Some Platitudes Concerning Drama," 46). For the most part, Galsworthy practiced the third course. He believed that presenting the truth as he saw it—undistorted and unbiased—would produce in his audience or readers "a sort of mental and moral ferment, whereby vision may be enlarged, imagination livened, and understand[ing] promoted" (quoted in Gillett [2], xi). Galsworthy's deliberate detachment was part of his artistic philosophy: as an artist, his job was to present the situation, not to solve it. His plays always deal ''in particular instances, and leave it to others to draw any general conclusions they may wish'' (Taylor, 116). ''For him the task lies in the unrolling of the problem, not in its solution. The unrolling of the problem should serve to make us think and reflect, to make us realise, to awaken our interest in what is hitherto unknown to us, or viewed in a wrong light. We ought to understand, not to condemn, to try to approach one another, and be conciliatory'' (Schalit, 219).

Coats claimed that Galsworthy's plays fit into five types of social tragedy (quoted by Gindin [2], 205). The first is the play of family relationships, like *Joy;* the second is the tragedy of social injustice, like the contrast between the rich and poor in *The Silver Box.* For Coats, the third type is the drama of social deterioration in which ''characters, after making a mistake, are hounded to disaster.'' *The Fugitive* and *Justice* serve as examples. The fourth type is the tragedy of idealism in ''which a character consciously chooses martyrdom,'' as in *The Mob* and *Escape.* The last category is the tragedy of ''caste feeling, like *Strife, The Skin Game,* and *Loyalties,* in which the finally unresolvable problem originates in some kind of inflexibly held social division.''

Generally, Galsworthy's plays are thesis plays. According to Sternlicht, he borrowed from Ibsen's problem plays, simplified them, and divested them of ''preaching and propaganda'' (101). His dramatic technique remains fairly consistent: ''He presents a near-balanced view of the play's problem or thesis through a highly dramatic situation supported by extremely realistic dialogue, seemingly uncontrived and nonpoetic and thus considered radical in its day. The denouement is left partially open and tinged with irony because Galsworthy sees a play, like life itself, more prone to questions than to answers. He eschews the deus ex machina ending for neatness's sake or the contrived finales of the 'well-made play' '' (Sternlicht, 102). His device of choice is that of contrast or, as some critics call it, ''parallelism'' (Henderson, 476), where he sets up a polemic between the privileged and the underprivileged ''with a chance conjunction of events in the plot'' (Scrimgeour, 67). Every character or action in the play relates to the theme—''There is nothing here, as in life, of the random or the irrelevant'' (Scrimgeour, 73).

Galsworthy has been compared often to Chekhov because like Chekhov, Galsworthy ''does not seek to mirror life but to present scientific, disinterested yet empathic observations of its forces, in a mode of presentation that does not dress up or suppress the truth, but holds it naked and unavoidable before us'' (Borreca, 487). The main difference between the two is that while Chekhov avoided the well-made-play model, Galsworthy embraced it. It is this adoption where Borreca sighted the fundamental weakness of Galsworthy's drama. Others point to Galsworthy's form of choice as a hindrance of another kind. Henderson called Galsworthy a ''phenomenon manqué, a craftsman endowed with all the arts but one—to breathe into the dramatic character a living soul'' (471). He compared Galsworthy's technique to that of a sculptor or painter, moving clay figures around, all surface, no substance. West felt that Galsworthy's inability to grow as a dramatic writer stemmed from his initial foray into the medium. Having his first play accepted for production really hindered his development: "This instant collapse of the walls of Jericho apparently gave Galsworthy the wholly mistaken idea that he had no need to learn more than he already knew about the theatre, and that there was no important distinction to be made between the novelistic and the dramatic" (xxi).

In all, Galsworthy wrote twenty-two full-length plays and many short ones. He achieved both literary and commercial success. The subject matter of his plays attacked most of the social problems of his time: "the unfair justice system, the repression of women in family and society, tensions between parents and children, exploitation of labor, anti-Semitism, poverty, strikes, jingoism, and others" (Sternlicht, 101). For all the criticism about his technique, his plays are valuable dramaturgically (because he was the one in a position to blend the nineteenth century with the "new drama") as well as historically (they still chronicle a particular moment in time). Many of them still have the power to move the reader, for despite his protestations to the contrary, bits of his passion about the social injustices he saw around him creep into the scenarios. "The eminence of Mr. Galsworthy in the field of drama is and has been due to the dignity not of his thought, but to the dignity of his emotions" (Nathan, 195). We need to look past the particulars of Edwardian England and realize that by dealing with the specific, Galsworthy's plays demonstrate the idea that "we are all human beings and not physiological specimens, and all reform uninspired by sympathy and understanding is dead wood in our tree" (Gillett [2], xvi).

ARCHIVAL SOURCES

The Galsworthy Memorial Collection at the University of Birmingham is the principal collection of materials; see *John Galsworthy: A Catalog of the Collection* (Birmingham: University of Birmingham Library, 1967). Other materials are held by the Houghton Library at Harvard University; the Bodleian Library, Oxford University; and Scribners Archive, Firestone Library, Princeton University.

PRIMARY BIBLIOGRAPHY

Plays

A Bit O' Love. London: Duckworth, 1915.
The Eldest Son. London: Duckworth, 1912.
Escape. London: Duckworth, 1926.
Exiled. London: Duckworth, 1929.
A Family Man. London: Duckworth, 1922.
The Forest. London: Duckworth, 1924.

The Foundations. London: Duckworth, 1920.
The Fugitive. London: Duckworth, 1913.
Justice. London: Duckworth, 1910.
The Little Dream. London: Duckworth, 1911.
Loyalties. London: Duckworth, 1922.
The Mob. London: Duckworth, 1914.
Old English. London: Duckworth, 1924.
The Pigeon. London: Duckworth, 1912.
The Roof. London: Duckworth, 1929.
The Show. London: Duckworth, 1925.
The Skin Game. London: Duckworth, 1920.
Windows. London: Duckworth, 1922.
The Winter Garden. London: Duckworth, 1935.

Anthologies

The Galsworthy Reader. Introduction by Anthony West. New York: Charles Scribner's
    Sons, 1967.
John Galsworthy: Five Plays (*Strife, Justice, The Eldest Son, The Skin Game, Loyalties*).
    Introduction by Benedict Nightingale. London: Methuen, 1984.
Plays. New York: Charles Scribner's Sons, 1928.
Plays. London: Duckworth, 1929.
Plays: The Silver Box, Joy, Strife. London: Duckworth, 1909.
Representative Plays by John Galsworthy. Introduction by George P. Baker. New York:
    Charles Scribner's Sons, 1924.
Six Short Plays. London: Duckworth, 1921.
Ten Famous Plays by John Galsworthy. Introduction by Eric Gillett. Reprint. London:
    Duckworth, 1952. Reprint. New York: AMS Press, 1976.

Collected Works

The Devon Edition of the Novels, Tales, and Plays of John Galsworthy. 22 vols. New
    York: Charles Scribner's Sons, 1926–29.
The Manaton Edition of the Works of John Galsworthy. 30 vols. London: Heinemann,
    1923–36. [Galsworthy wrote the prefaces to the plays.]

Essays and Articles on Drama and Theater

Candelabra: Selected Essays and Addresses. London: Heinemann, 1933.
''Some Platitudes Concerning Drama.'' In *The Inn of Tranquillity: Studies and Essays.*
    New York: Charles Scribner's Sons, 1912. Reprinted in *Playwrights on Play-*
    writing, ed. Toby Cole. New York: Hill & Wang, 1982.

SECONDARY BIBLIOGRAPHY

Archer, William. *The Old Drama and the New: An Essay in Re-valuation.* New York:
    Dodd, Mead, 1926. Reissued New York: Benjamin Blom, 1971.

Bache, William B. "*Justice:* Galsworthy's Dramatic Tragedy." *Modern Drama* 3.2 (Sept. 1960): 138–42.

Barker, Dudley. *The Man of Principle: A View of John Galsworthy.* London: George Allen & Unwin, 1967.

Beerbohm, Max. "Justice." In *Around Theatres,* 2:731–34. New York: Alfred A. Knopf, 1930.

Borreca, Art. "Galsworthy's Realism: A Revaluation." *Modern Drama* 34.4 (Dec. 1991): 483–93.

Burgess, Anthony. "Seen Any Good Galsworthy Lately?" *New York Times Magazine* (16 Nov. 1969): 57–64.

Coats, R. H. *John Galsworthy as a Dramatic Artist.* London: Duckworth, 1926.

Coudriou, Jacques. "The Social Aspect of John Galsworthy's Theatre." *Cahiers Victoriens et Édouardiens* nos. 9–10 (1979): 151–63.

Dupont, V. *John Galsworthy: The Dramatic Artist.* Paris: Didier, 1942.

Dupré, Catherine. *John Galsworthy.* New York: Coward, McCann & Geoghegan, 1976.

Eaker, J. Gordon. "Galsworthy and the Modern Mind." *Philological Quarterly* 29.1 (Jan. 1950): 31–48.

Ervine, St. John G. "John Galsworthy." In *Some Impressions of My Elders,* 113–160. New York: Macmillan, 1922; London: George Allen and Unwin, 1923.

Evans, Gareth Lloyd. "John Galsworthy and the Language of Man and Society." In *The Language of Modern Drama,* 65–81. London: Dent, 1977.

Fan, Ada Mei. "In and out of Bounds: Marriage, Adultery, and Women in the Plays of Henry Arthur Jones, Arthur Wing Pinero, Harley Granville-Barker, John Galsworthy, and W. Somerset Maugham." Ph.D. diss., University of Michigan, 1989. *DAI* 49 (1989): 1808A.

Ford, Ford Madox. "Galsworthy." In *Portraits from Life,* 124–42. Boston: Houghton Mifflin, 1937. Reprint. Westport, CT: Greenwood Press, 1974.

Fréchet, Alec. *John Galsworthy: A Reassessment.* Trans. Denis Mahaffey. Totowa, NJ: Barnes & Noble, 1982.

Fricker, Robert. "*Justice.*" In *Das moderne englische Drama: Interpretationes,* ed. Horst Oppel, 3rd ed., 113–129. Berlin: Schmidt, 1976.

Garnett, Edward, ed. *Letters from John Galsworthy, 1900–1932.* London: Cape, 1934.

Gillett, Eric. [1] "Galsworthy's Place in the Theatre." *Listener* (15 Jan. 1936): 125–36.

———. [2]. Introduction to *Ten Famous Plays by John Galsworthy.* London: Duckworth, 1952. Reprint. New York: AMS Press, 1976.

Gindin, James. [1]. *John Galsworthy's Life and Art: An Alien's Fortress.* Ann Arbor: University of Michigan Press, 1987.

———. [2]. "John Galsworthy." In *Dictionary of Literary Biography,* vol. 10, *Modern British Dramatists, 1900–1945,* ed. Stanley Weintraub, pt. 1, 194–206. Detroit: Gale Research, 1982.

Glasspool, Charles Stanley. "The Theme of Social Justice in the Drama of John Galsworthy." Ph.D. diss., University of Michigan, 1979. *DAI* 39 (1979): 4217A.

Hamilton, Robert. "Galsworthy the Playwright." *Contemporary Review* (Oct. 1952): 220–24.

Henderson, Archibald. "John Galsworthy." In *European Dramatists,* 467–79. Englewood Cliffs, NJ: Prentice-Hall, 1926.

Holloway, David. *John Galsworthy.* London: Morgan-Grampian, 1968.

Innes, Christopher. [1]. "Granville Barker and Galsworthy: Questions of Censorship." *Modern Drama* 32.3 (Sept. 1989): 331–44.

———. [2] *Modern British Drama, 1890–1990.* Cambridge: Cambridge University Press, 1992.

Lewisohn, Ludwig. "The Quiet Truth." In *The Drama and the Stage,* 168–73. New York: Harcourt, Brace, 1922.

Markovic, Vida. *The Reputation of Galsworthy in England, 1897–1950.* Belgrade: Faculty of Philology of the University of Belgrade, 1969.

Marrot, H. V. *The Life and Letters of John Galsworthy.* New York: Charles Scribner's Sons, 1936.

McDonald, Jan. "John Galsworthy." In *The "New Drama": 1900–1914: Harley Granville-Barker, John Galsworthy, St. John Hankin, John Masefield,* 103–147. New York: Grove Press, 1986.

Nathan, George Jean. *The Magic Mirror.* New York: Alfred A. Knopf, 1960.

Nicoll, Allardyce. *English Drama, 1900–1930: The Beginnings of the Modern Period.* Cambridge: Cambridge University Press, 1973.

Nightingale, Benedict. Introduction to *John Galsworthy: Five Plays.* London: Methuen, 1984.

Noonkester, Myron C. "Galsworthy on Adaptation." *Notes and Queries* 37.4 (Dec. 1990): 434.

Perrine, Laurence. "The Theme of Galsworthy's *Loyalties.*" *English Record* 27.3–4 (1976): 20–27.

Schalit, Leon. *John Galsworthy: A Survey.* London: Heinemann, 1929.

Scrimgeour, Gary J. "Naturalist Drama and Galsworthy." *Modern Drama* 7.1 (May 1964): 65–78.

Shatzky, Joel L. "Shaw, Barker, and Galsworthy: The Development of the Drama of Ideas, 1890–1910. Ph.D. diss., New York University, 1971. *DAI* 31 (1971): 4180A.

Simon, Elliott M. "John Galsworthy: The Individual and the Institution." In *The Problem Play in British Drama, 1890–1914,* 242–286. Salzburg: Institut für Englische Sprache und Literatur, 1978.

Smith, Philip E., II. [1]. "Galsworthy's Strife: The Dramatic Art of Ethical Naturalism." *Studies in the Humanities* 6.1 (June 1977): 37–43.

———. [2]. "John Galsworthy's Plays: The Theory and Practice of Dramatic Realism." Ph.D. diss., Northwestern University, 1970. *DAI* 30 (1970): 4465A–66A.

Stern, Faith E. B. "John Galsworthy's Dramatic Theory and Practice." Ph.D. diss., Stanford University, 1971. *DAI* 32 (1971): 986A.

Sternlicht, Sanford. "The Playwright of Conscience." In *John Galsworthy,* 101–112. Boston: Twayne, 1987.

Taylor, John Russell. *The Rise and Fall of the Well-made Play.* New York: Hill & Wang, 1967.

West, Anthony. Introduction to *The Galsworthy Reader.* New York: Charles Scribner's Sons, 1967.

Wilson, Asher Boldon, ed. [1]. *John Galsworthy's Letters to Leon Lion.* The Hague: Mouton, 1968.

———. [2]. "Oscar Wilde and *Loyalties.*" *Educational Theatre Journal* 11.3 (Oct. 1959): 208–11.

BIBLIOGRAPHIES

Marrot, H. V. *A Bibliography of the Works of John Galsworthy.* London: Elkin Mathews & Marrot, 1928.

Mikhail, E. H. *John Galsworthy the Dramatist: A Bibliography of Criticism.* Troy, NY: Whitston Pub. Co., 1971.

Stevens, Earl E., and H. Ray Stevens. *John Galsworthy: An Annotated Bibliography of Writings about Him.* De Kalb: Northern Illinois University Press, 1980.

William Schwenck Gilbert
(1836–1911)

MARY LINDROTH

William Schwenck Gilbert is best remembered for his collaboration with Arthur Sullivan on fourteen comic operas, also known as the Savoy operas after the theater that housed the last eight of the Gilbert and Sullivan operas. Today, Gilbert's reputation rests on the librettos he wrote for the Gilbert and Sullivan operas. This legacy, however, represents only a tiny percentage of the some seventy plays that Gilbert wrote and that were produced during his lifetime.

William Schwenck Gilbert was born on 18 November 1836 in London, England. His father was a retired naval surgeon and a novelist. Gilbert's childhood was particularly memorable because of an incident in which, at the age of two, he was kidnapped while on vacation with his parents in Italy and ransomed for twenty-five pounds. That Gilbert would become a playwright was not at first apparent. Indeed, his education suggested that he would pursue either a military or a legal career. He was educated at Boulogne, France, and at Great Ealing College. He then attended King's College, London, with the intent of obtaining a commission in the Royal Artillery, but when the Crimean War ended, so did Gilbert's aspirations. Gilbert then obtained a clerkship in the Education Department of the Privy Council Office, which he held from 1857 through 1862. Gilbert also studied law at this time. In 1863 he was called to the bar and for the next two years practiced law. Even when Gilbert began his writing career in earnest, he did not give up his military and legal aspirations. He held a commission in the Fifth West Yorkshire Militia and in the Royal Aberdeen Highlanders, and from 1893 on he was a justice of the peace for the county of Middlesex.

In 1867 he married Lucy Blois Turner, who was fourteen years younger than he. Before this time, however, he had begun a writing career, which consisted of writing dramatic pieces and dramatic criticism for magazines such as *London*

Society, Cornhill Magazine, the *Observer,* and *Illustrated Times.* He also wrote comic verses for *Fun* using his childhood nickname "Bab." Gilbert began writing plays at the instigation of T. W. Robertson. His first play, entitled *Uncle Baby,* opened at the Lyceum Theatre on 31 October 1863. Gilbert himself, however, never acknowledged this play. The first acknowledged produced play was *Dulcamara; or, The Little Duck and the Great Quack* (1866), an operatic burlesque of Gaetano Donizetti's opera *L'Elisir d'amore* (1832). Gilbert claimed to have written this play in ten days and to have rehearsed it in a week for its production at St. James's Theatre on 29 December 1866, which continued for 120 nights afterward. After *Dulcamara,* Gilbert wrote a series of operatic burlesques in the tradition of J. R. Planche, concluding with *The Pretty Druidess; or, The Mother, the Maid, and the Misteltoe Bough,* which opened on 19 June 1869. Gilbert also experimented with other forms and wrote short dramatic farces such as *Allow Me to Explain* (1867), farces under his nom de farce F. Latour Tomline such as *The Blue-legged Lady* (1874), and six "entertainments" such as *Ages Ago: A Ghost Story* (1869) for German Reed's Royal Gallery of Illustrations.

The 1870s were the years of Gilbert's most creative and productive output and account for some of his most popular and critical successes. In addition to such Gilbert and Sullivan operas as their first collaboration *Thespis; or, The Gods Grown Old* (1871) or such favorites as *H.M.S. Pinafore; or, The Lass That Loved a Sailor* (1878), Gilbert wrote fairy comedies such as *The Palace of Truth* (1870), *Pygmalion and Galatea* (1871), and *The Wicked World* (1873) that captivated audiences. He also wrote successful farces such as *Tom Cobb; or, Fortune's Toy* (1875) and *Engaged* (1877). Gilbert's less successful plays were his serious plays that mixed sentiment and satire as well as comedy and seriousness. Gilbert's serious plays include *Charity* (1874), *Sweethearts* (1874), *Broken Hearts* (1875), *Dan'l Druce, Blacksmith* (1876), and *Gretchen* (1879).

During the 1880s Gilbert, Sullivan, and Richard D'Oyly Carte worked together as librettist, composer, and theater manager to produce such immortal and well-beloved light operas as *Iolanthe; or, The Peer and the Peri* (1882) and *The Mikado; or, The Town of Titipu* (1885). After *The Gondoliers; or, The King of Barataria* (1889) Gilbert and Sullivan terminated their partnership as a result of a financial dispute. They worked together only two more times after this breach, and their last joint effort was *The Grand Duke: or, The Statutory Duel* (1896). The 1880s were also marked by comedies such as *Foggerty's Fairy* (1881) and *Comedy and Tragedy* (1884) as well as a melodrama entitled *Brantinghame Hall* (1888).

Unlike most dramatists of the nineteenth century, Gilbert exercised control over all aspects of playwriting, directing, and producing. He was one of the first, for example, to publish his plays, and four different volumes of his *Original Plays* appeared between 1876 and 1911. Gilbert also invested money to build the Garrick Theatre, which opened in 1889. It was in this theater that Gilbert's *The Fairy's Dilemma* opened on 3 May 1904. After 1904, however, Gilbert retired from the theater world and lived the life of a gentleman on his estate, Grim's Dyke. He was knighted as a playwright and not as a dramatist, much to his chagrin, on 30 June 1907. He died on 29 May 1911 in Harrow Weald, England, of a heart attack suffered after trying to save a woman from drowning in the lake on his estate.

Selected Biographical Sources: Baily; Browne; Dark and Grey; Orel.

MAJOR PLAYS, PREMIERES, AND SIGNIFICANT REVIVALS: THEATRICAL RECEPTION

The Palace of Truth. 1870. A fairy comedy in three acts based on Madame de Genlis's *Le Palais de la verité.* Opened 19 November at the Haymarket (London) for 230 performances. Revivals: Prince's Theatre (London), January 1884; Mohawk Drama Festival (directed by Charles Coburn and Percival Vivian), Schenectady, New York, 1937.

Gilbert's first fairy play follows the fortunes of the married King Phanor and Queen Altemire as well as the betrothed Princess Zeolide and Prince Philamir as they are forced—without realizing it—to speak the truth. While the play's title proclaims it a fairy comedy, fairies, as such, do not appear in the play, although there is a magical talisman without which one cannot lie. The reviewer for *Theatre* ("Mr. Gilbert as a Dramatist") focused on the adaptation as being somewhat derivative but defended the play from charges of being too artificial or fanciful. Archer [2] commended the play as satire well done. Cook [1], however, criticized the lack of sympathy created for the characters and noted that the actors' appearance in "medieval costume" was inconsistent since the costume suggested romance while the characters revealed themselves as self-seeking and shallow beings. An unsigned *Theatre* review (*"Palace of Truth"*) of the 1884 revival at the Prince's Theatre, on the other hand, defended and praised Gilbert's dramatic characters by criticizing the actors' misreadings of their lines.

Pygmalion and Galatea. 1871. Mythological comedy in three acts. Opened 9 December at the Haymarket (London) for 230 performances. Revivals: Lyceum (London), December 1883; Lyceum, March 1888; and Comedy (London), June 1900.

A greater commercial success, this mythological comedy focuses on the marriage between Pygmalion and Cynisca. After it demonstrates the depth of their love for one another, that love is put to the test when one of Pygmalion's statues, Galatea, molded in the likeness of a younger Cynisca, comes to life. Critics responded by arguing over whether Gilbert meant the play to be a sincere revelation of emotion or a satiric unmasking of false emotion. This ambiguity bothered many critics. The 1877 *Theatre* article ("Mr. Gilbert as a Dramatist"), for example, acknowledged a poignancy in Galatea's expression of love to point to an uncomfortable feeling that Gilbert might be "laughing in his sleeve at our emotion.'' Archer [2] proclaimed this play to be vulgar and blamed it on Gilbert's attempt to appeal to the Haymarket audience and the Haymarket management. Cook [2], on the other hand, liked the play, called it "pleasant and acceptable," and praised it as inventive, fresh, and clever, but also criticized it for being too slight to bear the burden of three acts. A *Theatre* review (*"Pygmalion and Galatea"*) of the 1883 revival concentrated on how the part of Galatea was acted and pondered the question of whether she was meant to be warm or cold, which led the reviewer to then ponder who breathed life into the role—the playwright or the actress.

The Wicked World. 1873. Fairy comedy in three acts. Opened 4 January at the Haymarket (London) for 200 performances.

This fairy comedy does include fairies and is set on a cloud. It satirizes the marriage institution when the female fairies, who have never known love, invite human knights to their cloud and not only experience love and the desire for marriage but also experience jealousy. Unlike many reviews that were won over by the charm of the play, the *Pall Mall Gazette* reviewed this play as "coarse" and "foul" (quoted in Orel, 51). This indictment resulted in part because Selene, the Fairy Queen, verbally assaults the character of Sir Ethnais at the end of act 2. Cook [3] praised the ingenuity of its story but argued that it was not dramatic because the characters lacked sympathy. Gilbert (under the pen name F. Latour Tomline) collaborated with Gilbert à Beckett on a burlesque version entitled *The Happy Land* that opened at the Court on 3 March 1873. Its political satire led the Lord Chamberlain to censor it.

Charity. 1874. Play in four acts. Opened 3 January at the Haymarket (London) for 80 performances. Revivals: Fifth Avenue Theater (New York), March 1874 and 1895.

This play about a "tramp" named Ruth Tredgett who is shunned by society in a hypocritical fashion was not popular with audiences and received a mixed reception, mostly negative, from its critics. While most were willing to acknowledge and support the risk Gilbert took by using the comedy form to explore a serious issue, many, like Archer [2], proclaimed it a failure. Archer objected to the burlesque element in a play that strove to be serious, thus leading to his indictment of the play as "unpleasant." Archer also objected to too many coincidences that strained the laws of probability. Sichel, on the other hand, who dubbed Gilbert the English Aristophanes, was not bothered by the presence of coincidence. Sichel discussed the exchange between Mr. Smailey and his former victim, Ruth, wherein Smailey acknowledges the coincidence of their meeting again after so many years. Sichel noted that Ruth's "inverting power" of irony "deals breezily with the cant of coincidence." For Sichel, the scene was dramatically effective, though improbable, because it revealed hypocrisy.

Tom Cobb; or, Fortune's Toy. 1875. Farcical comedy in three acts. Opened 24 April at St. James's Theatre (London).

Tom Cobb is a play of mistaken identity set in Ireland. An alive Tom Cobb assumes the identity of a dead Tom Cobb to avoid his debtors and is then forced to assume the identity of a duke and finally of a major-general. Each assumption of identity gets the hapless man into further farcical predicaments until finally it is discovered that the dead Tom Cobb is a long-lost relative with lots of money. Archer [2] noted that this play was not a success with audiences in order to then argue that it was a better play than the more popularly received *Engaged* because where *Engaged* was bitter, *Tom Cobb* was pleasant.

Broken Hearts. 1875. Fairy play in three acts. Opened 9 December at the Court (London). Two special performances in 1882 and 1885. Also opened in New York.

This fairy play takes place on an island where four women with broken hearts have isolated themselves from all men except for the deformed dwarf, Mousta. Trouble begins when Prince Florian and his magic cloak, which allows the wearer to become invisible, arrives. The play's sentiment and style were censured, and Scott dubbed it "Broken Parts" (quoted in Orel, 50). Arthur Clements and Frederick Hay wrote a burlesque entitled *Cracked Heads* that was performed at the Strand (London) on 2 February 1876. Despite the burlesque and the negative critical reception, Gilbert considered this play and *Gretchen* to be his finest works.

Dan'l Druce, Blacksmith. 1876. A new and original drama in three acts. Opened 11 September at the Haymarket (London). Revivals: Booth Theatre (New York), January 1877; Court (London), March 1884; the Prince of Wales's Theatre (London), February 1894.

Set in the seventeenth century, complete with "thee" and "thou," this play involves Roundheads, Cavaliers, a blacksmith, and a foundling child. Despite its being labeled "original," its first act is suggested by George Eliot's *Silas Marner* and involves a natural father's and an adoptive father's struggle for a daughter's love. The play was a favorite with character actors, but critics like Archer [2] complained that the play was undeveloped and that the first act was really a prologue while the remaining two acts were sketches. Archer, however, did see some merit in the character of Dorothy and used that character to reveal some of the best and worst examples of Gilbert's dramatic skill. Sichel suggested that the play was unsuccessful because it did not include irony and practiced the conventions it should have been satirizing. Arthur Clements wrote a burlesque entitled *Dan'l Tra-duced, Tinker* that opened at the Strand (London) on 27 November 1876.

Engaged. 1877. Farcical comedy in three acts. Opened 3 October at the Haymarket (London). Revivals: New York, 1878; Strand (London), July 1878; Court (London), November 1881; Haymarket (London), February 1886.

This farce, set on the border between Scotland and England, deals with Cheviot Hill's unfortunate tendency to engage himself to as many women as possible at the same time. Cheviot Hill, his friend Belvawney, and Hill's three fiancées, Belinda Treherne, Minnie Symperson, and Maggie MacFarlane, are all equally motivated by money and not by love. The introductory note written by Gilbert insisted that the play ''be played with the most perfect earnestness and gravity throughout,'' and as a result the play received diametrically opposed reviews from critics either praising it or denigrating it.

Gretchen. 1879. Play in four acts. Opened 24 March at the Olympic (London). Revivals: New York, 18 October 1886 and 1890.

In Gilbert's translation of the Faust theme, Faust is a priest who has sworn off women until Mephisto shows him the beautiful Gretchen. What follows is a tragedy of seduction and betrayal that ends with Gretchen dying. Considered by Gilbert to be one of his finest works, it had only a three-week run in London. Adams ([2], 438) defended the play as ''powerful,'' while most others, Archer [2] included, condemned it for lacking any skill in the analysis of human emotions since what was ethereal in the original was now ''commonplace'' and shallow. Alfred E. T. Watson did not help the reputation of the play when he included in his memoirs the tale of the occasion when Gilbert read the play aloud at his estate and Watson promptly fell asleep (quoted in Orel, 10).

Comedy and Tragedy. 1884. Opened 26 January at the Lyceum (London) (double-billed with a revival of *Pygmalion and Galatea*). Revival: Haymarket (London), April 1890.

A *Theatre* review (''*Comedy and Tragedy*'') called this ''a capital little play'' because of the opportunities it provided an actress to act in both the comic and tragic modes while the hero and villain of the piece duel over her reputation. The review went on to criticize Mary Anderson's portrayal because her comedy was labored and not delicate, and because her tragedy was artificial and not powerful.

ASSESSMENT OF GILBERT'S CAREER

The 1880s and 1890s were the heyday of Gilbert productions. Today it is assumed that that heyday consisted mainly of the Gilbert and Sullivan operas. As a result, scholarship on Gilbert's librettos has overshadowed scholarship on his fairy plays, farces, melodramas, sentimental dramas, and tragedies. A look at production records for these years (Adams [1], Allen, Mullen, Rowell [3]), however, demonstrates that Gilbert's nonmusical plays were produced as often and with as great acclaim as the operas. Still, assessment of Gilbert's dramatic contribution exclusive of the Savoy operas has suffered. In part, this has to do with a nagging suspicion that Gilbert's plays are important only insofar as they reveal the ideas, plots, and devices that will reappear in the Savoy operas. Like the operas, Gilbert's fairy comedies and farces create topsy-turvy worlds through devices such as a veil that make its wearer invisible; a talisman or flower with magical properties; mistaken identities; and coincidences to reveal men and women as selfish and shallow beings who hide behind social masks, polite manners, and good behavior. Some critics, such as Duployen and Stedman [1], read the plays to reveal how Gilbert was working toward the Savoy operas. Gilbert's nonmusical plays, however, merit interest in their own right.

Another factor contributing to the imbalance in Gilbert scholarship is that Gilbert wrote in the period between Sheridan and Shaw. It is a critical commonplace, as a look at surveys of the English drama will show, that this period did not produce anything of dramatic merit. Such a critical commonplace is exacerbated by the general critical assessment of Gilbert's day. One frequently repeated assessment is that he valued humor over drama. The judgment proclaimed in an 8 May 1904 unidentified review of *The Fairy's Dilemma* that the play "is good sport . . . not . . . drama" (quoted in Orel) is an assessment that haunted Gilbert throughout his playwriting career, especially in the dramatic criticism of Cook. Another frequent objection and one that was voiced in particular by Scott was that Gilbert privileged caricature over character. Finally, critics like Filon and Archer [2] hinted that he wrote such a prodigious number of plays simply to meet the demand for the variety that a growing, increasingly middle-class audience insisted upon.

Finally, the biggest hurdle confronting Gilbert scholarship is that Gilbert's plays have not been revived. According to Rowell ([1], 22) the only modern-day revival of a nonmusical Gilbert play was a production of *Engaged* at the National Theatre (London). As a result, it appears that Gilbert's nonmusical plays can only be interesting for what they reveal about an antiquated Victorian world and an antiquated Victorian drama. Studies appearing since Gilbert's death, however, albeit few in comparison to the Gilbert and Sullivan scholarship, suggest that it is time for a reappraisal of Gilbert's entire dramatic output.

For some critics, such as Filon, Gilbert's plays help to define an "original" and "English" drama. More recently Huberman has argued that *Tom Cobb* is the very first full-length English farce and that *Engaged* is important not because it is characteristic Gilbert or because it is controversial but because it is farce in a way that had never existed before. For other critics, such as Sutton, Gilbert's dramatic work reveals an incredible variety of dramatic forms such as entertainments, extravaganzas, burlesques, and pantomimes as well as full-length plays in the guise of fairy comedies, farces, sentimental dramas, and melodrama. Sutton's work is the most complete analysis of Gilbert's dramatic output and examines the two worlds created out of a topsy-turvy vision—that of "romantic illusion" and of everyday reality. Sutton's study reveals the intricate and complex ways in which all of Gilbert's plays dramatize the permeable boundaries between real and fantastic worlds.

The fantastic worlds of Gilbert's fairy plays interested Filon, Archer, Scott, and Cook, who suggested that Gilbert's three early fairy plays, *Palace of Truth, Pygmalion and Galatea,* and *Wicked World,* each written in blank verse, fared best with audiences in part because their satire was not set in the contemporary world but in a world of make-believe. This perspective, however, is somewhat confining. A look at the performance history of Gilbert's plays illustrates that many of Gilbert's more serious and controversial plays that were set in the contemporary world such as *Charity, Broken Hearts, Dan'l Druce, Engaged,* and *Comedy and Tragedy* had successful runs in the provinces as well as in the United States. Indeed, in a review of a new collection of Gilbert plays, Hankey took the opportunity to reconsider the plays from the perspective of audience reception and examined the extremes of delight and disgust that both the satirical *Engaged* and the fantastical *The Palace of Truth* evoked amongst audiences and critics. Bargainnier [1] reexamined another play that was less than successful with audiences—*Charity,* the melodrama denounced as immoral. Bargainnier's reexamination suggested that *Charity* failed because neither audiences nor critics were prepared to understand the form of the play. Bargainnier proposed that it was a problem play before its time, which form Arthur Wing Pinero and George Bernard Shaw would later perfect and make successful.

In 1982 Rowell [1] addressed and counteracted the unbalanced attention to Gilbert's plays by publishing a volume of plays not included in the Savoy opus. In the introduction Rowell foregrounded Gilbert's dramatic skill by exploring the Robertson connection and the dramatic qualities of showing rather than telling that Gilbert inherited. One of the plays Rowell included is *Engaged,* which is by far the most talked-about play in recent scholarship, partly because it is arguably Gilbert's most characteristic play and partly because of the influence it had on Shaw's *Arms and the Man* (Bargainnier [2]) and Oscar Wilde's *The Importance of Being Earnest* (see Hudson). Filon approached *Engaged* from a Robertsonian perspective and focused on the cruel caricature of mankind in the play. More recently, Fisher has argued, contrary to Filon's assertion, that Gilbert is not like Robertson, Byron, or Alberty since his mix of comedy, melodrama, and farce emphasizes the world of art and not the world of life. Stanton examined *Engaged* in the tradition of French well-made plays, and Cardullo uncovered a structure of disjuncture, contradiction, and reversal within the play.

Although not revived, Gilbert's plays, exclusive of his librettos, should be read, studied, and performed. In addition to what his plays reveal about the state of Victorian drama, Victorian audiences, and Victorian critics, they interrogate the very essence of drama and theatricality. As a reading of his plays forcibly demonstrates and as Hankey, Sutton, Rowell, and Fisher, among others, have foregrounded in their analyses, there is an extraordinary metadramatic quality in all of Gilbert's work. Each play's unique and dynamic reflection on dramatic conventions challenges the assumption that Gilbert's drama is highly artificial or conventional and thus flat.

ARCHIVAL SOURCES

Scrapbooks, clippings, reviews, and photographs are contained in the Billy Rose Collection of the New York Public Library. William S. Gilbert papers are housed at the British Library.

PRIMARY BIBLIOGRAPHY

Anthologies

The Best Known Works of W. S. Gilbert. New York: Grosset & Dunlap, 1932.

Foggerty's Fairy and Other Tales. London: Routledge, 1890.

Gilbert before Sullivan: Six Comic Plays by W. S. Gilbert. Ed. Jane W. Stedman. Chicago: University of Chicago Press, 1967.

New and Original Extravaganzas. Ed. Isaac Goldberg. Boston: John W. Luce, 1931.

Original Plays: First Series. London: Chatto & Windus, 1925.

Original Plays: Second Series. London: Chatto & Windus, 1922.

Original Plays: Third Series. London: Chatto & Windus, 1911.

Original Plays: Fourth Series. London: Chatto & Windus, 1911.

Plays and Poems of W. S. Gilbert. Reprint of the 1932 edition. New York: Random House, 1946.

Plays by W. S. Gilbert. Ed. George Rowell. Cambridge: Cambridge University Press, 1982.

Individual Plays Found in Collections

Dan'l Druce, Blacksmith. In *The Golden Age of Melodrama: Twelve 19th Century Melodramas,* ed. Michael Kilgarriff. London: Wolfe, 1974.

Engaged. In *British Plays of the Nineteenth Century: An Anthology to Illustrate the Evolution of the Drama,* ed. J. O. Bailey. New York: Odyssey, 1966; *English Plays of the Nineteenth Century,* vol. 3, *Comedies,* ed. Michael R. Booth. Oxford: Clarendon, 1973; *The Magistrate and Other Nineteenth-Century Plays,* ed. Michael R. Booth. London: Oxford University Press, 1974.

Pygmalion and Galatea. In *Chief British Dramatists,* ed. J. B. Matthews and P. R. Lieder. Boston: Houghton Mifflin, 1924; *Great Modern British Plays,* ed. James William Marriott. London: Harrap, 1932.

Rosencrantz and Guildenstern. In *Nineteenth-Century Shakespeare Burlesques,* vol. 4, selected by Stanley Wells. London: Diploma Press, 1977; *Nineteenth-Century Dramatic Burlesques: A Selection of British Parodies,* ed. Jacob B. Solomon. Darby, PA: Norwood Editions, 1980.

Sweethearts. In *Representative Modern Plays,* ed. Richard Albert Cordell. Oxford: Clarendon, 1929; *Typical Plays for Secondary Schools,* ed. James Plaisted Webber and Hanson Hart Webster. Boston: Houghton Mifflin, 1929; *The Drama: Its History, Literature, and Influence on Civilization,* vol. 16, ed. Alfred Bates. London: Athenian Society, 1903–4.

Tom Cobb; or, Fortune's Toy. In *English Plays of the Nineteenth Century,* vol. 4, *Farces,* ed. Michael R. Booth. Oxford: Clarendon Press, 1973.

SECONDARY BIBLIOGRAPHY

Adams, William Davenport. [1]. *A Dictionary of the Drama: A Guide to the Plays, Playwrights, Players, and Playhouses of the United Kingdom and America, from the Earliest Times to the Present.* Vol. 1. Philadelphia: J. B. Lippincott, 1904.

————. [2]. "Mr. Gilbert as a Dramatist." *Belgravia* (Oct. 1881): 438–48.

Archer, William. [1]. "Conversation VI: With Mr. W. S. Gilbert." In *Real Conversations.* London: Heinemann, 1904.

————. [2]. "Mr. W. S. Gilbert." 1881. Reprinted in *W. S. Gilbert: A Century of Scholarship and Commentary,* ed. John Bush Jones. New York: New York University Press, 1970.

Baily, Leslie. *Gilbert and Sullivan, Their Lives and Times.* New York: Viking, 1974.

Bancroft, Marie, and Squire Bancroft. *The Bancrofts: Recollections of Sixty Years.* 1909. New York: Benjamin Blom, 1969.

Bargainnier, Earl F. [1]. "Charity: W. S. Gilbert's 'Problem Play.' " *South Atlantic Bulletin* (Nov. 1977): 130–38.

————. [2]. "Mr. Gilbert and Mr. Shaw." *Theatre Annual* (1975): 43–54.

Beerbohm, Max. "Mr. Gilbert's Rentree (and Mine)." *Saturday Review* (14 May 1904): 619–20.

Brown, H. Rowland, and Rowland Grey. "The W. S. Gilbert of His Own Letters." *Cornhill Magazine* (Feb. 1922): 159–76.

Browne, Edith A. *W. S. Gilbert.* New York: John Lane, 1907.

Cardullo, Burt. "The Art and Business of W. S. Gilbert's *Engaged.*" *Modern Drama* (Sept. 1985): 462–73.

Clinton-Baddeley, V. C. "W. S. Gilbert." In *The Burlesque Tradition in the English Theatre after 1660.* London: Methuen, 1952. Reprint. Methuen Library Reprints, 1973.

"Comedy and Tragedy." *Theatre,* n.s. (1 March 1884): 143–44.

Cook, Dutton. [1]. *"The Palace of Truth."* In *Nights at the Play: A View of the English Stage.* London: Chatto & Windus, 1883.

————. [2]. *"Pygmalion and Galatea."* In *Nights at the Play: A View of the English Stage.* London: Chatto & Windus, 1883.

————. [3]. *"The Wicked World."* In *Nights at the Play: A View of the English Stage.* London: Chatto & Windus, 1883.

Danton, George H. "Gilbert's *Gretchen.*" *Germanic Review* (Apr. 1946): 132–41.

Dark, Sidney, and Rowland Grey. *W. S. Gilbert, His Life and Letters.* London: Methuen, 1923.

DuBois, Arthur E. "W. S. Gilbert, Practical Classicist." *Sewanee Review* (Jan. 1929): 94–107.

Duployen, Richard. "The Three Princesses." *Gilbert and Sullivan Journal* (Sept. 1971): 376–77.

Ellis, James D. "The Counterfeit Presentment: Nineteenth-Century Burlesques of *Hamlet.*" *Nineteenth Century Theatre Research* (Summer 1983): 29–50.

Filon, Pierre. "Gilbert." In *The English Stage, Being an Account of the Victorian Drama.* Trans. Frederic Whyte. New York: Dodd, Mead, 1897.

Fisher, Judith L. "W. S. Gilbert: The Comedic Alternative." In *When They Weren't Doing Shakespeare: Essays on Nineteenth-Century British and American Theatre,* ed. Judith L. Fisher and Stephen Watt. Athens: University of Georgia Press, 1989.

Fitzgerald, Percy. "Mr. Gilbert's Humour." *Theatre,* n.s. (1 Dec. 1881): 339–41.

Garson, R. W. "The English Aristophanes." *Revue de Littérature Comparée* 46 (1972): 177–93.

"Gilbert, Sir William Schwenck." In *British Authors of the Nineteenth Century,* ed. Stanley J. Kunitz. New York: H. W. Wilson, 1936.

"Gilbert, Sir William Schwenck (1836–1911)." In *The New Theatre Handbook and Digest of Plays,* ed. Bernard Sobel. New York: Crown, 1959.

"Gilbert, William Schwenck (1836–1911)." In *The Oxford Companion to the Theatre,* ed. Phyllis Hartnoll. 4th ed. New York: Oxford University Press, 1983.

"Gilbert, W(illiam) S(chwenck) 1836–1911 (Bab)." In *Contemporary Authors,* vol. 104, ed. Frances C. Locher, 166–67. Detroit: Gale Research, 1982.

"Gilbert without Sullivan." *Living Age* (1 July 1911): 50–53.

Goldberg, Isaac. [1]. *Sir Wm. S. Gilbert, A Study in Modern Satire: A Handbook on Gilbert and the Gilbert-Sullivan Operas.* Boston: Stratford, 1913.

———. [2]. *The Story of Gilbert and Sullivan; or, The "Compleat" Savoyard.* 1928. New York: AMS Press, 1970.

———. [3]. "W. S. Gilbert, 1836–1936." *Stage* (Nov. 1936): 101–3.

Granville-Barker, Harley. "Exit Planche—Enter Gilbert." Parts 1, 2. *London Mercury* (Mar.–Apr. 1932): 457–66, 558–73.

"The Grievances of the Dramatists." *Theatre,* n.s. (1 Mar. 1879): 71–75.

Grushow, Ira. "W. S. Gilbert." In *Critical Survey of Drama,* ed. Frank N. Magill, vol. 2. Englewood Cliffs, NJ: Salem Press, 1985.

Hankey, Julie. "Quiet, Unpumped, and Everyday." *Times Literary Supplement* (20 Aug. 1982): 901.

Head, Thomas G. "Gilbert, Sothern, and *The Ne'er-do-Weel.*" *Nineteenth Century Theatre Research* (Autumn 1976): 63–72.

Hindle, E. B. "W. S. Gilbert, Playwright and Humorist." *Manchester Quarterly* (Jan. 1885): 55–85.

Hollingshead, John. *Gaiety Chronicles.* London: Constable, 1898.

How, Harry. "Mr. W. S. Gilbert." In *Illustrated Interviews.* London: George Newnes, 1893.

Huberman, Jeffrey H. *Late Victorian Farce.* Ann Arbor, MI: UMI Research Press, 1986.

Hudson, Lynton. "Cyclones and Anticyclones." In *The English Stage, 1850–1950.* Westport, CT: Greenwood Press, 1972.

Isaacs, Lewis M. "W. S. Gilbert." *Bookman* (Oct. 1902): 150–57.

Jones, John Bush. [1]. "Gilbertian Humor: Pulling Together a Definition." *Victorian Newsletter* (Spring 1968): 28–31.

———, ed. [2]. *W. S. Gilbert: A Century of Scholarship and Commentary.* New York: New York University Press, 1970.

Knapp, Shoshana. "George Eliot and W. S. Gilbert: *Silas Marner* into *Dan'l Druce.*" *Nineteenth Century Literature* (Mar. 1986): 438–59.

Krutch, Joseph Wood. "The Creative Muddle." *Nation* (24 Oct. 1936): 480+.

Lawrence, Elwood P. "*The Happy Land:* W. S. Gilbert as Political Satirist." *Victorian Studies* (Dec. 1971): 161–83.

Matthews, Brander. "Notes on W. S. Gilbert." In *Papers on Playmaking.* New York: Hill & Wang, 1957.

Meisel, Martin. "Political Extravaganza: A Phase of Nineteenth-Century British Theatre." *Theatre Survey* (1962): 19–31.

Moulan, Frank. "The Humor of Gilbert and Shaw." *Theatre* (Mar. 1920): 158–60.

"Mr. Gilbert as a Dramatist." 1877. Reprinted in *W. S. Gilbert: A Century of Scholarship and Commentary,* ed. John Bush Jones, 7–16. New York: New York University Press, 1970.

"Mr. Gilbert's New Play." *New York Times* (31 Dec. 1871): 5.

Mullin, Donald, comp. *Victorian Plays: A Record of Significant Productions on the London Stage, 1837–1901.* New York: Greenwood Press, 1987.

"Musings without Method." *Blackwood's Magazine* (July 1911): 121–28.

Nettleton, George Henry. "A Visit to Sir William S. Gilbert." *Nation* (3 Aug. 1911): 96–97.

Nicoll, Allardyce. "Gilbert and Albery: Plays of the Seventies." In *A History of English Drama, 1660–1900,* vol. 5, *Late Nineteenth Century Drama, 1850–1900.* 2nd ed. Cambridge: Cambridge University Press, 1962.

Orel, Harold, ed. *Gilbert and Sullivan: Interviews and Recollections.* Iowa City: University of Iowa Press, 1994.

"*Palace of Truth.*" *Theatre,* n.s. (18 Jan. 1884): 88–91.

Pascal, Roy. "Four Fausts: From W. S. Gilbert to Ferruccio Busoni." *German Life and Letters* (July 1957): 263–65.

Pearson, Hesketh. [1]. *Gilbert: His Life and Strife.* New York: Harper, 1957.

———. [2]. "William Schwenck Gilbert." In *Lives of the Wits.* New York: Harper, 1962.

"*Pygmalion and Galatea.*" *Theatre,* n.s. (1 Jan. 1884): 48–50.

Reynolds, Richard R. "Gilbert's Fun with Shakespeare." *Mosaic* (Summer 1976): 167–72.

Righton, Edward. "A Suppressed Burlesque—*The Happy Land.*" *Theatre* (Aug. 1896): 63–66.

Rowell, George. [1]. Introduction. In *Plays by W. S. Gilbert,* ed. George Rowell. Cambridge: Cambridge University Press, 1982.

———. [2]. *Theatre in the Age of Irving.* Totowa, NJ: Rowman & Littlefield, 1981.

———. [3]. *The Victorian Theatre, 1792–1914: A Survey.* 2nd ed. Oxford: Clarendon Press, 1978.

Sahai, Surendra. "William S. Gilbert." In *English Drama, 1865–1900.* New Delhi: Orient Longman, 1970.

Sawyer, Newell W. "Robertson, Gilbert, and a New Social Consciousness." In *The Comedy of Manners from Sheridan to Maugham.* New York: A. S. Barnes, 1961.

Scott, Clement. Review of *Engaged* by W. S. Gilbert. *Theatre* (Oct. 1877): 64.

Sichel, Walter. "The English Aristophanes." 1911. Reprinted in *W. S. Gilbert: A Century of Scholarship and Commentary,* ed. John Bush Jones. New York: New York University Press, 1970.

"Sir William Schwenck Gilbert." In *The Dictionary of National Biography, The Concise Dictionary, Part II, 1901–1950.* London: Oxford University Press, 1961.

"(Sir) W(illiam) S(chwenck) Gilbert, 1836–1911." In *Twentieth-Century Literary Criticism,* ed. Sharon K. Hall, vol. 3. Detroit: Gale Research, 1980.

Stanton, Stephen S. "Ibsen, Gilbert, and Scribe's *Bataille de Dames.*" *Educational Theatre Journal* (Mar. 1965): 24–30.

Stedman, Jane W. [1]. "General Utility: Victorian Author-Actors from Knowles to Pinero." *Educational Theatre Journal* (Oct. 1974): 289–301.

———. [2]. "The Victorian After-Image of Samuel Johnson." *Nineteenth Century Theatre Research* (Summer 1983): 13–27.

Stephens, John Russell. "Political and Personal Satire." In *The Censorship of English Drama, 1824–1901.* New York: Cambridge University Press, 1980.

Sutton, Max Keith. *W. S. Gilbert.* Boston: Twayne, 1975.

"The Theatre." *New York Times* (16 Nov. 1871): 5.

Thorndike, Ashley H. "Sir William Schwenck Gilbert." In *English Comedy*. New York: Macmillan, 1929.

Review of *Tom Cobb, or Fortune's Toy* by W. S. Gilbert. *Athenaeum* (May 1875): 597.

Review of *Tom Cobb, or Fortune's Toy* by W. S. Gilbert. *Theatre* (May 1875).

"Two Victorian Humorists: Burnand and the Mask of Gilbert." *Times Literary Supplement* (21 Nov. 1936): 935–36.

Vandiver, E. P., Jr. "W. S. Gilbert and Shakespeare." *Shakespeare Association Bulletin* (July 1938): 139–45.

"W. S. Gilbert." *Bookman* (July 1911): 463–65.

"W. S. Gilbert—The Pervasive Spirit of Topsy-turveydom." *Current Literature* (July 1911): 86–87.

Wearing, J. P. *The London Stage, 1890–1899: A Calendar of Plays and Players*. Vol. 1, *1890–1896;* Vol. 2, *1897–1899*. Metuchen, NJ: Scarecrow Press, 1976.

Wilson, A. C. "W. S. Gilbert." *Manchester Quarterly* (1925): 277–97.

Wilson, Edmund. "Gilbert without Sullivan." *New Yorker* (12 Apr. 1947): 110–16.

Woodfield, James. "The Censorship Saga." In *English Theatre in Transition, 1889–1914*. London: Croom Helm, 1984; Totowa, NJ: Barnes & Noble, 1984.

"Work of W. S. Gilbert." *Nation* (8 June 1911): 586–87.

BIBLIOGRAPHY

Allen, Reginald. *W. S. Gilbert: An Anniversary Survey and Exhibition Checklist with Thirty-Five Illustrations*. Reprinted from *Theatre Notebook* (1961): 118–28. Charlottesville: Bibliographical Society of the University of Virginia, 1963.

Dillard, Philip H. *"How Quaint the Ways of Paradox!" An Annotated Gilbert and Sullivan Bibliography*. Metuchen, NJ: Scarecrow Press, 1991.

Searle, Townley. *Sir William Schwenck Gilbert: A Topsy-turvy Adventure*. London: Alexander-Ouseley, 1931.

Harley Granville-Barker
(1877–1946)

JAMES FISHER

Harley Granville-Barker, one of the most versatile theater men of the early twentieth-century British stage, was, at various times, and often simultaneously, a successful playwright, actor, and director. At the height of his success in these areas, he withdrew from the center of the English theater to become a significant drama critic, scholar, and translator.

Harley Granville-Barker was born in London on 25 November 1877, the son of architect Albert James Barker and Mary Elizabeth Bozzi-Granville, who worked as a bird mimic and reciter. He was privately educated and coached in drama by his mother before he began an acting career in his early teens. He received training at Sarah Thorne's theatrical school at Margate, Kent, and continued through the 1890s to act in numerous companies throughout English theaters, eventually landing leading roles. In 1895 he joined Ben Greet's company, where he had the opportunity of working with other soon-to-be iconoclasts of the modern stage, including Edward Gordon Craig. There he also met actress Lillah McCarthy. They were married and began a fruitful stage partnership, with McCarthy playing leading roles in many productions directed by Granville-Barker. During this time he began playwriting in collaboration with Berte Thomas, but beginning with his own play, *The Marrying of Ann Leete,* his most important contributions to the stage began to attract attention.

Granville-Barker, like such contemporaries as Craig, William Archer, and, most significantly, George Bernard Shaw, worked to liberate the English theater from its slavish dependence on the attitudes, plays, and production practices of the nineteenth-century stage. Around the turn of the century Granville-Barker joined the newly established Stage Society, where he directed *The Marrying of Ann Leete* and acted for the first time in one of Shaw's plays, taking the role of Marchbanks in *Candida.* Over the next decade he acted in or directed many of Shaw's plays, and the two men developed a close bond that had a strong influence on them both. In 1904 Granville-Barker worked with Archer on a plan for an English National Theatre and continued his own playwriting with *The Voysey Inheritance, Prunella* (written with Laurence Housman), *Waste, The Madras House,* and *The Harlequinade* (written with Dion Clayton Calthrop). *Waste* caused a considerable controversy with its frank sexual content and political implications and was censored by the Lord Chamberlain's Office after its first performance. The play remained unlicensed until 1920, despite Granville-Barker's fierce battle to break the oppressive censorship prevalent in England at that time.

Granville-Barker remains best known for the Shakespearean productions he staged at the Savoy Theatre, *A Winter's Tale* and *Twelfth Night* in 1912 and *A Midsummer Night's Dream* in 1914. In these productions Granville-Barker restored the full texts of the plays and placed an emphasis on the poetic language, eliminating all remnants of well-worn stage business that had become part of the audience's expectations over the centuries. He encouraged a quick-paced delivery of lines and, borrowing from scenic practices pioneered by Craig, Max Reinhardt, and others, offered impressionistic images while aiming to integrate all production elements into a cohesive and unified whole. Barker's plan to give similar treatment to some of Shakespeare's tragedies was interrupted by the outbreak of World War I, an event that triggered significant changes in his personal life and work.

Granville-Barker left England for America to produce some plays with the Stage Society of America. While in New York he met Helen Huntington, wife of millionaire Archer M. Huntington, and they began a relationship that culminated in the end of both of their previous marriages. They were wed on 31 July 1918, and the following year, when the war had ended, Granville-Barker turned away from active participation in theatrical productions. Although he wrote a few more plays, most notably *The Secret Life* and *His Majesty,* he devoted himself to translating works by a number of European dramatists and to dramatic criticism and scholarship. He was a sought-after lecturer, and his most significant published criticism, *Prefaces to Shakespeare,* begun in 1927, resulted from a series of lectures and his own prewar productions.

Biographers and scholars have tended to see Granville-Barker's post–World War I career as an abandonment, even a repudiation, of his work as a pioneering dramatist and theatrical practitioner. However, it is more the case that his later work was simply an extension of his achievements in moving the English theater into the modern era. With his wife, Granville-Barker moved to Paris in 1930, but during the Nazi occupation they escaped to New York, where he worked for the British Information Services and lectured at Harvard, Princeton, and elsewhere. They returned to England at the end of the war, but ill health prevented Granville-Barker from chairing the National Theatre Committee and Governors of the Old Vic. In the spring of 1946 he returned to Paris, where he died on 31 August.

Selected Biographical Sources: Britton; Dymkowski; Kennedy [1]; Morgan [1]; Purdom; Salenius; Salmon; Whitworth.

MAJOR PLAYS, PREMIERES, AND SIGNIFICANT REVIVALS: THEATRICAL RECEPTION

The Weather-Hen; or, Invertebrata. 1899. Written in collaboration with Berte Thomas, 1897. Opened 29 June at Terry's Theatre (London).

A comedy in a prologue, two acts, and an epilogue, *The Weather-Hen* owes much to the social-problem plays of Henrik Ibsen, particularly *A Doll's House.* Hankin called it "extremely bold." However, Beerbohm [3] noted that this very boldness undermined its appeal to the public, "but the eccentric few find much that is good in it." Walkley [6] found the play's themes worn, but praised Granville-Barker and Thomas for their fresh handling of them, noting that "the authors have the sort of talent of which the theatre stands just now very much in need."

The Marrying of Ann Leete. 1902. Written in 1899. Opened 26 January at the Royalty Theatre (London) (Stage Society Production). Revival: 1975, Royal Shakespeare Company, London.

The Marrying of Ann Leete is a comedy in four acts about a "new woman." Ann is the daughter of Carnaby Leete, an aging and ill politician who hopes to revive his fortunes through a marital alliance between Ann and Lord John Carp. His eldest daughter had endured a similar fate, and the unhappy marriage that resulted leads Ann to embark on a voyage of self-discovery. When Leete fights a duel with Carp over Ann's honor and is wounded slightly, Carp proposes to Ann. She initially accepts, mostly out of duty to her father, but as she slowly realizes that to her father she is little more than barter, she announces that she will marry the gardener instead in an attempt to fulfill her destiny as a wife and a mother. The final scene shows the couple on their wedding night, a social experiment filled with complicated spiritual and sexual implications. Symons [3] was one of the few contemporary critics who seemed to understand and appreciate the subtleties of a play that seems remarkably ahead of its time. He noted that it represented a "new thing on the stage, full of truth within its own limits; but it is an episode, not a conclusion, much less a solution. Mr. Barker can write: he writes in short, sharp sentences, which go off like pistols, and he can keep up the firing, from every corner of the stage." Most critics agreed with Walkley [2], who cynically acknowledged the difficulty of writing a play in four acts "and throughout them all to keep the audience blankly ignorant of the meaning of it. . . . Granville Barker calls his piece a comedy. It might more suitably be termed a practical joke."

Prunella; or, Love in a Dutch Garden. 1904. Written in collaboration with Laurence Housman. Opened 23 December at the Court Theatre (London). Revivals: 24 April 1906, Court Theatre; 7 May 1907, Court Theatre; 13 April

1910, Duke of York's Theatre. American productions: Theatre Guild School (New York), May 1913; 27 October 1913, Little Theatre (New York); Everyman Theatre, December 1921 and January 1930; 15 June 1926, Garrick Theatre (New York). New act added for 1930 revival.

A play in three acts, *Prunella* is a bittersweet comedy drawn from the traditions of harlequinade and Pierrot plays. Granville-Barker directed and played the role of Pierrot himself in the first production. *Prunella* is not in the rambunctious and physical vein of harlequinade in any respect, and despite its touches of cynicism, it is essentially a slight and sentimental poetic love story, owing much to the nineteenth-century French vision of Pierrot. Critics were respectful, but somewhat puzzled by the play's combination of cynical modernity and childish fantasy. Since it was clearly not a typical harlequinade for children, they were at a loss to categorize the piece. Some, like the *Daily Express* (Review of *Prunella*), called it "imitation Bernard Shaw cynicism," while Walkley [3] labeled it "Funambulesque."

The Voysey Inheritance. 1905. Written 1903–5. Opened 7 November at the Court Theatre (London). Revivals: 12 February 1906, Court Theatre (London); 7 September 1912, Kingsway Theatre (London); 3 May 1934, Sadler's Wells Theatre (London); 27 June 1989, Cottesloe Theatre (National Theatre) (London). American production: December 1990, Long Wharf Theatre (New Haven, Connecticut). Television: 1979, BBC-TV.

A play in five acts, *The Voysey Inheritance* was the first Granville-Barker play to make use of a male protagonist. Weak and sensitive Edward Voysey inherits a family fortune, but slowly learns that it was built on a foundation of corruption. He considers repudiating the inheritance and exposing the truth, but realizes, with the support of his level-headed fiancée, Alice, that he will cause total ruin to his company, his family, and many innocent investors. When he reveals to George Booth, his late father's closest friend, that his father had bilked Booth out of a considerable fortune, Booth at first does not believe it. Thinking that Edward himself has stolen the money, Booth threatens to expose the scandal. However, when Edward convinces him that, by nature, he could not possibly have cheated Booth, the old man agrees to cooperate if he is reimbursed at a faster rate than other investors. Edward, staggered by yet another hypocrisy, considers repudiating his responsibilities, but Alice convinces him instead to manage the company so fairly and brilliantly that he can make up for the past by protecting the investors. Edward, in a deep personal and business "partnership" with Alice, proceeds into an uncertain future with a new sense of moral courage and purpose. Beerbohm [2] called the 1905 production of *The Voysey Inheritance* "the finest scene of grim, ironic comedy in modern English drama," and the *Observer* (Review of the *Voysey Inheritance*) found the 1912 revival to be "the finest comedy of modern times." When the play was notably revived in 1989 by the National Theatre of Great Britain in a highly praised production, critics were impressed particularly with the fact that the play seemed to mirror contemporary events. O'Neill wrote of this production that the play "asserted its claim across the years that Thatcherism, even if its passing has begun, was merely the latest manifestation of an inescapable national legacy. . . . [It was] full of good talk, lively characters, and surprising wit that affirmed J. B. Priestley's estimation of Barker as a dramatist 'who often takes Shavian themes but scores them for orchestra and not for Shaw's military band.' "

Waste. 1907. Written 1906–7. Opened 24 November at the Imperial Theatre (London) (Stage Society Production). The play was censored after one performance. Revivals: 1 December 1936, Westminster Theatre (London); winter 1985, the Pit Theatre, Barbican Centre, Royal Shakespeare Company. Television: 1979, BBC-TV.

A tragedy in four acts, *Waste* concerns Henry Trebell, a social reformer who drafts a bill calling for the disbanding of the Church of England and using its funds to establish a sweeping educational reform. Trebell's single-minded devotion to his cause and his manipulations to create a political alliance to put his plan into effect are compromised by his flirtation with the charming Amy O'Connell. When Amy, who is separated from her husband, discovers that she is carrying Trebell's child, she rushes to him to seek his assistance in terminating her pregnancy. When he reacts in horror to her suggestion, she is hurt by his inability to love and his uncompromising attitude and single-minded commitment to his work. Trebell persuades her to wait for him in another room while he meets with Lord Cantelupe, a powerful adversary. Instead, she rushes off to a back-alley abortion that results in her death. Trebell endeavors to keep the scandal secret as his plan moves into Lord Horsham's powerful cabinet council, wherein Granville-Barker effectively skewers the corrupt power of Edwardian politics. The council uses the scandal as an excuse for abandoning Trebell's plan. When he learns this, he commits suicide, not as an escape from failure or scandal, but as the appropriate conclusion to the failings of his private life. The *Athenaeum* (Review of *Waste*) called *Waste* "the most important event of our recent theatrical history," but the play was abruptly censored due in equal parts to the sexual and political controversy it aroused. Nearly eighty years later, Rich, reviewing the 1985 Royal Shakespeare Company revival, called *Waste* "a completely contemporary portrait of needlessly wasted public and private lives."

The Madras House. 1910. Written in 1909. Opened 9 March at the Duke of York's Theatre (London). Revival: 30 November 1925, Ambassadors Theatre (London); 22 June 1977, Olivier Theatre (National Theatre) (London). American production: 29 October 1921, Neighborhood Playhouse (New York) (transferred to the National Theatre).

A comedy in four acts, *The Madras House* is a complex play in which Philip Madras, a priggish and proper Edwardian gentleman, is planning the sale of Madras House, a store owned by his extended family, to an American. Philip's proprieties are strained to the limit by the hypocrisy he encounters in the sexual politics of his family and among his employees. When Marion Yates, one of the employees, admits to being pregnant, she is pressured to name the father, but refuses. Philip later learns that his father, Constantine, has fathered Marion's child, and he agrees to assume financial responsibilities; Marion, however, vehemently rejects his assistance and scorns his phallocentric attitudes. Philip's wife, Jessica, plans to leave him, pointing out his inability to accept and acknowledge her individuality as a person. Having matured in his beliefs, Philip sells Madras House and resolves with Jessica to repair their marriage and work together for the improvement of society. Critics were inclined to praise the acting more than the play, and many saw particular difficulties with the discursive fourth act, which seemed a disappointment after three comparatively lively acts. Archer [3] stated that the play was twenty minutes too long, and Beerbohm [1], similarly disposed, went so far as to advise his readers not to stay for the entire performance. Among more recent critics, Kennedy [1] has called it Granville-Barker's finest play, writing that if he "never sounds the clear brass notes of Shaw, he makes us far more conscious of the intricacies of sexual harmony and the importance of overtones to moral acts" (115).

The Harlequinade. 1913. Written in collaboration with Dion Clayton Calthrop. Opened 1 September at the St. James's Theatre (London). American production: 10 May 1921, Neighborhood Playhouse (New York) (transferred to the Punch and Judy Theatre on 14 June 1921).

Labeled an "excursion" in seven parts, *The Harlequinade* was originally presented on a double bill with George Bernard Shaw's *Androcles and the Lion.* A fanciful theatrical history told by a little girl named Alice and her Uncle Edward, it makes use of elements of classical mythology and commedia dell'arte to tell the story of man as symbolized by theatrical history. Critical response was dismissive, with Walkley [1] proclaiming that "the theatre audience is in no mood for these subtleties."

ADDITIONAL PLAYS, ADAPTATIONS, AND PRODUCTIONS

Among Granville-Barker's earliest works, *The Comedy of Fools* (written in 1895), *The Family of the Oldroyds* (written in 1895–96), and *Our Visitor to "Work-a-Day"* (1898–99) were written in collaboration with Berte Thomas and were unproduced. Other unproduced works include *Agnes Colander* (1900–1901), *Farewell to the Theatre* (1916), *The Secret Life* (1919–23), and *His Majesty* (1923–28). Granville-Barker also wrote one-acts, including *A Miracle Play* (written circa 1900; opened 23 March 1907 at Terry's Theatre, London), *Rococo* (written in 1911; opened 21 February 1911 at the Court Theatre, London), and *Vote by Ballot* (written in 1914; opened 16 December 1917 at the Court Theatre, London).

Granville-Barker's many translations and adaptations include Arthur Schnitzler's *Anatol* (1911), *The Morris Dance* (1913; adapted from Robert Louis Stevenson and Lloyd Osborne's *The Wrong Box*), Thomas Hardy's *The Dynasts*

(1914), Sacha Guitry's *Deburau* (1920), Jules Romains's *Doctor Knock* (1925) and *Six Gentlemen in a Row* (1927), and the following Spanish plays, all translated in collaboration with Helen Granville-Barker: Gregorio Martínez Sierra's *The Romantic Young Lady* (1923), *The Two Shepherds* (1921), *The Kingdom of God* (1923), *Wife to a Famous Man* (1923), and *Take Two from One* (1931); and Serafín and Joaquín Alvarez Quintero's *The Women Have Their Way* (1927), *A Hundred Years Old* (1927), *Fortunato* (1927), *The Lady from Alfaqueque* (1927), *Love Passes By* (1932), *Don Abel Wrote a Tragedy* (1932), *Peace and Quiet* (1932), and *Dona Clariñes* (1932).

ASSESSMENT OF GRANVILLE-BARKER'S CAREER

Harley Granville-Barker's reputation today is based less on his plays than on his theatrical innovations as a director and theorist and on his scholarly and critical output. During Granville-Barker's lifetime his own plays were seldom produced and were generally viewed as less-than-successful attempts to imitate the plays of George Bernard Shaw. Since his death, and particularly beginning in the mid-1970s, Granville-Barker's reputation as a dramatist has grown as the result of several acclaimed revivals of his plays as well as new scholarly and critical interest in his drama, his directing achievements, and his writings on the art of the theater.

Granville-Barker's earliest plays, written with Berte Thomas, including *The Family of the Oldroyds, The Weather-Hen,* and *Our Visitor to "Work-a-Day,"* were all concerned, in one way or another, with issues inspired by the dawning of feminism in turn-of-the-century England. Granville-Barker was the dominant partner in this collaboration, which was formed while he was a young actor touring the British provinces in the 1890s, and the plays were inspired in part by George Meredith's novels and the symbolist movement, particularly the plays of Maurice Maeterlinck. Only *The Weather-Hen* was actually produced, with only modest success. Granville-Barker's most produced plays during his lifetime, also collaborations, were two overtly theatrical works inspired by Pierrot plays, the harlequinade, and the traditions of commedia dell'arte: *Prunella: or Love in a Dutch Garden* (with Laurence Housman) and *The Harlequinade* (with Dion Clayton Calthrop).

However, Granville-Barker's lasting reputation as a dramatist rests firmly on four plays, *The Marrying of Ann Leete, The Voysey Inheritance, Waste,* and *The Madras House,* generally recognized as expertly constructed social-problem dramas in the Ibsenesque mold. These plays are second only to those of Shaw as scathing assaults on bourgeois hypocrisy and middle-class morality in Edwardian England. Shaw clearly influenced Granville-Barker's drama of ideas, but Granville-Barker's own innovation was the focus he placed on the "interior action" of his characters. Each of these plays features a central character forced to face an unpleasant truth about himself or herself, ultimately leading to a crisis testing his or her moral and spiritual courage.

Although critics have found some of these plays to be inordinately discursive and subtle to the point of obscurity, Granville-Barker's themes and the inherent reality of his characters and their situations firmly establish his place among the giants of the early twentieth-century stage. Whether examining the emergence of the "new woman" in *The Marrying of Ann Leete,* presenting the deep-seated corruption of Edwardian politics in *Waste,* tracing the way that the sins of a father may be visited on his children in *The Voysey Inheritance,* or portraying the sexual mores of the era in *The Madras House,* Granville-Barker's unique and advanced dramaturgy is set on the brink of the shattering transition from the nineteenth century into the modern era. Granville-Barker's greatest accomplishment as a dramatist may well be the quality of his dialogue. Through his frank discussions of sexual and gender politics, his boldly modern views of the class struggle and political corruption, and his unblinking assault on social and moral hypocrisy, Granville-Barker emerges as a powerful voice from an extraordinary age in British drama.

During this time, Granville-Barker also staged numerous important contemporary dramas for the Stage Society and three Shakespearean plays (between 1912 and 1914) that contributed mightily to strides made by Edward Gordon Craig and William Poel in modernizing the treatment of Shakespeare's work on stage. As a dramatist and a director, Granville-Barker was a significant proponent of the importance of the actor, and he seemed equally comfortable in the dramatic and comic veins, writing in his essay "The Heritage of the Actor" that for him, "the antics of Harlequin are not essentially different from the art that shows us Oedipus."

Following World War I, Granville-Barker turned his attentions away from theatrical production and his own playwriting (although he returned to both on occasion) to translate works by Gregorio Martínez Sierra and the Alvarez Quintero brothers in collaboration with his second wife, Helen, and, on his own, plays by Eugène Brieux, Jules Romains, Arthur Schnitzler, and Sacha Guitry. His most significant achievement as a critic and scholar was his series of *Prefaces to Shakespeare,* which he labored over between 1927 and his death in 1946. Granville-Barker's reputation as a major dramatist of the early twentieth century has been recognized only in recent years, but it is safe to assume that it will remain so, enhancing a career of similar innovation in theatrical production and criticism.

ARCHIVAL SOURCES

Manuscripts and letters related to Granville-Barker can be found in the British Library; the Enthoven Collection of the Theatre Museum; the Beerbohm Tree Collection, University of Bristol Theatre Collection; the Bernard F. Burgunder Collection, Department of Rare Books, Cornell University Library; the Department of Rare Books and Special Collections, the University of Michigan Library (Ann Arbor); the Harry Ransom Humanities Research Center, University of

Texas at Austin; the Lincoln Center Library of the Performing Arts, New York Public Library; the Berg Collection, New York Public Library; the Bodleian Library, Oxford University; Harvard University Library; Yale University Library; and the Lord Chamberlain's Office.

PRIMARY BIBLIOGRAPHY

Plays

The Harlequinade. With Dion Clayton Calthrop. London: Sidgwick & Jackson, 1918.
His Majesty. London: Sidgwick & Jackson, 1928.
The Madras House. London: Sidgwick & Jackson, 1910.
The Marrying of Ann Leete. London: Sidgwick & Jackson, 1909.
Prunella; or, Love in a Dutch Garden. With Laurence Housman. London: A. H. Bullen, 1906. Revised. London: Sidgwick & Jackson, 1930.
The Secret Life. London: Chatto & Windus, 1923.
The Voysey Inheritance. London: Sidgwick & Jackson, 1909. Revised. London: Sidgwick & Jackson, 1913. Second Revision. London: Sidgwick & Jackson, 1934.
Waste. London: Sidgwick & Jackson, 1909. Revised. London: Sidgwick & Jackson, 1927.

Anthologies

Contemporary Plays (includes *The Voysey Inheritance*). Ed. T. H. Dickinson and J. R. Crawford. Boston Houghton Mifflin, 1925.
Edwardian Plays (includes *The Madras House*). Ed. G. Weales. New York: Hill & Wang, 1962.
Modern American and British Plays (includes *Waste*). Ed. S. M. Tucker. New York: Harper & Brothers, 1931.
Plays by Harley Granville Barker. Cambridge: Cambridge University Press, 1987.
Plays of To-day. Vol. 2 (includes *Prunella*). London: Sidgwick & Jackson 1925–30.
Rococo, Vote by Ballot, Farewell to the Theatre. London: Sidgwick & Jackson, 1917.
Three Plays. London: Sidgwick & Jackson, 1909.
Three Short Plays. Boston: Little, Brown, 1917.

Books, Essays, and Articles on Drama and Theater

"Alas, Poor Will!" *Listener* (3 Mar. 1937): 387–89, 425–26.
Associating with Shakespeare. London: Humphrey Milford for the Shakespeare Association, 1932.
"At the Moscow Art Theatre." *Seven Arts* (1917): 659–61.
"The Canadian Theatre." *Queen's Quarterly* (Autumn 1936): 256–67.
"The Casting of *Hamlet*: A Fragment." *London Mercury* (Nov. 1936): 10–17.
"The Coming of Ibsen." In *The Eighteen-Eighties,* ed. Walter de la Mare. Cambridge: Cambridge University Press, 1930.
"The Coming of Ibsen." *Theatre Arts Monthly* (Oct./Nov. 1930): 866–74, 931–39.

A Companion to Shakespeare Studies. Ed. Granville-Barker and G. B. Harrison. Cambridge: Cambridge University Press, 1934; New York: Macmillan, 1934.

The Eighteen-Seventies. Ed. Granville-Barker. Cambridge: Cambridge University Press, 1930.

The Exemplary Theatre. London: Chatto & Windus, 1922.

"Exit Planché—Enter Gilbert." In *The Eighteen-Sixties,* ed. John Drinkwater. Cambridge: Cambridge University Press, 1932.

"From Henry V to Hamlet." In *Proceedings of the British Academy, 1924–1925.* London: Humphrey Milford, 1925.

"The Future of the Comédie-Française . . . A Letter to M. Copeau." *Observer* (1 Sept. 1929): 11.

"Georgiana." *English Review* (Feb./Mar. 1909): 420–31, 690–99.

"The Golden Thoughts of Granville Barker, Author, Mime, and 'Producer.' " *Play Pictorial* (Jan. 1912): iv.

Granville Barker and His Correspondents. Edited and annotated by Eric Salmon. Detroit: Wayne State University Press, 1986.

"*Hamlet* in Plus Fours." *Yale Review* (Oct. 1926): 205.

"Help for *Unpopular* Literature." *Author* (Winter 1931): 56–57.

"The Heritage of the Actor." *Quarterly Review* (July 1923): 53–73.

"Hints on Producing a Play." *Amateur Dramatic Year Book* (1928–1929): 6–16.

"Introduction." In *The Boy David,* by J. M. Barrie. London: Peter Davies, 1938.

"Introduction." In *Little Plays of St. Francis,* by Laurence Housman. London: Sidgwick & Jackson, 1922.

"Introduction." In *One Man's View,* by Leonard Merrick. London: Hodder & Stoughton, 1918.

"Introduction." In *Plays,* by Gregorio Martínez Sierra. London: Chatto & Windus, 1923.

"Introduction." In *Plays,* by Leo Tolstoy. Transl. L. Maude and A. Maude. London: Humphrey Milford, 1928.

"Introduction." In *The Players' Shakespeare.* London: Ernest Benn, 1923.

"Introduction." In *Portraits of a Lifetime,* by Jacques-Émile Blanche. Transl. and ed. Walter Clement. London: J. M. Dent, 1937.

"Introduction." *Three Plays* by Maurice Maeterlinck. Transl. A. Sutro and William Archer. London and Glasgow: Gowans & Gray, 1911.

"J. E. Vedrenne." *Author* (Apr. 1930): 75.

"J. M. Barrie as a Dramatist." *Bookman* (Oct. 1910): 13–21.

Julius Caesar: The Forum Scene. London: 1911.

"A Letter to Jacques Copeau." *Theatre Arts Monthly* (Oct. 1929): 753–59.

" 'Max', Mr. Granville Barker, and the National Theatre." *Drama* (Apr. 1923): 121–22.

"A National Theatre." *The Times* (10 Feb. 1930): 13, 14.

"A National Theatre." *The Times* (11 Feb. 1930): 15, 16.

A National Theatre. London: Sidgwick & Jackson, 1930.

"The National Theatre." *Drama* (Dec. 1930): 34–36.

A National Theatre: Scheme and Estimates. With William Archer. London: Duckworth, 1907.

"A Note upon Chapters XX and XXI of 'The Elizabethan Stage.' " *Review of English Studies* (Apr. 1925): 231–35.

"Notes on Rehearsing a Play." *Drama* (July 1919): 2–5.

"Notes on the Prize Design for a National Theatre." *Drama* (July 1924): 229–33.

On Dramatic Method. London: Sidgwick & Jackson, 1931.

On Poetry in Drama. London: Sidgwick & Jackson, 1937.

"On Translating Greek Tragedy." In *Essays in Honour of Gilbert Murray,* ed. J.A.K. Thomson and A. J. Toynbee, 237–47. London: Allen & Unwin, 1936.

"On Translating Plays." In *Essays by Divers Hands,* vol. 5, ed. John Drinkwater, 19–42. London: Humphrey Milford Press, 1925.

"The Perennial Shakespeare." *Listener* (20 Oct. 1937): 823–26, 857–59.

The Perennial Shakespeare. London: British Broadcasting Corporation, 1937.

"Plans for a National Theatre." *Drama* (Dec. 1929): 43–46.

"Plans for a National Theatre." *Theatre Arts Monthly* (Aug. 1935): 635–38.

"A Pleasant Walk." *Cornhill Magazine* (Apr. 1946): 52–57.

Prefaces to Shakespeare. 2 vols. Princeton, NJ: Princeton University Press, 1946–47.

Prefaces to Shakespeare. 4 vols. London: Batsford, 1963.

Prefaces to Shakespeare. 5 vols. London: Batsford, 1968–71 (a sixth volume, containing articles and prefaces to the acting editions, was published in 1974).

Quality. London: Humphrey Milford, 1938.

"Reconstruction in the Theatre." *The Times* (20 Feb. 1919): 11.

The Red Cross in France. London: Hodder & Stoughton, 1916; New York: George H. Doran, 1916.

"Repertory Theatres." *New Quarterly* (Nov. 1909): 491–504.

"Review: *Designs by Inigo Jones for Masques and Plays at Court.* With Introduction and Notes by Percy Simpson and C. F. Bell." *Review of English Studies* (Apr. 1925): 231–35.

"Review: *The Frontiers of Drama* by Una Ellis-Fermor." *Review of English Studies* (Apr. 1946): 144–147.

"Review: *The Physical Conditions of the Elizabethan Public Playhouses* and *Restoration Stage Studies* by W. J. Lawrence." *Review of English Studies* (Apr. 1928): 229–37.

Scheme and Estimates for a National Theatre. With William Archer. New York: Duffield & Co., 1908.

"The School of 'The Only Possible Theatre.' " *Drama* (May/June/July 1920).

"Shakespeare and Modern Stagecraft." *Yale Review* (July 1926): 703–24.

"Shakespeare's Dramatic Art." In *A Companion to Shakespeare Studies,* ed. Harley Granville-Barker and G. B. Harrison, 45–87. Cambridge: Cambridge University Press, 1934, 1959.

"Some Tasks for Dramatic Scholarship." *Essays by Divers Hands,* n.s. (1923): 17–38.

"Some Victorians Afield." *Theatre Arts Monthly* (Apr./May 1929): 256–64, 361–72.

Souls on Fifth. Boston: Little, Brown, 1916.

"Souls on Fifth." *Fortnightly Review* (1917): 336–47, 525–36.

"The Spirit of France." *The Times* (19 July 1928): 3–4.

"The Stagecraft of Shakespeare." *Fortnightly Review,* n.s. (July 1926): 1–17.

The Study of Drama. Cambridge: Cambridge University Press, 1934.

"Tennyson, Swinburne, Meredith—and the Theatre." In *The Eighteen-Seventies,* 161–91. Cambridge: Cambridge University Press, 1929.

"The Text of a Speech at a Complimentary Dinner to Dr. C. E. Wheeler." *British Homoeopathic Journal* (Jan. 1939): 65–66.

"Le Théâtre Britannique d'aujourd'hui." *France–Grande Bretagne* (Apr. 1934): 105–17.

"The Theatre in Berlin." *The Times* (19 Nov. 1910): 6.
"The Theatre in Berlin." *The Times* (21 Nov. 1910): 12.
"A Theatre That Might Be." *Theatre Arts Monthly* (June 1945): 370–77.
"The Theatre: The Next Phase." *English Review* (Apr./July 1910): 631–48.
"The Theatre: The Next Phase." *Forum* (Aug. 1910): 159–70.
"Three Victorians and the Theatre." *Fortnightly Review* (May 1929): 655–72.
"Two German Theatres." *Fortnightly Review* (Jan. 1911): 60–70.
"University Drama." *Drama* (Autumn 1946): 11–16.
The Use of the Drama. Princeton, NJ: Princeton University Press, 1945, London: Sidgwick & Jackson, 1946.
"Verse and Speech in 'Coriolanus.' " *Review of English Studies* (Jan. 1947): 1–15.
"A Village Shakespeare Stage." *Drama* (Dec. 1924): 257.
"William Archer." *Drama* (July 1926): 176–78, 182.

SECONDARY BIBLIOGRAPHY

Archer, William. [1]. *The Old Drama and the New.* New York: Heinemann, 1923.
———. [2]. *Play-Making.* London: Chapman & Hall, 1912.
———. [3]. "Review of *The Madras House.*" *Nation* (10 Mar. 1910): 910.
———. [4]. "The Theatrical Situation." *Fortnightly Review* (1910): 736–50.
———. [5] "The Vedrenne-Barker Season, 1904–1905." Pamphlet printed for the Royal Court Theatre, London, 1905.
Arrell, D. H. "The Old Drama and the New Conceptions of the Nature of Theatrical Experience in the Work of William Archer, G. B. Shaw, W. B. Yeats, E. G. Craig, and H. Granville Barker." Ph.D. diss., University of London, 1976.
Barbour, Charles M. "Up against a Symbolic Painted Cloth: *A Midsummer Night's Dream* at the Savoy, 1914." *Educational Theatre Journal* (Dec. 1975): 521–28.
Beerbohm, Max. [1]. "Review of *The Madras House.*" *Saturday Review* (19 March 1910): 362–63.
———. [2]. "Review of *The Voysey Inheritance.*" *Saturday Review* (11 Nov. 1905): 621.
———. [3]. "Review of *The Weather-Hen.*" *Saturday Review* (14 July 1899): 71.
Braun, Edward. *The Director and the Stage.* London: Methuen, 1982.
Bridges, Robert. *The Influence of the Audience: Considerations Preliminary to the Psychological Analysis of Shakespeare's Character.* New York: Stanley Morison, 1926.
Bridges-Adams, W. [1]. "Granville Barker and the Savoy." *Drama,* n.s., no. 52 (Spring 1959): 28–31.
———. [2]. *The Lost Leader: W. Bridges Adams on Harley Granville Barker.* London: Sidgwick & Jackson, 1954.
Britton, L. J. "The Achievement of Harley Granville Barker." Master's thesis, University of Wales, 1954–55.
Callahan, David. "Harley Granville Barker and the Response to Spanish Theater, 1920–1932." *Comparative Drama* (Summer 1991): 129–47.
Downer, Alan S. "Harley Granville Barker." *Sewanee Review* 55 (1947): 627–45.
Dukore, Bernard F. [1]. *Bernard Shaw, Director.* Seattle: University of Washington Press, 1971.

————. [2]. "*The Madras House* Prefinished." *Educational Theatre Journal* (1972): 135–38.

Dymkowski, Christine. *Harley Granville Barker: A Preface to Modern Shakespeare.* Washington, DC: Folger Books, 1986.

Fisher, James. "Harlequinade: Commedia dell'arte on the Early Twentieth-Century British Stage." *Theatre Journal* (Mar. 1989): 30–45.

Fox, Maureen E. "Dramatic Technique in the Major Plays of Harley Granville Barker." Ph.D. diss., University of Toronto, 1975.

Glick, Claris. "An Analysis of Granville Barker's Criticism of Shakespeare." Ph.D. diss., University of Texas, 1956.

Greif, Karen. " 'If This Were Play'd upon a Stage': Harley Granville Barker's Shakespeare Productions at the Savoy Theatre, 1912–1914." *Harvard Library Bulletin* (Apr. 1980): 117–45.

Griffiths, Trevor. "Tradition and Innovation in Harley Granville Barker's *A Midsummer Night's Dream*." *Theatre Notebook* (1976): 78–87.

Hankin, John. "Review of *The Weather-Hen*." *Academy* (15 July 1899): 67.

Holder, Heidi J. " 'The Drama Discouraged': Judgment and Ambivalence in *The Madras House*." *University of Toronto Quarterly* 58 (1988–1989).

Hunt, Hugh. "Granville Barker's Shakespearean Productions." *Theatre Research* (1969): 44–49.

Inkster, Leonard. "Shakespeare and Mr. Granville Barker." *Poetry and Drama* (Mar. 1913): 22–26.

Innes, Christopher. "Granville Barker and Galsworthy: Questions of Censorship." *Modern Drama* 32.3 (Sept. 1989): 331–45.

Jackson, Anthony. "Harley Granville Barker as a Director of the Royal Court Theatre, 1904–1907." *Theatre Research* (1972): 126–38.

Kelly, Helen M. T. *The Granville-Barker Shakespeare Productions: A Study Based on Promptbooks.* Ann Arbor, MI: University Microfilms, 1965.

Kennedy, Dennis. [1]. *Granville Barker and the Dream of Theatre.* Cambridge: Cambridge University Press, 1985.

————. [2]. "Granville Barker's Sexual Comedy." *Modern Drama* 23 (1980): 75–82.

Mazer, Cary M. "Actors or Gramophones: The Paradoxes of Granville Barker." *Theatre Journal* (1984): 5–23.

McCarthy, Lillah. *Myself and My Friends.* London: Thornton Butterworth, 1933.

Mehra, Manmohan. *Harley Granville-Barker: A Critical Study of the Major Plays.* Calcutta, India: Naya Prokash, 1981.

Morgan, Margery M. [1]. *A Drama of Political Man: A Study in the Plays of Harley Granville Barker.* London: Sidgwick & Jackson, 1961.

————. [2]. "Edwardian Feminism and the Drama: Shaw and Granville Barker." *Cahiers Victoriens et Édouardiens*, nos. 9–10 (1979): 63–85.

Norton, Roger C. "Hugo von Hofmannsthal's *Der Schwierige* and Granville Barker's *Waste*." *Comparative Literature* 14 (Summer 1962): 272–79.

O'Neill, Michael C. "Review of *The Voysey Inheritance*." *Theatre Journal* 42.3 (Oct. 1990): 377.

Palmer, John. [1]. "Mr. Barker's Dream." *Saturday Review* (14 Feb. 1914): 202–3.

————. [2]. "Mr. Granville Barker's Inheritance." *Saturday Review* (14 Sept. 1912): 325–26.

———. [3]. "Shakespeare's 'The Winter's Tale.' " *Saturday Review* (28 Sept. 1912): 391–92.

———. [4]. "Twelfth Night." *Saturday Review* (23 Nov. 1912): 637–39.

Review of *Prunella*. *Daily Express* (24 Dec. 1904): 5.

Purdom, C. B. *Harley Granville Barker: Man of the Theatre, Dramatist, and Scholar.* London: Rockliff, 1955. Reprint. Westport, CT: Greenwood Press, 1971.

Rich, Frank. "The Stage: Three Plays in West End." *New York Times* (2 July 1985): C9.

Ritchie, Harry M. "Harley Granville Barker's *The Madras House* and the Sexual Revolution." *Modern Drama* (1972–73): 150–58.

Rutledge, F. P. *Harley Granville Barker and the English Theatre.* Dublin: National University of Ireland, 1950–1951.

Salenius, Elmer W. *Harley Granville Barker.* Boston: Twayne, 1982.

Salmon, Eric. *A Secret Life: Harley Granville Barker.* London: Heinemann, 1981, 1983.

Sharp, Cecil. *The Songs and Incidental Music Arranged and Composed for Granville Barker's Production of A Midsummer Night's Dream at the Savoy Theatre in January, 1914.* London: Simpkin Marshall, Hamilton, Kent, 1914.

Shaw, George Bernard. [1]. *Bernard Shaw's Letters to Granville Barker.* Ed. C. B. Purdom, with commentary and notes. London: Phoenix House, 1956.

———. [2]. "Granville Barker: Some Particulars." *Drama* (1946): 7–14.

Stowell, Sheila. " 'A Quaint and Comical Dismay': The Dramatic Strategies of Granville Barker's *The Voysey Inheritance.*" *Essays in Theatre* 5 (1987).

Symons, Arthur. [1]. "Granville Barker: Some Particulars." *Drama,* n.s. (Winter 1946): 7–14.

———. [2]. *Plays, Acting, and Music.* New York: E. P. Dutton & Company [1903].

———. [3]. "Review of *The Marrying of Ann Leete.*" *Academy* (1 February 1902): 123.

Thomas, Noel. "Harley Granville Barker and the Greek Drama." *Educational Theatre Journal* (1955): 294–300.

Trousdale, Marion. "The Question of Harley Granville-Barker and Shakespeare on the Stage." *Renaissance Drama,* n.s. 4 (1971): 3–36.

Review of *The Voysey Inheritance*. *Observer* (8 Sept. 1912): 10.

Walkley, A. B. [1]. "Review of *The Harlequinade.*" *The Times* (2 Sept. 1913): 6.

———. [2]. "Review of *The Marrying of Ann Leete.*" *The Times* (28 Jan. 1902): 7.

———. [3]. "Review of *Prunella.*" *The Times* (24 Dec. 1904): 10.

———. [4]. "Review of *The Voysey Inheritance.*" *The Times Literary Supplement* (10 Nov. 1905): 384.

———. [5]. "Review of *Waste.*" *The Times* (27 Nov. 1907): 8.

———. [6]. "Review of *The Weather-Hen.*" *The Times* (1 July 1899): 16.

Review of *Waste*. *Athenaeum* (30 Nov. 1907): 699.

Whitworth, Geoffrey. *Harley Granville Barker, 1877–1946: A Reprint of a Broadcast.* London: Sidgwick & Jackson, 1948.

Williams, Gary J. "A Midsummer Night's Dream: The English and American Popular Traditions and Harley Granville Barker's 'World Arbitrarily Made.' " *Theatre Studies* (1976/77): 40–52.

Wilson, J. Dover. "Memories of Barker and Two of His Friends." In *Elizabethan and Jacobean Studies Presented to Frank Percy Wilson,* ed. Herbert Davis and Helen Gardner. Oxford: Clarendon Press, 1959.

Woodfield, James. *English Theatre in Transition, 1889–1914.* London and Sydney: Croom Helm, 1984; Totowa, NJ: Barnes & Noble, 1984.

BIBLIOGRAPHIES

Davis, Mary Louise. "Reading List on Harley Granville Barker." *Bulletin of Bibliography* (1912–1913): 130–31.
May, Frederick, and Margery M. Morgan. "A List of Writings." In *Harley Granville Barker,* by C. B. Purdom, 293–309. London: Rockcliff, 1955.

Graham Greene
(1904–1991)

LAWRENCE JASPER

Graham Greene was one of the most distinguished figures of twentieth-century letters, and his internationally acclaimed novels are justly regarded today as the greatest part of his achievement. But for a brief period in midcareer, he turned his literary gifts and his moral and ethical preoccupations to the legitimate stage. Beginning with such challenging and provocative plays as *The Living Room* (1953) and *The Potting Shed* (1957), he compiled a notable record of critical and popular success in both England and America.

Henry Graham Greene was born on 2 October 1904 in Berkhamsted, England, to Marion Raymond Greene (a first cousin of Robert Louis Stevenson) and Charles Henry Greene (headmaster of Berkhamsted School and a teacher of English, history, and Latin classics). Although the circumstances of Greene's first years of life were not exceptionally unhappy, he was a painfully sensitive child. He was shy, withdrawn, and given to nightmares and strange imaginings, and he constantly sought his privacy. Greene noted in his essay "The Lost Childhood" that these traits amounted to an affliction when at age seven he became a boarder at his father's school, for not only did the boy's physical awkwardness, odd voice, and partial lisp mark him as a figure for ridicule, but the total absence of solitude made his life at the school unbearable. Also, as the headmaster's son, Greene could be suspected of being a spy—a fact that was cruelly exploited by a few of his classmates, causing Greene to feel isolated, disliked, distrusted, and wary of humiliation. It was during these grade-school years, the author has explained, that he first gained insight into "human wickedness" and the torment of divided loyalties.

During a turbulent adolescence, marked by suicide attempts, escapes from home and school, and early (at sixteen) psychiatric treatment, Greene eventually found less destructive forms of "escape": he took theater trips to London and steeped himself in turn-of-the-century romance fiction. Tales of treachery and violence, such as Marjorie Bowen's *The Viper of Milan,* had a special appeal. Greene has left detailed accounts of how these melodramas, along with the injuries of his childhood, helped to give shape to his own literary pilgrimage. The primary focus of his fiction and drama was on the corruption and unhappiness of the human condition. With his fixation on the "night side of life," to use his own apt description (*British Dramatists,* 24), Greene created a peculiar psychological landscape haunted by spiritual torment—by failure, evil, guilt, fear, suffering, and betrayal.

In the fall of 1922 Greene departed the troubling confines of Berkhamsted for the more spacious prospects of Balliol College, Oxford, and he relished his newfound freedom. He grew in confidence, his keen intellect came to the fore, and he gained fruitful apprenticeships both in the crafts of writing and in the practical aspects of the theater. He was elected president of the Oxford Modern Poetry and Drama Society, which gave him introductions to a number of literary and theatrical figures of the time, such as Edith Sitwell, Walter de la Mare, and the playwrights Emlyn Williams and Clifford Bax (who helped Greene find his first literary agent). Greene also became the editor of the *Oxford Outlook* in 1924, writing its fiction and drama reviews. He organized the first "Oxford Poets Symposium" (consisting of Greene, A. L. Rowse, and other classmates reading original poems on the newly formed BBC Radio). He also published a book of verse, *Babbling April* (1925), and completed his first (unpublished) novel.

Greene's fascination with the theater propelled him through the whole range of theatrical experience: as playwright, actor, and entrepreneur. In his freshman year he entered two playwriting competitions—"narrowly missing" in one, and in the other, more formal one, receiving important encouragement from the judges, who included Harley Granville-Barker. Later, he organized, produced, and performed in his own undergraduate theater company, appearing in such roles as Banquo in *Macbeth* and "a young bounder" in *The Importance of Being Earnest.* Although not all of the company's production ambitions were realized, Greene spoke at this time of his attraction to the plays of G. B. Shaw, with which one of his own plays, *The Complaisant Lover,* would later be favorably compared.

Before graduating from Oxford with his degree in modern history in 1925, Greene had a fateful meeting with Vivien Dayrell-Browning, the woman who became his wife in 1927 (and would later bear him two children), and who was solely responsible for his conversion to Roman Catholicism in 1926. Greene had initially undertaken his religious studies to appease his converted Catholic fiancée, but the issues raised in his instruction—especially those concerning sin, damnation, and salvation—would have a profound effect on the ethical arguments in his mature fiction and in the three plays, *The Living Room, The Potting Shed,* and *Carving a Statue.*

In 1929, while Greene was working as a subeditor at *The Times* of London, his third (but first published) novel, *The Man Within,* achieved moderate success; and he spent the next two decades establishing his reputation with such successful "detective thrillers" as *The Orient Express* (1933) and *This Gun for Hire* (1936) and with a series of internationally acclaimed literary novels—his so-called Catholic novels—*Brighten Rock* (1938), *The Power and the Glory* (1940), *The Heart of the Matter* (1948), and *The End of the Affair* (1951).

But the would-be playwright also remained actively involved in projects directly related to theater and drama during this period. From 1935 to 1939, for example, he functioned as film critic for the *Spectator,* graduating to the post of literary editor and drama critic in 1940. In 1937 he cofounded and served as film critic for the satirical magazine *Night and Day.* The year 1942 saw the publication of his brief, perceptive history of drama entitled *British Dramatists.* In 1939 the BBC broadcast his radio drama *The Great Jowett,* about a celebrated Oxford don; and between 1940 and 1967 Greene wrote nine screenplays (seven based on his own novels and short stories), achieving his greatest cinematic success with his original script for *The Third Man* (1949), a film acclaimed as the most popular in British screen history (Forman, 18).

Buoyed by the enormous success of his recent screenplay and "in need of a rest" from his novels (Preface, ix), Greene at last turned his attention directly to the theater. Although his attempted stage adaptation of *The Heart of the Matter* was a failure in 1950, Greene returned in 1953 with *The Living Room,* a naturalistic study of sin, guilt, and suicide. It led to a spirited controversy— and a yearlong London production—with its unorthodox treatment of sexuality and religion. This was followed in 1957 by the successful New York premiere of *The Potting Shed,* an equally controversial play about the loss and recovery of faith. Greene achieved a near-record-breaking London triumph with his third play, *The Complaisant Lover* (1959), a comedy with serious undertones about the moral failure of adultery. All three plays received both London and New York productions, and all were included in the Burns Mantle *Best Plays of the Year* volumes.

After a five-year hiatus from the theater, during which he experimented with prose comedy and political fiction and became an effective *franc-tireur* on international issues, Greene returned to London with his fourth play, *Carving a Statue* (1964). This tragicomedy, his most experimental and thematically ambitious work, was also his least successful on the stage. Its failure was devastating to the author, and he printed an extraordinary "epitaph" for the play in its published edition, speaking of how "tormenting" it was to write and exasperating to produce. He chided the critics for misunderstanding the work and then declared, in words that signaled his withdrawal from the stage: "I make my living in another field" ("Epitaph for a Play," 7).

Although more than a decade later Greene would offer *The Return of A. J. Raffles* (1975), an adaptation of E. W. Hornung's turn-of-the-century novel, *The Amateur Cracksman,* the results were disappointing; and a lesser fate awaited his inconsequential farce, *For Whom the Bell Chimes* (1980), and its curtain raiser, *Yes and No.* The mild reception of these last stage efforts precipitated Greene's permanent retirement from playwriting, his energy and patience for the theater exhausted, at the age of seventy-five.

In the 1980s Greene grew more reflective; he wrote a final volume of autobiography, collected his letters, and made selections from his "dream diary" for publication. Although his creative output gradually slowed during this period, his fifth collection of short stories appeared only weeks before his death. In December 1989 the author was diagnosed with a rare blood disease, and since he had long been estranged from his wife and son, he moved to be near his daughter in Vevey, Switzerland, where on 3 April 1991 a career that had touched seven decades came to a close.

In addition to his honorary degrees from Oxford, Cambridge, and the University of Edinburgh, Greene received the following honors and awards: Honorary Member of the American Institute of Arts and Letters, 1961; John Dos Passos Prize (United States), 1980; Commander of the Order of Arts and Letters (France), 1984; Companion of Literature, Royal Society of Arts and Literature (Great Britain), 1984; and British Order of Merit, 1986.

Selected Biographical Sources: Cassis; Greene, "The Lost Childhood," "The Revolver in the Corner Cupboard," *A Sort of Life, Ways of Escape;* Mockler; Shelden; Sherry.

MAJOR PLAYS, PREMIERES, AND SIGNIFICANT REVIVALS: THEATRICAL RECEPTION

The Living Room. 1953. Opened 16 April at Wyndham's Theatre (London) for 307 performances. Produced and directed by Peter Glenville. Revived 17 November 1954 at Henry Miller's Theatre (New York) for 22 performances.

Greene achieved a highly controversial success with this theological problem play about a young, recently orphaned, Catholic woman who is sent to live with elderly relatives in a bizarre household where blind adherence to religious orthodoxies has banished love and compassion, and where an obsessive fear of death has led to the closure of all rooms where death has occurred. After the young woman reveals her affair with a married man—a non-Catholic psychologist—she is cruelly betrayed and humiliated, forced to choose between her lover and her faith; and when she is finally unconsoled by the hollow platitudes of her uncle, a Catholic priest, she commits suicide in the one remaining "living room" of the macabre house, uttering a childhood prayer.

Virtually all reviewers graciously welcomed the esteemed novelist's entry into the West End theater; and while most applauded the play as a whole, their opinions on its individual merits varied widely. Tynan [1] hailed the work as not only the best new play of the London season, but as "easily the best first play of the last half-century" (see Beaton, 55). Stephens [1] termed it "a work of genius," and the superlatives "magnificent," "powerful," and "haunting" were affixed by Trewin [5], Lambert [2], and *The Times* (Review of *The Living*

Room), among others. Findlater's more moderate estimation was that the play was at times difficult, even "infuriating," but he admired its "uncommon literary skill" and found it "poignant, exciting, and vibrantly alive." He also labeled as singularly obtuse those few detractors, such as Worsley [1], who dubbed the play a "baffling failure." The more pointed criticisms focused on the play's daring subject matter and uneven structure. Although Hamilton faulted "Greene's remorseless, obsessive drive into the dark," and Worsley [1] objected to what he saw as the author's customary "sentimental addiction to failure," the vast majority soundly applauded Greene's courageous efforts to make the drama a vehicle for ideas, to examine questions of moral conduct and religious faith. *The Times* reviewer, conveying the sentiments of most, declared that the growing moral/spiritual awareness of the characters "gives the work a momentousness all too rare on the stage." But Tynan [1] likewise spoke for the majority in faulting the nature and effect of the play's conclusion. The suicide of the young girl in the penultimate scene of the play was described as "melodramatic," an "improbable dramatic expedient," and as Hamilton ventured, it seemed to arise merely from the author's thematic requirement for a "final act of expiation." The other most noted structural flaw was the play's final, "anticlimactic" scene of debate (e.g., Lambert [2], Trewin [5], Tynan [1], and Worsley [1]). But Tynan added that if in Greene's ambitious first play he "stumbles at the highest level, he is wonderfully sure-footed on the way up." Trewin [5] concurred, predicting correctly that these "minor flaws" would easily be overlooked in "one of the most provocative plays of its time."

The 1954 New York production became a short-lived cause célèbre. Kronenberger [1] (4–6), Gibbs, Bentley (200–203), Hayes [1, 3], and Clurman [2] strenuously defended the significance of what Bentley called the play's attempt to "define the lives of people in religious, not simply sociological or psychological, terms." Kronenberger thought that the "quality of the writing and the tragic vision of life merited unalloyed respect." Bentley, Clurman, and Hayes were less sanguine on the play's craftsmanship, but Bentley felt that the "shockingly" inept American production had "ruined the play," and Hayes indicted the philistinism of the majority of reviewers (including Atkinson [2, 4], John Mason Brown, Chapman [2], Coleman [1], Hawkins, Kerr [4], McClain [3], and Watts [2]) who found the issues of the drama "too depressing," "too hifalutin'," and/or "irrelevant." Kronenberger, who selected the drama for his *Best Plays* volume, summed up the apathetic reception on what he described as a "frivolous" New York stage: "One real value of *The Living Room* was that its black-bordered script brought darkness to light places, bestowing a real dignity on a Broadway that is much too fond of greeting cards."

The Potting Shed. 1957. Opened 29 January at the Bijou Theatre (New York) for 143 performances. Produced by Carmen Capalbo and Stanley Chase. Directed by Carmen Capalbo. Revived 5 February 1958 at the Globe Theatre (London) for 101 performances.

Greene combined his religious preoccupations and his proven facility with the detective-thriller genre in this faintly autobiographical story involving a priest who had once made a desperate pact with God: bartering his faith for the life of his fourteen-year-old nephew, James, who had attempted suicide in a gardener's "potting shed." The boy was restored to life, though he remembered nothing. Immediately, however, he was sent away to boarding school and ostracized ever afterward by his parents, who secretly wished to suppress the scandal of an apparent "miracle," since the boy's father was a famed rationalist author in the mode of Bertrand Russell. The play recounts James's return after thirty years of mental and spiritual misery and his detectivelike search for the truth. With the aid of the priest without faith, the traumatic secret of the past is uncovered, the family conflicts are resolved, and meaning and faith are restored to the two men's lives.

After viewing this "psychological detective story," as Greene termed it, the New York critics appeared much more positively disposed toward his talents for the stage. His forceful and literate dialogue and the characterization of the priest, for example, were universally admired. But *The Potting Shed* gave evidence that the novelist was still struggling with the dramatic form, and critics again attacked or defended the play largely around the issue of its kinetic structure and the nature and effect of its conclusion. Most critics, such as Atkinson [1, 3], Chapman [3], Coleman [2], Kerr ([1], 146–149 and [5]), Watts [1], and the *Theatre Arts* reviewer (Review of *The Potting Shed*), noted that Greene's deft manipulation of familiar detective-thriller devices had brought a high theatricality to the better part of three acts; but many, including Hewes [3] and Kronenberger ([2], 12–13) agreed with McClain [1] that since the major reversal and discovery occurs in act 2, the concluding act appeared anticlimactic, even "redundant." Others, like Donnelly, Gassner ([2], 155–157) and the critic for *Theater Arts,* noted that in the playwright's use of the structural expedients of melodrama, he had to some extent sacrificed the development of character and theme. Similarly, Kronenberger and Clurman [3], two of the strongest defenders of Greene's first play, objected that the playwright's sudden provision of a "theological solution" to this detective story had sounded a false note, as had the precipitous conversion of the two principals. Clurman condemned the "moral hypocrisy" of the ending and dismissed the play as "bogus."

The 1958 London premiere was only moderately successful and gave rise to many of the same observations as its New York counterpart: the civilized and probing dialogue (Darlington, Trewin [3], Tynan [3], Worsley [2]), scenes of high theatricality (Darlington, Hobson [1], *The Times* ["Globe Theatre: 'The Potting Shed' "]), a plot marred by anticlimax (Darlington, *The Times*), and an implausible, "inauthentic" resolution (Brahms, Darlington, Hope-Wallace [2], Stephens [2], Trewin [3]). Lambert [1] and Stephens preferred the elemental power of *The Living Room;* and Lambert agreed with Brahms, Inglis, and Worsley in faulting the "muddled" and "bloodless" production of the play.

The Complaisant Lover. 1959. Opened 18 June at the Globe Theatre (London) for 402 performances. Produced and directed by John Gielgud. Revived 1 November 1961 at the Ethel Barrymore Theatre (New York) for 101 performances.

Greene's most popular work for the stage was a startling departure: in essence, a drawing-room comedy that concludes on a note of sardonic humor. In scenes verging on the farcical, the play at first exploits a stock love triangle, in which a boring, bumbling, buffoonish husband receives a letter from his wife's paramour, a jealous type intent on precipitating a divorce. But in a suddenly somber scene, the cuckold is immediately driven to tears and to the brink of suicide. He quickly recovers, however, and then cannily proposes a ménage à trois, which satisfies his desire to keep his wife, assuages his wife's guilt, and completely disconcerts the third party, who reluctantly becomes "the complaisant lover."

London critics and audiences enthusiastically hailed Greene's first comedy. Forster, Frank, and Thompson pronounced it the best play of the season and Greene's most entirely successful play to date. Most, including Trewin [2], Stephens [3], Wilson, Hobson [2], Pritchett, and Brien, praised the author's attempt to suffuse his light drawing-room comedy with serious insights concerning domestic versus romantic love. Stephens termed it a "dangerous mixture" and claimed that in Greene's "daring, paradoxical treatment of a serious theme" he had surpassed even G. B. Shaw. Hobson spoke for most in praising the "magnificent" scene of the husband's sad discovery and its inspired performance by Sir Ralph Richardson. Forster added that Greene's sophisticated, many-layered comedy had "miraculously transformed the tired trivia" of the love triangle "into a sin-and-tonic work of art"; but Forster also detected that even with the inspired performances, the play's final transition from the nearly farcical to the serious tête-à-tête in act 2 was "a little wobbly and abrupt": "as Bully Bottom crumbles into Uncle Vanya." The play's dialogue drew unanimous praise for its verve, grace, and deftness. Frank, for example, placed Greene "second only to Tchekhov as a writer of natural dialogue." But Tynan ([2], 84–85), while finding a "startling casual candour" in Greene's dialogue, complained that "mastery of dialogue" was "no substitute for mastery of characterization," and he joined Jones in observing an unresolved liability that would be borne out by later commentators on the play: the thinly drawn comic characters seemed "inconsistent" when abruptly required to convey the serious sentiments of the play's final scene.

The 1961 Broadway reception was a disappointment after the comedy's London success. Although the critics Gilbert, Hewes ([1], [2], 5) Kerr [2, 3], and Chapman [1] celebrated the play's "sophisticated" modern look at an age-old dilemma, they were countered by many others, including Clurman [1], Gassner [1], Nadel, and the *Theatre Arts* correspondent (Review of *The Complaisant Lover*), who felt that the theme and final bargain were in various degrees "distasteful"; and a number of others, like Taubman, McClain [2], and Watts [3], found the theme disappointingly "thin." Once again, however, Greene's fluent, graceful, witty language was virtually unanimously praised, as were the pleasures of individual scenes, such as the uproarious bedroom farce in act 1, scene 2. But the play's seriocomic style drew many more serious detractors among New York's critics—including Gilman, McCarten, McClain [2], and Taubman—than the London production had. Similarly, more faulted key characterizations that seemed "superficial," "inconsistent," and "unbelievable" (e.g., Mannes, Nadel, Taubman, and Watts [3]). The majority of reviewers concluded, with Hewes [1, 2], that the latter two flaws of the work had been compounded in the New York production, since the buffoonish, cuckolded husband was played not by Sir Ralph Richardson, but by the handsome and virile Sir Michael Redgrave.

Carving a Statue. 1964. Opened 17 September at the Haymarket Theatre (London) for 52 performances. Produced and directed by Peter Wood.

Leaving West End domestic comedy far behind, Greene launched into his most experimental work: a tragic tale of an untalented sculptor who has devoted fifteen years to the making of an immense statue of God the Father, sacrificing everything except his dreams to the task, though he has no notion of how to complete it. His friends, his son's happiness, and an innocent girl's life are all destroyed in the process; and the play ends with the sculptor abandoning the first statue when he is struck with a new obsession: if he cannot encompass God in his work, he will try to recreate Lucifer.

This amorphous play provoked scathing columns from Hobson [3], Holland, Holstrom, Hope-Wallace [1], Rutherford, Trewin [4], and *The Times* ("See-Saw of Pride and Contrition"). Bryden alone insisted on the right of the "greatest contemporary English novelist" to such experimentation, but he, too, joined the consensus: the play was deemed "steadily untheatrical," a "laboured parable without development or resolution." Reviewers noted that the action was often "gratuitous," "shamelessly padded," rife with "melodramatic clichés," and, "at times, intolerably crude." The play was repeatedly labeled "unintelligible," its characters neither "comically nor tragically alive," and its dialogue "overladen with heavy-handed symbols." Holstrom's view, that the "play shows no sign of a redeeming talent," accurately summarized the critical onslaught. But the embittered author insisted on having the last word on the play that he regarded as his "favorite" (Harwood, 747). Greene admitted that the drama was flawed, but in his spirited counterattack he claimed that the critics' opinions had been narrow-minded and undigested ("Epitaph for a Play"). After this debacle, however, he never attempted another serious work for the stage.

ADDITIONAL PLAYS, ADAPTATIONS, AND PRODUCTIONS

Greene's only other original plays—the two brief comedies, *For Whom the Bell Chimes* and its twenty-minute curtain raiser, *Yes and No* (Leicester, 20

March 1980)—added little to his critical reputation. Aire's reaction to the longer play may be taken as representative: "The piece is lacking in basic stagecraft," "too weak to rank as satire, too silly to count as theatre, and too technically difficult even to find a home in the village hall." *Yes and No* proved equally disappointing. The author's 1950 collaboration (with Basil Dean) on the dramatization of his own novel, *The Heart of the Matter,* was closed by the producers during Boston previews. Greene also offered a loose adaptation of E. W. Hornung's turn-of-the-century novel, *The Amateur Cracksman,* that premiered as *The Return of A. J. Raffles* (London, 1975); but this too failed to find an audience. Most called it "tiresome" (e.g., Hurren and Nightingale); panned its "laboured jokes and plot" (Panter-Downes); and concluded, with Peereboom, that it "would not be worth mentioning if it were written by somebody else." On the other hand, the filmed adaptations of Greene's plays and fiction, many of which were completed by the author himself, were generally much more successful, and these have received generous critical attention in the volumes by Adamson and Phillips.

ASSESSMENT OF GREENE'S CAREER

Graham Greene entered the British theater at a time of stagnation between two periods of heightened theatrical activity, and much was expected from the esteemed author who had been lured from his accustomed genre. But the evidence reveals that Greene had recurrent difficulties in adapting his literary talents to the stage, and that he chose to remain largely aloof from the exploration of the new styles and themes that so thoroughly defined the "angry decade." These observations are fundamental to any assessment of Greene's work for the theater.

In the 1940s the British theater had offered a measure of relief from the ugly realities of war and its aftermath. The brief flowering of verse drama from Eliot and Fry had, in Tynan's ([3], 270) apt description, provided "imagined worlds where austerity's paraphernalia could be forgotten," and "reminders that words could be put to other public uses than those of military propaganda, news bulletins, and government regulations." Also during the immediate postwar period a tremendous upsurge in interpretive energy had been poured into productions of the classics—the impulse of a "battered Europe," said Brook, "a reaching back towards a memory of lost grace" (43). But by the early 1950s both of these trends seemed to have expended their momentum, leaving a theater dominated by diversions and entertainments of a lesser order: the drawing-room comedy, the detective thriller, and the farce. At the same time, however, as the economy revived, everyday reality became less unpleasant, and the public recovered its former taste for plays about the facts of contemporary life.

It was in this context, in this "theatre starved of ideas," as Taylor ([2], 21) has described it, that Greene's provocative first play, *The Living Room,* was produced. Contemporary surveys of the drama, like those of Trewin ([1], 214) and Beaton and Tynan (55) spoke in glowing terms of the playwright's conspicuous arrival amid the pallid offerings of the early years of the decade. According to Trewin, the play was "bristling with problems, ethical and emotional, and amply satisfies the modern desire for soul searching," and he spoke in hopeful terms of the promise the playwright held for the future. Tynan ([2], 21–23) was even more optimistic, declaring Greene "a potentially great dramatist."

But one of the most renowned prose stylists of his generation did not become a major playwright. After *The Living Room* he produced only two other successful plays, and while they are the offerings of an accomplished writer, they lack the confident craft and finesse of his more celebrated novels. As others have justly argued (e.g., Bryden, Davis, Goetz, Hayes [2, 3], and Lumley), the strictures and economies of the dramatic form forced Greene to sacrifice some of the finest attributes of his fiction: the allusive montages of description and commentary in his narration; the sudden, "cinematic" shifts of perspective between character, scene, and the larger frame of the story. Greene advanced the development of the twentieth-century novel with such prosaic abilities, but they steadfastly resisted dramatic investiture. As Greene himself remarked (Preface, vii), his greatest playwriting challenge (and most persistent weakness) was the development of an adequate kinetic structure in a genre "which depends for communication on dialogue alone."

Consequently, the plots of Greene's dramas frequently appear awkward and halting, the conclusions somewhat forced. As Tynan ([2], 21–23) has accurately observed about the *The Living Room:* "Having tied a modern knot, Greene cuts it with a old-fashioned theatrical axe." *The Potting Shed* represents an advancement in dramatic craftsmanship over its predecessor, primarily in its manipulation of suspense and its piecemeal revelations, but Atkinson's [1] observation at the play's premiere remains valid nonetheless: it has the occasional cumbrousness of "a nineteenth-century thesis drama . . . a form no longer fresh." Greene's best theatrical technique is found in *The Complaisant Lover*—a departure from the "well-made-play" tradition of West End naturalism in favor of the equally well-worn tradition of domestic comedy. The play has a much more subtle delineation of plot than the author's previous efforts, and some of its scenes have retained their humor. But the play does not differ greatly from other "boulevard" comedies of the period, and its "blending" of styles was never completely satisfactory, once separated from Ralph Richardson's initial assay of the principal role. Significantly, the only patent failure among Greene's serious efforts for the stage, *Carving a Statue,* has as its chief flaw his least well-managed fable: it is underdeveloped, poorly articulated, and cluttered with irrelevant incident. Critics Barbour, Cottrell, Gassner [2], Lumley, Sharrock, and Turnell can be included in the consensus on this central aspect of Greene's uneven dramaturgy.

Another principal criticism leveled at Greene—especially by his countrymen—in the surveys of British drama that have emerged since the late 1950s was not that he had insufficiently mastered the exigencies of dramatic form, but rather that he had failed to rise with the tide of determined experiment and innovation that began in 1956 with Osborne's *Look Back in Anger*. It was in this sense a "cultural critique": it marked Greene as an "outsider" and his works as anachronistic and irrelevant. In Elsom's generally accurate assessment, the new, post-war generation of playwrights and their "theme of social alienation came to dominate the drama" (77) and theatre in the last half of the decade. One result, as Hinchliffe has explained, was that Greene's typical themes—such as the clash between divine law and human law in *The Living Room* and *The Potting Shed*—were perceived by the "new wave" of dramatists (and critics) as "too large or remote to be useful either in life or the theatre" (26).

Greene increasingly came under attack by critics who compared him unfavorably to the new, predominately working- or middle-class playwrights. Buckle, for example, in a joint review of *The Complaisant Lover* and Behan's *The Hostage,* which opened side by side in the West End in June 1959, contrasted the two playwrights and their plays in a manner that reflected the gathering critique: "The one [Greene's], was written by the Senior Classics Master for the delight of rich and doting parents; the other [Behan's], was inspired by stolen hooch, improvised by the common scholarship boy and banged out just for the hell of it. The Greene play is all intelligence, the Behan all blood and guts; and the latter is my choice every time." A few months later, in a joint review of *The Complaisant Lover* and Shaffer's *Five Finger Exercise,* Brien was more vitriolic, attacking the well-to-do Greene as an unwelcome interloper on the prevalent issues confronting the middle class: "Mr. Greene is looking through the key hole. He patronizes his people and sneers at what he regards as their pathetic suburban chatter." On the other hand, said Brien, "Mr. Shaffer was inside his family and he knows what real horror and passion and humour can be found imbedded in middle class small talk." Finally, Hobson's [5] remarkable 1959 article "Youth Changes Direction" further clarified the altered nature of the theater and its new critical expectations. After reporting that the character of the London theater had "almost entirely changed" in the previous few years, Hobson declared that although Greene, along with Rattigan and T. S. Eliot, had provided "admirable plays" in the past, "they spoke, and speak, for themselves alone"; and, unlike the "new renaissance of young British playwrights, their work is based on beliefs that in a sense are private to themselves." Then, in the unmistakable argot of the revolutionary, Hobson complained that such beliefs did "not fling open on a new road that suddenly seems to lead to unexpected and unknown peace and spiritual wealth." The majority of later commentators, including Allsop, John Russell Brown [1], Chiari, Elsom, Hinchliffe, Popkin, Trussler, and Tynan [2, 3], have agreed with Hobson that Greene, in key respects, "had failed the revolution."

But if a persistent tendency in recent accounts of the British stage has been to devalue Greene's plays for his having declined to reflect the sociopolitical causes of the moment, other critics, perhaps more removed from the "revolution"—most of them are non-British—have generally been more appreciative, their analyses more balanced. Such critics as Adler, DeVitis, Goetz, Raynor,

Walling, and Weales, for example, have contributed insightfully to this body of criticism, especially regarding the playwright's forceful and literate dialogue and his richly drawn characters that demand and reward fine acting, such as the despairing priest in *The Living Room* and the haunted man who returns from the dead in *The Potting Shed.* These scholars have been most appreciative of the author's spiritual and moral passion. Raynor's description of Greene's achievement may be taken as a fitting summation of the views of this group of critics and as a testament to those aspects of the author's signature plays, *The Living Room* and *The Potting Shed,* that survive the specific infelicities of structure and transcend the tides of sociopolitical revolutions: "They translate into terms of theater the strangeness and haunting power of his novels. They are plays of faith in which men are able to see that they live inescapably and often terrifyingly in the presence of God" (214).

ARCHIVAL SOURCES

Extensive materials, including manuscripts, reviews, photos, and correspondence, can be found in the Humanities Research Center of the University of Texas, Austin, and the Lauinger Library of Georgetown University.

PRIMARY BIBLIOGRAPHY

Plays

Carving a Statue. London: Bodley Head, 1964.
The Complaisant Lover. London: Heinemann, 1959; New York: Viking, 1961.
The Great Jowett (a radio play). London: Bodley Head, 1981.
The Living Room. London: Heinemann, 1953; New York: Viking, 1954.
The Potting Shed. New York: Viking, 1957; Revised version. London: Heinemann, 1958.
The Return of A. J. Raffles. London: Bodley Head, 1975; New York: Simon & Schuster, 1976.
Yes and No, and For Whom the Bell Chimes. London: Bodley Head, 1983.

Anthologies

Collected Plays. (Includes *The Living Room, The Potting Shed, The Complaisant Lover, Carving a Statue, The Return of A. J. Raffles, The Great Jowett, Yes and No, For Whom the Bell Chimes.*) London: Penguin, 1985.
Three Plays. (Includes *The Living Room, The Potting Shed, The Complaisant Lover.*) London: Mercury, 1961.

Selected Nonfiction

British Dramatists. London: Collins, 1942. Reprinted in *The Romance of English Literature.* New York: Hastings House, 1944.

"Epitaph for a Play." In *Carving a Statue,* 7–8. London: Bodley Head, 1964.
"The Lost Childhood." In *'The Lost Childhood' and Other Essays,* 141–48. London: Eyre & Spottiswoode, 1951.
Preface. In *Three Plays,* vii–xiii. London: Mercury, 1961.
"The Revolver in the Corner Cupboard." In *'The Lost Childhood' and Other Essays,* 173–76. London: Eyre & Spottiswoode, 1951.
A Sort of Life (autobiography). London: Bodley Head, 1971.
Ways of Escape (autobiography). London: Bodley Head, 1980.

SECONDARY BIBLIOGRAPHY

Adamson, Judith. *Graham Greene and Cinema.* Norman, OK: Pilgrim, 1984.
Adler, Jacob H. "Graham Greene's Plays: Technique versus Value." In *Graham Greene: Some Critical Considerations,* ed. Robert O. Evans, 219–30. Lexington: University of Kentucky Press, 1963.
Aire, Sally. Review of *For Whom the Bell Chimes* and *Yes and No. Plays and Players* (Apr. 1980): 29.
Allsop, Kenneth. *The Angry Decade: A Survey of the Cultural Revolt of the Nineteen-Fifties.* Wendover, England: John Goodchild, 1985.
Armstrong, William A., ed. *Experimental Drama.* London: Bell, 1963.
Atkinson, Brooks. [1]. " 'Potting Shed': World Debut of Second Graham Greene Play." *New York Times* (10 Feb. 1957): 2:1.
———. [2]. "Theatre: Graham Greene's 'Living Room.' " *New York Times* (18 Nov. 1954): 41.
———. [3]. "Theatre: Greene's 'The Potting Shed.' " *New York Times* (30 Jan. 1957): 32.
———. [4]. "Theatre: 'The Living Room.' " *New York Times* (28 Nov. 1954): 2:1.
Barbour, Thomas. "Playwrights or Play-Writers." *Hudson Review* (Autumn 1954): 470–75.
Beaton, Cecil, and Kenneth Tynan. *Persona Grata.* London: Wingate, 1953.
Bentley, Eric. *What Is Theatre?* New York: Atheneum, 1968.
Brahms, Caryl. Review of *The Potting Shed. Plays and Players* (Mar. 1958): 11.
Brien, Alan. "Christmas Cavil." *Spectator* (18 Dec. 1959): 907–8.
Brook, Peter. *The Empty Space.* New York: Atheneum, 1969.
Brown, Ivor. "Greene Fields." *Observer* (19 Apr. 1953): 11.
Brown, John Mason. "Parish Greene." *Saturday Review* (18 Dec. 1954): 24–25.
Brown, John Russell. [1]. Introduction. In *Modern British Dramatists: A Collection of Critical Essays,* ed. John Russell Brown, 1–14. Englewood Cliffs, NJ: Prentice-Hall, 1968.
———, ed. [2]. *Modern British Dramatists: New Perspectives.* Englewood Cliffs, NJ: Prentice-Hall, 1984.
Bryden, Ronald. "Somebodaddy." *New Statesman* (25 Sept. 1964): 462.
Buckle, Richard. Review of *The Hostage* and *The Complaisant Lover. Plays and Players* (Aug. 1959): 13.
Cassis, A. F. *Graham Greene: Life, Work, and Criticism.* Fredericton, Canada: York, 1994.
Chambers, Colin, and Mike Prior. *Playwrights' Progress: Patterns of Postwar British Drama.* Oxford: Amber Lane, 1987.

Chapman, John. [1]. " 'The Complaisant Lover' a Silky and Stylishly Acted Sex Comedy." *Daily News* (2 Nov. 1961).

———. [2]. " 'The Living Room' Lacks Power to Make It an Absorbing Tragedy." *Daily News* (18 Nov. 1954).

———. [3]. " 'The Potting Shed': A Mystical and Intellectually Provocative Play." *Daily News* (30 Jan. 1957).

Chiari, J. *Landmarks of Contemporary Drama.* London: Herbert Jenkins, 1965.

Clurman, Harold. [1]. Review of *The Complaisant Lover. Nation* (25 Nov. 1961): 437.

———. [2]. Review of *The Living Room. Nation* (4 Dec. 1954): 496–97.

———. [3]. Review of *The Potting Shed. Nation* (16 Feb. 1957): 146–47.

Coleman, Robert. [1]. " 'The Living Room' Opens at the Henry Miller." *Daily Mirror* (18 Nov. 1954).

———. [2]. " 'The Potting Shed' Is a Study of Faith." *Daily Mirror* (30 Jan. 1957).

Review of *The Complaisant Lover. Theatre Arts* (Jan. 1962): 15, 71.

Cornish, Roger, and Violet Ketels, eds. *Landmarks of Modern British Drama.* Vol. 1, *The Plays of the Sixties.* New York and London: Methuen, 1985.

Cottrell, Beekman W. "Second Time Charm: The Theatre of Graham Greene." *Modern Fiction Studies* 3:3 (Autumn 1957): 249–55.

Darlington, W. A. "Do You Believe in Miracles?" *Daily Telegraph and Morning Post* (24 Feb. 1958): 11.

Davis, Elizabeth. *Graham Greene: The Artist as Critic.* Fredericton, Canada: York, 1984.

DeVitis, A. A. *Graham Greene.* Rev. ed. Boston: Twayne, 1986.

Donnelly, Tom. "A Detective Story for Grown-Ups." *New York World-Telegram* (30 Jan. 1957): 18.

Elsom, John. *Post-War British Theatre.* London: Routledge & Kegan Paul, 1976.

Findlater, Richard. "Graham Greene as Dramatist." *Twentieth Century* (June 1953): 471–73.

Forman, Denis. *Films, 1945–1950.* London: Wingate, 1952.

Forster, Peter. "Sin and Tonic." *Spectator* (3 July 1959): 7.

Frank, Elizabeth. "Brighter Greene without a Shadow." *News Chronicle* (19 June 1959): 3.

Gassner, John. [1]. "Broadway in Review." *Educational Theatre Journal* (Mar. 1962): 67.

———. [2]. *Theatre at the Crossroads.* New York: Holt, 1960.

Gibbs, Wolcott. "Mr. Greene's Tragedy." *New Yorker* (27 Nov. 1954): 86.

Gilbert, Justin. " 'Lover' Squares Triangle Amusingly." *New York Mirror* (2 Nov. 1961).

Gilman, Richard. "The Stage: Mixture Almost as Before." *Commonweal* (24 Nov. 1961): 233–34.

"Globe Theatre: 'The Potting Shed.' " *The Times* (6 Feb. 1958): 12.

Goetz, Germaine. "Greene the Dramatist." *Essays in Graham Greene* 1 (1987): 127–68.

Hamilton, Ian. "Theatre: 'The Living Room.' " *Spectator* (24 Apr. 1953): 512.

Harwood, Ronald. "Time and the Novelist—Graham Greene Interviewed." *Listener* (4 Dec. 1975): 747–49.

Hawkins, William. " 'The Living Room' Furnished by Britain." *New York World-Telegram and Sun* (18 Nov. 1954): 30.

Hayes, Richard. [1]. "No Living Rooms." *Commonweal* (10 Dec. 1954): 278.

———. [2]. "The Stage: A Novelist's Theater." *Commonweal* (15 Mar. 1957): 613–14.

———. [3]. "The Stage: 'The Living Room.' " *Commonweal* (24 Dec. 1954): 333–34.

Hayman, Ronald. *British Theatre since 1955: A Reassessment*. Oxford: Oxford University Press, 1979.

Hewes, Henry. [1]. "An Adult Look at Adultery." *Saturday Review* (2 Dec. 1961): 36.

———. [2]. *The Best Plays of 1961–1962*. New York: Dodd, Mead, 1962.

———. [3]. "Resurrection Will Out." *Saturday Review* (16 Feb. 1957): 26–27.

Hinchliffe, Arnold P. *British Theatre, 1950–70*. Oxford: Blackwell, 1974.

Hobson, Harold. [1]. "Annus Mirabilis." *The Sunday Times* (9 Feb. 1958): 23.

———. [2]. "The Greatest of These . . ." *The Sunday Times* (21 June 1959): 21.

———. [3]. "Harold Hobson on Zeffirelli and Greene." *The Sunday Times* (20 Sept. 1964): 31.

———. [4]. *Theatre in Britain*. Oxford: Phaidon, 1984.

———. [5]. "Youth Changes Direction." *The Sunday Times* (28 June 1959): 21.

Holland, Mary. "The Greene Image of God." *Observer* (20 Sept. 1964): 27.

Holstrom, John. "Sans Everything." *Plays and Players* (Nov. 1964): 40–41.

Hope-Wallace, Philip. [1]. " 'Carving a Statue' at the Haymarket." *Guardian* (18 Sept. 1964): 13.

———. [2]. " 'The Potting Shed': A Moral Drama." *Guardian* (6 Feb. 1958): 5.

Hurren, Kenneth. "Return of the Native." *Spectator* (13 Dec. 1975): 770.

Inglis, Brian. "Dungeons of the Mind." *Spectator* (14 Feb. 1958): 203.

Innes, Christopher. *Modern British Drama, 1890–1990*. Cambridge: Cambridge University Press, 1992.

Jones, Mervyn. "Two Unhappy Families." *Observer* (21 June 1959): 17.

Kerensky, Oleg. *The New British Drama*. London: Hamish Hamilton, 1977.

Kerr, Walter. [1]. *Pieces at Eight*. New York: Simon & Schuster, 1957.

———. [2]. *The Theater in Spite of Itself*. New York: Simon & Schuster, 1963.

———. [3]. "Theater: 'The Complaisant Lover.' " *New York Herald Tribune* (2 Nov. 1961).

———. [4]. "Theater: 'The Living Room.' " *New York Herald Tribune* (18 Nov. 1954).

———. [5]. "Theater: 'The Potting Shed.' " *New York Herald Tribune* (30 Jan. 1957).

Kitchin, Laurence. *Drama in the Sixties: Form and Interpretation*. London: Faber, 1966.

Kronenberger, Louis, ed. [1]. *Best Plays of 1954–1955*. New York: Dodd, Mead, 1955.

———, ed. [2]. *Best Plays of 1956–1957*. New York: Dodd, Mead, 1957.

Lambert, J. W. [1]. Review of *The Potting Shed*. *Drama: The Quarterly Theatre Review* (Summer 1958): 18–19.

———. [2]. "Wages of Sin." *The Sunday Times* (19 Apr. 1953): 9.

Review of *The Living Room*. Times (17 Apr. 1953): 2.

Lumley, Frederick. *New Trends in 20th Century Drama: A Survey since Ibsen and Shaw*. New York: Oxford University Press, 1972.

Mannes, Marya. Review of *The Complaisant Lover*. *Reporter* (7 Dec. 1961): 62.

Marowitz, Charles, Tom Milne, and Owen Hale, eds. *New Theatre Voices of the Fifties and Sixties*. London: Eyre Methuen, 1981.

Marowitz, Charles, and Simon Trussler, eds. *Theatre at Work*. London: Methuen, 1967.

Matlaw, Myron. *Modern World Drama*. New York: Dutton, 1972.

McCarten, John. Review of *The Complaisant Lover*. *New Yorker* (11 Nov. 1961): 117–18.

McClain, John. [1]. "A Fine Play for 2 Acts—But 3d Lags." *New York Journal American* (30 Jan. 1957): 20.

————. [2]. "Graham Greene Play Has Middling Merit." *New York Journal American* (2 Nov. 1961).

————. [3]. "Problem Play Stirs Debate." *New York Journal American* (18 Nov. 1954): 22.

Mockler, Anthony. *Graham Greene: Three Lives.* Angus, Scotland: Hunter Mackay, 1994.

"Mr. Greene Promises No More Miracles." *Life* (1 Apr. 1957): 68.

Nadel, Norman. " 'Lover' Opens at Barrymore." *New York World-Telegram and Sun* (2 Nov. 1961).

Nightingale, Benedict. "Through the Slips." *New Statesman* (12 Dec. 1975): 764.

Panter-Downes, Mollie. "Letter from London: 'The Return of A. J. Raffles.' " *New Yorker* (26 Jan. 1976): 100–101.

Peereboom, John J. "Playing with Words: The London Drama Scene." *Dutch Quarterly Review* 6:4 (1976): 331.

Phillips, Gene D. *Graham Greene: The Films of His Fiction.* New York: Teachers College Press, Teachers College, Columbia University, 1974.

Popkin, Henry. Introduction. In *Modern British Drama,* ed. Henry Popkin, 7–25. New York: Grove Press, 1964. First paperbound edition, 1969. Originally published as *The New British Drama,* 1964.

Review of *The Potting Shed. Theatre Arts* (Apr. 1957): 15.

Pritchett, V. S. "Take Away Sin." *New Statesman* (27 June 1959): 886, 888.

Raynor, Henry. "Graham Greene." In *Contemporary Dramatists,* ed. D. L. Kirkpatrick, 4th ed., 211–14. Chicago: St. James Press, 1988.

Rewak, William J. "The Potting Shed: Maturation of Graham Greene's Vision." *Catholic World* (Dec. 1957): 210–13.

Rusinko, Susan. *British Drama, 1950 to the Present: A Critical History.* Boston: Twayne Publishers, 1989.

Rutherford, Malcolm. "God Only Knows." *Spectator* (25 Sept. 1964): 402.

"See-Saw of Pride and Contrition." *The Times* (18 Sept. 1964): 15.

Sharrock, Roger. "Unhappy Families: The Plays of Graham Greene." In *Graham Greene: A Revaluation,* ed. Jeffrey Meyers, 68–92. New York: St. Martin's Press, 1990.

Shelden, Michael. *Graham Greene: The Man Within.* London: Heinemann, 1994.

Sherry, Norman. *The Life of Graham Greene.* Vols. 1 and 2. London: Jonathan Cape, 1989–94.

Stephens, Frances, ed. [1]. *Theatre World Annual,* no. 4. London: Rockliff, 1953.

————, ed. [2]. *Theatre World Annual,* no. 9. London: Rockliff, 1958.

————, ed. [3]. *Theatre World Annual,* no. 11. London: Barrie & Rockliff, 1960.

Taubman, Howard. "Theatre: Comedy about a Triangle." *New York Times* (2 Nov. 1961): 43.

Taylor, John Russell. [1]. *Anger and After: A Guide to the New British Drama.* London: Eyre Methuen, 1978.

————. [2]. *The Angry Theatre: New British Drama.* Revised and expanded ed. New York: Hill & Wang, 1969.

————. [3]. "Dramatists and Plays since 1880." In *1880 to the Present Day,* ed. Hugh Hunt, Kenneth Richards, and John Russell Taylor. Vol. 7 of *The Revels History of Drama in English.* London: Methuen, 1978.

————. [4]. *The Rise and Fall of the Well-made Play.* New York: Hill & Wang, 1967.

Thompson, John. "This Play Brings Greatness to the Theatre." *Daily Express* (19 June
    1959): 11.
Trewin, J. C. [1]. *Dramatists of Today*. London: Staples Press, 1953.
———. [2]. "In Retrospect: 'The Complaisant Lover.' " *Illustrated London News* (15
    Aug. 1959): 32.
———. [3]. "Miracle Play." *Illustrated London News* (22 Feb. 1958): 314.
———. [4]. "Places of Play." *Illustrated London News* (3 Oct. 1964): 520.
———. [5]. "A Sense of Sin." *Illustrated London News* (2 May 1953): 704.
Trussler, Simon. *The Cambridge Illustrated History of British Theatre*. London: Cam-
    bridge University Press, 1994.
Turnell, Martin. *Graham Greene*. Grand Rapids, MI: Eerdmans, 1967.
Tynan, Kenneth. [1]. "The Season in London." In *Best Plays of 1952–1953*, ed. Louis
    Kronenberger, 34–35. New York: Dodd, Mead, 1953.
———. [2]. *Tynan on Theatre*. Harmondsworth: Penguin, 1964.
———. [3]. *A View of the English Stage, 1944–1963*. London: Davis-Poynter, 1975.
Walling, Gerald C. *Graham Greene: A Study of Four Dramas*. New York: Peter Lang,
    1991.
Watts, Richard, Jr. [1]. "Graham Greene's Absorbing Drama." *New York Post* (30 Jan.
    1957): 64.
———. [2]. "Graham Greene's Horror Drama." *New York Post* (18 Nov. 1954).
———. [3]. "Mr. Greene Looks at a Triangle." *New York Post* (2 Nov. 1961).
Weales, Gerald. *Religion in Modern English Drama*. Philadelphia: University of Penn-
    sylvania Press, 1961.
Wilson, Cecil. "Still Tears As Greene Turns to Comedy." *Daily Mail* (19 June 1959):
    3.
Worsley, T. C. [1]. "The Drama of Defeat." *New Statesman and Nation* (25 Apr. 1953):
    483–84.
———. [2]. "The English-Theater-at-Its-Best." *New Statesman* (15 Feb. 1958): 196.
Worth, Katharine. *Revolutions in Modern English Drama*. London: Bell, 1973.

BIBLIOGRAPHIES

Brennan, Neil, and Alan Redway. *A Bibliography of Graham Greene*. New York: Oxford
    University Press, forthcoming.
Cassis, A. F. *Graham Greene: An Annotated Bibliography of Criticism*. Metuchen, NJ:
    Scarecrow Press, 1981.
Miller, Robert H. *Graham Greene: A Descriptive Catalog*. Lexington: University Press
    of Kentucky, 1978.
Vann, J. D. *Graham Greene: A Checklist of Criticism*. Kent, OH: Kent State University
    Press, 1970.
Wobbe, R. A. *Graham Greene: A Bibliography and Guide to Research*. New York:
    Garland, 1979.

Cicely Hamilton

(1872–1952)

SUE THOMAS

Born Cicely Mary Hammill in London on 15 June 1872, Hamilton, who changed her name when she became an actress around 1892, was the first child of Denzil and Maude Hammill. The early loss of her mother and her father's peripatetic military and diplomatic employment and untimely death in 1891 disrupted family life. Hamilton was educated in boarding schools in Malvern and Bad Homburg. She worked as a pupil-teacher and translator before gaining employment in provincial fit-up theater and Edmund Tearle's touring company, supplementing her income by hack writing. Around 1903, feeling herself to be in a professional rut, she moved to London, keen to write for the stage. Her first success was *Diana of Dobson's* (1908).

Her political outlook at this time was actively feminist, tinged with socialist sympathies. She helped found the Actresses' Franchise League, the Women Writers' Suffrage League, and the Women's Tax Resistance League and was a founding member of the editorial board of *The Englishwoman.* She distinguished herself as a satirist. *How the Vote Was Won* (coauthored by Christopher St. John) and *A Pageant of Great Women* were very popular suffrage plays. She performed in Play Actors' and Pioneer Players' productions and for nearly two years played Mrs. Knox in Bernard Shaw's *Fanny's First Play,* her most acclaimed role. Her *Just to Get Married* (1910) was modestly successful.

From November 1914 to May 1917 she was a clerk at the Scottish Women's Hospital Unit at Royaumont, frequently organizing entertainments. She then joined Lena Ashwell's Concerts at the Front company at Abbeville. There she developed a repertory company (with Gertrude Jennings). She worked with Concerts at the Front around Winchester in 1918–19 and in Amiens and the occupied Rhineland in 1919.

After 1919 Hamilton earned her principal income as a free-lance journalist, contributing mainly to the independent *Time and Tide,* and from travel writing. She continued her feminist activism, working for the Six Point Group, the Open Door Council, and, on the issue of birth control, the New Generation League. Her political principles were libertarian liberal, marked by an abhorrence of the collective mind and irresponsible democracy; her leanings were Conservative and consistently antipacifist without being militaristic.

Her only moderately successful post–World War I play was *The Human Factor* (*The Old Adam*). She continued her association with the theater as an occasional producer; *Time and Tide* drama critic (1925–26); popular historian with Lilian Baylis of the Old Vic; a memorializer of the work of women in theater through obituaries, book reviews, and a series of annual digests (in the *Woman's Leader* covering 1925–30); a reader of play scripts for the Society of Authors and a member of its drama committee; and an occasional lobbyist.

She died in London on 6 December 1952. Aside from her plays, she had authored under her own name twenty-four books, including six novels, three of them—*Diana of Dobson's, Just to Get Married,* and *A Matter of Money*—novelizations of plays. Her play *Phyl* had been fictionalized as a serial in the *Common Cause,* 21 November 1913–6 February 1914. She is best known today as the author of the feminist tract *Marriage as a Trade* (1909).

Hamilton's many emotionally sustaining friendships with women, some of whom were probably lesbians, have been cited by Whitelaw to place her within a lesbian continuum. There is no evidence of a sexually expressed lesbianism on Hamilton's part. Women provided her key career breaks in theater and journalism and were prominently associated with her involvements in experimental theater. Hamilton vigorously celebrated and defended spinsterhood. In ''The Sins We Do Not Speak Of: An Attempt to Consider an Ugly Subject Dispassionately,'' *Time and Tide* (1928): 1035 (not mentioned by Whitelaw), Hamilton categorized lesbianism with ''lusts of the flesh'' and indecent ''excesses.'' A deeply religious woman, she described lesbianism and homosexuality as a ''doubly accursed'' state and anticipated the amelioration of social condemnation only.

Selected Biographical Sources: Hamilton, *Life Errant* and uncollected journalism; Whitelaw.

MAJOR PLAYS, PREMIERES, AND SIGNIFICANT REVIVALS: THEATRICAL RECEPTION

Diana of Dobson's. 1908. Opened 12 February at the Kingsway Theatre (London) for 143 performances. Managed by Lena Ashwell and produced by Norman McKinnel. Kingsway Theatre, opening 11 January 1909, for 32 performances. Produced by Norman McKinnel. Produced by Charles Frohman at the Savoy Theatre (New York) 5 September 1908.

This play, which offered realistic representations of the living-in system for shopworkers and homelessness, and sharp observations of the economic and social relations of the lower and upper classes and the economic basis of marriage, was widely and, for the most part, enthusiastically reviewed. The *Illustrated London News* reviewer (Review of *Diana of Dobson's*) congratulated Hamilton on her handling of "very serious issues in a cheerful comedy manner; it gives us the realistic qualities of the problem-drama while avoiding alike propagandism and pessimism." The first act, set in a worker's dormitory, and the confrontation between heroine and hero at the end of the third act earned high praise: "Distinctly amusing . . . fresh and diverting" (Review of *Diana of Dobson's, The Times*). The *Athenaeum* reviewer (Review of *Diana of Dobson's*) was impressed by Hamilton's individuation of the working women. Reviewers for *Reynolds News*, the *Pall Mall Gazette*, the *Illustrated Sporting and Dramatic News*, and *Stage* (all entitled Review of *Diana of Dobson's*) expressed reservations about the plausibility of her characterization of Captain Bretherton. The play failed in New York and was promptly withdrawn. Reviewers found the material stale (see Review of *Diana of Dobson's, New York Dramatic News* and *New York Times*) and suggested that Carlotta Nillson was miscast as Diana (see Review of *Diana of Dobson's Theatre* and *New York Dramatic News*). "Four acts of lamentation and improbability," wrote Woolf.

How the Vote Was Won. 1909. (with Christopher St. John, one act). First matinee performance at the Royalty Theatre, 13 April. Edith Craig took it on a provincial tour of suffrage societies for the Actresses' Franchise League in late 1909–10, and it was one of the staple plays of the Pioneer Players. First performed in the United States at Maxine Elliott's Theatre as part of a Votes for Women matinee on 31 March 1910, it was also extraordinarily popular in North America before World War I (see Hale, Kayssar, and La Follette).

This fantasy of mass conversion of recalcitrant men to the suffrage cause, a variant of *Lysistrata* based on a satirical essay of Hamilton's published in the *Woman's Franchise,* no. 20 (14 November 1907), and as a pamphlet, was described by the *Era* reviewer (Review of *How the Vote Was Won*) as "extremely amusing." The reviewer for the *Pall Mall Gazette* (Review of *How the Vote Was Won*) commented: "The fact that it is so acutely controversial is not at all against it—is in fact, a virtue rather than a defect, for the Theatre of Ideas is upon us. All that really matters is that it is clever and witty."

A Pageant of Great Women. 1909. (one act). Opened at the Scala Theatre (London) for one matinee performance in a women's suffrage program on 12 November. Produced by Edith Craig. It, too, was taken on Craig's 1909–10 tour for the Actresses' Franchise League. Craig eventually organized it on a free-lance basis and included it among the staple plays of the Pioneer Players.

In this realization of a cartoon by W. H. Margetson developed in collaboration with Edith Craig, a roll-call of famous women is used to defeat the arguments of Prejudice against Woman before Justice. Reviewers for the *Era* and *Stage* (both entitled Review of *The Homecoming* and *A Pageant of Great Women*) found the Scala Theatre program propagandist, but *The Times* review (Review of *A Pageant of Great Women*) commented on its "real and sustained interest" and the "intense earnestness and absolute good taste" with which suffragist ideals were presented.

Just to Get Married. 1910. Opened on 8 November at the Little Theatre (London), running for 31 performances. Produced by Cavendish Morton and directed by Gertrude Kingston. Revived for 30 performances at the Little Theatre, commencing 17 January 1911. Directed by Gertrude Kingston. New York Playhouse Company at Maxine Elliott's Theatre (New York), 1912, 24 performances.

Reviewers generally recognized the continuity between Hamilton's arguments in *Marriage as a Trade* and the dilemma of the uneducated and untrained Georgiana Vicary, brought up in dependent gentility. "But patrons are not bored by a stage sermon," wrote the *Athenaeum* reviewer (Review of *Just to Get Married*), who was disappointed only by the "fairy tale" conclusion. *The Times* review (Review of *Just to Get Married*) offered mixed praise and condemnation: "The first two acts were so good, so shrewd in observation of personal details, so true in their picture of the well-to-do family, so deadly in their indictment of the system, so adroit in their mixture of witty comedy with dead earnest tragedy—for it was indeed almost that—that a feeble third act could not destroy their merit." Strachey defended the last act by arguing that it accorded with the comic genre. P. J. acknowledged that Hamilton was trying "to get away from the ordinary stage types." The reviews of *Just to Get Married* from the North American tour that preceded the New York run praised highly both Hamilton's craft and Grace George and Lyn Harding in the leading roles. The New York reviews were more mixed. The reviewer for the *New York Morning Telegraph* (Review of *Just to Get Married*) described the play as "very English," a mixture of "insipidity, incoherence, platitude and spasmodic sentimentality." The *New York Times* reviewer (Review of *Just to Get Married*) found it "very slight." Dale thought it "so gracefully written and so delicately acted that nobody can afford to overlook it." Hamilton's "humor is direct and frank, her knowledge of certain phases of life considerable, and she has a wholesome capacity for telling obvious truths pointedly, and for denoting character with consistency and vigor, if not much invention or subtlety. Her present work is a tract rather than a drama—except for one very excellent scene," wrote the *New York Evening Post* reviewer (Review of *Just to Get Married*).

The Human Factor. 1924. Opened at the Repertory Theatre (Birmingham) on 8 November; produced and directed by Barry V. Jackson as *The Old Adam* at the Kingsway Theatre (London) from 17 November 1925 to 16 January 1926 (67 performances).

"It is odd," wrote the reviewer in the *Illustrated London News* (Review of *The Old Adam*), "that it should be from a woman that we obtain one of the most thoughtful plays we have had of late about war, and one the least pacifist in its moral." R. J. described it as "Erewhonian satire, based on a debatable thesis about the innate and eternal combativity of the human race." Hamilton's witty satirical style was compared (favorably) with Bernard Shaw's by Omicron and A.H.W. [2]. Reviewers delighted particularly in the humorous characterizations of the fisherman admiral and the cabinet members. The mingling of comedy and pathos in the final act drew mixed responses. For instance, R. J. saw how the mingling was essential to her point; *The Times* reviewer (Review of *The Human Factor*) of the original production felt that it prevented a "very bright play indeed" being "a very distinguished piece of work"; Doubleday found it "poignant"; H. H. "so effective." A.H.W. [2] criticized Hamilton's characterizations of women, finding the female doctor "an almost exact replica of the gaunt 'unsexed' creatures of the second-rate caricaturist in the early days of the suffrage movement." "The author of this play," she wrote, "knows well how to amuse without this sort of thing."

ADDITIONAL PLAYS, ADAPTATIONS, AND PRODUCTIONS

Hamilton also wrote eight one-act plays, a two-scene play, three full-length plays for adults, two full-length plays for children, a Nativity play, and three adaptations and devised an antisuffrage waxworks. Hamilton's short plays are *The Traveller Returns,* produced in London as *The Sixth Commandment* (1906); *The Sergeant of Hussars* (1907), produced as *The Captain of Hussars* in the United States in 1908 (see "Miss Lena Ashwell Interviewed"); *Mrs. Vance* (1907); *The Pot and the Kettle,* coauthored by Christopher St. John (1909); *The Homecoming* (1910), revived as *After Twenty Years* (1914); the two-scene *Jack and Jill and a Friend* (1911), revived as *Jack and Jill* (1912); *The Constant Husband* (1912); *The Lady-Killer* (1914); and *Mrs. Armstrong's Admirer,* first performed at Abbeville and revived in London (1920). The most successful of these was *The Sergeant of Hussars,* which ran for 59 performances as curtain raiser for Charles Reade's *The Lyons Mail* at the Shaftesbury Theatre (1908–9). An antisuffrage waxworks (described as "a brilliant success") was taken on Edith Craig's 1909–10 tour for the Actresses' Franchise League, and as *The Waxworks* became part of the Pioneer Players repertoire. A description of the play, now lost, is given in "Dramatic Propaganda."

The Cutting of the Knot (1911), revived as *A Matter of Money* (1913); *Phyl* (1913, revived 1918); and *The Brave and the Fair* (1920) had brief and undistinguished runs. Hamilton's adaptation of Edgar Jepson's story *Lady Noggs* (1913) had 50 performances at the Comedy Theatre; her adaptation and co-production of Carl Zuckmayer's *Katherina Knie* as *Caravan* (1932) was disastrous, closing after 5 performances. Her adaptation with Elizabeth Robins of Robins's novel *"Where Are You Going To . . . ?"* was refused a license in 1914. *The Child in Flanders,* a Nativity play originally performed at Abbeville (1917), was revived annually by the Lena Ashwell Players "for some years," notably in London in 1919, 1921, and 1925. A recent first production of *The Beggar Prince,* a full-length play for children, was mentioned in "Personalities and Powers: Cicely Hamilton." Whitelaw (83–84) mentioned a 1926 production and performances on an Old Vic tour during the 1940s. Trewin noted a run at the Embassy Theatre, opening on 26 December 1929; A.H.W. [1] gave the title of this production as *The Fairy Prince* and mentioned an earlier run at the Kingsway Theatre. Hamilton herself produced the 1929 revival. Her other children's play is *Mr Pompous and the Pussy-Cat.* No performance details are known.

ASSESSMENT OF HAMILTON'S CAREER

Cicely Hamilton's plays and playwriting career have been occluded in conventional theatrical histories. In part the occlusion was produced by the demise or redirection after the outbreak of World War I of the feminist theaters and companies for which she wrote between 1907 and 1914, her productivity as a writer of one-act plays, and her failure to attract and cultivate an adult comic audience after World War I. She also achieved greatest popularity in provincial theater—*Diana of Dobson's,* the copyright on which she had sold for one hundred pounds, was toured continuously for twenty years—and in a women's suffrage theater poised on the threshold of an amateur/professional divide. During the late 1910s and early 1920s she felt a need to write about war. Drama and literature on this subject became readily marketable only after 1928 with the successes of R. C. Sherriff's *Journey's End* and Robert Graves's *Goodbye to All That,* but they were successes that validated combatant masculine experience. Valuable bibliographical detail of Hamilton's plays in performance has been provided by Nicoll, Holledge, Trewin, Whitelaw, and Wearing's general bibliographies of the London stage from 1900 to 1939 and scholars working on Edith Craig's Pioneer Players (Cockin, Dymkowski). Hamilton's postwar work in children's theater is very poorly documented.

Nicoll's appraisal of Hamilton was formulated in terms of a dubious dichotomy between minority and feminized popular elements. Inventiveness and originality were judged to lie in the minority elements—the realistic scenes in the shop assistants' dormitory and on the Embankment in *Diana of Dobson's,* the science-fiction scenario of *The Old Adam*—and not very great dramatic talent in the conservative artifice of the "sentimentally novelette material" of romance. In her own day Hamilton's shift in *The Old Adam* to the worlds of government, science, and the military, conventionally coded as masculine, was rewarded in *The Times* (reviewed as *The Human Factor*) by the dropping of the epithet "little," consistently used in earlier reviews in summations of praise. Trewin's discussion of Hamilton is more extended than Nicoll's, but his critical judgments recirculated Nicoll's dichotomy. So, too, did Blodgett's in her analyses of *Diana of Dobson's* and *Just to Get Married,* although she used slightly different terminology. For her, Hamilton's admirably realistic representations of the material conditions of women's work and marriage were "compromised" by romantic entanglements and endings. Implicitly and anachronistically Blodgett demanded of the plays positive role models for 1990s western middle-class feminists.

Hamilton's heroines, Diana Massingberd and Georgiana Vicary, were deemed inauthentic in their renunciations of autonomy for love.

The critical denigration of Hamilton's strategic deployment of romance plots has, in Clark's formulation in a different context, "covered over the transgressive content of the sentimental, its connection to a sexual body, and its connection to the representations of consciousness." Hamilton's representations of gender in romance scenarios do not simply "acquire meaning by reinforcing the values of [heterosexual] love and marriage, of emotional vulnerability and domesticity, and by making them appear natural, inevitable, and desirable as culturally legible signs of 'femininity' " (Cohan and Shires). Her use of romance as a generic layer in her prewar plays facilitates sharp, frequently witty critiques of the economic positionings of working and dependent women within early twentieth-century capitalistic and educational practices, the social and economic coercion of women into barter of sex and motherhood for an often relatively amenable livelihood within the institutions of marriage and the mistress, and the highly ambiguous moral positionings of women as a product of their economic vulnerability and, in *Mrs Vance* and *The Constant Husband,* of the qualities middle-class men find desirable in a wife. Hamilton is more interested in culturally materialist than psychological semiotics, although she works to connect the two. A prime instance is her characterization of Phyllis Chester in *Phyl.* Phyl, a struggling governess by trade, angered by class condescension and depressed by her social isolation, longs for the hedonism of an upper-middle-class lifestyle, motivated in large part by intense feelings of matrophobia for the sister who raised her, who has become angelically resigned to poverty and drudgery.

Hamilton's representations of female sexual desire are fairly coy—left, for instance, as a subtext in the relationship between Diana Massingberd and Captain Bretherton, realized in the color in the cheeks and joy of life of Phyl after she has become Jack Folliott's mistress and in the pathetic fallacy of the storm that drenches and muddies Georgiana Vicary. Phyl is represented reveling in the costumes Folliott buys for her, staging her class transformation for his connoisseur's sexual gaze, playing to the sexualized rescue fantasies of both of them. The stage image of the dirty and bedraggled Georgiana proposing to Adam Lankester soon after having jilted him on the eve of their wedding implies an authorial attitude to the moral justice of their marriage. The image is complex, also suggesting that Adam accepts her for herself and not for the upper-class finery in which her aunt has invested to produce Georgiana as a marriageable sexual object.

In Hamilton's *Time and Tide* theater reviews she demonstrated a keen sense of the generic conventions within which authors and cast were working, reworkings of mythic romances in representations of sexual relationships, and the uses to which stage types were put. The mobilized conventions, myths, and types were seen to provide intelligibility, a catering to public taste in a necessarily commercial theater, and scope for the dramatist to exploit and challenge the audience's comfortable familiarity with aspects of the theatrical material.

The tactical use of renovated stage types and generic plots and motifs drawn from drama and literature to develop feminist themes is central to the effects and achievements of many of Hamilton's own plays. It is an integral part of her effort to use her freedom to express the "sincerity" she felt necessary to overcome the "flat" technique and "stunted ideas" that had historically diminished the artistic achievements of women ("Our Work"). Stowell's [1, 2, 3] detailed studies of the generic layers and types of Hamilton's early plays are impressively informed by comparisons with other contemporary British dramatic treatments of similar themes or material. Her readings, though, pay scant attention to sexually desiring female subjectivity and overlook the narrative implications of Hamilton's use of a Jewish male stereotype in exploitative entrepreneur Sir Jabez Grinley (*Diana of Dobson's*) and a colonial stereotype in Adam Lankester.

In comic drama, prose satire, and fiction Hamilton was an effective social commentator through future fantasy. In this genre she worked in particular to develop propositions about collective psychology, some of them contestable empirically and as being structured by stereotypes. In *The Old Adam* she used what Leed (41) in *No Man's Land* would later term "community of August" feelings of war excitement as evidence of a human combative instinct expressed in the "energy, furious energy" (41) of enlistment, support for the war effort, the professional woman battling patriarchal bureaucracy, and pacifist campaigning. The thesis produced dramaturgical difficulties in the last act. Hamilton had to compress in a very brief time frame what she interpreted as two historical cycles represented in much "community of August" sentiment and in one character a recognizably late or postwar despair, part of a reaction of grief for a son killed in the war. After World War I Hamilton began to theorize history as comprising cycles of a sometimes questionably "progressive" action and reaction.

Scholarly assessment of Hamilton as a dramatist is still hampered by the lack of a thorough bibliography of her creative output and journalism, which would enable a more complete historical contextualization of the ideas informing her plays, and the want of wide-ranging studies of competing narrativizations of courtship, adultery, and female desire between 1905 and 1925, which might give a fuller sense of the cultural work performed by her full-length plays in their day. Single plays have been reprinted in recent anthologies, but there is no collected edition of her plays that might give contemporary scholars a better sense of her dramatic range. It is highly unlikely that Hamilton's plays could recapture a general theatrical audience: they are, perhaps, too well grounded in the culturally material specificities of the gender relations of their time and place, too topical in their comic and occasionally melodramatic effects.

ARCHIVAL SOURCES

Copies of Hamilton's unpublished plays—with the exception of *The Cutting of the Knot (A Matter of Money)*—and her adaptation with Elizabeth Robins of Robins's "*Where Are You Going To . . . ?*" are held among the Lord Chamberlain's Plays, British Library. Opinions on the unlicensed adaptation are in the Lord Chamberlain's Plays Correspondence Files, 1900–1968. The few manuscript materials held in the United Kingdom are listed in the *Location Register of Twentieth-Century English Literary Manuscripts and Letters.* Some letters from Hamilton are held in the Harry Ransom Research Center, University of Texas at Austin, and the Elizabeth Robins Papers, Fales Library, New York University. The Robins Papers also contain correspondence about the adaptation of *"Where Are You Going To...?"* Reviews of the New York Playhouse Company tour and the New York production of *Just to Get Married* are collected in the 1911 Grace George scrapbook, Billy Rose Theatre Collection, New York Public Library. This collection also holds the promptbook for Charles Frohman's production of *Diana of Dobson's,* U.S. reviews of *Diana of Dobson's,* and, in the Robinson Locke Collection, an envelope of newspaper clippings about Hamilton.

PRIMARY BIBLIOGRAPHY

Plays

The Beggar Prince. In *The Beggar Prince and Four Other Modern Plays,* by Cicely Hamilton, K. Ranee Corlett, Allan Ogilvie, Stuart Ready, and Frederick Williams. Glasgow: Collins, 1936. Published separately, London: C. H. Fox, [1944].

The Child in Flanders. London, Samuel French, 1922. Reprinted in *One-Act Plays of To-day,* 2nd series, ed. J. W. Marriott. London: Harrap, 1924; *Fifty One-Act Plays,* ed. C. M. Martin. London: Victor Gollancz, 1934.

Diana of Dobson's. London: Samuel French, 1925. Reprinted in *New Woman Plays,* ed. Linda Fitzsimmons and Viv Gardner. London: Methuen, 1991.

How the Vote Was Won, a Play in One Act. With Christopher St. John. Chicago: Dramatic Publishing Co., [1910]; London: Edith Craig, 1913. Reprinted in *A Century of Plays by American Women,* ed. Rachel France. New York: Richards Rosen, 1979; *How the Vote Was Won and Other Suffragette Plays,* ed. Dale Spender and Carole Hayman. London: Methuen, 1985; *Anthology of British Women Writers,* ed. Dale Spender and Janet Todd. London: Pandora, 1989.

Jack and Jill and a Friend. London: Samuel French, 1911; New York: Samuel French, 1914. Reprinted in *Fifty More Contemporary One-Act Plays,* ed. Frank Shay. New York: D. Appleton & Co., 1928.

Just to Get Married: A Comedy in Three Acts. London and New York: Samuel French, 1914.

Mr Pompous and the Pussy-Cat, a Play for Children in Three Acts. London: Samuel French, [1948].

Mrs Vance. Englishwoman 1 (1909): 62–71.

The Old Adam: A Fantastic Comedy. Oxford: Basil Blackwell, 1926; New York: Brentano's, 1927.

A Pageant of Great Women. [London]: Suffrage Shop, 1910; London: M. Lawson for

the Suffragette Fellowship, 1948. Reprinted in *Sketches from the Actresses' Franchise League,* ed. Viv Gardner. Nottingham: Nottingham Drama Texts, 1985.
The Pot and the Kettle. With Christopher St. John. London: E. Craig, n.d.

Autobiography

Life Errant. London: J. M. Dent, 1935.

SECONDARY BIBLIOGRAPHY

Ashwell, Lena. *Myself a Player.* London: Michael Joseph, 1936.
Blodgett, Harriet. "Cicely Hamilton, Independent Feminist." *Frontiers* 11.1–2 (1990): 99–104.
Clark, Suzanne. *Sentimental Modernism: Women Writers and the Revolution of the Word.* Bloomington: Indiana University Press, 1991.
Cockin, Katharine. "New Light on Edith Craig." *Theatre Notebook* 45.3 (1991): 132–43.
Cohan, Steven, and Linda M. Shires. *Telling Stories: A Theoretical Analysis of Narrative Fiction.* London: Routledge, 1988.
Dale, Alan. Review of *Just to Get Married. New York American* (2 Jan. 1912).
Review of *Diana of Dobson's. Athenaeum* (22 Feb. 1908): 236.
Review of *Diana of Dobson's. Illustrated London News* (22 Feb. 1908): 266.
Review of *Diana of Dobson's. Illustrated Sporting and Dramatic News* (7 Mar. 1908): 19.
Review of *Diana of Dobson's. New York Dramatic News* (19 Sept. 1908).
Review of *Diana of Dobson's. New York Times* (6 Sept. 1908): 2:7.
Review of *Diana of Dobson's. Pall Mall Gazette* (13 Feb. 1908): 4.
Review of *Diana of Dobson's. Reynolds News* (16 Feb. 1908): 4.
Review of *Diana of Dobson's. Stage* (13 Feb. 1908): 23.
Review of *Diana of Dobson's. Theatre* (Oct. 1908): xxi.
Review of *Diana of Dobson's. The Times* (13 Feb. 1908): 10.
Doubleday, Anne. Review of *The Human Factor. Time and Tide* (21 Nov. 1924): 1141–42.
"Dramatic Propaganda." *Common Cause* (11 Nov. 1909): 404.
Dymkowski, Christine. "Entertaining Ideas: Edy Craig and the Pioneer Players." in *The New Woman and Her Sisters: Feminism and Theatre, 1850–1914,* ed. Viv Gardner and Susan Rutherford. Hemel Hempstead: Harvester Wheatsheaf, 1992.
H., H. Review of *The Old Adam. Observer* (22 Nov. 1925): 11.
Hale, Beatrice Forbes-Robertson. "The Drama and Suffrage." *Woman Voter* 5.2 (Feb. 1914): 7–8.
Holledge, Julie. *Innocent Flowers: Women in the Edwardian Theatre.* London: Virago, 1981.
Review of *The Homecoming* and *A Pageant of Great Women. Era* (26 Nov. 1910): 21.
Review of *The Homecoming* and *A Pageant of Great Women. Stage* (24 Nov. 1910): 18.
Review of *How the Vote Was Won. Era* (15 May 1909): 14.
Review of *How the Vote Was Won. Pall Mall Gazette* (15 Apr. 1909).

Review of *The Human Factor.* (produced later as *The Old Adam*). *The Times* (10 Nov. 1924): 10.

J., P. "The Little Theatre." *Saturday Review* (12 Nov. 1910): 607–8.

J., R. "War without Armaments." *Spectator* (5 Dec. 1925): 1019–20.

Review of *Just to Get Married. Athenaeum* (12 Nov. 1910): 601–2.

Review of *Just to Get Married. New York Evening Post* (2 Jan. 1912).

Review of *Just to Get Married. New York Morning Telegraph* (2 Jan. 1912).

Review of *Just to Get Married. New York Times* (2 Jan. 1912): 9.

Review of *Just to Get Married. The Times* (9 Nov. 1910): 12.

Kayssar, Helene. *Feminist Theatre: An Introduction to Plays of Contemporary British and American Women.* Basingstoke: Macmillan, 1986.

La Follette, Fola. "Suffragetting on the Chautauqua." *Ladies Home Journal* (Jan. 1916): 27, 51.

Leed, Eric J. *No Man's Land: Combat and Identity in World War I.* Cambridge: Cambridge University Press, 1979.

"Miss Edith Craig." *Vote* (12 Mar. 1910): 232–33.

"Miss Lena Ashwell Interviewed." *Pall Mall Gazette* (8 Feb. 1908): 1–2.

Nicoll, Allardyce. *English Drama, 1900–1930: The Beginnings of the Modern Period,* 366–67. Cambridge: Cambridge University Press, 1973.

Review of *The Old Adam. Illustrated London News* (28 Nov. 1925): 1104.

Omicron. Review of *The Old Adam. Nation and Athenaeum* (28 Nov. 1925): 321.

"Our Work." *Vote* (14 June 1910): 62.

Review of *A Pageant of Great Women. The Times* (13 Nov. 1909): 12.

"Personalities and Powers: Cicely Hamilton." *Time and Tide* (26 Jan. 1923): 83–84.

Stowell, Sheila. [1]. "Drama as a Trade: Cicely Hamilton's *Diana of Dobson's.*" In *The New Woman and Her Sisters: Feminism and Theatre, 1850–1914,* ed. Viv Gardner and Susan Rutherford. Hemel Hempstead: Harvester Wheatsheaf, 1992.

———. [2]. "Re[pre]senting Eroticism: The Tyranny of Fashion in Feminist Plays of the Edwardian Age." *Theatre History Studies* 11 (1991): 51–62.

———. [3]. *A Stage of Their Own: Feminist Playwrights of the Suffrage Era.* Ann Arbor: University of Michigan Press, 1992.

Strachey, Marjorie. Review of *Just to Get Married. Englishwoman* 8 (1910): 212–16.

Trewin, J. C. "Cicely Hamilton." In *Dictionary of Literary Biography,* vol. 10, *Modern British Dramatists, 1900–1945,* ed. Stanley Weintraub, pt. 1, 212–215. Detroit: Gale Research, 1982.

W., A. H. [1]. Review of *The Fairy Prince. Woman's Leader* (10 Jan. 1930): 386.

———. [2]. Review of *The Old Adam. Woman's Leader* (27 Nov. 1925): 348.

Wearing, J. P. *The London Stage, 1900–1909: A Calendar of Plays and Players.* Vol. 2. (1900–1909). Metuchen, NJ: Scarecrow Press, 1981.

Whitelaw, Lis. *The Life and Rebellious Times of Cicely Hamilton: Actress, Writer, Suffragist.* London: Women's Press, 1990.

Woolf, Rennold. "Diana of Dobson's Is A. H. Woodsy." *New York Daily Telegraph* (6 Sept. 1908).

BIBLIOGRAPHY

Thomas, Sue. "Cecily Hamilton on Theatre: A Preliminary Bibliography." *Theatre Notebook* 49 (1995): 99–107.

St. John Hankin
(1869–1909)

TED BAIN

Controversy was apparent when the three-volume edition of St. John Hankin's *Dramatic Works* was published in 1912, three years after he took his own life at the age of thirty-nine. Drinkwater's critical introduction opened with a two-page paragraph attempting to discount the relevance of Hankin's death and his unpopularity among many of his peers. Indeed, Hankin's life and his work seem to have served as a subversive response to the intolerance of Edwardian society.

St. John Emile Clavering Hankin was born in Southampton on 25 September 1869 to Charles Wright Hankin, the director of the King Edward VI Grammar School of Southampton, and Mary Louisa Perrot Hankin, who owned an independent fortune and from whom (according to Hankin's widow) he was presumed to have inherited much of his charm and ability. During Hankin's lifetime his father suffered a nervous breakdown and became an invalid. His mother died a month before his suicide.

Hankin matriculated at Malvern Public School, Worcester, in 1883, and at Merton College, Oxford, in 1886, where he studied classics. After Oxford he worked in London as a private tutor and as a journalist, contributing an undetermined number of unsigned articles to the *Saturday Review.*

In 1893 Hankin coauthored with Nora Vynne a one-act play, *Andrew Paterson.* In 1894 he joined the *Indian Daily News* in Calcutta and returned within the year to his parents' home in London after contracting malaria. From 1897 to 1899 he wrote about seventy drama reviews for *The Times,* and from 1898 to 1903 over one hundred short satiric pieces for *Punch,* some of which were reprinted in 1901 as *Mr. Punch's Dramatic Sequels.*

In 1901 Hankin married Florence Routledge, the daughter of the publisher George Routledge. Florence was ten years older than Hankin, and by all indications their childless marriage was a happy one. (None of Hankin's unpublished writings remain to suggest otherwise.) After the wedding Hankin devoted his time to writing plays and participated in the running of the Stage Society as "Hon.-Librarian" for the 1903–4 season and on the Council of Management from 1902 until his death.

Hankin's first full-length play, *The Two Mr. Wetherbys,* was performed in 1903 by the Stage Society, London. Several of his poetic parodies written for periodicals were republished in 1904 as *Lost Masterpieces and Other Verses.* He was chronically ill, however, and retired to Campden, Gloucestershire, in 1905.

His last years of declining health coincided with the first productions of his major plays. The Court Theatre (London) staged *The Return of the Prodigal* in 1905 and *The Charity That Began at Home* in 1906. The Stage Society (London) presented *The Cassilis Engagement* in 1907 and *The Last of the De Mullins* in 1908. Also in 1908 the performance of *The Burglar Who Failed* at the Criterion (London) was the first appearance of a Hankin play in a commercial theater.

Suffering from the progressive and debilitating symptoms of neurasthenia, Hankin made out his will late in 1908 and drowned himself at the baths at Llandrindod Wells, Wales, on 15 June 1909. Arguably, his final action signified a rational, dispassionate, and unsentimental alternative to invalidism and epitomized the intellectual resolve of his plays' most notable characters.

Selected Biographical Sources: Drinkwater; Evans; Moses; Phillips [2]; Woods.

MAJOR PLAYS, PREMIERES, AND SIGNIFICANT REVIVALS: THEATRICAL RECEPTION

The Two Mr. Wetherbys. 1903. Opened 15 March at the Imperial Theatre (London) for 2 performances. Produced by the Stage Society. Revivals: Madison-Square Theatre (New York), 23 August 1906; Scottish Repertory Theatre, Royalty Theatre (Glasgow), 2 November 1906; Melbourne Repertory Theatre, Turn Verein Hall, 26 June 1911; Birmingham Repertory Theatre, for 7 performances, 18 September 1915; Repertory Theatre (Liverpool), 1917–18 season; Little Theatre (Bristol), 9 March 1925.

Beerbohm [5] praised the 1903 Stage Society production as a "pure and delicate comedy" and ranked it the best, but least appreciated, of three recent London openings discussed in his *Saturday Review* critique. Chambers agreed that the play was pleasing enough to be a commercial production, but the *Athenaeum* ("The Week: At the Imperial") dismissed the play as "almost destitute of originality."

The Return of the Prodigal. 1905. Opened 22 September at the Court Theatre (London) for 6 performances; reopened 29 April 1907 at the Court for 13 performances. (Replaced by Elizabeth Robins's *Votes for Women!* after eleven days of a scheduled four-week run.) Other London productions: Miss Horniman's

Company, Coronet Theatre, 22 May 1912; Globe Theatre, 24 November 1948; Thorndike Theatre (Leatherhead), 23 January 1973.

Regional revivals: Miss Horniman's Company, Gaiety Theatre (Manchester), 11 May 1908; reopened 15 March 1909 and 19 September 1910 at the Gaiety; Pilgrim Players, Edgbaston Assembly Rooms, Birmingham, for 4 performances, 11 March, 30 September, and 7 October 1911, and 3 February 1912 (Matthews reported 5 performances); Scottish Repertory Theatre, Royalty Theatre (Glasgow), 16 October 1911; Repertory Theatre (Liverpool), 7 February 1912; Miss Horniman's Company, His Majesty's Theatre (Montreal), 29 February 1912; Miss Horniman's Company, Gaiety Theatre (Manchester), 3 March 1913; Birmingham Repertory Theatre, 13 September 1913 and 16 April 1914; Birmingham Repertory Company, West Pier Theatre (Brighton), 16 March 1915; Birmingham Repertory Company, Theatre Royal (Leamington Spa), 23 March 1915; Birmingham Repertory Theatre, 15 May 1915; Birmingham Repertory Theatre, 13 February 1920 and 3 February 1923; Birmingham Repertory Company, Prince's Theatre (Manchester), 8 June 1923; Little Theatre (Bristol), 7 April 1924. (The first five Birmingham Repertory Theatre revivals totaled 48 performances.)

The first Court Theatre performance was reviewed in the *Academy* ('' 'The Return of the Prodigal' at the Royal Court Theatre'') as amusing because of the good acting; in the *Athenaeum* (Review of *The Return of the Prodigal*) it was described as ''laboriously excogitated'' but suitable for ''the public taste.'' The *Sketch* (''The Stage from the Stalls'') objected to the unappealing cynicism of a play in which a ''cheery young man does mean things with an air which defies and paralyses the moral judgement.'' Beerbohm [4], however, argued that the play was not obligated to offer any moral solution to the social problems it depicted, though he did criticize the inconsistency of a subversive and strong-minded title character who admits a failed desire to be respectable and prosperous. Four years later, Beerbohm [3] described the play as Hankin's ''most gracefully and lackadaisically acute.''

After the 1948 Globe revival with John Gielgud, Trewin ([3], 63) noted that most of his colleagues reacted with the ''testiest annoyance'' and speculated that the play disappointed spectators because ''it has no part to tear a cat in.'' Recalling the same production, Tanitch explained, ''The major mistake was to let Cecil Beaton loose on his favourite period: the play couldn't be seen for the over-dressing, lost in all the theatrical plumage.''

The Charity That Began at Home. 1906. Opened 23 October at the Court Theatre (London) for 8 performances. Revivals: Miss Horniman's Company, Gaiety (Manchester), 9 November 1908 and 16 September 1912; Repertory Theatre (Liverpool), 24 February 1913; the Melbourne Repertory Company, the Playhouse, 26 August 1917; Birmingham Repertory Theatre, for a total of 37 performances, 30 January 1915, 25 March 1916, and 9 June 1917.

Baumann strongly condemned the play's 1906 performance at the Court as pretentious and absurd, but praised Ben Webster's performance as Verreker and Hankin's understanding of the "outward refinement and inward ruffianism" of the "rising generation." The *Academy* (" 'The Charity That Began at Home' at the Court Theatre") applauded the play's depiction of "real" people in "actual experience," but could not be excited by the play or its characters because of Hankin's "eclectic feebleness."

The Cassilis Engagement. 1907. Opened 10 February at the Imperial Theatre (London) for 2 performances. Produced by the Incorporated Stage Society. Other London productions: Merrie Andrews Dramatic Society amateur production, Court Theatre, 17 January 1913; Guildhall School of Music, 22 February 1956.

Regional revivals: Scottish Repertory Theatre, Royalty Theatre (Glasgow), 4 April 1910 and 30 January 1911; Liverpool Repertory Company, at the Gaiety Theatre (Manchester), 22 March 1911, and at the Liverpool Playhouse, 20 March 1911 and 15 April 1912; Liverpool Repertory Theatre, Liverpool Playhouse, 26 February 1915; Birmingham Repertory Theatre Company, for a total of 97 performances, 22 March 1913 and 24 January 1914; at the Grand Theatre (Wolverhampton), 23 February 1915; at the Grand Theatre (Croydon), 2 March 1915; at the West Pier Theatre (Brighton), 9 March 1915; at the Theatre Royal (Leamington Spa), 27 March 1915, 22 January 1916, 25 November 1916, and 15 September 1917; Birmingham Repertory Theatre, 25 October 1919; 1 October 1921, 18 August 1923, and 25 January 1926; Birmingham Jewish Arts Society, Alexandra Theatre (Birmingham), 18 December 1928; Birmingham Repertory Theatre, 8 March 1949.

Beerbohm [1] objected to the play's cruel depiction of snobbishness, to the Borridges' "perfect contentment" in vulgarity, and to their "ease" in an upper-class country house. He also criticized the heavy pacing of the 1907 Stage Society performance, an observation corroborated in the *Academy* review ("Mr. St. John Hankin's Comedy at the Stage Society"). The *Athenaeum* ("The Week") reviewed the play as "simple and primitive" and suggested that its action could be shortened to three acts.

Phillips ([2], 66) pointed out that the short-lived London production received "tepid reviews," but that after Hankin's death the play found great popularity in provincial repertory theaters. Goldie (48–49) recalled the 1911 Liverpool Repertory revival as a "brilliant comedy" in which Estelle Winwood as Ethel Borridge showed "great charm and promise." Trewin ([1], 24) described the play as "a kind of theatre mascot" for the Birmingham Repertory Theatre, where it was produced repeatedly and, according to its general manager Bache Matthews (149), was always "sure of a general welcome whenever it is revived."

The Burglar Who Failed. 1908. (one act). Opened 27 October at the Criterion Theatre (London) for 55 performances. Revivals: Birmingham Repertory Theatre, 18 February 1914 and 2 March 1918.

The Times review of the London opening ("Criterion Theatre") described the plot of a pitiful burglar who is subdued and lectured by a schoolgirl on how to make an honest living, and it conveyed Hankin's wish to attribute the idea to H. M. Harwood.

The Last of the De Mullins. 1908. Opened 6 December at the Haymarket Theatre (London) for 2 performances. Produced by the Incorporated Stage Society. Revivals: Miss Horniman's Company, Gaiety Theatre (Manchester), 18 August 1913; Birmingham Repertory Theatre, 2 March 1918.

Shaw wrote to Granville-Barker that Lillah McCarthy's 1908 performance as Janet De Mullin was amplified by other weak or miscast performances and "appealed with extraordinary gusto to every unmarried woman of twenty-eight to go straight out and procure a baby at once without the slightest regard to law or convention," which created a predictably alienating effect in the audience (quoted in Purdom, 142). Beerbohm [2] described Janet De Mullin as a tedious and jarring invention in a good cause and suggested that her preference for independence rather than familial duty, for motherhood rather than virginity, could have been more plausibly declared on her behalf by another (read: male) character. Agate (101) pointed out the realism of the play's depiction of moral authority as a privilege afforded by economic status.

The Constant Lover. 1912. (one act). Opened 30 January at the Royalty Theatre (London) for 14 performances. Other London productions: Everyman Theatre, 7 August 1922; Theatre Club (New Boltons), 28 March 1952; Hovenden Theatre Club, 19 February 1962.

Regional revivals: Birmingham Repertory Theatre, 14 June 1913 and 6 June 1914; Repertory Theatre (Liverpool), 16 November 1915; Little Theatre (Bristol), 31 March 1924; Birmingham Repertory Theatre, 6 September 1949; Liverpool Repertory Company, 25 November 1953; the Welsh Theatre Company, Grand Theatre (Swansea), 4 November 1969.

A 1913 *New Statesman* review ("St. John Hankin") of Hankin's published works identified *The Constant Lover* as the shortest, lightest, and most moving of his plays.

ADDITIONAL PLAYS, ADAPTATIONS, AND PRODUCTIONS

Andrew Paterson (written with Nora Vynne) was performed 22 June 1893 at the Bayswater Bijou Theatre (London), Victoria Hall. *The Three Daughters of M. Dupont* (translation of Eugène Brieux, *Les Trois Filles de M. Dupont*) was performed 25 March 1905 as a Stage Society (London) production. *Thompson* (completed by George Calderon) was performed 22 April 1913 at the New Royalty Theatre (London), and revived at the Birmingham Repertory Theatre, 17 February 1917. *The Times* review ("Thompson") of the 1913 opening praised the "nimble wit" of this "slender story."

ASSESSMENT OF HANKIN'S CAREER

"Infinitesimal" was how Hankin described his own chances of success in the London theater of his day. He cited the noncommercial nature of his work as the reason. The significant number of Hankin revivals in Manchester and Birmingham repertory theaters, however, suggests otherwise. Trewin's history of the Birmingham Repertory Theatre ([1], 58) referred to *The Cassilis Engagement* as that theater's "constant winner" and mentioned repeatedly Birmingham's continuing admiration for Hankin's comedy.

Why were Hankin's plays so much more popular in the regional theaters than in London? Perhaps his unflinching satiric portrayal of a high society turned against itself too closely implicated the more privileged audiences found in the country's largest and most influential city. The same plays may have held a stronger comic appeal for audiences of outsiders in the provinces.

Nonetheless, Hankin's lesser reputation as a writer for the London stage persists. Along with George Bernard Shaw, Harley Granville-Barker, and John Galsworthy, Hankin is known as one of the principal "new" authors produced during the Vedrenne-Barker management of the Court Theatre from 1904 to 1907. Of these four playwrights, Hankin's plays received the fewest performances, and their form of social criticism has since been the least regarded.

Hankin's relatively quiet appeal to London audiences is not surprising. Both of his Court Theatre plays, *The Return of the Prodigal* and *The Charity That Began at Home,* feature an intellectual dandy figure who performs as social critic, a brilliant, amusing, yet often-detested perfectionist who must ultimately recoil from the circumstances of life that fail to meet his standards. Many of Hankin's characters are less playful versions of the subversive dandies of Wilde's comedies, whose authority of manner is ironically derived from the social values they reject. Modeled after such detached observers as Wilde's Henry Wotton (*The Picture of Dorian Gray*) or Henry James's Gabriel Nash (*The Tragic Muse*), the principal Hankin figure assumes superiority through abstention. But unlike the characters of Wilde and James, who measure their lives by the rule of aesthetic pleasure, Hankin's characters suffer the practical consequences of Edwardian social standards favoring mediocrity and corruption over intelligence and integrity. Within the Hankin comedy, therefore, failure becomes an oppositional virtue.

Eustace Jackson of *The Return of the Prodigal* is one of the Edwardian theater's first intellectual dandy characters, an incorrigible but stylish failure who behaves with a languid and polished air of indolence. An unproductive family embarrassment who has been sent abroad in the vain hope that he will achieve financial independence, Eustace returns to extort from his father a living allowance in exchange for his cynical promise to "go away and live quietly."

To his affluent relatives, Eustace's lordly conduct is an unanswerable impertinence. Ironically, the status of his moralizing family is contingent on perpetuating the misfortunes of an exploited working class. Mirroring his upbringing,

Eustace is coldly polite, manipulative, and unscrupulous, but distinguishes himself by his perfect lack of hypocrisy. From the experience of suffering, he is inclined to prey on predators rather than on innocent victims. His own moral form of rebellion involves mimicry of the very values he despises.

The pessimism of the Hankin dandy figure is inherent in Eustace's compliance with the despicable conventions of his family's world. His cynical respect for the detestable, along with his renunciation of emotion as superfluous, aspires to the highest condition achievable in a world of philistine values. After years of hostile rebuke, Eustace is effectively immune to his indignant detractors, and his penetrating critical observations seem to flow effortlessly in direct response to censorious charges against him.

The Hankin dandy's pained sophistication also prevails in *The Charity That Began at Home,* a satire on the philanthropic idealism of a patrician widow and daughter whose country home serves as a haven for incompetent servants and house guests whom no one else will entertain. Among the guests is Hugh Verreker, an imperturbable cynic who recounts his past sufferings with such poised objectivity that he wins the affections of the naïve daughter of the house. An unforeseen betrothal is announced, other members of the household are outraged, and Verreker unselfishly withdraws from the match, to much relief. In his cool benevolence, Verreker reveals no sentimental remorse over his aborted romance. As a champion of values lost in the world around him, his expression of feeling is a studied display of what others should feel, not an indulgence in an irrational emotion.

Hankin's conception of the dandy's well-reasoned capacity for feeling is best rendered in his final play, *The Constant Lover,* a one-act duet in which an irresponsible young lawyer, Cecil Harburton, scandalizes others by declaring, without shame or guile, his "constant" love for many women. Harburton's rational preference for constancy rather than fidelity demonstrates the unsentimental compassion that is the ultimate form of the dandy's self-expression. Although his time is filled with charming encounters, Harburton ultimately lives in untroubled solitude, placidly regretting the inevitable coming of middle age when he will no longer be able to resist conventional dullness and stupidity.

In an intolerant world emotional disengagement masks the awareness of life's cruelty, fragility, and competitiveness. The taste and intelligence of the Edwardian dandy figure are therefore in irreconcilable opposition to narrow-mindedness and callous expediency. The values of the uncorrupted dandy who must subsist in a corrupted world are necessarily short-lived. He achieves a temporary notoriety before he is ultimately subsumed in the comforts of the upper-class society from which he originates. The intellectual dandy's critical standards are directed against the privileges of class distinction, paradoxically the only circumstances under which his potential for refinement and sophistication can be realized. The social commentary of Hankin and other Edwardian dandy writers is therefore limited to the faults and foibles of a terrible but necessary high society, beyond which existed chaos and vulgarity. The gallant gesture of defiance of Hankin's dandy characters who deplore, but cannot change, the reprehensible nature of privilege is also implicit in Hankin's satiric portrayals of the savage inhumanity of an insulated high society.

Though Hankin regretted Wilde's commercial degradation of his talent, he loved Wilde's portrayals of "foolish pompous domineering old ladies" ("The Collected Plays of Oscar Wilde," 194). He acknowledged *The Importance of Being Earnest*'s Lady Bracknell as an "immortal creation" and replicated her grand aristocratic manner in several of his own characters. In *The Return of the Prodigal* Lady Faringford, like Lady Bracknell, flaunts her conservatism with steady condescension, ignoring the social context that renders it absurd, articulating myopic views on music and education with a splendid touch of arrogance. More overtly than Wilde, however, Hankin also satirically attacked the stylish malevolence of uninformed snobbishness.

This double-edged, mortal humor is integral to *The Cassilis Engagement*, which involves the ill-fated engagement between an aristocratic simpleton and an opportunistic lower-class girl, a prospective union that horrifies the young man's country circle. Rather than provoke an elopement, his mother intelligently sanctions the engagement and invites the fiancée and her grotesque mother for a prolonged visit at her handsomely furnished Leicestershire house. Predictably, the young couple comes to recognize the incompatibility between classes and dissolves the engagement. Although the play insinuates a rationale for class distinctions, it favors neither class and draws merciless parodies of crude ambition, irate snobbishness, and sterile refinement. One may be amused by the mother's quiet domination of her fiendish upper-class circle, but there is nothing gentle about the passivity with which she awaits the inevitable demise of her son's passion.

The wolfish humor of *The Cassilis Engagement* is contemporary with the comic writings of H. H. Munro ("Saki"), who along with Hankin is known (but much more widely) for his literary dissections of the affairs, peccadilloes, and high-born attitudes of the Edwardian leisure class. Hankin and Saki are uniquely compatible in both period and style. Coupled with their satire is a serious homage paid to flippancy, extravagance, heartless egocentricity, and well-bred cynicism, and to the imminent failure of talent offered to a vulgar, uncomprehending society.

Arguably, Hankin and Saki are the Edwardian link in an esoteric literary chain that began in the novels of Edward Bulwer-Lytton and other Victorian writers, who portrayed dandy figures whose aloof demeanor masked a heroic idealism. Subsequently the fictional dandy figure was appropriated and "unsentimentalized" by nineteenth-century French novelists (including Gautier, Sue, and Balzac) who depicted the dandified hero's humanitarian actions as oppositional— that is, performed in service of a critical response to a particular social establishment.

From a comparable critical perspective, Hankin introduced to the stage a muted and cynical form of Edwardian dandyism, incorporating what was perhaps the most unpopular disposition of his time: an open regard for eugenics and social Darwinism, along with a wry awareness of the impossibility of any tranquil panegyric for society. Although his antiheroic wit was not met with wide acclaim, Hankin's influence can be seen in the theatrical successes of a generation later. It was evident in the detestable charm of Frederick Lonsdale's 1920s characters who coincide unwittingly with or comment ironically on upper-class pretensions. The same influence is also recognizable in Noël Coward's mockery of the fallacy of social equality, a recurrent theme throughout his work from *Easy Virtue* (1925) to *Relative Values* (1951).

While the influence of Hankin's major plays remains largely unrecognized, the intent behind his minor works is comparably overlooked. *The Two Mr. Wetherbys* has been hastily dismissed as a marital farce with an implausible resolution and as a weak imitation of Wilde's style (Phillips [2], 40). Not so readily acknowledged is the play's possible association with what Hankin termed Ibsen's tragedy that "makes you chuckle" ("Mr. Bernard Shaw as Critic" 164). Hankin's unique attempt to address comically the destructiveness of marital reprobation may be aimed at the core of those malignant relationships cited as the significant background to Ibsen's domestic problem plays (if one is to believe, among others, Mrs. Alving in *Ghosts* and Mrs. Sorby in *The Wild Duck*).

The Last of the De Mullins has been regarded as an ineffective use of the stage as a pulpit. The play depicts a single mother's return to the village of her aristocratic family, where she refuses first an opportunity of marriage to her son's father, then an offer of a legitimate adoptive home for her son under her parents' roof. The heroine's proclamation that she will not surrender to duty the fulfillments of motherhood has been criticized both for its shrill didacticism and its chilly rhetoric (Phillips [2], 78; Palmer, 220). Curiously, this disparaged passage echoes Elizabeth Robins's dramatic representation of maternal attachment as the exclusive concern of women. Before Hankin, no other male playwright had presented such a notion. (Robins was the only woman playwright produced at the Court Theatre, and her play *Votes for Women!* was substituted during an aborted run of *The Return of the Prodigal* in 1907.)

Over the seventy-five years since his death, Hankin has received little critical attention. Rarely are his works performed. The cold humor and submerged passion of his plays seem to have a limited appeal that has relegated him to a lower echelon of English dramatists. Or perhaps the smallness of human nature observed in the plays has been ascribed to the author himself. In either case, the lingering assessment of Hankin could stand some revision. Palmer in his 1913 *New York Times* review of Hankin's posthumously published *Dramatic Works* remarked, "Mr. Hankin is not great. . . . Hankin is not the man who has realized everything, forgotten nothing, and from a great height looks dispassionately down upon humanity." The critic may have inadvertently epitomized Hankin in an attempt to describe what he was not.

ARCHIVAL SOURCES

The University of Illinois Library at Urbana-Champaign holds five manuscripts in the author's hand: "The Propagandist as Playwright," two pieces of fiction, and two essays.

PRIMARY BIBLIOGRAPHY

Plays

Andrew Paterson: A One-Act Play. With Nora Vynne. *Theatre* (1 July 1893): 34–40.
The Cassilis Engagement. In *Representative British Dramas: Victorian and Modern,* ed. Montrose J. Moses. Boston: Little, Brown, 1918. Also in *Contemporary Plays,* ed. Thomas H. Dickinson and J. R. Crawford. Boston: Houghton Mifflin, 1925; *Late Victorian Plays,* ed. George Rowell. London: Oxford University Press, 1968.
The Charity That Began at Home: A Comedy for Philanthropists. London: Martin Secker, 1906.
The Constant Lover: A Comedy of Youth in One Act. London and New York: Samuel French, 1912; *Theatre Arts Magazine* 3 (1919): 67–77. Also in *One-Act Plays of To-day,* 4th series, ed. J[ames] W. Marriott. London: Harrap, 1928.
The Last of the De Mullins: A Play without a Preface. London: A. C. Fifield, 1909. Also in *Twentieth Century Plays,* vol. I, ed. F. W. Chandler and R. A. Cordell. New York: T. Nelson, 1934.
The Return of the Prodigal: A Comedy for Fathers. New York and London: Samuel French, 1907; Richards Press, 1949. Also in *Edwardian Plays,* ed. Gerald Weales. New York: Hill & Wang, 1962.
Thompson: A Comedy in Three Acts (completed by George Calderon). London: Secker, 1913; New York: Mitchell Kennerley, 1913; Samuel French, [1924].
The Two Mr. Wetherbys: A Middle-Class Comedy. New York and London: Samuel French, 1921.

Anthologies

Dramatic Sequels. (*Mr. Punch's Dramatic Sequels,* without "Dramatic Prologue" to Pinero's *The Notorious Mrs. Ebbsmith.*) London: Martin Secker, [c. 1925]; New York: Minton, Balch, 1926.
The Dramatic Works of St. John Hankin. 3 vols. (All full-length and one-act plays except *Thompson,* and six essays.) Ed. John Drinkwater. London: Martin Secker, 1912; New York: Mitchell Kennerley, 1912.
Mr. Punch's Dramatic Sequels. London: Bradbury, Agnew, [1901].
The Plays of St. John Hankin. 2 vols. (All full-length and one-act plays.) Ed. John Drinkwater. London: Martin Secker, 1923; New York: George H. Doran, 1923.
Three Plays with Happy Endings. (*The Cassilis Engagement, The Charity That Began at Home, The Return of the Prodigal.*) London and New York: Samuel French, [1907].

Parodies

44 dramatizations in *Punch* (June 1898–Dec. 1903).
"The Actor-Manager Explains." *Punch* (6 July 1904): 2.
"Another 'Real Conversation.' " *Punch* (19 June 1901): 462.
"Hamlet for Ladies." *Punch* (31 May 1899): 256.
"Hamlet's Soliloquy (New Style)." *Punch* (21 Jan. 1903): 44; (1 May 1907): 307.
"The 'Iris' Club." *Punch* (11 Dec. 1901): 422.
"The Modern Dramatist to His Muse." *Punch* (6 Jan. 1909): 10.
"Mr. Punch's Dramatic Recipes: I—How to Write a Celtic Drama." *Punch* (14 June 1899): 285.
"Mr. Punch's Dramatic Recipes: II—How to Write a 'Gleeful Plenitude.' " *Punch* (5 July 1899): 1.
"Mr. Punch's Dramatic Recipes: III—How to Write an Anglo-Indian Drama." *Punch* (12 July 1899): 16.
"Mr. Punch's Dramatic Recipes: IV—How to Be an Actor-Manager." *Punch* (16 Aug. 1899): 76.
"Mr. Punch's Dramatic Recipes: V—How to Be a Dramatic Critic." *Punch* (23 Aug. 1899): 88.
" 'The Tempest' in a Tea-cup." *Punch* (9 May 1900): 330.

Essays and Articles on Drama and Theater

"The Censorship of Plays." *Academy* (29 Feb. 1908): 514–15.
"The Collected Plays of Oscar Wilde." *Fortnightly Review* (1 May 1908): 791–802. Reprinted in *The Dramatic Works of St. John Hankin,* 3:181–201.
"How to Run an Art Theatre for London." *Fortnightly Review* (1 Nov. 1907): 814–18. Reprinted in *The Dramatic Works of St. John Hankin,* 3:171–79.
"Mr. Bernard Shaw as Critic." *Fortnightly Review* (1 June 1907): 1057–68. Reprinted in *The Dramatic Works of St. John Hankin,* 3:149–70.
"The Need for an Endowed Theatre in London." *Fortnightly Review* (1 Dec. 1908): 1038–47. Reprinted in *The Dramatic Works of St. John Hankin.* 3:203–21.
"The Propagandist as Playwright." Handwritten, n.d, 14 pp.
"Puritanism and the English Stage." *Fortnightly Review* (1 Dec. 1906): 1055–64. Reprinted in *The Dramatic Works of St. John Hankin,* 3:131–48.
"Shakespeare for Amateurs." *Academy* (5 Mar. 1898): 264–65.

Reviews

8 reviews (signed) in *Academy* (1899, 1905–7).
70 drama reviews (unsigned) in *The Times* (1897–99).

SECONDARY BIBLIOGRAPHY

Agate, James E. "A Note on Repertory." In *Alarums and Excursions,* 81–101. New York: George H. Doran, 1922.
Baumann, Arthur A. "Pshaw!" *Saturday Review* (27 Oct. 1906): 512.

Beerbohm, Max. [1]. " 'The Cassilis Engagement.' " *Saturday Review* (16 Feb. 1907): 199–200. Reprinted in *Last Theatres, 1904–1910,* 276–79. New York: Taplinger, 1970.

———. [2]. " 'The Last of the De Mullins.' " *Saturday Review* (12 Dec. 1908): 726–27. Reprinted in *Last Theatres, 1904–1910,* 413–15. New York: Taplinger, 1970.

———. [3]. "A Note on St. John Hankin." *Saturday Review* (26 June 1909): 810. Reprinted in *Last Theatres, 1904–1910,* 473–74. New York: Taplinger, 1970.

———. [4]. " 'The Return of the Prodigal.' " *Saturday Review* (7 Oct. 1905): 463–64. Reprinted in *Around Theatres,* 2:166–72. London: William Heinemann, 1924.

———. [5]. "Three Plays." *Saturday Review* (21 Mar. 1903): 356–57. Reprinted in *More Theatres, 1898–1903,* 546–50. New York: Taplinger, 1969.

Chambers, E. K. "A Romance and a Comedy." *Academy* (21 Mar. 1903): 282–83.

" 'The Charity That Began at Home' at the Court Theatre." *Academy* (27 Oct. 1906): 422–23.

"Criterion Theatre." *The Times* (28 Oct. 1908): 15.

Dickinson, Thomas H. *The Contemporary Drama of England.* Boston: Little, Brown, 1917.

Drinkwater, John. "Introduction." In *The Dramatic Works of St. John Hankin,* 1:3–28. London: Martin Secker, 1912; New York: Mitchell Kennerley, 1912.

Evans, T. F. "St. John Hankin." In *Dictionary of Literary Biography,* vol. 10, *Modern British Dramatists, 1900–1945,* ed. Stanley Weintraub, pt. 1, 218–26. Detroit: Gale Research, 1982.

Goldie, Grace Wyndham. *The Liverpool Repertory Theatre, 1911–1934.* Liverpool: University Press of Liverpool, 1935.

Howe, P. P. "St. John Hankin and His Comedy of Recognition." *Fortnightly Review* (Jan. 1913): 165–75. Reprinted in *North American Review* (Jan. 1913): 78–89; "St. John Hankin," in *Dramatic Portraits,* 163–83. 1913. Reprint. Port Washington, NY: Kennikat Press, 1969.

Hudson, Lynton. *The English Stage, 1850–1950.* London: Harrap, 1951.

Kemp, Thomas C. *Birmingham Repertory Theatre: The Playhouse and the Man.* 2nd ed. rev. Birmingham: Cornish Brothers, 1948.

Lane, Harry. "The Cassilis Engagement: Hankin's 'Comedy for Mothers.' " *English Studies in Canada* 8 (Dec. 1982): 437–51.

Laurence, Dan H., ed. *Bernard Shaw: Collected Letters, 1898–1910.* London: Max Reinhardt, 1972.

Matthews, Bache. *A History of the Birmingham Repertory Theatre.* London: Chatto & Windus, 1924.

McDonald, Jan. *The "New Drama," 1900–1914.* New York: Grove Press, 1986.

Meyerstein, E.H.W. "St. John Hankin." *English* 7 (Spring 1949): 175–79.

Morgan, A[rthur] E[ustace]. "Hankin." In *Tendencies of Modern English Drama,* 111–120. New York: Charles Scribner's Sons, 1924.

Moses, Montrose J., ed. Introduction to *The Cassilis Engagement.* In *Representative British Dramas,* 535–37. 1918. Rev. ed. Boston: D.C. Heath, 1931.

"Mr. St. John Hankin." *Athenaeum* (26 June 1909): 768.

"Mr. St. John Hankin's Comedy at the Stage Society." *Academy* (16 Feb. 1907): 169.

Nethercot, Arthur H. "The Quintessence of Idealism; or, The Slave of Duty." *PMLA* 62 (1947): 844–59.

Palmer, John. "A New Vanbrugh: St. John Hankin's Contribution to Recent English Drama." *New York Times* (13 Apr. 1913): 220.

Phillips, William H. [1]. "The Individual and Society in the Plays of St. John Hankin." *Shavian* 4 (Spring 1972): 170–74.

———. [2]. *St. John Hankin: Edwardian Mephistopheles.* Rutherford, NJ: Fairleigh Dickinson University Press, 1979.

Pogson, Rex. *Miss Horniman and the Gaiety Theatre, Manchester.* London: Rockliff, 1952.

Purdom, C. B., ed. *Bernard Shaw's Letters to Granville Barker.* New York: Theatre Arts Books, 1957.

Review of *The Return of the Prodigal. Athenaeum* (30 Sept. 1905): 444.

" 'The Return of the Prodigal' at the Royal Court Theatre." *Academy* (30 Sept. 1905): 1010.

Rowell, George, and Anthony Jackson. *The Repertory Movement: A History of Regional Theatre in Britain.* Cambridge: Cambridge University Press, 1984.

Salmon, Eric, ed. *Granville Barker and His Correspondents: A Selection of Letters by Him and to Him.* Detroit: Wayne State University Press, 1986.

"St. John Hankin." *New Statesman* (21 July 1913): 450–51.

"The Stage from the Stalls." *Sketch* (4 Oct. 1905): 452.

Tanitch, Robert. "A Comedy for Fathers." *Spectator* (14 Dec. 1991): 51.

" 'Thompson.' " *The Times* (23 Apr. 1913): 10.

Trewin, J[ohn] C[ourtenay]. [1]. *The Birmingham Repertory Theatre, 1913–1963.* London: Barrie & Rockliff, 1963.

———. [2]. *The Edwardian Theatre.* Totowa, NJ: Rowman & Littlefield, 1976.

———. [3]. *The Theatre since 1900.* London: Andrew Dakers, 1951.

"The Week." *Athenaeum* (16 Feb. 1907): 207.

"The Week: At the Imperial." *Athenaeum* (21 Mar. 1903): 379.

Weintraub, Stanley, ed. *Desmond MacCarthy's The Court Theatre, 1904–1907.* Coral Gables, FL: University of Miami Press, 1966.

Wilson, A[lbert] E[dward]. *Edwardian Theatre.* London: A. Barker, 1951.

W[oods], G[abriel] S. "Hankin, St. John Emile Clavering." In *The Dictionary of National Biography, 1901–1911,* ed. Sir Sidney Lee, 196. London: Oxford University Press, 1912.

BIBLIOGRAPHY

Phillips, William H. *St. John Hankin: Edwardian Mephistopheles.* Rutherford, NJ: Fairleigh Dickinson University Press, 1979.

W. Stanley Houghton
(1881–1913)

TED BAIN

Stanley Houghton wrote almost exclusively for the Manchester Gaiety Theatre, England's first provincial repertory theater, and, along with two of his contemporaries, Harold Brighouse and Allan Monkhouse, is remembered as one of the principal regional playwrights of the Manchester school. In 1912 Houghton's one famous play, *Hindle Wakes,* appeared to launch him in a promising career, but he died a year later at the age of thirty-two. His other works have since been relatively neglected.

William Stanley Houghton (pronounced Hawton), the only son of John Hartley Houghton, a Manchester merchant, was born in Ashton-upon-Mersey, Cheshire, on 22 February 1881. In his youth he suffered ill health and grew up an avid, though not especially strong, participant in cricket, tennis, and golf. As Brighouse ([1], xii) put it, "Perhaps at his favorite games enthusiasm outran discretion."

Through his early years his family moved often, and he was educated at Bowdon College, the Stockport Grammar School, the Wilmslow Grammar School, and the Manchester Grammar School, which B. Iden Payne, his future producer, also attended. Although recognized as a talented student, he did not enter university. In 1897, at the age of fifteen, he began full-time work in his father's cotton retail business in Manchester, where he served as a salesman until 1912.

For most of his adult life, according to Brighouse [1], Houghton "burnt the candle at both ends" (xi), dividing himself between a career in the cotton trade and a long apprenticeship as a writer and theater practitioner. He was a long-standing member of the Manchester Athenaeum Dramatic Society, acting in over seventy roles and serving occasionally as producer and secretary between 1901 and 1912. Within this amateur group he was known for his serious devotion to acting, through which he learned much of the playwright's craft (Brighouse [1], Wisenthal).

In 1905 and 1906 he was an unpaid weekly theater critic for the *Manchester City News* and wrote about sixty reviews of second-tier performances. From 1907 to 1912 he contributed drama and book reviews as well as occasional sketches to the *Manchester Guardian,* where he was reputed to be a stern but fair critic and a strong supporter of those writers he felt were most deserving of recognition.

Brighouse [1] observed that Houghton was not politically active: he professed socialism, practiced liberalism, but "was, as every artist must be, the looker-on." Viewing Houghton as the disengaged observer might help to explain why he was able to move continually between the working world of the Cotton Exchange and the leisure world of the men's clubs. It would appear that recreational pursuits were as important as his professional labors. Besides holding membership in the Manchester Athenaeum, he was in 1908 a founding member of the Swan Club, a luncheon club for daily discussion of food and art. In 1912 he became a member of the Savage Club and the Dramatists' Club.

Houghton's career ended soon after he became acclaimed outside of Manchester. The success of *Hindle Wakes* and the Haymarket (London) production of *The Younger Generation* enabled him to leave the cotton trade in 1912, after which he spent an unproductive year in London. Illness and the rush of critical recognition are cited as possible distractions. After returning briefly to Manchester, he moved to Paris, where he began a play, *The Weather,* and a novel, *Life.* Neither was completed before successive bouts of influenza and appendicitis forced him on to Venice, where he underwent two surgical operations. He returned again to Manchester, where he died of meningitis on 10 December 1913 and was cremated.

In 1915 Annie Horniman, founder of the Gaiety Theatre, unveiled his memorial tablet in the Manchester reference library. Also in 1915 a Houghton memorial scholarship was established for a Manchester Grammar School student to attend Manchester University.

Selected Biographical Sources: Brighouse [1, 2]; Gooddie; Morley; Mortimer; Pogson; Wisenthal.

MAJOR PLAYS, PREMIERES, AND SIGNIFICANT REVIVALS: THEATRICAL RECEPTION

The Dear Departed. 1908. (one act). Opened 2 November at the Gaiety Theatre (Manchester) as a curtain raiser for Bernard Shaw's *Widowers' Houses;* stayed in the Gaiety repertoire, sharing the bill with other full-length plays through 1909 on three different programs opening 8 February, 19 April, and 1 November. Revived June 1909 at the Coronet Theatre (London); and 28 May 1913 at the Criterion Theatre (London) for 288 performances. The play is still favored in amateur societies. Contracts in the Stanley Houghton Collection, University of Salford Library, refer to performances in New York, Norway, Sweden, and Denmark (Hilda Englund), 1909.

The program note for the first production attributed the idea to a story of de Maupassant. Pogson suggested that the play was immediately popular for its humor and its authentic representation of Lancashire life by the "well-nigh perfect cast" of the first Gaiety production (58).

Independent Means. 1909. Opened 23 September at the Gaiety Theatre (Manchester); revived 26 September 1910 at the Gaiety. Toured by Iden Payne's company in 1913–14. According to Brighouse ([1], xliii) there was no performance in London. A television version was made by Granada TV in the early 1960s.

Independent Means was Houghton's first long play, a leisure-class satire best known for its portrayal of a casual suffrage activist who proves to be a little more employable than her feckless husband. Pogson (84) described it as a neatly constructed comedy of contemporary manners, whose nondidactic and "somewhat shallow" characterizations suited the public taste but disappointed the critics.

The Master of the House. 1910. (one act). Opened 26 September at the Gaiety Theatre (Manchester) on a program with *Independent Means;* reopened 28 November 1910 at the Gaiety, sharing the bill with Harold Brighouse's *Dealing in Futures.* Revival: Kingsway Theatre (London), for 1 performance, 10 February 1935.

Brighouse ([1], xlvi) viewed *The Master of the House* as an interesting but faulty experiment in the gruesome, but Houghton was more critical of the acting in the first production and pointed to the play's success when Fred Ovens was played in England and America by Whitford Kane. *The Times* review ("Kingsway Theatre") of the 1935 London revival described the play as a "not particularly fortunate" performance of a "grimly ironical tale, which makes rather mechanical play with a corpse."

The Younger Generation. 1910. Opened 21 November at the Gaiety Theatre (Manchester); reopened twice, on 8 May 1911 and 29 April 1912, at the Gaiety. Revived May–June 1912 by Miss Horniman's Company at the Coronet Theatre (London); reopened with some cast changes, November 1912, at the Haymarket Theatre (London) and transferred 10 February 1913 to the Duke of York's Theatre (London) for 131 performances. The Haymarket and Duke of York's productions were under management of Frederick Harrison. Touring performances in America, under management of Charles Frohman; in the provinces under management of Iden Payne. Revivals: Lyric (Hammersmith), for 22 performances, January–February 1919, produced by Stanley Drewitt. A television version was made by Granada TV in the early 1960s.

Reviews of the 1912 London productions were mixed. In the *Academy* ("A Triple Bill at the Haymarket") Houghton was described as a "wise sociologist" in depicting the typical clash between the generations. The *Athenaeum* ("Dramatic Gossip") criticized the humor as almost farcically extravagant, but allowed that the author's knack for "individualizing" each of his characters kept in evidence the theme of "the revolt of youth against the restraining influences of age." The *Illustrated London News* (" 'The Younger Generation.' At the Haymarket") ranked the play as a light comedy not in the serious vein of *Hindle Wakes*. Similarly, *The Times* reviewer ("The Haymarket Theatre") described *The Younger Generation* as less daring than *Hindle Wakes,* but still "pleasant enough as entertainment," especially for "the majority of unsophisticated playgoers."

Fancy Free. 1911. (one act). Opened 6 November at the Gaiety Theatre (Manchester). Revivals: Kingsway (London), for 9 performances, October 1917; International One-Act Play Theatre Company, Kingsway (London), for 1 performance, 3 February 1935.

According to Brighouse ([1], xlviii), the first performance, Iden Payne's Manchester production, fell flat with the audience and the press, and the *Manchester Guardian* review denigrated the characters for morals approximating "canine promiscuity." A contract in the Houghton Collection refers to a 1912 U.S. performance by William A. Brady; the play was performed successfully in 1912 at the Tivoli Music Hall (London) after the Stage Society's production of *Hindle Wakes;* from February to June 1913 *Fancy Free* shared a bill at the Princess Theatre (New York).

The *Athenaeum* review (Review of *The Works*) in 1914 of Houghton's collected works dismissed him as "but a poor imitator of greater genius" and cited as an example *Fancy Free,* "which by no means flattered Oscar Wilde." In the same year, however, Ellis's appreciation of Houghton in the *English Review* described the same play as "a miniature gem which combines the polished artifice of Oscar Wilde with the gay, non-moral wit of some audacious *boulevardier.*"

Hindle Wakes. 1912. Opened 16 June at the Aldwych Theatre (London) for 2 performances. Staged by the Horniman Company and the Incorporated Stage Society. Transferred on 16 July 1912 to the Playhouse (London), then on 28 September 1912 to the Court Theatre (London) for 108 performances.

Opened in repertory 28 October 1912, 16 December 1912, 8 September 1913, and 15 December 1913 with Miss Horniman's Company at the Gaiety Theatre (Manchester); also through the 1913–14 season by the Horniman Company at the Coronet Theatre (London) and on New York and provincial tours. According to Brighouse ([1], l–li), the success of *Hindle Wakes* was immediate; in 1913 five companies played it in the provinces, setting new records at many theaters in Yorkshire and Lancashire, including the Gaiety. The total number of performances in the eighteen months from the first production to the time of Houghton's death was 1,838.

Contracts and letters in the Houghton collection refer to royalties from *Hindle*

Wakes from the African Theatres Trust Ltd. in South Africa, 1914; to performances in Calcutta, 1916; and to the film rights to *Hindle Wakes* from Gaumont, 1931. Revivals: Miss Horniman's company at the Duke of York's Theatre (London), on a double bill with Brighouse's *Converts* for 33 performances, September 1915; Court Theatre (London) for 18 performances, December 1916; Everyman (London) for 18 performances, August 1927; London Repertory Company, Regent Theatre (London), for 6 performances, November 1927; Theatre Royal, Stratford East, for 14 performances, April 1953, produced by Joan Littlewood.

Brighouse made a novel out of the play for Reader's Library, which sold half a million copies and was serialized. Morley's (98) biography of Sybil Thorndike noted her performance as Mrs. Hawthorn in the "first talking version" of *Hindle Wakes* on film, directed by Victor Saville in 1931.

The first Stage Society (London) performance was directed and produced by Lewis Casson. The cast included Sybil Thorndike as Beatrice, Edyth Goodall as Fanny, and twenty-six-year-old Herbert Lomas as Jeffcote senior. (Lomas played the same role in a 1950 Arts Theatre revival [London].) *The Times* review ("The Stage Society") remarked that "despite its cynicism and occasional grossness, the play won favour by the truthfulness of its homely detail and the sincerity of its players," whose "angular, rough-tongued Lancashire ways" were "an agreeable novelty." In the *Illustrated London News* ("'Hindle Wakes.' At the Playhouse") the play was described as a "sound, strong, breezy work . . . illustrating a phase of life which is far more genuinely English than those scenes of London drawing-rooms, and sending out a flashlight over the gulf that separates working-class from burgess notions of morality." After the play had run for several months, the same publication ("'Hindle Wakes.' Transferred to the Court") added that "Stanley Houghton's brilliant comedy shows us how possible it is to make a study of provincial manners amusing at the same time that it is absolutely faithful. And Miss Horniman's Manchester players teach us how happily an ensemble can be secured among artists from such a system as that as repertory theatre keeps constantly working together." The *English Review* ("Play of the Month") cited *Hindle Wakes* as one of the "real sources of the arts" to be found in the provinces. Palmer [1], however, consistently referred to the play as "Hindley Wakes" and objected to its subversively "Shavian" outcome, which was not worked out "within the limits of commonly-accepted moral convention." Palmer had praise, however, for the first act, which had begun to show that "new plays are independently being written for a barbarous place like Manchester fully equal to the best new London work."

Phipps. 1912. (one act). Opened 19 November at the Garrick Theatre (London) for 2 performances. Produced by Arthur Bourchier. Revivals: Chicago, 1913, by Iden Payne; film version titled *Nearly Divorced,* 1929.

The Times ("The Garrick Theatre: 'Phipps' ") described Bourchier's 1912 production as a "worldly little trifle." A *Theatre* review (Review of *Phipps*) of a 1914 American production condemned the play as an "immature and foolish fragment." In the same year the *Athenaeum* review (Review of *The Works*) of Houghton's collected works labeled his insights as "commonplace" and speculated that *Phipps* would be the most persistently revived of his plays.

Pearls. 1912. (one act). Opened 20 December at the Pavilion (Glasgow). Revivals: Coliseum (London), 6 January 1913; Drury Lane (London) for 1 performance, 27 April 1915.

Pearls was originally titled *The Minion of the Law*. It was written in October 1912 for actor-manager Arthur Bourchier and his wife Violet Vanbrugh, who performed it at the Coliseum and other music halls. The manuscript is on microfilm in the Stanley Houghton Collection, University of Salford Library.

Trust the People. 1913. Opened 6 February at the Garrick Theatre (London) for 44 performances. Written in 1912 for Arthur Bourchier; manuscript on microfilm in the Stanley Houghton Collection, University of Salford Library.

According to Brighouse ([1], lv–lvii) *Trust the People* was considered a failure for different reasons: because of Houghton's supposed hurried writing, because Houghton had made a transparent attempt to write a popular play, or because of Houghton's illness. The *Illustrated London News* review (" 'Trust the People' ") charged that the play's political satire was "notoriously" implausible and objected to the "monstrous notion" of a prime minister who proposes to use party funds to silence a blackmailer. The review added that Houghton was "too ambitious in breaking from the provincial environment in which he moves with such ease" and that it was "not wise of him as yet to try to do without the help of Lancashire." Similarly, *The Times* review ("Garrick Theatre: 'Trust the People' ") stated that the play was mostly "manufactured theatricalism" or "sheer nonsense," but was partially redeemed in the last act by "a little bit of real and keenly felt Lancashire domesticity." Palmer [2] concurred that the play was artistically and morally insincere and even suggested that Houghton had possibly "bargained with the devil for full houses."

The Perfect Cure. 1913. Opened 17 June at the Apollo Theatre (London) for 4 performances. Produced by Charles Hawtrey and withdrawn after 4 nights. Houghton thought that the production was badly cast (except for Hawtrey). The play toured the provinces under E. T. Heys's management. A contract in the Houghton Collection refers to a 1912 performance by Frederick Harrison of *The Cure*.

In response to the 1913 London performance, *The Times* ("Mr. Houghton's New Comedy") praised the well-performed portrayal of a remarkably selfish father as consistent with Houghton's familiar theme of the younger generation's revolt against the old. The *Illustrated London News* (" 'The Perfect Cure' ") described the play as a "true and delightful comedy" and noted that it was set in a London suburb, disproving the reviewer's previous notion that Houghton was "helpless without a Lancashire setting." The *Academy* review (" 'The Perfect Cure' at the Apollo Theatre''), however, described the play as disappointingly implausible, rejecting its notion of adult children who do not desire to get out in the world and of parents who are not anxious to let them go.

The Hillarys. (written with Harold Brighouse). 1915. Opened 30 April at Kelly's Theatre (Liverpool); also 2 June 1915 at the Criterion Theatre (London) for 18 performances. A contract in the Houghton Collection refers to a performance by African Theatres Trust Ltd. in South Africa, 1915.

The *Illustrated London News* review ('' 'The Hillarys' '') of the Criterion production described the play's scenario as ''only too exactly'' like that of Hankin's *The Cassilis Engagement,* but nevertheless a badly needed wartime entertainment. *The Times* reviewer ('' 'The Hillarys' at the Criterion'') agreed that the play's presentation of ''the superficial commonplaces'' of love was a pleasant diversion.

ADDITIONAL PLAYS, ADAPTATIONS, AND PRODUCTIONS

Maria (one act) was written around 1900. *After Naseby* (one act), *The Last Short* (one act), and *The Blue Phial* (one act) were written around 1901. These four plays are no longer extant.

Adam Moss: Bachelor was written around 1901. *Midnight Visitors: A Nocturne* (one act) and *The General's Word* (one act), the latter under the pseudonym William Stanley, were written around 1906. The manuscripts of these three plays are in the Stanley Houghton Collection, University of Salford Library. *The Intriguers* (written with Frank Nasmith) was performed 19 October 1906 at the Athenaeum Society (Manchester). The manuscript is on microfilm in the Stanley Houghton Collection, University of Salford Library.

The Reckoning (one act) opened 22 July 1907 at the Queen's Theatre (Manchester). Brighouse [1] mentioned that it was revived as a music-hall sketch. The manuscript is on microfilm in the Lord Chamberlain's Stage Plays, the British Library. *Marriages in the Making* was written January–April 1909. Though it was not performed, Brighouse ([1], xliii) described it as a light comedy of slight texture, which did not live up to its first act, but was amusing to the end. *The Fifth Commandment* (one act) was first performed at the Little Theatre (Chicago) in 1913. It opened 14 July 1914 with Miss Horniman's Company at the Gaiety Theatre (Manchester) and was revived 28 November 1914 by the Birmingham Repertory Theatre for 7 performances. *Ginger* was first performed 19 July 1913; a contract in the Stanley Houghton Collection, University of Salford Library, refers to performances by Esmé Percy and K. Graeme. The manuscript is on microfilm in the Houghton Collection. Mortimer (482) identified the play as a comedy inspired by H. G. Wells's *Kipps,* 1905. *The Weather* was written in 1913 in Paris. The incomplete manuscript (18 pages) is in the Stanley Houghton Collection, University of Salford Library. *The Old Testament and the New* (one act) was first performed 22 June 1914 at the Gaiety

Theatre (Manchester). *Partners* opened 15 April 1915 at the Prince's Theatre (Manchester). One year before its first performance, Brighouse ([1], xlviii–xlix) introduced the play as the full-length version of *Fancy Free* and speculated that its last act was too long.

ASSESSMENT OF HOUGHTON'S CAREER

During his brief career Houghton's performed works exhibited three contrasting personalities. The first, Houghton the socially conscious son of a Lancashire cotton trader, commented mordantly on the bourgeois materialism that was corrupting provincial communities. *The Dear Departed* was Houghton's first performed play, a tight one-act satire in which grasping relatives eye their inheritances and attempt to hurry through the appropriate period of mourning for the family patriarch. In the local setting of *The Dear Departed,* the preoccupation with money implicitly creates a condition of enslavement, satirically indicting characters who follow society's prescriptions rather than their own consciences. His second play, *Independent Means,* offers a softened and trivialized version of the same mercenary impulses, as seen in a spoiled young couple who must redeem themselves in work after their benefactor loses his fortune and falls dead.

The second, Houghton the flamboyant exquisite, was said by Ellis in a 1914 tribute to have "paraded pleasant signs of dandyism" (though Brighouse ([1], xii) denied the notion, perhaps to curb any possible insinuations) and was featured in a Max Beerbohm caricature as being lionized by the London critics. In the witty one-act *Fancy Free,* a flippant portrayal of London society, Houghton's Wildean tendencies are most apparent. *Fancy Free* depicts an open-marriage contract between two sophisticated dilettantes that is put to the test when they discover each other conducting affairs at the same hotel. Houghton similarly captured the corrupted affections of high society in *Phipps,* another one-act comedy, but was arguably less than successful in an attempt to stretch *Fancy Free* into a three-act version, *Partners.*

The third, Houghton the dutiful employee in his father's business for fourteen years, inimitably portrayed the weight of familial duty and the malevolence of parental oppression. The first act of *Hindle Wakes* is in itself a masterpiece, a disturbing scenario of the misplaced priorities of controlling parents who manipulate their daughter into a lie by withholding the news of her close friend's death.

Perhaps *Hindle Wakes* (1912) was Houghton's last note on a lingering theme. Annie Horniman's company had already, in the fall of 1910, performed two Houghton comedies about a father's inescapable tyranny, shown as macabre in the one-act *The Master of the House* and as bumptious in *The Younger Generation.* Another related play, *The Perfect Cure* (1913), was a full-length adaptation of the powerful one-act *The Fifth Commandment* (written in 1911), which was not performed in Houghton's lifetime. Both versions depict a parent who feigns infirmity in order to block the marital prospects of a grown daughter.

All three of these phases in Houghton's drama display an accomplished mix of comic detachment with what Brighouse ([1], xl) called "sincere observation." For example, much came from Houghton's observation of the Lancashire community of textile workers, in which women weavers and spinsters had become more employable than male laborers. With financial security, working women could also claim forms of social independence that were previously exclusive to men. In *Hindle Wakes,* therefore, Fanny Hawthorn is able to shrug off the label of fallen woman without trepidation.

Although *Hindle Wakes* was immensely popular, in the wake of Houghton's premature death it was largely dismissed as a slight but well-crafted play. A typical assessment was offered by Dickinson in 1917: "[*Hindle Wakes*] is well done in that it is laconic and commonplace. But it is a perfect example of the 'little play.' It is neither ugly nor beautiful. The play represents the step beyond which it is impossible to go in art, in that it introduces whims and pleasure as guides in the great decisions of life. Without calling upon passion or jealousy or the demand for self-realization, it shows a slangy youngster having 'her little fancy.' The story of such a play could be told in ten words as well as in three acts" (219–20).

Evidently, the relevance of Houghton's social observations became less of a concern to many critics than his supposed "place" within theatrical genealogy. In the *Dictionary of National Biography* (Charlton), Houghton is remembered as an imitator of better-known playwrights, such as Ibsen, Shaw, and Wilde, from whom he derived "unfortunately with an adroitness that belongs less to genius than to his besetting sin, mere showmanship."

Although Brighouse and other contemporaries once regarded Houghton as the leading talent of the Manchester school, his recognition has since diminished. Currently, his minor reputation may be part of a general critical preference. After all, the significance of Horniman's Manchester Gaiety Theatre as something more than a local theatrical interest has been largely overlooked since World War I. Houghton's career may provide an ideal case for reevaluating the conventional criteria for defining "important" as necessarily distinct and separate from "regional" drama.

ARCHIVAL SOURCES

Houghton's papers are located at the University of Salford Library. They include photographs of original commercial productions as well as unpublished manuscripts. Three other collections have material relevant to Stanley Houghton's career: (1) the seventeen-volume collection of press cuttings of Annie Horniman and (2) the Allan Monkhouse Collection, both at the John Rylands University of Manchester Library (Deansgate), and (3) the Harold Brighouse

Collection at the Eccles Public Library, Greater Manchester. The Brighouse Collection includes a bound typescript of *The Hillarys.*

PRIMARY BIBLIOGRAPHY

Plays

The Dear Departed. New York and London: Samuel French, 1910. Also in *More One-Act Plays by Modern Authors,* ed. Helen Louise Cohen. New York: Harcourt, Brace, 1927; *Seven Famous One-Act Plays.* New York: Penguin, 1937; *Twenty-Four One-Act Plays.* New York: Everyman's Library, 1939.

Fancy Free. London: Samuel French, 1912.

Hindle Wakes: A Play in Three Acts. London: Sidgwick & Jackson, 1912. Also in *Contemporary Drama: English and American,* ed. Thomas H Dickinson and J. R. Crawford. Boston: Little, Brown, 1925; *Modern American and British Plays,* ed. Samuel Marion Tucker. New York and London: Harper, 1931.

Independent Means, a Comedy in Four Acts. New York: Samuel French, [1911]. Also in *Granada's Manchester Plays,* ed. Gerald Savory. Manchester: Manchester University Press, 1962.

The Master of the House. In *One-Act Plays of To-day,* 3rd series, ed. J[ames] W[illiam] Marriott. London: Harrap, 1949.

The Younger Generation: A Comedy for Parents in Three Acts. London: Sidgwick & Jackson; New York: Samuel French, [1910]. Also in *Granada's Manchester Plays,* ed. Gerald Savory. Manchester: Manchester University Press, 1962.

Anthologies

Five One Act Plays. (*The Dear Departed, Fancy Free, The Fifth Commandment, The Master of the House, Phipps.*) London: Samuel French, 1913.

The Works of Stanley Houghton. 3 vols. (*The Dear Departed, Fancy Free, The Fifth Commandment, Hindle Wakes, Independent Means, Marriages in the Making, The Master of the House, The Old Testament and the New, Partners, The Perfect Cure, Phipps, The Younger Generation,* his novel, and other prose pieces.) Ed. and intro. Harold Brighouse. London: Constable, 1914.

Essays and Articles on Drama and Theater

Almost 200 theatre and book reviews for *The Manchester Guardian* (1907–mid-1912). Also short stories and sketches.

"Our Amateur Actors." *Manchester Guardian* (31 Aug. 1905): 4.

SECONDARY BIBLIOGRAPHY

Agate, James. Review of *The Works of Stanley Houghton. Manchester Playgoer* (July 1914): 26.

Brighouse, Harold, ed. [1]. "Introduction." In *The Works of Stanley Houghton,* I:ix–lix. London: Constable, 1914.

———. [2]. *What I Have Had.* London: Harrap, 1953.

Charlton, Henry Buckley. "Houghton, William Stanley." In *The Dictionary of National Biography, 1912–1921,* ed. H.W.C. Davis and J.R.H. Weaver, 271–73. London: Oxford University Press, 1927.

Dickinson, Thomas H. *The Contemporary Drama of England.* Boston: Little, Brown, 1917.

"Dramatic Gossip." *Athenaeum* (30 May 1912): 544.

Ellis, Anthony L. "Stanley Houghton: The Man and His Work." *English Review* (16 Jan. 1914): 275–76.

Gaberthuel, Marcel. "William Stanley Houghton, 1881–1913: Eine Untersuchung seiner Dramen." Ph.D. diss. University of Freiburg, 1969.

"The Garrick Theatre: 'Phipps.' " *The Times* (20 Nov. 1912): 10.

"Garrick Theatre: 'Trust the People.' " *The Times* (7 Feb. 1913): 8.

Gooddie, Sheila. *Annie Horniman: A Pioneer in the Theatre.* London: Methuen, 1990.

"The Haymarket Theatre: 'The Younger Generation.' " *The Times* (20 Nov. 1912): 8.

" 'The Hillarys.' At the Criterion." *Illustrated London News* (12 June 1915): 748.

" 'The Hillarys' at the Criterion." *The Times* (3 June 1915): 11.

Review of *Hindle Wakes: A Play in Four Acts. Bookman* 43 (1912): 80.

" 'Hindle Wakes.' At the Playhouse." *Illustrated London News* (20 July 1912): 88.

" 'Hindle Wakes.' Transferred to the Court." *Illustrated London News* (5 Oct. 1912): 486.

Hudson, Lynton. *The English Stage, 1850–1950.* London: Harrap, 1951.

Kemp, Thomas C. *Birmingham Repertory Theatre: The Playhouse and the Man.* 2d ed., rev. Birmingham: Cornish Brothers, 1948.

"Kingsway Theatre: Three One-Act Plays." *The Times* (11 Feb. 1935): 10.

Littlewood, Robin. "The Plays and Prose of Stanley Houghton." *Daily Chronicle* (July 1914).

Matthews, Bache. *A History of the Birmingham Repertory Theatre.* London: Chatto & Windus, 1924.

Montague, C. E. (Obituary) *Manchester Guardian* (9 June 1914).

Morley, Sheridan. *Sybil Thorndike: A Life in the Theatre.* London: Weidenfeld & Nicolson, 1977.

Mortimer, Paul. "W. Stanley Houghton: An Introduction and Bibliography." *Modern Drama* 28 (Sept. 1985): 474–89.

"Mr. Houghton's New Comedy: 'The Perfect Cure' at the Apollo Theatre." *The Times* (18 June 1913): 10.

Palmer, John. [1]. " 'Hindley [sic] Wakes' and the Stage Society." *Saturday Review* (22 June 1912): 774–75.

———. [2]. " 'Trust the People.' " *Saturday Review* (15 Feb. 1913): 202–3.

" 'The Perfect Cure.' At the Apollo." *Illustrated London News* (21 June 1913): 952.

" 'The Perfect Cure' at the Apollo Theatre." *Academy* (28 June 1913): 819.

Review of *Phipps. Theatre* (Dec. 1914): 267.

"Play of the Month: 'Hindle Wakes.' " *English Review* (11 June 1912): 655–56.

Pogson, Rex. *Miss Horniman and the Gaiety Theatre, Manchester.* London: Rockliff, 1952.

Savory, Gerald, ed. *Granada's Manchester Plays.* Manchester: Manchester University Press, 1962.

Scott, Dixon. "The Real Stanley Houghton." In *Men of Letters.* London: Hodder & Stoughton, 1923.

Smigel, Libby. "Fallen Women and Male Pratfalls: The Social Comedy of Stanley Houghton." Paper presented at the East Central Theatre Conference, February 1993.

"The Stage Society: 'Hindle Wakes.' " *The Times* (18 June 1912): 10.

Trewin, J[ohn] C[ourtenay]. *The Edwardian Theatre.* Totowa, NJ: Rowman & Littlefield, 1976.

"A Triple Bill at the Haymarket: 'The Younger Generation.' " *Academy* (30 Nov. 1912): 703.

" 'Trust the People.' At the Garrick." *Illustrated London News* (15 Feb. 1913): 196.

Wilson, A[lbert] E[dward]. *Edwardian Theatre.* London: A. Barker, 1951.

Wisenthal, J. L. "Stanley Houghton." In *Dictionary of Literary Biography,* vol. 10, *Modern British Dramatists, 1900–1945,* ed. Stanley Weintraub, pt. 1, 231–34. Detroit: Gale Research, 1982.

Review of *The Works of Stanley Houghton. Athenaeum* (25 July 1914): 127.

Review of *The Younger Generation. Theatre* 18 (1913): 145–46.

" 'The Younger Generation.' At the Duke of York's." *Illustrated London News* (15 Feb. 1913): 196.

" 'The Younger Generation.' At the Haymarket." *Illustrated London News* (23 Nov. 1912): 750.

BIBLIOGRAPHY

Mortimer, Paul. "W. Stanley Houghton: An Introduction and Bibliography." *Modern Drama* 28 (Sept. 1985): 474–89.

Laurence Housman
(1865–1959)

PAMELA MONACO

When most people hear the name "Housman" today, they think of Laurence Housman's brother, A. E. Housman, but Laurence Housman was a well-known writer during his own lifetime. A highly prolific writer of plays, novels, essays, and poetry, Laurence Housman is most often remembered for the play *Victoria Regina* and for being the most censored British dramatist.

Born on 18 July 1865 in Bromsgrove, Worcestershire, England, Laurence Housman was the sixth of seven children born to Edward and Sarah Jane Housman. Always a religious household, the Housmans turned to Catholicism in 1869 when Sarah Jane was diagnosed with breast cancer, and Housman would waver between Catholicism and religious doubt for most of his life. After their mother's death in 1871, Housman's sister Clemence took over much of the caretaking for Housman, and the two became inseparable for the rest of their lives. In 1883 Housman and Clemence left for London to study art at Lambeth and South Kensington. Housman's earliest professional work was as an illustrator for others' books, most notably for Christina Rossetti's *Goblin Market*. His first published written work was the short story "Green Gaffer," published in the July 1890 *Universal Review*. Housman developed a love for writing and within five years published several works, including a volume on *The Writings of William Blake* (1893) and two collections of moralistic fairy tales. By the end of the 1890s Housman had finished three books of verse. However, *An Englishwoman's Love Letters,* published anonymously in 1900 and believed by readers to be fact rather than fiction, was Housman's first commercial success. In addition, from 1899 to 1907 Housman served as the art critic for the *Manchester Guardian.*

Housman's dramatic career—and his battles with the Lord Chamberlain's Office—began in 1902 with the Nativity play *Bethlehem,* which had to be privately produced because of the ban on plays that presented sacred figures on the stage. In 1923 this play was finally given a public performance without any textual changes. This was the first of over thirty confrontations Housman would have with the censor's office. Housman's next play, *Prunella; or, Love in a Dutch Garden,* a Pierrot play, was written with Harley Granville-Barker and proved to be one of his most successful. Although Housman would continue to work with Granville-Barker and wrote a number of plays based on Granville-Barker's suggestions, they wrote only this play together.

Over the next fifteen years Housman wrote some of his less memorable plays. Three of the plays, *The Vicar of Wakefield* (1906), *Lysistrata* (1910), and *Alice in Ganderland* (1911), were adaptations, none of which were well received. Many thought that *Lysistrata* was written as a challenge to see if it could get past the censor; it did, but to the delight of few. It and *Alice in Ganderland* are representative of propaganda plays Housman wrote in support of his favorite causes, in this case the suffrage movement. Housman wrote *Lysistrata* for Gertude Kingston's Little Theatre after the play he initially gave to her, *Pains and Penalties,* was banned by the censor. In this case, the offense was not the presentation of religious figures on stage but the defense he offered for Queen Caroline against the charges of adultery brought by King George IV. Although offered in a private performance, *Pains and Penalties* would not receive a public performance, even though the ban was lifted ten years later after Housman made one change: the removal of the word "adultery." By the time the ban was lifted, interest in the play had waned. During this period Housman had five other plays produced: *The Oxford Historical Pageant* (1907), *The Chinese Lantern* (1908), *A Likely Story* (1910), *The Lord of Harvest* (1910), and *Bird in Hand* (1918), all for very limited runs.

The next success Housman had in drama was with his *Little Plays of St. Francis.* He published the first of this collection, *As Good as Gold,* in 1916. His devotion to the saint inspired him to write numerous other one-act plays about St. Francis, and in 1922 he published his first series of *Little Plays of St. Francis,* with a preface by Granville-Barker. Despite the plays' focus on a religious personage, the censor approved of them. These plays were never mounted on the professional stage, but they proved overwhelmingly popular with amateur and church groups. The plays were frequently produced as part of the Glastonbury Festival, for which Housman would often direct and act. For approximately twenty-five years, from 1925 to 1951, the Dramatic Society of London annually presented these plays at Christmas. Only during World War II did the society discontinue these performances. In response to the interest in these plays, Housman eventually wrote more than sixty one-act plays on the life of St. Francis. Housman believed that this play cycle was his finest work. During this period Housman also wrote a number of plays based on the classics, including *Apollo in Hades, Death of Alcestis,* and *The Doom of Admetus,* published together as the trilogy *The Wheel.*

Although Housman would continue to write plays until shortly before his death, he would have only one more critical success. While Housman was at work on the St. Francis plays, he was also busy writing plays about another compelling interest, historical figures. Because of the ban on presenting plays about Queen Victoria on stage while any of her close relatives were still alive, Housman could not get a license for any of the plays in his series about Queen Victoria. This did not prevent Housman from publishing closet dramas on Queen Victoria, nor did it prevent amateur groups from mounting productions of some of the one-act plays in the play cycle. In 1935 Housman selected ten episodes from his cycle and arranged them into a chronological overview of Queen Victoria's life, calling the composite play *Victoria Regina*. Because of the ban, the play was given a private staging at the Gate Theatre in 1935, but Edward VIII declared that beginning with the one hundredth anniversary of Victoria's coronation, presentations of Victoria could appear on the British stage. In December 1935 Gilbert Miller produced the play in New York with Helen Hayes as Queen Victoria to great success. One hundred years and a day after Victoria's coronation, on 21 June 1937, *Victoria Regina* was produced at London's Lyric Theatre to critical and popular acclaim. Housman continued to write plays about Queen Victoria, eventually writing over fifty plays on her life.

Housman continued to write religious, historical, and propaganda plays during the last quarter century of his life, but none met with much success. He relied on the Old Testament for material for his *Palestine Plays* (1942), of which one play, *Jacob,* was given a production in 1942. Several more series of plays on Queen Victoria were published, including *Palace Scenes* (1937), *The Golden Sovereign* (1937), *Gracious Majesty* (1941), and *Happy and Glorious* (1943). His social interest in prison reform and nonviolence, which had inspired his 1930 play *The New Hangman,* prompted him in 1935 to write another play against the death penalty, *Judge Lynch*. The last play produced before his death was *The Family Honour,* a farce based on family legend, presented in 1950 at the New Lindsay Theatre Club. Laurence Housman died on 21 February 1959 at the age of ninety-three in a nursing home in Glastonbury near the home in Street that he and Clemence had moved to in 1924. He was a Quaker at the time of his death.

Selected Biographical Sources: Banks; Engen; Housman, *The Unexpected Years;* Mix.

MAJOR PLAYS, PREMIERES, AND SIGNIFICANT REVIVALS: THEATRICAL RECEPTION

Bethlehem, A Nativity Play. 1902. Opened 18 December at the Great Hall of the Imperial Institute (London) for 45 performances. Directed by Edward Gordon Craig. Music by Joseph Moorat. Revival: Revised version, written in collaboration with Rutland Boughton, Regent Theatre (London), December 1923.

With songs, verse, and dialogue, this play depicts the birth of Jesus and was thus banned from the professional stage. Reviews of this production on the private stage were mixed. *The Times* review (Review of *Bethlehem*) noted the continuous music throughout and declared the play "wholly English." As with many other critics of later plays, this reviewer did not think that the play was drama as much as it was a "series of tableaux." Weales wrote of the published version that it was too poetic and overly simplistic. Two songs from the original production, "Noel" and "The World Is Old Tonight," have been published in *The English Book of Hymns.*

Prunella; or, Love in a Dutch Garden. 1904. Written in collaboration with Harley Granville-Barker. Opened 23 December at the Court Theatre (London) for 28 performances. Produced by J. E. Vedrenne and H. Granville-Barker. Music by Joseph Moorat. Revivals: Court Theatre, 24 April 1906, 7 May 1907, April 1910 Duke of York's Theatre; and May 1913; Theatre Guild School (New York), May 1913; Everyman Theatre, December 1921 and January 1930; Garrick Theatre (New York), June 1926. New act added for the 1930 revival.

Most critics and audiences responded favorably to this fantasy play based on the Pierrot tradition. The reviewer for *Sketch* (Review of *Prunella*) declared this one of the "thrills" of the winter season. Archer [1] agreed, calling it "original and exquisite." Archer [2] also had particular praise for the gradual development of dramatic tension. Beerbohm went so far as to declare it "one of the most important of English plays" (466). *The Times* reviews (Review of *Prunella*, 1910, 1930) called for heightened fantasy in the staging of the play and declared that the added act in the 1930 revival emphasized the obvious and thus made the play more artificial and less graceful. Most critics commented on the serious message of the play (Review of *Prunella, The Times,* 1906; Archer [1]; Review of *Prunella, World;* Review of *Prunella, Stage*). New York reviews were less favorable, complaining about the lack of action ("A Play Without a Punch") and English sentimentalism (Boyce). Granville-Barker played Pierrot in the original production.

The Chinese Lantern. 1908. Opened 16 June for 6 matinee performances at the Haymarket Theatre (London). Music by Joseph Moorat.

Most reviews were critical of this play about a young man who strives to express his artistic ambitions. Several reviews criticized Housman's tendency to moralize and felt it particularly inappropriate to attach a strong philosophical message to a fantasy (Review of *The Chinese Lantern* by *The Times* and *Athenaeum;* Fyfe [1]). Because *Prunella* is also a fantasy with a moral center, unfavorable comparisons between *The Chinese Lantern* and *Prunella* were made. Fyfe [1] declared that the difference between the two was probably due to Granville-Barker's involvement with the earlier play. Most critics felt that the play lacked cohesion and fell apart after the first act. Once again, heavy editing was recommended. *The Times* (Review of *The Chinese Lantern*), however, stated that this was the first presentation of the Chinese on the British stage and called for more plays about China.

Pains and Penalties: The Defense of Queen Caroline. 1911. Opened 26 November at the Savoy (London) for 1 performance. Produced by Laurence Housman and Edith Craig. Performed by Edith Craig's Pioneer Players.

As with many of Housman's other plays, the censor's ban apparently contributed to the interest in the play. The reviewer for *Sketch* (Review of *Pains and Penalties*) wrote about the senselessness of banning plays, and the reviewer for *The Times* (Review of *Pains and Penalties*) reported that the theater was filled because of the ban. Farjeon found the play interesting but felt that its artistic merits alone would not create much interest. He declared that public audiences would have little interest in the play because of the old heroine, the absence of a hero, and the lack of dramatic effect. The episodic structure was faulted for rendering the play undramatic. *The Times* complained of the blend of artistic imagination and historical fact.

Mr. Gladstone's Comforter. 1929. Opened 31 October at the Lyric (Hammersmith) for 20 performances (doubled-billed with *Beau Austin*). Produced by Sir Nigel Playfair.

Reviews were mixed, with even the favorable reviews critical of the lack of a dramatic climax. Agate and Jennings took exception to the lack of historical accuracy, with Agate declaring the play a fantasy. Most reviews commented on the use of dialogue to re-create historical figures with the consequent episodic structure. Only Ivor Brown believed that this structure added to the effectiveness of the play.

Victoria Regina. 1935. Opened 5 January at the Gate Theatre (London) for 23 performances. Revivals: Broadhurst Theatre (New York), December 1935; return engagement after a summer break in August 1936. Lyric Theatre (London), 21 June 1937; Renaissance Theatre (Berlin), April 1938; Martin Beck Theatre (New York), October 1938.

Victoria Regina was Housman's most popular and successful play with both critics and audiences. Certain Housman traits were criticized again—the play was episodic, dialogue driven, and too much a blend of historical fact and imaginative fiction. In this case, however, these flaws were generally excused and at times seen as clever devices. Almost all the reviews praised the choice of playlets that were combined for production. MacCarthy called the play "ingeniously presented" and praised the choice of plays that focused on one theme and thus gave the episodic presentation continuity. Wyatt commented that the play offered a more complete portrait of Victoria and was better than that found in the recently published biography by Lytton Strachey. Isaacs and Malcolm declared that the episodic form was well suited to the topic; Malcolm suggested that others learn from Housman's example and called for Housman to bring more royal figures to the stage. In particular, critics seemed to like the love story that portrayed Victoria as both woman and monarch. Repplier and Atkinson [1] stated that Housman's ability to make the subject of Victoria interesting was proof of a master at work. Atkinson [2] and John Mason Brown both noted that the plays were written for a publisher and not a producer, Brown finding that the play lacked emotion and both agreeing that it was too language driven at the expense of action. Brown and Atkinson [3] also found fault with the last two scenes that highlight Victoria as an old woman, for they noted that the scenes seemed designed to add theatrical touches of fantastic makeup rather than to highlight any thematic point. *The Times* review (Review of *Victoria Regina*, 1938) and Atkinson [3] suggested that the producers of the various productions take advantage of the other plays Housman had written on Victoria and offer different programs of other Victoria plays. Only Hobhouse expressed distaste for the play. He criticized Housman's use of "rumor" to supplement facts and felt that Victoria came across as "Vicky the Pooh." Only he expressed regret that the ban had been lifted. Trask reported that the Berlin production contained a number of alterations to make the play acceptable for the German public; all references to Disraeli were deleted and all of Housman's suggestions about Albert's Jewish parentage were removed. In addition, two actresses were employed to play Victoria.

ADDITIONAL PLAYS, ADAPTATIONS, AND PRODUCTIONS

Many of Housman's plays were closet dramas that were never produced on the stage. None of his classical dramas, such as *The Death of Orpheus* (1921) or *The Death of Socrates* (1925), were performed. Several of his one-act fantasy and farce plays were produced, including *The Fairy* (1921) in Glastonbury, *A Fool and His Money* (1927) in New Milton, and *Bird in Hand* (1918) in London. His one-act propaganda play, *The Lord of Harvest,* was doubled-billed with the one-act *A Likely Story* at the Court Theatre in London in 1910, but most of his other propaganda plays, such as *The New Hangman* (1930) and *Judge Lynch* (1935), plays protesting the death penalty, were never produced. His 1923 play *Echo de Paris: A Study from Life,* based on his encounter with Oscar Wilde, was also not produced. Housman wrote or contributed to several pageant plays, a form compatible with Housman's episodic style of drama: *The Oxford Historical Pageant,* a collaborative effort, was produced in 1907 in Oxford, and Housman's *St. Martin's Pageant* was produced in 1921 in Westminster and in London in 1922. In addition to the almost perennial presentation of *Little Plays of St. Francis* from 1925 to 1951 (except for the years 1941–46), Housman also had the religious dramas *Nunc Dimittis* and *Jacob* produced in 1933 and 1942, respectively. In addition, Housman wrote three adaptations that were staged. With Liza Lehrman providing music, Housman wrote the light opera *The Vicar of Wakefield* (1906) based on Goldsmith's novel. It was produced in November 1906 in Manchester and the next month, after extensive editing, in London; Housman disclaimed any responsibility for the revision. Housman's two other adaptations, a modernized version of Aristophanes' *Lysistrata* (1910) and a revision of *Alice in Wonderland* called *Alice in Ganderland* (1911), were both expressions of his support for the suffrage movement. Most reviewers complained that *Lysistrata* was too tame and *Alice in Ganderland* was an uneven blend of parody and heavy-handed moralism. During the last decade of Housman's life only two of his plays were given productions: *The Family Honour* (1950) and *Consider Your Verdict* (1950). Almost all of the aforementioned productions had very short runs of less than a week. In 1918 a silent film of *Prunella* directed by Jules Raycourt was released. Housman's 1907 play *The Change Ringers* and his 1914 play *The Pied Piper* were not published.

CRITICAL ASSESSMENT OF HOUSMAN'S DRAMATIC CAREER

No critical evaluation of Housman's dramatic career has yet been done. Recent scholarship on Housman has focused on his poetry, his letter writing, and his illustrations. Although the 1935 *Time* magazine review of *Victoria Regina* ("Helen Millennial") declared Housman a "literary lightweight," Housman's contributions to the British stage should not be overlooked.

Greene credited Housman with the invention of the play cycle, a series of short plays all revolving around a single person. Use of this structure resulted in two of Housman's most successful dramas, *Victoria Regina* and *Little Plays of St. Francis*. Because these plays were written as separate playlets united together and because they relied on conversation rather than action to reveal character, the plays were criticized as being episodic and undramatic. Not many play cycles are written today, but Housman's dramatic structure has clearly influenced today's most popular entertainment form, television. No critical study has been done on Housman's use of the play cycle, whether he altered this structure over time, or how other playwrights may have adapted his structure.

Housman's reliance on conversation rather than action for character development stems from his desire to reveal the human qualities of his historical and religious subjects. A principal criticism of these conversations was their historical inaccuracies. Housman defended his combination of imagination and fact, saying that it was often necessary to bridge the gaps between what was known. He also pointed out that his speculation about Prince Albert's Jewish background was based on reports by several sources who attested to its truth. Housman was also criticized for his tendency to pontificate in his plays. Despite the flaws, Housman's use of conversation as a means of character delineation deserves closer examination. The emphasis on language over action that is a hallmark of our present drama results in plays imbued with more naturalistic conversation than found in Housman's plays, but Housman's contribution to the development of this type of drama has not been studied. Likewise, Housman's poetic drama and his development of historical and religious drama clearly anticipate the works of T. S. Eliot and Christopher Fry. In addition, Darlington noted Housman's variation of the choral character in *Jacob*. The character of The Voice that functions as both commentator and Jacob's conscience may be a type of split protagonist used for a stream-of-consciousness presentation.

Nicoll [2] has written about the tendency of historical plays written in the early part of this century to "revivify the past" without political commentary on the present day, of which *Victoria Regina* is the perfect example (733). The relationship of Housman's historical plays to that of other historical plays of the time may give us greater insight into both Housman's work and that of other playwrights of the period.

Perhaps Housman's most important contributions are his religious plays. Even though Housman's religious drama was never professionally produced, Housman did help revive religious drama. Nicoll ([1], 237) suggested the importance of *Little Plays of St. Francis* because of their structure and their role in the development of amateur theater groups of the time. Only Weales has written about Housman's religious drama, which he found to be simplistic. Careful study of Housman's religious works and other writings shows that the so-called simplicity derives from Housman's own feelings about spirituality. For Housman, organized religion was an impediment to a spiritual life that could best be developed through one's own personal relationship with God. Further assessments may be able to more fully evaluate Housman's spiritual values and explore the connection between these values and his drama.

One other connection that should be more fully explored is that between Housman and Harley Granville-Barker. Although they only wrote one play together, Granville-Barker had a long-lasting relationship with Housman. Granville-Barker's influence on Housman's playwriting has never been evaluated.

ARCHIVAL SOURCES

The most extensive collection of manuscripts of plays, produced and unproduced, as well as some of Housman's other writings and drawings, is available at the Street Library branch of the Somerset County Library. Other manuscript materials, prints, and drawings are housed at the Huntington Library and Art Gallery and the British Library and its Manuscript Department.

PRIMARY BIBLIOGRAPHY

Plays

Alice in Ganderland. London: Woman's Press, 1911.
Angels and Ministers: Four Plays of Victorian Shade and Character. (Includes *The Queen: God Bless Her; His Favorite Flower; The Comforter. Possession* added to the 1922 edition.) London: Jonathan Cape, 1921; New York: Harcourt, Brace, 1922.
As Good as Gold: A Play in One Act. London and New York: Samuel French, 1916.
Bethlehem: A Nativity Play. London and New York: Macmillan, 1902; Boston: Baker International Play Bureau, 1927.
Bird in Hand. London and New York: Samuel French, 1916.
Bond of Fellowship. London: Sidgwick & Jackson, 1935.
The Chinese Lantern. New York: Samuel French, 1920.
The Comments of Juniper. (Includes *The Peacemakers; The Mess of Pottage; Brother*

Ass; The Makers of Miracles; The Order of Release; The Last Comment.) London: Sidgwick & Jackson, 1926.

Cornered Poets. (Includes *The Fire-Lighters; The Messengers; Charles! Charles!; The Cutty-Stool; Elegy of a Country Churchyard; Sal Volatile; The Mortuary.*) London: Jonathan Cape, 1929; New York: Cape & Smith, 1929.

The Death of Socrates: A Dramatic Scene. London: Sidgwick & Jackson, 1925; Boston: Small, Maynard, 1925.

Dethronements: Imaginary Portraits of Political Characters. (Includes *The Kingmaker; The Man of Business; The Instruments.*) London: Jonathan Cape, 1922; New York: Macmillan, 1923.

Echo de Paris: A Study from Life. London: Jonathan Cape, 1923; New York: Appleton, 1924.

False Premises: Five One Act Plays. Oxford: Blackwell, 1922.

Family Honour: A Comedy of Four Acts and an Epilogue. London: Jonathan Cape, 1950.

Followers of St. Francis: Four Plays of the Early Franciscan Legend. London: Sidgwick & Jackson, 1923.

Four Plays of St. Clare. (Includes *Good Beauty; Kind Comfort; Weaker Vessels; Holy Terror.*) London: Sidgwick & Jackson, 1934.

The Golden Sovereign. (Includes *Angels and Ministers, Possession, Dethronements, Echo de Paris, Palace Plays, Cornered Poets,* and *Palace Scenes.*) London: Jonathan Cape, 1937; New York: Charles Scribner's Sons, 1937.

Gracious Majesty. London: Jonathan Cape, 1941.

Happy and Glorious: A Dramatic Biography. London: London Reprint Society, 1943. Rpt. London: Jonathan Cape, 1945.

Judge Lynch. In *Twenty-Five One-Act Plays of 1935,* ed. John Bourne. London: Lovat, Dickson, & Thompson, 1935.

Little Plays of St. Francis: A Dramatic Cycle from the Life and Legend of St. Francis of Assisi. London: Sidgwick & Jackson, 1922. Reprint. Great Neck, NY: Core Collection Books, 1979.

Little Plays of St. Francis: A Dramatic Cycle from the Life and Legend of St. Francis of Assisi. 2nd series. London: Sidgwick & Jackson, 1930.

Little Plays of St. Francis: A Dramatic Cycle from the Life and Legend of St. Francis of Assisi. 3 vols., illustrated. London: Sidgwick & Jackson, 1935.

The Lord of Harvest: A Morality in One Act. London and New York: Samuel French, 1916.

Lysistrata. London: Woman's Press, 1911.

Nazareth: A Morality in One Act. London and New York: Samuel French, 1916.

The New Hangman: A Play in One Act. London and New York: Putnam, 1930.

Nunc Dimittis: An Epilogue to "Little Plays of St. Francis." London: Dramatic Society of University College of London, 1933.

Old Testament Plays. London: Jonathan Cape, 1950.

The Oxford Historical Pageant, June 27–July 3, 1907. Oxford: Oxford Pageant Company, 1907.

Pains and Penalties: The Defence of Queen Caroline. London: Sidgwick & Jackson, 1911.

Palace Plays. London: Jonathan Cape, 1930.

Palace Scenes: More Plays of Queen Victoria. London: Jonathan Cape, 1937.

Palestine Plays. (Includes *Abraham and Isaac; Jacob; Ramoth Gilead; The Burden of*

Nineveh.) London: Jonathan Cape, 1942; New York: Charles Scribner's Sons, 1943.

Possessions: A Peep-Show in Paradise. London: Jonathan Cape, 1921.

Prunella; or, Love in a Dutch Garden. With Harley Granville-Barker. London: A. H. Bullen, 1906; New York: Brentano's, 1906; London: Sidgwick & Jackson, 1911, 1930 (revised edition); Boston: Small, Maynard, 1939 (revised edition). Also in *Plays of To-Day,* vol. 2. 1925. Reprint. Freeport, NY: Books for Libraries Press, 1970.

The Queen's Progress: Nine Palace Plays. 2nd series. London: Jonathan Cape, 1932.

Samuel, The King-maker: A Play in Four Acts. London: Jonathan Cape, 1944.

Six O'Clock Call. (Acting Version). London: Jonathan Cape, 1938.

The Vicar of Wakefield. London: W. S. Johnson, 1906.

Victoria and Albert: Palace Plays. 3rd series. London: Jonathan Cape, 1933.

Victoria Regina: A Dramatic Biography. London: Jonathan Cape, 1934; New York: Charles Scribner's Sons, 1935.

Ways and Means. London: H.F.W. Deane & Sons, 1928.

The Wheel: Three Poetic Plays on Greek Subjects (*Apollo in Hades, Death of Alcestis, The Doom of Admetus*). London: Sidgwick & Jackson, 1910; New York: Samuel French, 1920.

Ye Fearful Saints!: Plays of Creed, Custom, and Credulity. (Includes *Consider Your Verdict; The Time Servers; The She-Ass and the Tired Colt; The Gods Whom Men Love Die Old; The New Hangman; The Waiting Room; Old Bottles; The Wrong Door; In This Sign Conquer.*) London: Sidgwick & Jackson, 1932.

Other Writings

The "Little Plays" Handbook: Practical Notes for Producers of "Little Plays of St. Francis," "Followers of St. Francis," and "The Comments of Jupiter." London: Sidgwick & Jackson, 1927.

The Unexpected Years. London: Jonathan Cape, 1937.

"Victoria Regina." *Stage* (Jan. 1936): 41–43.

SECONDARY BIBLIOGRAPHY

Agate, James. Review of *Mr. Gladstone's Comforter. The Sunday Times* (3 Nov. 1929): 6.

Review of *Alice in Ganderland. The Times* (28 Oct. 1911): 10.

Archer, William. [1]. "Christmas Entertainments." *World* (27 Dec. 1904): 1111.

———. [2]. *Play-Making: A Manual of Craftsmanship.* Boston: Small, Maynard, 1923.

Atkinson, Brooks. [1]. "Good Queen Vicky." *New York Times* (9 Oct. 1938): 10:1.

———. [2]. Review of *Victoria Regina. New York Times* (27 Dec. 1935): 15.

———. [3]. Review of *Victoria Regina. New York Times* (5 Jan. 1936): 9:1.

Banks, Olive. *The Biographical Dictionary of British Feminists, 1900–1945,* 2:99–102. New York: New York University Press, 1990.

Beerbohm, Max. *Around Theatres.* 1930. New York: Greenwood Press, 1968.

Review of *Bethlehem. The Times* (20 Dec. 1923): 10.

Boyce, Neith. "Love in a Dutch Garden." *Harper's Weekly* (10 Jan. 1914): 27.

Brook, Donald. *Writers' Gallery,* 61–66. London: Rockliff, 1944. Reprint. Port Washington, NY: Kennikat Press: 1970.

Brown, Ivor. Review of *Mr. Gladstone's Comforter. Saturday Review* (9 Nov. 1929): 541–42.

Brown, John Mason. *Two on the Aisle: Ten Years of the American Theatre in Performance.* New York: Norton, 1938.

Review of *The Chinese Lantern. Athenaeum* (27 June 1908): 800.

Review of *The Chinese Lantern. Sketch* (24 June 1908): 362.

Review of *The Chinese Lantern. The Times* (17 June 1908): 14.

Church, Richard. "Mr. Housman's Queen Victoria." *Spectator* (15 Sept. 1933): 349.

"The Curtain Went Up." *Stage* (Feb. 1936): 6.

Darlington, W. A. Review of *Jacob. New York Times* (14 June 1942): 8:1.

Davies, A. Emil. Review of *Possessions: A Peep-Show in Paradise. New Statesman* (21 Jan. 1922): 454.

Engen, Rodney K. *Laurence Housman.* Stroud, Gloucestershire: Catalpa Press, 1983.

Farjeon, Herbert. "Pains and Penalties." *World* (5 Dec. 1911): 866.

Review of *A Fool and His Money. The Times* (22 Feb. 1935): 10.

Fyfe, H. Hamilton. [1]. Review of *The Chinese Lantern. World* (24 June 1908): 1192.

———. [2]. Review of *Prunella. World* (1 May 1906): 775.

Granville-Barker, Harley. Preface. In *Little Plays of St. Francis: A Dramatic Cycle from the Life and Legend of St. Francis of Assisi,* by Laurence Housman, rev. ed., vii–xv. London: Sidgwick & Jackson, 1926.

Greene, Ellin. Afterward. In *The Rat-Catcher's Daughter,* by Laurence Housman, ed. Ellin Greene, 164–69. New York: Athenaeum, 1974.

"Helen Hayes Plays the Royal *Victoria Regina* Royally." *Newsweek* (28 Dec. 1935): 25–26.

"Helen Millennial." *Time* (30 Dec. 1935): 22–23.

"Henley on Hammersmith." *Saturday Review* (9 Nov. 1929): 541–42.

Hobhouse, Christopher. Review of *Victoria Regina. Spectator* (25 June 1937): 1187.

"Incident at the Savoy Theatre." *The Times* (27 Nov. 1911): 8.

Isaacs, Edith J. R. "At Its Best: Broadway in Review." *Theatre Arts Monthly* (Feb. 1936): 93–105.

Jennings, Richard. Review of *Mr. Gladstone's Comforter. Spectator* (9 Nov. 1929): 662.

Kalisch, Alfred. "The Vicar of Wakefield." *World* (18 Dec. 1906): 1249.

Kenyur-Hodgkins, Ian G. *Laurence Housman, 1865–1959, Clemence Housman, 1861–1955, Alfred Edward Housman, 1859–1936.* London: National Book League, 1975.

Review of *A Likely Story. The Times* (28 May 1910): 12.

Review of *The Lord of Harvest. The Times* (28 May 1910): 12.

Review of *Lysistrata. Athenaeum* (5 Oct. 1910): 465.

Review of *Lysistrata. Illustrated London News* (15 April 1910): 506.

Review of *Lysistrata. Saturday Review* (15 Oct. 1910): 480–81.

Review of *Lysistrata. Sketch* (19 Oct. 1910): 46.

Review of *Lysistrata. The Times* (12 Oct. 1910): 10.

MacCarthy, Desmond. "Victoria Rediviva." *New Statesman and Nation* (3 July 1937): 14.

Malcolm, Ian. Review of *Victoria Regina. Quarterly Review* (Oct. 1937): 263–77.

Mix, Katherine Lyon. "Laurence Housman." In *Dictionary of Literary Biography,* vol. 10, *Modern British Dramatists, 1900–1945,* ed. Stanley Weintraub, pt. 1, 235–42. Detroit: Gale Research, 1982.

Morgan, Charles. "*Victoria Regina.*" *New York Times* (11 July 1937): 10:1.

Review of *Mr. Gladstone's Comforter. Illustrated London News* (9 Nov. 1929): 662.

Review of *Mr. Gladstone's Comforter. Saturday Review* (9 Nov. 1929): 541–42.

Review of *Mr. Gladstone's Comforter. Spectator* (19 Nov. 1929): 662.

Review of *Mr. Gladstone's Comforter. The Times* (1 Nov. 1929): 14.

Nicoll, Allardyce. [1]. *English Drama, 1900–1930: The Beginnings of the Modern Period.* Cambridge: Cambridge University Press, 1973.

———. [2]. *World Drama from Aeschylus to Anouilh.* 1949. London: Harrap, 2nd ed. 1976.

Review of *Pains and Penalties. Sketch* (6 Dec. 1911): 266.

Review of *Pains and Penalties. The Times* (27 Nov. 1911): 8.

Review of *Pains and Penalties. World* (5 Dec. 1911): 866.

"A Play without a Punch." *Literary Digest* (15 Nov. 1923): 944–45.

Review of *Prunella. Illustrated London News* (23 April 1920): 604.

Review of *Prunella. Sketch* (4 Jan. 1905): 420.

Review of *Prunella. Stage* (26 April 1906): 17.

Review of *Prunella. The Sunday Times* (1 Jan. 1922): 4.

Review of *Prunella. The Times* (24 Dec. 1904): 10.

Review of *Prunella. The Times* (25 Apr. 1906): 12.

Review of *Prunella. The Times* (14 Apr. 1910): 12.

Review of *Prunella. The Times* (27 Dec. 1921): 6.

Review of *Prunella. The Times* (31 July 1930): 12.

Review of *Prunella. World* (14 May 1907): 857.

Repplier, Agnes. "The Brothers Housman." *Atlantic Monthly* 165.1 (Jan. 1940): 46–50.

Trask, Claire. Review of *Victoria Regina. New York Times* (17 Apr. 1938): 10:2.

Review of *The Vicar of Wakefield. Athenaeum* (15 Dec. 1906): 782.

Review of *The Vicar of Wakefield. Sketch* (19 Dec. 1906): 306.

Review of *The Vicar of Wakefield. The Times* (12 Dec. 1906): 4.

Review of *Victoria Regina. Illustrated London News* (3 July 1937): 48.

Review of *Victoria Regina. Literary Digest* (11 Jan. 1936): 19.

Review of *Victoria Regina. New York Times* (22 June 1937): 26.

Review of *Victoria Regina. Stage* (Jan. 1936): 41–43.

Review of *Victoria Regina. The Times* (22 June 1937): 14.

Review of *Victoria Regina. The Times* (3 Jan. 1938): 10.

Weales, Gerald. *Religion in Modern English Drama.* Philadelphia: University of Pennsylvania Press, 1961.

Wyatt, Euphemia Van Rensselaer. Review of *Victoria Regina. Catholic World* (Feb. 1936): 598–99.

BIBLIOGRAPHIES

Catalogue of the Ian Kenyur-Hodgkins Collection of Laurence Housman. Oxford: Warrack Perkins, 1978.

Kemp, Ivor. *Laurence Housman, 1865–1959: A Brief Catalogue of the Collection of Books, Manuscripts, and Drawings Presented to the Street Library.* Street: Somerset County Library, 1967.

Henry Arthur Jones
(1851–1929)

COLETTE LINDROTH

Self-made man, family man, prolific writer, robust defender of England, contentious rebel—in many ways dramatist H. A. Jones embodies the popular idea
of the Victorian/Edwardian man of letters. Born on 20 September 1851 in
Grandborough, Buckinghamshire, the son of a farmer, Jones in both his background and attitudes represented the "backbone of England." His was a story
of opportunities seized and made the most of; nothing in his early life suggested
that he would become one of the best-known dramatists of the late nineteenth
century.

Jones's position at birth was humble, especially in terms of intellectual opportunity. He received his education in the local grammar school in Grandborough, but left at the age of thirteen to work as a clerk in Bradford, employed
by a commercial firm owned by an uncle whom he disliked all his life. The
limitations of his possibilities did not daunt him, however. Rather, he seized the
opportunity for self-education, reading widely (Shakespeare, Milton, and the
Jacobean and Elizabethan poets and dramatists were his special favorites) and
writing incessantly. During these years of authorial apprenticeship he turned his
hand to poetry, fiction, and drama indiscriminately.

He left his uncle's employ when he was eighteen and journeyed to London,
where he immediately immersed himself in the theater. Falling in love alter-
nately with beautiful actresses and the theater itself, he concluded that the stage
was his world. He went to the theater as often as five times a week, going to
some plays again and again; it was here, he later said, that he learned all there
was to know about the perfect dramatic structure that was to become synonymous with his name.

His eventual fame was not his for the asking, however. For years he worked
at mundane jobs to support himself, writing feverishly, attending as many plays

as time and his pocketbook allowed, and sending scripts around for consideration by theater managers. Finally he succeeded in catching the attention of Wy-
bert Rouseby, the manager of the Theatre Royal in Exeter, who produced *Hearts
of Oak* and *It's Only Round the Corner* in 1879. In the same year *A Clerical
Error,* which Jones said had been previously rejected by every theater manager
in London, was accepted by Wilson Barrett and produced at the Court Theatre
in London. Jones's long career was launched.

The modest success of these first short pieces was eclipsed by the spectacular
response to *The Silver King* in 1882. Written in collaboration with H. A. Herman, this rousing melodrama played for more than a year in its original run and
was frequently revived for twenty years or more in England, on the Continent,
and in the United States. From this point on Jones was a significant voice in
the English theatrical world.

From the first Jones refused to be limited to any one type of drama. Although
much of his success rested with his ability to produce gripping, persuasive, fast-
moving melodrama, he soon began experimenting with other, less safely crowd-
pleasing genres. In 1884 his *Saints and Sinners* provoked criticism and
controversy for daring to treat religious themes on the stage, and *Judah,* in 1890,
startled critics and audiences alike with its originality and its daring use of
psychology. *The Dancing Girl* (1891) was also found provocative in its frank
approach to questions of sexual behavior.

Jones was also successful in other, less controversial modes. In the last decade
of the nineteenth century and the first years of the twentieth century he distinguished himself in the creation of satiric drawing-room comedies, including *The
Case of Rebellious Susan* and *Mary Goes First,* a form in which much of his
enduring fame was gained. In all of these genres Jones's skill at producing the
"well-made play" was always in evidence.

But a list of Jones's popular stage successes does not entirely capture his
significance in the nineteenth-century dramatic scene. Jones also influenced the
stage history of his time and for succeeding generations in a series of private
and public controversies for which he was famous during his lifetime and
through which he became one of the most influential shapers of modern drama.
His plays themselves, especially his moral melodramas, may seem dated, but in
his battles for artistic freedom and financial independence for the dramatist he
was a true pioneer.

His most significant battles had to do with his insistence that stage literature
was just that—literature, and deserving of publication just as much as fiction,
poetry, or essays. For a variety of reasons, including erratic copyright laws,
plays were published privately and for a limited audience in the nineteenth
century. Jones helped change that, insisting in *The Renascence of the English
Drama* (1895), *The Foundations of a National Drama* (1913), and *The Theatre
of Ideas* (1915), as well as in numerous speeches and magazine and newspaper
articles, that dramatic literature must be written to be read as well as performed.
He worked tirelessly for the day when published dramas would be available to

posterity in libraries, as well as to the relatively few playgoers who could see stage performances. Here he was fighting two battles of great significance: one to secure more orderly copyright privileges for the playwright, and another to remove English drama from the low estate to which it had fallen during his time. The first battle ended in 1891 with the passage of the Anglo-American Copyright Law. From that time on his plays were published as they were produced. The other battle took longer, for it involved altering the taste of his era.

For years Jones contended that drama was not simply three hours of pleasing entertainment for the masses, but was serious literature that must deal realistically with significant social issues and must inspire, challenge, even shock its audience out of complacency as well as entertaining that audience. Drama, he insisted, must be restored to its rightful position as a great art form that would "assert the value and dignity of human life," one that is "full of meaning and importance."

His insistence that drama confront contemporary reality brought Jones into the forefront of the struggle against censorship, both official and unofficial, a struggle that continued throughout his life. Official censorship was an obvious constraint on the dramatist's freedom, but the demands of "Mrs. Grundy," a timid popular audience that responded with hostility to assaults on convention and decorum, were a subtler and more significant one. Jones campaigned against this timidity throughout his life in books, articles, speeches, and especially in "To Mrs. Grundy," a preface appended to *The Case of Rebellious Susan.* Here Jones challenged the British audience to accept unflinching realism on stage, to look with "a wise, sane, wide-open eye upon all things." The essay also attacked Grundyism for hating "all the great eternal things in literature and art [so much] that if our English Bible itself were to be now first presented to the British public, you would certainly start a prosecution against it for its indecency and its frightful polygamistic tendencies." Jones fought for the dramatist's right to present religious and sexual themes realistically throughout his long career.

In these battles Jones was joined by famous men who were also his good friends, H. G. Wells and George Bernard Shaw. During World War I, however, he found himself at odds with these men, battling what he considered their indefensible pacifism while England was at war. The rupture between Jones, Shaw, and Wells was convulsive to all concerned, since the three had been close friends on both artistic and personal levels for years, but Jones, moved by narrow, emotional patriotism, was horrified by what he felt to be "dangerous and fallacious political creeds." In 1915 the rupture became public when Shaw was asked to resign from the Dramatists' Club because of his attitudes toward the war and Jones, rather than defending his friend, attacked him in a letter charging that Shaw's writings had "done great harm" to England's cause. In *My Dear Wells* the attack was even more unrestrained, accusing Shaw of providing fodder for German propaganda.

Although the rupture was mended after the war and Shaw always maintained that on his part at least their friendship had remained constant, these heated exchanges not surprisingly cooled the friendship among these men. They also helped develop Jones's reputation for irascibility, a reputation established early in his career with a series of conflicts with actor-managers who produced many of his plays. One thing remained constant throughout his life, however: Jones's devotion to principle, whether in artistic or political matters, was outspoken and uncompromising.

The years after World War I were difficult for Jones, not only because of the strains caused by the war. He had to a considerable extent outlived his enormous popularity, and there was a stridency to his writings, both dramatic and journalistic, in these years. His health was also increasingly fragile, leading to a series of mental and physical breakdowns that taxed both him and his family. On 7 January 1929 he died at his home in Hampstead of pneumonia.

Selected Biographical Sources: Cordell; Griffin; Doris Arthur Jones.

MAJOR PLAYS, PREMIERES, AND SIGNIFICANT REVIVALS: THEATRICAL RECEPTION

The Silver King. 1882. Opened at Princess's Theatre (London) on 16 November for 289 performances. J. W. Comyns Carr produced.

The popular melodrama that started Jones's successful stage career, *The Silver King* deals with ideas of sin, redemption, and the possibility of a second chance, ideas Jones worked with throughout his life. Although long on coincidence and short on probability, the play is vivid and fast-moving, proceeding swiftly to its ending of sin punished and virtue rewarded.

As the play opens, Wilfred Denver, a man with a weakness for drink and gambling, is desperate. Broke, unemployed, jeered in the local tavern, he realizes his degradation but pleads with his loyal wife, Nelly, not to let the children know how far he has fallen. In a complicated bit of plotting he becomes implicated in a murder committed by Herbert Skinner, a villain with a smooth exterior. Because he was so drunk, Denver thinks that he himself has done it. Appalled with himself, he flees to Bristol to try to start a new life.

When Denver mysteriously reappears, he gives a friend money to give Nelly and their children without revealing where the money came from. Finally coincidence steps in—an old acquaintance happens to see Denver and persuades him to show himself to Nelly. All is revealed: Denver has become wealthy mining in Nevada and, subdued and repentant, wants only to pay for his crimes. In a flurry of coincidences the truth comes out—a former ally confesses that Skinner committed the murder. Denver's good name is restored, as are his wife and family as the curtain falls on a happy ending.

The play received tumultuous popular response, with a run whose length was unusual for the era, and was frequently revived. While some critics found the melodrama and coincidences overdone, they too applauded the moral tone and rousing action and expressed the feeling that an important new voice was being heard on the English stage.

The Dancing Girl. 1891. Opened at the Haymarket Theatre (London) on 15 January for 266 performances. Produced by Herbert Beerbohm Tree.

Like several other of Jones's plays, *The Dancing Girl* deals with an attempt to live a double life and also with the Victorian double standard of sexuality for men and women. Set in an isolated seaside village, the play treats several polar opposites—city/country, honesty/deception, rigid morality/sexual freedom. Drusilla Ives, the "dancing girl" of the title, has left her strict Quaker home to live in London, where she performs under the name of "Diane Valrose." In this identity she has been courted by Valentine Danecourt, the Duke of Guisebury. A complicated plot brings them both to St. Endellion, where Drusilla's father, David, a strict Quaker, still lives. The scandal of Drusilla's double life threatens to erupt, and the main characters are pulled in several directions that dramatize personal conflicts between good and evil.

In a complicated ending resolution of a sort is reached. Valentine has lost his wealth but has become a hero, erecting a seawall that saves lives in a shipwreck. He and the other residents of St. Endellion are living lives of quiet virtue and restraint. Finally he receives news of Drusilla, who has gone to New Orleans, where she found the excitement she had craved, but also met her death. As is so often the case in Jones's plays, virtue has triumphed, and straying from its path has resulted in death.

Critical reception to *The Dancing Girl* was generally favorable, with special praise for the ways in which Jones managed to create a complicated plot and still move the drama briskly to its surprising and exciting conclusion. There were some complaints about improbability in the incidents, however.

The Case of Rebellious Susan. 1894. Opened at St. James's Theatre (London) on 3 October for 164 performances. Charles Wyndham produced.

One of several plays in which Jones explored the question of the sexual double standard for men and women, this play counsels, as do his others on this theme, that while it is unjust, it is also inevitable, and women would be well advised to accept the situation with as much grace as possible. Susan defiantly vows revenge when she discovers that her husband has been unfaithful, and sets out to punish him with the same kind of behavior he has been indulging in. Other characters in the play, although sympathetic, counsel resignation; faced with Susan's enraged shout that men are "brutes," her wise friend Lady Darby only replies, "I'm afraid they are; but I don't see what we're to do except take them as we find them and make the best of them."

An idealistic young couple is mocked for trying to achieve equality in marriage; the husband is an ineffectual cipher and the wife turns into a raging virago. Lady Darby, on the other hand, a patient wife who has long turned a blind eye to her husband's countless infidelities, is attractive, admirable, and wise. Reluctantly, Susan adopts Lady Darby's resigned approach, accepting her husband's promise that he will not repeat his misbehavior (a promise almost certain to be broken), and the play ends with female acceptance of male frailty.

The Case of Rebellious Susan was popular with both critics and the audience, praised for its stinging wit and its candid presentation of modern marriage and its problems. While some critics protested against the negative picture of men, the general reception was favorable.

Michael and His Lost Angel. 1896. Opened at the Lyceum Theatre (London) on 15 January for 10 performances. Produced by Johnston Forbes-Robertson.

Michael and His Lost Angel occupies a unique position among Jones's works: it is one of his few complete failures, receiving what Jones himself called "savage" treatment both from critics and a booing opening-night audience. Still, it remained one of his favorite plays, one that he insisted was much better than many that became very popular. Dealing with sin, redemption, hypocrisy, and honesty, it develops some of his favorite themes.

The Reverend Michael Feversham is an intensely spiritual, rather rigid young cleric who, as the play begins, has insisted, kindly but firmly, that one of his parishioners, Rose Gibbard, publicly proclaim her sin against chastity. Michael himself is attracted against his will to Audrie Lesden, a woman who keeps secret an early, unsuccessful marriage. Both Michael and Audrie are fascinated by a portrait of Michael's dead mother, who had told him before her death that she would look after him as his "good angel" in heaven.

Michael succumbs to temptation with Audrie, but they both pay for it with an agony of guilt, and Michael begins to realize how unfair he had been to Rose Gibbard as he and Audrie concoct a story to hide their transgression. Begging her to be his "good angel" and agree that they must separate, Michael tears himself away. By the play's end Michael, who has fled to the Continent and led a life of penitence, has died. Audrie has come to repent at his deathbed (she too is dying), and Rose, who has become an Anglican nun, presides over the final scene of repentance, forgiveness, and presumed redemption.

Michael and His Lost Angel received savagely negative reviews from the critics both in England and in the United States. Critics seemed puzzled by Jones's aim in writing the play; some complained that it was too didactic, others that it was immoral, but all agreed that it was a disaster on the stage, a "miserable mistake" that should never have been attempted.

Mrs. Dane's Defence. 1900. Opened at Wyndham's Theatre (London) on 9 October for 207 performances. Charles Wyndham produced.

One of Jones's best-known and longest-running plays, *Mrs. Dane's Defence* deals with the issue of sexual morality and the ill effects of any kind of sexual impropriety on a woman's life. The double standard is in fine form here, since Mrs. Dane, although an attractive woman with great appeal both to the audience and to other characters in the play, is seen as justifiably punished for bearing a child out of wedlock and then telling lies about her situation. The responsibility of the father is never even made an issue.

As the play opens, potential scandal is brewing; a careless comment about Mrs. Dane suggests that she was known under a different name in Vienna, and that her conduct there had been scandalous. In the face of lurid gossip Mrs. Dane steadfastly maintains her innocence, insisting that it's all a case of mistaken identity. She gives Sir Daniel Carteret, an experienced lawyer, a detailed account of her blameless life, but he remains unconvinced.

Finally, amidst a tangle of conflicting stories and charges made and retracted, the truth is revealed. "Mrs. Dane" was indeed guilty of the behavior gossip attributed to her. In her own defense she pleads her naïveté, her grief and remorse over the outcome, and her blameless life since then. Sir Daniel expresses his pity but insists that his nephew Lionel, who was engaged to her, must be told and the marriage must not take place. A sympathetic woman pleads her case, insisting that Mrs. Dane has paid for her "sin," but Sir Daniel remains adamant. Mrs. Dane must leave, driven by "the hard law . . . that we can't escape from." Mrs. Dane leaves in despair, with everyone more or less agreeing that, despite the sadness of it all, this is for the best. From sexual indiscretion there is no appeal for a woman.

Mrs. Dane's Defence was treated with great seriousness by the critics, who praised its courageous look at "risky" material as well as its sound morality. While some cautioned that Jones went too far in his description of Mrs. Dane's past, others proclaimed it the best play he had written.

The Hypocrites. 1906. Opened at the Hudson Theatre (New York) on 30 August. Produced by Charles Frohman.

This play, like many of Jones's, explored the hypocrisy of "polite" Victorians who insisted that everyone but themselves live up to rigorous moral standards, especially in sexual matters. The lines of conflict are quickly drawn. The Wilmores, although one of the local "great families," are heavily mortgaged; their hope of financial and social survival depends on their son, Lennard, making a "good" marriage to Helen Plugenet, the daughter of a baronet. Helen is an idealistic young woman, but Lennard is quickly revealed as having a somewhat checkered past. The Wilmores are making a fuss because Sheldrake, a local working man, has gotten a girl pregnant and refuses to marry her; they insist that he must.

The hypocrisy of the title is displayed when Lennard, in scenes of classic Victorian melodrama, is revealed to be guilty of the same behavior as Sheldrake. The Wilmores are as adamant that Lennard must not marry his lover, Rachel, as they were that Sheldrake must do so, and the double standard for the middle class as opposed to the working class is clearly drawn.

The resolution is again the stuff of melodrama. Inspired by Helen's nobility, Lennard suddenly (and for no apparent reason) gains the moral courage to do the right thing. He proclaims his love for Rachel, insists on marrying her, defies his parents, and refuses to marry for money instead of love and duty. At the end of the play the Empire has saved the day. Lennard will go to India to work on the railroad; his mother, finally reconciled to his behavior, will probably accompany them.

The Hypocrites was produced to great acclaim both in London and New York. American critics were especially enthusiastic about the biting satire that ''flays conventional morality'' and reveals real goodness. Some even mentioned ''shouts of praise'' that broke out in the audience on opening night. London critics were somewhat more reserved, but praised the candid and uncompromising view of society presented in the play.

Mary Goes First. 1913. Opened at the Playhouse (London) on 18 September for 151 performances. Produced by Marie Tempest.

One of the most deft and delightful comedies Jones ever wrote, *Mary Goes First* is also one of his least dated. The plot hinges on a matter of precedence— literally who shall ''go first'' to dinner, the wife of a knight or the wife of a baronet. While this is hardly a burning issue in the late twentieth century, the vanity and competitiveness driving that kind of ambition are timeless qualities.

The plot is slight, revolving around the dreadful Thomas Bodsworth, who has recently been knighted, and his even more dreadful wife, an overdressed, over-coiffured, ill-mannered example of nouveau riche vulgarity. Mary Whichello, a lively, witty woman, has until now been the acknowledged social leader of her circle, but with the Bodsworths' title she must defer to Mrs. Bodsworth. Mary's taunting of Lady Bodsworth is a comic masterpiece, but she finally goes too far; the lady in question overhears herself called ''an impropriety'' and, in a rage, threatens to sue unless a written apology is proffered by Mary. Mary refuses, and the play seesaws back and forth through the machinations of husbands, friends, lawyers, and the women.

Along the way Mary concocts a scheme through which her husband can secure a title even higher than the Bodsworths'. After much comic maneuvering justice is more or less done; Mary triumphs, title and all, and the curtain falls as she and the now-deferential Lady Bodsworth do a Gaston-Alphonse routine on their way to the dinner table. The impasse is resolved when Mary grabs her companion and simply shoves her through the door.

Critics were enthusiastic about *Mary Goes First,* praising its wit, its lively, convincing dialogue, and its lighthearted skewering of snobbery and pretension. The structure of the play, always one of Jones's strengths, was praised, as was the skillful stagecraft involved in the final scene.

ASSESSMENT OF JONES'S CAREER

As the author of more than fifty produced plays, most of which were hits in England and the United States and on the Continent, Jones was clearly a major figure on the English theatrical scene in the nineteenth century. From the first he was seen as instrumental in lifting British drama from the level of cheap spectacle and easy entertainment to which it had fallen. He was considered, with his contemporaries Arthur Wing Pinero and George Bernard Shaw, as forming the vanguard of new realism and sophistication for the drama. His ability to combine a message of social reform with skillfully plotted stories was commended throughout his career, and his mastery of the "well-made play" has always been acknowledged.

From the first he also received criticism, however, often for relying too heavily on the lurid conventions of melodrama, a problem of which he himself was aware. Having gained success and financial independence with the melodrama of *The Silver King,* he said that he intended to dedicate himself to experimentation, to pleasing himself "rather than the exigencies of a theatrical manager" and the demands of an unsophisticated audience. However, his next significant effort, *Saints and Sinners,* was itself melodramatic in structure, though considerably more sophisticated in its incorporation of social ideas. This fascination with the strong theatrical scene rather than the subtle one was to continue throughout his life. It is one of the reasons why modern scholars especially see Jones as dated. While he is considered one of the best of nineteenth-century dramatists, he is often contrasted to Shaw, who is clearly as much at home among modernists as he was among the Edwardians. Equally clearly Jones is not.

But it is not only as a playwright that Jones must be considered; he is significant as a theoretician as well, a man who broadened the number of topics that were felt appropriate for presentation on stage. One quality that friend and foe alike remarked on throughout Jones's career was his "Englishness," his ability to present the English middle class, particularly, as worthy of serious artistic attention. Throughout his life he defended English drama in comparison to that of the Continent, insisting that it was in England, rather than in Ibsen's Norway, for example, that true realism was developing. The relationship between him and Ibsen is indeed one of the factors to be studied in his career. He was inclined to scoff at Ibsen; in 1884 he wrote (with H. A. Herman) *Breaking a Butterfly,* a fairly clumsy effort intended as a comic commentary on *A Doll's House.* While he later pleaded the folly of youth to excuse this reductive and unsuccessful effort, he never entirely lost his scorn for Ibsen's play; he told friends that Ibsen should have presented Torvald breathing a sigh of relief when his spoiled, annoying Nora finally walked out of his life. Because they were both realists, Jones and Ibsen were often compared, usually in Ibsen's favor, but Jones denied all his life that he had been influenced by the Norwegian. His realism was entirely English, he insisted, a homegrown product independent of Continental influences.

If concern with material that is typically English is one of Jones's defining characteristics, another is his interest in certain moral themes that recur in his plays. The possibility of redemption after wrongdoing is one of his favorite ideas, developed in *The Silver King, Judah, Michael and His Lost Angel,* and many others. A powerful attack on English social ills, especially snobbery, is apparent in many of his best comedies, including *Dolly Reforming Herself, The Case of Rebellious Susan,* and *Mary Goes First.* Perhaps his favorite approach combines the attack on snobbery with a condemnation of the hypocrisy it so often produced. This two-pronged attack is evident in *Mrs. Dane's Defence, The Dancing Girl, Judah, The Masqueraders, The Lie, The Liars, The Hypocrites,* and others. It provides his strongest and most enduring social commentary, a commentary well worth studying even though his attitudes rarely transcend those of the era in which he wrote.

A study of his plays in connection with critics' judgments of them is especially rewarding, providing a survey of changing attitudes from the late nineteenth century to the present day. Most of his contemporaries admired his seriousness, his high moral tone, his courageous realism, and his deft touch with satire. Others condemned his too-frank approach to religious and sexual matters, finding even the titles of *Saints and Sinners* or *The Liars* ''not nice'' or complaining that religious ideas must not be presented on the stage at all. Later generations praised him for doing exactly these things. The reasons for these choices tell the reader as much about the era represented as they do about Jones.

Nor has Jones disappeared from contemporary scholarship. Again the focus of critical attention has changed, with his presentation of women receiving serious consideration. The picture of ''the new woman'' in Jones's plays is often studied, as is his picture of the double standard of sexual mores. In this regard Jones is often considered with his friend and contemporary, Arthur Wing Pinero. While Jones certainly does not present liberated women by contemporary standards, his investigations of the issues involved are challenging and historically illuminating.

As an essayist, too, Jones is deserving of study. His studies of censorship, his calls for a national theater and for reform of the actor-manager system, his demands for increased dignity for the drama, even his comments on the infant film industry, reveal a distinctive voice: confident, often contentious, sometimes strident, but always observant, well informed, highly principled, and vitally interested in drama and society.

ARCHIVAL SOURCES

Manuscripts, typescripts, and promptbooks of several of Jones's plays are held by the New York Public Library, Lincoln Center branch. The Harvard University Library, the Yale University Library, and the Bodleian Library have manuscripts of some of his plays. Collections of his correspondence are held in the collections of the British Library, the University of London Library, and the University of Chicago Library.

PRIMARY BIBLIOGRAPHY

Plays

The Bauble Shop. London: Samuel French, 1893.
A Bed of Roses. London: Samuel French, 1882.

Breaking a Butterfly. In collaboration with H. A. Herman. London: privately printed, 1884.

Carnac Sahib. London: Samuel French, 1899.

The Case of Rebellious Susan. London: Macmillan, 1897.

Chance the Idol. London: privately printed by the Chiswick Press, 1902.

The Chevaleer. London: Samuel French, 1904.

A Clerical Error. London: Samuel French, 1906.

The Crusaders. London: Macmillan, 1893. Also in *Representative Plays by Henry Arthur Jones.* New York: Macmillan, 1925.

The Dancing Girl. London: Samuel French, 1891. Also in *Representative Plays by Henry Arthur Jones.* New York: Macmillan, 1925.

The Deacon. London: Samuel French, 1893.

The Divine Gift. London: Duckworth, 1913. Also in *Representative Plays of Henry Arthur Jones.* New York: Macmillan, 1925.

Dolly Reforming Herself. London: privately printed, 1908. Also in *Representative Plays by Henry Arthur Jones.* New York: Macmillan, 1925.

Elopement. Ilfracombe: privately printed by John Tait, 1879.

The Galilean's Victory. (Original title *The Evangelist.*) London: privately printed by the Chiswick Press, 1907.

The Goal. London: printed at the Chiswick Press, 1898. Also in *Representative Plays by Henry Arthur Jones.* New York. Macmillan, 1925.

Grace Mary. London: printed at the Chiswick Press, 1898. Also in *Representative Plays by Henry Arthur Jones.* New York: Macmillan, 1925; *The Theatre of Ideas.* London: Chapman & Hall, 1915.

Hearts of Oak. London: Samuel French, 1885.

Her Tongue. In *The Theatre of Ideas.* London: Chapman & Hall, 1915.

The Heroic Stubbs. London: privately printed by the Chiswick Press, 1906.

The Hypocrites. London: Samuel French, 1908.

It's Only Round the Corner. London: Samuel French (Lacy's Acting Edition), 1883.

Joseph Entangled. London: Samuel French, 1906.

Judah. London: Macmillan, 1894. Also in *Representative Plays by Henry Arthur Jones.* New York: Macmillan, 1925.

The Liars. London: Macmillan, 1904. Also in *Representative Plays by Henry Arthur Jones.* New York: Macmillan, 1925.

The Lie. New York: George H. Doran, 1915; London: F. E. Morrell, 1923.

The Manoeuvres of Jane. London: Macmillan, 1904.

Mary Goes First. London: Samuel French, 1913. Also in *Representative Plays by Henry Arthur Jones.* New York: Macmillan, 1925.

The Masqueraders. London: Macmillan, 1899. Also in *Representative Plays by Henry Arthur Jones.* New York: Macmillan, 1925.

Michael and His Lost Angel. London: Macmillan, 1896. Also in *Representative Plays by Henry Arthur Jones.* New York: Macmillan, 1925.

The Middleman. London: Samuel French, 1907. Also in *Representative Plays by Henry Arthur Jones.* New York: Macmillan, 1925.

Mrs. Dane's Defence. London: Macmillan, 1905. Also in *Representative Plays by Henry Arthur Jones.* New York: Macmillan, 1925.

An Old Master. London: Samuel French, 1883.

The Physician. London: Macmillan, 1899.

The Princess's Nose. London: privately printed by the Chiswick Press, 1902.

Representative Plays by Henry Arthur Jones. Ed. Clayton Hamilton. 4 vols. New York: Macmillan, 1925.

The Rogue's Comedy. London: Macmillan, 1898.

Saints and Sinners. London: Macmillan, 1891. Also in *Representative Plays by Henry Arthur Jones.* New York: Macmillan, 1925.

The Silver King. In collaboration with H. A. Herman. London: Samuel French, 1907. Also in *Representative Plays by Henry Arthur Jones.* New York: Macmillan, 1925.

Sweet Will. London: Samuel French (Lacy's Acting Edition), 1893.

The Tempter. London: Macmillan, 1898. Also in *Representative Plays by Henry Arthur Jones.* New York: Macmillan, 1925.

The Triumph of the Philistines. London: Macmillan, 1899.

We Can't Be As Bad As All That. New York: privately printed, 1910.

Whitewashing Julia. London: Macmillan, 1905.

Books and Articles on Drama and Theater

''The Actor-Manager.'' *Fortnightly Review* (1 July 1890).

''The Bible on the Stage.'' *New Review* (July 1893).

The Censorship Muddle and a Way out of It. London: privately printed by the Chiswick Press, 1909.

''The Censorship of Plays.'' *Author* (1 May 1902).

''The Cornerstone of Modern Drama.'' *New York Times* (4 Nov. 1905): 4:1.

''The Drama and the Film.'' *Daily Telegraph* (29 Apr. 1919).

''A Few Hints to Young Playwrights.'' *Dramatic Times* (14 June 1919).

''The Film Play.'' *The Times* (21 Feb. 1922).

''The First Night Judgment of Plays.'' *Nineteenth Century* (July 1889).

''The Forbidden Word.'' *Yorkshire Post* (4 Oct. 1920).

The Foundations of a National Drama. London: Chapman & Hall, 1913.

''The Heroines of the Film.'' *The Times* (29 and 30 Aug. 1921). Also published in *New York Times* (28 and 29 Aug. 1921).

''How Plays Are Written.'' *Pall Mall Gazette* (8 Oct. 1884).

''Literary Critics and the Drama.'' *Nineteenth Century* (Apr. 1903).

''Middleman and Parasites.'' *New Review* (June 1893).

''Motion Pictures and the Speaking Stage.'' *Photoplay* (May 1921).

My Dear Wells: A Manual for the Haters of England. New York: Dutton, 1921.

''Our Puerile Stage Plays.'' *National News* (4 May 1919).

Patriotism and Popular Education. London: Chapman & Hall, 1919.

''The Reading of Modern Plays.'' *London Daily Mail* (29 Sept. 1906).

''The Recognition of the Drama by the State.'' *Nineteenth Century* (Mar. 1904).

''Religion and the Stage.'' *Nineteenth Century* (Jan. 1885).

The Renascence of the English Drama. London: Macmillan, 1895.

''The Theatre and the Mob.'' *Nineteenth Century* (Sept. 1883).

The Theatre of Ideas. London: Chapman & Hall, 1915.

''The Triumphant Film.'' *Sunday Express* (25 July 1920). Also published in *Photoplay* (May 1921).

''Why English Drama Is Crowded Out.'' *Evening News* (3 May 1919).

SECONDARY BIBLIOGRAPHY

Archer, William. *The Old Drama and the New: An Essay in Re-valuation.* New York: Dodd, Mead, 1926; Benjamin Blom, 1971.

Bloom, Harold, ed. *Twentieth-Century British Literature,* 3:1454–59. New York: Chelsea House, 1986.

Booth, Michael R. *English Melodrama.* London: H. Jenkins, 1965.

Breed, Paul F., and Florence M. Sniderman, eds. *Dramatic Criticism Index,* 358–59. Detroit: Gale, 1972.

Bullock, J. M. "Henry Arthur Jones." *Book Buyer* (Apr. 1898): 225–28.

Carlson, Susan. "Two Genres and Their Women: The Problem Play and the Comedy of Manners in the Edwardian Theatre." *Midwest Quarterly* (Summer 1985): 413–24.

Cordell, Richard A. *Henry Arthur Jones and the Modern Drama.* New York: Ray Long & Richard R. Smith, 1932.

Davies, Acton. "The Playwright and His Profits." *Munsey's Magazine* (Oct. 1905): 74–83.

Dickinson, Thomas H. "Henry Arthur Jones." In *The Contemporary Drama of England.* Boston: Little, Brown, 1917; 1925.

Filon, Pierre. *The English Stage, Being an Account of the Victorian Drama.* Trans. Frederic Whyte. New York: Dodd, Mead, 1897. Reprint. New York: Benjamin Blom, 1969.

Fisher, Judith L. "The 'Law of the Father': Sexual Politics in the Plays of Henry Arthur Jones and Arthur Wing Pinero." *Essays in Literature* (Fall 1989): 203–23.

Foulkes, Richard, ed. *British Theatre in the 1890s: Essays on Drama and the Stage.* Cambridge: Cambridge University Press, 1992.

Griffin, Penny. *Arthur Wing Pinero and Henry Arthur Jones.* New York: St. Martin's Press, 1991.

Hamilton, J. Angus. "Henry Arthur Jones." *Munsey's Magazine* (May 1894): 174–78.

"Henry Arthur Jones." In *The McGraw-Hill Encyclopedia of World Drama,* 2: 426–30. New York: McGraw-Hill, 1972.

"Henry Arthur Jones." *Nation* (22 July 1915): 128.

Jenkins, Anthony. *The Making of Victorian Drama.* Cambridge: Cambridge University Press, 1991.

Jones, Doris Arthur. *Taking the Curtain Call: The Life and Letters of Henry Arthur Jones.* New York: Macmillan, 1930.

Kaplan, Joel H. "Henry Arthur Jones and the Lime-Lit Imagination." *Nineteenth-Century Literature* (Winter 1987): 115–41.

Morgan, A. E. *Tendencies of Modern English Drama.* London: Constable, 1924.

Nicoll, Allardyce. [1]. *English Drama, 1900–1930: The Beginnings of the Modern Period,* 337–39. Cambridge: Cambridge University Press, 1973.

———. [2]. *A History of English Drama, 1660–1900,* vol. 5, *Late Nineteenth Century Drama, 1850–1900,* 161–72. 2nd ed. Cambridge: Cambridge University Press, 1962.

"Our Omnibus-Box." *Theatre* (London) (1 Sept. 1886): 174–75.

Rowell, George, ed. *The Victorian Theatre: A Survey.* Oxford: Clarendon Press, 1967.

Taylor, John Russell. *The Rise and Fall of the Well-made Play.* New York: Hill & Wang, 1967.

Wallis, Bruce. "*Michael and His Lost Angel:* Archetypal Conflict and Victorian Life."
    Victorian Newsletter (1978): 20–26.
Wiley, Catherine. "The Matter with Manners: The New Woman and the Problem Play."
    In *Women in Theatre,* 109–27. Cambridge: Cambridge University Press, 1989.
Williams, Harold. *Modern English Writers.* London: Sidgwick & Jackson, 1925.
Wisenthal, J. L. "Henry Arthur Jones." In *Dictionary of Literary Biography,* vol. 10,
    Modern British Dramatists, 1900–1945, ed. Stanley Weintraub, pt. 1, 259–68.
    Detroit: Gale Research, 1982.

BIBLIOGRAPHY

Wearing, J. P. "Henry Arthur Jones: An Annotated Bibliography of Writings about
    Him." *English Literature in Transition, 1880–1920* 2.2, no.3 (1979): 160–228.

D. H. Lawrence
(1885–1930)

ROBERT WILCHER

D. H. Lawrence never saw any of his plays on the stage; and of the eight that he completed, only two were performed and three published during his lifetime. His reputation as a writer, which has grown steadily since his early death at the age of forty-four, has been based primarily on his achievements in prose fiction, travel sketches, and poetry. Nevertheless, since they were rediscovered in the 1960s, several of his early plays have become established as a permanent part of the repertoire of British theater, and Lawrence himself has been recognized as a dramatist of considerable stature.

David Herbert Richards Lawrence was born on 11 September 1885 in the coal-mining village of Eastwood in Nottinghamshire. He was the fourth child and third son of Arthur John Lawrence, a collier, and Lydia Beardsall, who had been a schoolteacher before her marriage in 1875. His mother's resentment at the social and economic circumstances of her married life and the diversion of her possessive love from her poorly educated husband to her sons, first Ernest until his death in 1901 and then the younger "Bert," created tensions within the household that provided material for much of Lawrence's early writing. It was during his childhood at Eastwood that Lawrence had his first experience of drama, when he watched touring theatrical troupes perform in a large tent. After attending the local Board School, he won a scholarship to Nottingham High School in 1898, where he continued as a pupil until 1901. He was employed for three months as a clerk in a factory in Nottingham, but a serious bout of pneumonia cut this short, and as soon as he was well enough, he began a new career as a pupil-teacher at the British School in Eastwood. Between 1903 and 1905 he went three days a week for training to the Pupil-Teacher Centre in Ilkeston, a few miles south of Eastwood. During this period he had begun to write poetry and had started work on the novel that was to become *The White*

Peacock. In September 1906 he enrolled as a student in the Teachers' Training Department at Nottingham University College. After obtaining his certificate in 1908, he left the Midlands to take up a post in Croydon, just south of London, at Davidson Road School, where he taught for the next four years. He had enjoyed visits to the London theatre during his student days in Nottingham, where he saw Galsworthy's *Strife,* and he again began to frequent the theaters and concert halls of the capital. While at Davidson Road, he also became involved in school drama, painting scenery and taking a hand in rehearsals. The publication of *The White Peacock,* soon after the death of his mother in December 1910, and the completion of a second novel, together with another attack of pneumonia, led him to resign his teaching post early in 1912 and determine to earn his living as a writer.

By this time Lawrence had completed at least three plays, one of which— probably a version of *The Widowing of Mrs. Holroyd*—had been rejected by Harley Granville-Barker and, through the good offices of Edward Garnett, was being considered for production by Iden Payne. The earliest of his works for the stage seems to have been *A Collier's Friday Night,* which Lawrence himself claimed to have started as early as 1906, but which more probably belongs to 1909. The third of these early plays was *The Merry-Go-Round,* which he began during his mother's final illness in 1910. Negotiations with Iden Payne came to nothing, partly because Lawrence departed suddenly for Germany in May 1912 in the company of Frieda Weekley (née von Richthofen), daughter of German aristocrats and wife of a professor at the University of Nottingham. Shortly before leaving England, he informed Garnett that he had written a comedy, which was presumably *The Married Man.* In May the second novel, *The Trespasser,* was published, and by September the runaway couple had rented a villa on Lake Garda in Italy, where they stayed until April 1913, by which time Lawrence had finished the manuscript of *Sons and Lovers* and dramatized the predicament he found himself in with Frieda and her family in *The Fight for Barbara.* This play, together with *The Merry-Go-Round* and *The Married Man,* were sent to Garnett in England, who returned them with unfavorable comments in February 1913. The previous month Lawrence was warning Garnett that yet another new play would soon be on its way to him. Described as ''neither a comedy nor a tragedy,'' this must have been *The Daughter-in-Law.* During the rest of 1913 Lawrence was working on his next novel, *The Rainbow,* and revising *The Widowing of Mrs. Holroyd,* which was the first of his plays to appear in print in 1914.

Lawrence and Frieda eventually married in July 1914 and spent the war years in England. In the autumn of 1918 Lawrence returned to drama with *Touch and Go,* a play that deals with the futile contest between labor and capital in a Midlands mining area and involves characters derived from *Women in Love.* Hopes that it would be produced by the People's Theatre Society were not fulfilled, but it was issued as part of a People's Theatre series in 1920 with a preface specially written by Lawrence. By then he and Frieda had left for Italy and the extended travels that took them to Australia, San Francisco, and New Mexico over the next five years. They were already abroad when *The Widowing of Mrs. Holroyd* was at last staged by an amateur company in Altrincham near Manchester in March 1920. It was in New Mexico that Lawrence again turned his attention to drama, first with two fragmentary scripts—*Altitude,* a light-hearted satire on the guests assembled by Mabel Dodge Luhan on her ranch at Taos; and the opening scene of *Noah's Flood.* This latter piece was evidently abandoned in favor of another biblical subject, *David,* which was completed in 1925 and published in 1926. Lawrence was again in Italy with Frieda when *The Widowing of Mrs. Holroyd* received its professional premiere in December 1926 and *David* was produced in May 1927. There were no further performances before his death at Vence in France on 2 March 1930, and it was not until Peter Gill's productions in the 1960s that Lawrence at last came into his own as a playwright.

Selected Biographical Sources: Carswell; Chambers; *The Letters of D. H. Lawrence,* vols. 1–7; D. H. Lawrence, "Nottingham and the Mining Country-side"; Frieda Lawrence; Moore [1, 2]; Nehls; Sagar [3]; Worthen [1, 2].

MAJOR PLAYS, PREMIERES, AND SIGNIFICANT REVIVALS: THEATRICAL RECEPTION

The Widowing of Mrs. Holroyd. 1920. (written 1910). Staged 9–13 March at the Unitarian Schools, Dunham Road, Altrincham. Produced by the Altrincham Garrick Society. First professional production on 12, 13, and 19 December 1926 at the Kingsway Theatre (London). Produced by Esmé Percy with the amalgamated 300 Club and Stage Society. Revivals: Granada TV, 23 March 1961, in a version adapted by Ken Taylor and directed by Claude Whatham; Royal Court Theatre (London), March 1968, as part of the Lawrence Season directed by Peter Gill; BBC2 TV, 14 October 1995. There is evidence that the play was first staged in Los Angeles 26–31 December 1916. Details will appear in the Cambridge volume of Lawrence's plays, which is being prepared by John Worthen and Hans-Wilhelm Schwarze.

For Carswell, who reviewed the 1920 production anonymously for *The Times* (Review of *The Widowing of Mrs. Holroyd,* 12 Mar. 1920), the simplicity with which Lawrence presented "an every-day situation" in "every-day speech" made "an intense impression on the mind and the emotions"; but although she found it a "fine and stimulating play," she considered that not enough knowledge was provided about the early days of the Holroyd marriage to explain the wife's expression of grief and guilt at the end. In a later account in *The Savage Pilgrimage,* Carswell recorded her feeling that "in a play so realistically written and produced a body-washing scene was theatrically unacceptable" (142). Several reviews of the 1926 production also expressed reservations about the ending: Omicron [2] deplored "the collapse of the third act," which "left the emotional core of the play unresolved" in its obsessive concentration on the corpse of the miner; and H. H. criticized the prolonged laying-out sequence for its "disastrous dissipation of the play's vital heat." MacCarthy's praise for the way in which Lawrence had "austerely kept his gift for lyrical expression within the bounds of naturalism" contrasted with the adverse view of *The Times* (Review of *The Widowing of Mrs. Holroyd,* 14 Dec. 1926) that the "economy in the use of dialogue" amounted to "a purposeful rejection of colour." There was disagreement, too, about the overall effect of the play: *The Times* found it "stagnant and tormented," whereas MacCarthy felt that it was "remarkable for the vigour and credibility of its passions," and H. H. responded to the power of "this tense little tragedy." Taylor's adaptation for television was praised by The *Times* ("Lawrence Play Skilfully Adapted to Television") for managing the "big scenes . . . without deteriorating into melodrama," and this first postwar revival was put into perspective with the comment that the play "is typical Lawrence of the *Sons and Lovers* period, both in setting and in subject." For reviewers of the 1968 production, the final sequence was the crowning achievement of the Royal Court's Lawrence Season: Wardle [4] observed that "there is nothing in the earlier plays that matches the last scene"; Gray likened the widow's lament to "those great choric threnodies in Greek tragedy"; Nightingale [1] found her words "painful and unnerving to hear, every one the authentic language of intolerable stress"; and Hobson was moved by "the grandeur and the reconciliation of the quiet close," which "in the depths of its grief and the dignity of its sorrow, none of the masters of ritual has surpassed and few have equalled." The 1995 television production elicited a similar response from Truss, who commented that after "an hour of emotional slow-build," the last twenty minutes of the play "were utterly heart-breaking; a true catharsis."

David. 1927. Staged 22–23 May at the Regent Theatre (London). Produced by Robert Atkins for the 300 Club and Stage Society.

The only production of Lawrence's last play was not well received. *The Times* (Review of *David*) noted "the peculiar intensity of language" with which the dramatist had "filled out the story of Saul, rather than of David," but judged the result to be "neither drama nor poetry." Only the oath of friendship between David and Jonathan and David's singing to allay the perturbation of the king's mind by evil spirits stirred this reviewer to "more than curiosity at Mr. Lawrence's experiment." Omicron [1] had no patience with the archaism of the biblical style and considered that "the play lacked all dramatic movement."

My Son's My Son. 1936. Opened 26 May at the Playhouse Theatre (London). Produced by Leon M. Lion. Revivals: Golders Green Hippodrome (London), August 1936; Blancheteatern (Stockholm), March 1937, translated by Ebba Low and directed by Harry Roeck Hansen.

Announced as an unrevised play by D. H. Lawrence completed by Walter Greenwood, this was in fact an adaptation of *The Daughter-in-Law* that conflated the four acts into three, modified the dialect, and changed the ending. While some were grateful to Greenwood for the theatrical skill with which he furnished the supposedly unfinished play with a conclusion, the reviewer in *The Times* (Review of *My Son's My Son*) was aware of what was lost when the tension that had "bound together the rest of the play" gave way to a radically different kind of tension and the situation created in the first two acts was resolved with "a melodramatic flourish." Modiano [2] reported that the success of the Stockholm production, which was performed more than 70 times in 1937–38, was due to the Swedish public's readiness for Lawrence's working-class realism.

A Collier's Friday Night. 1965. (written 1906–9). Sunday-night "production without decor" 8 August at the Royal Court Theatre (London). Directed by Peter Gill. Revival: Royal Court Theatre, February 1968, as part of the Lawrence Season directed by Peter Gill.

The Sunday-night premiere of Lawrence's first play was "the only good theatre of the week" for Benedictus, who was moved by "its affecting picture of the young and what they grow into." *The Times* reviewer ("The Economics of Affection") considered it "astonishing" in its freedom from "self-justification," in the "fair-mindedness" with which it portrayed the collier father, and in its "strong sense of fun" and recognized behind the apparent naïveté of its construction an "inventive use of common domestic incident to provide shape and suspense." When it was revived in 1968, Wardle [5] commented on the detachment with which the young dramatist had been able to "present an unsentimental study of the mechanics of domestic love" and saw it as a model of "what naturalism should be: the art of riveting the attention by telling the truth about ordinary life." Several other reviewers drew attention to the play's lack of a conventional plot, Bryden [1] commending it as "simply a slice out of the life of a family" and Young insisting that it was by no means "shapeless," with its "fine arching span that reaches from the first sight of Mrs Lambert waiting for her family's return to our last glimpse of her as she goes up to bed, all her family duties completed." A dissenting note was struck by Shorter with the verdict that although it was "remarkable and lively," it did not go anywhere and merely confirmed his view that "Lawrence was never much of a playwright." Gray compared its treatment of human relationships unfavorably with that in *Sons and Lovers* and blamed the lack of complexity and thematic integration on "the constricting form" of the conventional play.

The Daughter-in-Law. 1967. (written in 1913). Opened January 17 at the Traverse Theatre (Edinburgh). Directed by Gordon McDougall. Revivals: Royal Court Theatre (London), March 1967, directed by Peter Gill; Royal Court Theatre (London), March 1968, as part of the Lawrence Season directed by Peter Gill; Hampstead Theatre (London), August 1985, directed by John Dove.

The Times ("Original Play by Lawrence Revived") admired the "truthfulness and warmth of its best scenes" at the Traverse, but criticized the "rather long drawn out" exposition in the first act and "the sometimes distracting naturalism." The play was given a more enthusiastic reception at the Royal Court, where Bryden [2] considered it neither too naturalistic nor too slow and thought that it made "most of our post-war essays in working-class drama look flimsy." It was the "absolute verisimilitude" of the stage activity—"preparing, cooking, serving and eating meals, the miner washing off the grime after a day in the pit"—that Marcus found "most remarkable," and the marital rows that came "blazingly to life" left him feeling that Lawrence might have become a great dramatist "if he had been able to see a performance as good as this." Wardle [2] was "amazed that such a work could have been neglected" and declared that "the Derbyshire dialect rings with a common humanity which is the most precious sound in the theatre." Reviewing it alongside *Roots,* Jones came to the conclusion that given the opportunity, Lawrence "could have been as skilful a playwright as Wesker." For Edwards, the 1985 production offered "a beautifully sure and precise slice of life and marital strife" in "a poetically rich and often funny local idiom"; while Woddis, in spite of reservations about Lawrence's sexual politics and the unfamiliar dialect, acknowledged that it was the work of "a masterly playwright and a painfully honest analyst of his own obsessions."

The Fight for Barbara. 1967. (written 1912). Opened 9 August at the Mermaid Theatre (London). Directed by Robin Midgley.

The Fight for Barbara is based on the elopement of Lawrence and Frieda, but is by no means simply autobiographical. The performance was prefaced by readings from letters and other writings that created a sense of the real people behind the stage characters. Pritchett [1] felt that it illustrated "the old truth that true stories are not enough," but admitted that the "central comedy often carries well"; Dawson was unconvinced by its dramatic qualities and thought that it "would have made a short story"; Taylor considered that the insight it might give into Lawrence's private life was "rather a flimsy reason for staging the play now," but grudgingly admitted that the prefatory material turned a "dull act of literary piety" into "an unexpectedly fascinating couple of hours in the theatre." A more positive response came from Kimpel and Eaves, who praised the balance of passion and humor in the scenes between the runaway couple and the genuinely dramatic "interaction between two fully conceived and equally presented antagonists." Wardle [1] also saw it as "essentially a duet for the lovers," which demonstrated "the power of genius to transfigure what in another man would be narcissistic special pleading" and kept the volatile emotions "always anchored in hard detail."

Touch and Go. 1973. (written in 1918). Opened 6 October at the Questors Theatre (Ealing, London). Directed by Peter Whelan for the Questors Theatre Company (amateur). First professional production at the Oxford Playhouse (Oxford) and the Royal Court Theatre (London), November 1979, directed by Gordon McDougall.

The amateurs who first tried this play out on the stage declared in their house magazine, *Questopics* ("About *Touch and Go*"), that it was "superbly actable," with dialogue "full of unexpected twists and turns, ironies and humors of real speech," and that its theme of the futile war between labor and capital spoke "directly to us today." Reviews of the 1979 production were divided over the success of what de Jongh recognized as "the only play in which Lawrence related public and private lives." De Jongh himself, while admitting that as a play it was flawed, felt that the clash of will between the colliery owner and the striking miners in the final scene was "one of the most thrilling episodes in early 20th century drama" and applauded Lawrence's attempt to forge links between industrial politics and unresolved sexual passions. O'Connor, on the other hand, condemned it as a collection of "undigested raw elements" that had only been deemed worthy of revival because its "abrupt stereotyped action" contained "some crude similarities" to the current political situation. Barber admired the "verve" of the writing and respected the "impassioned belief" of the play's message, but thought that Lawrence had been "unable here to give his burning sincerity a convincing dramatic shape"; and Nightingale [2] was put off by its "political naivety," contrasting the analyses mouthed by "a some-times verbose and precious elite" with Lawrence's earlier vital evocations of working-class living.

The Merry-Go-Round. 1973. (written 1910). Opened 7 November at the Royal Court Theatre (London). Directed by Peter Gill. Revival: Octagon Theatre (Bolton), April 1980, directed by Wilfred Harrison.

As Hebert pointed out, the 1973 production, which was adapted by Gill from Lawrence's original text, toned down the grotesquely farcical Polish baron and baroness to a colorless clergyman and his wife, kept the entertaining pet goose offstage for practical reasons, and generally reinforced the elements of natural-ism. For Wardle [3], there was considerable continuity with the other colliery plays in the "full naturalistic apparatus" and the "clamped-down intensities" generated by "powerfully self-willed characters," even though Lawrence had for once set "his ruling obsessions in comic perspective" and allowed "the farcical wheels" to accelerate toward the end. The refusal to push the situation through to a tragic crisis irritated several of the reviewers: Nightingale [3] felt cheated by the convenient comic pairings into which the potentially disastrous rivalries were resolved "with a most uncharacteristic smirk and shrug"; Russell Davies saw the ending as a "bizarre truce" imposed upon the play's conflicts; and Hurren felt that the finale was "so hopelessly facetious" that the dramatist could not have "seriously envisaged a stage production." Billington was ex-ceptional in regarding this "comedy laced with pain and passion" as further evidence of Lawrence's unique ability among British dramatists of his day to deal "intelligently with personal relationships" and to express emotion "through physical ritual as much as through words." According to Cecil Davies, the premiere of Lawrence's original text in 1980 confirmed that it was "thor-oughly viable in the theatre" and revealed that in its bold mixture of styles, it was technically "a progressive, forward-looking, experimental play" (152).

AN ADDITIONAL PLAY AND DRAMATIC FRAGMENTS

The Married Man exists only in a text that appears to begin in the middle of a scene. It was written during the spring of 1912 and drew for its plot upon a visit Lawrence had made earlier that year to a philandering friend in the country who was in a similar predicament to that of the married man of the title. There is no record of its having been produced on the stage. The two fragments, *Altitude* and *Noah's Flood,* belong to the periods Lawrence spent in New Mexico in 1924 and 1925.

ASSESSMENT OF LAWRENCE'S CAREER

A serious assessment of Lawrence's work as a dramatist only began in the late 1960s in the wake of Peter Gill's productions of the three colliery plays at the Royal Court Theatre. There are passing references to *The Widowing of Mrs. Holroyd* in early accounts of his achievement by Kuttner, Garnett, and Shanks and more substantial appreciations of the printed texts of *Touch and Go* by Lowell, who highlighted the timeliness of Lawrence's political message in both preface and play, and of *David* by Sackville West, who praised the clarity of thought, the depth of restrained feeling, and the well-managed archaism of this austere drama. Carswell gave some prominence to *The Widowing of Mrs. Holroyd, Touch and Go,* and *David* in her early chronicle of Lawrence's career as a writer. The publication of *A Collier's Friday Night* prompted O'Casey to an enthusiastic review in which he discerned the force, humor, and dramatic feeling of a play worthy of production and lamented the lack of encouragement for a man who might have become a great dramatist.

Among the more substantial responses to the Lawrence season at the Royal Court in 1968, Nightingale [1], Gray, and Moe all commented on the wealth of environmental and domestic detail that gave such a keen sense of reality to the personal relationships in the colliery plays, and both Nightingale and Moe drew attention to the freshness and stageworthiness of the dialogue. In an attempt to place Lawrence in the context of his own age, Moe likened the compassionate resignation of the mother-in-law in the final scene of *The Widowing of Mrs. Holroyd* to Maurya in Synge's *Riders to the Sea,* and Nightingale contrasted the convincing evocation of the miners' world with the middle-class sensationalism of Galsworthy's *Strife.*

In an early academic assessment of the drama, Waterman compared *The Widowing of Mrs. Holroyd* with ''Odour of Chrysanthemums'' and judged the ending of the play to be more powerful. Williams, adding a section on Lawrence to the revised edition of his influential study of naturalistic theater, divided the six pre-1914 plays into two groups: in the three colliery pieces, which have close connections with *Sons and Lovers* and the early mining stories, the young dramatist had looked to the examples of Chekhov and Synge and had succeeded in embodying the rhythm of ordinary life in a language that captured the shape and sound of a particular way of living; and in *The Married Man, The Merry-Go-Round,* and *The Fight for Barbara,* he had dealt with relationships in a lighter, more slangy tone, which drew no more than a disapproving glance from his modern critic. By the time Lawrence wrote *Touch and Go,* which Williams saw as an extension of material in *Women in Love,* he had become separated from his early environment, and the naturalist mode no longer suited his changed purpose of presenting attitudes toward and arguments about mining life. This relative evaluation of the plays was reinforced by an influential article in which Sagar [2] highlighted the immediacy of the colliery plays with their living, rooted speech, regretted the lack of a comparable authenticity in *Touch and Go,* passed over *The Merry-Go-Round* as a romp fit only for the amateur dramatic society, condemned *The Married Man* for its leaden wit and callow moralizing, and discounted *The Fight for Barbara* as being largely of biographical interest. *David,* ignored by Williams, was judged as a text that might be made to live in a fine production, but Sagar was generally dissatisfied with this attempt to adapt a biblical story for the modern stage.

In the first book-length study of Lawrence as a dramatist, Sklar [2] began the process of examining the nature of Lawrence's early naturalism in more detail and approaching the nonnaturalistic plays with a more sympathetic understanding of the theatrical effects he was aiming at. She concluded that the colliery plays offer much more than accurately observed slices of working-class life. In Lawrence's hands the naturalist mode is an artistic means of investing everyday activities like bread making with thematic significance and of actualizing emotion through the contrast between spoken and unspoken feelings. Instead of dismissing the other early plays for their triviality, Sklar recognized that they share an ironical view of sexual relationships and that each, in its different way, is a conscious experiment with dramatic form. *The Merry-Go-Round* combines realism and fantasy as it moves out from the intimate closed sets of miners' kitchens into the bustling life of the village and creates the sprightly rhythm of a country dance for its comedy of changing partners. A production that adopted the stylization of the Restoration comic theater and rendered the characters as types rather than fully rounded human beings might well reveal a comedy of manners of considerable subtlety lurking in the text of *The Married Man,* with its sexual cat-and-mouse games and its spontaneous sense of fun. *The Fight for Barbara* marks the culmination, for Sklar, of Lawrence's experiments with the comic possibilities of drama. She detected a Shavian flavor in the bite of the dialogue and was reminded of the comedies of Noël Coward in Lawrence's closest approach to the methods of the well-made play. Shaw was also invoked in connection with the debate in the second act of *Touch and Go,* a play that contains the elements of a modern tragedy in its portrayal of characters caught in an irresolvable conflict of social and economic interests. Finally, Sklar saw in *David* a heroic attempt to realize on stage the effects of religious ritual and responded positively to its archetypal conception of character, its episodic form, and the intensity of its stylized language.

More recent studies have elaborated the lines of approach laid down by these pioneering critics. Stovel [1, 2] argued that the colliery plays not only handled some of the same autobiographical material as the early fiction but that the process of writing them helped Lawrence to develop his distinctively dramatic qualities as a novelist. While many added to the chorus of admiration for the authenticity with which Lawrence rendered working-class domestic life, Coniff argued that naturalism was too restrictive for the expression of his vision and emphasized both the highly formal structure of *The Widowing of Mrs. Holroyd* and the element of symbolism that enriches its superficially realistic surface; and Hartman pursued the symbolic resonance of the threshold and the sense of touch in the same play. Scheckner added *Touch and Go* to the three earlier plays in his investigation into the contradictory attitudes toward industrial strife and the class struggle that Lawrence was never able to resolve.

Reading the three comedies as attempts at comedy of manners, Galenbeck concluded that although Lawrence was attracted to the conventions of patterned plot, word play, hierarchy of class-conscious characters, and ironically happy ending as means of exploring the relations between the sexes, he was unable to endorse the affirmation of society that is the ultimate goal of this kind of drama. Cecil Davies argued that Lawrence was consciously in revolt against current theatrical fashions in all his plays and examined the innovative features of *The Merry-Go-Round,* with its mixing of dramatic styles and its frequent changes of scene that challenge the methods of a period of box sets and naturalistic detail. In the Bolton production the kind of multiple set commonly used by Piscator in the 1920s proved to be effective, whether or not Lawrence himself had such a device in mind, and demonstrated that in this as in other respects he was in advance of the British theater of his own day. For Ian Clarke, *The Fight for Barbara* was best understood in the context of the society drama written for the late Victorian and Edwardian commercial theater by Henry Arthur Jones and Arthur Wing Pinero. Taking Pinero's *The Notorious Mrs. Ebbsmith* as an example of the serious dramatic treatment of an unorthodox sexual relationship, he showed how Lawrence exploited the plot situations and character stereotypes of the genre in order to question rather than endorse the dominant codes of social and moral behavior.

David has also had its recent champions. Gamache stressed the Nietzschean and apocalyptic elements in the contest between Saul and David and suggested that Lawrence was reaching toward a more Brechtian mode of dramatic presentation in his last play; and Brunsdale saw its composition as a crucial event in Lawrence's development as a writer, which enabled him to discard the religious primitivism of his middle period and embrace the possibility of human regeneration through the self-sacrifice of love.

While the belated assessment of Lawrence's drama as a body of work in its own right and as part of his total achievement is still in its early stages, it is already clear that the colliery plays have gained a secure place for themselves both in the theater and in the history of twentieth-century drama. It remains to be seen whether the comedies and later plays will stand the test of repeated performance and vindicate the claims that have tentatively been advanced for them.

ARCHIVAL SOURCES

Information about the location of manuscripts and typescripts of individual plays can be found in the bibliography compiled by Warren Roberts and in the checklist compiled by Lindeth Vasey in Keith Sagar's *D. H. Lawrence: A Calendar of his Works*. Most of the material relating to Lawrence's plays is held by the University of Texas at Austin and the University of California at Berkeley.

PRIMARY BIBLIOGRAPHY

Plays

Altitude. A fragment published in *Laughing Horse* no. 20 (Summer 1938): 12–35.
A Collier's Friday Night. London: Secker, 1934.
The Daughter-in-Law. First published in *The Complete Plays of D. H. Lawrence*. London: Heinemann, 1965.
David. London: Secker, 1926 (reprinted 1927); New York: Alfred A. Knopf, 1926; London: New Adelphi Library, 1930.
David: A Play. New York: Haskell House, 1974.
Keeping Barbara. Argosy 14 (Dec. 1933): 68–90. Retitled *The Fight for Barbara*. *The Married Man*. Virginia Quarterly Review 16 (Autumn 1940): 523–47.
The Merry-Go-Round. Virginia Quarterly Review (Christmas Supplement) (Winter 1941): 1–44.
Noah's Flood. A fragment published in *Phoenix: The Posthumous Papers of D. H. Lawrence,* ed. Edward D. McDonald. New York: Viking, 1936; London: Heinemann, 1936.
Touch and Go. London: C. W. Daniel, 1920; New York: Seltzer, 1920.
The Widowing of Mrs. Holroyd. New York: Kennerley, 1914; London: Duckworth, 1914; New York: Seltzer, 1921.

Anthologies

The Complete Plays of D. H. Lawrence. (The Widowing of Mrs. Holroyd, David, The Married Man, The Daughter-in-Law, The Fight for Barbara, Touch and Go, The Merry-Go-Round, A Collier's Friday Night, Altitude: A Fragment, Noah's Flood: A Fragment.) London: Heinemann, 1965 (reprinted 1970); New York: Viking, 1966.
The Plays of D. H. Lawrence. (The Widowing of Mrs. Holroyd, Touch and Go, David.) London: Secker, 1933.

The Plays of D. H. Lawrence. (*The Widowing of Mrs. Holroyd, Touch and Go, David.*)
London: Heinemann, 1938.

Three Plays by D. H. Lawrence. (*A Collier's Friday Night, The Daughter-in-Law, The
Widowing of Mrs. Holroyd.*) Introduction by Raymond Williams. Harmondsworth: Penguin, 1960 (reprinted in Penguin Classics, 1985).

The Widowing of Mrs. Holroyd and The Daughter-in-Law. Introduction by Michael Mar-
land. London: Heinemann, 1968.

Selected Short Stories, Novels, and Articles

"Nottingham and the Mining Countryside." In *Phoenix: The Posthumous Papers of D.
H. Lawrence,* ed. Edward D. McDonald. New York: Viking, 1936; London: Heinemann, 1936.

"Odour of Chrysanthemums." *English Review* (June 1911). Reprinted in *The Prussian
Officer and Other Stories.* London: Duckworth, 1914.

The Rainbow. London: Methuen, 1915; New York: Huebsch, 1915.

Sons and Lovers. London: Duckworth, 1913; New York: Kennerley, 1913.

The Trespasser. London: Duckworth, 1912; New York: Kennerley, 1912.

The White Peacock. New York: Duffield, 1911; London: Heinemann, 1911.

Women in Love. New York: Seltzer, 1920; London: Secker, 1921.

Essays and Articles on Drama and Theater

"By the Lago di Garda: III. The Theatre." *English Review* 15 (Sept. 1913): 202–34.
Reprinted in *Twilight in Italy.* London: Duckworth, 1916; New York: Huebsch,
1916.

"Indians and Entertainment." *New York Times Magazine* (26 Oct. 1924). Reprinted in
Mornings in Mexico. London: Secker, 1927; New York: Alfred A. Knopf, 1927.

Preface to *Touch and Go.* First printed with *Touch and Go* in 1920. Reprinted in *Phoenix
II: Uncollected, Unpublished, and Other Prose Works by D. H. Lawrence,* ed.
Warren Roberts and Harry T. Moore. London: Heinemann, 1968.

Letters

The Collected Letters of D. H. Lawrence. Ed. Harry T. Moore. 2 vols. New York: Viking,
1962; London: Heinemann, 1962.

The Letters of D. H. Lawrence, 1901–1913. Vol. 1. Ed. James T. Boulton. Cambridge:
Cambridge University Press, 1979.

The Letters of D. H. Lawrence, 1913–1916. Vol. 2. Ed. George J. Zytaruk and James T.
Boulton. Cambridge: Cambridge University Press, 1981.

The Letters of D. H. Lawrence, 1916–1921. Vol. 3. Ed. James T. Boulton and Andrew
Robertson. Cambridge: Cambridge University Press, 1984.

The Letters of D. H. Lawrence, 1921–1924. Vol. 4. Ed. Warren Roberts, James T. Boulton, and Elizabeth Mansfield. Cambridge: Cambridge University Press, 1987.

The Letters of D. H. Lawrence, 1924–1927. Vol. 5. Ed. James T. Boulton and Lindeth
Vasey. Cambridge: Cambridge University Press, 1989.

The Letters of D. H. Lawrence, 1927–1928. Vol. 6. Ed. James T. Boulton and Margaret H. Boulton, with Gerald M. Lacy. Cambridge: Cambridge University Press, 1991.
The Letters of D. H. Lawrence, 1928–1930. Vol. 7. Ed. Keith Sagar and James T. Boulton. Cambridge: Cambridge University Press, 1993.

SECONDARY BIBLIOGRAPHY

"About *Touch and Go.*" *Questopics,* no. 84 (Sept. 1973). Reprinted in Sagar and Sklar.
Aldington, Richard. *D. H. Lawrence: A Complete List of His Works together with a Critical Appreciation.* London: Heinemann, 1935.
Barber, John. Review of *Touch and Go. Daily Telegraph* (12 Nov. 1979): 15.
Benedictus, David. "Gobstoppers." *Spectator* (13 Aug. 1965): 209.
Billington, Michael. Review of *The Merry-Go-Round. The Guardian* (8 Nov. 1973): 10.
Brunsdale, Mitzi M. "D. H. Lawrence's *David:* Drama as a Vehicle for Religious Prophecy." *Themes in Drama* 5 (1983): 123–37. Reprinted in Ellis and De Zordo.
Bryden, Ronald. [1]. "Mesmerising Lawrence." *Observer* (3 Mar. 1968): 31.
———. [2]. "Strindberg in the Midlands." *Observer* (19 Mar. 1967): 25.
Carlson, Susan. *Women of Grace: James's Plays and the Comedy of Manners,* 127–37. Studies in Modern Literature, no. 48. Ann Arbor, MI: UMI Research Press, 1985.
Carswell, Catherine. *The Savage Pilgrimage: A Narrative of D. H. Lawrence.* London: Chatto & Windus, 1932.
Chambers, Jessie [E. T.]. *D. H. Lawrence: A Personal Record by E. T.* 1935. 2nd ed., ed. Jonathan D. Chambers. New York: Barnes & Noble, 1965.
Chatarji, Dilip. "The Dating of D. H. Lawrence's *A Collier's Friday Night.*" *Notes and Queries,* n.s. 23 (Jan. 1976): 11.
Clark, L. D. *The Minoan Distance: The Symbolism of Travel in D. H. Lawrence.* Tucson: University of Arizona Press, 1980. (*David,* 342–46.)
Clarke, Ian. "*The Fight for Barbara:* Lawrence's Society Drama." In *D. H. Lawrence in the Modern World,* ed. Peter Preston and Peter Hoare. Basingstoke: Macmillan, 1989.
Coniff, Gerald. "The Failed Marriage: Dramatization of a Lawrentian Theme in *The Widowing of Mrs. Holroyd.*" *D. H. Lawrence Review* 11 (1978): 21–37.
Review of David. *The Times* (24 May 1927): 14.
Davies, Cecil. "D. H. Lawrence: *The Merry-Go-Round,* a Challenge to the Theatre." *D. H. Lawrence Review* 16 (1983): 133–63.
Davies, Russell. Review of *The Merry-Go-Round. Plays and Players* (Jan. 1974): 50–51.
Dawson, Helen. "Running off with Lawrence." *Observer* (13 Aug. 1967): 15.
de Jongh, Nicholas. "Vein of Riches." *Guardian* (10 Nov. 1979): 13.
Delany, Paul. *D. H. Lawrence's Nightmare: The Writer and His Circle in the Years of the Great War.* New York: Basic Books, 1978.
Draper, R. P., ed. *D. H. Lawrence: The Critical Heritage.* London and Boston: Routledge & Kegan Paul, 1970.
"The Economics of Affection." *The Times* (9 Aug. 1965): 5.
Edwards, Christopher. "Seeing Is Believing." *Spectator* (24 Aug. 1985): 30.
Ellis, David, and Ornella De Zordo, eds. *D. H. Lawrence: Critical Assessments.* Vol. 4. Mountfield, East Sussex: Helm Information, 1992.

French, Philip. ''Major Miner Dramatist.'' *New Statesman* (22 Mar. 1968): 390. Reprinted in Jackson and Jackson.

Galenbeck, Susan Carlson. ''A Stormy Apprenticeship: Lawrence's Three Comedies.'' *D. H. Lawrence Review* 14 (1981): 191–211.

Gamache, Lawrence B. ''Lawrence's *David:* Its Religious Impulse and Its Theatricality.'' *D. H. Lawrence Review* 15 (1982): 235–48.

Garnett, Edward. ''Art and the Moralists: Mr. D. H. Lawrence's Work.'' *Dial* (16 Nov. 1916): 377–81. Reprinted in Draper.

Gray, Simon. ''Lawrence the Dramatist.'' *New Society* (21 Mar. 1968). Reprinted in *D. H. Lawrence: A Critical Anthology,* ed. H. Coombes. Harmondsworth: Penguin, 1973.

H., H. Review of *The Widowing of Mrs. Holroyd. Outlook* (24 Dec. 1926): 629.

Hanson, Barry. ''D. H. Lawrence Season of Plays: Rehearsal Logbook.'' *Plays and Players* (Apr. 1968). Reprinted in Sagar and Sklar.

Hartman, Geoffrey H. ''Symbolism versus Character in Lawrence's First Play.'' In *Easy Pieces,* 81–88. New York: Columbia University Press, 1985.

Hebert, Hugh. ''The Whipper-in: An Interview with Peter Gill.'' *Guardian* (7 Nov. 1973): 12.

Hobsbaum, Philip. *A Reader's Guide to D. H. Lawrence.* London: Thames & Hudson, 1981.

Hobson, Harold. Review of *The Widowing of Mrs. Holroyd. The Sunday Times* (17 Mar. 1968): 49.

Holderness, Graham. *D. H. Lawrence: History, Ideology, and Fiction.* Dublin: Gill and Macmillan, 1982; Atlantic Highlands, NJ: Humanities Press, 1982. (*Touch and Go,* 211–14.)

Hurren, Kenneth. ''Sister's Three.'' *Spectator* (17 Nov. 1973): 646–47.

Jackson, Dennis, and Fleda Brown Jackson, eds. *Critical Essays on D. H. Lawrence.* Boston: G. K. Hall, 1988.

Jansohn, Christa. ''Books, Music, and Paintings in *A Collier's Friday Night.*'' *Cahiers Victoriens et Édouardiens,* no. 32 (Oct. 1990): 61–79.

Jones, D.A.N. ''Somebodies.'' *New Statesman* (24 Mar. 1967): 415–16.

Kauffmann, Stanley. ''Three Cities.'' *New Republic* 169 (15 Dec. 1973): 22, 33–34.

Kimpel, Ben D., and T. C. Duncan Eaves. ''*The Fight for Barbara* on Stage.'' *D. H. Lawrence Review* 1 (1968): 72–74.

Kumar, Shrawan. ''D. H. Lawrence's Relationship: *A Collier's Friday Night.*'' In *Essays on D. H. Lawrence,* ed. T. R. Sharma, 162–67. Meerut, India: Shalabh Book House, 1987.

Kuttner, Alfred. Review of *Sons and Lovers. New Republic* (10 Apr. 1915): 255–57. Reprinted in Draper.

Laird, Holly. ''Heroic Theater in David.'' In *Critical Essays on D. H. Lawrence,* ed. Dennis Jackson and Fleda Brown Jackson, 203–9. Boston: G. K. Hall, 1988.

Lambert, J. W. ''Plays in Performance.'' *Drama* 89 (Summer 1968): 19–30.

Lawrence, Frieda. ''*Not I, But the Wind . . .* '' New York: Viking, 1934.

''Lawrence Play Skilfully Adapted to Television.'' *The Times* (24 Mar. 1961): 18.

Lowell, Amy. ''A Voice Cries in Our Wilderness (D. H. Lawrence).'' 1926. In *Poetry and Poets: Essays.* Boston: Houghton Mifflin, 1930.

MacCarthy, Desmond. Review of *The Widowing of Mrs. Holroyd. New Statesman* (18 Dec. 1926): 310.

Mahnken, Harry E. "The Plays of D. H. Lawrence: Addenda." *Modern Drama* 7 (1965): 431–32.

Malani, Hiran. *D. H. Lawrence: A Study of His Plays.* Atlantic Highlands, NJ: Humanities Press, 1982.

Marcus, Frank. "The Dominant Sex." *Plays and Players* (May 1967): 19.

Modiano, Marko. [1]. *Domestic Disharmony and Industrialization in D. H. Lawrence's Early Fiction.* Uppsala, Sweden: Acta Universitatis Upsaliensis, 1987. (*A Collier's Friday Night,* 47–50; *The Daughter-in-Law,* 71–76; *The Widowing of Mrs. Holroyd,* 69–71.)

———. [2]. "An Early Swedish Stage Production of D. H. Lawrence's *The Daughter-in-Law.*" *D. H. Lawrence Review* 17 (1984): 49–59.

Moe, Christian. "Playwright Lawrence Takes the Stage in London." *D. H. Lawrence Review* 2 (1969): 93–97.

Moore, Harry T. [1]. *D. H. Lawrence: His Life and Works.* 1951. 2nd ed. New York: Twayne, 1964.

———. [2]. *The Intelligent Heart: The Story of D. H. Lawrence.* New York: Farrar, Straus & Young, 1954; revised as *The Priest of Love: A Life of D. H. Lawrence.* New York: Farrar, Straus & Giroux, 1974.

Review of *My Son's My Son. The Times* (27 May 1936): 14.

Nath, Suresh. [1]. *D. H. Lawrence: The Dramatist.* Ghaziabad, India: Vimal Prakashan, 1979.

———. [2]. "Symbolism in the Plays of D. H. Lawrence." In *Essays on D. H. Lawrence,* ed. T. R. Sharma, 168–82. Meerut, India: Shalabh Book House, 1987.

Nehls, Edward. *D. H. Lawrence: A Composite Biography.* 3 vols. Madison: University of Wisconsin Press, 1957–59.

Nightingale, Benedict. [1]. "On the Coal Face." *Plays and Players* (May 1968): 18–21, 51.

———. [2]. "A Passion Unresolved." *New Statesman* (16 Nov. 1979): 778–79.

———. [3]. "The Trouble with Harry." *New Statesman* (16 Nov. 1973): 748–49.

Nin, Anais. "Novelist on Stage." In *Critical Essays on D. H. Lawrence,* ed. Dennis Jackson and Fleda Brown Jackson, 212–14. Boston: G. K. Hall., 1988.

Niven, Alastair. *D. H. Lawrence: The Writer and His Work.* 'Writers and Their Work' series. Harlow, Essex: Longman, 1980; New York: Charles Scribner's Sons, 1980.

O'Casey, Sean. "A Miner's Dream of Home." *New Statesman and Nation* (28 July 1934). Reprinted in *Blasts and Benedictions,* ed. Ronald Ayling, 222–25. London: Macmillan, 1967; and in Jackson and Jackson, 209–11.

O'Connor, Garry. Review of *Touch and Go. Financial Times* (8 Nov. 1979): 23.

Omicron. [1]. Review of *David. Nation and Athenaeum* (28 May 1927): 261.

———. [2]. Review of *The Widowing of Mrs. Holroyd. Nation and Athenaeum* (18 December 1926): 422.

"Original Play by Lawrence Revived." *The Times* (28 Jan. 1967): 13.

Panichas, George A. [1]. *Adventure in Consciousness: The Meaning of D. H. Lawrence's Religious Quest.* Studies in English Literature, 3. The Hague: Mouton, 1964. (*Touch and Go,* 33–35; *David,* 136–50.)

——— [2]. "D. H. Lawrence's Biblical Play *David.*" *Modern Drama* 6 (1963): 164–76.

Pinion, F. B. *A D. H. Lawrence Companion: Life, Thought, and Works,* 265–75. London: Macmillan, 1978.

Pritchett, V. S. [1]. "Keep It Going." *New Statesman* (18 Aug. 1967): 211–12.

———. [2]. "Lawrence's Laughter." *New Statesman* (1 July 1966): 18–19.

Roston, Murray. *Biblical Drama in England from the Middle Ages to the Present Day.* London: Faber & Faber; Evanston, IL: Northwestern University Press, 1968.

Sackville West, Edward. Review of *Reflections on the Death of a Porcupine* and *David. New Statesman* (10 July 1926): 360–61. Reprinted in Draper.

Sagar, Keith. [1]. *D. H. Lawrence: A Calendar of His Works: With a Checklist of the Manuscripts of D. H. Lawrence by Lindeth Vasey.* Manchester: Manchester University Press, 1979.

———. [2]. "D. H. Lawrence: Dramatist." *D. H. Lawrence Review* 4 (1971): 154–82.

———. [3]. *D. H. Lawrence: Life into Art.* New York: Viking, 1985.

———. [4]. "The Strange History of *The Daughter-in-Law.*" *D. H. Lawrence Review* 11 (1978): 175–84.

Sagar, Keith, and Sylvia Sklar. "Major Productions of Lawrence's Plays." In *A D. H. Lawrence Handbook,* ed. Keith Sagar. Manchester: Manchester University Press, 1982.

Scheckner, Peter. *Class, Politics, and the Individual: A Study of the Major Works of D. H. Lawrence,* 70–87. Rutherford, NJ: Fairleigh Dickinson University Press, 1985. (*The Widowing of Mrs. Holroyd, Touch and Go, A Collier's Friday Night.*)

Shanks, Edward. "Mr. D. H. Lawrence: Some Characteristics." *London Mercury* 8 (May 1923): 64–75. Reprinted in Draper.

Shorter, Eric. "Lawrence Play Takes Too Long Pondering." *Daily Telegraph* (1 Mar. 1968): 19.

Sinzelle, Claude M. *The Geographical Background of the Early Works of D. H. Lawrence.* Paris: M. Didier, 1964.

Sklar, Sylvia. [1]. "*The Daughter-in-Law* and *My Son's My Son.*" *D. H. Lawrence Review* 9 (1976): 254–65.

———. [2]. *The Plays of D. H. Lawrence: A Biographical and Critical Study.* London: Vision, 1975.

Spurling, Hilary. "Old Folk at Home." *Spectator* (22 Mar. 1968): 378–79.

Stovel, Nora Foster. [1]. "D. H. Lawrence and 'The Dignity of Death': Tragic Recognition in 'Odour of Chrysanthemums,' *The Widowing of Mrs. Holroyd,* and *Sons and Lovers.*" *D. H. Lawrence Review* 16 (1983): 59–82.

———. [2]. "D. H. Lawrence, from Playwright to Novelist: 'Strife-in-Love' in *A Collier's Friday Night* and *Sons and Lovers.*" *English Studies in Canada* 13 (1987): 451–67. Reprinted in Ellis and De Zordo.

Taylor, John Russell. Review of *The Fight for Barbara. Plays and Players* (Oct. 1967): 40.

Truss, Lynne. Review of *The Widowing of Mrs. Holroyd. The Times* (16 Oct. 1995): 43.

Wardle, Irving. [1]. "Forgotten Play Shows Power of Genius." *The Times* (10 Aug. 1967): 5.

———. [2]. "Lawrence Play with a Strindberg Touch." *The Times* (17 Mar. 1967): 12.

———. [3]. Review of *The Merry-go-Round. The Times* (8 Nov. 1973): 13.

———. [4]. "Not an Ordinary Relationship." *The Times* (15 Mar. 1968): 13.

———. [5]. "Pay Day for Young Lawrence." *The Times* (1 Mar. 1968): 12.

Waterman, Arthur E. "The Plays of D. H. Lawrence." *Modern Drama* 2 (1960): 349–57.

Review of *The Widowing of Mrs. Holroyd. The Times* (14 Dec. 1926): 12.

Williams, Raymond. *Drama from Ibsen to Brecht.* London: Chatto & Windus, 1952. Previously published as *Drama from Ibsen to Eliot.* London: Chatto & Windus, 1952.

Woddis, Carole. "*The Daughter-in-Law.*" *Plays and Players* (Oct. 1985): 32–33.

Worthen, John. [1]. *D. H. Lawrence: A Literary Life.* New York and London: Macmillan, 1989.

———. [2]. *D. H. Lawrence: The Early Years, 1885–1912.* Cambridge: Cambridge University Press, 1991.

Young, B. A. Review of *A Collier's Friday Night. Financial Times* (1 Mar. 1968): 28.

BIBLIOGRAPHIES

Hepburn, James G. "D. H. Lawrence's Plays: An Annotated Bibliography." *Book Collector* 14 (Spring 1965): 78–81.

Rice, Thomas Jackson. *D. H. Lawrence: A Guide to Research.* New York and London: Garland, 1983.

Roberts, Warren. *A Bibliography of D. H. Lawrence.* London: Hart-Davis, 1963; 2nd ed. Cambridge: Cambridge University Press, 1982.

John Masefield
(1878–1967)

RONALD E. SHIELDS

Remembered today primarily for his poetry and novels, John Masefield during the first three decades of this century wrote dramas for the professional stage, verse dramas, and several plays as part of the religious-drama movement. Although some were considered promising by critics and public alike, Masefield's theatrical voice has not been influential. Together with his friends and fellow poets Gordon Bottomley and Laurence Binyon, Masefield is assessed today as a transitional literary figure, a spokesman for the British national spirit, and a minor participant in several failed theatrical traditions.

John Masefield was born in Ledbury, Herefordshire, on 1 June 1878, the son of George Edward and Carol Parker Masefield. Masefield's mother died in childbirth, and his father, a successful solicitor, died shortly thereafter following treatment for mental illness. Orphaned at age six, the young Masefield was cared for by relatives in a country home in Herefordshire. After running away from King's School in Warwick, the young boy of thirteen was allowed to join the crew of a training ship, the *Conway.* After voyages to South America and around Cape Horn, he tired of life at sea and jumped ship in New York City.

Disinherited by his family because of his seemingly irresponsible behavior, he stayed in New York and lived a dismal existence in Greenwich Village. During this time he began to write poetry. He returned to England in 1897, worked as a bank clerk, began to publish, and spent time in Bloomsbury with William Butler Yeats, John Millington Synge, and Lady Gregory. From his contact with this circle, Masefield developed a close friendship with the poet and verse dramatist Laurence Binyon and became enamored with the verse-speaking skills of Florence Farr, an artistic follower of Yeats. His first book of poems, *Salt-Sea Ballads,* published in 1902, received both popular and critical acceptance.

Masefield married Constance Crommelin in 1903. While working for the *Manchester Guardian*, he began to write plays for the professional stage. Between 1907 and 1916 Masefield wrote ten plays, including some of his most important dramas; several were staged by Harley Granville-Barker. His tawdry one-act melodrama *The Campden Wonder* was produced in 1907. *The Tragedy of Nan,* considered one of his finest efforts, premiered in 1908 and became a modest popular success; *The Witch,* an adaptation, followed in 1910. Following the commercial promise of these melodramas in the style of Synge, Masefield wrote historical dramas in the style of Shaw's *Caesar and Cleopatra.* These plays (*Pompey the Great, Philip the King, The Faithful*) failed to please.

In the years between the wars Masefield identified himself with the theatrical reformers E. G. Craig, Bottomley, and Yeats, who all worked in theory and practice to alter the substance, style, and purpose of theatrical art. Responding to his difficulties in producing his plays and pleasing the public, Masefield condemned the professional stage for producing trite plays with old ideas and talents. In an essay published as a preface to scene designs by Craig, Masefield envisioned a time when lovers of poetry and drama would build and support theaters for themselves. To do so, he argued, would acquaint new audiences with the power of the spoken word and strengthen the national spirit. Little did he know that he would answer the call himself.

Amateur theatricals and verse-speaking festivals occupied the time and talents of the entire Masefield family during these years. He eventually settled his family at Hillcrest, his home in Boar's Hill near Oxford, where his neighbors included Gilbert Murray, Robert Graves, Robert Bridges, and a circle of students from Oxford University, including the American Corliss Lamont. Beginning in 1919, Masefield and his wife organized a group of local citizens supportive of cultural and educational events in the area. At the same time he seized the chance to promote amateur performers (including his daughter and students from Oxford) in stagings of classic verse dramas. In 1922 the group, now called the Hill Players, added semiprofessional performers to its numbers as guest performers.

Masefield also joined with other poets and educators in support of verse speaking. He adjudicated verse-speaking festivals in Scotland and heard the talents of Marjorie Gullan's students from Glasgow. These performances sparked a desire to plan his own verse-speaking festivals beginning in 1923, known as the Oxford Recitations. These annual festivals, held first at Oxford University and later at Boar's Hill, attracted large numbers of student participants and their teachers from all over Scotland and England; poets who served as adjudicators for the event included Binyon, Murray, and Bottomley. Working together, poets, student performers, and their teachers refined a vocal delivery style sensitive to poetic nuance and form, ''the poet's elocution'': a highly musical and rhythmic approach to verse speaking, as taught by Elsie Fogerty and Marjorie Gullan in the tradition of the legendary stage voices of Florence Farr and Marion Terry.

In 1924 Masefield secured funds from the Lamont family to build a private theater in his garden, called the Music Room. With the building completed, the Masefields prepared a steady schedule of events—lectures, poetry readings, the annual verse-speaking festival, and continued performances by the Hill Players were all featured on the small wooden stage, considered by Bottomley as one of the finest in England. Here Masefield staged several of his own plays, translations, and adaptations (*Tristan and Isolt, A King's Daughter, Esther, Berenice, The Trial of Jesus*) and invited Bottomley to premiere his experimental choric verse dramas in 1929.

As an adjudicator, producer of community drama, and performer (he occasionally appeared as an actor with the Hill Players), Masefield contributed to the popularity of amateur theatricals and verse speaking between the wars. During the 1920s he produced and wrote dramas to his own poetic tastes and for special audiences, without the worry of creating a commercial success. Masefield's translation of Racine's *Esther* and his adaptation of *Berenice*, along with his plays on biblical subjects (*Esther, Good Friday, A King's Daughter*, and *The Trial of Jesus*), were theatrical experiments in verse not written for the professional stage. After his appointment as poet laureate, Masefield gradually turned away from drama, as both writer and producer. He sold the property at Boar's Hill, moved to Pinbury Park, near Cirencester in Gloucestershire, and began his career as the Queen's Poet.

As a writer his awards were many: he was a recipient of the Hanseatic Shakespeare Prize from Hamburg University in 1938, named poet laureate in 1930, and given the Royal Birthday Honours in 1935. Throughout his life, particularly during and after his Oxford Recitations, he never failed as an advocate for poetry through the spoken word. He died on 12 May 1967 and was buried in the Poets' Corner, Westminster Abbey, London.

Selected Biographical Sources: Bottomley; Dwyer; Fisher; Lamont; Maine; McCarthy; Nevinson [2]; Shields; Smith; Sternlicht.

MAJOR PLAYS, PREMIERES, AND SIGNIFICANT REVIVALS: THEATRICAL RECEPTION

The Campden Wonder. 1907. Opened 8 January at the Court Theatre (London) for 8 performances; directed by Harley Granville-Barker and presented as a double bill with Cyril Harcourt's *The Reformer.*

Masefield's first play to be staged, the story of a shocking miscarriage of justice (complete with triple hangings implied offstage), created a successful scandal. The critic for *The Times* (Review of *The Tragedy of Nan*), when reviewing *The Tragedy of Nan*, referred back to *The Campden Wonder* as Masefield's effort simply "to outdo the fat boy in Pickwick as a source of horror." The play was produced along with a light comedy and poorly presented; a reviewer for the *Manchester Guardian* (Review of *The Campden Wonder*) gave the author slightly more credit than the production.

The Tragedy of Nan. 1908. Opened in London on 24 May at the New Royalty Theatre, produced by the Pioneers, featuring Lillah McCarthy and directed by Harley Granville-Barker; moved to the Haymarket as a matinee the following month. Opened in New York at the Thirty-ninth Street Theatre as a series of special matinee performances in February 1920.

The Tragedy of Nan is a Cinderella story gone wrong: Forced to live her life in shame of her father's supposed guilt, Nan falls in love with a weak, selfish man. She sets out to test his love and is rejected; consequently, she stabs her love and then throws herself into the river. Drawing connections between the idea of Nan's father's guilt and a similar theme in Ibsen's work, the reviewer for *The Times* (Review of *The Tragedy of Nan*) accepted the twists and turns of the plot and praised Masefield's skill at character exposition. The play was judged superior to his earlier effort, with special praise for Lillah McCarthy's haunting portrayal as Nan. Woollcott valued the play as an actor's vehicle, a popularity based on histrionics. Although he called the play imaginative and dramatic, he chided the cast and director of the American premiere for their excess and called for restraint. In recent years Dwyer (72) argued that Masefield salvaged the extreme plot of *The Tragedy of Nan* primarily through the evocation of local color elements in language, setting, and character. Smith (95) speculated that McCarthy, who had recently married Granville-Barker, brought attention and resonance to the play because of her reputation as an interpreter of Shaw.

The Faithful. 1914. Opened 4 December at the Birmingham Repertory Theatre. The American premiere was on 13 October 1919 at the Garrick Theatre, presented by the Theatre Guild with scenery by Lee Simonson (see Brugière).

Masefield's lyrical drama, set in Japan, presents a morality play as ritualized drama. Despite the obvious experimental and poetical nature of the script, it was deemed a failure at the Garrick. Lewisohn, writing for the *Nation* urged the Theatre Guild to reject such future dramas of a lyrical and fantastic theme; although Simonson provided atmospheric sets for the stage, his efforts could not compensate for the play's shortcomings. Theatrical realism was urged instead. Lewisohn saw the play as emotionally reductive and distant, devoid of character warmth and motivation, and implausible in action. In contrast, Coatsworth, writing for *New Republic* saw the poetic simplicity of the dramatic fable as its strength, specifically the thematic richness of the cultural forces within the play that shape belief, ritual, revenge, and duty. Nevertheless, she judged the Theatre Guild production a complete failure in acting, staging, period style, and emotional tone.

ADDITIONAL PLAYS, ADAPTATIONS, AND PRODUCTIONS

Masefield's additional plays for the professional stage range from comic short one-acts to blazing melodrama to noble tragedy. Describing critical responses to Masefield's two dramas on historical figures, Cunliffe (183) noted that the plays were considered pompous and dreary. *Pompey the Great* opened on 4 December 1910 at London's Aldwych Theatre, produced by the London Stage Society; a revised version was presented by the Manchester University Dramatic Society in 1915. *Philip the King* opened on 5 November 1914 at the Royal Opera House, Covent Garden, London, directed by Harley Granville-Barker. In addition, Masefield wrote two one-acts. *The Sweeps of Ninety-Eight* opened on 7 October 1916 at the Birmingham Repertory Theatre, triple-billed with John Drinkwater's *The God of Quiet* and George Bernard Shaw's *The Inca of Perusalem;* Masefield's *The Locked Chest* premiered 28 April 1920 at the St. Martin's Theatre, London.

The Witch, an adaptation of H. Wiers-Jenssen's *Anne Pedersdotter,* opened on 10 October 1910 at the Glasgow Repertory Theatre. The London premiere, featuring Lillah McCarthy and directed by Granville-Barker, opened in late January 1911, with a limited run through 17 February. The American premiere was on 18 November 1926 at the Greenwich Village Theatre, directed by Hubert Osborne, with settings and costumes by Livingston Platt. This melodrama spins forward toward the final curtain as a tale of suspected witchcraft, forbidden sex, and domestic hate. The critic for the London premiere (Review of *The Witch*) noted Masefield's skill at adapting the play for modern audiences, specifically the ways in which the element of witchcraft contributed to the play's emotional complexity by merging the supernatural with the sexual. Lillah McCarthy was praised for her expressive use of gesture and stillness in the lead role; Granville-Barker was urged to bring more light up on the scene. Reviewing the Greenwich Village production, Atkinson wryly reduced the plot to medieval witch burning as *Desire under the Elms*—a melodramatic and theatrical mixture of soaring emotions with enough calculated plot twists to challenge any actor.

Masefield's contributions to religious drama include *Good Friday,* which opened on 25 February 1916 at the Garrick Theatre, London, and *The Coming of Christ,* written at the invitation of Bishop Bell for Canterbury Cathedral and premiered on 28 April 1928. Smith (192) argued that the religious themes and subjects in these plays should be seen as autobiographical: Masefield's early years as an agnostic and his later journey toward a questioning faith. In recent years, the literary critic William Spanos has noted a fundamental moral weakness in Masefield's religious plays, a quality also condemned in Bottomley's *The Acts of Saint Peter.* Spanos (142–43) rejected Masefield's representation of the Christian faith in all of his religious dramas, specifically Masefield's depiction of unrelenting pessimism, underlying naturalism, and facile conversion—the human condition apparently untouched by the reality of the redemptive function of the Incarnation.

As noted and reviewed in various local and national papers, Masefield produced four of his dramas in and around Boar's Hill with his amateur players: *Esther,* an adaptation of Racine (directed by Penelope Wheeler and performed by Masefield's Hill Players), opened on 5 May 1921 at Wootton; the Hill Players also premiered *A King's Daughter* on 25 May 1923 at the Oxford Playhouse. In the newly constructed Music Room at Boar's Hill ("Masefield's Poetic Theatre"), the Hill Players presented *The Trial of Jesus* on 9 May 1925 (Lamont, 24). The play was revived on 26 March 1932 at the Everyman Theatre in London by the Citizen House Players, Bath. Thouless (48) saw Masefield's *Esther* as a successful experiment in verse drama, particularly in his use of choric interludes. Thouless continued by praising *A King's Daughter,* Masefield's drama about Jezebel, as a bold reworking of the biblical tale: Jezebel presented as a heroine and a victim of the evil designs of others (see also Nevinson [1], 235). Critics characterized the performances of *The Trial of Jesus* as impressive, but saw Masefield's use of choric interludes as ineffective (quoted in Cunliffe (184); see also Spanos (142)). Finally, Masefield's greatest critical artistic success at Boar's Hill, *Tristan and Isolt,* opened in the Music Room on 21 October 1927, following its premiere by the Lena Ashwell Players in February 1927 at the Century Theatre, Bayswater. Reviewers for the *Oxford Times* (Review of *Tristan and Isolt*) and *The Times* (*"Tristan and Isolt"*) praised the emotional strength and characterizations within Masefield's production and his skill as producer and concluded that the drama held the audience, composed primarily of individuals from Oxford, in rapt attention during all of the three-hour performance.

ASSESSMENT OF MASEFIELD'S CAREER

The degree to which Masefield experimented with and influenced popular as well as innovative theatrical forms and styles of presentation has yet to be fully assessed. Masefield showed some promise as a commercial playwright, a promise unfulfilled in the years that followed. His early plays were given some noteworthy productions and received supportive critical receptions, but they were rarely revived (Bhatnager, 10–15; Montague, 202). In recent years, Dwyer has stood alone in her attempts to reacquaint this and future generations with Masefield's plays. Dwyer's assessment (69) of Masefield's entire theatrical canon as an undiscovered treasure for the stage has yet to be proven onstage for this or any generation.

Masefield wrote at least ten prose dramas and seven verse plays between 1909 and 1948, an uncertain figure given that Masefield destroyed aborted efforts and left others unpublished (Smith, 225–227; Dodds, 1, 21). Although *The Campden Wonder, The Tragedy of Nan,* and *The Witch* were written to appeal to popular theatrical taste, *Philip the King, The Faithful, Pompey the Great, Tristan and Isolt,* and his plays on biblical subjects were written as challenges to popular taste, experiments in verse drama, or for particular audiences (see Montague, Morgan, Muir, Nevinson [2], Spanos, Thouless). Working to bring works of serious artistic intent to the commercial stage, Masefield ultimately failed; consequently, he devoted his energies as a playwright to private theatricals and community drama. In short, a complete assessment of Masefield's dramas must examine his entire theatrical canon within the context of his intended audiences and his shifting attitudes toward the role of theater in society.

Another difficulty for Masefield scholarship today involves a critical understanding of his plays and his theatrical career within and beyond his influential work as a poet and novelist. Most Masefield scholarship has focused on the thematic and personal connections between his early plays and his other writings and associates at that time (see Bhatnager, Fisher, Sternlicht). The influence of Yeats, Synge, and Lady Gregory on Masefield's early plays has been carefully traced by literary critics as well as biographers to explain Masefield's use of verse drama, regional themes and characters, and the one-act-play genre, respectively (see Dwyer, 69–70; Smith, 78–79). Recent scholarship has uncovered Masefield's neglected contributions as an important writer in Arthurian literature, specifically his verse tragedy, *Tristan and Isolt* (Dodds). His failed experiments in verse drama (*The Faithful*) and historical drama (*Pompey* and *Philip the King*) need similar reappraisal. Overall, Masefield's plays have been sorely neglected in recent years as suitable subjects for the study of theatrical genre (melodrama, historical drama, and verse drama). Given the modest commercial popularity of his early work and the stature of the professional artists who worked on those stagings, his plays and performances from this period should be critiqued as part of the development and decline of these traditional theatrical genres.

But this is not to say that Masefield's major contributions as a theater artist can be adequately addressed within scholarship limited to the professional or popular stage. Like his friend and fellow verse dramatist Gordon Bottomley, Masefield's theatrical reputation must include a serious reappraisal of his neglected contributions in the area of community drama. Turning his back on the professional stage, Masefield's work in the theater between the wars can best be understood not only as experiments in dramatic technique but as an attempt to create new audiences for the stage, audiences sensitive to poetic nuance (see Bottomley, 20–21; Nevinson [2], 64; Smith, 186). At first the press coverage of Masefield's private theatricals at Wootton and Boar's Hill was limited. However, with the popularity of the annual Oxford Recitations and the construction of his private theater, an increasing number of reviews covering Masefield's theatricals at Boar's Hill appeared in major British publications and occasionally in America as well (Shields, 16–18). The extensive publicity surrounding these events contributed to Masefield's growing reputation as a populist writer and supporter of community drama. Although he was praised as a populist writer, his plays produced at Boar's Hill were not themselves products of a populist theatre.

Masefield scholarship today must discuss this paradox, reassess the forces that created his public reputation as a populist figure, and explicate Masefield's plays and productions from the perspective of social and cultural history. More needs to be done to understand Masefield's role in the changing public attitudes toward amateur theatricals and the professional stage during his time, particularly in those years leading up to his appointment as poet laureate. These areas of cultural and literary interpretation have yet to be explored. To do so may prompt interest in his plays for production and provide a clearer understanding of the connections between his literary reputation, shifting cultural attitudes toward the arts, his personal life, and his public role as poet laureate.

ARCHIVAL SOURCES

Major collections of Masefield's manuscripts and unpublished personal and professional papers are housed at the following: the Bodleian Library, Oxford University; Fisk University; the State University of New York at Buffalo; the University of Vermont; the Harry Ransom Humanities Research Center, at the University of Texas, Austin; Yale University Library; the Houghton Library, Harvard University; and the Berg Collection, New York Public Library.

PRIMARY BIBLIOGRAPHY

Plays

Berenice. London: Heinemannn, 1922.
The Coming of Christ. New York: Macmillan, 1928.
Easter: A Play for Singers. London: Heinemann, 1929.
End and Beginning. London: Heinemann, 1933.
Esther. London: Heinemann, 1922.
The Faithful. London: Heinemann, 1915.
Good Friday. Letchworth: Garden City Press, 1916; New York: Macmillan, 1916; London: Heinemann, 1917.
A King's Daughter. New York: Macmillan, 1923.
Melloney Holtspur. London: Heinemann, 1922.
The Tragedy of Pompey the Great. London: Grant Richards, 1909.
The Trial of Jesus. London: Heinemann, 1925.
Tristan and Isolt. London: Heinemann, 1927.
The Witch (based on *Anne Pedersdotter* by H. Wiers-Jenssen). Boston: Little, Brown, 1917.

Anthologies

Collected Plays of John Masefield. New York: Macmillan, 1919.
Collected Works: Verse and Prose Plays. (Vols. 3–4). New York: Macmillan, 1925.
The Locked Chest, and The Sweeps of Ninety-Eight (two one-acts). New York: Macmillan, 1917.
John Masefield. Edited and introduced by David Llewellyn Dodds. Cambridge: D.S. Brewer, 1994. Series title: *Arthurian Poets: Arthurian Studies 32.* (*Tristan and Isolt, When Good King Arthur.*).
Plays. Vols. 1–2. London: Heinemann, 1936.

Books on Drama and Theater

A Macbeth Production. London: Heinemann, 1945.
The Oxford Recitations. New York: Macmillan, 1928.
So Long to Learn: Chapters of an Autobiography. New York: Macmillan, 1952.

SECONDARY BIBLIOGRAPHY

Atkinson, Brooks J. "The Play: From the Norwegian." *New York Times* (19 Nov. 1926):
    6.
Bhatnager, L. K. *John Masefield, the Poetic Dramatist.* Meerut, India: Shalabh Book
    House, 1983.
Bottomley, Gordon. *A Stage for Poetry.* Kendal, England: Titus Wilson & Son, 1948.
Brugière, Francis (photographer). A photograph of *The Faithful* as produced by the the-
    atre Guild. *Theatre Arts Magazine* (Jan. 1920): 2.
Review of *The Campden Wonder. Manchester Guardian* (9 Jan. 1907): 6.
Clark, George Herbert. "John Masefield and Jezebel." *Sewanee Review* 32 (1924): 242.
Coatsworth, Elizabeth J. Review of *The Faithful. New Republic* (12 Nov. 1919): 326.
"A Country House Theatre: Mr. Masefield's Innovation at Boar's Hill, Oxford." *Country
    Life* (8 Aug. 1925): 233.
Craig, E. G. *Scene.* London: Oxford University Press, 1923.
Cunliffe, John W. *Modern English Playwrights.* Port Washington, NY: Kennikat Press,
    1969.
Dodds, David Llewellyn. "Introduction." In *Arthurian Poets: Arthurian Studies 32.* Ed-
    ited and introduced by D. L. Dodds, 1–29. Cambridge: D.S. Brewer, 1994.
Drew, Fraser Bragg. "The Irish Allegiances of an English Laureate: John Masefield and
    Ireland." *Eire-Ireland* 4 (1968): 24–34.
Dwyer, June. *John Masefield.* New York: Ungar, 1987.
Review of *The End of the Beginning. The Times* (18 Mar. 1934): 10.
Fisher, Margery. *John Masefield.* New York: Henry Z. Walck, 1963.
Review of *A King's Daughter. Oxford Times* (12 Nov. 1924): 10.
Knight, G. Wilson. "Masefield and Spiritualism." In *Mansions of the Spirit,* ed George
    A. Panichas, 259–88. New York: Hawthorn Books, 1967.
Lamont, Corliss. *Remembering John Masefield.* New York: Tenth Avenue Editions, 1991.
Lewisohn, Ludwig. "The Theatre Guild: Review of *The Faithful." Nation* (8 Nov. 1919):
    591–92.
Maine, Basil. *The Best of Me.* London: Hutchinson, 1937.
Mallik, Upendra Nath. *John Masefield, a Playwright.* Patna, India: Janaki Prakashan,
    1983.
"Masefield's Poetic Theatre." *Living Age* (3 Jan. 1925): 69.
"Masefield's Theatre at Boar's Hill." *New York Times* (18 May 1930): sec. v, pp. 3,
    16.
McCarthy, Lillah. *Myself and My Friends.* London: Thornton Butterworth, 1933.
Review of *Melloney Holtspur. The Times* (11 July 1923): 10.
Montague, Charles E. "Mr. Masefield's Tragedies." In *Dramatic Values,* 197–206. Gar-
    den City, NY: Doubleday, 1925.
Morgan, Charles. "John Masefield's Passion Play: A Review of *The Trial of Jesus."
    New York Times* (17 Apr. 1932): 3:1.

"Mr. Masefield as a Playwright." *Nation* (22 Mar. 1919): 432.

Muir, Kenneth. "Verse and Prose." In *Contemporary Theatre,* 97–116. London: Edward Arnold Publishers, 1962.

Nevinson, Henry W. [1]. "*A King's Daughter:* The Tragedy of Jezebel." *New Statesman* (2 June 1923): 235–36.

———. [2]. "An Oxford Experiment." *Saturday Review of Literature* (23 Aug. 1924): 64.

Shanks, Edward. "Review of *Melloney Holtspur.*" *Outlook* (21 July 1923): 54.

Shields, Ronald E. "Like a Choir of Nightingales: The Oxford Recitations, 1923–1930." *Literature in Performance* 3 (Nov. 1982): 15–26.

———. "Voices Inside a Poet's Garden: John Masefield's Theatricals at Boar's Hill." *Text and Performance Quarterly* 16 (1996).

Smith, Constance Babington. *John Masefield: A Life.* New York: Macmillan, 1978.

Spanos, William V. *The Christian Tradition in Modern British Verse Drama: The Poetics of Sacramental Time.* New Brunswick, NJ: Rutgers University Press, 1967.

Sternlicht, Sanford. *John Masefield.* Boston: Twayne, 1977.

Strong, L.A.G. *John Masefield.* London: Longmans, 1964.

Thouless, Priscilla. *Modern Poetic Drama.* Oxford: Basil Blackwell, 1934.

Towse, J. Rankin. [1]. "Mr. Masefield's Tragedy: *The Faithful.*" *Nation* (17 Nov. 1915): 668.

———. [2]. "Plays by Masefield." (A Review of *The Tragedy of Nan* and Other Plays). *Nation* 102 (1 June 1916): 602–3.

Review of *The Tragedy of Nan. The Times* (26 May 1908): 57.

Review of *Tristan and Isolt. Oxford Times* (25 Feb. 1927): 7.

"*Tristan and Isolt:* Mr. Masefield's Production at Boar's Hill." *The Times* (22 Oct. 1927): 10.

West, Rebecca. Review of *The Faithful. Living Age* (21 June 1919): 719–22.

White, Newman Ivey. "John Masefield—An Estimate." *South Atlantic Quarterly* (1927): 189–200.

Williams, Charles. "John Masefield." In *Poetry at Present.* Oxford: Clarendon Press, 1930.

Review of *The Witch. The Times* (1 Feb. 1911): 187.

Woollcott, Alexander. Review of *The Tragedy of Nan. New York Times* (22 Feb. 1920): 6.

BIBLIOGRAPHIES

Handley-Taylor, Geoffrey. *John Masefield, O.M.: The Queen's Poet Laureate.* London: Cranbrook Tower Press, 1960.

Simmons, Charles H. *A Bibliography of John Masefield.* New York: Columbia University Press, 1930.

Wight, Crocker. *John Masefield: A Bibliographical Description of His First, Limited, Signed, and Special Editions.* Boston: Library of the Boston Athenaeum, 1986.

Williams, I. A. [*a bibliography of his works.*]. Norwood, PA: Norwood Editions, 1977.

W. Somerset Maugham
(1874–1965)

ROBERT F. GROSS

Although William Somerset Maugham is now best remembered as the author of narrative fiction (*Of Human Bondage, Cakes and Ale,* and *The Razor's Edge* being his most famous novels), he first won wealth and renown as a playwright. In fact, his early reputation was so strongly associated with the stage that J. B. Priestley observed in 1930 that Maugham's fame in the theater kept him from winning appropriate recognition for his novels.

Maugham was born on 25 January 1874 at the British embassy in Paris, where his father worked as a solicitor. Although his was a happy and affectionate family, it was not long-lived. His mother died of tuberculosis when he was barely eight years old, and his father died of cancer two and a half years later. Maugham was sent to live with an uncle, a middle-aged vicar, and his German-born wife. One result of these traumatic experiences of separation was the development of a stutter, an impediment that plagued Maugham for the rest of his life.

At the age of sixteen Maugham was sent to Heidelberg, where he attended lectures and immersed himself in fin de siècle culture. He developed an interest in the writings of Arthur Schopenhauer, an admiration for the operas of Richard Wagner, and an enthusiasm for works of such iconoclasts of the modern theater as Henri Becque, Hermann Sudermann, and Henrik Ibsen. He went so far as to translate a German edition of *Ghosts* into English in an attempt to learn Ibsen's dramatic technique. By the time Maugham returned to England in 1892, he had chosen to study medicine as a hedge against poverty, but had set his ambitions on a writing career.

Maugham's stage experience began modestly with the 1902 Berlin premiere of his curtain raiser, *Marriages Are Made in Heaven,* which ran for 8 performances in a cabaret theater. Showing a young man who agrees to be financially supported by his new wife through a generous settlement she had received from a former lover, the comedy exhibits the worldliness and materialism that mark much of his later work. This was followed by an equally sardonic drama in the Ibsenite vein, *A Man of Honour,* in which a young man, driven by idealism, marries a Cockney barmaid when he learns that he has made her pregnant. His ideals are not, however, enough to compensate for the differences between them, and the marriage quickly deteriorates into misery, from which he is delivered by his wife's suicide. Playing briefly in London in both 1903 and 1904, *A Man of Honour* drew some praise from critics, but did nothing to help the young playwright gain a foothold in the commercial theater. Indeed, it would not be until 1907 that another play of Maugham's would be performed. In the meantime he continued to write and suffered repeated rejection from London producers.

His fortunes suddenly turned with the production of *Lady Frederick* (1907), chosen by a producer who needed a play to fill a theater that was unexpectedly empty. No one predicted that it would run for 422 performances. Suddenly, many of Maugham's previously rejected plays found producers; *Mrs. Dot, Jack Straw,* and *The Explorer* were soon all running in London alongside *Lady Frederick.* Audiences were not taken with the melodramatic posturings of *The Explorer,* but the other three plays quickly established Maugham as a skillful comic entertainer whose work showcased the talents of star comedians. *Penelope* (1909) remains the most deft and carefully constructed of these early entertainments.

Following on these successes, Maugham's next plays mixed comic formulas with weightier concerns. *Smith* (1909) and *The Land of Promise* (1913) contrasted London decadence with colonial virtue (Rhodesia and Canada, respectively). Both *Landed Gentry* (performed under the title *Grace*) and *The Tenth Man* (both 1910) give bleak pictures of domesticity and business among the landed gentry, and both are uneasy compromises between difficult issues and formulaic dramaturgy. *Love in a Cottage* (1918) fell into a similar muddle as it tried to portray the evils of wealth while more persuasively dramatizing the miseries of poverty. *Caesar's Wife* (1919) was by far the most successful of these experiments, as Maugham minimized plot complications and moved away from melodramatic touches to achieve a greater subtlety of expression. *The Unknown* (1920), an excursion into the play of ideas, ultimately lapses into melodrama, but not before painting a stark and painful picture of the loss of religious faith in the wake of the First World War.

In 1913 Maugham became the lover of Syrie Bernardo, a stylish and intelligent woman of the Mayfair set, and she soon became pregnant. But by the time of their marriage in 1915, Maugham had become involved with the love of his life, the energetic Gerald Haxton, whose outgoing manner nicely balanced Maugham's introversion. The nearly thirty years of their relationship, until Gerald's death in 1944, were the years of Maugham's best writing; all his major works, with the exception of *Of Human Bondage* (1915), were produced during those years. This relationship was, however, incompatible with his marriage to

Syrie (who may have blackmailed him into marriage in the first place), and the two were divorced in 1929, after years of rancorous separation.

After meeting Gerald Haxton, Maugham turned to a series of witty comedies. With *Our Betters* (written 1915, produced 1917) he produced a work that exhibited a depth of insight not seen in his earlier entertainments. It was followed by three of his most assured comedies—*The Unattainable* (1916), *Home and Beauty* (1919), and *The Circle* (1921). Maugham's next essay into comedy, *The Camel's Back* (1923), a bitter farce, was not nearly so successful, but *The Constant Wife* (1926), the most brittle and consistently sophisticated of his comedies, showed him back at the top of his form. His final comedy, *The Breadwinner* (1930), which showed a middle-aged husband telling off his wife and children and setting off to live his own life, was much looser in structure than *The Constant Wife,* but no less complete in its attack on the nuclear family.

Two melodramas of the 1920s returned to the world made famous by Maugham's short stories of British émigrés in Asia, with a mixture of exotic atmosphere, illicit love, and violence. The first, *East of Suez* (1922), is an uneasy mixture of story and spectacle, while the second, *The Letter* (1927), is an expertly wrought suspense drama about adulterous love and murder on a Malay plantation.

By the end of the 1920s Maugham had wearied of the theater. He felt that he was no longer in touch with his audience and was no longer interested in writing the kinds of plays they expected of him. His three last plays—*The Sacred Flame* (1930), *For Services Rendered* (1932), and *Sheppey* (1933)—he explained, were written for himself. In the first, a hybrid of murder mystery and thesis play about euthanasia, he consciously adopted a more heightened style of speech for his characters. In the second, he returned to the setting and themes of *The Unknown,* but treated them with more complexity of character and richness of incident. Finally, *Sheppey* mixed comedy, morality play, and satire in the bleak tale of a barber who tries to follow the teachings of Jesus and is declared insane by his family. As Maugham predicted, none of these plays pleased his audiences, though they remain some of his most intriguing theatrical works.

In the following decade Maugham continued to be prolific, publishing essays, short stories, novels, memoirs, and a travel book. After his last novel, *Catalina,* appeared in 1948, Maugham limited himself largely to essays and occasional pieces. The last decades of his life were marked by increasing emotional instability. In 1962 the *Sunday Express* serialized a memoir, *Looking Back,* in which Maugham shocked and offended many of his friends with his vitriolic attacks on his ex-wife. The following year Maugham made headlines when he tried to adopt his lover, Alan Searle, and disinherit his daughter, Liza, on the grounds that she was illegitimate. Increasingly ill and senile, he lived ''out his last days in a nightmare'' (Coward [1], 607), which only ended on 15 December 1965 with his death from pneumonia.

Selected Biographical Sources: Calder [2]; Morgan; Sanders.

MAJOR PLAYS, PREMIERES, AND SIGNIFICANT
REVIVALS: THEATRICAL RECEPTION

Lady Frederick. 1907. Opened 16 October at the Royal Court Theatre (London) for 422 performances, directed by W. Graham Browne. Revivals: 9 November 1908, Hudson Theatre (New York), directed by William Seymour; 21 November 1946, Savoy Theatre (London), directed by Murray Macdonald; 24 June 1970, Vaudeville Theatre (London), directed by Malcolm Farquhar.

This glittering, artificial comedy of wit and intrigue, in which a respectable English family tries to thwart the romance between its young heir and a much older, thoroughly charming adventuress, was Maugham's first stage success. Turner praised the play as a "witty, original and exquisitely-wrought study of a fascinating personality." In contrast to its great popular success in London, its New York premiere was greeted tepidly: "This is a story of theatre, not of real life," a reviewer from the *Nation* ("Drama") pronounced disapprovingly. Although Potter found the play in its 1946 revival pointless and the relocation of an Edwardian play to an 1880s setting annoying, he concluded, "Miss Coral Browne admirably carried the play" in the title role. In 1970 Wardle [3] found the play reactionary in its politics and loathsome in its characters, and Farquhar's production disturbingly uncritical in its approach. For Hurren, the play was flat and dated.

Penelope. 1909. Opened 9 January at the Comedy Theatre (London) for 246 performances. Revivals: 13 December 1909, Lyceum Theatre (New York), directed by Dion Boucicault; 9 September 1953, Arts Theatre (London), directed by Walter Hudd.

A comedy of manners in which a clever wife, upon learning of her husband's infidelity, wins him back by encouraging the affair to run its course, *Penelope* has been praised as one of Maugham's most charming comedies. Although Archer [2] criticized the play as implausible and slightly cynical, he admitted that it was "amusing." Grein [1] enjoyed the play's worldliness and charm. Woollcott [2] praised the play in its New York premiere, blaming tired moments on the actors rather than the playwright. The 1953 London revival caused an anonymous critic for *The Times* ("Arts Theatre: *Penelope* by W. Somerset Maugham") to observe that although the play no longer shocked, it still gave satisfaction through its cleverness, while *Plays and Players'* R. B. noted that the younger actors in the production were having trouble adapting to Maugham's style.

The Unattainable. 1916. Opened 8 February at the New Theatre (London) for 141 performances. Directed by Dion Boucicault. Revivals: 20 September 1916, Empire Theatre (New York), directed by W. Somerset Maugham; 12 June 1926, Playhouse (London), directed by Athole Stewart; 22 March 1949, Arts Theatre (London), directed by Joan Swinstead.

First performed under the title *Caroline,* this comedy proceeds from a simple premise. Caroline Ashley has lived as a grass widow in London, enjoying her love affair with bachelor Robert Oldham. When her husband's obituary suddenly appears in *The Times,* she and Robert find their idyllic relationship threatened as everyone now expects them to marry. They are only saved by a clever friend, who announces that the death notice was incorrect. Grein [5] praised Maugham's deftness at spinning out such an amusing play from such a slight premise: "He is as crafty as old Scribe and he writes ever so better." S. W. [1], on the other hand, savaged the New York production, saying that Maugham had a wonderful comic idea that he had let degenerate into farce.

Our Betters. 1917. Opened 12 March at the Hudson Theatre (New York) for 112 performances, directed by J. Clifford Burke. Revivals: Globe Theatre (London), 12 September 1923, directed by Stanley Bell; 20 February 1928, Henry Miller's Theatre (New York), directed by Reginald Bach; 3 October 1946, Playhouse (London), directed by Jack Minster.

Reviewers and audiences were both shocked and titillated at this sardonic comedy about American heiresses married to European aristocrats. Although this play is usually listed as one of Maugham's highest dramatic achievements, its sardonic tone has rendered it a far less popular candidate for revival than *The Circle.* The *Nation*'s S.W. [2] represented the overall reaction of the New York critics when he concluded that "the piece leaves an unpleasant taste in the mouth without convincing one of its sincerity." MacCarthy [3] was more approving in his reaction to the London premiere, saying that it was evidence of the author's continuous progress as a playwright and praising it as "mercilessly amusing." Only five years later, however, Atkinson [2] found the Broadway revival dated and attributed its success to the skilled comic playing of Ina Claire and Constance Collier rather than to the script itself. By 1946 the play was so far removed from current manners that reviewers approached it as a period piece, though Smiles defended the play, noting that most of the actors had failed to accommodate themselves to Maugham's style, performing far too quickly and casually.

Caesar's Wife. 1919. Opened 27 March at the Royalty Theatre (London) for 241 performances, directed by Wilfred Eaton. Revival: 24 November 1919, Liberty Theatre (New York), directed by B. Iden Payne.

Inspired by *La Princesse de Clèves,* this stoic, understated drama of a wife who falls in love with a young diplomat, only to renounce him for the good of his career and, by extension, "the Empire," has been admired for its grace and careful construction, but has not enjoyed any revivals, perhaps because of its imperialist rhetoric. *The Times* ("Royalty Theatre: *Caesar's Wife*") praised the initial production as "a triumphantly tactful evening," though Archer [1] found the husband too noble to be believed and the psychology superficial. Broun, reviewing the Broadway production, found it an interesting experiment in which dramatic conflict was almost completely internalized.

Home and Beauty. 1919. Opened 8 October under the title *Too Many Husbands* at the Booth Theatre (New York) for 15 performances, directed by Clifford Brooke. Revivals: 30 August 1919, Playhouse (London), directed by Charles Hawtrey; Aldwych Theatre (London), 24 November 1942, directed by Val Gielgud; Arts Theatre (London), 31 August 1950, directed by Roy Rich; National Theatre (London), 8 October 1968, directed by Frank Dunlop; Eisenhower Theatre (Washington, D.C.), 2 June 1979, directed by José Ferrer.

In a farcical variant on the *Enoch Arden* situation, a soldier who was believed dead returns to London to discover that his wife has married his best friend. The two men find themselves only too eager to retreat from their marriages, and the wife finds herself a third and far wealthier replacement for them. Woollcott [1] found the New York premiere delightful, but conceded that for American audiences, the play was somewhat foreign in its sensibility. In London Huxley admired the way the humor all followed consistently from the play's initial premise. The successful 1950 revival still struck Stephens with its modernity. Later revivals have not been nearly so well received. The National Theatre's production drew notice to the play's bitterness (Marcus) and misogyny (Billington). Although Rosemary Harris was praised for her interpretation of Victoria, the 1979 revival was criticized for its verbosity and lack of strong direction (Coe, Lardner).

The Circle. 1921. Opened 3 March at the Haymarket Theatre (London) for 181 performances, directed by J. E. Vedrenne. Revivals: 12 September 1921, Selwyn Theatre (New York), directed by Clifford Brooke; February 1931, Vaudeville Theatre (London), directed by Raymond Massey; 18 April 1938, the Playhouse (New York), directed by Bretaigne Windust; 1944 (London); 20 July 1976 at the Chichester Festival, continued at the Haymarket Theatre (London), directed by Peter Jews; 20 February 1986 by the Mirror Repertory Company (New York), directed by Stephen Porter; 20 November 1989, Ambassador Theatre (New York), directed by Brian Murray.

This high comedy, which contrasts a young woman who leaves her husband for a planter in the Malay States with her mother-in-law, who left her own husband years ago for another man, is widely considered Maugham's dramatic masterpiece and is by far the most frequently revived. It was hailed from the first as Maugham at his best (Woollcott [3], MacCarthy [1]), and each major revival has occasioned comment on its seeming indestructibility. "What a cunning play this is," exclaimed Wardle [1] of the 1976 Chichester revival. The 1989 Broadway revival found Simon praising its "superabundance of charm." Levine has written a particularly interesting article on the play, focusing on the various implications of the title.

The Constant Wife. 1926. Opened 29 November at Maxine Elliott's Theatre (New York) for 295 performances, directed by Gilbert Miller. Revivals: 6 April 1927, Strand Theatre (London), directed by Basil Dean; 19 May 1937, Globe Theatre (London), directed by Richard Bird; 8 December 1951, National Theatre

(New York), directed by Guthrie McClintic; 19 September 1973, Albert Theatre (London), directed by John Gielgud.

This witty and extremely unsentimental comedy, although admired by critics, has proved difficult to produce successfully. The premiere production starred Ethel Barrymore in a performance that Maugham praised as the best he had ever seen in any of his plays. "If ever there was a patrician performance," cheered Benchley, "here it is." The London production, by contrast, was a fiasco. Brown pronounced the play "heartless" and Fay Compton seriously miscast in the leading role. Ten years later the play fared only slightly better on the London stage. Atkinson [1] found Katharine Cornell's 1951 performance too romantic and sincere, and Wilson found Ingrid Bergman's 1973 portrayal of Constance too Swedish for the play's London setting.

For Services Rendered. 1932. Opened 1 November at the Globe Theatre (London) for 78 performances. Revival: National Theatre (London), 1 May 1979, directed by Michael Rudman.

In this deeply pessimistic domestic drama, a family in Kent serves as a microcosm in which the economic, social, and ethical crises of England after the First World War play themselves out. Critical reaction was sharply divided, with Pollock praising it as "unquestionably the biggest play written since Ibsen's heyday," while Fleming and Grein [4] believed that the play's strategy of heaping misfortunes on a single family and attributing them all to the war resulted in a weak argument. Wardle [2] found the 1979 revival successful in bringing out all the play's undercurrents and likened it to *Home and Beauty* in its depiction of the selfishness of respectable English society.

Sheppey. 1933. Opened 14 September at Wyndham's Theatre (London), directed by John Gielgud, for 83 performances. Revival: 18 April 1944, Playhouse (New York), directed by Cedric Hardwicke.

Adapted by Maugham from one of his first published short stories, "A Bad Example" (1899), *Sheppey* has tended to confuse audiences and annoy critics. The story of a London barber who wins a sweepstakes and resolves to use it to help the poor, thus scandalizing his family, who plot to have him declared insane, *Sheppey* is a mixture of domestic comedy, mordant satire, and, most unusual for Maugham, nonrealistic dramaturgy. While MacCarthy [2] described it as a very grim comedy, Grein [2] was offended by the extreme bitterness with which the play treated religious material. "There are sanctities that should be safe from such assaults," he explained. The play fared even less well in its New York production, where Nichols found much of the writing aimless and marked by odd shifts in mood, despite revisions by the playwright.

ADDITIONAL PLAYS, ADAPTATIONS, AND PRODUCTIONS

Maugham adapted only three foreign plays to the English-speaking stage. In 1909 his reworking of Ernest Grenet-Dancourt's *The Noble Spaniard* ran for 55

performances, with Charles Hawtrey in the role of a vainglorious Spanish nobleman who is foiled in his courtship of a clever, young, French widow. Although its initial run was short, it has enjoyed popularity with amateur theater
groups. Much less successful was Maugham's adaptation of Molière's *Le Bourgeois Gentilhomme, The Perfect Gentleman,* which ran for a mere 8 performances in 1913. His 1933 adaptation of Luigi Chiarelli's *grottesca* drama *The
Mask and the Face* was only slightly more successful in its single production
by the Theatre Guild.

On the other hand, Maugham's fiction has often been adapted to the stage,
sometimes to enormous popular acclaim. Indeed, *Rain* (1922), John Colton and
Clemence Randolph's adaptation of Maugham's short story "Miss Thompson,"
is now better known than any of Maugham's own plays. Maugham's tale of the
brassy prostitute and her disastrous meeting with the sexually repressed Reverend Davidson became the basis for the play that ran for 648 performances on
Broadway, enjoyed similar success abroad, and was the basis for three films,
with Gloria Swanson, Joan Crawford, and Rita Hayworth each starring in the
role of Sadie Thompson. *The Moon and Sixpence,* Maugham's novel inspired
by the life of Paul Gauguin, was first dramatized by Edith Ellis, whose dialogue
was so poor that Maugham revised much of it. Despite Maugham's intervention,
however, its 1925 West End run was only mildly successful. Maugham had an
even bigger hand in Barlett McCormack's 1931 adaptation of *The Painted Veil;*
he wrote to Gladys Cooper that less than thirty lines of his adaptor's script
survived in the final version. Maugham may have had a hand in the 1941 adaptation of his novel of backstage life, *Theatre,* credited to Guy Bolton. According to a pre-Broadway review, Maugham was working on the play, although
later scholarship has not verified that claim, and Stott [1] has rejected it.
Maugham later remarked that he much preferred Marc-Gilbert Sauvajon's
French adaptation of *Theatre, Adorable Julia,* to Bolton's version. Zoë Akins's
1933 adaptation of "The Human Element," telling of a British socialite's love
for her chauffeur, remains unpublished and unperformed, as does Romney
Brent's adaptation of Maugham's "The Vessel of Wrath," *Man-Hunt. Before
the Party* (1949), Rodney Ackland's adaptation of Maugham's short story of
the same name, in which a desperate and embittered wife slays her alcoholic
husband with a parang, met with difficulties in the transition from a tersely
written tale into a full-length play. As the reviewer for the *New Statesman and
Nation* observed, "Mr. Ackland's second act is a failure, because, artistically,
it is unnecessary" (*"Before the Party"*).

Attempts to adapt Maugham's work to the musical stage have met only with
failure. Vernon Duke's musical adaptation of *Rain, Sadie Thompson* (1944),
with book and lyrics by Rouben Mamoulian and Howard Dietz, complete with
dancing natives and dream ballet, ran for less than two weeks on Broadway.
An operatic version of *The Moon and Sixpence* by composer John Gardner
enjoyed a brief run at Sadler's Wells Opera in 1957 and quickly vanished into
obscurity. Maugham's first novel, *Liza of Lambeth,* a naturalistic study of Lon-

don slum life, seems an unlikely property for a musical comedy, but the project was undertaken, with book and lyrics by William Rushton and Berry Stringle and music by Cliff Adams. Produced in London in 1976, it opens as "a chorus of battered females lift up their skirts to complain about 'usbands'" and unsuccessfully tries to reconcile squalor and misery with musical-comedy conventions (Curtis). Given this history of unsuccessful attempts, it may be just as well that composer Richard Adler (of *Damn Yankees* fame) never attained his ambition of turning *Of Human Bondage* into a musical comedy (Behrman).

There is a special category of plays in which a character appears who is modeled on Maugham himself. S. N. Behrman wrote two plays named *Jane,* both adapted from Maugham's short story of the same name: first, as a farce for the London stage (1947), and, later, as a high comedy for Broadway (1952). In both, Maugham appears as the witty and detached author, William Tower, who is separated from his socially ambitious, interior designer wife, suggested by Syrie Bernardo. In a stage direction Behrman (297) went so far as to suggest that the actor playing Tower should read the works of Maugham, especially his autobiographical volume, *The Summing Up.* Noël Coward fashioned three characters on Maugham. *Point Valaine* (1934) is not only dedicated to Maugham and has a plot that reads like a conscious imitation of a Maugham short story, telling of British expatriate Linda Valaine's torrid and tortured affair with a malevolent Russian headwaiter, who ends up throwing himself to the sharks, but also presents Mortimer Quinn, a bachelor British author, whose world travels and "dry aloofness" mirror Maugham's own public persona. In *South Sea Bubble* (1956) he appears in the guise of John Blair-Kennedy, "a novelist of some repute" (Coward [3], 1) who is interested in traveling and learning about the outposts of the Empire. The most important portrait, however, is found in *A Song at Twilight* (1966), in which Coward himself originally played the role of Hugo Latymer, an elderly, closeted homosexual author, who has marred his talent and injured his private life by refusing to come to terms with his sexual preference. Coward ([2], 4) stressed the similarity to Maugham in his performance, even making himself up to resemble the celebrated author.

ASSESSMENT OF MAUGHAM'S CAREER

Maugham candidly admitted that he wrote his plays not for posterity, but for the present. In *The Summing Up* he argued that prose drama was a popular and topical form, "scarcely less ephemeral than a news sheet" (122). A playwright needs to be able to recognize a good story, a revelatory detail, and must be able to put a story over in such a way that it will hold and move an audience. Economy is essential to a good play; digressions are fatal. A playwright must always remember that the group intelligence of an audience is far less than that of its most intelligent members, and must avoid overly intellectual content: "The only ideas that can affect them when they are welded together in that unity which is an audience, are those commonplace, fundamental ideas that are almost feelings. These, the root ideas of poetry, are love, death and the destiny of man'' (131).

Maugham's attitude toward the theater was one of thoroughgoing pragmatism. When he found in rehearsal that the final act of *The Unattainable* was ineffective, he asked the director for permission to rewrite it and produced a new version of it within twenty-four hours. When director Basil Dean asked for permission to cut some dialogue from *East Of Suez,* Maugham replied, "Why not? The theatre is a workshop." He had little patience with the noncommercial theater and with the rise of the director and the play of ideas and had no interest in twentieth-century experiments in dramatic form. The purpose of theater was to entertain, not instruct. "Politics is the refuge of third-rate playwrights," he once told Clare Booth Luce (quoted in Smith).

As a result of this conservatism, Maugham did not fare well with the critical establishment, and his plays tended to be received better by audiences than reviewers, who accused Maugham of a facile and even cynical view of the theater. Oliver's dismissal of the playwright—"as clever and as shallow as they come"—encapsulates much of the negative criticism that has been aimed at Maugham ever since the beginning of his career. Even admirers of Maugham's narrative fiction have been inclined to dismiss the plays as trivial. "Examined as a whole, Maugham's plays are largely superficial and do not warrant extensive thematic analysis," concluded Calder ([2], 167) and scholars have tended to agree with him. Despite the great amount published on Maugham's life and literary output, volumes devoted to the author's entire oeuvre usually relegate his dramatic output to a single chapter, in which the published plays are quickly summarized and evaluated, along with a few comments on major themes. Only three volumes have been devoted entirely to Maugham's drama. The earliest, Dottin's *Le Théâtre de W. Somerset Maugham* (1937), still remains the most thoughtful study of Maugham's dramatic development. Savini's *Das Weltbild in William Somerset Maughams Dramen* (1939) is little more than an essay, arguing that Maugham's plays generally dramatize the conflict between Victorian and postwar values. Barnes's *The Dramatic Comedy of William Somerset Maugham* (1968) provides useful assessments of most of the comedies. All three works move briskly through the plays, with little close reading or protracted analysis.

Dottin may have best accounted for the general critical neglect of Maugham's plays when he observed that the very ease and apparent simplicity of Maugham's style can lead readers astray: "En réalité, lecteurs et spectateurs superficiels sont victimes de la simplicité, du naturel, de la facilité du style et du dialogue" (258). Interpretive difficulties do not leap off the pages of these scripts—Maugham aspires to ease and clarity and generally achieves it. As a result, he does not present overt challenges to interpretation, but seeks to give the appearance of elegant finish. If Ibsen is the John Donne of modern drama, Maugham is its Robert Herrick.

From the first, Maugham used the form of the well-made play as the vehicle for a highly unsentimental and materialistic view of life. This *Weltanschauung* is best understood, as Naik (3) pointed out, as a tension between humanitarian and cynical views of experience. MacCarthy [1] has best described the cynical side of Maugham's sensibility. Viewed as a whole, Maugham's stage writing is at its best when it balances the cynical and humanitarian impulses within a scene or character: the good-hearted Lady Frederick disillusioning her young admirer by initiating him into the mysteries of her dressing table (*Lady Frederick*); Robert and Caroline realizing that they are too set in their ways to move from romance to cohabitation (*The Unattainable*); Lady Grayston deploying brilliant tactical maneuvers to salvage her reputation after a disastrous indiscretion (*Our Betters*); or Winnie realizing to her chagrin that she is too much a creature of her middle-class background to accept her working-class suitor (*Loaves and Fishes*).

Maugham learned to achieve this balance in comedy early on; it took him much longer to effect it in drama. His first assured drama, *Caesar's Wife,* eschews cynicism entirely in favor of an almost Corneillean exercise in Stoic virtue. *The Letter* is a satisfying melodrama that largely ignores both cynicism and humanitarianism in favor of a traditional, middle-of-the-road approach to a tale of adultery and murder. It functions as a detective play in which, as Taylor (101) has pointed out, Maugham's need to keep the audience ignorant of certain facts ultimately precludes any depth of vision. Only at the very end of his playwriting career, with *The Sacred Flame, For Services Rendered,* and *Sheppey,* did his double optic manifest itself successfully in noncomic work, creating various unsettling combinations of bitterness and pathos. For Dottin, these final dramas rank among Maugham's finest theatrical works.

Whether in comedy or drama, however, Maugham's thematic concern remains the same. He is an anatomist of physical, emotional, and ideological constraints—the title of his best-known novel, *Of Human Bondage,* could easily be taken as the title for his collected works. Sexual desire (*East of Suez, The Letter*), religious belief (*The Unknown*), patriotism (*For Services Rendered*), Christian morality (*The Sacred Flame*), and the class system (*Landed Gentry, Loaves and Fishes*) are presented as painful constraints upon the individual (Calder [1] passim). Marriage, however, is most frequently the predominant image of bondage. In *Penelope, Landed Gentry, The Land of Promise, The Unattainable, Home and Beauty, Caesar's Wife, East of Suez, Our Betters, The Circle, The Constant Wife,* and *The Breadwinner,* marriage is defined by a lack of freedom. In the most lighthearted of these, such as *Home and Beauty* and *The Unattainable,* characters are able to avoid the matrimonial trap altogether, and in *The Constant Wife* and *The Breadwinner,* the protagonists' refutations of domestic bondage are so complete that Dottin has referred to them as "attaques bolchevisantes contre la famille" (13). In *The Circle* Elizabeth is able to escape her marriage, but only by running off with another man, a precarious solution at best, as the pathetic example of her mother-in-law demonstrates. In *Penelope* a clever woman is able to contrive a degree of freedom within her marriage, though without ever questioning the double standard (Carlson [1]). A few plays suggest that submission to the bonds of marriage can confer a degree of nobility, if not necessarily happiness (*Landed Gentry, Caesar's Wife, The Land of Promise*). Finally, in the bleakest and most melodramatic plays of marriage, such as *East of Suez* and *For Services Rendered,* any illusion of a successful escape seems impossible, and the sole liberator is death (*The Sacred Flame, Sheppey*).

Given Maugham's largely negative view of the constraints upon individual freedom, critics have been divided on the challenge he presents to the status quo. For Carlson ([1], 417) and Innes, the plays include transgressions but ultimately serve as conservative forces, reinforcing the established order. For Barnes (129), on the other hand, the plays provide a destabilizing force, in which social order is irrevocably disrupted. The Carlson-Innes approach ultimately explains the early comedies, from *Lady Frederick* to *Penelope,* much better, while Barnes's approach more successfully accounts for the later comedies, from *The Unattainable* to *The Breadwinner,* with their increasingly eccentric social configurations. In the late melodramas no accommodation to the established order is either possible or desirable for an intelligent and vital person. This line of development is consistent with Innes's conclusion that Maugham's playwriting career charts a growing inability to acquiesce to the expectations of his audience.

Although the themes of Maugham's plays often advocate freedom, their forms are anything but free. Indeed, his few forays away from a realistic, well-made form—such as the use of heightened speech in *The Sacred Flame* or the symbolic coming of death in *Sheppey*—are timid gestures in comparison to the contemporaneous experiments of, say, Ernst Toller, Luigi Pirandello, or Eugene O'Neill. For Maugham, playwriting requires submission to a rigorous craft, which demands absolute self-abnegation in obedience to its rules. "However brilliant a scene may be," he explained, "however witty a line or profound a reflection, if it is not essential to his play, the dramatist must cut it" (*The Summing Up,* 125). This leads us to a paradox at the center of Maugham's dramatic work, for although his characters may aspire to be free, the dramatic action never depicts them in their liberty. The dramatic action takes place in the world of constraints, and freedom, in an undefined elsewhere. When Teddy and Elizabeth leave for the Federated Malay States (*The Circle*), Constance takes off for her romantic fling (*The Constant Wife*), or Charles Battle quits his odious wife and children (*The Breadwinner*), the final curtain descends. Freedom remains a utopian notion, set in an unrepresentable elsewhere, while both dramatic action and dramatic authorship take place in bondage. In this respect, *Caesar's Wife,* with its ultimate renunciation of happiness in favor of duty, may be Maugham's most uncompromising metatext on the playwright's work, while a comedy of escape, like *The Breadwinner,* may reflect his own chafing at the restraints of drama.

Maugham scholarship is in a curious state. On the one hand, there are excellent biographies (Morgan, Calder [2]) and bibliographies (Mander and Mitchenson, Sanders, Stott [1]), and some excellent, although critically conservative, overviews of his entire output (Calder [1], Naik). At the same time, only very scant attention has been paid to his plays, and the development of critical theory has only manifested itself in Carlson's excellent feminist considerations of his comedies. Aside from the occasional references to Ibsen or Wilde, no attempts have been made to seriously investigate influences on Maugham's playwriting. While his contemporaries were quick to point out *The Tenth Man's* indebtedness both to Henri Bernstein's *La Rafole* and Ferdinand Fabre's *Les Ventres dorés* (Grein [3]) and *Penelope*'s relationship to Victorien Sardou's *Divorçons* (''*Penelope* Only Mildly Amusing''), no theatrical historian has yet attempted to reconstruct the dramatic context within which Maugham worked and his relationship to playwrights both commercial, like Bernstein, and experimental, like Sudermann. Tintner's investigation of the influence of Henry James on *Our Betters* remains the single example of source scholarship in the study of Maugham's drama. Similarly, although Morley has noted the influence of *The Breadwinner* on Noël Coward's *Fumed Oak* and *Our Betters* on *The Vortex,* no scholarship has provided careful evaluation of Maugham's place in the development of modern drama, and modern comedy in particular. To what extent are the comedies of Noël Coward, Frederick Lonsdale, Philip Barry, and S. N. Behrman indebted to Maugham? To what extent does a 1920s drama of domestic claustrophobia like Sidney Howard's *The Silver Cord* owe more to Maugham than to Ibsen? Many such questions must be posed and answered before Maugham's role in theatrical modernism will be adequately understood.

Finally, recent developments in deconstructive, Marxian, and psychoanalytic criticism may provide valuable techniques to critics who wish to look beneath the apparent simplicity and finish of Maugham's plays to find the personal and social forces that led to such a need to repress and contain dangerous ambiguities and aporias. Maugham's dramatic asceticism cannot be dismissed as mere facility, any more than Jean Racine's or Samuel Beckett's. It is a finely wrought defense mechanism in a period of rapid change, and that it proved so popular for a time tells us that it was not merely a personal aberration. To dismiss Maugham as ''as clever and as shallow as they come'' (Oliver) is to ignore a sophisticated playwright whose work is far more complex than he would have us suspect.

ARCHIVAL SOURCES

Most of the drafts of Maugham's plays can be found in the library of the Royal National Theatre, London, including an early, unperformed and unpublished comedy, *The Middle of Next Week,* and an early draft of *Mrs. Dot,* entitled *Worthley's Entire* (which is also in the Theatre Collection of the New York Public Library). The drafts of *Lady Frederick* and *Penelope* are in the Library at the University of Texas, Austin. The Berg Collection at the New York Public Library and the Library of Congress possess copies of a number of unperformed and unpublished plays, including *Mrs. Beamish* (which also exists in a later revision, entitled *Under the Circumstances*), *The Keys to Heaven, The Road Uphill,* and *The Force of Nature,* as well as the performed but unpublished plays *Mlle. Zampa, Love in a Cottage,* and *The Camel's Back.* Maugham was also an indefatigable letter writer, and many manuscript collections contain letters by him. The most substantial collection is at the University of Texas, Austin, but there are also important collections at Yale University, Stanford University, Indiana University, and the New York Public Library.

PRIMARY BIBLIOGRAPHY

Plays

The Bread-winner. London: Heinemann, 1930; *The Breadwinner.* Garden City, NY: Doubleday, Doran, 1931.
Caesar's Wife. London: Heinemann, 1922; New York: George H. Doran, 1923.
The Circle. London: Heinemann, 1920; New York: George H. Doran, 1921.
The Constant Wife. New York: George H. Doran, 1927; London: Heinemann, 1927.
East of Suez. London: Heinemann, 1922; New York: George H. Doran, 1922.
The Explorer. London: Heinemann, 1912; Chicago: Dramatic Publishing Company, 1912.
For Services Rendered. London: Heinemann, 1932; Garden City, NY: Doubleday, Doran, 1933.
Home and Beauty. London: Heinemann, 1923.
Jack Straw. London: Heinemann, 1912; Chicago: Dramatic Publishing Company, 1912.
Lady Frederick. London: Heinemann, 1912; Chicago: Dramatic Publishing Company, 1912.
The Land of Promise. London: Bickers & Sons, 1913; Ottawa: George A. Popham, 1914; New York: George H. Doran, 1922; London: Heinemann, 1922.
Landed Gentry. London: Heinemann, 1913; Chicago: Dramatic Publishing Company, 1913.
The Letter. London: Heinemann, 1927; New York; George H. Doran, 1927.
Loaves and Fishes. London: Heinemann, 1924; New York: Samuel French, 1926.
A Man of Honour. London: Chapman & Hall, 1903; *Fortnightly Review* (Mar. 1903); Chicago: Dramatic Publishing Company, 1912.
Marriages Are Made in Heaven. In *The Venture.* Vol. 1. London: Pear Tree Press, 1903.
Mrs. Dot. London: Heinemann, 1912; Chicago: Dramatic Publishing Company, 1912.
The Noble Spaniard. London: Evans Brothers, 1953.
Our Betters. London: Heinemann, 1923; New York: George H. Doran, 1924.
Penelope. London: Heinemann, 1912; Chicago: Dramatic Publishing Company, 1912.
The Perfect Gentleman. Theatre Arts 39.1 (Nov. 1955): 49–64.
The Sacred Flame. Garden City, NY: Doubleday, Doran, 1928; London: Heinemann, 1929.
Sheppey. London: Heinemann, 1933; Boston: W. H. Barker, 1949.
Smith. London: Heinemann, 1913; Chicago: Dramatic Publishing Company, 1913.
The Tenth Man. London: Heinemann, 1913; Chicago: Dramatic Publishing Company, 1913.

The Unattainable. London: Heinemann, 1923.
The Unknown. London: Heinemann, 1920; New York: George H. Doran, 1920.

Anthologies

Collected Plays. 3 vols. (Volume 1: *Lady Frederick, Mrs. Dot, Jack Straw, Penelope, Smith, The Land of Promise;* Volume 2: *Our Betters, The Unattainable, Home and Beauty, The Circle, The Constant Wife, The Breadwinner;* Volume 3: *Caesar's Wife, East of Suez, The Sacred Flame, The Unknown, For Services Rendered, Sheppey.*) London: Heinemann, 1952.

Plays. 6 vols. (Volume 1: *Lady Frederick, Mrs. Dot, Jack Straw;* Volume 2: *Penelope, Smith, The Land of Promise;* Volume 3: *Our Betters, The Unattainable, Home and Beauty;* Volume 4: *The Circle, The Constant Wife, The Breadwinner;* Volume 5: *Caesar's Wife, East of Suez, The Sacred Flame;* Volume 6: *The Unknown, For Services Rendered, Sheppey.*) London: Heinemann, 1931–34.

Selected Plays. (*Sheppey, The Sacred Flame, The Circle, The Constant Wife, Our Betters.*) Harmondsworth: Penguin, 1963.

Six Comedies. (*The Unattainable, Home and Beauty, The Circle, Our Betters, The Constant Wife, The Breadwinner.*) Garden City, NY: Garden City Publishing, 1937.

Three Comedies. (*The Circle, Our Betters, The Constant Wife.*) New York: Washington Square Press, 1969.

Three Dramas. (*The Letter, The Sacred Flame, For Services Rendered.*) New York: Washington Square Press, 1968.

Essays and Articles on Drama and Theater

"A Few Comments on the Younger Dramatists." In Noël Coward, *Bitter-Sweet and Other Plays.* Garden City, NY: Doubleday, Doran, 1929.

"Gladys Cooper." *Plays and Players* 1.3 (Dec. 1953): 4.

"Somerset Maugham Interviewed for *Stage.*" *Stage* 1.1 (Nov. 1940): 48–49.

The Summing Up. Garden City, NY: Doubleday, 1950.

SECONDARY BIBLIOGRAPHY

Archer, William. [1]. Review of *Caesar's Wife. Weekly Review* (4 June 1919): 110.

———. [2]. "*Penelope* and Popularity." *Nation* (16 Jan. 1909): 606–7.

"Arts Theatre: *Penelope* by W. Somerset Maugham." *The Times* (11 Sept. 1953): 2.

Atkinson, Brooks. [1]. "*The Constant Wife:* Katharine Cornell Appears in One of Somerset Maugham's Comedies." *New York Times* (16 Dec. 1951): 11:1, 3.

———. [2]. "Worldly Sinners." *New York Times* (4 Mar. 1928): 9:1.

B., R. "*Penelope.*" *Plays and Players* (Oct. 1953): 16.

Barnes, Ronald E. *The Dramatic Comedy of William Somerset Maugham.* The Hague: Mouton, 1968.

"*Before the Party* at St. Martins." *New Statesman and Nation* (5 Nov. 1949): 514.

Behrman, S. N. *People in a Diary: A Memoir.* Boston: Little, Brown, 1972.

Benchley, Robert. "Something Good." *Life* (16 Dec. 1926): 19.

Billington, Michael. "Good Comedy But Poor Farce." *The Times* (9 Oct. 1968): 9.

Broun, Heyward. "Repressed Emotion Is the Keynote in *Caesar's Wife*." *New York Tribune* (25 Nov. 1919): 11.

Brown, Ivor. "Heartless House." *Saturday Review* (16 Apr. 1927): 598–99.

Calder, Robert. [1]. *W. Somerset Maugham and the Quest for Freedom*. Garden City, NY: Doubleday, 1973.

———. [2]. *Willie: The Life of W. Somerset Maugham*. New York: St. Martin's Press, 1989.

Carlson, Susan L. [1]. "Two Genres and Their Women: The Problem Play and the Comedy of Manners in the Edwardian Theatre." *Midwest Quarterly* (Summer 1985): 413–24.

———. [2]. "Women in Comedy: Problem, Promise, Paradox." In *Drama, Sex, and Politics,* ed. by James Redmond, 159–71. Cambridge: Cambridge University Press, 1985.

Coe, Richard L. Review of *Home and Beauty. National Theatre Review* (Aug. 1979): 31.

Coward, Noël [1]. *The Noel Coward Diaries*. Ed. Graham Payn and Sheridan Morley. Boston: Little, Brown, 1982.

———. [2]. *Point Valaine*. New York: Doubleday, Doran, 1935.

———. [3]. *South Sea Bubble*. London: Heinemann, 1956.

Curtis, Anthony. "*Liza of Lambeth*." *Plays and Players* (Aug. 1976): 30.

Dottin, Paul. *Le Théâtre de W. Somerset Maugham*. Paris: Librairie Académique Perrin, 1937.

"Drama." *Nation* (12 Nov. 1908): 470–72.

Fleming, Peter. "The Theatre: *For Services Rendered* by W. Somerset Maugham. At the Globe Theatre." *Spectator* (11 Nov. 1932): 659.

Grein, J. T. [1]. Review of *Penelope. The Sunday Times* (10 Jan. 1909): 9.

———. [2]. "Somerset Maugham's New Play." *Illustrated London News* (30 Sept. 1933): 498.

———. [3]. Review of *The Tenth Man. The Sunday Times* (27 Feb. 1910): 4.

———. [4]. "Two Gifted Pessimists." *Illustrated London News* (26 Nov. 1932): 854.

———. [5]. Review of *The Unattainable. The Sunday Times* (13 Feb. 1916): 4.

Hurren, Kenneth. "*Lady Frederick*." *Plays and Players* (Aug. 1970): 27.

Huxley, Aldous. "A Good Farce." *Athenaeum* (26 Sept. 1919): 956.

Innes, Christopher. "Somerset Maugham: A Test Case for Popular Comedy." *Modern Drama* (Dec. 1987): 549–59.

Lardner, James. "*Home and Beauty:* Marriage and Maugham from A to B." *Washington Post* (4 June 1979): B:1, 9.

Levine, Robert T. "The Weight of a Title: An Analysis of Maugham's *The Circle*." *Theatre Annual* (1984): 1–13.

MacCarthy, Desmond. [1]. "Drama: *The Circle*." *New Statesman* (19 Mar. 1921): 704–5.

———. [2]. "Mr. Maugham's New Play." *New Statesman and Nation* (16 Sept. 1933): 325–26.

———. [3]. "Somerset Maugham: *Our Betters*." *New Statesman* (6 Oct. 1923): 738–39.

Marcus, Frank. "Farce with a Bitter Heart." *Sunday Telegraph* (13 Oct. 1968).

Morgan, Ted. *Maugham*. New York: Simon & Schuster, 1980.

Morley, Sheridan. *A Talent to Amuse: A Biography of Noël Coward.* Boston: Little, Brown, 1985.

Naik, M. K. *W. Somerset Maugham.* Norman: University of Oklahoma Press, 1966.

Nichols, Lewis. "The Play: Edmund Gwenn in the Leading Role of a Slowish Somerset Maugham Play Called *Sheppey* Opening at the Playhouse." *New York Times* (19 Apr. 1944): 2:27.

Oliver, Edith. "The Theatre: Off-Broadway." *New Yorker* (3 Mar. 1986): 84–85.

"*Penelope* Only Mildly Amusing." *New York Times* (14 Dec. 1909): 11.

Pollock, John. "Theatre." *Saturday Review* (London) (12 Nov. 1932): 6.

Potter, Stephen. "Theatre." *New Statesman and Nation* (30 Nov. 1946): 396.

Priestley, J. B. "A Letter from England." *Saturday Review of Literature* (New York) (1 Nov. 1930): 299.

"Royalty Theatre: *Caesar's Wife.*" *The Times* (28 Mar. 1919): 9.

Sanders, Charles. "W. Somerset Maugham." In *Dictionary of Literary Biography,* vol. 10, *Modern British Dramatists, 1900–1945,* ed. Stanley Weintraub, pt. 2, 22–42. Detroit: Gale Research, 1982.

Savini, Gertrud. *Das Weltbild in William Somerset Maughams Dramen.* Erlangen: Junge & Sohn, 1939.

Simon, John. "Serene *Circle,* Soggy *Tempest.*" *New York* (4 Dec. 1989): 166–68.

Smiles, Sam. "*Our Betters.*" *New Statesman and Nation* (12 Oct. 1946): 263.

Smith, Jack. "Experts Recall Somerset Maugham." *New York Journal-Tribune* (12 Sept. 1966).

Stephens, Frances. *Theatre World Annual.* Vol. 2. London: Rockliff, 1951.

Taylor, John Russell. *The Rise and Fall of the Well-made Play.* New York: Hill & Wang, 1967.

Tintner, Adeline R. "W. Somerset Maugham vs. Henry James." *Antiquarian Bookman* (7 Nov. 1983): 3092–3120.

Turner, Reginald. Review of *Lady Frederick. Academy* 73 (2 Nov. 1907): 96–97.

W., S. [1]. "Drama." *The Nation* 103, no. 2675 (5 Oct. 1916): 330–32.

———. [2]. "Review of Plays: Our Betters." *The Nation* 104, no. 2699 (22 Mar. 1917): 350.

Wardle, Irving. [1]. "*The Circle* at Chichester." *The Times* (21 July 1976): 9.

———. [2]. "*For Services Rendered.*" *Plays and Players* (June 1979): 19–21.

———. [3]. "The Small Society." *The Times* (25 June 1970).

Wilson, Sandy. "*The Constant Wife.*" *Plays and Players* (Nov. 1973): 44–45.

Woollcott, Alexander. [1]. "A Delightful Maugham Farce." *New York Times* (9 Oct. 1919): 16.

———. [2]. "The Drama: Marie Tempest in *Penelope* at the Lyceum Theatre." *New York Herald Tribune* (14 Dec. 1909): 7.

———. [3]. "The Play: Maugham Much Magnified." *New York Times* (13 Sept. 1921): 12.

BIBLIOGRAPHIES

Bason, Frederick T. *A Bibliography of the Writings of William Somerset Maugham.* London: Unicorn Press, 1931.

Henry, W. H., Jr. *A French Bibliography of W. Somerset Maugham.* Charlottesville: Bibliographical Society of the University of Virgina, 1967.

Mander, Raymond, and Joe Mitchenson. *Theatrical Companion to Maugham: A Pictorial Record of the First Performances of the Plays of W. Somerset Maugham.* London: Rockliff, 1955.

Sanders, Charles. *W. Somerset Maugham: An Annotated Bibliography of Writings about Him.* De Kalb: Northern Illinois University Press, 1970.

Stott, Raymond Toole. [1]. *A Bibliography of the Works of W. Somerset Maugham.* London: Kaye & Ward, 1973.

———. [2]. *Maughamiana: The Writings of W. Somserset Maugham.* London: Heinemann, 1950.

Allan Monkhouse

(1858–1936)

LIBBY SMIGEL

Allan Monkhouse is remembered for his drama criticism for the *Manchester Guardian* and for his plays produced at Annie Horniman's Manchester Gaiety Theatre. Along with Stanley Houghton and Harold Brighouse, he is considered one of the three principal playwrights of the so-called Manchester school.

Allan Noble Monkhouse was born on 7 May 1858 to John W. S. Monkhouse and Mary Brown Monkhouse at Barnard Castle, Durham. Following his education in England's private schools, he entered the Manchester cotton trade. His first wife, Lucy Dowie, died in 1894, the second year of their marriage. In 1902 he married Elizabeth Dorothy Pearson, by whom he had two daughters and two sons.

He joined the *Manchester Guardian* in 1902 as an editor and drama critic. For the rest of his life Monkhouse sustained a high reputation as a critic and continued to work for the *Guardian,* as well as contribute to the *New Statesman,* while writing novels and—after Annie Horniman's Gaiety Theatre repertory company was formed in Manchester—plays.

His first play, *Reaping the Whirlwind,* a domestic tragedy in one act produced in 1908, was the first local-written drama produced by the Horniman company. His next two works, also produced at the Manchester Gaiety, were problem plays suggesting the range of Monkhouse's work. *The Choice* (1910) portrayed the calamity of war, while *Mary Broome* (1911) addressed domestic tyranny. A few years later, Monkhouse's affinity with the Manchester theater allowed him to try his hand at a topical burlesque, *Nothing like Leather* (1913), which spoofed the Gaiety company in a performance featuring Horniman as herself.

Monkhouse was also among a group of theater practitioners and critics who, in 1910, lectured at the Playgoers' Club in Liverpool and prompted the community to start the Liverpool Repertory Theatre Company at the Playhouse in

1911. His comedy *The Education of Mr. Surrage* (1912) was given its first performance by that new company. Because the play's theme of family differences between generations is often considered the signature of the Manchester-school playwrights, *The Education of Mr. Surrage* has been subjected to unfavorable comparisons with Houghton's *Hindle Wakes* and Brighouse's *Hobson's Choice* (Nicoll, 281). Nonetheless, the play has endured enough to see a revival broadcast in 1950 by the BBC Home Service.

Following the First World War, Monkhouse achieved critical recognition, but limited public exposure, for his bitter antiwar drama *The Conquering Hero* (1924), his domestic problem plays *The Hayling Family* (1924) and *Sons and Fathers* (1926), and his plays on labor unrest, *First Blood* (1925) and *The Rag* (published 1928). Monkhouse died on 10 January 1936, at his home in Disley.

Selected Biographical Sources: Brighouse; Mikhail [1].

MAJOR PLAYS, PREMIERES, AND SIGNIFICANT REVIVALS: THEATRICAL RECEPTION

Reaping the Whirlwind. 1908. (one act). Opened 28 September at the Gaiety (Manchester) on a double bill with Charles McEvoy's *David Ballard.* Revival: Miss Horniman's company, His Majesty's Theatre (Montreal), February 1912.

This tragic twist on the love-triangle theme was received favorably in Manchester, but unfamiliarity with serious curtain raisers produced an indifferent response from Montreal audiences and critics (see Pogson, 121). Nicoll (280) saw "no particular value" in the play.

Mary Broome. 1911. Opened 9 October at the Gaiety (Manchester). Produced by Stanley Drewitt. Revival: Miss Horniman's company, Coronet (London), 6 performances, May 1912. Television adaptation by Gerald Savory, Granada TV, 1960.

A witty young man with literary aspirations is forced by his father to marry the maid he has impregnated, but she emigrates to Canada with a working-class partner when her child dies and her husband shows no concern. The *New Statesman* ("Mr. Monkhouse's Mary Broome") lauded the first act as a "masterpiece of pointed compression," but as for the whole play, "psychologically, nothing happened." The absence of a clear didactic message caused Firkins to write, "It is not a serious, not an artistic, hardly a moral, play." The *Pall Mall Gazette,* however, discerned that the laying bare of motives and character caused the discomfort of the reception (see Pogson, 153–54). Agate (235) included the play in his list of "the theatrical play about real people." Sutton [2] wrote that despite the play's "keen dialogue," the second act was "aesthetically improper and shocking"—a comedy of bad manners (138–39). Rowell and Jackson (44) noted the originality and sensitivity of the reworking of the plot of the attraction between an heir and a maidservant.

The Education of Mr. Surrage. 1912. Opened 4 November at the Playhouse Repertory Theatre (Liverpool). Revivals: Gaiety (Manchester), performed by the Liverpool Repertory Company, November 1912; Birmingham Repertory Theatre, 10 performances, produced by John Drinkwater, September 1916; Century Theatre (London), October 1925. BBC broadcast, July 1950.

What should have been a delicate domestic comedy of the differences in moral attitudes between generations was given a heavy-handed first production in Liverpool, which Monkhouse good-naturedly tolerated (Goldie, 81–82). Agate (94) said that the play contained "the comic rhythm in things tragic," as it warned us "to laugh with care."

Nothing like Leather. 1913. (one act). Opened 29 September at the Gaiety (Manchester).

This farce, which took as its topic of satire the Gaiety Theatre management and actors and the *Manchester Guardian* theater critic, was a screaming success as the opener of the theatre season (Pogson, 157–158).

The Grand Cham's Diamond. 1918. (one act). Opened 21 September at the Birmingham Repertory Theatre on a triple bill with *One Day More* (Conrad) and *The Bear* (Chekhov). Produced by John Drinkwater. Revivals: Arts Theatre (London), double-billed with Monkhouse's *Cecilia,* 6 performances, March 1933. BBC broadcast, 1927.

Rowell and Jackson called it a "broadly comic and Cockney extravaganza" (44).

The Conquering Hero. 1924. Opened 23 February at Albert Hall (Leeds). Produced by Basil Dean. Revivals: Aldwych (London), 1 performance, produced by Play Actors, 23 March 1924; transferred to Queen's (London), 3 April 1924; transferred to St. Martin's (London), 60 performances, produced by Milton Rosmer, 28 April 1924; Liverpool Repertory Theatre, 1924–25 season, with William Armstrong producing and acting the lead role; Royalty (London), 1 performance, performed by the "G" Club, 11 March 1934.

A remarkable play about the war written during the war, it is considered by most to be Monkhouse's masterpiece. Sutton ([2], 146) compared it to Granville-Barker's *The Secret Life,* saying that the one shows the disillusion of a mind warped by war, while *The Conquering Hero* shows the "warping process in operation." Armstrong, reviewing the published version of the play, called it an excellent psychological study. The *Review of Reviews* critic ("Drama of the Month") voiced the "liveliest contempt and dislike" for Christopher Rokeby, the humanist who questions participating in the war.

The Hayling Family. 1924. Opened 26 October at the Aldwych (London) for 1 performance. Produced by Lewis Casson. Performed by Play Actors.

A mordant depiction of a tyrannical father whose selfishness destitutes his family found favor from *The Times* ("Play Actors at the Aldwych") for the first act, but Monkhouse was accused of letting the emotion of the situation overtake the play. Sutton ([2], 141) classed the play as a "drama of retrospect," similar to Ibsen's, in which the action is precipitated from some cause from the past, a truth revealed or silence broken.

First Blood. 1925. Amateur production. Stockport Garrick Society. Revivals: Little Theatre (Leeds), January 1926; Gate Theatre (London), December 1926.

Describing the play's dialogue as "pertinent, crisp, and natural," Brown [3] found the quarrel between two workers and an employer's son in the first act to be particularly well crafted and performed. The end of the play, however, was unconvincingly "jerky."

Sons and Fathers. 1926. Opened 24 January at the Royal Academy of Dramatic Art (London) for 1 performance by the RADA Players. Directed by Milton Rosmer.

John Gielgud played Dick Southern, the virtuous family man and businessman who at every crossroad surrenders his high standards rather than cause suffering for his family. Nicoll (276) proffered this play as an example where Manchester writers showed a similarity to Irish dramatists in the theme of sacrificing personal comfort for the sake of a larger good or dream. Brown [2] called the dialogue "natural, vivid, and fully expressive of fine shades of meaning."

Cecilia. 1932. Opened 14 November at the Repertory Theatre (Liverpool) as part of its "twenty-first anniversary" coming of age. Revival: Arts Theatre (London), for 6 performances, double-billed with *The Grand Cham's Diamond*, March 1933.

A self-absorbed actress leaves her husband for a Hollywood director and returns humiliated to his protection. While praising the acting, *The Times* (Review of *Cecilia*) felt that the play as a whole lacked "atmosphere." The *Saturday Review* (Review of *Cecilia*) criticized the quietly "conventional ending," where Monkhouse might have otherwise exploited the potential for a "big scene."

ADDITIONAL PLAYS, ADAPTATIONS, AND PRODUCTIONS

The Choice (one act) opened 6 June 1910 at the Gaiety (Manchester); it was revived at the Gaiety on a bill with Stanley Houghton's *The Dear Departed* and Sackville-Martin's *Cupid and the Styx* in March 1912. *Resentment* opened 8 October 1912 at the Temperance Hall, Sheffield, produced by Ben Iden Payne's company. *The Stricklands* opened on 5 February 1920 at the Lyceum Theatre (New York). *O Death Where Is Thy Sting?* opened 13 March 1928 at the Arcadia Theatre (Scarborough); it was revived by the Arts League of Service Travelling Theatre in the same year. *The Wiley One* was produced in 1929 by the Arts League of Service Travelling Theatre. *The King of Barvender*, a musical drama, was produced in 1930 by the Arts League of Service Travelling Theatre. *Paul Felice* opened 15 September 1930 at the Repertory Theatre, Liverpool.

There are no records of professional productions of *Shamed Life* and *Night Watches* (first published in *War Plays,* 1916). *The Rag* (published in 1928), a dramatic treatment of two rival newspapers, was reviewed in a *Saturday Review* notice (''Awaiting Production''), but there seems to have been no professional production.

ASSESSMENT OF MONKHOUSE'S CAREER

While the Manchester Gaiety Theatre provided Monkhouse with his greatest opportunity to develop as a dramatist, he had previously established himself as a novelist, editor, and critic. As a critic he was familiar with some of the best acting in England and had a reputation as a proficient and astute observer, known for his appreciation of subtle acting technique and his broad knowledge of contemporary and Shakespearean drama. Brown [1] described Monkhouse as an English post-Ibsenite who observed the playwriting of such Continental dramatists as Ibsen and Brieux but was an ''English mind going the English way.'' Although Monkhouse was to become known as a principal writer of the Manchester ''school,'' he was not a provincial playwright per se. His plays dealt with more than regional foibles, imparting a universal view of the carnivorousness of human nature and the castigation and destruction of people through silence.

Monkhouse's best plays are not the ones that received a positive critical response, perhaps because of their unsettling depictions of problems that, if seriously acknowledged, would disrupt the spectators' popular belief in their social order. For example, several of Monkhouse's plays challenge the legitimacy of familial love and duty. In *The Hayling Family* the devotion of a wife and children to ''save'' a tyrannical wastrel of a father ends bitterly in the entire family's financial ruin as well as in the sacrifice of the wife's life. In *Resentment* a father's diffidence in summoning a doctor (to counter his wife's obsessive concern) is punished by the woman's barring him from his dying child's bedside. In *Mary Broome* a father tries to control his frivolous son by using financial threats to make him marry the woman he has made pregnant.

Using ironic dialogue and wit, Monkhouse portrayed the frightening irreconcilability of family strife. His domestic plays demonstrate the impossibility of teaching a lesson, of effecting change in the recalcitrant ones, or of making amends without exacting or suffering punishment. Monkhouse pursued other themes with this characteristic ironic tone and uncompromising perspective. His plays about labor struggles—*The Rag* and *First Blood*—provide a critical view of capitalists' ''responsibility'' to their employees, and his plays about war— *The Conquering Hero, Shamed Life,* and *The Choice*—offer comparably cynical looks at cowardice, duty, or morality. The unremittingly dark humor underlying his serious dramas led Nicoll (281) to dismiss them as being ''too talky'' and without enough humor, despite the wide critical acknowledgment of Monkhouse's deft command of dialogue (see Swinnerton, 217–225; Moses, 808; and individual reviews). Criticism that the characterizations were "static" is best explained by understanding that this was a deliberate choice: Monkhouse intended to portray the unchangeable and intractable natures that caused or underlay so many social and familial problems. This understanding of human nature is pervasive in Monkhouse's novels as well, especially *Dying Fires* (1912).

Contemporary objections also arose from the so-called immorality of some of his characters and from the controversial implications raised in some of his plays. Like Houghton's *Hindle Wakes, Mary Broome* was criticized for the female's renunciation of the match to make an "honest" woman of her, though the critics often couched their objections in ambiguous terms (Firkins). The *Review of Reviews* ("Drama of the Month") may have disliked *The Conquering Hero* more for the disturbing questions Christopher Rokeby raised about patriotism and what was being fought than for the character himself.

Critics preferred the conventional humor of *The Education of Mr. Surrage,* in which members of a younger generation are subverted in their adulation of offbeat artists who take advantage of their hospitality by a practical bourgeois father who steps in to "manage" the artists into productive, honorable citizens. The clever but predictable formula of the generation-gap comedy posed no threat to self-satisfied critics. Monkhouse achieved similarly positive response for *The Grand Cham's Diamond,* a bit of a farce parodying the sensational thrillers of the day.

Swinnerton (225) attributed the lackluster critical and audience response to Monkhouse's work to its "literary" qualities, but verbal elegance can hardly be the whole story. Agate and Brown seem to come closet to understanding what Monkhouse's dramaturgy is all about, perhaps because they were his friends as well as associates. Agate (96) observed that Monkhouse knew "his stage better than to preach from it," which responded to critics looking for a moral resolution. Brown [2] saw Monkhouse as a fine mind honoring the theater by staging fine issues, and [1] with an unashamed quietism holding his audience—however small—spellbound. Monkhouse's work, perhaps more so than that of any other Edwardian dramatist, deserves to be reevaluated and revived.

ARCHIVAL SOURCES

Monkhouse's papers and correspondence are housed in the Allan Monkhouse Collection in the Library of John Rylands University of Manchester (Deansgate). Other correspondence is held by the Bodleian Library at Oxford, the Eton School Library, and the Churchill College Archives and King's College Library at Cambridge. Annie Horniman's seventeen-volume collection of press clippings is also available at John Rylands University. Papers of Monkhouse's Gaiety Theatre colleagues, Stanley Houghton and Harold Brighouse, are located respectively at the University of Salford Library and the Eccles Public Library, Greater Manchester.

PRIMARY BIBLIOGRAPHY

Plays

Cecilia. London: Gollancz, 1932.

The Conquering Hero. London: Benn, 1923. Also in *Modern British Dramas,* ed. Harlan H. Hatcher. New York: Harcourt, Brace, 1941.

The Education of Mr. Surrage. London: Sidgwick & Jackson, 1913.

First Blood. London: Benn, 1924; Boston: Phillips, 1924. Also in *Representative British Dramas: Victorian and Modern,* rev. ed., ed. Montrose J. Moses. Boston: Heath, 1931.

The Grand Cham's Diamond. London: Gowans & Gray, 1924; Boston: LeRoy Phillips, 1924.

The King of Barvender. London: Gowans & Gray, 1927. Also in *One-Act Plays of Today,* 5th series, ed. J[ames] W[illiam] Marriott. London: Harrap, 1951.

Mary Broome. London: Sidgwick & Jackson, 1912; Boston: Luce, 1913. Also in *Granada's Manchester Plays,* ed. Gerald Savory. Manchester: Manchester University Press, 1962.

Night Watches. In *The Atlantic Book of Modern Plays,* ed. Sterling Andrus Leonard. Rev. ed. Boston: Little, Brown, 1934.

Nothing like Leather. Rev. ed. London: Gowans & Gray, 1930; Boston: Baker International Play Bureau, 1930.

O Death Where Is Thy Sting? London: Gowans & Gray, 1926; Boston: International Play Bureau, 1926.

Paul Felice. London: Gollancz, 1930.

The Rag. London: Sidgwick & Jackson, 1928.

Sons and Fathers. London: Benn, 1925.

Anthologies

Four Tragedies. (*The Hayling Family, Reaping the Whirlwind, Resentment, The Stricklands.*) London: Duckworth, 1913.

War Plays. (*The Choice, Night Watches, Shamed Life.*) London: Constable, 1916.

Essays and Articles on Drama and Theater

Articles and reviews in the *Manchester Guardian.*

Allan Monkhouse. London: Harrap, 1926.

Books and Plays. London: Mathews & Lane, 1894.

The Manchester Stage, 1880–1900. London: Constable, 1900.

"The Words and the Play." *Essays and Studies* 11 (1925): 32–48.

SECONDARY BIBLIOGRAPHY

Agate, James. *Alarums and Excursions.* New York: George H. Doran, 1922.

Armstrong, Martin. "Four Plays." *Spectator* (17 Nov. 1923): 742–44.

"Awaiting Production." *Saturday Review* (19 Jan. 1929): 79–80.

Brighouse, Harold. *What I Have Had: Chapters in Autobiography.* London: Harrap, 1953.

Brown, Ivor. [1]. "A Fine Mind." *Saturday Review* (29 Mar. 1924): 321.

———. [2]. "Some Sinners and a Saint." *Saturday Review* (30 Jan. 1926): 118–19.

———. [3]. "The Theatre: Ancient and Modern." *Saturday Review* (11 Dec. 1926): 728.

Review of *Cecilia. Saturday Review* (25 Mar. 1933): 289.

Review of *Cecilia. The Times* (16 Mar. 1933): 12.

" 'The Conquering Hero,' by Allan Monkhouse, at the Queen's." *Spectator* (12 Apr. 1924): 594–95.

" 'The Conquering Hero': Play Actors at the Aldwych." *The Times* (24 Mar. 1924): 10.

" 'The Conquering Hero': War Play at the Queen's Theatre." *The Times* (4 Apr. 1924): 10.

Cunliffe, John W. *Modern English Playwrights: A Short History of the English Drama from 1825.* New York and London: Harper, 1927.

Dobrée, Bonamy. "Plays of Yesterday." *Nation* (2 Jan. 1926): 502.

"Drama of the Month." *Review of Reviews* (May–June 1924): 504.

Firkins, O. W. " 'Mary Broome' at the Neighborhood Playhouse." *Review* (3 Jan. 1920): 18.

"The 'G' Club: The Conquering Hero." *The Times* (13 Mar. 1934): 12.

Goldie, Grace Wyndham. *The Liverpool Repertory Theatre, 1911–1934.* Liverpool: University Press of Liverpool, 1935.

Gooddie, Sheila. *Annie Horniman: A Pioneer in the Theatre.* London: Methuen, 1990.

Review of *The Grand Cham's Diamond. The Times* (16 Mar. 1933): 12.

Hudson, Lynton. *The English Stage, 1850–1950.* London: Harrap, 1951.

Kemp, Thomas C. *Birmingham Repertory Theatre: The Playhouse and the Man.* 2d ed., rev. Birmingham: Cornish Brothers, 1948.

Matthews, Bache. *A History of the Birmingham Repertory Theatre.* London: Chatto & Windus, 1924.

Mikhail, E. H. [1]. "Allan Monkhouse." In *Dictionary of Literary Biography,* vol. 10, *Modern British Dramatists, 1900–1945,* ed. Stanley Weintraub, pt. 2, 46–49. Detroit: Gale Research, 1982.

———. [2]. *English Drama, 1900–1950: A Guide to Information Sources,* 259. Detroit: Gale Research, 1977.

Moses, Montrose J. "Allan Monkhouse and C. K. Munro." In *Representative British Dramas: Victorian and Modern,* rev. ed., 805–9. Boston: Heath, 1931.

"Mr. Monkhouse's Mary Broome." *New Statesman* (12 Dec. 1931): 748.

Nicoll, Allardyce. *English Drama, 1900–1930: The Beginnings of the Modern Period.* Cambridge: Cambridge University Press, 1973.

"Play Actors at the Aldwych: 'The Hayling Family.' " *The Times* (27 Oct. 1924): 10.

Pogson, Rex. *Miss Horniman and the Gaiety Theatre, Manchester.* London: Rockliff, 1952.

Review of *The Rag. Saturday Review* (19 Jan. 1929): 79.

Rowell, George, and Anthony Jackson. *The Repertory Movement: A History of Regional Theatre in Britain.* Cambridge: Cambridge University Press, 1984.

Savory, Gerald, ed. *Granada's Manchester Plays: Television Adaptations of Six Plays Recalling the Horniman Period at the Gaiety Theatre, Manchester.* Manchester: Manchester University Press, 1962.

Short, Ernest. *Sixty Years of Theatre,* 125, 238. London: Eyre & Spottiswoode, 1951.

Sutton, Graham. [1]. "The Plays of Allan Monkhouse." *Fortnightly Review* (Oct. 1924): 547–57.

———. [2]. *Some Contemporary Dramatists.* London: Leonard Parsons, 1924.

Swinnerton, Frank. *The Georgian Scene: A Literary Panorama.* New York: Farrar & Rinehart, 1934.

Trewin, J[ohn] C[ourtenay]. [1]. *The Edwardian Theatre.* Totowa, NJ: Rowman & Littlefield, 1976.

———. [2]. *The Theatre since 1900.* London: Andrew Dakers, 1951.

Wilson, A[lbert] E[dward]. *Edwardian Theatre.* London: A. Barker, 1951.

Arthur Wing Pinero
(1855–1934)

ARTHUR GEWIRTZ

Generally recognized as the leading dramatist of his day until George Bernard Shaw displaced him, Sir Arthur Pinero was the complete theater man. Actor, playwright, director, he had his firm hand in every particular of the production of his plays—decor, lighting, and costumes as well as stage management and each actor's presentation of his or her character. Thus, in his playwriting, he not only helped change the course of the British theater toward the end of the nineteenth century, as most scholars agree, but strongly in control of his own dramas from first to last, he pointed the way to the type of director who was to become a major force in the Western theater of the twentieth century.

Born in London in 1855 of a family that, though of Jewish-Portuguese ancestry, was thoroughly Anglicized, Arthur Wing Pinero lived a middle-class life for his first ten years. His father, John Daniel Pinero (the spelling of the family name had been changed from Pinheiro by the playwright's grandfather), followed in the family practice of law, but with rather less success than his father and brother. Nevertheless, he was able to provide well enough for his family until he suffered business reverses probably stemming from his own negligence. As a result, at the age of ten, Arthur was removed from school and placed in his father's office to pursue a career in law. Upon his father's retirement, after a brief stint working in a library, he returned to law, helping to support his family. When his father died, he continued financial aid to his mother, but after a while the family no longer required his income. He then abandoned law for the stage.

He did not enter upon the theater altogether as a novice. Starting at the age of fifteen, still clerking in the law office, he took evening elocution lessons at Birkbeck Scientific and Literary Institution, now part of the University of London. Students at Birkbeck gave recitals and plays not only in London but in outlying cities such as Bristol, Edinburgh, and Liverpool as well; Pinero's efforts were rewarded with a readership at the institution.

Actually, he had evinced his interest in the theater even earlier. From a young age he attended the theater assiduously, attracted most to the serious Shakespeare productions of Samuel Phelps and Henry Irving and to the cup-and-saucer presentations of Tom Robertson dramas by Squire and Marie Bancroft. The latter were to have an important influence on Pinero's own work because in their quiet, realistic fashion they were a sharp contrast to the contemporary fustian in writing and acting. Also, Pinero wrote plays that he diligently sent around to producers who regularly rejected them—vociferously on at least one occasion (Dunkel, 95).

Now at the Theatre Royal at Edinburgh he was actually going to embark on a career that he had seemingly desired all of his life. He was only a general utility man—or a bit-part actor—in a stock company, changing parts from week to week. Here he received invaluable training for his future. He was retained at Edinburgh until, unfortunately, the theater burnt down, but he was then hired for the Royal Alexandria Theatre in Liverpool. At both theaters he not only had an opportunity of playing a variety of small parts but was able to observe the work of major actors who starred in their famous vehicles with the support of the stock players. While he was at the Alexandria Theatre, a dramatization of Wilkie Collins's novel *Miss Gwilt* was tried out with Pinero in a small role, and he duly went on with it when the play opened in London, an unexpected failure. Nevertheless, he was hired to play Claudius in support of Henry Irving in a touring version of *Hamlet.* Despite bad notices, one reviewer calling Pinero the worst Claudius he had ever seen, Irving hired the young actor for his regular London company. He stayed with Irving for five years, playing lesser roles than Claudius, and then in 1881 he transferred to the Bancrofts, now at the Theatre Royal, Haymarket (London). Again, the stage experience at both London playhouses and with great personalities of the theater gave him the kind of practical experience that is comparable to that of Shakespeare, Molière, and Ibsen.

The practice of long runs at both Irving's Lyceum and the Bancrofts' Haymarket theaters gave Pinero the opportunity to return to playwriting, a chance he seized with a vengeance. Between 1877 and 1881 he produced ten long and short plays; one of them, the three-act *The Squire,* was a signal success in London but was a failure when given in New York. In 1882 Pinero quit acting to devote himself wholly to playwriting. He continued to be a prolific dramatist, writing sixteen plays between 1882 and 1893, some of them great successes and a few of them landmarks in English drama.

His greatest financial triumph was *Sweet Lavender,* a sentimental comedy produced at Terry's Theatre (London) on 21 March 1888 for a run of 684 performances. The company's star, Edward Terry, played the role of Dick Phenyl, making it his most famous part. Also important commercially but more impressive artistically are the plays known as the Court farces. These plays, *The*

Magistrate, The Schoolmistress, and *Dandy Dick,* were performed at the Royal Court Theatre (London) in Sloane Square between 1885 and 1887.

The first of these, *The Magistrate,* was greeted rapturously by audiences and critics alike. Contemporary farces produced on the English stage were translations or copies of French farces with the sauce of sex removed or were altogether knockabout buffoonery. Pinero thoroughly Anglicized the form. While sex may skirt the outer edges of *The Magistrate,* the play is not dependent on it. Rather than relying on ''adulterous autonoma,'' Pinero attempted to ''create probable characters in possible situations'' (Dawick, 129–30). Thus one may say that he created the farce of character. Further, the structure of the play is strong, and it even suggests certain social satire. Later English farce writers were to take Pinero as their model. *The Magistrate* played at the Court 363 times; there were three road companies in England; Pinero took his only trip to America to make sure that the American production would be performed correctly; productions were offered in Australia, India, and South Africa; the farce was given in German as *Der blaue Grotte,* playing in many places in Germany and Austria, and was given as well in Prague. While the other two Court farces did not fare quite as well as the first, Pinero made good money on them all.

The financial independence resulting from the commercial success of *Sweet Lavender* and the Court farces enabled Pinero to write his most daring play to date, *The Second Mrs. Tanqueray,* produced at St. James's Theatre (London) in 1893. Undoubtedly, the courage to write such a play was partially inspired by William Archer, the translator of Ibsen and a great critical crusader for a ''new drama,'' who early on found in Pinero the man who might help create an artistic and thoughtful native drama. Archer became one of Pinero's chief proponents and defenders.

Pinero had already written a strong play in *The Profligate,* produced at the Garrick Theatre (London) in 1889; John Hare, the manager of the theater, however, asked the author to alter the original ending so that it could be happy. Although Pinero honored the request, he resorted to his original ending when he printed the play. But with *The Second Mrs. Tanqueray* he had the play all his own way. The effect of the piece was sensational. Pinero, in handling, with apparent realism, the subject of the woman with a past, in suggesting that it was immoral to maintain a double standard of sexual behavior for men and women, and in implying that society was uncharitable toward the plight of women in difficult circumstances and that its sexual repression was perhaps the cause of unhappy marriages and wandering husbands, brought onto the serious English stage subjects and thoughts never before heard there aloud. Further, he did this in a drama that had Pinero's usual solid structure and characters, especially that of the heroine, Paula Tanqueray, of unusual psychological complexity. In addition, Pinero wrote the play in a political atmosphere in which changes in law about the status of women were being debated. While Pinero did not address himself directly to the political debate, the sympathy he showed toward Paula must have been a forceful contribution to it. The play was not only a critical but a financial success as well and showed that serious drama of such import as this could attract a fashionable audience in the English theater.

In the midst of all his prolific production—we must remember that he directed his plays as well—Pinero married Myra Hamilton, a widow with two children, in 1883. Mrs. Hamilton, an actress known as Myra Holme, gave up her career soon after the marriage. There were no children from the union, but Pinero acted as a father to both of Myra's children.

With the acclaim accorded to *The Second Mrs. Tanqueray,* Pinero took his place as the preeminent British dramatist. Shaw and a few like-minded critics may have differed about the worth of Pinero's pieces—though Shaw was prominent in the successful attempt to gain Pinero a knighthood in 1909—but few others until well into the next decade contended Pinero's central place in the panoply of British playwrights. Pinero's varied productions continued apace. In the ensuing decade and a half his serious plays included *The Notorious Mrs. Ebbsmith* (1895), *Iris* (1901), and *Mid-Channel* (1909). Some social comedies were *The Benefit of the Doubt* (1895), *The Gay Lord Quex* (1899), and *His House in Order* (1906), his longest-running play since *Sweet Lavender.* He wrote a bleak satiric drama, *The Thunderbolt,* which received a short run in its original production in 1908, but a number of modern critics admire it. His nostalgic-sentimental comedy, *Trelawney of the "Wells,"* first performed in 1898, remains ever popular.

It is commonly thought that the quantity and quality of Pinero's production fell off after the first decade of the twentieth century. Actually, in the final two decades of his life he wrote eleven full-length plays, some of them unproduced. A few, such as *The "Mind the Paint" Girl* (1912) and *The Big Drum* (1915), were fairly successful. Another, *The Freaks* (1918), received good notices and fine patronage but suffered from the "effects of two air-raids in its opening days" (Griffin, 162). *The Enchanted Cottage* (1922) is a fantasy, a comparatively new mode for Pinero, and *Dr. Harmer's Holidays,* produced only in Washington, D.C., in 1931, also shows Pinero in a new theatrical style, with short Brechtian-type scenes. Thus Pinero's energy and perhaps his quality did not diminish. According to one modern critic, Pinero did not "grow old-fashioned. He simply became unpopular," his ideas too pessimistic for one part of his audience and too critical of society for another (Griffin, 20).

Selected Biographical Sources: Dawick; Dunkel; Griffin; Lazenby.

MAJOR PLAYS, PREMIERES, AND SIGNIFICANT REVIVALS: THEATRICAL RECEPTION

The Squire. 1881. Produced at St. James's Theatre (London) 29 December for 170 performances. An impressive cast that included William and Madge Kendal, John Hare, and Brandon Thomas helped the play to its success. Opened in New York at Daly's Theatre on 10 October 1882 for 47 performances.

This play, Pinero's first "serious" drama, about a female squire who inadvertently and secretly enters into a bigamous marriage, was warmly received (Dawick, 96–97). But the charge that Pinero had plagarized from J. Comyns Carr's *The Mistress of the Farm* (a dramatization of Thomas Hardy's *Far from the Madding Crowd*), considerably reduced his pleasure in the success. The controversy flared for a while but eventually petered out, leaving Pinero embittered about the whole subject of plagiarism (Dawick, 97–104).

The Magistrate. 1885. Produced at the Court Theatre (London) 21 March for a run of 363 performances. Opened in New York at Daly's Theatre on 7 October 1885 for 75 performances. It was revived at the Old Vic (London), 18 March 1959; at the Festival Theatre (Chichester), 21 May 1969; at the Cambridge Theatre (London), 18 September 1969; and at the National Theatre (Lyttleton) (London), 24 September 1986. A musical, *The Boy,* based on the farce opened at the Adelphi Theatre (London) 14 September 1917 and ran 803 times.

This farce is about a woman who, to enhance her successful attempt at a second marriage, reduces her age by five years but thus has to pass off her nineteen-year-old son as fourteen. Fyfe wrote that in *The Magistrate* Pinero "recreated the farce of character. The farce of intrigue had, in 1885, long held the stage unchallenged. . . . This order of farce Pinero drove from the English-speaking stage" (30–31). Smith reinforced Fyfe's point when he said that Aeneas Posket (the husband in the farce) "is a more rounded character than we often find in farce, idiosyncratic, unconventional and believable" (25). Rowell [1] was taken by the "humanity and warmth" of the characters, "especially when they are compared with other favourite farces of the period" (2). Griffin attributed the continued popularity of the play to the central character, who is "too good-natured and weak to resist the blandishments" of his stepson and thus ends up in "absurd situations" (176–77). Beerbohm [3] thought the play "perfect" of its kind (20).

The Schoolmistress. 1886. Opened at the Court Theatre on 27 March for a run of 291 performances. Played in New York 28 times starting on 7 December 1886 at the Standard Theatre. Revived in London at the Savoy Theatre, 8 April 1964.

This play about the principal of Volumnia College for young ladies who is also a musical-comedy star had the audience laughing from the rise of the curtain to the last line (Dawick, 139). Some modern critics believe that the humor possesses serious material. Rowell [1], for example, thought that "much of the humour derives from the struggles of the menfolk to throw off their silken chains. . . . in the end feminine enterprise triumphs" (3). Griffin found that "underneath the absurdity of many of the situations . . . , Pinero has some serious observations to make on marriage . . . [on] the dilemma which faces young women who, educated like men and behaving with the independence and freedom of men, find the position difficult, indeed impossible, to maintain in the face of love and possible marriage" (139).

Dandy Dick. 1887. Given at the Court Theatre (London) 262 times starting 27 January. Produced in New York at Daly's Theatre 5 October 1887, it achieved a run of only 32 performances. It was revived at the Mermaid Theatre (London), 18 August 1965; at the Festival Theatre (Chichester), 25 July 1973; at the Garrick Theatre (London), 17 October 1973.

The audience and reviewers enjoyed themselves—although some journalists revised their opinions later—at this farce about a dean of the Church of England who, hard pressed financially, places his money on what looks like a sure thing (Dawick, 144). But the long run indicates that audiences had no such second thoughts. Beerbohm [3], however, who as a youngster loved the play, liked it less in a 1900 revival. Although he still found it an "amusing farce—a good piece of work," he denigrated what he thought to be its dated conventions. However, he believed that the painful old-fashioned style would in time become interestingly quaint (238). Indeed, later critics and audiences have made Beerbohm a true prophet. Smith, for instance, lauded the farce's language and the characterization of the dean's two daughters (39–40), two features that Beerbohm hated in 1900. Other critics have admired the convincing central portrait of the Reverend Augustus Judd. Fyfe, for example, thought that it conformed perfectly to his formulation of Pinero's farce of character: "possible people doing improbable things" (36). Griffin, writing some sixty years later, equally admired the creation of Judd but described the workmanship somewhat differently. For her, Pinero's formula for both this play and *The Magistrate* is that they centrally display "probable characters placed in possible circumstances which, because of their own sentiments and foibles, gradually become more and more involved and ridiculous" (138). In both cases convincing characters become involved in incongruous doings.

Sweet Lavender. 1888. Played at Terry's Theatre (London) 684 times beginning 21 March. Produced at the Lyceum Theatre (New York) 13 November 1888. Revived at the Ambassadors Theatre (London) for 90 performances starting on 14 December 1920. The noted actor Edward Terry played Dick Phenyl (his greatest acting success) in this drama.

This play about the trials in true love's course of a laundress's illegitimate daughter and a banker's adopted son was Pinero's greatest commercial success. The first-night audience and the original reviewers enjoyed the play; Clement Scott, for example, found it "wholesome, pure, refreshing, a charming play" (quoted in Dawick, 154). Reviewing an 1899 revival, Beerbohm [3] thought its sentiment saccharine, its plot silly, and its characters unreal, yet these elements were managed so dextrously that they were almost convincing, causing the spectator to smile or laugh as long as the curtain was up (117–18). Pinero himself seems to have taken a wryer view of the play than Beerbohm (Wearing [1], 113). The author thus agreed with Archer ([2], 287), Fyfe (54), and Dawick, who thought that it was "an almost cynical blending of scenes of undiluted sentimentality with others in Pin[ero]'s distinctive comic vein'' (152). Griffin, as did other critics, noted the play's relationship to the work of Tom Robertson, pointing particularly to its "affinities with *Caste,* in its exploration of the barriers to 'true love' set up by social class'' (168).

The Profligate. 1889. Opened at the Garrick Theatre (London) on 24 April for a run of 129 performances.

This drama about a womanizer whose past catches up with him was Pinero's attempt to "continue that assertion of individuality which had begun when he wrote *The Squire*'' (Fyfe, 94). Pinero insisted that he did not know Ibsen when he wrote this play, but whether or not he did, "he sensed . . . that there was a climate receptive to serious ideas, in the theatre as well as in novelwriting'' (Griffin, 144). Almost thirty-five years after its original production Archer [2] wrote that the drama "now seems terribly antiquated; but we were quite right in hailing it, in April, 1889, as the strongest piece of original drama that the stage had seen for many a long year'' (290). The first production was weaker than the printed text, which reflected Pinero's original intent, because the theater manager was so frightened of its tragic ending that he insisted that it be altered.

The Cabinet Minister. 1890. Opened at the Court Theatre (London) 23 April for a run of 199 performances. Played 6 times at Daly's Theatre in New York starting on 12 January 1892. Revived at the Albery Theatre (London) 21 November 1991.

Despite its puzzled reception by the opening-night audience and original reviewers who did not know when to laugh or cry, this farce about a cabinet minister's wife who foolishly borrows large sums of money from a socially ambitious moneylender achieved considerable success. Perhaps the first-nighters were confused because the author tried "to make it less farcical than its predecessors'' at the Court (Wearing [1], 98). But later critics also were unenthusiastic: Fyfe asserted that it did not really fit the formula of the earlier Pinero Court farces of " 'possible people doing improbable things' '' (47); Lazenby (56) and Griffin (140) both found the play "diffuse.''

The Times. 1891. Premiered at Terry's Theatre (London) 24 October, for 155 performances.

This comedy about a self-made, social-climbing linen draper who tries to buy his way into society received "lukewarm'' reviews (Dawick, 176) but nevertheless achieved a respectable commercial success. Later critics also dismissed the play, but regularly cited its importance in the history of play publication. A series of legal moves culminating in U.S. Senate ratification in 1891 of the International Copyright Act of 1887 prevented English plays from being performed in the United States without paying royalties to the authors. Now a play could be published simultaneously with its first performance without fear that other managers would use it to produce unauthorized stagings. Pinero in his "Introductory Note'' to *The Times,* the first drama to be published under the new conditions, asserted that if simultaneous publication and first performance became a custom, they "might dignify at once the calling of the actor, the craft of the playwright" (vi). Pinero thus attempted to be taken seriously both as a worker in the theater and as a writer of literature. He was successful in that *The Times* went into a second edition, started the fashion for publishing reading editions of plays, and importantly influenced Bernard Shaw, who "later used the practice virtually as a substitute for theatrical production" (Dawick, 177).

The Second Mrs. Tanqueray. 1893. This epoch-making drama ran 225 times at St. James's Theatre (London) from 27 May. It was brought to New York at the Star Theatre by the English company of Mr. and Mrs. Kendal, where it was successful (Carr, 113), thus allowing a number of stars—Olga Nethersole, Mrs. Patrick Campbell (the original Paula Tanqueray), Mrs. Leslie Carter, and Ethel Barrymore—to play the leading role over the next three decades. The unsuccessful Barrymore production, in 1924, finished the play in New York but not in the United States, for Tallulah Bankhead acted it in summer stock in 1940 (Carr, 106–30). In London it had a number of successful revivals: at the Playhouse in 1922 for 220 performances; at the Haymarket in 1950 for 206 performances; and at the National Theatre in 1981.

This drama about a respectable man who marries his mistress only to have his "pure" daughter unknowingly become engaged to one of his wife's former lovers was a great success from its very first night. In his first review Archer spoke of the tears that came to his eyes when Pinero came before the curtain and the "house rose at him." Here at least, he thought, was a man with the "will and talent to emancipate himself and give the artist within himself free play." Archer's praise for the drama can be taken for all who lauded it. He spoke of Pinero's "astonishing advance in philosophical insight and technical skill . . . as nearly as possible perfect," the masterly exposition, and the wit "without a trace of that elaborate conceit-hunting which has hitherto spoiled so much of Mr. Pinero's best work" (Rowell [2], 232–33). Archer did find some faults, yet for him, as for most other critics, the play was a breakthrough for English drama. But there were those, not only the old-fashioned reviewers, who were recalcitrant. Chief among them was Shaw [2], who at the play's publication two years later influentially attacked its exposition, which he thought lacked "vital action and real characters." More important, he found fault with the characterization of its central figure, which at a crucial moment in the drama is drawn from the point of view of Pinero and the prevailing society rather than from her own view sympathetically imagined by the author (36–39). This division on the play is held still by Pinero's recent critics: Griffin, who agreed with Archer as to the play's weight and epoch-making significance (212–47), and Innes, who, while understanding the play's historic value, yet sided with Shaw as to the play's technical and social conventionality (10–13).

The Notorious Mrs. Ebbsmith. 1895. Opened at the Garrick Theatre (London) 15 March for 86 performances. Opened in New York at Abbey's Theatre 23

December 1895 by John Hare heading an English company, but it played only 16 times. Mrs. Patrick Campbell, who originated the role of Agnes Ebbsmith, played it in New York 6 times in January 1902 at the Republic Theatre (Carr, 143).

This drama did not gain the success of *The Second Mrs. Tanqueray* largely because its central character was unconvincing in important ways. The critic who slashed deepest was Shaw [2], who said that Pinero did not know the type of woman, the "platform woman," that he attempted to create in this play. Agnes neither speaks like her, acts like her, nor thinks like her, and the scene in which she retrieves a Bible from the flames to which she consigned it is sheer claptrap (40–45). Archer [3] professed to admire the play, calling it an advance over *The Second Mrs. Tanqueray,* "technically by far the strongest thing our modern stage has to show" (77–78). But even he found fault with the language of the central character, implying that the author did not altogether understand her. Nevertheless, Archer, Pinero's always-staunch supporter, insisted that the flaws could be fixed by minor linguistic alterations. But the critic's defense of the dramatist could not extend to the Bible scene. That stuck even in his craw.

Trelawny of the "Wells." 1898. Opened at the Court Theatre (London) 20 January 1898 and played 135 times. In New York, at the Lyceum Theatre, opening 22 November 1898, it ran for 131 performances. In London the play had revivals in 1925, 1965, 1992, and 1993. New York had revivals in 1900, 1911, 1925, and 1927 (Carr, 172–86). The play was made into a musical that opened in London 3 August 1972.

This "comedietta," as Pinero termed it, the "most frequently revived" of the author's plays (Innes, 12), was about the contrast between the free spirits of the theater and stuffy upper-class society and about the change brought by Tom Robertson in theatrical style from the bombast of the earlier part of the nineteenth century to the surface realism that followed; Pinero explicated this second aspect of his drama in "The Theatre in the 'Seventies" (135–63). Although critics were divided in their response to the play, Grein, who saw in it a "field of humour and of true comedy" (Rowell [2], 273), and Shaw and Archer (Dawick, 240–242), who for once agreed in finding this Pinero play captivating, were indicative of the success this comedy was to find in the future.

The Gay Lord Quex. 1899. Opened in London at the Globe Theatre 8 April for a run of 300 performances. It was revived in London at the Alberry Theatre 16 June 1975. In New York it opened at the Criterion Theatre 12 November 1900 with its London company and played also at the Harlem Opera House for a total of 75 performances. The drama had a New York revival 12 November 1917 (Carr, 191–204).

This play about a manicurist who tries to rescue her foster sister from marriage with a womanizer received good reviews even though it was compared to risqué Restoration comedy. Especially admired was the play's technical facility (for example, Beerbohm [3], 130–32), particularly in its third act, which a modern critic called a "virtuoso feat of stagecraft, comparable with the 'Screen Scene' in Sheridan's *The School for Scandal*" (Dawick, 248). But Griffin, although admiring the play's construction, found it "not a particularly attractive one" because it "presents a world which is hypocritical, cynical and amoral," and "female virtue is cynically regarded" (157).

Iris. 1901. Opened at the Garrick Theatre (London) 21 September 1901 for 115 performances. Revived at the Adelphi Theatre 21 March 1925 for 150 performances. Its New York premiere came to the Criterion Theatre on 13 September 1902, where it played 77 times.

This play about a woman who comes to grief because she lacks character received good notices, but did not achieve the success the reviews indicated it should, perhaps because, as one critic noted, it was too harrowing for its audience (Dawick, 256). Even Beerbohm [1], who seems to have taken Shaw's place not only as the drama critic of the *Saturday Review* but as Pinero's chief scourge, found merit in the play, entitling his review "Mr. Pinero Progresses" (162). Nevertheless, he spent most of his piece showing what he found unconvincing in the drama. No such qualms attacked Walkley, who thought *Iris* to be a "very powerful, very painful, play, . . . a piece of literature" (174). Later critics tended to agree. Nicoll appraised the play as skillful and rightly drained of sentimentality, and although the type of woman represented by the heroine would not precisely exist in our time, one "might well find parallels within the freer range of present-day social life" (342). Griffin thought that "Pinero is unsparing in his picture of a young woman, unprotected by money or reputation, who is incapable of surviving in a hostile and uncaring world" (151).

Letty. 1904. London premiere at the Duke of York's Theatre 8 October, where it was presented 123 times. In New York it played at the Hudson 64 times starting 12 September 1904.

This drama about a poor clerk in a low stockbroker's office who, after sore temptation, is finally able to resist the advances of a gentleman appropriately named Letchmere received divided reviews. Walkley thought it not great but still "extremely interesting" (175). However, he criticized its "literary" language. Beerbohm [1] devoted two articles to the drama attacking its excesses of construction and language (281–90).

His House in Order. 1906. Opened at St. James's Theatre 1 February for a run of 430 performances. Revived at the New Theatre 6 July 1951 for 114 performances. Its premiere in New York on 3 September 1906 was at the Empire Theatre, where it played 127 times.

This play about a woman whose marriage is haunted by her husband's dead first wife was received with almost universal praise (Dawick, 284). Even Beerbohm [2] had a conflict between his higher and lower self, the former finding fault with the technical manipulation, the latter enjoying the drama's suspense and hoping the best for its heroine (220–25). Walkley had no such problem: to him "the play tells a plain tale plainly," although he still found some passages in which the characters talked in too literary a fashion (185–86). Later critics tended to have the same conflict as Beerbohm (Hamilton, vol. 3, 245; Fyfe, 245; Griffin, 158–59).

The Thunderbolt. 1908. Opened at St. James's Theatre (London) 2 September for 58 performances; revived at the Arts Theatre (London) 12 September 1945.

Labeled on the title page as *An Episode in the History of a Provincial Family,* the drama failed, Pinero thought, because the "drab in literature and drama is not for our climate" (Wearing [1], 213). It did receive respectful reviews, but when a critic says that the play stimulates rather than attracts, one can hardly expect the public to flock to it (Dawick, 298–99). Later critics, however, admired the play. Hamilton called it a "masterpiece of the sardonic mood" (vol. 4, 21), and Nicoll found it technically dextrous, its characterization of individuals and the family group effective, and the language "simple, concise and eminently natural" (343).

Mid-Channel. 1909. Opened 2 September at St. James's Theatre (London) for 58 performances; revived at the Royalty Theatre (London) 30 October 1922. In New York it played 96 times at the Empire Theatre from 31 January 1910.

This drama about a middle-aged couple whose marriage has gone sour was another failure for the author. Beerbohm [2] roundly condemned the play as taken from the stage rather than from life (480–83), and in an article three weeks later he was calling the drama *Mid-Gutter* (487–88). Shaw [1] seems to have found some virtue in the play and blamed its failure on the St. James's audience, which, he felt, was the object of Pinero's merciless satire accomplished with the "skill and ruthlessness of a scientific torturer.... There is not enough fun in Mid-Channel" (886–87). Modern critics find the subjects of the drama honestly depicted and the satire effective (Dawick, 300; Griffin, 151–53).

ADDITIONAL PLAYS, ADAPTATIONS, AND PRODUCTIONS

200 Pounds a Year, a one-act, was presented at the Globe Theatre (London) 6 October 1877 for 36 performances. *La Comete; or, Two Hearts,* a three-act drama, was given at the Theatre Royal, Croydon, 22 April 1878. *Two Can Play at That Game,* a one-act comedy, was presented at the Lyceum Theatre (London) 40 times starting 20 May 1878. *Daisy's Escape,* a one-act comedy, was presented 31 times at the Lyceum Theatre (London) starting 20 September 1879. *Hester's Mystery,* a one-act comedy-drama, was given 308 times at the Folly Theatre (London) starting 5 June 1880. *Bygones,* a one-act comedy, was presented at the Lyceum Theatre (London) 18 September 1880 and played 89 performances.

The Money-Spinner, a comedy, opened at St. James's Theatre (London) 8 January 1881 and played 98 times. In New York it began its run 21 January 1882 and was acted for four weeks. On 23 April 1891 Mr. and Mrs. Kendal, who introduced the play to London, brought it to New York at Palmer's Theatre (Carr, 7–12).

Imprudence, a farce, was given at the Folly Theatre (London) 27 July 1881 for 54 performances. *Bound to Marry,* a comedy, was unperformed. Its typescript is at the Garrick Club library, London. *Girls and Boys: A Nursery Tale,* a comedy, was offered at O'Toole's Theatre (London) 1 November 1882 for 53 performances. *The Rector: The Story of Four Friends* was given at the Court Theatre (London) 16 times starting 24 March 1883. *The Rocket,* in which the author "could be seen learning to structure a farce" (Griffin, 137), played for 51 performances at the Gaiety Theatre (London), where it opened on 10 December 1883. *Lords and Commons* was given at the Haymarket Theatre (London) 24 November 1883 and played 70 times. In New York it opened at Daly's Theatre 15 November 1884 and played 10 times. *Low Water* was acted 7 times at the Globe Theatre (London) starting 12 January 1884. *The Ironmaster,* translated from George Ohnet's *Le Maître des forges,* played 200 times at St. James's Theatre (London) beginning 17 April 1884.

In Chancery, a farce, played at the Gaiety Theatre (London) 36 times starting 24 December 1884. In New York it played 24 times at the Madison Square Theatre starting 8 June 1885. A musical version of the play, *Who's Hooper?,* was performed 350 times at the Adelphi Theatre (London) beginning 13 September 1919. *Mayfair,* an adaptation of Victorien Sardou's *Maison neuve,* was given at St. James's Theatre (London) 31 October 1885 and played 53 times.

The Hobby Horse was produced at St. James's Theatre (London) in 1883 for a run of 109 performances. Its original reception was hostile. Archer [4], writing about an 1897 revival, thought that its first reviewers "treated it rather churlishly," but he now found the play to be "delightful. I don't know when I've spent so refreshing an evening in the theatre" (137). Some thirty years later he called the comedy "amusing but not very significant" ([2], 287). This last opinion is now the prevalent one.

The Weaker Sex (1889), a play about two mothers, each of whom is in love with the same man as her daughter, prefigures, in the case of one mother in comic terms, in the case of the other in melodramatic terms, the tragic dilemma of *The Second Mrs. Tanqueray.* It is also a satire of the women's rights movement. Originally written in 1884, receiving its first production in Manchester in 1888 and its first London production in a revised version in 1889, its run of 61 performances suggests the low esteem in which both critics and audience held it.

Lady Bountiful (1891) played for 65 performances, starting 7 March, at the Garrick Theatre (London), and for 53 performances, starting 15 November 1891, at the Lyceum Theatre (New York). Modern critics, like most of the original reviewers, have found this novelistic drama unattractive.

The Amazons (1893) opened at the Court Theatre (London) on 7 March 1893, "pleased most of the audience and reviewers but enjoyed only a modest run" (Dawick, 184). Produced 19 February 1894 at the Lyceum Theatre in New York, it achieved a respectable run of 127 performances (Carr, 134). Fyfe (51) and Griffin (139) found this farce about a woman who brings up her three daughters as boys still pertinent.

The Benefit of the Doubt opened at the Comedy Theatre (London) 16 October 1895 and played only 74 times though praised by both Archer and Shaw. It may have been the acting that killed the play (Dawick, 218–19). In New York it fared even worse, with 30 performances at the Lyceum Theatre beginning 6 January 1896.

The Princess and the Butterfly; or, The Fantastics opened at St. James's Theatre (London) 29 March 1897 for a run of 97 performances. This play with five acts and five settings caused a rift between Pinero and George Alexander because the latter tried to cut corners. Archer praised the play's originality, while Shaw, liking it somewhat, thought it excessively long and wasteful (Dawick, 223–27). The drama was produced at the Lyceum Theatre in New York for 79 performances beginning 23 November 1897.

The Beauty Stone, a romantic opera, a collaboration with J. Comyns Carr and Arthur Sullivan, presented at the Savoy Theatre (London) 28 May 1898 for 50 performances, was a dismal failure (Dawick, 244).

A Wife without a Smile (1904) was produced at London's Wyndham's Theatre (London) on 12 October for a run of 77 performances and at New York's Criterion Theatre for 16 performances. Although the play was a failure, it caused a scandal. One of its characters tied a string to the springs of a couch, bore a hole through the floorboard, and attached a doll to the other end of the string so that if any strenuous activity, presumably erotic, occupied the couch, the doll would dance on the ceiling in the floor below. The play was denounced not only for artistic reasons but for the sexual implications, which Pinero repudiated, of the dancing doll. However, many felt about Pinero's claims of innocence as did Beerbohm [2], who wrote that it was unlikely that the author "never, in repeated rehearsals, foresaw that we might find an indelicate meaning which was bound to be staring all of us in the face" (96).

Preserving Mr. Panmure (1911) opened at the Comedy Theatre (London) on 9 January 1911 and ran for 99 performances. Pinero called it a "grimy little satire at best" (Wearing [1], 234).

The "Mind the Paint" Girl, another of Pinero's essays into backstage life, ran for 126 performances at the Duke of York's Theatre (London) from 17 February 1912. In New York it ran for 136 performances at the Lyceum Theatre starting 9 September 1912.

The Widow of Wasdale Head is a one-act fantasy that opened at the Duke of York's Theatre (London) 14 October 1912 and ran for 26 performances. In New York it ran for 136 performances at the Lyceum Theatre starting 9 September 1912. *Playgoers: A Domestic Episode,* a one-act comedy, opened at St. James's Theatre (London) 31 March 1913 and played 70 times. *The Bulkley Peerage: A Very Grand Guignolette,* a farcical sketch, had no professional performance but appeared in *Pearson's Magazine* 38 (December 1914): 654–58.

The Big Drum (1915) opened at St. James's Theatre (London) on 1 September
and ran for 111 performances. Although Griffin called this drama Pinero's "last
major play," possessing the "power and intensity of great comedy" (161), most
other critics did not agree. Nicoll, for example, said that it ineffectively contrasts
a number of rich social climbers with a novelist of integrity who, however,
speaks of his principles in "artificial terms" (341). At the request of the play's
producer, George Alexander, Pinero, after the first performance, made the original ending, which Pinero saw as a "piece of ironic comedy" (viii), presumably
happy.

Mr. Livermore's Dream: A Lesson in Thrift, a propaganda sketch, was given
12 performances at the Coliseum (London) starting 15 January 1917.

The Freaks opened at the New Theatre, London, on 14 February 1918 for a
run of 51 performances. Modern critics have been divided about the quality of
the play, Dawick calling it an "inconsequential comedy" (344) and Griffin
finding it a "funny (and sad) play" (162). Its main thesis, spoken by a leading
character, "Who is a Freak and who is normal in this world? Who shall decide?" (*The Freaks,* 107) seems to strike a contemporary note.

Monica's Blue Boy: A Wordless Play (music by Sir Frederick Cowen) was
produced at the New Theatre 8 April 1918 for 38 performances. It is unpublished; the typescript is at the Garrick Club library. *Quick Work: A Story of a
War Marriage* was produced at the Stamford Theatre, Stamford, Connecticut,
14 November 1919. *A Seat in the Park: A Warning,* a one-act comedy, was
produced at the Winter Garden, London, 21 February 1922.

The Enchanted Cottage (1922), a fantasy, opened in London on 1 March for
a run of 64 performances and was produced in New York at the Ritz Theatre
on 31 March 1923 an equal number of times. Unsuccessful in both cities, it was
nevertheless made twice into a successful film. Most modern critics agree with
Nicoll that this fantasy shows the "restricted boundaries of [Pinero's] dramatic
vision" (341). Griffin, however, thought that the "play is moving in its simple
sincerity" (171).

A Private Room, a comedy in one act, was produced for 23 performances at
the Little Theatre (London) starting on 14 May 1928.

Dr. Harmer's Holidays, a play in nine scenes, was produced at the Shubert-
Belasco Theatre in Washington, D.C., 16 March 1931. This drama about a
respectable physician who for several weeks once a year plunges into the depths
of degradation has divided modern critics. Dawick believed that the respectable
characters are so unattractive that one almost cannot blame Harmer for his desire
for a prostitute's company, an effect Pinero hardly intended (365–66). Griffin
called the play "powerful and strange . . . in technique and conception far in
advance of other English plays of the time," its episodic structure similar to
that of Brecht and Piscator (155).

Child Man, an unproduced farce written in 1929, again has divided recent
critics. If this play were produced, wrote Dawick, "audiences would probably
be more embarrassed than amused" (367). Griffin, on the other hand, believed

that this "savage satire on modern ideas about bringing up children and on family life . . . is as relevant now as it was in 1930, and . . . would stage well" (162).

A Cold June, a comedy, was presented at the Duchess Theatre (London) 29 June 1932 for 19 performances. *Late of Mockford's,* completed in 1934, was unperformed.

ASSESSMENT OF PINERO'S CAREER

Critics agree on Arthur Wing Pinero's historic importance to the English theater, that he and Henry Arthur Jones were pioneers in the 1880s and 1890s of the nineteenth century in bringing to the stage a new seriousness. Their plays dealt with realistic characters, that is, those with whom, by the authors' lights, the audience could readily identify as deriving from their everyday lives. Archer [2] gave the major credit to Pinero: "In so far as any one man can be called the regenerator of the English drama, that man is Arthur Pinero. . . . From December, 1881, when *The Squire* was produced, until September, 1901, which saw the production of *Iris,* his principal plays may be reckoned as milestones on the path of progress. . . . With the new century, however, . . . he no longer stood . . . alone. But [he] was the brilliant and even daring pioneer of a great movement" (286).

With some qualifications most modern critics agree with this assessment of Pinero's historic importance, but until the recent discerning works of Dawick and Griffin, they consigned him to the minor place of "important pre-Shavian." The ability of his dramas outside of the Court farces and *Trelawney of the "Wells"* to hold the stage or to maintain the attention of the serious scholar is now the central question about Pinero.

When one first examines his work, it is his prolific output and great variety that are impressive. For thirty years Pinero's plays came tumbling out of his pen: comedies, psychological studies, fantasies, farces, tragedies, satire, and sometimes combinations of a few of these forms. They were peopled by characters from every class of English life, lords and ladies, the upper middle class, provincial bourgeois, petty bourgeois in business, even those from the very poor East End of London. In Pinero there is a richness and profusion often the mark of a major writer.

Further, he followed in the tradition of the great English nineteenth-century novelists who wrote for the great public. He disdained the fringe dramatist who, he believed, avoided the hard job of interesting the major part of the theatergoing public in serious drama. He thus wrote for the stages of the West End, where he directed his plays with the firm, perhaps rigid, hand of the martinet; he had a grasp even the most brilliant actors and actresses accepted because of the thoroughness of his compositions and his complete understanding of their theater.

This sound knowledge of the uses of the stage in his time made many of his plays models of technique. Even his old enemy Max Beerbohm praised the dexterity of *His House in Order,* hating the play for its ability to manipulate, yet at the same time affected by that very manipulation. Others such as Walkley and Archer pointed to the fine construction of play after play. Later critics also admired his technical skill. Dawick, for example, called the third act of *The Gay Lord Quex* the equal of Sheridan's screen scene in *The School for Scandal.*

Nor were his methods confined to those of the late nineteenth- and early twentieth-century stages. The fantasy of *The Enchanted Cottage* has been derided as a poor imitation of Barrie, but in the decade in which it was written, the 1920s, when advanced dramatists experimented mainly in expressionistic forms, Pinero's play was "wholeheartedly Expressionistic" (Griffin, 171). Griffin also pointed to the advanced Brechtian technique of *Dr. Harmer's Holiday.*

But there were also adverse remarks about Pinero's construction. Shaw, for example, sneered at the waste of two characters in the first act of *The Second Mrs. Tanqueray.* Others have noticed the long arm of coincidence at work in his drama, even as late as *His House in Order* in 1906. Criticism of his excessively literary language was made not only by Shaw and Beerbohm but also by those more admiring of him, Walkley and even Archer. This flaw in his work may be felt less strongly today because his high-toned language somehow seems to belong with the stiff Victorian costumes.

But certain strictures are perhaps fatal to the endurance of his work. In addition to the techniques mentioned earlier, Shaw importantly attacked Pinero's ability to create his characters with that special gift of the great dramatist, imaginative sympathy. For Shaw, Pinero viewed his creations as society saw them, not as they saw themselves. We may infer, then, that in conceiving them at least in part from society's point of view, Pinero wished to reinforce society's notion of them. Therefore, no matter how much he may have seemed critical of society, no matter how much sympathy he may have shown his central characters, finally and essentially Pinero upheld society in its rigid, repressive, uncharitable views.

There is even more truth here than Shaw suggested. For instance, a modern reader cannot help but be repelled by the worship of the pure young girl in *The Second Mrs. Tanqueray* even though there is implied criticism of her. There is still far too much left untarnished for comfort. Also, the modern reader, following Archer, might well condemn as unbelievable Agnes Ebbsmith's retrieving from the fire the Bible she has tossed into it, but the incident may also be seen as a sop to the established church. Other works are equally disturbing and unfortunately sometimes laughable. *Letty* has an epilogue showing the title character, who has resisted a womanizer, some years later ensconced in a safe bourgeois marriage while the young blade who besieged her now suffers from some mysterious illness. *Mid-Channel*'s adulterous heroine, presumably to satisfy society's overt attitude toward a woman's sexual misconduct, plunges to her death.

Pinero's plays therefore often give the effect of being constricted, of shutting out the fresh air of new ideas. The sense of his plays sometimes being hermetically sealed is reinforced by their tight construction. Shaw [1] wrote to Pinero in 1909, "Why do you still struggle [to] *construct* plays?" (887). He added, "I never construct a play: I let myself rip." A few lines down he pointed out another failure he found in Pinero's work: "You bite hard; but you do not let yourself wag your tail. The fun is in you." but, Shaw implied, it was no longer in the plays he was writing now. But that fun was always absent from Pinero's so-called serious drama. He made himself out to be a stern moralist, and his dramas are stern to the point of a reader's exhaustion. Finally, what must surely be an admirable quality, his critical evenhandedness to all his characters—what Shaw, in describing the characters in *Mid-Channel,* called Pinero's merciless-ness—also turns against him, making him seem detached and disdainful. This, too, helps create the effect of airlessness in some of his dramas.

Yet in the same place where Shaw voiced the criticisms just mentioned, he called Pinero a genius. One must agree that if he is not a genius, he is a very large talent, and who is sure, or who cares, about the difference?

In the first place he has immense power. The very concentration that some-times makes his plays seem airless also lends them sheer power. Second, that very evenhandedness toward his characters that makes his work seem cold and detached also gives them a psychological complexity. Paula Tanqueray is a puppet either for gaining easy sympathy from the audience or for allowing society to feel complacent. Even Shaw until the end of the play found her convincing. Agnes Ebbsmith may be an invalid "platform woman," but we at this distance lack knowledge of the type just as Pinero did. For a modern au-dience, she, rent by conflicting emotions, is a vigorous and heartbreaking per-sonality for much of the play. Other characters are also figures of compelling interest: Sophie Fullgarney and Lord Quex in *The Gay Lord Quex* and Iris and Maldonado in *Iris,* for example. Moreover, Pinero did not lose his sense of humor when he gained preeminence as a dramatist. *The Gay Lord Quex* is a finely ironic comedy; *A Wife without a Smile* is amusingly naughty even without the dancing doll; even his late one-act piece *A Seat in the Park* is a droll romp for two excellent actors.

But what is perhaps most surprising and fascinating about Pinero is his knowl-edge of sexuality. His plays are permeated with it, and his understanding of it is many times greater than the puritan Shaw's. Critics sometimes wonder why Aubrey Tanqueray bothered marrying his mistress Paula. The answer seems clear. His first wife was cold, and Paula gave him such sexual pleasure that he did not wish to take the chance of losing her. Marriage assured his possession of her better than his supporting her, especially since he would thus be allowed to hide her in the country. Agnes Ebbsmith would not let herself know that she was besotted with sex. That obsession with sex is especially true of Iris, who does not care a rap what society will say as long as she can have her lover. When a man to whom she is not attracted forces her, because of her financial impecuniousness, to become his mistress, she freezes him out emotionally. That man is Maldonado, who, though she is unfeeling toward him, so wishes to possess her that he will marry her. When he discovers that she still loves another who has suddenly returned to her life, he becomes so angry that he wishes to do her bodily harm. But he stops himself, orders her out of his house, then tears up the room. There are few scenes, perhaps no scene, with that power in Edwardian drama. Further, almost all the plays of Pinero, whether or not out of his top drawer, are illuminated with his knowledge of the central place of sexuality in human conduct.

When as a youngster Pinero daily stood outside the Garrick Club envying the established actors who had earned the right to membership (Dawick, 3), he perhaps little thought of the interior division the habit indicated. On the one hand, he wished to become an actor, a member of a profession that, no matter what respectability it desired to gain, was still raffish, undoubtedly more raffish than he portrayed it in *Trelawny*. Yet that these actors had a club, an institution that imitated those of respectable society, showed their desire and Pinero's to join the prevailing powers.

Therein lay Pinero's conflict in his drama. His wish to leave law practice and join a profession so tenuous and bohemian as acting indicated his desire to leave the staidness of bourgeois life for the unleavened ways of the actor. To make the break, to leave the law, the profession of his ancestors, must have shown his deep dislike, perhaps his hatred, for that respectable life. But he knew its power to harm those who too much defied its rules. Hence in his drama there were those plays that at the same time slashed at society and placated it.

Yet there are dramas, beside the four that are usually revived, that are altogether honest and still stand up. These are *The Gay Lord Quex, Iris,* perhaps even the manipulative *His House in Order,* and the bleak *The Thunderbolt.* There are three late dramas, unsuccessful in their day, that are worth an airing: the sad, wise play that has special significance for us, *The Freaks;* the expressionistic, frightening, sardonic, yet charming fantasy, *The Enchanted Cottage;* and that brief tale of sexual repression and explosion, *Dr. Harmer's Holiday.* But we must not forget that *The Second Mrs. Tanqueray* has had a successful modern revival, and though it falls down, it can yet provide a powerful instrument on which a great actress might play; it might also serve as a reminder of how things used to be. Although less cogent than its predecessor, *The Notorious Mrs. Ebbsmith* might well possess current interest. In sum, then, Pinero still has the ability to interest us in the theater and in the study as well, where we can read him, among other reasons, with the fascinating discovery that he was writing in the age of Freud and thinking along many of the same lines.

ARCHIVAL SOURCES

Manuscripts for the plays are to be found in the British Library and in the library of the Garrick Club, London. Pinero material is widespread in England and in the United States. For a complete list of their repositories, see Dawick, xiii–xv.

PRIMARY BIBLIOGRAPHY

Plays

The Amazons. London: Heinemann, 1894; Boston: Baker, 1895.
The Beauty Stone. With J. Comyns Carr and Arthur Sullivan. London: Chappell, 1898.
The Benefit of the Doubt. London: Heinemann, 1895.
The Big Drum. London: Heinemann, 1915.
The Bulkley Peerage: A Very Grand Guignolette. Pearson's Magazine 38 (Dec. 1914): 654–58.
The Cabinet Minister. London: Heinemann, 1892; New York: Lovell, 1891; Birmingham: Oberon Books, 1987.
Child Man. In A. W. Pinero, *Two Plays.* London: Heinemann, 1930.
A Cold June. London: Chiswick Press, 1932.
Dandy Dick. London: Heinemann, 1893, 1956; Boston: Baker, 1893; London: Samuel French, 1936.
Dr. Harmer's Holidays. London: Chiswick Press, 1924. Also in A. W. Pinero, *Two Plays.* London: Heinemann, 1930.
The Enchanted Cottage. London: Heinemann, 1922; Boston: Baker, 1925.
The Freaks. London: Heinemann, 1922.
The Gay Lord Quex. London: Heinemann, 1900; New York: Russell, 1900. Also in *Social Plays of Arthur Wing Pinero,* ed. Clayton Hamilton, vol. 2. New York: Dutton, 1918.
Hester's Mystery. London: T. H. Lacy, 1893.
His House in Order. London: Heinemann, 1906. Also in *Social Plays of Arthur Wing Pinero,* ed. Clayton Hamilton, vol. 3. New York: Dutton, 1919, 253–449.
The Hobby Horse. London: Heinemann, 1892; Boston: Baker, 1892.
Imprudence. London: Walter Smith, 1881.
In Chancery. London: Samuel French, 1905.
Iris. London: Heinemann, 1902. Also in *Social Plays of Arthur Wing Pinero,* ed. Clayton Hamilton, vol. 2. New York: Dutton, 1918, 231–423.
Lady Bountiful. London: Heinemann, 1891; Boston: Baker, 1892.
Late of Mockford's. Typescript, 1934.
Letty. London: Heinemann, 1904. Also in *Social Plays of Arthur Wing Pinero,* ed. Clayton Hamilton, vol. 3. New York: Dutton, 1919.
The Magistrate. London: Heinemann, 1892; Boston: Baker, 1892; London: Samuel French, 1936. Also in *English Plays of the Nineteenth Century,* vol. 4, *Farces,* ed. Michael R. Booth. Oxford: Clarendon Press, 1973; *Pinero: Three Plays,* introduction by Stephen Wyatt. London: Methuen, 1985.
Mayfair. London: J. Miles, 1885.
Mid-Channel. London: Heinemann, 1911. Also in *Social Plays of Arthur Wing Pinero,* ed. Clayton Hamilton, vol. 4. New York: Dutton, 1922, 289–506; *Modern British Dramas,* ed. Harlan Hatcher. New York: Harcourt, Brace, 1941.
The "Mind the Paint" Girl. London: Heinemann, 1913.
The Money-Spinner. London: T. H. Lacy, 1900; London: Samuel French, 1910.
Mr. Livermore's Dream. London: Chiswick Press, 1917.
The Notorious Mrs. Ebbsmith. London: Heinemann, 1895. Also in *Social Plays of Arthur*

Wing Pinero, ed. Clayton Hamilton, vol. 1. New York: Dutton, 1917, 197–362; *The "New Drama,"* introduction by Carl M. Selle. Coral Gables, FL: University of Miami Press, 1963; *British Plays of the Nineteenth Century,* ed. J. O. Bailey. New York: Odyssey, 1966.

Playgoers: A Domestic Episode. London: Samuel French, 1913. Also in *Fifty One-Act Plays,* ed. Constance M. Martin. London: Gollancz, 1921.

Preserving Mr. Panmure. London: Heinemann, 1912; Chicago: Dramatic Publishing, 1910.

The Princess and the Butterfly; or, The Fantastics. London: Heinemann, 1898.

A Private Room. London: Samuel French, 1928.

The Profligate. London: Heinemann, 1891.

Quick Work: A Story of a War Marriage. London: Chiswick Press, 1918.

The Rocket. London: Samuel French, 1905.

The Schoolmistress. London: Heinemann, 1894. Also in *Plays by A. W. Pinero,* ed. George Rowell. Cambridge: Cambridge University Press, 1986.

A Seat in the Park: A Warning. London: Samuel French, 1922.

The Second Mrs. Tanqueray. London: Heinemann, 1895. Also in *Social Plays of Arthur Wing Pinero,* ed. Clayton Hamilton, vol. 1. New York: Dutton, 1917, 47–195; *Pinero: Three Plays,* introduction by Stephen Wyatt. London: Methuen, 1985; *English Drama in Transition,* ed. Henry F. Salerno. New York: Pegasus, 1968; *English Plays of the Nineteenth Century,* vol. 2, *Dramas, 1850–1900,* ed. Michael R. Booth. Oxford: Clarendon Press, 1969; *Plays by A. W. Pinero,* ed. George Rowell. Cambridge: Cambridge University Press, 1986.

The Squire. London: Samuel French, 1905.

Sweet Lavender. London: Heinemann, 1893; Boston: Baker, 1893.

The Thunderbolt. London: Heinemann, 1909. Also in *Social Plays of Arthur Wing Pinero,* ed. Clayton Hamilton, vol. 4. New York: Dutton, 1922, 31–276; *Plays by A. W. Pinero,* ed. George Rowell. Cambridge: Cambridge University Press, 1986.

The Times. London: Heinemann, 1891; Boston: Baker, 1892.

Trelawny of the "Wells." London: Heinemann, 1899; Chicago: Dramatic Publishing, 1925; London: Samuel French, 1936. Also in *Pinero: Three Plays,* introduction by Stephen Wyatt. London: Methuen, 1985; *Plays by A. W. Pinero,* ed. George Rowell. Cambridge: Cambridge University Press, 1986.

The Weaker Sex. London: Heinemann, 1894.

The Widow of Wasdale Head. In *Representative One-Act Plays by British and Irish Authors,* ed. Barrett H. Clarke. Boston: Little, Brown, 1921.

A Wife without a Smile. London: Heinemann, 1905.

Essays and Articles on Drama and Theater

Pinero wrote many pieces on drama and the theater, a complete listing of which may be found in Dawick, 410–11. The following may be of special interest.

"Prefatory Letter." In William Archer, *The Theatrical "World" of 1895.* 1896. Reprint. New York: Benjamin Blom, 1971.

"Robert Browning as a Dramatist." *Transactions of the Royal Society of Literature,* 2nd ser. 31 (1912): 255–68.

Robert Louis Stevenson: The Dramatist. A Lecture Delivered to the Members of the

Philosophical Institution of Edinburgh at the Music Hall in Edinburgh on Tuesday, 24th February, 1903. London: Chiswick Press, 1903. Reprinted in *Papers on Playmaking,* ed. Brander Matthews. New York: Hill & Wang, 1957.
"The Theatre in the 'Seventies." In *The Eighteen-Seventies: Essays by Fellows of the Royal Society of Literature,* ed. Harley Granville-Barker. New York: Macmillan, 1929.

SECONDARY BIBLIOGRAPHY

Archer, William. [1]. *English Dramatists of Today.* London: T. Fisher Unwin, 1886.
———. [2]. *The Old Drama and the New.* Boston: Small, Maynard, 1923.
———. [3]. *The Theatrical "World" of 1895.* With a Prefatory Letter by Arthur W. Pinero. 1896. Reprint. New York: Benjamin Blom, 1971.
———. [4]. *The Theatrical 'World' of 1897.* 1898. Reprint. New York: Benjamin Blom, [1969].
Bailey, J. O., ed. *British Plays of the Nineteenth Century: An Anthology to Illustrate the Evolution of the Drama.* New York: Odyssey, 1966.
Beerbohm, Max. [1]. *Around Theatres.* London: Rupert Hart-Davis, 1953.
———. [2]. *Last Theatres, 1904–1910.* New York: Taplinger, 1970.
———. [3]. *More Theatres, 1898–1903.* New York: Taplinger, 1969.
Booth, Michael. *Theatre in the Victorian Age.* Cambridge: Cambridge University Press, 1991.
Borsa, Mario. *The English Stage of To-day.* Trans. Selwyn Brinton. London: John Lane, 1908.
Carr, William Patterson. "The Plays of Sir Arthur Wing Pinero on the New York Professional Stage." M.A. thesis, University of Washington, 1948.
Cordell, Richard A. *Henry Arthur Jones and the Modern Drama.* New York: Ray Long & Richard R. Smith, 1932.
Davis, Cecil W. "Pinero: The Drama of Reputation." *English* 14 (Spring 1962): 13–17.
Dawick, John. *Pinero: A Theatrical Life.* Niwot: University Press of Colorado, 1993.
Dent, Alan. *Mrs. Patrick Campbell.* London: Museum Press, 1961.
Donaldson, Frances. *The Actor-Managers.* London: Weidenfeld & Nicolson, 1970.
Duncan, Barry. *The St. James's Theatre.* London: Barrie & Rockliff, 1964.
Dunkel, Wilbur Dwight. *Sir Arthur Pinero: A Critical Biography with Letters.* 1941. Reprint. Port Washington, NY: Kennikat Press, 1967.
Ervine, St. John. *The Theatre in My Time.* London: Rich & Cowan, 1933.
Fyfe, Hamilton. *Sir Arthur Pinero's Plays and Players.* New York: Macmillan, 1930.
Granville-Barker, Harley, ed. *The Eighteen-Seventies: Essays by Fellows of the Royal Society of Literature.* New York: Macmillan, 1929.
Griffin, Penny. *Arthur Wing Pinero and Henry Arthur Jones.* New York: St. Martin's Press, 1991.
Hamilton, Clayton, ed. *The Social Plays of Arthur Wing Pinero* (4 vols.) New York: Dutton, 1917–1922.
Innes, Christopher. *Modern British Drama, 1890–1990.* Cambridge: Cambridge University Press, 1992.
Kaplan, Joel H. "Edwardian Pinero." *Nineteenth Century Theatre* 17 (Summer and Winter 1989): 20–49.

Lazenby, Walter. *Arthur Wing Pinero.* New York: Twayne, 1972.

Legatt, Alexander. "Pinero: From Farce to Social Drama." *Modern Drama* 17 (Sept. 1974): 329–44.

Mason, A.E.W. *Sir George Alexander and the St. James's Theatre.* London: Macmillan, 1935.

Miner, Edmund J. [1]. "The Limited Naturalism of Arthur Pinero." *Modern Drama* 19 (June 1976): 147–59.

———. [2]. "The Novelty of Arthur Pinero's Court Farces." *English Literature in Transition, 1880–1920* 19.4 (1976): 299–305.

———. [3]. "The Theme of Disillusionment in the Drama of Arthur Pinero." *Contemporary Review* 226 (Apr. 1975): 184–90.

Nicoll, Allardyce. *English Drama, 1900–1930: The Beginnings of the Modern Period.* Cambridge: Cambridge University Press, 1973.

Rowell, George, ed. [1]. *Plays by A. W. Pinero.* Cambridge: Cambridge University Press, 1986.

———. ed. [2]. *Victorian Dramatic Criticism.* London: Methuen, 1971.

Sawin, Lewis. *Alfred Sutro: A Man with a Heart.* Niwot: University Press of Colorado, 1989.

Selle, Carl M. "Introduction." In *The "New Drama."* Coral Gables, FL: University of Miami Press, 1963.

Shaw, George Bernard. [1]. *Bernard Shaw: Collected Letters, 1898–1910.* Ed. Dan H. Laurence. New York: Viking, 1985.

———. [2]. *Dramatic Opinions and Essays with an Apology.* Vol. 1. New York: Brentano's, 1925.

Smith, Leslie. *Modern British Farce: A Selective Study of British Farce from Pinero to the Present Day.* Totowa, NJ: Barnes & Noble, 1989.

Sutro, Alfred. *Celebrities and Simple Souls.* London: Duckworth, 1933.

Thompson, Fred, Clifford Grey, Howard Talbot, and Ivor Novello. *Who's Hooper? A Musical Play in Two Acts.* Founded on Sir Arthur Pinero's Farce "In Chancery." London: Ascherberg, Hopwood & Crew, [1919].

Trewin, J. C. [1]. *The Edwardian Theatre.* Oxford: Basil Blackwell, 1976.

———. [2]. *The Theatre since 1900.* London: Andrew Dakers, 1951.

Walkley, A. B. *Drama and Life.* 1908. Reprint. Freeport, NY: Books for Libraries Press, 1967.

Wearing, J. P. [1]. *The Collected Letters of Sir Arthur Pinero.* Minneapolis: University of Minnesota Press, 1974.

———. [2]. *The London Stage, 1890–1899* (2 vols.); *1900–1909* (2 vols.); *1910–1919* (2 vols.); *1920–1929* (3 vols.). Metuchen, NJ: Scarecrow Press, 1976, 1981, 1982, 1984.

Webster, Margaret. *The Same Only Different.* New York: Alfred A. Knopf, 1969.

Woodfield, James. *English Theatre in Transition, 1889–1914.* London: Croom Helm, 1984; Totowa, NJ: Barnes & Noble, 1984.

BIBLIOGRAPHY

Weaver, Jack W., and Earl J. Wilcox. "Arthur Wing Pinero: An Annotated Bibliography of Writings about Him." *English Literature in Transition* 23 (1980): 231–59.

J. B. Priestley
(1894–1984)

LINCOLN KONKLE

In addition to theater critics, time has not been very kind to J. B. Priestley, who would find this the cruelest cut of all since it was the ontological nature of time and its epistemological ramifications regarding the human condition that formed the philosophical center of his vast and varied oeuvre. Priestley wrote plays, novels, short stories, autobiographies, travel literature, television and film scripts, essays, critical studies of English literature, and discourses on Western civilization. Of some 150 books he published over six decades, 28 were novels, 5 of which, along with 1 collection of short stories, remain in print. His drama has met an even more obscure though less deserved fate: of 48 plays produced on the stage over thirty-two years, 39 of which were published, none are in print (except for acting editions, of which there are 8 available from Samuel French and 1 from Dramatists Play Service). Furthermore, no play of Priestley's is included in the major anthologies of modern drama published as textbooks for college courses in the United States. However, though Priestley's plays were absent from the New York stage for forty years, ten years after his death J. B. Priestley has been rediscovered in America, as evidenced by the 1994 revival of *An Inspector Calls,* which won four Tony Awards and enjoyed an extraordinarily long run for a serious nonmusical drama on Broadway in the 1990s. Similarly, while Priestley's plays suffered a twenty-year hiatus from the West End, four or five remained in the British repertory.

John Boynton Priestley was born on 13 September 1894 to an English schoolmaster and an Irish mother who died when he was two. His father remarried, and John was largely raised by his stepmother. The backdrop for Priestley's childhood was the northern city of Bradford in the former county of Yorkshire. Bradford was a medium-sized industrial city; however, just outside the city limits lay the pastoral and mysterious Midlands moors, which have been romanticized in English poetry and fiction from the Middle Ages to the present. Having left school and worked as a clerk at a wool firm in his hometown for three years, in 1914 Priestley volunteered for military duty and was wounded three times during World War I, but always returned to action. After the war Priestley studied literature, modern history, and political science for three years (1919–22) at Cambridge. He met Pat Tempest, a librarian and lover of music, and they married in 1921. In 1922 Priestley turned down a teaching position and went to London to begin his career as a free-lance writer of essays and criticism. In three years he published five books and Pat bore him two daughters, but then fortune turned; his wife and his father died of cancer within a year of each other (1924–25). In 1926 Priestley married Mary Holland Wyndham Lewis, with whom he had two more daughters and a son. The need to support his family drove Priestley to write at a furious pace; by 1929 he had produced seventeen books of fiction, criticism, and collections of essays. The enormous commercial success of his fourth novel *The Good Companions* (1929) freed him from financial pressures, but he continued to write and publish at an astounding rate.

Sales of his novels also allowed Priestley to venture into the theater, though conservatively at first with an adaptation of *The Good Companions* (1931) coauthored by play-doctor Edward Knoblock. Priestley's first solo-authored play, *Dangerous Corner* (1932), was a ''whodunit'' that received early negative reviews, causing its backers to withdraw their support. Refusing to accept defeat, Priestley and his agent A. D. Peters formed the production company English Plays Limited with their own money and allied themselves with the Duchess Theater (London), which would be the site of many premieres of Priestley's plays. Ultimately, *Dangerous Corner* went on to become his most widely produced work for the stage.

During the 1930s Priestley wrote no fewer than seventeen plays (along with nine novels), ranging in subject from the dissolution of families in *Eden End* (1934) and *Time and the Conways* (1937) to marriage farces such as *Laburnum Grove* (1933); from the infinite repetition of life cycles in *I Have Been Here Before* (1937) to the state of the soul beyond bodily death in *Johnson over Jordan* (1939). He experimented with nonrealistic dramaturgy in *Music at Night* (1938), despite a rigidly realistic commercial theater, and worked with such great stage and film actors as John Gielgud in *The Good Companions* (1931), Ralph Richardson in *Cornelius* (1935) and four other plays, Laurence Olivier in *Bees on the Boatdeck* (1936), and Sybil Thorndike in *The Linden Tree* (1947). Priestley himself acted in 12 performances of *When We Are Married* (1938), playing a drunken photographer when the actor cast in the role was injured in an automobile accident twenty-four hours before opening night. In 1937 Priestley went on a lecture tour in the United States and got a taste of screenwriting in Hollywood (a bad taste, evidently, since he had his name removed from the movies' credits).

Only the Second World War could slow Priestley's literary and theatrical output, but he became an even more famous public figure from his nightly BBC broadcasts called "Postscripts," which had the formidable task of bolstering the morale of the British populace in the face of Hitler's European campaign and bombing of London. After the war Priestley served as a U.K. delegate to the UNESCO conferences and helped to start the nuclear disarmament movement in Great Britain. Despite this commitment to fight the good fight during the 1940s on the political stage, Priestley still managed to produce five of his most successful and provocative plays: *They Came to a City* (1943), *Ever since Paradise* (1946), *An Inspector Calls* (1946), *The Linden Tree* (1947), and *Summer Day's Dream* (1949). He also published six novels in this turbulent decade.

In 1952 his second marriage ended in divorce; soon after he wedded anthropologist Jacquetta Hawkes, with whom he had collaborated on the "platform play" *Dragon's Mouth* (1952). The negative reception of this and other plays led to Priestley's diminished interest in the theater; however, he still wrote teleplays for the BBC and published novels, critical studies, autobiographies, and travel literature. In the 1960s Priestley produced a long contemplative history, *Literature and Western Man* (1960), and his own philosophical treatise on time, *Man and Time* (1964). His final theatrical venture was to collaborate with Iris Murdoch to adapt her novel *A Severed Head* for the stage (1963). The 1970s brought him several honors, including a doctor of letters from Bradford University (which had also named its new library and computer center after Priestley), freeman of the city of Bradford, and the Order of Merit (an honor more exclusive than a knighthood, which he had refused). In 1984, following surgery for colon cancer, he contracted pneumonia; a month before his ninetieth birthday J. B. Priestley died at his home in Stratford-upon-Avon.

Selected Biographical Sources: Atkins; Braine; Brome; Cooper; DeVitis and Kalson.

MAJOR PLAYS, PREMIERES, AND SIGNIFICANT REVIVALS: THEATRICAL RECEPTION

Dangerous Corner. 1932. Opened 17 May at the Lyric Theatre (London) for 151 performances. Produced by Tyrone Guthrie. Opened 27 October in New York at the Empire Theatre for 206 performances. Reopened 1933 at the Waldorf Theatre (New York) for 90 performances. Revivals: 1988 at the Shaw Festival, Niagara-on-the-Lake, Ontario.

This murder mystery has been a crowd pleaser ever since its precarious debut, but critics found it lacking in substance. Most reviewers deemed *Dangerous Corner* a failure; however, with regard to the repetition of the first act's beginning but with a variation that prevents the unfolding of tragedy, Agate said, "If this is not a brilliant device, I do not grasp the meaning of either word" (113). Even Priestley later saw *Dangerous Corner* as "merely an ingenious box of tricks" (*The Plays of J. B. Priestley,* 1:viii).

Eden End. 1934. Opened 13 September at the Duchess Theatre (London) for 162 performances. Produced by Irene Hentschel. Opened 1935 in New York at the Masque Theatre for 24 performances. Revivals: 1948 at the Duchess Theatre (London) for 100 performances; 1974 at the National Theatre (London) to commemorate J. B. Priestley's eightieth birthday; August 1994 at the Shaw Festival, Niagara-on-the-Lake, Ontario.

Although *Eden End* received mixed reviews when it opened in London, since then theater critics and scholars whose taste in drama runs toward realism and a gloomy mood à la Chekhov have praised it as the Priestley play par excellence. "The atmosphere of mutability [provides] the play's chief power" (Evans, 90). A number of sources report Priestley citing this as his favorite and/or best play.

Time and the Conways. 1937. Opened 26 August at the Duchess Theatre (London) for 225 performances. Produced by Irene Hentschel. Opened in New York in 1938 at the Ritz Theatre with Jessica Tandy as Kay for 32 performances. Revivals: West End, 1990.

Despite the prosaic title, this profoundly moving family portrait juxtaposes the optimism of youth and the sadness of unfulfilled dreams. Although this is the first of Priestley's "time plays," the theories of time are irrelevant here, as Atkins explained: "If Priestley had never read Ouspensky and Dunne, if indeed Ouspensky and Dunne never existed, then the play still could have been written just as it stands" (80). It is difficult to disagree with Braine's assessment of *Time and the Conways:* "Of all Priestley's plays this is the most deeply satisfying" (85).

I Have Been Here Before. 1937. Opened 22 September at the Royalty Theatre (London) for 210 performances. Produced by Lewis Casson. Opened in 1938 in New York at the Guild Theatre for 20 performances. Revivals: 26 May 1947 at the Theatre Royal (Bristol) for 16 performances.

The most explicit presentation of Priestley's synthesis of Dunne and Ouspensky's theories of time, the play suffered by comparison to *Time and the Conways* in most reviews; however, Verschoyle [1] wrote that *I Have Been Here Before* was "still an oasis in the theatrical desert."

Music at Night. 1938. Performed 2 August at the Malvern Festival. Opened 10 October 1939 at the Westminster Theatre.

In Priestley's first experiment with dramatic form, he continued to explore metaphysical issues. DeVitis and Kalson regarded this as "a significant achievement through language and a major break-through in theatrical form" (181); it "engages the intellect and sways the emotion" (184).

When We Are Married. 1938. Opened 11 October at St. Martin's Theatre (London) for 175 performances. Produced by Basil Dean. Opened in 1939 in New York at the Lyceum Theatre for 150 performances. Revivals: 1939 at the Prince's Theatre (Bradford) for 102 performances.

Many critics cite this "shouting Yorkshire farce" (Trewin, 117) as Priestley's best comedy, written in the spirit of Chaucer, not Shaw (Evans, 170). Fleming found it "continuously amusing" but a "minor work."

Johnson over Jordan. 1939. Opened 22 February at the New Theatre (London) for 40 performances. Produced by Basil Dean. Reopened 21 March at the Saville Theatre (London); closed 26 May.

Priestley's most ambitious work for the theater, this modern *Everyman* closed so quickly because of the immense cost of staging such a "dream play." *The Times* review (Review of *Johnson over Jordan*) gave Priestley credit for trying something new, but Verschoyle [2] absolutely deplored *Johnson over Jordan.* Cooper claimed, "The third act can stand against any other parallel kind of fantasy-morality play" (130); however, while Trewin found the end extraordinary, overall "its expressionistic-symbolic mumbo irritates" (116). Given the perspective of time, DeVitis and Kalson hailed it as "a landmark occasion in the London theatre" (185).

They Came to a City. 1943. Opened 21 April at the Globe Theatre (London) for 280 performances. Produced by Irene Hentschel.

Given the chaos embroiling the world at the time, the hope for utopia within this play was a remarkable achievement of the imagination and will. "It has no pretensions to being anything but a piece of sincere propaganda for Priestley's belief in the perfectibility of man" (Evans, 193). Trewin, while admitting that "the dramatist is preaching, deliberately preaching," also pointed out that "wartime audiences did not reject the sermon as arid" (116).

Ever since Paradise. 1946 (written 1939). Opened 4 June at the New Theatre (London) for 165 performances. Produced by Priestley.

Tossing realistic theater aside, Priestley dramatized the war between the sexes with three married couples who act out and comment upon their trials and tribulations. Initial reviews were mixed, as are scholarly assessments. Atkins found it too "thirtyish" (233) in its going out of the way to avoid adultery and marital breakup, and he compared the happy ending to the tied-up heroine being pulled off the railroad tracks at the last second. However, the play is not without its supporters. Evans found it "the most sophisticated of Priestley's comedies. . . . The method is similar to that of Thornton Wilder's in *Our Town*" (170). Klein called *Ever since Paradise,* along with *Johnson over Jordan* and *Music at Night,* "the Great Experimental Triptych" (144).

An Inspector Calls. 1946. Opened 1 October at the New Theatre (London) for 41 performances. Produced by Basil Dean. Opened 21 October 1947 in New York at the Booth Theatre for 95 performances. Revivals: 1973, Mermaid Theatre (London); 1992 at the National Theatre (London); 27 April 1994 in New York at the Royale Theatre (New York); closed June 1995.

Despite its less-than-successful debut, this detective thriller is generally regarded as Priestley's best synthesis of his social criticism of the English class system and his mastery of riveting theatrical craftsmanship; for example, Atkins (216) called it a perfect play. In 1946 reviewers in London and New York saw *An Inspector Calls* as a gimmicky melodrama similar to *Dangerous Corner.* However, the critical and commercial success of the 1994 revival of *An Inspector Calls* proves the timelessness of the play's message and the theatrical effectiveness of Priestley's dramaturgy: the production received both the Olivier (London) and the Tony (New York) for best revival of a play and won additional awards for directing, acting, set design, and lighting.

The Linden Tree. 1947. Opened 15 August at the Duchess Theatre (London) for 422 performances. Produced by Michael Macowan. Opened 7 March 1949 in New York at the Theatre Royale for 8 performances.

A return to the Chekhovian drama of *Eden End, The Linden Tree* was Priestley's most commercially and critically successful play at home (it won the Ellen Terry Award for best play in 1947), but abroad the critics repudiated it as a too-talky, dull "conversation piece" (Atkinson).

Summer Day's Dream. 1949. Opened 8 September at St. Martin's Theatre (London) for 43 performances. Produced by Michael Macowan.

In *They Came to a City* utopia was a shadowy possibility beyond the walls of the city; in this "post-atomic pastoral" (Young, 50) Priestley shows us a brave new world in Great Britain twenty-five years into the future (1975). *The Times* critic (Review of *Summer's Day Dream*) found it "an overlong atmosphere play," but Evans respected it as "perhaps the most avowedly idealistic play that Priestley has written" (205).

ADDITIONAL PLAYS, ADAPTATIONS, AND PRODUCTIONS

Space does not permit a comprehensive listing of J. B. Priestley's forty-eight produced plays (see Klein for a complete list); however, there are a few additional produced and published plays worth noting since some critics and scholars have included them in their assessments of Priestley's better plays. *Laburnum Grove* (comedy) opened 28 November 1933 at the Duchess Theatre (London) for 335 performances, and in New York in 1935 for 101 performances. *Cornelius* (a satire on business) opened 20 March 1935 at the Duchess Theatre (London). *Desert Highway* (a war play) opened 13 December 1943 at the Theatre Royal (Bristol). *Dragon's Mouth* (a Jungian allegory written with Jacquetta Hawkes) was performed 13 April 1952 at the Malvern Festival and opened 13 May at the Winter Garden Theatre (London). In addition, Klein referred to twelve typed manuscripts of complete plays never performed or published that are in the possession of J. B. Priestley's widow, Jacquetta Priestley (3).

ASSESSMENT OF PRIESTLEY'S CAREER

J. B. Priestley was the torch carrier of British theater and drama during the 1930s and 1940s. While T. S. Eliot's foray into drama looked backward in time to classical Greek tragedy, Priestley looked forward, or rather he attempted to advance audiences, critics, and English drama itself past the limited realistic dramaturgy and high (and dry) drawing-room comedy dominating the London stage at that time (i.e., Somerset Maugham, Noël Coward). He made innovative experiments in theatrical form and introduced theories of time as a subject suitable for dramatic treatment. Although Priestley was a social (some say socialist) critic in and out of the theater, his vision of time and life was nonetheless optimistic and affirmative.

Given the paucity of artistic as opposed to purely commercial ventures on the London stage of the 1930s and 1940s, it is all the more puzzling why Priestley and his plays have faded into obscurity. In scholarly studies of modern drama little or no mention is made of Priestley. Braine observed, "My personal impression is that he hasn't been blacklisted by the literary pundits but whitelisted; it's as if he didn't exist" (54). Priestley fares a bit better in studies of modern British drama, still warranting a chapter or a paragraph or two in which he is recognized as one of the few original voices in the British theater after Shaw and before Osborne (Innes, Dietrich, Lumley); however, he is not even mentioned in Roy's *British Drama since Shaw* (1972). For a more developed description of Priestley's decline in status as a dramatist, see Klein (257–58).

Part of the problem may be that critics are unsure as to his proper generic placement. Dietrich called Priestley a minor playwright "better known as a novelist and essayist, and as a public and media personality" (225–26); however, most of the book-length studies of Priestley have claimed that his greatest achievement is in drama (Evans, Klein, Cooper, Atkins). DeVitis and Kalson stated it best: "As a novelist he is a minor figure among giants performing miracles; as a dramatist he stands alone" (116). Most of the journalistic and academic criticism on Priestley evaluates individual plays or his dramaturgy as a whole based upon the criteria of realistic theater and drama, but Priestley himself said, "All of my plays are principally fantasies" (Cooper, 154). They were, however, fantasies designed not merely to entertain, but also to cause audiences to reflect upon the social conditions that had given rise to two world wars and a global economic depression within the space of thirty years. Though uneven in quality, Priestley's plays have been unanimously praised by critics and scholars for their variety of subject, genre, and dramaturgical form: "It would probably amaze the majority of today's younger theatergoers (and writers) to be told that J. B. Priestley has been one of the major experimentalists in the 20th-century English Theatre" (Atkins, 237). Some of his plays belong to the English tradition of the Shavian debate of ideas (e.g., *Ever since Paradise, Summer Day's Dream*); some are character and mood pieces in the manner of Chekhov (e.g., *Eden End, The Linden Tree*); some experiment with nonrealistic theatrical technique in a manner similar to Strindberg's *A Dream Play* and Wilder's *Our Town* (e.g., *Johnson over Jordan, Music at Night*); some fall into the murder-mystery genre à la Agatha Christie (e.g., *Dangerous Corner, An Inspector Calls*); and some attempt little more than to provoke laughter and goodwill in the audience (e.g., *Laburnum Grove, When We Are Married*). As Hobson said, "People never quite knew what to expect when they went to see a Priestley play" (109).

The assortment of tones and techniques in his drama is responsible for the sometimes contradictory image of Priestley one finds in reviews and studies of British literature and drama. For example, Trewin described him as both "John Boynton Priestley" and "Jack Priestley," the "experimenter" and the "hearty good fellow" (113). Priestley liked neither of these views and rejected other labels attached to him and/or his plays (e.g., man of letters, dramatist of ideas, socialist, Marxist, expressionistic, epic theater, naturalistic, committed drama, engaged drama). Apparently he did not object to the more literary term romanticist, though he is clearly a classicist in form, following in the tradition of Ben Jonson rather than Shakespeare.

Brome, the author of the only birth-to-death biography of Priestley, called him "a secular preacher" (481), yet such a label belies the entertainment purpose of many of his plays, especially the comedies. Lumley claimed that "humor is Priestley's forte" (302); however, Evans noted that "Priestley is, in fact, less remembered as a comic dramatist, than as one who exploited unusual themes in an often unusual manner" (151). Priestley reminded Evans of Dickens, "where so often the purposefulness of the comic spirit is blunted by the demands of the merely entertaining" (164); on the other hand, "His comedy is, in the end, always aspiring toward the artificial reconciliations of the forest of Arden" (Evans, 177).

Surprisingly, only Atkins noticed the importance of gender in Priestley's comic vision: "While reading Priestley's work in its totality one soon becomes aware of a Female Champion, half gallant, half protective" (273). Priestley thought that the women's movement was the one major example of social progress in the twentieth century; at the same time, he worried that the feminine principle was in danger of being lost. Atkins quoted this statement from Priestley's nonfiction work, *British Women Go to War:* "The world has long been suffering from an overdose of the masculine values and a lack of the feminine principle, with its realistic outlook and its care for the individual human being" (277). Klein also listed "men and women" as one of three major ideas/issues in Priestley's plays, but he did not elaborate on the tone or points that Atkins saw in the entire oeuvre. Even limited to the plays, a feminist reading of Priestley's portrayal of men and women and the comments his characters make on gender differences would be of interest.

Utopia was a possibility in Priestley's view of the evolution of civilization: he "believed in the perfectibility of man"; however, DeVitis and Kalson insisted that his view was not "Pollyanna's," but rather that "his vision is based on a Jungian concept of the oneness of all men" (118, 9, 125). Throughout his career Priestley consistently criticized the West's capitalistic system based upon materialistic goals, but he also never accepted Marxism or communism because of their "denial of anything that suggests any other dimension to man beyond the

beliefs of dialectical materialism'' (DeVitis and Kalson, 181). Though not religious in the usual sense, Priestley welcomed the presence of religion in society
as long as it helped individuals make their lives purposeful and contributed to
the humanistic progress of civilization.

Whether writing as dramatist, novelist, or essayist, Priestley was sharing with
audiences and readers his fascination with ''Time which, for him, transcends
our ordinary notions of the clock'' (Brown, 5). Priestley's ''Time Plays'' (usually referring to *Time and the Conways* and *I Have Been Here Before,* but
sometimes also to either *Dangerous Corner* or *An Inspector Calls*) offer ''a new
immortality'' (Evans, 56); that is, you can spiral up, spiral down, or stay in the
same old groove. In the four plays mentioned Priestley dramatized friends and
families experiencing *déjà vu,* ''What-Might-Have-Been,'' precognitive
dreams—all stemming from a theory of temporal reality and existence similar
to reincarnation. Although scholarship has not revealed Priestley encountering
Buddhism in any significant way in his life, the influence of J. W. Dunne's *An
Experiment with Time* (1927) and P. D. Ouspensky's *A New Model of the Universe* (1931) upon Priestley has been well documented.

In addition, DeVitis and Kalson cited E. A. Abbott's *Flatland: A Romance
of Many Dimensions by a Square* (1884) as making Priestley think about dimensions and perception much earlier than his reading of Dunne and Ouspensky.
Another influence so obvious that it is rarely mentioned is Priestley's writer
friend, H. G. Wells. Indeed, one cannot help wondering why Priestley did not
write science fiction, though *Summer Day's Dream* could be classified as such
and contemporary studies have described his interest in time in terms more
appropriate for science fiction: for example, Evans called Priestley a ''time-
traveller'' (59) (see also Innes, 370, and Braine, 142). Even if one finds Priestley's ideas about time to be the stuff dreams are made of, they nevertheless
make fascinating food for thought and are effective for delivering his social
lessons. Anyway, how much Priestley believed in the conceptualization of time
in the plays is open to debate. In a note at the beginning of *I Have Been Here
Before,* Priestley said that it ''does not follow because I make use of [Ouspen-
sky's theories] that I necessarily accept them'' (*The Plays of J. B. Priestley,* 1:
202). Innes believed that ''Priestley never found a satisfactory dramatic form
for his metaphysical view of life'' (374), but Atkins claimed that Priestley ''persuaded his audiences to feel the passage of time in a new way'' (240–41). Also,
Innes saw Priestley as anticipating ''Beckett's focus on time'' (428).

Perhaps it is partly the focus on such an abstract subject as the nature of time
that is responsible for Priestley's main fault as a dramatist: his characters are
mostly types and lack depth; but this is also probably caused by the rapidity of
composition of the plays. (Priestley claimed to have written *Dangerous Corner*
in one week.) Evans expressed the problem with regard to *Dangerous Corner,*
but it applies to many of the plays: ''The characters are merely types, merely
to serve the plot, none of them made to dramatize an acutely observed individual
psychology'' (75). On the other hand, as asserted by Hobson, ''J. B. Priestley

turned the theatre-goer's attention to the common man and woman'' (104). For example, in *Cornelius* (1935), ''This was the first time that the stage grasped the full magnitude and terror of unemployment'' (74). To be fair, Hobson also said, *''Cornelius* is a moving play of a businessman boldly facing danger, but it ends in cloud-cuckoo land'' (74). If Priestley is too much a ''happy-ending man'' (Atkins, 12), he makes up for it by the implicit and explicit criticism of selfish, materialistic, and spiteful behavior of his representative characters throughout his plots before their propitious resolutions. Furthermore, Priestley's ''style is direct, forceful—even heroic. . . . His intentions are clear, for to be understood is, for Priestley, to engage in the most rewarding skill of all—to live vitally in community'' (DeVitis and Kalson, 231).

However high or low one ranks his individual plays, Priestley must be given credit for his artistic integrity and service to the theater; as Nightingale said ''His achievement is to have kept the theatre alive and thinking at times when it was threatening to expire of frivolity, smugness, and commercialism'' (227). Despite the fact that in the past twenty years six book-length studies of J. B. Priestley have been published, there has been scant interpretation of individual plays or novels. ''Priestley is one of England's national treasures'' (DeVitis and Kalson, 230), but for thirty years he and most of his plays have been a buried treasure. Now, with the successful run of *An Inspector Calls* in London and New York, perhaps theater artists and audiences will rediscover Priestley and let his plays live again on the stage, thus in a way affirming Priestley's philosophy of time: What goes around comes around.

ARCHIVAL SOURCES

Manuscripts and letters are collected at the Harry Ransom Humanities Research Center at the University of Texas at Austin. See Lucetta Teagarden, *A Writer's Life: J. B. Priestley: An Exhibition of Manuscripts and Books* (Austin: Humanities Research Center, University of Texas at Austin, 1963). As noted earlier apparently a considerable collection of manuscripts and other material is in the possession of Priestley's surviving family.

PRIMARY BIBLIOGRAPHY

The following represents a small portion of J. B. Priestley's publications; see Day's bibliography for a complete listing.

Plays

The Plays of J. B. Priestley. 3 vols. London: Heinemann, 1948–50.

Novels

Angel Pavement. London: Heinemann, 1930.
Bright Day. London: Heinemann, 1946.

The Good Companions. London: Heinemann, 1929.
The Image Men. London: Heinemann, 1968.
Lost Empires. London: Heinemann, 1965.
The Magicians. London: Heinemann, 1954.
The Shapes of Sleep. London: Heinemann, 1962.

Autobiographies

Instead of the Trees: A Final Chapter of Autobiography. London: Heinemann, 1977.
Margin Released: A Writer's Reminiscences and Reflections. London: Heinemann, 1962.
Midnight on the Desert: A Chapter of Autobiography. London: Heinemann, 1937.
Rain upon Godshill: A Further Chapter of Autobiography. London: Heinemann, 1939.

Essays

Essays of Five Decades. Chosen and introduced by Susan Cooper. London: Heinemann, 1969.

SECONDARY BIBLIOGRAPHY

Agate, James. *First Nights.* New York: Benjamin Blom, 1971.
Atkins, John. *J. B. Priestley: The Last of the Sages.* London: Calder, 1981.
Atkinson, Brooks. Review of *The Linden Tree. New York Times* (8 Mar. 1949): 319.
Braine, John. *J. B. Priestley.* London: Weidenfeld & Nicolson, 1978.
Brome, Vincent. *J. B. Priestley.* London: Hamish Hamilton, 1988.
Brown, Ivor. *J. B. Priestley.* London: Longmans for the British Council, 1957; rev. ed., 1964.
Cooper, Susan. *J. B. Priestley: Portrait of an Author.* London: Heinemann, 1970.
DeVitis, A. A., and Albert E. Kalson. *J. B. Priestley.* Boston: Twayne, 1980.
Dietrich, Richard F. "1930–1950: Waiting for Beckett." In *British Drama, 1890 to 1950: A Critical History.* Boston: Twayne, 1989.
Evans, Gareth Lloyd. *J. B. Priestley—The Dramatist.* London: Heinemann, 1964.
Fleming, Peter. Review of *When We Are Married. Spectator* 161 (21 Oct. 1938): 651.
Haun, Harry. "A Visionary Inspector." *Playbill* 12.10 (31 July 1994): 10–12.
Hobson, Harold. *Theatre in Britain: A Personal View.* Oxford: Phaidon, 1984.
Hughes, David John. *J. B. Priestley: An Informal Study.* London: Hart-Davis, 1958.
Innes, Christopher. "J. B. Priestley (1894–1984): Temporal Dislocation and Transcendence." In *Modern British Drama, 1890–1990,* 367–78. Cambridge: Cambridge Universal Press, 1992.
Review of *Johnson over Jordan. The Times* (23 Feb. 1939): 12.
Klein, Holger. *J. B. Priestley's Plays.* Basingstoke: Macmillan, 1988.
Lob, Ladislaus. *Mensch und Gesellschaft bei J. B. Priestley.* Bern: Francke, 1962.
Lumley, Frederick. *Trends in 20th Century Drama: A Survey since Ibsen and Shaw.* London: Rockliff, 1956.
Nightingale, Benedict. "J. B. Priestley." In *A Reader's Guide to Fifty Modern British Plays.* London: Heinemann, 1982.
Pogson, Rex. *J. B. Priestley and the Theatre.* Clevedon, Somerset: Triangle Press, 1947.

Rogers, Ivor A. "The Time Plays of J. B. Priestley." *Extrapolation* 10 (Dec. 1968): 9–16.

Skloot, Robert. "The Time Plays of J. B. Priestley." *Quarterly Journal of Speech* (Dec. 1970): 426–31.

Smith, Grover, Jr. "Time Alive: J. W. Dunne and J. B. Priestley." *South Atlantic Quarterly* (Apr. 1957): 224–33.

Review of *Summer Day's Dream. The Times* (9 Sept. 1949): 2.

Trewin, J. C. "Bradford Enchanted." In *Dramatists of Today.* London: Staples Press, 1953.

Verschoyle, Derek. [1]. Review of *I Have Been Here Before. Spectator* 159 (1 Oct. 1937): 529.

———. [2]. Review of *Johnson over Jordan. Spectator* 162 (3 Mar. 1939): 349.

Williamson, Audrey. *Theatre of Two Decades.* London: Rockliff, 1951.

Young, Kenneth. *J. B. Priestley.* London: Longmans for the British Council, 1977.

BIBLIOGRAPHY

Day, Alan Edwin. *J. B. Priestley: An Annotated Bibliography.* New York and London: Garland Publishing, 1980.

Terence Rattigan
(1911–1977)

ROBERT F. GROSS

Terence Rattigan was an extremely popular playwright who drew on the English well-made-play tradition to fashion works in a range of genres, from romantic comedy to historical drama. He is most highly respected, however, for the psychological dramas that he wrote in the late 1940s and early 1950s: *The Browning Version* (1948), *The Deep Blue Sea* (1952), and *Separate Tables* (1954). In these plays Rattigan's strong theatrical instincts and understated dialogue seem particularly well suited to depictions of middle-class men and women who suffer as they try to balance their need for self-respect with the demands of their passions.

Rattigan was born on 10 June 1911 to Vera Houston Rattigan and Frank Rattigan, a British diplomat. It was assumed that young Terence would follow in his father's footsteps professionally, and his courses of study at Harrow and Trinity College were interspersed with summers spent studying foreign languages in France and Germany, providing experiences that would take dramatic form in his early plays, *Black Forest* (1935) and *French without Tears* (1936). His interest in the theater, however, soon took precedence over his family's plans for him. With an Oxford roommate, Philip Heimann, he wrote a comedy of college life, *First Episode* (1933), which received some encouraging reviews and a run of 80 performances on the West End. This was enough to determine Rattigan's course in life. His father graciously offered to support the young playwright for two years, with the understanding that he would return to a career in diplomacy or banking if the experiment was unsuccessful. In the second year Rattigan established himself in the West End with the tremendously successful romantic comedy *French without Tears*.

The next few years showed Rattigan trying unsuccessfully to follow up on his first success. *After the Dance,* a drama showing the demise of Noël Coward's

340 Robert F. Gross

"Bright Young Things" as they succumb to age, inertia, and alcohol, brought Rattigan some favorable notice in 1939, but failed to draw audiences. *Follow My Leader* (1938), a political farce, fell afoul of the censors, who delayed production for two years, by which time it already seemed passé. *Grey Farm,* an adaptation of a novel by Hector Bolitho, written in collaboration with the author, finally found its way to Broadway in 1940, where it met with universal condemnation from the critics, who found it a ludicrously overwrought melodrama.

In 1942 Rattigan enjoyed his second West End success with *Flare Path,* a play that mixed comedy and pathos to tell the story of three RAF pilots and their wives. The play, which drew on Rattigan's own experiences in the RAF, appealed to the prevailing patriotic mood and ran for 679 performances. Rattigan followed this by *While the Sun Shines* (1943), an even more popular farce about wartime London, and *Love in Idleness* (1944), a vehicle for the talents of Alfred Lunt and Lynn Fontanne. In 1944 all three of these plays were running on the West End, and Rattigan was being hailed as the preeminent commercial dramatist of his generation. He also found himself much in demand as a screenwriter.

With the appearance of *The Winslow Boy* in 1946, Rattigan began to be recognized by both critics and audiences as a more substantial and insightful playwright than they had hitherto suspected. This recognition increased with *The Browning Version* (1948) and *Adventure Story* (1949), a highly ambitious attempt to dramatize the life of Alexander the Great. The more troubled and psychologically probing plays of the 1950s were influenced, in part, by the suicide of Kenneth Morgan, an ex-lover of Rattigan's, who had fallen in love with a bisexual man. When the relationship deteriorated in 1949, Morgan committed suicide. The circumstances of Morgan's death not only provided the impetus for *The Deep Blue Sea* (which in its initial form was a play about a gay man) but led to an intensified awareness of the destructive potential of passion in much of Rattigan's later work. Morgan's name appears in a number of places in the plays of this period, as in Mary Morgan, the heroine of *The Sleeping Prince* (1953). The plays from *The Winslow Boy* through *Separate Tables* (1954), while not all successful, established Rattigan's reputation as a superb craftsman and insightful observer of human passions.

An abrupt shift in the London theater, however, quickly began to affect Rattigan's fortunes. The opening of the Royal Court Theatre and the introduction of a new, more bluntly honest generation of playwrights suddenly made Rattigan's work look old-fashioned. His reputation was not helped by his critical pronouncements, which seemed to attack experimentation and intellectual sophistication in the theater, and to defend a realistic drama of character. Although his drama about T. E. Lawrence, *Ross* (1960), enjoyed great popularity on the West End, despite mixed reviews, *Variation on a Theme* (1958), *Joie de Vivre* (1960), and *Man and Boy* (1963) met with fierce attacks from the critics and indifference from the public. Thoroughly discouraged with these responses, he turned to screenwriting for the next seven years, returning to the theater with *A Bequest to the Nation* (1970), a historical drama about Lord Nelson. Response to the play as a whole was tepid, despite general admiration for its flamboyant and highly theatrical presentation of Emma Hamilton. Neither *In Praise of Love* (1973), a pair of one-acts, nor his final drama, *Cause Célèbre* (1977), enjoyed the reception accorded to the best of his earlier work. Terence Rattigan died 30 September 1977 after a two-year struggle with cancer of the bone marrow.

Selected Biographical Sources: Darlow and Hodson; Ruskino; Young.

MAJOR PLAYS, PREMIERES, AND SIGNIFICANT REVIVALS: THEATRICAL RECEPTION

French without Tears. 1936. Opened 6 November at the Criterion Theatre (London) for 1,030 performances. Directed by Harold French. Revivals: Henry Miller's Theatre (New York), 28 September 1937; Young Vic Company (London), August 1973.

Despite negative notices from the weekly reviewers, led by a scathing attack from Agate ("This is not a play. It is not anything. It is nothing."), this comedy of adolescent affection in a French crammer's school proved to be a great popular success. Later critics, such as Darlow and Hodson (86), have praised it for its balance of sprightly comedy and poignancy. Hobson [1] went so far as to compare its mixture of gaiety and impending darkness with *Love's Labour's Lost.*

Love in Idleness. 1944. Opened 19 September at the Lyric Theatre (London) for 213 performances. Directed by Alfred Lunt. Transferred (under the title *O Mistress Mine*) to the Empire Theatre (New York), 23 January 1946. Directed by Alfred Lunt.

This comedy, which tells the story of a young radical who comes to London to discover that his widowed mother has taken up residence with a wealthy government minister, garnered great praise for Alfred Lunt and Lynn Fontanne and poor notices for Rattigan, who was accused of writing a thin and superficial play (Atkinson [2]). Later critics, however, have seen it as an important step forward in Rattigan's development. Young (60) noted that this is the first play of Rattigan's in which mature people are taken seriously. Taylor (150) found the play more emotionally genuine and probing than Rattigan's earlier work.

The Winslow Boy. 1946. Opened 23 May at the Lyric Theatre (London) for 476 performances. Directed by Glyn Byam Shaw. Revivals: Empire Theatre (New York), 29 October 1947; Roundabout Theatre (New York), October 1980.

Described by Ruskino (61) as Rattigan's "first solid achievement," this fictionalized version of the 1908 Archer Shee case was the first of Rattigan's plays to gain serious critical attention. The reviewers for *The Times* ("Lyric Theatre: *The Winslow Boy* by Terrence Rattigan") and *New Statesman and Nation* ("At the Theatre") both found the first act dazzling and the second act, with its romantic subplot, a letdown. Other critics, such as Worsley [2] and Taylor (151), have found the well-made pyrotechnics of the first act somewhat empty. Carlin has suggested that the most interesting ambiguity in the play is that the audience never really knows whether Ronnie Winslow is guilty or not.

Playbill. (consisting of the one-acts *The Browning Version* and *Harlequinade*). 1948. Opened 8 September at the Phoenix Theatre (London) for 245 performances. Directed by Peter Glenville. Revivals: Coronet Theatre (New York), 12 October 1949.

Harlequinade, a farcical one-act about a troupe of actors rehearsing *Romeo and Juliet,* looks back to the techniques of Rattigan's early comedies. *The Browning Version,* however, was the first psychologically probing drama of his maturity. Critics have agreed that this study of an emotionally starved pedant is a milestone in Rattigan's development. Trewin (187) and Ruskino (67–68) both called attention to the play's compact and unified structure. Foulkes (379) saw the play as establishing the triangle to be found repeatedly in Rattigan's later work, with a woman caught between two men, one older, one younger, and argued that Millie is the first of Rattigan's "nymphomaniacs," a type that includes (according to Foulkes) Hester Collyer and Alma Rattenbury.

The Deep Blue Sea. 1952. Opened 6 March at the Duchess Theatre (London) for 513 performances. Directed by Frith Banbury. Revivals: Morosco Theatre (New York), 5 November 1952; Théâtre Graumont (Paris), December 1953; Guilford, 1971; Cambridge Arts Theatre, 1977; Greenwich Theatre (London), October 1981; Theatre Royal, Haymarket (London), May 1988.

This play has been highly praised for its portrait of Hester Collyer, a solicitor's wife who is desperately attracted to Freddie Page, an ex–RAF pilot, and is tempted to commit suicide as their relationship disintegrates. Ruskino (82) has described Hester as "a modern existentialist heroine," and Hill ([2], 41) has proclaimed her a forerunner of the women's movement. Worsley [1] has argued that Hester is less a character than a personification of obsession. The combination of psychological insight and fine craftsmanship has made it one of Rattigan's most enduring plays, as Billington and Self's reviews of revivals attest. Tynan ([2], 19) argued that Rattigan betrayed a brilliant play by giving the audience every reason to believe that Hester should commit suicide, and then showing her surviving. Carlin overingeniously pointed to the play's German doctor and Hester's gas heater as evidence that the play is really about the Holocaust.

Separate Tables. 1954. Opened 22 December at St. James's Theatre (London) for 726 performances. Directed by Peter Glenville. Revival: Music Box Theatre (New York), 25 October 1956.

This set of closely related one-acts, set in a residential hotel, has remained one of Rattigan's most famous works, having been well received in revivals and film and television adaptations. Ruskino (93) considered it his best drama. The first play, dealing with the reunion of an aristocratic fashion model and the alcoholic husband who had almost beaten her to death, was considered the weaker of the two, though Ruskino (93) has seen it as a psychological study equal to Strindberg's *The Dance of Death* and *Miss Julie.* Barker and Tynan ([2], 80) both observed that the play relies less on the observation of life than on the canny use of theatrical types. Gross has interpreted the play as an expression of British fears and aspirations in the postwar era.

Variation on a Theme. 1958. Opened 8 May at the Globe Theatre (London) for 132 performances. Directed by John Gielgud.

This reworking of *La Dame aux camélias,* showing an ailing adventuress's infatuation for an emotionally unstable ballet dancer, elicited some of the most venomous reviews in Rattigan's career. Both Hobson [2] and Tynan [1] accused the play of poorly disguising a gay relationship as a heterosexual one. Taylor (156) repeated this criticism, but saw the play's central problem as one of tone: it both wants to spoof Dumas's notion of romantic love and embrace it. Worsley [2, 3] has been virtually alone in defending it, finding it Rattigan's harshest and most uncompromising play and faulting director John Gielgud for failing to give the play the bite it demands.

Ross. 1960. Opened 12 May at the Theatre Royal, Haymarket (London), for 762 performances. Directed by Glyn Byam Shaw. Revival: Eugene O'Neill Theatre (New York), 26 December 1961.

Although this dramatic biography of T. E. Lawrence was one of the most popular of Rattigan's postwar plays, critical response to it was cool. Brustein (23) argued that it did nothing to illuminate Lawrence's genius and became sidetracked in the "totally irrelevant" issue of his sexuality. Pryce-Jones found the play insufficiently dramatic, and Panter-Downes considered its episodic structure too much like that of an old movie. For Hobson [3], the play's comic moments were effective, while the passages of high drama were hurt by Rattigan's understated prose. Carlin, despite his reservations about the writing, argued that it was worth examining for Rattigan's use of Lenin as his protagonist's alter ego.

Man and Boy. 1963. Opened 4 September at the Queen's Theatre (London) for 69 performances. Directed by Michael Benthall. Transferred on 12 November 1963 to the Brooks Atkinson Theatre (New York).

In a plot suggested by the downfall of confidence man Ivar Krueger, Rattigan explored the twisted relationship between an extravagant, amoral father and the son who both rejects him and hungers for his love. Leonard and Young both faulted the play for improbabilities and weak construction. Taubman focused on what he considered the main structural weakness, the son's inarticulateness in his final confrontation with his father. Bryden argued that Rattigan was too inhibited to deal satisfactorily with the passions that attracted him to the story in the first place. Taylor (158), on the other hand, praised this as one of Rattigan's best plays. Here, he argued, Rattigan moved beyond the certainties of the well-made structure to a mysterious web of implications. Favorable reactions by

Campbell and Curtis to a 1971 Anglia Television production of the play suggest that many of the negative responses to the original production were due to flaws in casting and direction.

ADDITIONAL PLAYS, ADAPTATIONS, AND PRODUCTIONS

Four of Rattigan's early, unpublished plays were collaborations. The earliest, *First Episode* (1933), written with Philip Heimann, was also the first to be produced. Darlow and Hodson found it particularly interesting for its treatment of male homosexuality. *Grey Farm* (1934), an adaptation of the novel of the same name by Hector Bolitho, written with the novelist, was a brooding piece about a murderous psychopath and his son, which failed to find favor with either audiences or critics during its brief New York run in 1940. *A Tale of Two Cities* (1934), adapted from Charles Dickens's novel with John Gielgud, was shelved until a BBC radio production in 1950. *Follow My Leader,* a satirical farce about the Third Reich, written by Anthony Maurice, ran afoul of the Lord Chamberlain's Office in 1938 and had to wait until 1940 for its premiere, by which time it already seemed out of date.

Rattigan's sole unpublished later stage play was also a collaboration. *Joie de Vivre,* an attempt to both update *French without Tears* and transform it into a musical comedy (with lyrics by Paul Dehn and music by Robert Stolz), was the greatest public fiasco of Rattigan's career, running for only 4 performances on the West End in 1960 and receiving uniformly negative notices.

Of Rattigan's solo efforts, only one remains unpublished and unperformed. *Black Forest* (1935), a play about English tourists vacationing in a German hotel, which Rattigan later described as ''a turgid drama about tangled emotions,'' has been treated at greatest length by Young, who concurred with the playwright's judgment, finding it superficial and stereotyped. He noted, however, that its open-ended structure looks forward to Rattigan's mature work.

After the Dance (1939), which shows Noël Coward's generation clashing with the more earnest and ruthless youth of Rattigan's contemporaries, ran for 60 performances on the West End. Ruskino praised the play as an underrated character study in the style of Chekhov, but anonymous reviewers in *The Times* (''St. James's Theatre: *After the Dance* by Terence Rattigan'') and *New Statesman and Nation* (''*After the Dance* at the Criterion'') found it awkwardly plotted and embarrassingly derivative of Sardou and Ibsen. *Flare Path* (1942), whose story of romance and peril among RAF pilots was best described by Trewin as ''well-made and uncompromisingly sentimental,'' but a play whose eccentric yet egalitarian society foreshadows the rooming house of *Separate Tables.*

While the Sun Shines (1943), a comedy of wartime London, best described by Nichols as an amalgam of Noël Coward and P. G. Wodehouse, enjoyed a long run on the West End, but failed to please Broadway audiences. *Who Is Sylvia?* (1950), which shows a diplomat spending his entire adulthood pursuing women who resemble someone he kissed when he was seventeen (all of whom are played by the same actress), met with little praise from reviewers, who found its premise thin, though Taylor praised it for its charm and deft touches. Rattigan's Ruritanian comedy, *The Sleeping Prince* (1953), pleased audiences as a vehicle for Laurence Olivier and Vivien Leigh in London, but was received far more coolly when presented on Broadway with Michael Redgrave and Barbara Bel Geddes. It is best known through Rattigan's own cinematic adaptation, *The Prince and the Showgirl.*

Other than *Ross,* none of Rattigan's forays into historical drama were enthusiastically received. His favorite play, *Adventure Story* (1949), based on the life of Alexander the Great, was widely faulted for a weak second act and dialogue too small for its heroic subject matter. *A Bequest to the Nation* (1970), adapted from his television play, *Nelson—A Portrait in Miniature* (1966), presents Emma Hamilton as a slatternly wench who brings Lord Nelson an intense combination of social humiliation and sexual fulfillment. Another slave to passion, Alma Rattenbury, is the heroine of *Cause Célèbre* (1977), a treatment of a notorious British murder trial of the 1930s, which was first produced as a radio play.

Rattigan's remaining one-acts differ widely in style, content, and quality. *High Summer,* a one-act play that places domestic intrigue over the sale of the familial estate against a weekend of cricket matches, was originally meant to be part of *Playbill* and resurfaced in 1972 as a television play for the BBC. *All on Her Own* (1968), in which a widow struggles with her belief that she may have been responsible for her husband's death, is a haunting sketch. *In Praise of Love* (1973), like *Playbill,* is made up of two one-acts: *Before Dawn,* a coarse burlesque of *Tosca,* and *After Lydia,* a poignant drama in which a husband and wife indulge in an elaborate charade as they both pretend that the wife is not fatally ill. *After Lydia* was expanded into a full-length play for its 1974 premiere in New York and was performed under the title *In Praise of Love.* Darlow and Hodson argued (298) that *After Lydia* is one of the best plays from the second half of Rattigan's career.

ASSESSMENT OF RATTIGAN'S CAREER

Rattigan clearly articulated his theatrical aesthetic in the prefaces to his *Collected Plays,* a handful of essays, and a number of interviews given throughout his career. He explained that his early models were Shaw, Galsworthy, and Chekhov. He later repudiated much of Shaw's writing, arguing that the development of the play of ideas had had a deleterious effect on modern drama. The basis of all great drama, Rattigan insisted, was character, not theme. He believed that character was best conveyed through a realistic, colloquial style of dialogue, and that the most moving moments in drama were the result of simple, understated language, whether that of Lear lamenting the death of Cordelia, or Osvald's "Mother, give me the sun" at the end of *Ghosts.* Above all, he argued that a playwright could not write for posterity, but must write to move and please his contemporary audience. In short, he situated himself in the English realist tradition of bourgeois, commercial drama—Tom Robertson, Henry Arthur Jones, and Somerset Maugham. Theoretically, he opposed many of the trends that distinguished postwar European drama: the revival of poetic drama, led by Christopher Fry and T. S. Eliot, Brechtian drama, the theater of the absurd, and the more aggressive and loosely crafted realism of the Royal Court playwrights. He became notorious for his personification of the British theater-going public in the figure of Aunt Edna, a middle-class matron, who, Rattigan argued, had an infallible instinct for theater. While some saw this as an apology for a reactionary theater, Rattigan argued that this was not so: Aunt Edna's tastes were continually modified by her experiences. In one late essay he imagined her attending *Waiting for Godot* and even enjoying some of it. Although Rattigan was often pictured as an archconservative, his tastes were no more predictable than Aunt Edna's: he praised the plays of Harold Pinter and invested money in Joe Orton's *Entertaining Mr. Sloane.* Overall, however, his aesthetic was commercial and conservative, and an overwhelmingly negative response to that conservatism has dominated critical response to him from the mid-1950s to the present day.

From the premiere of *French without Tears* through *The Winslow Boy,* Rattigan was more popular with his audiences than with the critics, who took exception to the contrived happy ending of *Flare Path,* the superficial treatment of ideology in *Love in Idleness,* and the facile introduction of a love plot into *The Winslow Boy.* He was seen as an adroit entertainer, whose desire to please often undermined the integrity of his work. *The Browning Version* won admiration, not only for its tight structure and powerful use of understatement, but because the protagonist, Andrew Crocker-Harris, possessed a depth not seen in a previous Rattigan character. His portrait of Alexander the Great in *Adventure Story* was not well received, but continued to win respect for Rattigan as a playwright who was not content with merely pleasing. In 1953 Trewin reflected the opinion of many critics when he concluded that the author was an accomplished and versatile playwright who was "steadily widening his range" (123). The portraits of Hester Collyer in *The Deep Blue Sea* and Major Pollock in *Separate Tables* were taken as further proof of Rattigan's maturity. At the same time, some critics began to point out the limitations of even Rattigan's strongest efforts. Clurman argued that Rattigan's well-made style sacrificed ambiguity and richness of characterization in favor of clarity. Tynan ([2], 80) pointed out that Rattigan was always careful not to run the risk of alienating his middle-class audience's sensibilities.

The rise of the Royal Court, however, suddenly made Rattigan seem not only old-fashioned, but a prime example of everything that critics found reprehensible in the West End theater. Even when Rattigan tried to take advantage of the greater opportunity for openness, especially in the treatment of sexual themes, he was attacked for being old-fashioned and evasive. Suddenly, it seemed to be open season on Rattigan. The ferocity of these attacks is best seen in a 1963 two-part article in the *New Statesman and Nation.* Entitled "Terence and His Tycoons," it began with Bryden describing Rattigan as an emotionally be-numbed playwright who was not capable of dealing with the emotional material he chose. It then was followed by Brophy's denunciation of his screenplay for *The VIPs* as a manipulative work, "licking the boots of money and rank" (369). It is not surprising that such attacks drove Rattigan from the theater for almost a decade.

In a perceptive article Worsley [2] tried to account for the discrepancy be-tween Rattigan's modest, but real merits and the attacks he provoked. He con-cluded that Rattigan was being attacked as a member of a previous generation of playwrights, and as a representative of a privileged class. His subject matter, penchant for understatement, theatricality, and highly finished style were all construed as marks of an outmoded theatrical establishment. To the present day, much of the critical neglect of Rattigan in England is based on the objections first raised in the late 1950s.

In the United States Rattigan never enjoyed the esteem and success he knew in England. Some of this was due to unfortunate casting choices on Broadway: Margaret Sullavan in *The Deep Blue Sea* rather than Peggy Ashcroft; Barbara Bel Geddes instead of Vivien Leigh in *The Sleeping Prince;* Maurice Evans instead of Eric Portman in *Playbill;* and so on. In an article entitled "Sea-Change Problem" Rattigan himself theorized that realistic plays of character like his functioned on a recognition of national behaviors known in common by playwright, actors, and audiences. Outside of the society they depicted, he ex-plained, the plays often seemed stereotyped or overly exotic. Krutch's conclu-sion that a spectator's response to *The Winslow Boy* depends entirely on the extent to which one is able to enjoy "the current English preference for under-statement" can easily be extended to Rattigan's other work as well and suggests that it is as much the style as the content of Rattigan's plays that have limited their acceptance.

Critics have suggested different reasons for Rattigan's understated style. Bry-den argued that Rattigan was incapable of dealing with deep emotion. Darlow and Hodson, more generously, saw him as a shy man in a repressive society, who came to use implication to mediate between strong feeling and social in-teraction. Certainly, the problem how to express emotion without sacrificing social decorum is not only a stylistic problem for the playwright, but for his characters as well. The protagonists in *After Lydia, Ross,* and *The Browning Version* all suffer from their inability to express emotion directly. The denoue-ment of *Separate Tables* can be seen as a celebration of understatement, in which the happy ending is brought about by the fact that none of the people in the dining room choose to confront the Major. In this case, it is precisely the feared confrontation that does not occur that gives the final scene its theatrical power. By and large, even Rattigan's roles for stars such as Margaret Leighton, Glynis Johns, and Eric Portman are remarkably self-effacing roles. They ask the actors to move the audience through their ability to suggest strong emotion indirectly.

Only Emma Hamilton in *A Bequest to the Nation* impresses the audience through her emotional extravagance. Tynan ([2], 19) argued that Rattigan chose to write about essentially undramatic people. Although Tynan meant this as a negative criticism, it points toward one of Rattigan's great strengths: he is able to focus the audience's attention on characters who, in other hands, would be considered too genteel and repressed to hold the stage.

There have been attempts to ground Rattigan's style in his homosexuality. For Young, Rattigan's sexual preference was only another proof of his immaturity, which kept him from ever becoming a truly important dramatist, despite his strong theatrical instincts. Darlow and Hodson, with greater insight and less prejudice, saw the homophobia of the period, partly internalized by Rattigan himself, making it difficult for Rattigan to express certain feelings, especially those related to sexuality, in a straightforward manner. For Curtis, neither Rattigan nor his plays actually conformed to the dictates of his society; he was closer to Joe Orton in his sensibility than to Sir Harold Nicholson.

In his mature work Rattigan repeatedly returned to the power of sexual attraction to dominate and humiliate. Indeed, Worsley [2] went so far as to state that humiliation was the major theme of Rattigan's late work. While Hester Collyer, Major Pollock, T. E. Lawrence, and Lord Nelson all suffer from social opprobrium for their desires, they are, more importantly, victims of their own inability to accept their sexual proclivities. *Who Is Sylvia?* treats erotic obsessiveness comically, but there is more than a touch of melancholy in Mark and Oscar's lifetime pursuit of youthful romance. *Man and Boy,* perhaps Rattigan's most daring play, maps this dynamic of obsession and humiliation onto a father-son relationship. As Foulkes has pointed out, it was only with *Cause Célèbre* that Rattigan resolved these deep-seated ambivalences toward passion.

Critics such as Hill [1, 2] and Ruskino have worked to rebuild Rattigan's reputation in the face of general critical neglect and occasional attacks. Hill, the only critic in the early 1980s to give protracted and serious consideration to the playwright, did so by adopting the aesthetic values articulated by Rattigan himself, defending his meticulous use of structure and traditional values. Ruskino took Rattigan's emphasis on characterization as a starting point and frequently compared him to Chekhov. This line of defense, however, is not without its problems. Chekhov's brilliant uses of non sequiturs, of characters so immersed in their thoughts that they fail to hear each other, and of unsentimental juxtapositions of pathos and laughter, are not found in Rattigan's plays. His characters usually respond directly to what has just been said, and his juxtaposition of pathos and comedy tends to release dramatic tension, rather than intensify it. Clurman's observation that Rattigan's dramatic technique eschews ambiguity is accurate and strengthens the argument that Rattigan was working in a tradition of realism far removed from Chekhov.

By far the greatest amount of work done on Rattigan has been devoted to evaluating the merits of individual plays. The most valuable recent scholarship, by Darlow and Hodson, has been biographical. Little has been done to relate

Rattigan's work to that of other playwrights, his society, his ideology, or his theatrical milieu. Rattigan scholarship has yet to move out of the controversies of the 1950s and 1960s to a more considered understanding of this meticulous and reserved playwright. ''A wilful and self-conscious neo-classicist'' (Taylor) who worked within the dominant forms of his day, he was still able to imbue them with a highly individual and deeply conflicted sensibility.

ARCHIVAL SOURCES

Terence Rattigan's manuscripts are with the Rattigan estate in London.

PRIMARY BIBLIOGRAPHY

Plays

Adventure Story. London: Hamish Hamilton, 1950.
After the Dance. London: Hamish Hamilton, 1939.
All on Her Own. In *Best Short Plays, 1970,* ed. Stanley Richards. Philadelphia: Chilton, 1970.
A Bequest to the Nation. London: Hamish Hamilton, 1970; Chicago: Dramatic Publishing, 1971.
Cause Célèbre. London: Hamish Hamilton, 1978.
The Deep Blue Sea. London: Hamish Hamilton, 1952; New York: Random House, 1952.
Flare Path. London: Hamish Hamilton, 1942.
French without Tears. London: Hamish Hamilton, 1937; New York: Farrar & Rinehart, 1938.
High Summer. In *Best Short Plays, 1973,* ed. Stanley Richards. Radnor: Chilton, 1973.
In Praise of Love (After Lydia and *Before Dawn).* London: Hamish Hamilton, 1973.
In Praise of Love: A Comedy. New York: Samuel French, 1975.
Love in Idleness. London: Hamish Hamilton, 1945.
Man and Boy. New York: French, 1963; London: Hamish Hamilton, 1964.
Playbill (The Browning Version and *Harlequinade).* London: Hamish Hamilton, 1949; New York: Samuel French, 1950.
Ross. London: Hamish Hamilton, 1960; New York: Random House, 1962.
Separate Tables. London: Hamish Hamilton, 1955; New York: Random House, 1955.
The Sleeping Prince. London: Hamish Hamilton, 1954; New York: Random House, 1954.
Variation on a Theme. London: Hamish Hamilton, 1958.
While the Sun Shines. London: Hamish Hamilton, 1944.
The Winslow Boy. London: Hamish Hamilton, 1946; New York: Dramatists Play Service, 1946.

Anthologies

The Collected Plays of Terence Rattigan. Volume 1 (*French without Tears, Flare Path, While the Sun Shines, Love in Idleness, The Winslow Boy*); Volume 2 (*Playbill,*

Adventure Story, Who Is Sylvia?, The Deep Blue Sea); Volume 3 (*The Sleeping Prince, Separate Tables, Variation on a Theme, Ross, Heart to Heart*); Volume 4 (*Man and Boy, A Bequest to the Nation, In Praise of Love, Cause Célèbre*). London: Hamish Hamilton, 1953–78.

The Deep Blue Sea with Three Other Plays: Harlequinade, Adventure Story, The Browning Version. London: Pan Books, 1955.

Plays. Volume 1 (*French without Tears, The Winslow Boy, The Browning Version, Harlequinade*); Volume 2 (*Separate Tables, The Deep Blue Sea, Before Dawn, After Lydia*). London: Eyre Methuen, 1981–84.

The Winslow Boy with Two Other Plays: French without Tears and Flare Path. London: Pan Books, 1950.

Essays and Articles on Drama and Theater

"An Appreciation of His Work in the Theatre." In *Theatrical Companion to Coward,* ed. Raymond Mander and Joe Mitchenson. London: Rockliff, 1957.

"Aunt Edna Waits for Godot." *New Statesman and Nation* (15 Oct. 1955): 468–70.

"Concerning the Play of Ideas." *New Statesman and Nation* (4 Mar. 1950): 241–42.

"Drama without Tears." *New York Times* (10 Oct. 1937): 11:3.

"The Play of Ideas." *New Statesman and Nation* (13 May 1950): 545–46.

"Sea-Change Problem." *New York Times* (4 Dec. 1949): 2:6.

SECONDARY BIBLIOGRAPHY

"*After the Dance* at the Criterion." *New Statesman and Nation* (1 July 1939): 13–14.

Agate, James. "The Dramatic World: *French without Tears.*" *The Sunday Times* (8 Nov. 1936): 6.

"At the Theatre." *New Statesman and Nation* (1 June 1946): 393.

Atkinson, Brooks. [1]. "At the Theatre." *New York Times* (4 April 1953): 8:6.

———. [2]. "Circus with the Lunts." *New York Times* (1 Sept. 1946): 2:1.

Barker, Ronald. "*Separate Tables.*" *Plays and Players* (Nov. 1954): 25.

Billington, Michael. "*The Deep Blue Sea,* Arnauld, Guilford." *The Times* (7 July 1971): 7.

Brophy, Brigid. "Terence and His Tycoons: Part Two." *New Statesman and the Nation* (20 Sept. 1963): 368–69.

Brustein, Robert. "Theater: A Little Night Music." *New Republic* (2 Feb. 1962): 23.

Bryden, Ronald. "Terence and His Tycoons: Part One." *New Statesman and the Nation* (20 Sept. 1963): 368.

Campbell, Patrick. "*Man and Boy:* Anglia June 6." *Stage and Television Today* (10 June 1971): 11.

Carlin, M. M. "Lenin, Hitler, and the House of Commons, in Three Plays by Terence Rattigan: A Case for the Author of *French without Tears.*" *University of Cape Town Studies in English* (Oct. 1982): 1–18.

Clurman, Harold. "Theatre." *Nation* (10 Nov. 1956): 416.

Curtis, Anthony. "Professional Man and Boy." *Plays and Players* (Feb. 1978): 21–23.

Darlow, Michael, and Gillian Hodson. *Terence Rattigan: The Man and His Work.* London; New York: Quartet Books, 1979.

Foulkes, Richard. "Terence Rattigan's Variations on a Theme." *Modern Drama* 22 (Dec. 1979): 375–81.

Gross, Robert F. " 'Coming Down in the World: Motifs of Benign Descent in Three Plays by Terence Rattigan." *Modern Drama* 33 (Sept. 1990): 394–408.

Hill, Holly. [1]. "A First-Rate Playwright's Return to Prominence." *Wall Street Journal* (21 May 1981).

———. [2]. "Rattigan's Renaissance." *Contemporary Review* 240 (Jan. 1982): 37–42.

Hobson, Harold. [1]. "Agony and Ecstasy." *The Sunday Times* (5 Aug. 1973).

———. [2]. "Are Things What They Seem?" *The Sunday Times* (11 May 1958): 13.

———. [3]. "Theatre: The Symbolic Enigma." *The Sunday Times* (15 May 1960).

Hope-Wallace, Philip. "*The Deep Blue Sea:* Terence Rattigan's Fine New Play." *Manchester Guardian* (7 March 1952).

Krutch, Joseph Wood. "Drama." *Nation* (15 Nov. 1947): 537.

Leonard, Hugh. "Separate Fables." *Plays and Players* (Nov. 1963): 40.

"Lyric Theatre: *The Winslow Boy* by Terence Rattigan." *The Times* (24 May 1946): 7.

Nichols, Lewis. "*While the Sun Shines.*" *New York Times* (20 Sept. 1944): 21.

Panter-Downes, Mollie. "Letter from London." *New Yorker* (9 July 1960): 59–60.

Pryce-Jones, Alan. "The Desert and the Despot." *Observer* (15 May 1960).

Ruskino, Susan. *Terence Rattigan.* Boston: Twayne, 1983.

Self, David. "*Cause Célèbre/The Deep Blue Sea.*" *Plays and Players* (Sept. 1977): 30–31.

"St. James's Theatre: *After the Dance* by Terence Rattigan." *The Times* (22 June 1939): 14.

Taubman, Harold. "Theatre." *New York Times* (1 Dec. 1963): 2:1.

Taylor, John Russell. *The Rise and Fall of the Well-made Play.* New York: Hill & Wang, 1967.

Trewin, J. C. *Dramatists of Today.* London: Staples Press, 1953.

Tynan, Kenneth. [1]. "At the Theatre: Musing out Loud." *The Observer* (11 May 1958): 15.

Tynan, Kenneth. [2]. *Curtains.* London: Longmans, 1961.

Worsley, T. C. [1]. "The Expense of Spirit." *New Statesman and the Nation* (15 Mar. 1952): 301–2.

———. [2]. "Rattigan and His Critics." *London Magazine* (Sept. 1964): 60–72.

———. [3]. "*Variation on a Theme.*" *New Statesman and the Nation* (17 May 1958): 633–34.

Young, B. A. *The Rattigan Version: Sir Terence Rattigan and the Theatre of Character.* New York: Atheneum, 1988.

Elizabeth Robins
(1862–1952)

KATHERINE E. KELLY

Until recently, Elizabeth Robins, an American citizen who lived her entire professional life in England, had been remembered as the definitive interpreter of Ibsen's major female roles on the modern British stage. But following a surge of interest in recovering the contributions of women to British theater, scholars have discovered Robins's accomplishments as a stage manager, playwright, and polemicist.

Born in Kentucky on 6 August 1862, Elizabeth was the oldest living child of her banker father, Charles, and her ailing mother, Hannah. Hannah's deteriorating mental health required that Elizabeth move to Zanesville, Ohio, at the age of ten, where she was raised by her paternal grandmother, Jane Hussey Robins. She excelled in school compositions, directed family theatricals, and was worshipping a stage idol, the American actress Mary Anderson, by the time she reached her late teens. Discouraged from acting by her strict grandmother and scientifically minded father, Elizabeth nevertheless persisted in her dream of becoming a highly skilled and well-paid actress, leaving for New York in 1881 at eighteen years of age. Within two years she had met James O'Neill, father of the American playwright, who helped her secure a series of varied small roles in the company he first traveled with and later owned. She eventually played the role of Mercedes with great success in O'Neill's long-running *Count of Monte Cristo*. Highly ambitious and anxious to earn sufficient money to buy her mother a comfortable home, Robins looked for improving prospects in the acting profession. Moving to Boston in 1883, she met an actor who would later become her husband, and within a few years she moved back to New York to join the prestigious acting company of Lawrence Barrett and Edwin Booth. Her husband, George Parks, wanted Robins to retire from the stage, in spite of her strong drive to succeed. Financially and emotionally stretched, Parks suffered from exhaustion, which culminated in suicide in June 1887. Robins never re-married, but went on to become the successful and well-paid actress she had dreamed of becoming in Ohio.

The 1880s and 1890s were Robins's years of fame as an actress, when she played several of Ibsen's female roles to wide acclaim. Critic Clement Scott, typically anti-Ibsen, wrote of Robins's 1891 performance as Hedda Gabler, "She has almost ennobled crime. She has made a heroine out of a sublimated sinner. She has fascinated us with a savage." During the 1890s Robins also played Ibsen's Mrs. Linden from *A Doll's House,* Hilda Wangel from *The Master Builder,* Rebecca West from *Rosmersholm,* Agnes from *Brand,* Rita and Asta from *Little Eyolf,* and Ella Rentheim from *John Gabriel Borkman.* Playing these roles was both an asset and a liability for an actress earning her living from the stage. Robins's personal and professional friendships with William Archer, her intimate friend for many years, and Henry James, her long-time confidant, helped establish her credibility as a serious and intelligent interpreter of the Norwegian playwright many dismissed as perverse.

In order to proceed with her performance of Ibsen's *Hedda Gabler,* Robins had to secure the rights to produce the play, which led her to experiment with stage managing. Her first venture in management was arranged with American actress Marion Lea, another ambitious American making her career in London. William Heinemann had already secured both acting and publishing rights, which required that the actresses apply to him for permission to produce the play. After collaboratively rewriting the translation with William Archer, Robins and Lea negotiated three years' worth of acting rights and rented the Vaudeville Theatre. Following a two-week rehearsal period, the performance ran for one week in April and one week in June of 1891 to rave reviews, especially among the London literati. Robins and Lea joined again in November of 1891, renting the Criterion Theatre to produce Clement Scott's adaptation of Dumas *fils*'s *Denise.* Their final collaboration occurred in May 1892, when they produced Alfhild Agrell's *Karin* in Florence Bell's translation. Robins and the Charringtons (Charles Charrington and his actress wife Janet Achurch) comanaged a week of performances of Ibsen's *A Doll's House* and *Hedda Gabler* in October of 1892. On one final occasion, in February and March of 1893, Robins joined with Herbert Waring to produce Ibsen's *The Master Builder.*

In an even more ambitious if short-lived attempt to bring literary drama before interested audiences, Robins cofounded the New Century Theatre with William Archer in 1897. The New Century, a small theater catering to an intellectual coterie, was intended to realize Archer's and Robins's dream of a permanently endowed artistic (rather than commercial) theater. Robins played only a single role at the New Century, devoting most of her energies to directing and reading plays submitted for production. But she soon discovered that this activity was interfering with a growing desire to write.

In between acting and planning New Century productions, Robins translated from the Norwegian, wrote fiction and essays for profit and art, and began to write plays. Her first play, *Alan's Wife* (1893), was cowritten with Florence Bell but was produced and published anonymously because of its controversial treatment of infanticide. Her second and last published play, *Votes for Women!* (1907), written, according to Robins, "under the pressure of a strong moral conviction," has recently become one of the best known of the genre of suffrage dramas written widely throughout the United States and Europe during the late nineteenth and early twentieth centuries. Robins published several of her early full-length fictional works—*George Mandeville's Husband* (1894); *The New Moon* (1895); the collection of stories, *Below the Salt* (1896); and *The Open Question: A Tale of Two Temperaments* (1898)—under the pseudonym C. E. Raimond. She concealed her identity for at least two reasons: first, she still viewed her primary profession as the theater, while writing was a lifelong habit that might—or might not—make her money and bring her artistic satisfaction. Second, she recognized the liability of female authorship, brought home to her by William Archer's well-intended compliment that her writing was "masculine." Retiring as an actress in 1902, at the age of forty, she shifted her professional allegiance from the stage to the page. Beginning with *The Magnetic North* (1904), Robins's novel based upon the Alaska diaries of her brother Raymond and his partner Albert Schulte, she published in her own name.

Robins's six-week stay in Nome with her brother gave her firsthand experience with the Alaskan gold rush that found its way into the novel, a popular success in the male adventure genre. Critics praised *The Magnetic North* for its lifelike treatment of masculine life, comparing the novel to work by Jack London, Bret Harte, and Mark Twain. Her next novel, *A Dark Lantern* (1905), a fictional exposé of the rest cure for women, also appeared under her own name, receiving critical reviews from feminists Mona Caird and W. L. Courtney and conventional moralists like W. T. Stead. Referring to the social Darwinism of the period, Edward Garnett praised the heroine's pursuit of the "best and strongest" mate (Thomas, 8).

Throughout her lifetime Robins turned to fiction more often than drama, the former being easier to publish for profit than the latter. Publishers and producers had well-formulated views on the capabilities of women playwrights, with William Archer giving Robins typical advice in the early 1900s: "I don't think you have the power of concentration required for playwriting. Certainly you could find a novel far easier than a play" (Gates [2], 139). For the most part, Robins ignored Archer's assessment, continuing to sketch ideas and write plays on her own and with her friend, Florence Bell. But she knew that fiction would earn her a living far more readily than drama, and so, in the end, she wrote and published more fiction and nonfiction than plays.

In the year 1906 Robins was asked by the Kensington Branch of the National Union of Women's Suffrage Societies to present her views on the suffrage question. In the process of describing her position, Robins defined herself as "pro" suffrage and agreed to present in a public debate how she had been "converted" to support for the suffrage cause (John [1], 142–43). Beginning with her controversial play, *Votes for Women!* (1906–7) and its adaptation to novel form, entitled *The Convert* (1907), and continuing to the end of her life, Robins's fiction and nonfiction focused increasingly on questions of gender and power. *Come and Find Me!* (1906–7), the companion volume to the highly successful *The Magnetic North,* revised the adventure quest as the story of women's friendship, while *Where Are You Going To?* (1913), serialized in shorter form in the United States as *My Little Sister* (1912–13), gave a fictional account of white slavery, the abduction of young (in this case, middle-class) Caucasian women to houses of prostitution. Like *Votes for Women!* and *The Convert,* this novel blended documentary, fiction, and polemic in a provocative mix of conventions that aroused strong and mixed reactions.

Robins's nonfiction records the major centers of interest in her professional life—the women's movement and the stage. *Way Stations* (1913), a widely read and reviewed collection of many of her suffrage speeches with a commentary, chronicles her ''conversion'' to the suffrage movement, including her endorsement of suffragettes' militant tactics, and articulates British feminism viewed through the lens of the suffrage agitation. Robins published the most aggressive of her polemics, *Ancilla's Share: An Indictment of Sex Antagonism* (1924), anonymously, in part because she drew on personal friends and circumstances for her materials. Both a general and specific indictment of pervasive misogyny, *Ancilla's Share*'s polemic celebrates the peacemaking powers of women. Attacked by sexual-freedom advocate H. G. Wells as ''anti-sex'' and dismissed by younger artists as ''pre-war'' in style, the book undersold most of Robins's others. Robins's primary nonfiction works described the theater—*Ibsen and the Actress,* published by the Hogarth Press in 1928, *Theatre and Friendship: Some Henry James Letters* (1932), and the largely autobiographical *Both Sides of the Curtain* (1940). The works on Ibsen and the letters from Henry James did not sell well at the time, but have since attracted the interest of theater and cultural historians as valued records of theatrical practices.

By 1918 Robins was directing more of her fiction toward the popular U.S. magazine market, with its promise of steady fees from serialization. *Camilla* (1918) explores a young American woman's attitudes toward marriage and divorce, while the sensationalist spy novel *The Messenger* (1919) treats German espionage and the official censorship of British and American pacifists. Neither of these were positively reviewed. Her best postwar novel, *Time Is Whispering* (1923), tells the story of an apparently mismatched man and woman whose friendship develops against the backdrop of the peaceful cultivation of the English countryside. While experimenting with chronology in a minor way, the novel exhibits the wide gap separating Robins's prewar ''leisurely'' narrative style from that of the increasingly preferred modernists, like Virginia Woolf, whose experiments with narrative conformed more closely to avant-garde painting and music. Elizabeth Robins died in 1952 in Henfield, Sussex, leaving behind Backsettown Farms, a retreat and shelter for professional women established by Robins and Octavia Wilberforce in 1927 that continued operating into the late 1980s.

Selected Biographical Sources: Gates [2]; John [1].

MAJOR PLAYS, PREMIERES, AND SIGNIFICANT
REVIVALS: THEATRICAL RECEPTION

Alan's Wife. 1893. Cowritten with Florence Bell. Matinées performed 28 April and 2 May at Terry's Theatre (London). Produced by Herman de Lange, Independent Theatre Society.

This stage adaptation of Swedish author Elin Ameen's story "Befraid" tells the story of a young married woman's loss of her husband and subsequent decision to murder her sickly infant. In its controversial treatment of infanticide, "new womanhood," and gender, the play jumped directly into the new drama's controversial treatments of Darwinism, including mercy killing and the role of motherhood in race survival. Running only two performances at J. T. Grein's Independent Theatre, home of noncommercial and self-consciously artistic drama, *Alan's Wife* was at the time compared by Grein himself to Ibsen's *Ghosts.* Grein praised "this psychological and physical study of a woman's character" for its power, sadness, and simplicity. However, most critics, like the writer for *Era* (Review of *Alan's Wife*), were hostile, decrying the play's heroine as "a monster with whom we can feel no sympathy whatsoever. . . . She is simply an ignorant, cruel and presumptuous person." Some, however, supported the play, with Archer writing an overbearing forty-three-page introduction to the original published script defending it against its attackers as a contribution to the new realism. In defense of the plot's originality, Archer appended a letter from Thomas Hardy showing that *Tess of the d'Urbervilles* and the original Ameen story were written independently. Grein wrote an appreciative appendix to the published edition. The play's reception was dominated by moral outrage at the character and action of Jean, whose status as a tragic heroine was sharply disputed.

Votes for Women! 1907. Opened 9 April at the Court Theatre (London) for 21 performances. Produced by John Vedrenne and Harley Granville-Barker. Directed by Harley Granville-Barker. The American premiere was staged in Wallack's Theatre (New York) 15 March 1909 for 6 performances. Produced by Actors' Alliance of America. According to Stowell [2], the Royal Academy of Dramatic Art (London) staged a revival in 1987, and excerpts from *Votes for Women!* formed part of a program of suffrage drama performed in the (London) Theatre Museum's "Rough Magic" series in 1990 (8 n. 3).

Written and staged under the mounting pressure of the woman suffrage movement in England and the United States, *Votes for Women!* was the first full-length play to blend suffrage propaganda with the conventions of Edwardian drama. Responses to the play reflected its unusual blend of topicality and dramatic convention, with reviewers praising individual elements of the production but faulting its political nature. While the critic writing for the "anti" paper, *Era* (Review of *Votes for Women!*), complained that "Miss Robins has taken care to give the women all the best parts in the piece," the "pro" paper, *Votes for Women,* found Robins to be evenhanded in the play's conclusion: "In the last scene between Vida Levering and Geoffrey Stonor, . . . the point of view of both is put with almost poignant clearness" (582). The critic for *The Times* (Review of *Votes for Women!*) doubted the wisdom of Robins widening the play's treatment of "the woman question" to include not only the vote but also the sexual double standard (the widespread expectation that men are "naturally" promiscuous and women "naturally" chaste), seduction, abortion, and infanticide. Weaving typical Edwardian conventions—the woman with a past; the education of the ingenue; the Ibsenite discussion scene—together with a subject electrified by dozens of contemporary allusions, *Votes for Women!* drew large and enthusiastic London audiences. It did not fare as well in the provinces, where scenes of suffrage protest and the rhetoric of suffrage agitation were heard less often and less intensely. The play, widely considered to be the most influential piece of literary propaganda to come out of the suffrage movement, has drawn considerable contemporary interest from historians and feminist scholars as an illustration of the feminist maxim "The personal is political" (Marcus [1]; Stowell [2]; Hirshfield; Wiley [2]).

ADDITIONAL PLAYS, ADAPTATIONS, AND PRODUCTIONS

Robins' first completed full-length play written on her own, *The Mirkwater* (1895), combined suspense and mystery with an exploration of the sexual double standard. Although marred by melodrama and implausible turns of plot, the play demonstrated her ability to write a major male part for an actor-manager type like George Alexander, to whom she offered it. *The Silver Lotus* (1895–96), also featuring a major role for an actor-manager, developed a recurring theme in Robins's work—the death of children. The historical melodrama *Benvenuto Cellini* (1899–1900), another actor-manager vehicle, was never produced, but it helped Robins establish her professional identity apart from the Ibsen movement, which was under attack at the end of the century.

ASSESSMENT OF ROBINS'S CAREER

The contribution of Elizabeth Robins to theatrical and literary culture during the rise of the new drama is undergoing thorough review. Traditional histories of key figures and forces in the new or modern drama in England tended to repeat the canonical pronouncements of a small number of influential critics such as Allardyce Nicoll and Ashley Dukes, who pointedly overlooked the contributions made by women playwrights and stage managers to theatrical and dramatic culture. With the recovery of Edwardian women playwrights and stage managers now under way (Fitzsimmons and Gardner; Stowell [2]), and with the recent publication of two biographies of Robins (Gates [2]; John [1]), together with an exhaustive Robins bibliography (Thomas), a critical mass of evidence for women's presence in the making of modern drama is inviting further research.

The history of Robins commentary parallels the history of feminist scholarship in the United States and England. With a couple of notable exceptions, the scant attention paid to Robins prior to 1980 focused squarely on her acquaintance with successful male writers and her centrality as a promoter and interpreter of Ibsen's female roles in the London-based high-drama coterie. Marcus's [2] 1973 dissertation on Robins, followed by Cima's [3] 1978 dissertation, together with the articles developed from their student writings, anticipated the later 1980s and 1990s investigations of Robins's life and work. From her role as conveyor of Ibsen and friend of Henry James, William Archer, Bernard Shaw, and Harley Granville-Barker, she was next celebrated as an English feminist, arguing in her fiction and nonfiction for women's rights and exploring what was called "sex antagonism" in her most "angry" writings (see Marcus [1]). This was the Robins of some fiction and essays, particularly the essays like "Women's Secret" collected in *Way Stations* (1913) and *Ancilla's Share* (1924). Feminists' interest in Robins's likeness to contemporary activist women quickly gave way in the later 1980s and 1990s to a historically inflected study of her rootedness in late Victorian, Edwardian, and Georgian culture (Holledge, Marcus [3]). As scholars replaced Robins in her historical period, they began discovering her work as a producer, stage manager, and playwright (Fitzsimmons and Gardner; Stowell [2]; Wiley [1, 2]), a subject addressed early on by Cima [4]. The resulting portrait of Elizabeth Robins has become increasingly complex, as the titles of both recent biographies, Gates's *Elizabeth Robins, 1862–1952: Actress, Novelist, Feminist* and John's *Elizabeth Robins: Staging a Life, 1862–1952,* imply.

Robins's contribution to distancing her "self" from curious historians and onlookers is meticulously recorded in both Gates's and John's studies. Robins kept secrets, edited and destroyed correspondence, and deliberately misled the public about herself and her career on various occasions. Both biographers have reflected current skepticism about the possibility of recovering a single, coherent "self," the modern biographer's unspoken promise made to the reader. In putting before the reader the entire range of Robins's productivity, with John emphasizing the pre-London and Gates the post-London years, these biographies will change the nature and direction of Robins scholarship. In John's narrative the truly "feminist" Robins did not emerge until after her years as an Ibsen interpreter and only reluctantly, after her involvement in the suffrage movement. The feminist Robins grew more prominent as the literary Robins faded in importance. Gates stressed the protofeminist tendencies of even the young Robins, finding in her school compositions evidence of a growing awareness of gender inequities. Both biographers revealed their subject's constant concern with deriving an income from her writing, a fact that does not always receive the attention it should by commentators, and both explored her personal relationships—most of them begun as literary or theatrical associations—carefully and responsibly, revealing Robins's prominence among London literati and connoisseurs of the new drama from the 1880s to the 1920s. The biographies open up new areas of inquiry: Do Robins's unpublished plays reveal a writer distinct from the composer of *Alan's Wife* and *Votes for Women!?* How do the works of fiction elucidate the published and unpublished plays (and vice versa)? How seriously did Robins take Darwinism? How did Robins respond to the changing discourse on motherhood during her lifetime? On women's health? How was Robins both praised and dismissed by the young ''modernists'' like Virginia Stephens (later Woolf)? Was Robins's awareness of social class a constant, unchanging preoccupation, or were her relationships with socially well-placed people a source of tension in her life and writing? Both biographers, together with Thomas's exhaustive bibliography, offer a wealth of evidence to be consulted in developing answers to these questions.

The complex Elizabeth Robins emerging in contemporary scholarship reminds us of the differences between contemporary and early twentieth-century feminism, of the unreliability of traditional histories of theater and drama, and of the fragility of a writer's accounts of herself. Rather than appearing as an endnote in future histories of modern British drama, Robins may now be given the attention due a major actress, a pioneer stage manager, a playwright, and a polemicist for women's rights.

ARCHIVAL SOURCES

Fales Library, New York University, holds the Elizabeth Robins Papers. This major archive is divided into the following categories: Diaries, 1873–1952; General Correspondence, 1873–1952; Robins Family Papers, 1803–1933; Raymond Robins and Margaret Dreier Robins, 1887–1951; Florence Bell, 1891–1930; Octavia Wilberforce, 1916–1963; Literary Productions; Theater Productions; Photographic Materials; Legal and Financial Records, 1885–1951; Scrapbooks, 1871–1904; Printed Material; and Artifacts and Ephemera.

The Harry Ransom Humanities Research Center, University of Texas at Austin, holds extensive correspondence between Robins and a wide array of literary and political figures. The New York Public Library, Henry W. and Albert A. Berg Collection of English and American Literature, holds folders of agreements, correspondence (including a large collection of letters from John Masefield and other literary figures to Robins), forms, and various statements from theatrical agencies related to Robins's work. Smaller deposits of letters and other materials exist in various university libraries (see Thomas for a detailed list).

PRIMARY BIBLIOGRAPHY

Plays

Alan's Wife: A Dramatic Study in Three Scenes: First Acted at the Independent Theatre in London. Coauthored with Florence Bell. With an introduction by William Archer. London: Henry & Co., 1893. Text reprinted in *New Woman Plays,* ed. Linda Fitzsimmons and Viv Gardner. London: Methuen, 1991.

Votes for Women! A Play in Three Acts. Chicago: Dramatic Publishing Co. (Sergel's Acting Drama, no. 627), 1907; London: Mills & Boon, 1909. Text reprinted in *How the Vote Was Won and Other Suffragette Plays,* ed. Dale Spender and Carole Hayman. London: Methuen, 1985.

Votes for Women! (using as a source text Robins's drama as submitted to the Court Theatre in 1907). Ed. Joanne E. Gates, in *Modern Drama by Women, 1880s–1930s: An International Anthology,* ed. Katherine E. Kelly. London and New York: Routledge, forthcoming in 1996.

Essays, Articles, and Books on Drama and Theater

"Across America with 'Junius Brutus Booth.' " *Universal Review* 7 (July 1890): 375–92.

Both Sides of the Curtain. London: Heinemann, 1940.

"Henrik Ibsen." *Time and Tide* 9 (1928): 242.

"Henrik Ibsen: The Drama of Ideas." *The Times* (17 Mar. 1928): 13–14.

Ibsen and the Actress. London: Hogarth Press, 1928.

Introduction to *Rebel Women* by Evelyn Sharp. London: United Suffragists, 1915.

Introduction to *Uncle Tom's Cabin* by Harriet Beecher Stowe. Bath Classics. Bath: Cedric Chivers [c. 1909–10].

"The Need of the London Stage." *Review of Reviews* 19 (Jan.–June 1904): 292–93.

"On Seeing Madame Bernhardt's Hamlet." *North American Review* 171 (Dec. 1900): 908–19.

"Some Personal Opinions on the National Theatre, Elizabeth Robins." *Drama* (Dec. 1929): 41.

Theatre and Friendship: Some Henry James Letters with a Commentary by Elizabeth Robins. New York: G. P. Putnam's Sons, 1932.

Way Stations. New York: Dodd, Mead, 1913. (See especially "To the Women Writer's Suffrage League.")

Translations

Bjornson, Bjornstjerne. *Magnhild and Dust.* The Novels of Bjornsterne Bjornson, vol. 6, ed. Edmund Gosse. London: Heinemann, 1897.

———. "Mother's Hands." *New Review* 8 (1893): 281–89, 408–18, 517–26. Reprinted in *Captain Mansana and Mother's Hands.* The Novels of Bjornstjerne Bjornson, vol. 7, ed. Edmund Gosse. London: Heinemann, 1897.

SECONDARY BIBLIOGRAPHY

Review of *Alan's Wife*. *Athenaeum* (6 May 1893): 581–82.

Review of *Alan's Wife*. *Era* (6 May 1893): 8.

Review of *Alan's Wife*. *Illustrated Sporting and Dramatic News* (6 May 1893).

Review of *Alan's Wife*. *Stage* (4 May 1893): 12.

Review of the book *Alan's Wife*. *Sun* (27 Oct. 1893).

Review of *Alan's Wife*. *Theatre* (1 June 1893): 334–35.

Archer, William. Review of *Alan's Wife*. *Westminster Gazette* (6 May 1893). Reprinted in *Theatrical World for 1893*. London: Scott, 1893.

Auster, Albert. *Actresses and Suffragists: Women in the American Theater, 1890–1920*. New York: Praeger, 1984.

Austin, L. F. Review of *Alan's Wife*. *New Review* 8 (Jan.–June 1893): 717–18.

Bell, Florence E. "Elizabeth Robins." *Landmarks: A Reprint of Some Essays and Other Pieces Published between the Years 1894 and 1922*, F. Bell, 107–13. New York: H. Liveright, 1929.

Bryan, George B. *An Ibsen Companion: A Dictionary-Guide to the Life, Works, and Critical Reception of Henrik Ibsen*. Westport, CT: Greenwood Press, 1984.

Cima, Mary Gay Gibson. [1]. "Acting through the Barricades: A Search for Prototypes of Feminist Theatre." *Turn-of-the-Century Women* 3.2 (1986): 42–46.

———. [2]. "Discovering Signs: The Emergence of the Critical Actor in Ibsen." *Theatre Journal* 35 (1983): 5–22.

———. [3]. "Elizabeth Robins: Ibsen Actress Manageress." Ph.D. diss., Cornell University, 1978.

———. [4]. "Elizabeth Robins: The Genesis of an Independent Manageress." *Theatre Survey* 21.2 (1980): 145–63.

Cordwell, Sue. "Elizabeth Robins." In *Dictionary of British Women Writers,* ed. Janet Todd. London: Routledge, 1989.

Davis, Tracy. "Acting in Ibsen." *Theatre Notebook* 39.3 (1985): 113–23.

Egan, Michael. *Henry James: The Ibsen Years*. London: Vision, 1972.

Fitzsimmons, Linda, and Viv Gardner, eds. *New Women Plays*. London: Methuen, 1991.

Gardner, Viv, and Susan Rutherford, eds. *The New Woman and Her Sisters: Feminism and Theatre, 1850–1914*. Hemel Hempstead: Harvester Wheatsheaf, 1992.

Gates, Joanne E. [1]. "Elizabeth Robins and the 1891 Production of Hedda Gabler." *Modern Drama* 27.4 (Dec. 1985): 611–19.

———. [2]. *Elizabeth Robins, 1862–1952: Actress, Novelist, Feminist*. Tuscaloosa and London: University of Alabama Press, 1994.

———. [3]. "Elizabeth Robins: From *A Dark Lantern* to *The Convert*—A Study of Her Fictional Style and Feminist Viewpoint." *Massachusetts Studies in English* 6 (1978): 25–40.

———. [4]. "Stitches in a Critical Time: The Diaries of Elizabeth Robins, American Feminist in England, 1907–1924." *A/B: Auto/Biography Studies* 4.2 (1988): 130–39.

Gates, Joanne E., and Victoria Joan Messner, eds. " 'Elizabeth Robins' Alaska Diary, 1900." Unpublished. Held in the Fales Library, New York University.

Grein, J. T. Review of *Alan's Wife*. *Westminster Review* 139 (1893): 707–8.

Hirshfield, Claire. "The Suffragist as Playwright in Edwardian England." *Frontiers* (2) (1987): 1–6.

Holledge, Julie. *Innocent Flowers: Women in the Edwardian Theatre.* London: Virago, 1981.

John, Angela V. [1]. *Elizabeth Robins: Staging a Life, 1862–1952.* London and New York: Routledge, 1995.

———. [2]. "Robins, Elizabeth." In *The Dictionary of National Biography: Missing Persons,* ed. C. S. Nicholls. Oxford: Oxford University Press, 1993.

Kelly, Katherine E. [1]. "The Actresses' Franchise League Prepares for War: Feminist Theatre in Camouflage." *Theatre Survey* (May 1994): 121–37.

———, ed. [2]. *Modern Drama by Women, 1880s–1930s: An International Anthology.* New York and London: Routledge, forthcoming in 1996.

Klauber, Adolph. Review of *Votes for Women! New York Times* (16 Mar. 1909): 9.

M., W. "The Gruesome Grein." *Hawk* (10 May 1893): 16.

Marcus, Jane. [1]. "Art and Anger." *Feminist Studies* 4 (1978): 69–98. Reprinted in *Art and Anger: Reading like a Woman.* Columbus: Ohio State University Press for Miami University, 1988.

———. [2]. "Elizabeth Robins." Ph.D. diss., Northwestern University, 1973. Ann Arbor: UMI, 1973.

———. [3]. "Invincible Mediocrity: The Private Selves of Public Women." In *The Private Self: Theory and Practice of Women's Autobiographical Writings,* ed. Shari Benstock. London: Routledge, 1988; Chapel Hill: University of North Carolina Press, 1988.

———. [4]. "Transatlantic Sisterhood: Labor and Suffrage Links in the Letters of Elizabeth Robins and Emmeline Pankhurst." *Signs* 3 (1978): 744–55.

Matlaw, M. "Robins Hits the Road: Trouping with O'Neill in the 1800s." *Theatre Survey* 29 (Nov. 1988): 175–92.

Postlewait, Thomas. *Prophet of the New Drama: William Archer and the Ibsen Campaign.* Westport, CT: Greenwood Press, 1986.

Scott, Clement. Review of Robins's performance as Hedda Gabler. *Illustrated London News* (25 Apr. 1891): 551–52.

Shattock, Joanne. *The Oxford Guide to British Women Writers.* Oxford: Oxford University Press, 1993.

Shaw, Bernard. [1]. "The Censorship of the Stage in England." *North American Review* 169 (Aug. 1899): 251–62.

———. [2]. *Shaw on Theater.* Ed. E. J. West. New York: Hill & Wang, 1958.

Spender, Dale, ed. *Time and Tide Wait for No Man.* London: Pandora, 1984.

Squier, Susan M. "The Modern City and the Construction of Female Desire: Wells's *In the Days of the Comet* and Robins's The Convert." *Tulsa Studies in Women's Literature* 8 (Spring 1989): 63–75.

Stowell, Sheila. [1]. "Re[pre]senting Eroticism: The Tyranny of Fashion in Feminist Plays of the Edwardian Age." *Theatre History Studies* 11 (1991): 51–62.

———. [2]. *A Stage of Their Own: Feminist Playwrights of the Suffrage Era.* Ann Arbor: University of Michigan Press, 1992.

Review of *Votes for Women! Chicago Record-Herald* (30 May 1907).

Review of *Votes for Women! Daily Chronicle* (10 Apr. 1907).

Review of *Votes for Women! Daily Express* (10 Apr. 1907).

Review of *Votes for Women! Daily Mirror* (10 Apr. 1907).

Review of *Votes for Women! Daily News* (10 Apr. 1907): 12.
Review of *Votes for Women! Era* (13 Apr. 1907): 13.
Review of *Votes for Women! New York Dramatic Mirror* (27 Mar. 1909): 3.
Review of *Votes for Women! New York Herald* (16 Mar. 1909).
Review of *Votes for Women! Saturday Review* (13 Apr. 1907): 456–57.
Review of *Votes for Women! Sketch* (22 May 1907): 170.
Review of *Votes for Women! The Times* (10 Apr. 1907): 5
Review of *Votes for Women! Votes for Women* (23 Apr. 1907): 582.
W[alkley], A. B. [1]. Review of *Alan's Wife. Speaker* (6 May 1893): 512.
———. [2]. Review of *Alan's Wife. Star* (29 Apr. 1893).
Wiley, Catherine. [1]. "The Matter with Manners: The New Woman and the Problem Play." In *Women in Theatre,* ed. James Redmond. Themes in Drama, 11. Cambridge: Cambridge University Press, 1989.
———. [2]. "Staging Infanticide: The Refusal of Representation in Elizabeth Robins' *Alan's Wife." Theatre Journal* 42 (1990): 432–46.
Woodfield, James. "Elizabeth Robins, The New Century Theatre, and the Stage Society." In *English Theatre in Transition, 1889–1914,* J. Woodfield. London: Croom Helm, 1984; Totowa, NJ: Barnes & Noble, 1984.
Wyant, G. G. "Personal Portraits [Elizabeth Robins]." *Bookman* 37 (July 1913): 512–16.

BIBLIOGRAPHY

Thomas, Sue. *Elizabeth Robins (1862–1952): A Bibliography.* Victorian Fiction Research Guide 22. Queensland: University of Queensland, Australia, 1994.

George Bernard Shaw
(1856–1950)

TRAMBLE T. TURNER

G.B.S., the persona created by Bernard Shaw, was as well known in 1950 for his involvement in Fabian politics (and as a waspish writer of letters to newspapers) as for his forty-eight plays. (Shaw chose not to use George in signing himself, a practice that some critics believe resulted from his antipathy toward his father, George Carr Shaw.) While such plays as *Pygmalion* (1912, produced 1913) gained renewed fame through film (1938) and later adaptations such as *My Fair Lady* (1956), Shaw himself credited three plays with establishing his career. Curiously, the first of the three that gave Shaw his earliest commercial success, *John Bull's Other Island* (1904), had received little attention in America until the mid-1970s work of Jenckes [1, 2]. The play remains one of Shaw's most popular plays in England and Ireland.

Shaw was born to Lucinda Elizabeth (Bessie) Gurly Shaw and George Carr Shaw on 26 July 1856 in Dublin. Though connected to a wealthy family (and perhaps married for her financial expectations), Lucinda Gurly was disinherited by her wealthy, unmarried aunt mainly as a result of her marriage to the improvident George Shaw. (The declining fortunes of Joyce's and Shaw's Anglo-Irish fathers provide an interesting basis for comparisons.) Two years after his mother left Ireland—and her husband—for London, Shaw followed. Having completed his first novel, *Immaturity,* on 28 September 1879, Shaw went on to write four more novels (*The Irrational Knot, Cashel Byron's Profession, Love among the Artists,* and *An Unsocial Socialist*) that were, at the time, not accepted for publication.

After working as a music and art reviewer for papers such as the *World,* Shaw went on to become a drama critic at the *Saturday Review.* That forum enabled him to champion original, sparse stagings for Shakespearean revivals; to advocate the Ibsen productions of the Independent Theatre; to push for the establishment of a National Theatre; and to encourage a climate favorable to his own experiments in drama. His opportunity to write as a reviewer came when his mother's former voice teacher and companion, George John Vandeleur Lee, asked the young Shaw to write the reviews that Lee had contracted to write for the *Hornet.*

Shaw was an effective Hyde Park speaker, and his political involvement led to his appointment to the Executive Committee of the Fabian party on 2 January 1885. In that role Shaw can be credited with helping to found the British Labour party. His political involvements led to a trip to Russia in 1931. During his last decade Shaw was increasingly attracted to dictators and totalitarian leaders (such as Joseph Stalin) due to a growing discouragement with the abilities of democracy to bring about social reform. Nevertheless, in his ongoing efforts to redefine communism, he was capable of claiming that more social communism existed in England during the 1930s than in Russia.

Though such works as *Widowers' Houses, Arms and the Man, The Devil's Disciple,* and *Candida* were staged by innovative companies in England and the United States from 1892 to 1900, Shaw's position as the preeminent English-language dramatist of his time was assured in 1904 and 1905 through his collaborations with the Vedrenne-Barker company. The company's successful 1904 performance of *John Bull's Other Island* led to a command performance for King Edward V11 in 1905. That same year the company scored again with productions of *Man and Superman* and *Major Barbara.* In later prefaces Shaw was to cite these three plays as the basis for his burgeoning career. Noteworthy for first staging Shaw's plays, however, were the actress Florence Farr (*Arms and the Man*) and Miss Annie Horniman, who financed the enterprise as discreetly as she was later to do with the Abbey Theatre of Dublin. (Indeed, Shaw's works were often chosen for production by female directors in the first half of the century.)

Shaw's plays written during World War I (*The Inca of Perusalem, Heartbreak House, Augustus Does His Bit,* and *Annajanska*) reflect an increasingly clouded optimism about the efficacy of social and political organizations. By 1921, when he completed *Back to Methuselah,* Shaw's faith in the power of Creative Evolution and the Life Force to regenerate the world was projected increasingly further into the future with a millennial aspect. In 1926 he received the Nobel Prize for Literature for the year 1925.

The establishment of the Malvern Festival in 1929 served notice that Shaw was regarded as a national asset similar to the Bard about whom Shaw wrote so much. Thirty-three years later North America paid Shaw the same tribute when the Shaw Festival was established in Ontario by Brian Doherty at Niagara-on-the-Lake. The Shaw Festival at Niagara-on-the-Lake has served as both a research center and an arena for maintaining popular interest in Shaw's topicality.

For example, of the 1983 production of *The Simpleton of the Unexpected Isles,* Martin Knelman wrote in Toronto's *Saturday Night,* ''It was the Falklands war that triggered [Denise Coffey's] interest in *Simpleton,* which features in its bizarre plot the arrival of fleets from all over the British Empire to threaten battle over a tiny island . . . *Simpleton* gleefully lampoons the sort of crackpot Victorian reform Shaw himself so often seemed to personify'' (quoted in Margery Morgan, 95). Trussler has suggested another basis for the ongoing Shavian commercial success, as well as the ongoing critical analysis: "At his best . . . [Shaw] can peel away the thin veneer of national sensibilities and inhibitions so as to reveal both their deep emotional subtext and (another paradox) a profound sense of the closeness of the naturalistic and surreal'' (6). Shaw died on 2 November 1950 after sustaining injuries on Sunday, 10 September, when he fell while pruning a tree in his garden at Ayot St. Lawrence.

Selected Biographical Sources: Bertolini; Carr; Henderson [1, 2]; Holroyd [1]; Rosset; Stanley Weintraub [1, 2, 3, 4, 5].

MAJOR PLAYS, PREMIERES, AND SIGNIFICANT REVIVALS: THEATRICAL RECEPTION

Widowers' Houses. 1892. Opened 9 December at the Royalty Theatre (London) in a private production directed by Herman de Lange. First American production at Herald Square Theater, 7 March 1907, directed by Lee Shubert. First public English production: Miss Annie Horniman's Company at Midland Theatre (Manchester), 7 June 1909. Revivals: Abbey Theatre, 9 October 1916, directed by Milton Rosmer; Stage Society at the Malvern Festival, 19 August 1930, directed by H. K. Ayliff; Theatre Royal (Stratford), 15 March 1965, directed by Ronald Eyre; Bristol Old Vic, September 1981, directed by John Love.

Arms and the Man. 1894. Opened 21 April at the Avenue Theatre (London). Directed by G. Bernard Shaw. Revivals: Savoy Theatre, 30 December 1907, directed by G. Bernard Shaw and Harley Granville-Barker; Abbey Theatre, 25 October 1916; Old Vic Theatre, 16 February 1931, directed by Harcourt Williams, with John Gielgud as Saranoff, Ralph Richardson as Bluntschli, and Marie Ney as Raina; Old Vic Company, September 1944 at the New Theatre, (London) directed by John Burrell, with a cast of Laurence Olivier, Ralph Richardson, Margaret Leighton, and Sybil Thorndike; Gaiety Theatre (Dublin), 1947.

Archer [1], writing about the original production, argued that it was "impossible, in short, to accept the second and third acts . . . as either 'romantic comedy' or coherent farce.''

Candida. 1894. Opened 30 July 1897 at the Independent Theater (Aberdeen). Directed by Charles Charrington. Revivals: Browning Society, South Broad St. Theatre (Philadelphia), 18 May 1903; Court Theatre, 26 April 1904, Vedrenne-Barker company, directed by Harley Granville-Barker; Malvern Festival, 18 August 1930, directed by H. K. Ayliff; Abbey Theatre (Dublin), 30 September 1935; Roundabout Theater (New York), 2 February 1969, directed by Gene Feist; Longacre Theatre (New York), 6 April 1970, directed by Laurence Carr,

Albery Theatre (London) 23 June 1977; directed by Michael Blakemore; King's Head, 1987, directed by Frank Hauser; production revived at the Arts Theatre, 12 January 1988; Boulevard Theatre (Soho), 21 September 1988, directed by Rob Kennedy.

Of the 1987 revival David Nice wrote that "what Frank Hauser makes us realize is the presence of abysses threatening to open beneath order and logic" (quoted in Margery Morgan, 30).

The Devil's Disciple. 1897. Opened 1 October at Harmanus Bleeker Hall (Albany, New York). Directed by Richard Mansfield. Revivals: Prince of Wales's Theatre (Kennington) 26 September 1899; Coronet Theatre (Notting Hill Gate), 7 September 1900, directed by Shaw; Savoy Theatre, 14 October 1907, directed by Shaw and Harley Granville-Barker; the production moved to the Queen's Theater on 23 November 1907; Abbey Theatre, 10 February 1920, directed by Lennox Robinson; Old Vic Company at the Buxton Festival, 31 August 1939, and at the Streatham Hill Theatre, 4 October 1939; Old Vic Company at the Golders Green Hippodrome, 10 June 1940, directed by Milton Rosmer; the production moved to the Piccadilly Theatre on 24 July 1940; Opera House (Manchester), 20 February 1956, directed by Noël Willman; the production moved to the Winter Garden Theatre (London), on 18 November 1956; Shaw Theatre, 5 July 1971, directed by Michael Croft; RSC (Royal Shakespeare Company) at the Aldwych Theatre, 13 July 1976, directed by Jack Gold; Malvern Festival Theatre, August 1981, with Anthony Quayle as Burgoyne.

The Times (Review of *The Devil's Disciple*) found that the work "cannot be called a sympathetic play. It is full of that mordant satire with which we are familiar in Mr. Shaw's work and full, too, of that sense of insincerity, of mere posing which mars so much of it."

Captain Brassbound's Conversion. 1899. Opened at the Strand Theatre, 16 December 1900 in a private performance. Directed by Charles Charrington. Revivals: Court Theatre, 20 March 1906, directed by Shaw and Harley Granville-Barker; Little Theatre, 15 October 1912, directed by Shaw; Cambridge Theatre, 18 February 1971, directed by Frith Banbury; the production moved to the Ethel Barrymore Theatre (New York), 17 April 1972, directed by Stephen Poster; Haymarket Theatre, 10 June 1982, directed by Frank Hauser.

Mrs. Warren's Profession. 1902. Opened 5 January by the Stage Society (London) in a private performance. First licensed production: Prince of Wales's Theatre (Birmingham), 27 July 1925, by the Macdona Players. Directed by Esmé Percy. Revivals: Royal Court Theatre, 24 July 1956, directed by Terence O'Brien; Gaiety Theatre (Dublin), 1961, directed by Gerald Healy; National Theatre Company at the Old Vic Theatre, 30 December 1970, directed by Ronald Eyre; Abbey Theatre, 27 July 1977; National Theatre at the Lyttleton, 10 October 1985, directed by Anthony Page; Harrowgate Theatre, 23 February 1989, directed by Andrew Manley.

The 1902 private production by the Stage Society prompted Grein to object that if "Shaw had fully understood the nature of Mrs. Warren's profession he would have left the play unwritten or have produced a tragedy of heartrending power." By 1985, however, opinion had shifted. The writer for *Time Out* found the play to be an "uncompromising, progressive, political piece, full of passionate conviction. And, sadly, it has a lot to say which is as great an indictment of our society as it is testament to Shaw's power as dramatist. It is so rare to see such a serious and strong play about women" (quoted in Margery Morgan, 21).

John Bull's Other Island. 1904. Opened 1 November at the Royal Court Theatre (London), performed by the Vedrenne-Barker company. Directed by Shaw and Harley Granville-Barker, with Granville-Barker playing Father Keegan. Revivals: Abbey Theatre (Dublin), 26 September 1916, with annual revivals until 1931; Abbey Theatre, 10 March 1969; Irish Theatre Company, 1980, directed by Patrick Mason, with Cyril Cusack as Keegan.

Beerbohm's enthusiastic review included the comment, "Most of the fun comes of a slight exaggeration on the things that the character actually would say. But Mr. Shaw has also the art of extracting a ridiculous effect from every scenic situation."

Man and Superman. 1905 (written 1901–3). Opened 21 May at the Court Theatre in a private performance by the Stage Society (London) (with the *Don Juan in Hell* act omitted). Directed by Shaw, with Harley Granville-Barker and Lillah McCarthy in the cast. The same production was opened for public performance on 23 May 1905 by the Vedrenne-Barker company. Shaw directed with Granville-Barker's assistance. Revivals without act 3, scene ii: Hudson Theatre (New York), 5 September 1905, presented by Charles Dillingham; Abbey Theatre (Dublin), 26 February 1917; Everyman Theatre, 23 May 1921, directed by Edith Craig; Birmingham Theatre, 14 August 1945, directed by Peter Brook; Gate Theatre (Dublin), 1951, directed by Dan O'Connell; Theatre Royal (Bristol), 11 March 1968, Bristol Old Vic Company, directed by John Moody, with Peter O'Toole; Malvern Festival Theatre, August 1977; Birmingham Repertory Theatre, 27 September 1982, directed by Patrick Dromgoole, with Peter O'Toole; the production moved to the Haymarket Theatre (London), 16 November 1982. Revivals of act 3, scene ii alone: Arts Theatre, 24 March 1943, 3 July 1946, and 8 September 1952; Coronet Theatre (Los Angeles), July 1947; the production toured fifty-two American cities, including a Carnegie Hall performance, 22 October 1951; directed by Charles Laughton, with Laughton as the Devil, Agnes Moorehead, and Sir Cedric Hardwicke. Revivals with act 3 included: Little Theatre, 27 January 1928, directed by Esmé Percy; moved to the Garrick Theatre 13 February 1928; Old Vic, 21 November 1938, directed by Lewis Casson, starring Anthony Quayle; Royal Shakespeare Company at the Savoy Theatre, 16 August 1977, directed by Clifford Williams; National Theatre at the Olivier, 2 January 1981, directed by Christopher Monahan.

Of the 1905 production Walkley complained that the "action-plot is well-nigh meaningless without the key of the idea-plot; . . . it is because of this parasitic nature of the action-plot, because of its weakness, its haphazardness, its unnaturalness . . . that one finds the play as a play unsatisfying.'' Similarly, Archer [3] wrote that the play was evidence of ''one of the main reasons why Mr. Shaw will never be an artist in drama. It is that his intellect entirely predominates over, not only his emotions, but his perceptions.''

Major Barbara. 1905. Opened 28 November at the Royal Court Theatre, performed by the Vedrenne-Barker company. Directed by Shaw and Harley Granville-Barker. Revivals: Court Theatre, 1 January 1906, directed by Granville-Barker; Wyndham's Theatre, 5 March 1929, directed by Lewis Casson and Charles Macdona, with Sybil Thorndike; Old Vic Theatre, 4 March 1935, directed by Henry Cass; Theatre Royal (Bristol), 26 June 1956, directed by John Moody, including Peter O'Toole as Peter Shirley; the production moved to the Old Vic Theatre on 16 July 1956; Martin Beck Theatre (New York), 30 October 1956, directed by Charles Laughton, who played Undershaft. The cast included Glynis Johns, Cornelia Otis Skinner, and Eli Wallach; Royal Court Theatre, 28 August 1958, directed by George Devine, with a cast including Joan Plowright and Vanessa Redgrave; Royal Shakespeare Company (RSC) at the Aldwych Theatre, 19 October 1970, directed by Clifford Williams, with a cast including Judi Dench and Richard Pasco; National Theatre at the Lyttleton, 27 October 1982, directed by Peter Gill, with Sian Phillips as Lady Britomart.

The *Pall Mall Gazette* (Review of *Major Barbara*) greeted the play with the observation that it contained ''wit enough to make the fortune of half-a-dozen ordinary plays. The question is whether there is wit enough to save a three hours' discussion in the theatre. We doubt it.'' Similarly, Archer [2] complained that ''[t]here are no human beings in *Major Barbara:* there are only animated points of view.''

Beerbohm praised Shaw's creation of Dubedat's death bed scene in a 24 November 1906 *Saturday Review* entry: ''Mr Shaw has, moreover, been as anxious to make his death-bed pathetic as was Dickens to make Little Nell's. And, where Dickens failed, Mr. Shaw has succeeded. The pathos here is real. I defy you not to be touched by it, while it lasts'' (quoted in Margery Morgan, 57).

Caesar and Cleopatra. 1906 (written 1898). Opened, in German, 31 March at Neues Theater, Berlin. Produced by Max Reinhardt; directed by Hans Olden. Moved to the Deutsches Theater, 15 June 1906. First English-language production: New Amsterdam Theatre (New York), 30 October 1906. Directed by Shaw and Johnston Forbes-Robertson; moved to the Grand Theatre (Leeds), 16 September 1907, and to the Savoy Theatre (London), 25 November 1907 (with act 3 omitted). Revivals: Theatre Royal, Drury Lane, 14 April 1913, directed by Shaw and Forbes-Robertson; Birmingham Repertory Theatre, 9 April 1925, directed by H. K. Ayliff; moved to the Kingsway Theatre (London), 1925; Abbey Theatre, 24 October 1927; Malvern Festival Theatre, 24 August 1929, directed by Ayliff; Old Vic Theatre, 19 September 1932, directed by Harcourt Williams, with Peggy Ashcroft; Opera House (Manchester), 24 April 1951, directed by Michael Benthall, with Laurence Olivier and Vivien Leigh; the production moved to St. James's Theatre, 10 May 1951; Birmingham Repertory Theatre, 12 June 1956, directed by Douglas Seale, with Geoffrey Bayidon, Doreen Aris, and Albert Finney; the production moved to the Old Vic Theatre on 30 July 1957; Palace Theatre (New York), 24 February 1977, directed by Ellis Rabb, with Rex Harrison as Caesar; Shaw Festival Theatre, Niagara-on-the-Lake, 1983.

The Times (Review of *Caesar and Cleopatra*) commented on how Shaw "uses the play as a means of giving out to you everything that happens to come at the moment into his head. Well, fortunately, it is Mr Shaw's head, and the things that happen to come into it are generally amusing things."

The Doctor's Dilemma. 1906. Opened 20 November at the Royal Court Theatre. Directed by Shaw and Harley Granville-Barker. Revivals: St. James's Theatre, 6 December 1913, directed by Granville-Barker, with Lillah McCarthy; Everyman Theatre, 2 April 1923, directed by Norman Macdermott, starring Claude Rains and Cathleen Nesbitt; Haymarket Theatre, 4 March 1942, directed by Irene Hentschel, starring Vivien Leigh and Cyril Cusack; Gaiety Theatre (Dublin), 1947, with Cyril Cusack; Haymarket Theatre, 23 May 1963, directed by Donald MacWhinnie; Chichester Festival Theatre, 17 May 1972, directed by John Clements, with a cast including Joan Plowright and John Neville.

The Philanderer. 1907 (written 1893). Opened 5 February at the Royal Court Theatre. Directed by Shaw and Harley Granville-Barker. Revivals: Royal Court Theatre, 20 January 1930, directed by Esmé Percy; Mermaid Theatre, 27 January 1966, directed by Don Taylor. National Theatre at Lyttleton, 7 September 1978, directed by Christopher Monahan.

Getting Married. 1908. Opened 12 May at the Haymarket Theatre. Directed by Shaw. Revivals: Booth Theatre (New York), 6 November 1916, directed by William Faversham; Birmingham Repertory Theatre, 18 October 1923, directed by H. K. Ayliff; Everyman Theatre, 9 July 1924, directed by Norman Macdermott, with Claude Rains and Edith Evans; Malvern Festival Theatre, 1982.

The Shewing-Up of Blanco Posnet. 1909. Opened 25 August at the Abbey Theatre. Directed by Sara Allgood and Lady Gregory. Revivals: Everyman Theatre, 14 March 1921, directed by Edith Craig; production moved to the Queen's Theatre, 20 July 1921; Mermaid Theatre, 3 October 1961, directed by Frank Dunlop.

Fanny's First Play. 1911. Opened 19 April at the Little Theatre; the production moved to the Kingsway Theatre 1 January 1912 for a total of 622 performances. Revival: 1915, a production that failed to garner interest or reviews.

The 1911 production is often credited as Shaw's first commercial success. However, see the reference to the success of *John Bull's Other Island* in the introduction to this chapter.

Androcles and the Lion. 1912. Opened 25 November, in German, at the Kleines Theater in Berlin. Produced by Max Reinhardt; moved to Hamburg in July 1913. Revivals: Abbey Theatre, 4 November 1919; Old Vic Theatre, 24 February 1930, directed by Harcourt Williams, with John Gieglud as the Emperor; Gaiety Theatre (Dublin), July 1956, starring Cyril Cusack; Malvern Festival Theatre, 29 August 1966, directed by Bernard Hepton.

Pygmalion. 1913. (written 1912). Opened in German at the Hofburgtheater in Vienna 16 October 1913. Directed by Hugo Thimig. Revivals: His Majesty's Theatre, 11 April 1914, directed by Shaw, with Herbert Beerbohm Tree and Mrs. Patrick Campbell; Aldwych Theatre, 10 February 1920, directed by Shaw, with Mrs. Patrick Campbell; Court Theatre, 30 December 1929 and 13 April 1931, directed by Esmé Percy (who also played Higgins); Old Vic Theatre, 21 September 1937, directed by Tyrone Guthrie; Theatre Royal (Bristol), 12 March 1957, directed by John Harrison, with Wendy Williams and Peter O'Toole as Doolittle; Albery Theatre, 15 May 1974, directed by John Dexter, with Diana Rigg, Alec McCowen, and Bob Hoskins; Malvern Festival Theatre, August 1978; Shaftesbury Theatre, 10 May 1984, directed by Ray Cooney, with Peter O'Toole; production revived at the Plymouth Theatre (New York), 1987, with Sir John Mills as Doolittle.

Reviews of the 1974 production that starred Diana Rigg praised the return of the play, which had been held off the boards due to an agreement with the producers of *My Fair Lady*. Wardle [3] reported: "Great musical though it was, My Fair Lady has much to answer for in keeping this masterpiece off the stage for so long. And among the pleasures of John Dexter's magnificent revival (the first in the West End since 1953) is that of rediscovering how musical Shaw's own work is without any outside assistance."

O'Flaherty, V.C. 1920. Opened 21 June at the Thirty-ninth Street Theatre (New York); performed by the Deborah Bierne Irish Players. Opened 19 December 1920 by the Stage Society at the Lyric Theatre (Hammersmith). The first production, by amateurs, occurred on 17 February 1917 on the western front. The performance was given by officers of the 40th Squadron, R.F.C., at Treizennes, Belgium. Revival: the Mermaid Theatre, 14 September 1966, directed by Peter Gill, starring Ian McKellan.

Marcus observed of the 1966 revival that it "almost persuades one that it is major Shaw."

Heartbreak House. 1920 (written 1916). Opened 10 November 1920 by the New York Theatre Guild. Directed by Dudley Digges. Revivals: Royal Court Theatre, 18 October 1921, directed by Shaw and J. B. Fagan; Birmingham Repertory Theatre, 3 March 1923, directed by H. K. Ayliff; Queen's Theatre, 23 April 1932, directed by H. K. Ayliff, with Cedric Hardwicke and Edith Evans as Ariadne (repeating her role in the English premiere); Cambridge Theatre, 18 March 1943, directed by John Burrell; National Theatre at the Old Vic Theatre,

25 February 1975, directed by John Schlesinger, with Colin Blakely and Kate Nelligan; Malvern Festival Theatre, August 1981, with Anthony Quayle; Haymarket Theatre, 10 March 1983, directed by John Dexter, with Rex Harrison and Diana Rigg.

Tracing Shaw's dramatic heritage, Agate [1] wrote, "You have to get Ibsen thoroughly in mind if you are not to find the Zeppelin at the end of Shaw's play merely monstrous." In reviewing the 1983 revival, Nightingale dismissed previous complaints about the lack of structure in Shaw's plays: "Never mind the plot, which barely exists: feel the passion, which indisputably does."

Back to Methuselah. 1922 (written 1920). Produced by the New York Theatre Guild, 27 February–13 March: parts 1 and 2, 27 February; parts 3 and 4, 6 March; part 5, 13 March. Directed by Philip Moeller. Revivals: Birmingham Repertory Theatre, 9–12 October 1923, with one part performed each day except for October 11: part 3 (matinee), part 4 (evening), directed by H. K. Ayliff, with Edith Evans, Cedric Hardwicke, and Gwen Ffrangcon-Davies; moved to the Court Theatre 18–22 February (with Caroline Keith taking the Edith Evans role); Malvern Festival Theatre, 20–22 August 1929, directed by H. K. Ayliff; National Theatre at Old Vic Theatre, 31 July–1 August 1969, directed by Clifford Williams and Donald Mackochnie, with Joan Plowright as the Voice of Lilith; Shaw Theatre, 18–19 June 1984, directed by Bill Pryde; Shaw Festival, Niagara-on-the-Lake, 15 August 1986, directed by Denise Coffey.

Responses to contemporary revivals of this alternative creation tale that Shaw termed a "meta-biological Pentateuch" have been varied. Wardle [1] wrote that the work was "[w]ithout dramatic life or coherence." The 1984 production, however, led Hay to write that "Bill Pryde and his accomplished team of nine actors have already scotched the notion that it's an intractable masterpiece."

Saint Joan. 1923. Opened 28 December at the New York Theatre Guild. Directed by Philip Moeller. Revivals: New Theatre, 26 March 1924, directed by Shaw and Lewis Casson, with Sybil Thorndike and Ernest Thesiger; Regent Theatre, 14 January 1925, directed by Lewis Casson, with Sybil Thorndike and Ernest Thesiger; Lyceum Theatre, 24 March 1926; His Majesty's Theatre, 6 April 1931; Old Vic Company at the New Theatre, 3 December 1947, directed by John Burrell, with Celia Johnson and Alec Guinness; Arts Theatre (Cambridge), 20 September 1954, directed by John Fernald, with Siobhan McKenna and Kenneth Williams; the production moved to the Arts Theatre (London), 29 September 1954, and on to the St. Martin's Theatre, 9 February 1955; National Theatre at the Chichester Festival Theatre, 24 June 1963, directed by John Dexter, with Joan Plowright, Robert Stephens, and Max Adrian; the production moved to the Old Vic Theatre 30 October 1963; Abbey Theatre (Dublin), 5 December 1972; National Theatre at the Olivier, 16 February 1984, directed by Ronald Eyre, with Frances de la Tour, Cyril Cusack, and Michael Bryant.

Pirandello emphasized the audience's reaction to the play (which he perhaps overidealized): "I noted with great satisfaction the rapt attention, the shrewd and intelligent smiling, the hearty laughter and the sincere applause [during the first three acts] with which every shaft of wit or irony in this admirable and inimitable Shavian dialogue was welcomed by an audience keenly aware of the artistic treat that was spread before it.''

The Apple Cart. 1929. Opened 14 June at the Polsky Theatre (Teatr Polski) (Warsaw), in Polish. Directed by Karel Borowski. Opened 19 August 1929 at the Malvern Festival Theatre, directed by H. K. Ayliff, with Cedric Hardwicke and Edith Evans; the production moved to the Queen's Theatre (London) on 17 September 1929. Revivals: Theatre Guild, Martin Beck Theatre (New York), 24 February 1930; Garrick Theatre (Melbourne), 9 October 1933, directed by Gregan McMahon, who played Magnus, with Coral Browne as Orinthia; Cambridge Theatre, 25 September 1935, directed by Cedric Hardwicke; Haymarket Theatre, 7 May 1953, directed by Michael Macowan, with Noël Coward, Margaret Leighton as Orinthia, and Margaret Rawlings as Lysistrata; Haymarket Theatre, 20 February 1986, directed by Val May, with Peter O'Toole, Susannah York, and Dora Bryan as Amanda.

Sometimes subject to charges of writing star vehicles, Shaw found a forgiving attitude in Ervine: ''*The Apple Cart,* which is as disconnected as a revue, is not, of course, a play, but who cares whether it is or not? . . . what an entertainment!''

Too True to Be Good. 1932. Opened 29 February by the Theatre Guild at the National Theatre (Boston). Directed by Leslie Banks, with Beatrice Lillie and Claude Rains; the production moved to the Guild Theatre (New York), 4 April 1932; opened at the Malvern Festival Theatre on 6 August 1932, directed by H. K. Ayliff, with Ellen Pollock, Cedric Hardwicke, and Ralph Richardson; moved to the New Theatre (London) on 13 September 1932. Revivals: Lyric Theatre (Hammersmith), 31 October 1944, directed by Ellen Pollock; Lyceum Theatre (Edinburgh), 6 September 1965, directed by Frank Dunlop; the production moved to the Strand Theatre (London) on 22 September 1965; Riverside Studios, 5 November 1986, directed by Mike Alfreds.

Based on the original production, Peter Noble renewed the career-long response to Shaw's experimentalism and success: ''Shaw breaks all the rules of the theatre, yet none can be said to break them more successfully'' (quoted in Margery Morgan, 89). Charles Morgan was less sympathetic: ''Mr. Shaw's present work has, as a document, the interest and, as a play, the tedium, of an undigested notebook. Being formless, it produces neither dramatic illusion nor intellectual tension.'' The 1965 revival resulted in Wardle calling for a reevaluation of the last phase of Shaw's career: ''This is a good deal more than a star production of a minor Shaw play. It is a well calculated act of revaluation [*sic*] designed to open up his neglected last phase'' (quoted in Margery Morgan, 89).

On the Rocks. 1933. Opened 25 November at the Winter Garden Theatre (London). Directed by Lewis Casson. Revivals: Abbey Theatre, 9 July 1934; Daly's Theatre (New York), 15 June 1938; Mermaid Theatre, (London) 21 August

1975, directed by Bernard Miles; Chichester Festival Theatre, 5 May 1982, directed by Patrick Garland and Jack Emery.

A play that sometimes resulted in charges of fascism received a more sympathetic review from Martin, who observed that it "warns rather than advocates. Make up your mind, he [Shaw] says, that Parliament, as you now know it, cannot be the instrument of salvation." The 1982 revival garnered a balanced assessment from Wardle [2], who argued that the play "shows his anarchic comic gift doing spirited battle with his authoritarian opinions."

The Simpleton of the Unexpected Isles. 1935 (written 1934). Opened 18 February at the New York Theatre Guild, directed by Henry Wagstaffe Gribble; the Malvern Festival Theatre, 29 July 1935, directed by Herbert Prentis; the Comedy Theatre, October 1935, directed by Gregan McMahon. Revivals: Arts Theatre (London), 7 March 1945, directed by Judith Furse; Manchester Green Room, 30 January 1953; Shaw Festival, Niagara-on-the-Lake, June 1983, directed by Denise Coffey.

After publication of the play, *The Times Literary Supplement* (Review of *The Simpleton of the Unexpected Isles*) termed it "the most interesting that Mr Shaw has written since *The Apple Cart.*" The original Australian production at the Comedy Theatre (Melbourne) in October 1935 and the 1983 revival resulted in mixed praise. The *Sydney Bulletin* (Review of *The Simpleton of the Unexpected Isles*) called the play "a magnificent confusion."

The Millionairess. 1936 (written 1934). Opened 4 January in Vienna at the Burgtheater. (Carr cited the production as opening at the Akademie Theater.) Directed by Herbert Warnick. Opened 7 March 1936 at the King's Theater by the McMahon Players, Melbourne, Australia, directed by Gregan McMahon, starring Enid Hollins. Revivals: Malvern Festival Theatre, 26 July 1937, directed by Herbert M. Prentice; the Globe Theatre, 11 September 1940, directed by George Devine, starring Edith Evans; New Theatre (London), 27 June 1952, directed by Michael Benthall, with Katharine Hepburn, Robert Helpmann, and Cyril Ritchard; the production moved to the Shubert Theatre (New York), on 17 October 1952; Haymarket Theatre, 14 December 1978, directed by Michael Lindsay-Hogg.

The Times Literary Supplement (Review of *The Millionairess*) identified the play's connection with Shaw's political development: "Amid all the bombast of assertion incidental to its author's style, we are permitted to watch Mr Shaw feeling his way towards new territory and to understand the nature of his present confusion . . . he has delivered a genuinely constructive criticism of the excesses of democracy." The Melbourne critic for the *Argus,* however, called the play a "superb comedy—impudent, pungent, and devastating" while also attributing to the play "[l]ess preaching and dogmatizing . . . than in anything Shaw has written in ten years" (quoted in Margery Morgan, 97).

Geneva. 1938. Opened 1 August at the Malvern Festival; directed by H. K. Ayliff. Moved to the Saville Theatre (London), on 22 November 1938; moved again to the St. James's Theatre on January 27, 1939. Revivals: Comedy Theater (Melbourne), 10 July 1939, directed by Gregan McMahon; Henry Miller's Theatre, New York, 30 January 1940, produced by the Colbourne-Jones Company; Mermaid Theater, 4 November 1971, directed by Philip Grout.

While praising the playwright, Dent faulted the reception of the audience: "It let out indiscriminate whoops of laughter at things which Mr Shaw obviously meant for serious statements. The shrug with which this political exposition concludes is a genuinely despairing one." The 1971 revival resulted in a basically enthusiastic review from Lambert, who commented that "[t]he old man's impatient anarchy wore surprisingly well, despite one or two wincingly insensitive lines." The New York opening prompted Atkinson to lament that "Mr Shaw is not improving in his playwriting . . . he makes logic and wisdom about great matters very difficult to listen to."

In Good King Charles' Golden Days. 1939. Opened 12 August at the Malvern Festival. Directed by H. K. Ayliff; moved to the Streatham Hill Theatre, 15 April 1940, and then to the New Theatre (London), 9 May 1940. Revivals: King's Theatre (Melbourne), 9 December 1939, directed by Gregan McMahon; People's Palace (London), 25 October 1948, directed by Matthew Forsyth; Malvern Festival Theatre, 11 August 1949, directed by Ernest Thesiger; Downtown Theatre (New York), 24 January 1957.

Of the Malvern opening, Agate [2] wrote, "This play's business is the affair of the men. Is it long? Yes. Too long? No. . . . Will anybody miss the lack of action? Yes, the witless and the idle."

ADDITIONAL PLAYS, ADAPTATIONS, AND PRODUCTIONS

Other plays by Shaw include *The Admirable Bashville; or, Constancy Unrewarded* (1903); *How He Lied to Her Husband* (1904); *Passion, Poison and Petrification; or, The Fatal Gazogene* (1905); *Press Cuttings* (1909); *The Dark Lady of the Sonnets* (1910); *Overruled* (1912); *Great Catherine* (1913); *The Music-Cure* (1914); *The Inca of Perusalem* (1916); *Augustus Does His Bit* (1917); *Annajanska, the Bolshevik Empress* (1918), originally titled *Annajanska, The Wild Grand Duchess; Jitta's Atonement* (1924), a free adaptation and translation of *Frau Gittas Sühne* (a play by Shaw's German translator, Siegfried Trebitsch); *The Glimpse of Reality* (1927; written in 1909); *The Fascinating Foundling* (1928), subtitled *A Disgrace to the Author; Village Wooing* (1934); *The Six of Calais* (1934); *Cymbeline Refinished* (1937), originally titled *Cymbeline Up to Date: A Happy Ending; Bouyant Billions* (1948); *Shakes versus Shav* (1949), a puppet-play commissioned by Waldo Lanchester; *Farfetched*

Fables (1950), a play written for amateurs; and *Why She Would Not,* a comedy
that Shaw was writing in the year of his death, 1950.

ASSESSMENT OF SHAW'S CAREER

While theater companies have relied on Shaw's plays from 1904 to the present
for commercial success, that aspect of his reception led Susan Todd to complain
that "it seems unpleasantly ironic that he should have been, for so long now,
appropriated by the richest, glossiest, most commercial production companies
for what is called 'revival' " (quoted in Margery Morgan, 115). Nevertheless,
Holroyd and others have credited the Niagara-on-the-Lake Shaw Festival with
nurturing a new seriousness in Shaw studies. Aside from noting the "[f]ringe
of seminars, special tours, and projects for young people" that are a part of the
festival, Holroyd [1] commented that "[w]hat had begun at Malvern in the 1930s
was accomplished in Niagara fifty years later" (4:77).

From the first productions of Shaw's work, a repeated complaint has been,
as Walkley argued, that plays like *Widowers' Houses* are "not dramatic. I only
see a number of people arguing round a table. Indeed, Mr. Shaw's people are
not dramatic characters at all, they are embodied arguments." Walkley's 17
December 1892 notice in the *Speaker* also indicated the reputation of G.B.S. at
the century's end: "You have Mr. Shaw the musical critic, and Mr. Shaw the
novelist, and Mr. Shaw the Ibsenite exegete, and Mr. Shaw the Fabian, and Mr.
Shaw the vegetarian, and Mr. Shaw the anti-vivisectionist—and now there is
Mr. Shaw the dramatist" (quoted in Evans, 58, 55).

Recent trends in Shaw criticism have returned to some of those other facets
of Shaw and include studies of the significance of Shaw's music and art criticism
and of Shaw as a controversialist (witness Stanley Weintraub [4]). Shaw himself
encouraged analysis of his plays in terms of a musical structure: "My plays
bear very plain marks of my musical education. My deliberate rhetoric, and my
reversion to the Shakespearian feature of long set roles for my characters, are
pure Italian opera. My rejection of plot and denouement, and my adoption of a
free development of themes, are German symphony" (Shaw, *Collected Letters,*
3:374).

Gainor demonstrated how a feminist reading of the Shavian canon can produce new perspectives on such aspects of Shavian dramaturgy as cross-dressing
roles and implied homoeroticism. Bevir's work showed an indication of renewed
interest in the political dimensions of Shaw's thought.

That Jorge Luis Borges—a writer often mentioned among "other postmodern
writers from Joyce and Borges to Beckett and Calvino" (Kearney [2], 303)—
described Shaw as a major influence suggests the validity of reconsidering Shaw
as a postmodernist. In an interview with Seamus Heaney and Richard Kearney,
Borges spoke often of the influence Shaw had on his thinking, recalling how
when "I read George Bernard Shaw's *The Quintessence of Ibsenism,* I was so
impressed that I went on to read all of his plays and essays and discovered there

a writer of deep philosophical curiosity and a great believer in the transfiguring power of the will and of the mind'' (quoted in Kearney [1], 51–52). While his comment pointed toward the elements of Barthian jeu and Bakhtinian carnival present in Shaw's works, Borges also repeatedly stressed the significance of Shavian metaphysics.

To Kearney's question, ''Do you think it is just a happy accident that your early discovery of the creative power of the mind coincided with your admiration for Irish writers and thinkers such as Berkeley, Shaw, Wilde and Joyce, who had also made such a discovery?'' Borges replied, ''As an outsider looking on successive Irish thinkers I have sometimes been struck by unusual and remarkable repetitions. Berkeley was the first Irish philosopher I read. . . . Then followed my fascination for Wilde, Shaw and Joyce. And finally there was John Scotus Erigena, the Irish metaphysician of the 9th century. . . . In short, what Shaw calls the life-force plays the same role in his system as God does in Erigena's. . . . the coincidence of thought is there. I suspect it has less to do with nationalism than with metaphysics'' (quoted in Kearney [1], 53–54).

Such issues of repetition of ''rewriting and rebeginning'' involve what Kearney considered a critical turn in the conception of the postmodernist enterprise. ''Postmodernism would thus refuse to view itself as a mere afterword to modernity. Instead it assumes the task of reinvestigating the crisis and trauma at the very heart of modernity'' (Kearney [2], 32). By placing postmodernism as a recursive movement that reexamines and reinterprets basic cruxes within modernism, Kearney provided a basis for examining Shaw's work as an example of the roots of postmodernism in modernism. Stanley Weintraub [1] has recently called for such a reexamination of traditional Shaw scholarship.

Indeed, not only does *John Bull's Other Island* question concepts of Irish identity, but the Abbey Theatre's rejection of that work suggests the relevance to Shaw's response of one definition of modernism: ''Modernism is, consequently, suspicious of attempts to reestablish national literatures or resurrect cultural traditions'' (quoted in Kearney [2], 12). However, just as Joyce has been cited as both a high modernist and as a postmodernist (depending on the critic's definitions and choice of examples), so Shaw can be situated as an early postmodernist. While also taking into account Borges's praise of Shaw, Holroyd [1] paired his tribute with that of another author in order to emphasize Shaw's dramaturgic complexity: ''Borges praised him for creating superb characters on stage, Brecht for subverting character and introducing the spirit of alienation'' (4:78). To Kearney's question about the ''relationship with philosophy'' of Borges's ''works [that] are peppered with metaphysical allusions,'' Borges returned to Shaw's importance. His response speaks to the basis of Shaw's ongoing interest for critics: ''For me Schopenhauer is the greatest philosopher. He knew the power of fiction in ideas. This conviction I share, of course, with Shaw. Both Schopenhauer and Shaw exposed the deceptive division between the writer and the thinker'' (quoted in Kearney [1], 52).

One, of course, should not forget that Shaw's high comic strain can be traced to his Irish heritage. It is a matter of early development touched upon by Rosset. But tying Shaw to a more clearly Irish heritage—the standard inroad has been *John Bull's Other Island*—is often ignored in favor of looking at Shaw as a universal genius who happened to be Irish. Both his universalism and his Irishness deserve fresh new visits from the scholarly world, the current mass of Shavian scholarship notwithstanding.

ARCHIVAL SOURCES

Extensive manuscripts are housed at the University of Texas, Austin, in the Harry Ransom Humanities Research Center; at the British Library Shaw Archive; and in the Shaw Collection at the University of North Carolina at Chapel Hill. The latter includes Shaw's correspondence with Malvern Festival Theatre director H. K. Ayliff and with a number of actresses. The collection also contains Shaw corrections to page proofs for biographies of Shaw by Archibald Henderson (a Chapel Hill math professor).

PRIMARY BIBLIOGRAPHY

Agitations: Letters to the Press, 1875–1950. Ed. Dan H. Laurence and James Rambeau. New York: Frederick Ungar, 1985.

Bernard Shaw: Collected Letters. Ed. Dan H. Laurence. 4 vols. London: Max Reinhardt, 1965–88.

The Bodley Head Bernard Shaw. London: Bodley Head, 1970–74. (Considered the standard edition.)

SECONDARY BIBLIOGRAPHY

Agate, James. [1]. Review of *Heartbreak House. Saturday Review* (21 Oct. 1921).

———. [2]. Review of *In Good King Charles' Golden Days. The Sunday Times* (13 Aug. 1939).

Archer, William. [1]. Review of *Arms and the Man. World* (25 Apr. 1894).

———. [2]. Review of *Major Barbara. World* (5 Dec. 1905).

———. [3]. Review of *Man and Superman. World* (30 May 1905).

Atkinson, Brooks. Review of *Geneva. New York Times* (31 Jan. 1940): 15.

Beerbohm, Max. Review of *John Bull's Other Island. Saturday Review* (12 Nov. 1904).

Bertolini, John A. *The Playwrighting Self of Bernard Shaw.* Carbondale: Southern Illinois University Press, 1991.

Bevan, E. Dean. *A Concordance to the Plays and Prefaces of Bernard Shaw.* 10 vols. Detroit: Gale Research, 1971.

Bevir, M. "The Marxism of George Bernard Shaw, 1883–1889." *History of Political Thought* 13.2 (Summer 1992): 299–318.

Bloom, Harold, ed. [1]. *Major Barbara: Modern Critical Views.* New York: Chelsea, 1988.

———, ed. [2]. *Man and Superman: Modern Critical Views.* New York: Chelsea, 1987.

———, ed. [3]. *Pygmalion: Modern Critical Views.* New York: Chelsea, 1988.

————, ed. [4]. *Saint Joan: Modern Critical Views*. New York: Chelsea, 1987.

Bloomfield, Z. "American Response to George Bernard Shaw: A Study of Professional Productions, 1894–1905." *Theatre Studies* 36 (1991): 5–17.

Review of *Caesar and Cleopatra*. *The Times* (26 Nov. 1907).

Carr, Pat M. *Bernard Shaw*. New York: Frederick Ungar, 1976.

Dent, Alan. Review of *Geneva*. *Spectator* (5 Aug. 1938).

Review of *The Devil's Disciple*. *The Times* (27 Sept. 1899).

Dukore, Bernard F. [1]. *Bernard Shaw, Director*. Seattle: University of Washington Press, 1971.

————. [2]. *Bernard Shaw, Playwright*. Columbia: University of Missouri Press, 1973.

————, ed. [3]. *The Collected Screenplays of Bernard Shaw*. London: George Prior Publications, 1980.

Ervine, St. John. Review of *The Apple Cart*. *Observer* (25 Aug. 1929).

Evans, T. F., ed. *Shaw: The Critical Heritage*. London: Routledge & Kegan Paul, 1976.

Gainor, J. Ellen. *Shaw's Daughters*. Ann Arbor: University of Michigan Press, 1991.

Gibbs, A. M. *Shaw: Interviews and Recollections*. New York: Macmillan, 1990.

Gordon, David J. *Bernard Shaw and the Comic Sublime*. New York: St. Martin's Press, 1990.

Grein, J. T. Review of *Mrs. Warren's Profession*. *Sunday Special* (12 Jan. 1902).

Grene, Nicholas. [1]. *Bernard Shaw, a Critical View*. New York: St. Martin's Press, 1984.

————. [2]. "The Maturing of Immaturity, Shaw's First Novel." *Irish University Review* 20.2 (1990): 225–38.

Harrison, W. "*Geneva,* a Postwar Approach." *Journal of Irish Literature* 19.2 (1990): 52–57.

Hay, Malcolm. Review of *Back to Methuselah*. *Time Out* (21 June 1984).

Henderson, Archibald. [1]. *Bernard Shaw: Playboy and Prophet*. New York: Appleton, 1932.

————. [2]. *George Bernard Shaw: Man of the Century*. New York: Appleton-Century-Crofts, 1956.

Holroyd, Michael. [1]. *Bernard Shaw*. 4 vols. New York: Random House, 1988–92.

————, ed. [2]. *The Genius of Shaw*. New York: Holt, Rinehart & Winston, 1979.

Hummert, Paul A. *Bernard Shaw's Marxian Romance*. Lincoln: University of Nebraska Press, 1973.

Jenckes, Norma Margaret. [1]. "John Bull's Other Island: A Critical Study of Shaw's Irish Play in Its Theatrical and Socio-Political Context." Ph.D. diss., University of Illinois, Urbana-Champaign, 1974.

————. [2]. "The Rejection of Shaw's Irish Play: *John Bull's Other Island*." *Éire-Ireland* 10:1 (1975): 38–53.

Kearney, Richard. [1]. *Transitions: Narratives in Modern Irish Culture*. Manchester: Manchester University Press, 1988.

————. [2]. *The Wake of Imagination*. Minneapolis: University of Minnesota Press, 1988.

Lambert, J. W. Review of *Geneva*. *Drama* (Spring 1972): 27.

Laurence, Dan H., and Nicholas Grene, eds. *Shaw, Lady Gregory, and the Abbey*. Gerrards Cross: Colin Smythe, 1993.

Review of *Major Barbara*. *Pall Mall Gazette* (29 Nov. 1905).

Marcus, Frank. Review of *O'Flaherty, V.C. Plays and Players* (Nov. 1966): 15.

Martin, Kingsley. Review of *On the Rocks. New Statesman and Nation* (2 Dec. 1933).

Meisel, Martin. *Shaw and the Nineteenth-Century Theater.* Princeton: Princeton University Press, 1963.

Review of *The Millionairess. The Times Literary Supplement* (28 Mar. 1936).

Morgan, Charles. Review of *Too True to Be Good. The Times* (8 Aug. 1932).

Morgan, Margery. *File on Shaw.* London: Methuen, 1989.

Nightingale, Benedict. Review of *Heartbreak House. New Statesman* (18 Mar. 1983).

Pirandello, Luigi. Review of *Saint Joan. New York Times* (13 Jan. 1924).

Rosset, B. C. *Shaw of Dublin: The Formative Years.* University Park: Pennsylvania State University Press, 1964.

Review of *The Simpleton of the Unexpected Isles. Sydney Bulletin* (16 Oct. 1935).

Review of *The Simpleton of the Unexpected Isles. The Times Literary Supplement* (28 Mar. 1936).

Smith, Warren Sylvester. *Bishop of Everywhere.* University Park: Pennsylvania State University Press, 1982.

Trussler, Simon. "Introduction." In *File on Shaw,* by Margery Morgan. London: Methuen, 1989.

Walkley, A. B. Review of *Man and Superman. The Times Literary Supplement* (26 May 1905).

Wardle, Irving. [1]. Review of *Back to Methuselah. The Times* (4 Aug. 1969).

———. [2]. Review of *On the Rocks. The Times* (6 May 1982): 15.

———. [3]. Review of *Pygmalion. The Times* (17 May 1974).

Weintraub, Rodelle, ed. *Fabian Feminist: Bernard Shaw and Woman.* University Park: Pennsylvania State University Press, 1977.

Weintraub, Stanley. [1]. *Bernard Shaw: A Guide to Research.* University Park: Pennsylvania State University Press, 1992.

———. ed. [2]. *Bernard Shaw: An Autobiography, 1856–1898.* New York: Weybright & Talley, 1969. Reprint. London: Max Reinhardt, 1970.

———. ed. [3]. *Bernard Shaw: An Autobiography, 1898–1950: The Playwright Years.* New York: Weybright & Talley, 1970. Reprint. London: Max Reinhardt, 1971.

———. ed. [4]. *Bernard Shaw on the London Art Scene, 1885–1950.* University Park: Pennsylvania State University Press, 1989.

———. [5]. *Journey to Heartbreak: The Crucible Years of Bernard Shaw, 1914–1918.* New York: Weybright & Talley, 1971.

Weintraub, Stanley, and Rodelle Weintraub, eds. *Arms and the Man and John Bull's Other Island.* New York: Bantam, 1993.

BIBLIOGRAPHY

G. B. Shaw: An Annotated Bibliography of Writings about Him. Vol. 1 (1871–1930). Ed. J. P. Wearing; Vol. 2 (1931–1956). Ed. Elsie B. Adams and Donald C. Haberman; Vol. 3 (1957–1978). Ed. Donald C. Haberman, 1986. De Kalb: Northern Illinois University Press, 1986–87.

R. C. Sherriff
(1896–1975)

MARK A. GRAVES

Few playwrights in recent memory can attribute an enduring reputation to one example of their creative output, yet the production and premiere of *Journey's End* (1928), a play about a British squad in a dugout in World War I, catapulted its creator, R. C. Sherriff, to national and international prominence as an insightful chronicler of the Great War. He would go on to write and see produced over half a dozen other plays and would write novels and screenplays, but this war play best seals Sherriff's place in the history of twentieth-century British theater.

Although he penned an autobiography aptly titled *No Leading Lady* (1968)—reflecting criticism that his most enduring dramatic success contained no female characters—little is known of Sherriff's life before he entered the British armed forces at the age of eighteen. It is perhaps safe to assume that he lived the life of the typical middle-class British youth, since he set his plays in such a milieu. From a lower-middle-class family, he was born Robert Cedric Sherriff on 6 June 1986 to Herbert Hankin and Constance Winder Sherriff in Hampton Wick, Surrey, near Kingston-on-Thames and London. Sherriff's father, like his father before him, held a position with the Sun Insurance Company there, where Sherriff at the age of seventeen secured a job earning four pounds a week as an insurance clerk. A descendant of Lawrence Sherriff, who founded Rugby School in 1557 (at least as his uncle's family history asserted), yet denied a public-school education himself because of his family's economic circumstances, he graduated from Kingston Grammar School and concerned himself throughout his career with a particular stratum of the British class structure, the middle class.

Sherriff interrupted his fledgling insurance career by enlisting in the Ninth East Surrey Regiment at the outbreak of World War I. The letters he wrote to his parents in this period would serve as the basis of his most famous theatrical work, *Journey's End,* not to appear until 1928. In the intervening ten years from the war to the premiere of his first major production, Sherriff cowrote and co-directed amateur plays for the support of the local rowing club. While none of these early manuscripts still exist, two plays from this period, *Profit and Loss* and *Cornlow-in-the-Downs,* were produced at the Gables Theatre, in Surbiton, really nothing more than a small theater in an old private house his rowing club had stumbled on to present their fundraisers.

Still working as an agent for the Sun Insurance Company, Sherriff completed the manuscript of *Journey's End* in a matter of months once his term as captain of his club's rowing team expired. The material substance of the drama actually took shape from a rough outline for a novel Sherriff had sketched out but dis-carded years before. Realizing that the play exceeded the abilities of his amateur rowing club, Sherriff sent the play to the Curtis Brown theatrical agency, the recipient of four of his earlier manuscripts, all firmly but politely rejected for lack of an interested theater company to perform them. Undaunted, he wrote in his autobiography, "When you've spent a year on a play it's hard to throw it in a corner and forget about it" (41). The Brown agency forwarded the work to Geoffrey Dearmer of the Incorporated Stage Society. Dearmer encouraged Sherriff to send a copy to George Bernard Shaw, who saw the play as a "social document" rather than a drama, but on that basis alone urged, "[L]et it be produced by all means" (45).

Under the direction of James Whale after three directors had turned it down, the Stage Society production of the play opened for a few performances in December 1928 with a then-unknown Laurence Olivier in the role of Captain Stanhope. Met with delayed, but eventual, critical and popular success after a lukewarm reception on opening night, the play moved to the West End's Savoy Theatre (London) in early 1929 under the guiding hand of producer Maurice Brown and with Colin Clive playing Stanhope. Breaking all box-office records in London's West End, Sherriff's drama was soon translated into twenty-five foreign languages, and productions opened in New York, Berlin, Paris, and Tokyo—for a sum total of twenty-six countries launching productions around the world, with forty companies performing the drama in Germany alone. Film versions featured both Colin Keith-Johnson and Conrad Veidt as Stanhope. Sher-riff novelized the play in collaboration with Vernon Bartlett, but the novel did not enjoy success equal to its dramatic counterpart. Drafts for a dramatic sequel never saw publication or production.

Sadly, Sherriff would never compose another play that came close to equaling the fame or financial or critical success of *Journey's End.* Maurice Brown's production of Sherriff's *Badger's Green* (1930), a comedy about resistance to-ward progress in an English village, did not meet with critical approval. In despair, Sherriff looked to schoolteaching as an alternative profession and was admitted to New College, Oxford University, at the age of thirty-five to pursue a degree in history and enjoy notoriety as perhaps the oldest member ever of the rowing team. His academic life was interrupted almost immediately, however, for a year later, he wrote the moderately successful *The Fortnight in September* (1931), a novel about a middle-class British family on its annual seaside holiday. Further financial advancement came when, at James Whale's behest, Carl Laemmle of Universal Pictures, Hollywood, offered Sherriff a contract to write screenplays. While in this position, Sherriff collaborated with Philip Wylie on the screenplay of H. G. Wells's *The Invisible Man* (1933) and with Charles Kenyon on Erich Maria Remarque's sequel to *All Quiet on the Western Front, The Road Back* (1937). His other screen credits included the adaptation of James Hilton's *Goodbye, Mr. Chips* (1939), *Lady Hamilton (That Hamilton Woman)* (1941), and *Quartet* (1949), a screen adaptation of four short stories by W. Somerset Maugham.

While success and financial security would come from other avenues, Sherriff never abandoned playwriting as a source of creative fulfillment. During the 1930s and 1940s Sherriff's theatrical endeavors ran concurrently with his success as a screenwriter. In 1936 he collaborated with actress Jeanne de Casalis (the wife of Colin Clive) on *St. Helena,* based on Napoleon's last years on St. Helena Island. In 1948, with the successful production and touring of *Miss Mabel,* about a twin who murders her sister after forging the other's will for altruistic purposes, Sherriff turned to the mystery and suspense genre. *Home at Seven* (1950), with Ralph Richardson as a bank employee who cannot account for a twenty-four-hour period during which time a murder occurs in his proximity, ran in London for 342 performances. *A Shred of Evidence,* with a similar story line, appeared in 1960. Sherriff returned to his interest in history in *The Long Sunset* (1955) about a Roman family living in the English countryside during the Roman occupation of Britannia. Other plays in this period included *The White Carnation* (1953), a Christmas mystery story, *The Telescope* (1957), later adapted into a musical called *Johnny the Priest* in 1960, and other novels.

Besides writing for the stage and screen, Sherriff wrote a radio play called *Cards with Uncle Tom* (1958) and a television script, *The Ogburn Story* (1963). In 1968 Sherriff published his autobiography entitled *No Leading Lady.* The title also serves as a metaphor for his life, for Sherriff died unmarried on 13 November 1975 in London after enjoying lifelong interests in the theater, film, cricket, rowing, and archeology. He helped excavate a Roman villa near Angmering and the fort of Proscolite on Hadrian's Wall between writing projects, and he was appointed a fellow of the Royal Society of Literature.

Selected Biographical Sources: Bracco; Hill; Morsberger.

MAJOR PLAYS, PREMIERES, AND SIGNIFICANT REVIVALS: THEATRICAL RECEPTION

Journey's End. 1928. Opened 9 December at the Apollo Theater (London) for 2 scheduled performances only. Produced by Geoffrey Dearmer for the Incorporated Stage Society and directed by James Whale. Moved to the Savoy Theatre (London) on 1 January 1929 for a trial run. Repremiered at the Savoy on

21 January 1929. Moved to the Prince of Wales's Theater (London) on 3 June
1930. Played for a total of 594 London performances. Produced by Maurice
Brown and directed by James Whale. Opened at Henry Miller's Theatre (New
York) on 22 March 1929, running for 485 performances. Revivals: Empire Theater (New York), 18 September 1939, for 16 performances; off-off Broadway
(New York), 1968–69; Mermaid Theatre (London), later moving to the Cambridge Theatre (London) 1972; Whitehall Theatre (London), 1988.

The production of this play is a story of good fortune, happenstance, and
second thoughts. Critical interpretation of the play during its earliest productions
often surrounded discrepancies between the two companies performing the play
before its New York debut. In London the Stage Society staged the play with
Laurence Olivier in the lead as Stanhope. Olivier considered Stanhope his favorite role in the theater, a distinction he later revised to include Archie in *The
Entertainer.* Morsberger reported that in actuality, Olivier neither completely
fell in love with nor completely committed to Sherriff's production. In London
casting for *Beau Geste* took place concurrently with the production of Sherriff's
play, and Olivier hoped that the Stanhope character would best showcase him
for the other production. The producers of *Beau Geste* awarded Olivier his
desired role, but as fate would have it, Olivier's decision to abandon the role
of Stanhope once Sherriff's drama was restaged at the Savoy Theatre on the
West End was ill advised. *Beau Geste* enjoyed only a short run, while *Journey's
End* played for over a year and created instant fame for both its director, James
Whale, and its star, Colin Clive, who went on to reprise his role in the film
(Morsberger, 1786).

Critics marveled at the play's realism, innovative setting, and lyricism. Macdonell saw the appearance of the play as much more effective than all the
propaganda put forth by England's peace societies. Darlington [1] provided perhaps the best theatrical overview of the various London companies, best characterized by an anecdote involving his wife. On the second night of the Stage
Society performance, Darlington's wife reportedly asked him, "Was it like that
[in the trenches]?" Darlington, choking back tears in "horrible gulps," replied,
"Exactly like that." Despite his overt emotional response to the play, Darlington
ultimately concluded that knowing that the three principal youthful actors, including Olivier, could not have served in World War I exposed the theatricality
of their performance rather than its realism. Colin Clive's casting in Stanhope's
role in the Savoy production eliminated this irregularity, but it reemerged in the
Arts Theatre production to be exported to New York. Darlington ultimately
agreed with Littell that the New York–bound company eventually achieved the
"curiously sure understatement" required of the characters.

Once the play was staged at Henry Miller's Theatre in New York, critics
made inevitable comparisons to an American World War I play from a few
years earlier. Most critics generally weighed the features of *Journey's End* and
What Price Glory? (1924) and found Sherriff's version of the Great War different from and for the most part superior to its American counterpart. Littell

saw the New York production as "completely satisfying and memorable" and considered the play superior to America's *What Price Glory?* in its representation of the war as most men fought it. Brown called the play a true war play and pleasant in its own right and saw the play's "hungry, gallant adherence to gentility" as preferable to virulent tirades against war and expressions of self-pity at the circumstances the characters find themselves in. Van Doren called it probably the best war play seen so far, obliterating the memory of any other. Woollcott called it "[t]he best play written for the English stage in this century and the finest work yet wrought by an Englishman out of his war experience."

In contrast, Nathan [2] chose *What Price Glory?* as the superior of the two, despite the virtues of underdramatization and simple evocation of emotion in both dialogue and performance manifest in Sherriff's creation. Nathan cited Sherriff's lapses into "cheap theatrical fetches" just when his message was reaching its highest convictions and also his tendency to create stock English characters with their all-too-consistent civility and gentility as weaknesses in the play's universal presentation of war. Nathan conceded that the performances were perfectly enacted, however. Young [1] submitted a similarly mixed review of the drama, with an emphasis on lyricism as its principal virtue. He cited the poetic quality of the dialogue as setting the play on its own, but considered it a poetry of "human concern" rather than "human imagination," for many scenes in Young's opinion were as yet underwritten. With the exception of Stanhope, the characters resembled types from romantic fiction, rather than fully realized dramatic characters, although the actors gave solid performances, especially Colin Keith-Johnson as Stanhope. Whereas *Journey's End* was more familiar as fiction (ironic since its novelization did not sell well), *What Price Glory?* succeeded better as drama, Young concluded.

In its first revival subsequent to the time of its original production, Sherriff's drama did not fare well, its reception perhaps explainable in terms of the recent outbreak of another world war. In its first Broadway run Atkinson [4] had called the play "unpretentious" and had cited Sherriff's relative inexperience in the theater as a strength revealed through his "integrity of characterization . . . total lack of theatrical assumptions and the bare ruggedness of his dialogue." This same inexperience, however, resulted in a structure too loosely divided into arbitrary scene changes. Ten years after his initial support of the drama, in his review of the 1939 revival, Atkinson [1] called the play dated in comparison to *What Price Glory?,* perhaps because of its actual strength, its ability to reevoke an era and make World War I a central character in the drama rather than rendering it as mere backdrop. Unfortunately, the revival failed because it did not reflect what war was like at the time (an ironic remark, since World War II had started only a few weeks after the publication of Atkinson's observations). The reviewer for *Time* ("Old Play in Manhattan") saw the experience of a scant number of British officers in a dugout in 1918 as "inexpressive [and] minuscule" in comparison to the millions fighting in Europe again. Less virulent in his criticism of the play's nostalgic limitations, and perhaps most fairly weighing the merits of the play versus the anxiety of the era in which it was being revived, Krutch saw the play as emphasizing, particularly to American audiences, the gulf between American understanding of war and the English stiff-upper-lip, public-school-inspired heroism. Such a differing perspective resulted in the idealization of the characters, made only more apparent by fears for the outcome of the future that the war presently raging in Europe provoked.

Completely divorced from its historical context, the play enjoyed a successful run in a much more contemporary London, revealing the harshness of criticism unfairly lumped on the play by the influence of World War II. Barnes, reviewing the 1972 revival, suggested that while all the characters in the play represented "clichés with a precious touch of truth to them," the play was aging well, even if it could not be considered a classic yet. Real heroism existed in the play, and Sherriff neutralized the sentimentality of his dramatic situation through the play's tragic conclusion. Weinraub cited London reviewers from *The Times,* the *Observer,* and the *Guardian,* who saw the play as "a magnificent revival," "wonderfully effective," and "a fascinating document of war," respectively. Sherriff was still alive to see his drama staged almost fifty years after its original composition.

Badger's Green. 1930. Opened 12 June at the Prince of Wales's Theatre (London). Produced by Maurice Brown and staged by James Whale.

This comedy about an English village's resistance to progress in the form of real-estate development was perhaps unfairly overshadowed by the worldwide success of *Journey's End.* Inevitable comparisons to Sherriff's phenomenal success and simplicity in the war play were harsh and reflected the critical and popular disappointment many felt based upon the promise of his earlier theatrical endeavor. Wakefield noted internal similarities between Sherriff's wartime and peacetime works, principally in their depictions of "a group of men . . . united in their preparations to defeat a common enemy, but disunited by an incompatibility of temperament." Questioning the overwhelming and nearly uniform critical accolades *Journey's End* received versus the lack of critical support this play would receive, Wakefield cited Sherriff's characterization rather than plot as creating the play's interest for audiences. Dukes considered the play's theme "genuine" and its execution "shrewd and good-natured," but suggested that had *Journey's End* not scored a success for Maurice Brown, this play would never have been produced on its own merits alone.

St. Helena. (with Jeanne de Casalis). 1936. Opened at the Old Vic Theatre (London) 7 February. Transferred to Daly's Theater (London) for a total of 128 performances. Opened 6 October 1936 at the Lyceum Theatre (New York). Produced by Max Gordon and directed by Robert Sinclair.

Sherriff collaborated with actress Jeanne de Casalis (then wife of Colin Clive) on this dramatization of Napoleon's last days, originally composed and published in 1934. It marked his return to the theater after the success of his screen adaptation of H. G. Wells's *The Invisible Man,* considered by many as one of the most enduring science-fiction screenplays of all time. The play's 1936 production at the Old Vic rapidly dwindled to houses of less than a hundred until Winston Churchill lauded the play in the editorial pages of *The Times* as "a work of art of a very high order" (quoted in Sherriff, *No Leading Lady,* 304). Packed houses for two months prompted the reopening of the play at a larger West End theater, but box-office proceeds plummeted, perhaps because of reviews that saw the play as forced and self-conscious, but competently acted (Fleming [2]).

The American production of the play suffered from comparisons with the standing-room-only dramatization of the life of another historical figure, Laurence Houseman's *Victoria Regina,* like *St. Helena* a compilation of vignettes. Unlike Houseman's playlets, however, Isaacs saw in the juxtaposition of the Sheriff and de Casalis vignettes the same dramatic patterning. Each scene began with cheerfulness and ended in despair, stifling the emotional range of both the actors and the overall structure of Napoleon's life as it moved downward toward death. Still, "It is always true and often vivid, though seldom moving." Atkinson [3] called attention to the authors' respectful treatment of the subject matter, but criticized the drama for making a French dictator into "a middle-class Englishman with a knack for commanding." Ultimately, Atkinson [2] considered the play and writing "undistinguished." Nathan [1], Young [2], and the reviewer for *Time* ("New Play in Manhattan") saw the play as unnecessarily prolonged. Nathan located the problem in the authors' tendency to include long quotations from Napoleon that brought the play closer to literary drama than theatrical performance. Similarly, Young attributed the sagging of the last third of the play to the limitations of historical accuracy, restricting what the character of Napoleon was left to say. Vernon, in the lone positive review, saw the play as entertaining to anyone not requiring external action, but interested in Napoleon as a character instead.

Miss Mabel. 1948. Opened 23 November at the Duchess Theatre (London) and moved to the Strand (London), running for a combined total of 181 performances.

Fleming [1] responded, "Mr. Sherriff's invention and felicity never fail him, and we come away from the theatre conscious of having seen a piece of work which is, in its unambitious, unpretentious way, something of a minor tour de force." Darlington [2] wondered if Sherriff planned for his play to start out so badly so as to magnify its redemption by the end, but the playwright added no such twist in this story of an elderly woman whose murder of her twin sister is ultimately uncovered. Sherriff so masterfully crafted the play that just when it seemed at its clumsiest and most simplistic, the audience began arguing for Miss Mabel's exoneration, rather than her condemnation by the authorities. Trewin [3] questioned the complexity of the play and its propensity for "sentimental blurring.'' The characters also fell into types, although the actors portraying Miss Mabel (Mary Jerrold), the lawyer (Clive Morton), and the vicar (W. E. Holloway) stood out.

Home at Seven. 1950. Opened 7 March at Wyndham's Theatre (London) for 342 performances.

As reported in the *New York Times* (''Sherriff Play Opens''), London critics and audiences warmly welcomed Ralph Richardson in the role of Sherriff's protagonist who cannot account for his whereabouts during a twenty-four-hour period when a murder occurs in his proximity. The reviewer for *The Times* (''Home at Seven'') expressed satisfaction with a play that lived up to its modest intentions.

The White Carnation. 1953. Opened 5 January at the Theatre Royal (Brighton, England). Reopened April 1953 at the Globe (London).

Most criticism considered this play a failed attempt at a gothic drama. Tynan saw the play as combining too many clichés and techniques employed by dramatists from British theater history. Trading upon the supernatural elements in the play, he concluded, ''Amidst such a confusion of moods Mr. Sherriff's play hasn't an unearthly chance of success'' (48). Similarly, Trewin [1] considered the play a disappointment, with a convincing opening scene and closing scene but only padding in between. Both reviewers commented on Sherriff's talent for writing roles for Ralph Richardson, however.

The Long Sunset. 1955. Opened 30 August at the Birmingham Repertory Theatre (Birmingham, England). First broadcast on the Home Service of the British Broadcasting Corporation 23 April 1955. Revival: November 1961 at the Mermaid Theatre (London).

Gascoigne saw the play as the product of a middle-aged English playwright trying to evoke Roman-occupied Britain through between-the-wars language. He wrote, ''R. C. Sherriff requires his language to travel 1, 500 years. . . . It doesn't quite get there. . . . In its bland way the play is well put together and holds the attention.''

A Shred of Evidence. 1960. Opened 27 April at the Duchess Theatre (London). Later moved to the Fortune Theatre (London).

This play was the last new play of Sherriff's to appear during his career. As with *Home at Seven* a decade earlier, one review wrote that Sherriff relied on chance, middle-class moral conscientiousness and an unaccounted-for time period in the life of his ''ordinary'' man to create a play ''related with astonishing economy and tautness. . . . Sherriff . . . builds the play with a detailed care: it is an uncommon union of dramatist and actor'' (Trewin [2]).

ADDITIONAL PLAYS, ADAPTATIONS, AND PRODUCTIONS

Sherriff wrote a full-length play entitled *Windfall* about the changes a simple man endures who is goaded into buying an Irish sweepstakes ticket that wins.

It opened in February 1933 at the Embassy Theatre, Swiss Cottage, Hampstead, to negative reviews. He also wrote a playlet entitled *Two Hearts Doubled* published by Samuel French in 1934. His play about London's East End *The Telescope* (1957) was later adapted as a musical called *Johnny the Priest* in 1960. Cornelius attributed to him *Mr. Bridie's Hand* (1926), although that play has not been listed in significant directories of Sherriff's output.

ASSESSMENT OF SHERRIFF'S CAREER

Even by the standards of his own time, R. C. Sherriff wrote plays often dated in their theme and dramatic method, harkening back to the works of J. M. Barrie, whom he met and admired. While many of his contemporaries wrote dramas that examined the significant economic, political, social, and even sexual issues of their times, Sherriff stuck to what he knew best, the effect of random occurrence or the demands of the moment on the middle-class British citizen he knew so well. As his career evolved, he often paid the price in terms of both critical appeal and box-office proceeds for dramatizing a vision of English life so familiar to him.

One could argue with some conviction, however, that Sherriff was ahead of his time in dramatizing effectively the most significant event of his generation, the First World War. Had he not written another word after *Journey's End,* he would have still ensconced himself in the history of British theater because of his precise capturing of the postwar mood without reopening old wounds. Before Sherriff's *Journey's End* came before the footlights, no single British or European play centered on the Great War experience had struck a chord with audiences. As a result, British producers hesitated to stage works about the First World War since most of them amounted either to a patriotic rehashing of support for the war or antiwar tracts that failed to garner interest among a population still carrying the visible scars of the western front.

Like the lives of the characters it depicts, *Journey's End* was at the mercy of forces beyond anyone's control, in particular, timing. Since commercial producers were uncertain of its marketability, questions arose about the potential of the work's artistic merit to create a critical momentum adequate to launch the play in the mainstream theater. A significant share of the play's artistic success depended upon re-creating the claustrophobic environment of a British dugout undergoing a bombardment on the western front. In his autobiography Sherriff described both the hushed audience response to the final curtain at the play's premiere performance and how he often ducked outside the stage door rather than risk witnessing poorly timed sound effects and lighting attempting to replicate shells crashing to the ground. His remarks here not only echo commercial producers' concerns over audience reception of his play, but also describe the innovative, even radical, use of the dramatic space and effects the play demanded.

Sherriff had said that he wanted to write a play appealing to the average soldier still walking about on the streets and byways of Great Britain. In reference to Sherriff's goal, most critics focused on Sherriff's realism in the play, disagreeing about the political motivations in its message, as Bracco comprehensively summarized. Most assessments saw the central question of the drama as involving the difference between "[w]hat the war was like" as opposed to "[w]hat the war meant" (152). Bracco located the appeal of *Journey's End* for critics and audiences alike in its ability to provide a vision of how the war was experienced, strained through the veil of memory, rather than as a political or social document attempting to verify reality. Sherriff's play succeeded, then, because it did not force-feed critics or audiences an overt political message about the war as others had done. Onions saw the drama as failing as a serious work for exactly the reasons it was so appealing: the work never problematized the social values it affirmed and, in the process, reinscribed a romantic version of heroism so indicative of such values supposedly obliterated by the war itself (92).

Although the overwhelming majority of critics heralded the play as one of the best to appear on the British stage in years—Swaffer called it "the greatest of all war plays"—some critics questioned the universality of a war play where the characters seem so steeped in class-dictated British dialects, a criticism leveled at Sherriff's later play *The Long Sunset* as well. Such dialects required adjustments by American audiences accustomed to the gritty vernacular of *What Price Glory?* appearing on Broadway earlier in the 1920s. Nathan [3] even identified "a faint pansy aspect" in a play that handled its material well. Most critics and audiences, however, based upon the play's phenomenal run, considered the characters so carefully and skillfully drawn from life, even if they did become types, that their words sounded like actual speech rather than theatrical dialogue.

The remainder of Sherriff's career was overshadowed by the overwhelming success of *Journey's End,* even though he enjoyed financial and critical success as a screenwriter on films such as *The Invisible Man, Goodbye, Mr. Chips,* and *Lady Hamilton (That Hamilton Woman).* Still, Sherriff's first love was always theater, and no matter what financial gains he enjoyed writing for films, the stage and audiences principally benefited from his artistic insight. His interest in suburban British life—what he considered "the simple and the ordinary"—provided British theatergoers with a mirror on their own world that was largely flattering and typical, but not stereotypical. What binds his work together is his avowed goal as a dramatist to write about the characters and virtues that he knew about since he had lived their lives. "I wanted to write plays about these people themselves," he wrote. "I knew from my early plays that audiences enjoyed watching characters grappling with problems that might come their own way" (*No Leading Lady,* 207). In *Badger's Green,* for example, which most critics considered a failure, the civic leaders of a local village band together to preserve their way of life. Similarly, in *The Long Sunset* Sherriff humanized the Roman evacuation of Britannia at the end of the occupation by portraying the struggles of a representative Roman family against the forces that threaten its survival.

For Sherriff, a simple tilting of everyday events could result in mystery, intrigue, maybe even a hint of trickery that was always corrected by the simple values, grace, and motivations inherent in the nature of his characters. In *Miss Mabel,* for example, the title character weighs the moral implications of poisoning her cantankerous, selfish twin sister and forging the latter's will to benefit others. While the authorities catch onto Miss Mabel's crime, justice seems served in the recognition of the offense alone. Moreover, in both *Home at Seven* and *A Shred of Evidence* average men battle with their consciences, agonizing over turning themselves in for crimes that they cannot assure themselves they did not commit versus the changes such unsubstantiated confessions could mean for themselves, their loved ones, and all they have worked for. In *The White Carnation* a man awakens from what he believes was an alcohol-induced nap after an annual Christmas party but what was really a bomb blast to find himself a ghost haunting his own house. Even *St. Helena,* criticized as limited in its too-concentrated deference to history, focuses on the everyday events surrounding the last years of Napoleon's life. Despite the dialogue that critics have correctly assessed as closer to oratory than everyday speech, Sherriff enabled audiences to forget that the central character had conquered Europe instead of just living out life as an impoverished country gentleman. While ordinary comfort such as a dram after work at the neighborhood pub or tea in the parlor could be enjoyed, excess was seldom rewarded and the search for simple truth and hard work was always the key to his vision.

Anderson summed up Sherriff's contribution to British drama best: "Fond of celebrating quiet values of suburban England, he must be judged a dramatist of competence rather than originality" (408). By his fourth decade in the theater, he knew sadly that the public no longer found his brand of British existence entertaining or enriching. When his last two plays received polite, but nonetheless harshly critical reviews, he knew that his dramatic career was over. "The theatre had been my first love," he wrote in his autobiography," and I should have liked to have stayed with it until the end; but maybe it was better to go with a few unwritten plays inside you than hang on until you wrote yourself right out" (352).

Thus it is difficult to predict where Sherriff scholarship will proceed in the future. In all likelihood, Sherriff's reputation will rest on the creation of *Journey's End,* if recent revivals and critical attention are any measure. Besides the war play, his autobiography provides significant insight into British theater production in the years before World War II and could prove valuable for scholars interested in the British theater between the wars. While, relatively speaking, he created perhaps the most significant play about war to appear in the twentieth century, he also wrote a body of works that, while they may not be considered artistically superior, nonetheless offer insight into a certain British class structure and values not often represented in drama of the era.

ARCHIVAL SOURCES

Sherriff's letters to the League of Dramatists surrounding his membership in the society and personal letters to Vernon Bartlett are housed in the Indiana University Library, Bloomington, Indiana. Other documents, including letters to his parents and clippings involving his plays, are located in the Surrey Record Office, Surrey, England.

PRIMARY BIBLIOGRAPHY

Full-Length Plays

Badger's Green. London: Gollancz, 1930; London and New York: Samuel French, 1934.
Home at Seven. London: Gollancz, 1951.
Journey's End: A Play in Three Acts. London: Gollancz, 1929; New York: Coward-McCann, 1929.
The Long Sunset. London: Elek Books, 1955.
Miss Mabel. London: Gollancz, 1949.
A Shred of Evidence. London: Samuel French, 1961.
St. Helena. With Jeanne de Casalis. London: Gollancz, 1934; New York: Stokes, 1935.
The Telescope (later adapted in the musical *Johnny the Priest*). London: Samuel French, 1957.
The White Carnation. London: Heinemann, 1953; London: Samuel French, 1953.
Windfall. N.p., 1933.

One-Act Plays

Two Hearts Doubled. London and New York: Samuel French, 1934.

Screenplays

The Dam Busters. Associated British Pictures, 1954.
The Four Feathers. London Films, 1939.
Goodbye, Mr. Chips. MGM, 1939.
The Invisible Man. Universal, 1933.
Lady Hamilton (That Hamilton Woman). London Films, 1941; United Artists, 1941.
Odd Man Out. Paramount, 1947.
One More River. Universal, 1934.
Quartet. Gainsborough, 1949.
The Road Back. Universal, 1937.
This above All. Twentieth Century Fox, 1941.
Trio. Gainsborough, 1950.

Autobiography

No Leading Lady. London: Gollancz, 1968.

Prose Works (Including Novels and Children's Books)

Another Year. London: Heinemann, 1948; New York: Macmillan, 1948.
Chedworth. New York: Macmillan, 1944.
The Fortnight in September. London: Gollancz, 1931; New York: Stokes, 1932.
Greengates. London: Gollancz, 1936; New York: Stokes, 1936.
The Hopkins Manuscript. London: Gollancz, 1939; New York: Macmillan, 1939.
Journey's End. Adapted with Vernon Bartlett. London: Gollancz, 1930; New York: Stokes, 1930.
King John's Treasure. London: Heinemann, 1954; New York: Macmillan, 1954.
The Siege of Swayne Castle. London: Gollancz, 1973.
The Wells of St. Mary's. London: Heinemann, 1973.

SECONDARY BIBLIOGRAPHY

Anderson, Michael, ed. *Crowell's Handbook of Contemporary Drama.* New York: Crowell, 1971.
Atkinson, J. Brooks. [1]. "The Drama of the Last War." *New York Times* (24 Sept. 1939): 9:1.
———. [2]. "Napoleon's Last Years in Captivity the Subject of 'St. Helena.' " *New York Times* (11 Oct. 1936): 10:1.
———. [3]. "Napoleon's Last Years the Subject of 'St. Helena' and of Maurice Evans's Acting." *New York Times* (7 Oct. 1936): 82.
———. [4]. "The Price of Glory?" *New York Times* (23 Mar. 1929): 23.
Barnes, Clive. " 'Journey's End' Offers 1920's View of War." *New York Times* (21 July 1972): 9.
Bracco, Rosa Maria. *Merchants of Hope: British Middlebrow Writers and the First World War, 1919–1939.* Providence, RI: Berg, 1993.
Brown, John Mason. "Gentlemen at War." *Saturday Review of Literature* 5 (18 May 1929): 1021.
Cornelius, Samuel Denver. "A Production of R. C. Sherriff's Journey's End." M.A. thesis, Texas Tech University, 1977.
Darlington, W. A. [1]. " 'Keying Down.' " *Theatre Arts* 13 (July 1929): 493–97.
———. [2]. "One Up, One Down." *New York Times* (12 Dec. 1948): 4.
Dukes, Ashley. "The London Scene: The English Theatre Holds Its Own." *Theatre Arts* 14 (Aug. 1930): 738.
Fleming, Peter. [1]. "Miss Mabel." *Spectator* 181 (26 Nov. 1948): 694.
———. [2]. "St Helena." *Spectator* 156 (27 March 1936): 575.
Gascoigne, Bamber. "Brand Excalibur." *Spectator* 207 (24 Nov. 1961): 765–66.
Hill, Eldon. "R. C. Sherriff." In *Dictionary of Literary Biography,* vol. 10, *Modern British Dramatists, 1900–1945,* ed. Stanley Weintraub, pt. 2, 149–54. Detroit: Gale Research, 1982.
"Home at Seven." *The Times* (8 Mar. 1950): 2.

Isaacs, Edith J. R. Review of *St. Helena*. *Theatre Arts* 20 (Nov. 1936): 843–47.

Krutch, Joseph Wood. "Past and Present." *Nation* 149 (30 Sept. 1939): 355–57.

Littell, Robert. " 'Journey's End'." *Theatre Arts* 13 (July 1929): 325–30.

Macdonell, A. C. "Journey's End." *London Mercury* 19 (Jan. 1929): 314–15.

Morsberger, Robert E. "R. C. Sherriff." In *Critical Survey of Drama,* ed. Frank Magill, vol. 5. Englewood Cliffs, NJ: Salem Press, 1985.

Nathan, George Jean. [1]. "Art of the Night." *Saturday Review* 15 (31 Oct. 1936): 17.

———. [2]. "Drama of War." *American Mercury* 17 (June 1929): 245–47.

———. [3]. "The Ladies War." *American Mercury* 17 (July 1929): 376–77.

"New Play in Manhattan." *Time* (19 Oct. 1936): 44.

"Old Play in Manhattan." *Time* 28 (2 Oct. 1939): 38.

Onions, John. *English Fiction and Drama of the Great War, 1918–1939*. New York: St. Martin's Press, 1990.

"R. C. Sherriff." *The Times* (18 Nov. 1975): 17.

"Sherriff Play Opens: 'Home at Seven' Wins Approval of Critics in London." *New York Times* (8 Mar. 1950): 34.

Swaffer, Hannen. "Stark Reality of Journey's End." *Daily Express* (22 Jan. 1929).

Trewin, J. C. [1]. "Alas, Poor Ghost!" *Illustrated London News* 222 (11 Apr. 1953): 584.

———. [2]. "Four in Hand." *Illustrated London News* 236 (14 May 1960): 850.

———. [3]. "The Voice of the Prophet." *Illustrated London News* 213 (18 Dec. 1948): 712.

Tynan, Kenneth. *Curtains: Selections from the Drama Criticism and Related Writings,* 48. New York: Atheneum, 1961.

Van Doren, Mark. "Decent Death." *Nation* 123 (10 Apr. 1929): 434.

Vernon, Grenville. "St. Helena." *Commonweal* (23 Oct. 1936): 617.

Wakefield, Gilbert. "Mr. Sherriff in a Cricket Blazer." *Saturday Review* 149 (21 June 1930): 184.

Weinraub, Bernard. "London: Jolly Good 'Journey's End.' " *New York Times* (3 June 1972): 52.

Woollcott, Alexander. "Lest We Forget." In *The Portable Woollcott*, 318–26. New York: Viking Press, 1946.

Young, Stark. [1]. "Journey's End." *New Republic* 58 (10 Apr. 1929): 325–26.

———. [2]. "Literates." *New Republic* 88 (21 Oct. 1936): 314.

Alfred Sutro
(1863–1933)

ARTHUR GEWIRTZ

It is easy to see why Alfred Sutro, now virtually forgotten, was a successful dramatist in his day. His plots are clear, the drama's main issues are quickly drawn, the characters are sharply etched, the dialogue is crisp and pointed, and the leading roles are knowingly written for actors with personality, charm, and wit, of whom there were several of importance then on the stage.

But it is equally apparent why Sutro's work remains obscure today. While his characters are often lively, his wit is more than occasionally irreverent and amusing, and the problems of the dramas are sometimes trenchantly presented, the resolutions of the plays, however, regularly conform to the official morals of his day. It is not necessarily fatal for plays to take that turn, for many of the great dramatists, Shakespeare and Molière, for example, often confirmed society's views. But Sutro did it with little questioning, without a tough, probing examination of them. If characters must nobly sacrifice themselves, for example, they arrive at their decision too easily and often surprisingly. Sutro, willing to please his immediate audience, failed to please later spectators and readers.

Alfred Sutro was born in London on 7 August 1863, the son of Dr. Sigismund Sutro and Helena Cohen Sutro. By becoming a physician, Dr. Sutro broke a long family tradition of the eldest son in the family becoming a rabbi, in fact, chief rabbi: "There had been Chief Rabbis in the family without a break, for many hundreds of years" (*Celebrities and Simple Souls,* 134). Sigismund Sutro, emigrating to England from a small town near Heidelberg and taking his degree at Edinburgh, became a staunch admirer of all things English, and surely this must have affected Alfred's mild attitude toward the prevailing mores of the day. But his strong Jewish ancestry in no way intruded upon his drama.

The future playwright was educated at the City of London School and at Brussels. At the age of sixteen he became a clerk in the City, but eventually joined his brother in a successful business there. But under his father's influence, as "a mere youngster" (*Celebrities and Simple Souls,* 137) he became involved in running Working-Mens' Clubs in the East End. The experience provided him with the "profoundest respect for the working-man," which he "never . . . lost" (*Celebrities and Simple Souls,* 137), but that sympathy was to emerge in only a single play, the one-act *The Man on the Kerb.* All his other dramas involve characters in the middle or upper classes.

In April 1894 Alfred Sutro married Esther Isaacs in Paris. He was a friend of her brother Rufus, who introduced the pair. (Rufus Isaacs was to become prominent as a political figure, finally as Lord Chief Justice of England and the Marquis of Reading.) Esther Isaacs insisted, before she would consent to marry Alfred, that he leave business and turn his hand to art, she herself being a painter: "I wanted to write; and she, with the confidence of youth, assured me that I could" (*Celebrities and Simple Souls,* 11–12). Alfred conformed to her condition and quit the lucrative partnership with his brother, who, however, provided him with the small income that enabled the couple to live the life of artists in Paris. But in the first year of their marriage Esther met A. B. Walkley, the drama critic of *The Times,* fell in love, and conducted a long affair with him. Alfred did not discover the affair until sometime later and thereon, "perhaps even before," the couple "led parallel but separate lives" (Sawin, 24–25, 62–63).

In Paris Sutro met the Belgian playwright Maurice Maeterlinck, with whom he was to remain good friends all his life. Sutro's translations of Maeterlinck's dramas were among the first of the Englishman's productions to reach the stage. His translation of Maeterlinck's *Monna Vanna* caused something of a stir in 1902 when the Lord Chamberlain's Office refused it a license. Performed privately at the Bijou in Bayswater on 1 June, it also occasioned a letter to *The Times,* signed by many of the prominent dramatists of the day, condemning the censor. Sutro's rendering of the Belgian's *Aglavaine and Selysette* (1897) was acted at the Royal Court (London) during the pivotal Vedrenne-Barker seasons of 1904–7. He also translated the drama *The Death of Tintagiles* (1896), performed by the Stage Society on 29 April 1900 under the direction of Harley Granville-Barker, and the nondramatic works *The Treasure of the Humble* (1897) and *Life of the Bee* (1901) (Sawin, 25, 57).

Before the first of his full-length dramas was produced, Sutro also adapted other work. With the actor Arthur Bourchier he rendered into English Alexandre Bisson's *Monsieur le Directeur,* which opened on 7 September 1895 as *The Chili Widow;* alone he adapted Jules Renard's one-act *Poil de Carotte* as *Carrots,* performed in 1900 in Dublin and London (Sawin, 44–46). With George Meredith, Sutro adapted the former's novel *The Egoist,* a work that was never performed. During this same period he published a play, *The Cave of Illusion,* with an introduction by Maeterlinck (1900). Sutro's collection of "duologues" called *Women in Love* came out in 1902, and a gathering of short stories entitled *The Foolish Virgins* in 1904.

But his first splash, after ten years of trying to get a play produced, came with *The Walls of Jericho,* staged on 31 October 1904 at the Garrick Theatre (London) with Arthur Bourchier and Violet Vanbrugh in the leads. The play, both a critical and commercial success, achieved more than 400 performances in London and was given in New York in the next year; Sutro estimated that more than two million people had seen it ("Alfred Sutro on Society"). In the seasons that followed, the playwright produced both comic and serious dramas, most of them successful. Among them are *The Fascinating Mr. Vandervelt* (1906), *John Glayde's Honour* (1907), *The Perplexed Husband* (1911), *The Choice* (1919), and *The Laughing Lady* (1922). But the last play, a failure in New York, where it starred Ethel Barrymore, was an omen of things to come, for Alfred Sutro had no more successes in the theater. In the 1920s came such dramas as *Far above Rubies* (1924), *A Man with a Heart* (1925), and *Living Together* (1929). The last was Sutro's disastrous final full-length play. He received the sympathy of his contemporaries in the theater. Graham Robertson, for example, wrote in a letter: "What pulverising notices! The critics seem to have agreed not to have him at any price. . . . Well, it shows that all old folks of his and my date should 'evermore hold our peace' " (Sawin, 227). As far as the theater public knew, Sutro virtually did hold his peace. A one-act, *The Blackmailing Lady,* was published in 1929, but mainly Sutro went on to nondramatic work: a book of short stories, *About Women,* in 1931 and his memoirs, *Celebrities and Simple Souls,* in 1933, the year of his death.

Selected Biographical Sources: "Alfred Sutro Dies in England"; *Celebrities and Simple Souls;* Harding; Mason; McCarthy; Sawin.

MAJOR PLAYS, PREMIERES, AND SIGNIFICANT REVIVALS: THEATRICAL RECEPTION

The Walls of Jericho. 1904. Opened at the Garrick Theatre (London) on 31 October with Arthur Bourchier and Violet Vanbrugh; ran for well over 400 performances. Opened in New York at the Savoy Theatre on 25 September 1905 with J. K. Hackett.

This drama contrasting a strong, self-made man from Australia with the self-indulgent "smart set" to which his wife belongs was both a critical and commercial success. The reviewer in the *Illustrated London News* praised the piece as homegrown and lusty (Sawin, 71), while Borsa called Sutro a "rising star," who brought to his worn theme a "portion of an actual existing life" (65–66). But the *New York Times* reviewer ("Sutro Points a Moral") disagreed: "Its sociological questions are not of the kind that can be satisfactorily thrashed out in the course of an evening's entertainment." A more recent critic, however, remembered it as a play that was "efficient in its mood and better than most of Sutro's later work" (Trewin [1], 57).

Mollentrave on Women. 1905. Produced at St. James's Theatre (London) on 13 February 1905. The play ran for only 65 performances, perhaps because its star-manager, George Alexander, did not appear in it (Mason, 213). Marion Terry played Lady Claude, the leading female role.

Mollentrave on Women is about the author of a highly successful book with the same title, who, bungling the love and marital affairs of several persons, persuades himself that he has untangled those affairs that those persons themselves have straightened out. The meager 65 performances indicate that most viewers agreed with the negative appraisal from the *Illustrated London News* that found the play conventional, its characters flimsy, and its plot sentimentally entangled (Sawin, 74). By contrast, Beerbohm [1] called the comedy "A Philosophic Farce, . . . a serious satire . . . distinguished by real grace and charm of dialogue" (364–65). Almost a quarter of a century later Sutro used the figure of Mollentrave as the narrator of the stories in *About Women.*

The Perfect Lover. 1905. Opened at the Imperial Theatre (London) 14 October, where it ran for 85 performances. Opened in New York under the title *The Price of Money* on 29 August 1906 at the Garrick Theatre.

Beerbohm [2] thought that Sutro wrote this drama about a man conventionally facing a number of moral problems about marriage, money, and family as a way of gaining easy success after the failure of *Mollentrave on Women* (196–99). But the play ran only 20 times more than its predecessor. Nevertheless, the piece traveled to New York. The response of the *New York Times* reviewer ("Sutro Play Interesting") was similar to Beerbohm's: although there was artistry in the drama, the author was writing with his "fingers on what he takes to be the pulse of the public."

The Fascinating Mr. Vandervelt. 1906. The only play by Sutro that made its debut in New York, it appeared at Daly's Theatre on 22 January. The highly admired English actress Ellis Jeffreys acted the leading the role of Lady Clarice. In London the play received its first performance at the Garrick Theatre on 26 April, where it played 94 times with Arthur Bourchier and Violet Vanbrugh in the major parts. C. Aubrey Smith, who brightened many Hollywood films in the 1930s and 1940s as an old, staunch, starchy, upright Englishman, here played a young, staunch, starchy, upright Englishman.

This comedy concerns the womanizing Mr. Vandervelt, who tries and fails to marry the wise and witty Lady Clarice. The *New York Times* devoted a good deal of space to the play, with both an opening-night review and a Sunday "think" piece. In the first of these ("Sutro Reveals a Very Agreeable Comedy Vein") the critic thought that even though the play could have stood condensation of the first two acts, it was still far above the current spate of comedies. On Sunday the *New York Times* ("The Stage and Its Plays") offered "general felicitation" and noted the comedy's "graceful, technical skill" and its wit that grew out of its characters. On the other hand, the critic went on to say that although the play showed a "kind of negative triumph of virtue," there was no "very positive flaying of vice." In London Beerbohm [1] found Sutro the most "literary" dramatist since Oscar Wilde and asserted that more than any other contemporary playwright he had a "fine sense of words, and a delicate ear for cadences"; the story might be old, but it was accomplished with "much skill" (422–23).

John Glayde's Honour. 1907. Opened at the St. James's Theatre (London) on 3 August for a run of 138 performances. George Alexander, the star-manager of the theater, played the leading role. In New York J. K. Hackett took the part for its run at Daly's Theatre starting on 23 December.

This play about a successful American financier who nobly gives up the wife he had neglected throughout his marriage garnered more praise than blame. The *Athenaeum* found it truly reflective of life on the fast track of profit and pleasure. Maeterlinck thought it the best play Sutro had written. His friend and fellow dramatist Israel Zangwill, although finding the drama not as original as *Mollentrave on Women,* nevertheless liked it (Sawin, 86–87). However, its "ordinary" (Mason, 181) run in London (compared to a blockbuster like that of *The Walls of Jericho*) was perhaps due to the negative reception by some critics. Beerbohm [1], while admitting the "mastery" Sutro demonstrated in the play's structure and the "dialogue of the finest quality," yet found the leading character unconvincing and therefore centrally detrimental to the drama (282–85). *The Times* ("St. James's Theatre") thought that Sutro's passion for nobility showed in his picture of Glayde, but that it was a "lime-light" nobility, merely showy sacrifice. In the following year Borsa reflected the negative criticism in calling the play "artificial, exaggerated, and imbued with . . . a want of realism" (67). The *New York Times* reviewer ("Artificial Play"), declaring the drama "rather . . . gripping," yet pointed to a "peculiarly unresponsive" first-night audience and declared himself fatally unconvinced by the central figure. Nicoll many years later found this effort by the author "largely a replica of *The Walls of Jericho*" (373), but Sutro's recent biographer thought that the characters and issues of the play are more complex than they seem superficially to appear (Sawin, 85–86).

The Perplexed Husband. 1911. Opened on 21 September 1911 at Wyndham's Theatre (London) with Gerald du Maurier, the star-manager, in the leading role, the comedy ran for 155 performances. In New York its debut was at the Empire Theatre on 2 September 1912, with John Drew in the central part and Mary Boland in an important supporting role.

This play about a husband who must face his wife's new feminism resulting in part from her attending a performance of Ibsen's *A Doll's House* was a success in both its London and New York incarnations. *The Times* ("Mr. Sutro's New Play") said that the "play won't bear thinking about. . . . Nevertheless, *The Perplexed Husband,* we are sure, gave a good deal of pleasure to a good many people," for it had "lightness, dexterity . . . and a nimble wit." Others praised its strong structure (Sawin, 129). The *New York Times* reviewer ("Perplexed Husband") wrote that its general idea was "exquisite, its texture gossamer, its philosophy sound, . . . and written in English which, though choice, is suggestive of the real speech of the people who use it.''

The Clever Ones. 1914. Produced at Wyndham's Theatre (London) on 23 April, it ran for 92 performances, with the star-manager Gerald du Maurier and Marie Lohr in the leading roles. Edmund Gwenn, who delineated many types of father in Hollywood films of the 1930s and 1940s (as well as the screen's most famous Santa Claus), here already portrayed a father. Opened in New York on 28 January 1915 at the Punch and Judy Theatre.

The reception of this satiric piece about a family of clever advanced women was generally good though not overwhelming, as the length of its run suggests. The *Athenaeum* reviewer, for example, believed that the play did not fulfill the promise of its first act, though the drama still reflected, albeit in an exaggerated fashion, society's features (Sawin, 145). The *New York Times* ("'The Clever Ones'") agreed, saying that though the comedy could "boast of several very entertaining scenes . . . its pace grows languid with the progress of the play.''

The Choice. 1919. Opened at Wyndham's Theatre (London) on 8 September with the star-manager Gerald du Maurier and Viola Tree in the leading roles and ran for more than 300 performances.

This play about the choice that a powerful industrialist must make between love and what he regards as duty was obviously received well. Du Maurier, who decided on this as his first post–World War I drama, selected a Sutro play because the author knew what the public wanted and was able to give it to them (Harding, 108). *The Times* ("The Choice") thought the drama, both for its story and its "ultra-modern types," of "high interest, very neatly written and brilliantly played." Du Maurier in the central role "showed his affection for the woman he loved by smacking her on the jaw and turning his back" (du Maurier, 206–7). At the end, however, he nobly renounces her so that she can marry the man she truly loves.

The Laughing Lady. 1922. Opened at the Globe Theatre (London) on 17 November, running for 164 performances; its cast included Marie Lohr, Violet Vanbrugh, Godfrey Tearle, and Edith Evans in a supporting role. Its New York debut at the Longacre Theatre was on 12 February 1923 with Ethel Barrymore in the starring role.

This play about a divorcée, brutally questioned in court by her husband's lawyer, who then falls in love with her, was a success in London but a failure in New York. Critics in London thought the play well made and seething with excitement; reviewers particularly praised Edith Evans in her secondary part (Sawin, 178–80). By contrast, Corbin in the *New York Times,* treating the play with disdain in both his opening-night review [1] and in a Sunday article [2], said that it came out of a "dateless yesterday": this play, like current British drama generally—and unlike current American drama—went back to the Wilde of *Lady Windermere's Fan* when Victorian morals were guarded, where passion must be pure.

ADDITIONAL PLAYS, ADAPTATIONS, AND PRODUCTIONS

The Chili Widow, adapted (with Arthur Bourchier) from the French *Monsieur le Directeur* by Alexandre Bisson, had its premiere at the Royalty Theatre (London) on 7 September 1895. It was well received but lost money because Bourchier kept it open after large audiences stopped coming (Sawin, 17, 23). *The Death of Tintagiles,* translated from the French of Maurice Maeterlinck, appeared in the *Pageant* in 1896 and was staged in St. George's Hall, London, 22 July 1902. *Aglavaine and Seylesette,* translated in 1897 from the French of Maurice Maeterlinck, appeared at the Royal Court (London) during the pivotal reign of Harley Granville-Barker and J. D. Vedrenne for 6 performances, starting on 15 November 1904. *The Egoist,* an adaptation with George Meredith of the latter's novel of the same name, 1898, was never performed and was not printed until 1920, when it was edited by Clement Shorter in a highly incorrect edition; it was printed correctly and edited by Lewis Sawin in 1981.

Carrots, a translation of the one-act French play *Poil de Carotte* by Jules Renard, was performed on 18 October 1900 in Dublin and on 21 November 1900 at the Prince of Wales's Theatre, Kensington. *The Cave of Illusion* (1900) was not produced but was published with an introduction by Maeterlinck, who thought that the play demonstrated what was best in modern drama: that is, moral perplexity without a solution. *Women in Love,* published in 1902, consists of eight duologues. Those performed were: *A Maker of Men,* produced on 27 January 1905 at St. James's Theatre (London) for a run of 84 performances and again at the Kingsway Theatre (London) on 9 October 1907 for 36 performances; *The Correct Thing,* given at the Drury Lane Theatre (London) on 29 June 1905 and also at a benefit performance in New York on 9 September 1905, where Margaret Anglin starred in this "virile little drama" ("Sutro's Strong Playlet"); *Ella's Apology* at Bloomesbury Hall (London), 11 August 1906; *Mr. Steinman's Corner* presented at His Majesty's Theatre (London) on 4 June 1907; and *The Gutter of Time* at the Pavilion, Eastbourne, 3 August 1908.

The Barrier was produced at the Comedy Theatre (London) on 10 October 1907 for 51 performances. Beerbohm [2] called this an "exciting comedy," the fourth act of which, however, should have been curtailed and attached to the third (327–29). *The Builder of Bridges* opened at St. James's Theatre (London) on 11 November 1908 for a run of 96 performances; it was given first in New York at the Hudson on 26 October 1909. It was poorly received on both sides of the Atlantic, though it enjoyed a good run in London. Both Beerbohm ([2], 406–9) and the reviewer in the *New York Times* ("Sutro Play Success)" found the characters unconvincing. *Making a Gentleman,* a comedy opening at the Garrick Theatre (London) on 11 October 1909, received mixed reviews. The *Athenaeum* thought the characters not sharply drawn (Sawin, 114), whereas

Beerbohm [2] asserted that while the characters were not fresh, the author had "breathed plenty of life into them" (487).

Monna Vanna, translated from the French of Maurice Maeterlinck in 1902, was presented at the Royal Court Theatre (London) for one matinee performance on 1 June 1911 and on 21 July 1914 at the Queen's Theatre (London). *The Firescreen* was produced at the Garrick Theatre (London) on 2 February 1912 for 61 performances with Arthur Bourchier and Violet Vanbrugh in the leads. A contemporary report found the play "artistic to a fault" ("London 'Boos' ''), but a modern critic called it a "strong play" (Sawin, 133). *Five Little Plays* (1912) is a collection of five one-acts, three of which were staged: *The Man on the Kerb,* produced at the Aldwych Theatre (London) on 24 March 1908; *The Man in the Stalls,* presented at the Palladium on 2 October 1911; and *The Bracelet,* produced in repertory in Liverpool on 26 February 1912. *The Two Virtues* opened at the St. James's Theatre (London) on 5 March 1914. Although the play was initially thought to be a hit ("The Two Virtues a Hit"), it ran for only 67 performances. *Uncle Anyhow* was presented at the Haymarket Theatre (London) on 1 March 1918; it was originally printed as *Rude Min and Christine* in 1915 and was produced as *The Two Miss Farndons* at the Gaiety in Manchester on 21 May 1917.

Freedom, written in 1914 for Harley Granville-Barker was never produced, but was printed in 1916. Sutro explained in the foreword that when the play was slated for production during World War I, the "Germans were at the gates of Paris—and it was obviously not the time to put upon the stage a play which dealt exclusively with questions of sex," by which he meant gender, for it then seemed irrelevant. Then, in the war women had shown themselves so capable of meeting large challenges that it seemed an "impertinence" to even publish a play showing them concerned with a minor issue.

The Great Redding Street Burglary, a propaganda one-act of World War I vintage, was produced at the Coliseum (London) on 31 July 1916. *The Marriage . . . Will Not Take Place,* a one-act, was produced at the Coliseum on 13 August 1917. *The Trap,* a one-act, Sutro's only thriller (Sawin, 168), was produced at the Coliseum (London) on 11 March 1918. *The Great Well* opened on 19 December 1922 at the New Theatre (London) for a run of 70 performances. *The Times* (Review of *The Great Well*) thought this an oft-told tale that Sutro, "an old theatrical hand," had turned into one that pleased the house on opening night. Sawin called the play "distressingly overwrought" (182).

Far above Rubies was produced at the Comedy Theatre (London) on 27 March 1924 for 41 performances, with a cast including Marie Lohr, Marie Tempest, Herbert Marshall, Ralph Forbes, and Mervyn Johns. *The Times* ("Comedy Theatre") thought that the play did not stand among Sutro's "happiest inspirations." Referring to one character in the play who calls another a perfect housekeeper, wife, and mother, a Sutro correspondent wrote to the author, "I would *murder* a man who said it to me" (Sawin, 188). Such a remark surely indicated how the tide was turning against the author.

A Man with a Heart was given first at Wyndham's Theatre (London) on 14

March 1925 with Gerald du Maurier in the leading role. *The Times* (Review of *A Man with a Heart*) reported that the story was the same as that of *Francillon,* a forty-year-old play by Dumas *fils,* but Sutro, adding only sentimentality, lacked Dumas's wit or cynicism. (Sutro apparently liked the plot so much that he used it also in "The Dangar Case," one of the stories in his collection *About Women.*) The play's star was disappointed by the playwright, who had never previously failed him (Harding, 137).

The Desperate Lovers opened at the Comedy Theatre (London) on 28 January 1927. This was another failure for Sutro in these years. Morgan wrote that the comedy possessed "no spirit . . . no lightheartedness." *Living Together* made its London debut on 14 January 1929 at Wyndham's Theatre. *The Times* (Review of *Living Together*) observed, "There is a freshness of a kind in the story but little in its treatment. . . . The construction . . . is almost pathetically weak." An utter failure (Sawin, 225), it was Sutro's last produced full-length play. *The Blackmailing Lady,* a one-act, printed in 1929, was performed (Sawin, 227). A number of "lost" Sutro plays were performed but never printed.

ASSESSMENT OF SUTRO'S CAREER

Alfred Sutro's is a paradigm of the career of many modern dramatists. Beginning with a string of unproduced plays written according to the "dictates of his conscience" (Beerbohm [2], 196) and translations of a favorite of the avant-garde, Maurice Maeterlinck, he then succumbed to the lure of fame and fortune to write dramas that would suit the public.

His first staged play, *The Walls of Jericho,* had the audience sympathize with a rough-and-ready Australian while it belittled high society. But since high society purchased the most expensive seats, not all its representatives were demeaned. The Australian's wife, one of the prime representatives of the smart set, is, after all, faithful to her husband, really loves the son she seems to neglect, and follows her husband to Australia. Her brother finally marries the woman he seduces and really loves and goes off to Australia to run a farm. Tradition is affirmed when a sympathetic character insists: "We women cry out at tyranny, but in our hearts we admire the tyrant. They call us complex, we are as elementary as the tide beneath the moon. Govern us, we cry to our husbands— and if you do, we scratch, but our soul is at peace" (49). The play was an immense success. Although none of his other dramas reached the popularity of *Jericho,* many of them garnered profits for three of the most prominent actor-managers of the day: George Alexander, Arthur Bourchier, and Gerald du Maurier. As well, he provided generous roles for other leading players, such as Violet and Irene Vanbrugh, Marie Lohr, and Dennis Eadie in London and John Drew, Mary Boland, and J. K. Hackett in New York.

The modern reader, however, finds Sutro to be repetitive and disappointing. For example, as Nicoll pointed out (373), the "magnanimous strong-man hero" in *John Glayde's Honour* (1907) repeats the one in *The Walls of Jericho.* He also appears in *The Builder of Bridges* (1908) and as late as *The Choice* (1919), one of the most popular of Sutro's dramas. These pieces are based on the domestic difficulties of the leading figure, whose wife or beloved has in one way or another betrayed him or fallen out of love with him. Apparently following the Sutro dictum that "the code of honor . . . is something the artist . . . must ennoble if he can" ("Alfred Sutro on Society"), these figures, instead of condemning their women, which presumably would accord with society's code of honor, improbably forgive them or surrender them to the men the women love.

Domestic difficulties are central to other plays as well and are often the result of husbands who are uncaring of their wives. While *Freedom*'s Miriam Chambers has been unfaithful to her husband simply because she could not tolerate the restraints of the marriage bonds, Gabrielle Molyneux of *The Cave of Illusion* (1900) turns to another man because her husband has made a servant girl pregnant; Lillian Tremblett in *The Perfect Lover* (1905) runs off with another man because her husband treats her brutally; Sophie Pelling of *The Perplexed Husband* (1911) becomes estranged from her husband because she, like Nora Helmer of *A Doll's House,* feels as though her husband has treated her as his plaything; in *The Laughing Lady* (1922) and *A Man with a Heart* (1925) the husbands are still neglecting their wives, the first by always being off in foreign parts and the other by inveterate womanizing. Even some of his one-acts dramatize similar situations.

In writing of *The Cave of Illusion,* Shaw [1] asked, "*When* will people realize that [of all] undramatic and stupid no-thoroughfares of subjects adultery is quite the worst? Sutro could write quite a decent play if he could only get away from it" (178). Not all of Sutro's plays have adultery at the core, but many, if they are not about adultery, hover at its edge and might as well be about it. The modern reader, for all his desire to understand the mores of another time, still gets tired of a subject archaic for him and little adorned by wit or penetrated by special insight.

Sutro did show a good deal of sympathy for the plight of women at the time. In an interview he defended their lying to stave off the male's brutal code of honor ("Alfred Sutro on Society"). In *John Glayde's Honour* he demonstrated that point of view. The title character's ennobling (but unconvincing) recognition of his part in his wife's adultery is demonstrated when he turns over his wife (with a monetary provision) to her lover so that the latter may marry her and she may never lie and betray again. In *Ella's Apology, The Gutter of Time,* and *Freedom* the wives argue the case for their infidelity, and in other plays the husbands' various kinds of neglect try to make us understanding of the wives' behavior. But the women's actions are often stupid, as Nicoll noted, and the heroines of *The Perplexed Husband, The Two Virtues, The Barrier,* and *Far above Rubies* "are all diverse mirror-images of the same person as she turns her face this way and that" (373). The audience really cares little about them or the situations they have made for themselves.

Most tiresome is Sutro's apparent inability to escape from the morals of his time. In *The Perfect Lover* the modern reader is pained by a long harangue from a supposedly sympathetic character urging a wife to return to her brutal husband simply because she is his wife (fortunately, she does not). In *The Laughing Lady* Lady Marjorie Colladine is persuaded to return to her idiot of a husband because he is her husband. In *A Man with a Heart* Nancy East, upon learning of her husband's uncontrollable womanizing, runs off with his best friend, Captain Christopher Evesham, who has always loved her. But it turns out that she never had sex with the captain, and at the play's end there is a loving embrace and reconciliation of the married couple. (In the story "The Dangar Case," which has the same plot and characters as *A Man with a Heart,* the ending is much more ambiguous.) Even in a comedy like *The Fascinating Mr. Vandervelt* the sophisticated and witty heroine, Lady Clarice, who seems to regard society's morals with a worldly-wise humor and skepticism, ends by marrying the starchy Colonel Raynor, an absolute supporter of society's uprightness. Sutro frequently satirizes society's blemishes, but never so much as to injure the commercial value of his dramas.

Critics roundly condemned Sutro's final produced full-length play, *Living Together,* but a reader today might find it one of his most interesting. He takes up what we know was (and still is) a contemporary question: Why marriage? He shows two couples living together without benefit of clergy, but only those with tough hearts survive. For they live in an essentially anarchic world, and pleasing only their own desires, indifferent to the fates of their cohabitants, they achieve their aims. The others are badly hurt or must lump it. Nor is there an indication that marriage at this stage of society's development is any better, for these same piratical types would pursue their aims with or without marriage, as Sutro has shown in more conventional dramas. This play ends with honest questions about both living together and marriage rather than with a soothing happy ending. Sutro's critics in the 1920s may have found his handling of the theme old-fashioned, but what seemed old-fashioned then seems honest now. The dramatist's technique is not as efficient here as in most of his dramas, yet it is too bad that critics then thought him so dated as to be beneath consideration. He may have lacked the sharpness of the young Noël Coward or the acerbic, sometimes acrid humor of his contemporary, the ever-adaptable W. Somerset Maugham, yet *Living Together* is thought-provoking and sensitive. With encouragement, Sutro might have gone on to other stimulating work.

ARCHIVAL SOURCES

Manuscripts, letters, and other documents are in the possession of Winton Dean; Colonel and Mrs. Jon Sutro; the British Library; the Cambridge University Library; the Central Zionist Archive, Jerusalem; the Humanities Research Center, University of Texas, Austin; the Library of the University of California, Los Angeles; the Houghton Library, Harvard University; Northwestern University Library; the Beinecke Library, Yale University; the William Perkins Library,

Duke University; the Norlin Library, University of Colorado; and the Elmer
Holmes Bobst Library, New York University (Sawin, ix, x).

PRIMARY BIBLIOGRAPHY

Plays

The Barrier. New York: Samuel French, 1908.
The Blackmailing Lady. London: Samuel French, 1929.
The Bracelet. New York: Samuel French, 1912. Also in *Five Little Plays.*
The Builder of Bridges. New York: Samuel French, 1909.
The Cave of Illusion. London: George Allen, 1900.
The Choice. London: Duckworth, 1919.
The Clever Ones. London: Chiswick Press, 1912.
The Correct Thing. New York: Samuel French, 1905. Also in *Women in Love.*
The Desperate Lovers. London: Duckworth, 1927.
Ella's Apology. New York: Samuel French, 1902. Also in *Women in Love.*
Far above Rubies. London: Duckworth, 1924.
The Fascinating Mr. Vandervelt. New York: Samuel French, 1907.
The Firescreen. London: Samuel French, 1912.
Five Little Plays. New York: Brentano's, 1913.
Freedom. New York: Brentano's, 1916.
A Game of Chess. New York: Samuel French, 1902. Also in *Women in Love.*
The Great Well. London: Duckworth, 1922.
The Gutter of Time. New York: Samuel French, 1902. Also in *Women in Love.*
John Glayde's Honour. London: William Heinemann, n.d.
The Laughing Lady. London: Duckworth, 1922.
Living Together. London: Duckworth, 1929.
A Maker of Men. New York: Samuel French, 1902. Also in *Women in Love.*
A Man with a Heart. London: Duckworth, 1925.
A Marriage Has Been Arranged. London: Samuel French, 1904. Also in *Five Little Plays.*
The Marriage . . . Will Not Take Place. London: Samuel French, 1917.
Mollentrave on Women. London: Samuel French, 1905.
Mr. Steinman's Corner. London: Samuel French, 1902. Also in *Women in Love.*
The Open Door. London: Samuel French, 1912.
The Perfect Lover. London: Samuel French, 1905. Also published as *The Price of Money.*
    London: Samuel French, 1906.
The Perplexed Husband. London: Samuel French, 1913.
Rude Min and Christine. London: Chiswick Press, 1915. (See *Uncle Anyhow,* which is
    another title of this play.)
The Salt of Life. London: Samuel French, 1905. Also in *Women in Love.*
The Two Virtues. London: Duckworth, 1914.
Uncle Anyhow. London: Samuel French, 1919.
The Walls of Jericho. London: Samuel French, 1906.
Women in Love. London: George Allen, 1902.

Translations and Adaptations

Aglavaine and Selysette. Translation of the play by Maurice Maeterlinck. London: George Allen, 1904.

Alladine and Palomides. Translation of the play by Maurice Maeterlinck. London: Gowans & Gray, 1907; New York: Dodd, Mead, 1914.

Carrots. Translation of Jules Renard's *Poil de Carotte.* New York: Samuel French, 1904.

The Chili Widow. Adaptation with Arthur Bourchier of Alexandre Bisson's *Monsieur le Directeur.* Not published.

The Death of Tintagiles. Translation of the play by Maurice Maeterlinck. London: Gowans & Gray, 1911; New York: Dodd, Mead, 1914. Also in *The Pageant* (a serial), London: Henry and Co., 1896.

The Egoist. Adaptation with George Meredith of the novel by Meredith. London: Privately printed by C. Shorter, 1920. Corrected edition, ed. Lewis Sawin. Athens: University of Ohio Press, 1981.

Monna Vanna. Translation of the play by Maurice Maeterlinck. London: George Allen, 1904. Also in *Joyzelle,* trans. A. Teixeira de Mattos; Maeterlinck, Maurice. *Monna Vanna,* trans. Alfred Sutro. New York: Dodd, Mead, 1907.

Stories and Memoir

About Women. London: Duckworth, 1931.

Celebrities and Simple Souls. London: Duckworth, 1933.

The Foolish Virgins. London: Chatto & Windus, 1904.

SECONDARY BIBLIOGRAPHY

"Alfred Sutro Dies in England at 70." *New York Times* (13 Sept. 1933): 19:1.

"Alfred Sutro on Society and the Smart Set." *New York Times* (13 Oct. 1907): 5:5.

"Alfred Sutro on the Playwright's Responsibilities." *New York Times* (21 Jan. 1906): 4:4.

"Artificial Play for J. K. Hackett." *New York Times* (24 Dec. 1907): 7:3.

Beerbohm, Max. [1]. *Around Theatres.* London: Rupert Hart-Davis, 1953.

———. [2]. *Last Theatres, 1904–1910.* New York: Taplinger, 1970.

Borsa, Mario. *The English Stage of To-day.* Trans. and ed. Selwyn Brinton. London: John Lane, Bodley Head, 1908.

"The Choice." *The Times* (9 Sept. 1919): 8.

" 'The Clever Ones' by Alfred Sutro." *New York Times* (29 Jan. 1915): 9:3.

"Comedy Theatre." *The Times* (28 Mar. 1924): 12.

Corbin, John. [1]. Review of *The Laughing Lady. New York Times* (13 Feb. 1923): 25: 1.

———. [2]. "The Stage in February—A Group of Plays." *New York Times* (18 Feb. 1923): 7:1.

du Maurier, Daphne. *Gerald: A Portrait.* Garden City, NY: Doubleday, Doran, 1935.

Review of *The Great Well. The Times* (20 Dec. 1922): 8.

Harding, James. *Gerald du Maurier, the Last Actor-Manager.* London: Hodder & Stoughton, 1989.

Review of *Living Together. The Times* (30 Jan. 1929): 12b.

"London 'Boos' for 'The Easiest Way.' " *New York Times* (11 Feb. 1912).

Review of *A Man with a Heart. The Times* (16 Mar. 1925): 12b.

Mason, A.E.W. *Sir George Alexander and the St. James's Theatre.* London: Macmillan, 1935.

McCarthy, Lillah. *Myself and My Friends.* New York: Dutton, 1933.

Mohrle, Barbara Anne Pauley. *"The Egoist:* The Novel as a Drama.'' M.A. thesis, University of Texas at Arlington, July 1981.

Morgan, Charles. "The London Theatre." *New York Times* (20 Feb. 1927): 7:1.

"Mr. Sutro's New Play." *The Times* (13 Sept. 1911): 3:5.

Nicoll, Allardyce. *English Drama, 1900–1930: The Beginnings of the Modern Period.* Cambridge: Cambridge University Press, 1973.

"Perplexed Husband Play of Rare Charm." *New York Times* (3 Sept. 1912): 11:5.

Sawin, Lewis. *Alfred Sutro: A Man with a Heart.* Niwot: University Press of Colorado, 1989.

Shaw, Bernard. [1]. *Collected Letters, 1898–1910.* Ed. Dan H. Laurence. New York: Viking, 1985.

———. [2]. *Dramatic Opinions and Essays with an Apology.* Vol. 1. New York: Brentano's, 1925.

"St. James's Theatre." *The Times* (12 Mar. 1907): 9.

"The Stage and Its Plays." *New York Times* (28 Jan. 1906): 4:3.

"Sutro Play Interesting But Not Convincing." *New York Times* (30 Aug. 1906): 7:2.

"Sutro Play Success But Not a Great One." *New York Times* (27 Oct. 1909): 11:4.

"Sutro Points a Moral and Adorns a Tale." *New York Times* (26 Sept. 1905): 6:1.

"Sutro Reveals a Very Agreeable Comedy Vein." *New York Times* (23 Jan. 1906): 9:1.

"Sutro's Strong Playlet." *New York Times* (9 Sept. 1905): 9:2.

"Timely Topics of the Theatre—New Play-Bills." *New York Times* (31 Oct. 1909): 5:14.

Trewin, J. C. [1]. *The Edwardian Theatre.* Oxford: Basil Blackwell, 1976.

———. [2]. *The Theatre since 1900.* London: Andrew Dakers, 1951.

"The Two Virtues a Hit." *New York Times* (6 Mar. 1914): 4:2.

Wearing, J. P. [1]. *The London Stage, 1900–1909: A Calendar of Plays and Players.* 2 vols. Metuchen, NJ: Scarecrow Press, 1981.

———. [2]. *The London Stage, 1910–1919: A Calendar of Plays and Players.* 2 vols. Metuchen, NJ: Scarecrow Press, 1982.

———. [3]. *The London Stage, 1920–1929: A Calendar of Plays and Players.* 2 vols. Metuchen, NJ: Scarecrow Press, 1984.

Woodfield, James. *English Drama in Transition, 1889–1914.* London: Croom Helm, 1984; Totowa, NJ: Barnes & Noble, 1984.

Oscar Wilde

(1854–1900)

ELIZABETH M. RICHMOND-GARZA

Oscar Fingal O'Flahertie Wills Wilde is remembered as much for his flamboyant personality as he is for his seductive and witty literary production. As the epitome of the aestheticist movement of fin de siècle London, Wilde managed most successfully to bring together his brilliant capacity to fabricate character and to satirize the mores of Victorian society in his plays, especially *The Importance of Being Earnest,* which in many ways initiates what we conveniently call "modern British drama."

Oscar Wilde was born on 16 October 1854 in Dublin to a young doctor, William Wilde, a talented but witty profligate, and Jane Francesca Elgee, an idealistic and strong woman who was known for her patriotic poetry and writings under the pen name of "Speranza." After his father's knighthood in 1864 and early death in 1876, Wilde was largely under the influence of his learned but eccentric mother. Both parents shared a devotion to culture and bohemian society, and Wilde and his older brother Willie were included in their parents' literary and intellectual gatherings before the family disintegrated.

Wilde entered the Portora Royal School, Enniskillen, in 1864, where he avoided athletics and socializing to concentrate on study. He excelled in Latin and Greek, to which, along with English, French, and Italian literature, his mother had introduced him as a child, and developed a talent for copying famous literary styles, a facility not always admired by his later critics. He discovered Benjamin Disraeli, whose debonair style, mannerisms, and linguistic wit he continued to emulate for much of his life. In 1871 he matriculated at Trinity College, Dublin, where he studied with Ireland's finest Greek scholar and Dublin's greatest society wit, Rev. John Pentland Mahaffy, and won, among other awards, the Berkeley Gold Medal for Greek. In 1874 he continued his brilliant academic work in classics and his studied aesthetic self-fashioning at Magdalen College,

Oxford, where he cultivated acquaintances with John Ruskin and Walter Pater, who shared his devotion to the expression of beauty through the arts and religion. He finished his career at Oxford with the flourish of winning the Newdigate Prize for Poetry for his poem *Ravenna* and moved with the portrait artist Frank Miles to London, where he courted the favor of the theatrical set, including Lillie Langtry, Ellen Terry, Helena Modjeska, Sarah Bernhardt, and Henry Irving.

His "aestheticist" way of dressing and brilliant wit quickly made him fashionable. He emblematized the *ars pro arte* movement begun by Ruskin, Pater, James McNeill Whistler, and others and was even caricatured in *Punch*. Dandyism was never the whole of his intellectual and artistic concern but was highly advantageous to him as he sought prestige in London. The initiating event of his theatrical career was the 1881 premiere of W. S. Gilbert and Arthur Sullivan's *Patience*, a delightful satire of the "aesthetic movement." While the play was not specifically directed at Wilde, its success when it moved to New York was secured by Wilde's agreement to give lectures and to accompany the D'Oyly Carte production with, as he said to the customs agent in Manhattan, nothing to declare but his genius. In America he also made new friends like Oliver Wendell Holmes, Sr., Henry Wadsworth Longfellow, Louisa May Alcott, and Walt Whitman.

Upon his return to Europe in 1883, he began to work on plays, starting with *The Duchess of Padua* for the American actress Mary Anderson. With only one volume of poems in print, in 1884 he married Constance Lloyd and had two sons in the next two years. Three years later, to secure their income, he took up a two-year editorship of *Woman's World* and wrote his *Fairy Tales,* several essays and short pieces, and *The Portrait of Dorian Gray.* In spite of the essays he had written, the most important collection being *Intentions,* which contains "The Decay of Lying" and "The Critic as Artist," it was not until 1892 with the production of *Lady Windermere's Fan* that his literary and theatrical career would really begin. A succession of plays followed this initial success, beginning in 1891 with the writing of *Salomé,* which, like *The Duchess of Padua,* was written in Paris. When it was denied a London license, Wilde was so furious he left for Paris to premiere the play there and threatened to renounce his citizenship. *Salomé* was quickly followed by *A Woman of No Importance,* written in the summer of 1892, and *An Ideal Husband,* written in October 1893, both of which were great successes in London. He reached the apex of his career in 1895 when, while *An Ideal Husband* was still drawing audiences in Lewis Waller's production, *The Importance of Being Earnest* opened in George Alexander's St. James's Theatre. Only days after the premiere of his best play, however, Wilde became embroiled in a criminal libel suit against the Marquess of Queensberry, the father of Lord Alfred Douglas, Wilde's longtime friend and companion, who had publicly accused him of being a homosexual. Wilde lost this ill-advised action and was sentenced to two years hard labor in the Reading Gaol. While in prison he wrote *De Profundis,* which is addressed to Douglas, although he never acknowledged it. After his release on 19 May 1897, Wilde immediately departed for the Continent, where he spent the last three years of his life in rather fragile health, poverty, and some loneliness, revising manuscripts and letters for publication in London. Whether from mussel poisoning (as Wilde claimed) or syphilis (as Ellmann [1], 88–89, claimed) or some other cause, Wilde died on 30 November 1900. He was received into the Catholic church on his deathbed, and although he was originally buried in Bagneux, his remains were moved to the Père Lachaise Cemetery in Paris.

Selected Biographical Sources: Ellmann [1]; Knox; Page; Wilde, *Letters.*

MAJOR PLAYS, PREMIERES, AND SIGNIFICANT REVIVALS: THEATRICAL RECEPTION

Vera: or, The Nihilists. 1883. Opened 20 August at the Union Square Theatre (New York) and closed one week later on 28 August.

Instead of the translation of one of Euripides' plays, perhaps *Hercules* or *Phoenissae,* which Wilde had been negotiating with Macmillan, by 1880 Wilde was undertaking this unorthodox play about the contemporary attempts of the Russian nihilists to assassinate Czar Alexander II. The play, with its provocatively "republican sentiments" according to a letter by Wilde to Clara Morris, the American actress (*Letters,* 59), could not open in London, although it had been accepted by the Adelphi Theatre, for a premiere on 17 December 1881 because Wilde was unable to find a suitable cast. The delay proved fortuitous since in March 1881 the czar had in fact been assassinated and his daughter was a member of the English royal family. The events were vigorously covered by the London press, and the play might easily have offended the Prince of Wales. The premiere in New York, which did not share what George S. Sala called the London audience's taste for "Russian accessories" and "fervid utterances about Freedom and the People," was not very successful, and the *New York Tribune* (Review of *Vera*) declared it a "foolish, highly peppered story of love, intrigue and politics."

The Duchess of Padua. 1891. Opened 21 January, produced at first anonymously by Lawrence Barrett under the title *Guido Ferranti,* and ran for a very short run at the Broadway Theatre (New York) (it closed on 14 February) before going on tour with Minna Gale as the Duchess in repertory with *Romeo and Juliet* (although *The Duchess of Padua* was not performed very often).

Like Wilde's first play, with which *The Duchess of Padua* shares many thematic and dramatic similarities, this second play, which was considered, but rejected, by the American actress Mary Anderson for a New York production in 1883, met with tepid reviews. Wilde himself had decided not to dedicate the play to Adela Schuster because "it is unworthy of her and unworthy of me" (*Letters,* 75n). The play reprises much of Percy Bysshe Shelley's *The Cenci* in an experiment that Wilde confided to Mary Anderson offers its audience not a representation of modern life but ''the essence of art . . . the modern idea under an antique form'' (*Letters,* 135–42). Winter named the author and gave a mixed review of the play. The play was an early example of the theatrical antiquarianism (gothic setting, red symbolic decor, and tolling last bell) to which Wilde referred in ''The Truth of Masks.''

Lady Windermere's Fan. 1892. Opened 20 February at St. James's Theatre (London) and ran until 29 July. After a provincial tour it returned to St. James's Theatre on 31 October.

The play was written in 1891, the year in which Elizabeth Robins brought Ibsen's *Hedda Gabler* to London and enthralled Wilde, as well as others, with a new style of drama that abandoned romantic tragedy for what Ibsen called ''photographing his contemporaries.'' One reviewer of the opening scene of *Lady Windermere's Fan* remarked ''that morning room, with its brown panels, was a triumph. It looked so like a room, and so unlike a stage imitation of one'' (quoted in Worth [2], 75). The realism was enhanced by the stylish audience members, who in turn, according to one reviewer, looked as though they belonged on a stage. This story of a woman with a past and her sheltered daughter who mistakes her for her husband's mistress, an adaptation of French *théâtre du boulevard* and of the eighteenth-century Irish comedy of Sheridan and Goldsmith, provoked intense responses from critics who sympathized with the plight of Lord Windermere and vigorously criticized Lady Windermere for wishing to destroy her husband. The review in the *Pall Mall Gazette* (Review of *Lady Windermere's Fan*), however, saw it as little more than a reworking of material already explored by Sardou and Dumas *fils,* and the *Daily Telegraph* (Review of *Lady Windermere's Fan*) also published an unfavorable review. Indeed, the critical debate was sufficiently warm that on 27 February Wilde himself published a letter in the *St. James's Gazette,* insisting that he had not rewritten the play in response to criticisms.

A Woman of No Importance. 1893. Opened 19 April at the Haymarket Theatre (London) and ran until 16 August.

Described on the title page as ''A new and original play of modern life'' and in a letter by Wilde as ''a woman's play,'' *A Woman of No Importance* followed the success of *Lady Windermere's Fan* quickly and starred Mrs. Bernard Beere, who had originally been cast as Vera, as Mrs. Arbuthnot and Herbert Beerbohm Tree as Lord Illingworth. It brings into stark contrast the worlds of melodrama and hedonism in the static world of Hunstanton, and its bitterness about the revenge of women assured it a less favorable critical reception than Wilde's earlier success. The review in the *Illustrated London News,* for example, while admitting the legitimacy of Wilde's representation of the ''woman's revolt,'' concluded that Haymarket audiences would probably resent the play's hostile presentation of men: ''It is not her [Mrs. Beere's] fault that she has to strike Mr. Tree in the face with his own glove, a climax which is a great injustice to both'' (quoted in Worth [2], 125). Max Beerbohm claimed on opening night to have heard "hoots and hisses" as well as applause from the audience (see Ellmann, [2], 360). Clearly Wilde's experiments, which parallel those of Chekhov in particular, aimed at a risky and even radical combination of tragedy and wit, of seriousness and lightness.

An Ideal Husband. 1895. Opened 3 January at the Theatre Royal, Haymarket, (London), where it played until 5 April, when Wilde was arrested. Moved to the Criterion Theatre for a very brief run a few days later. Opened on 12 March 1895 at the Lyceum Theatre in New York.

The play reverses the concern of Wilde's previous two plays, with actor-manager Lewis Waller in the lead as Lord Chiltern, by considering the problem of the man with a past and the impossibility of its own title. There is a woman with a past in the play, Mrs. Cheveley, but she is a savage satirical voice who not only is a match for her male opponent but also forces her audience to see the relations between social propriety and real political power. The play is far less sentimental in its characterizations and, at the same time, insists on the connections of these characters to the House of Commons, the Argentine Canal scheme, Westminster, St. James', and the European scene as a whole. In spite of the great popularity Wilde enjoyed at this point in his career, the play received mixed responses. While it was praised for its clever dialogue, its "Oscarisms," it was attacked as slight by critics like G. B. Shaw, who referred in his review to the critics who "protest that the trick is obvious, and that such epigrams can be turned out by the score by anyone lightminded enough to condescend to such frivolity" (quoted in Worth [2], 150). Oddly, Wilde's play endured several invidious comparisons, among them one to Henry James's *Guy Domville,* which had opened almost simultaneously at the St. James's Theatre. Archer [1], however, even though a bit critical of the play's flamboyance, continued his praise of Wilde, and Shaw ultimately insisted on its excellence and on the primitiveness of the English audience that was annoyed at being so exquisitely amused by an Irishman at its own expense. Soon after the play's opening two favorable interviews with Wilde were published in the *Sketch* and the *St. James's Gazette.*

The Importance of Being Earnest. 1895. Opened 14 February at the St. James's Theatre (London), where it played until 5 April when Wilde was arrested. Played for another month with his name removed from the bills and programs. Revived at the St. James's Theatre (London) in 1902 and in 1909. Revived at the National Theatre (London) in 1982.

Wilde's most successful play opened only a few weeks before he made his libel charge against the Marquess of Queensberry. Indeed, after the verdict came down against Wilde, his name was obliterated from the posters for both *The Importance of Being Earnest* and *An Ideal Husband,* which was still playing at the Haymarket. Charles Wyndham alone at the Criterion, *An Ideal Husband*'s new home, kept the name on the bills. Although some modern critics have disapproved of the play's dandyism and selfishness, Wilde's "The Soul of Man under Socialism" defended its principle of pleasure seeking. Even the seriousness of George Alexander in the role of Algernon, about which Wilde himself had worried, prompted praise from critics like G. B. Shaw. With more ambivalence Archer [2] damned it and praised it as "delightful to see": "What can a poor critic do with a play that raises no principle, whether of art or morals, creates its own canons and conventions, and is nothing but an absolutely willful expression of an irrepressibly witty personality?" Even Beerbohm [1], who declared the play a farce about one young man having a fling in the city while another does so in the country, considered it a theatrical triumph. The farce of identity has enjoyed multiple revivals and transformations. Worth [2] even argued that much of the drama written since the play's premiere is in many ways a variation on its satirical comedy of identities (180–82). In its practicing critics she included dramatists as varied as Charles Wood, Joe Orton, and Tom Stoppard.

Salomé. 1896. Opened in French on 11 February at Théâtre de l'Oeuvre, Paris. First performed in English in London from 10 to 13 May 1905 by the New Stage Club at the Bijou Theatre. Revived at the Festival Theatre (Cambridge) in 1931 and at the Gate Theatre (London) also in 1931.

The play had gone as far as rehearsals at the Palace Theatre in London, with Sarah Bernhardt to play the lead in her Cleopatra dress and with blue hair, when the license was refused because, as Wilde remarked, "no actor is to be permitted to present under artistic conditions, the great and ennobling subjects taken from the Bible" (quoted in Mikhail [3], 187). When Wilde threatened to leave England, Archer [1], who had defended Henrik Ibsen's plays, reproached England for risking the loss of so liberating and talented an author. The Parisians, with A. Lugné-Poe as director and Herod and Lina Munte as Salomé, eagerly took the occasion to show their greater sophistication, and the play premiered in Paris while Wilde was in prison. It was favorably reviewed by the Paris press, including Henri Bauer of the *Echo de Paris,* while at the same time in London appeared almost simultaneously a sympathetic interview with Wilde in the *Pall Mall Budget* and a savage attack in *The Times* (Review of *Salomé*) on the play's ferocity as "morbid, bizarre, repulsive, and very offensive." Even modern critics debate the nature of this play, which combines an interest in total theater techniques, satirical modern theater, and symbolist mysticism and, as Jullian suggested, is only fully intelligible when pronounced in French with an English accent. Even those who disliked the play, like W. B. Yeats, could not escape its spell.

ADDITIONAL PLAYS, ADAPTATIONS, AND PRODUCTIONS

La sainte courtisane, written in 1895 and never performed, is among those fragments that Wilde began before the trial. The play cleverly presents a dialogue between a hermit and a courtesan who reciprocally convert each other and exchange lives. Wilde confessed in 1895 that he was able to write only the lines for the courtesan (Worth [2], 183), and the fragment, subtitled *The Woman Covered with Jewels,* remains the unfinished comic analog to the tragic version of the attraction of passionate opposites portrayed in *Salomé.*

A Florentine Tragedy is also a fragment written in 1895. Although incomplete, it was first performed as a curtain-raiser for a 10 June 1906 production of *Salomé* at King's Hall (London). It had an opening scene written by T. Sturge Moore.

Like the other fragment, although rather darker in tone, this unfinished play is an ironic treatment of potentially tragic material. The play was written in reverse from the final confrontation scene in which, after the discovery by a bourgeois husband of his wife's adultery and his murder of her young aristocratic lover, the wife falls in love at last with her now far more interesting spouse. The manuscript was stolen from Wilde's Tite Street house at the time of his arrest, and although he tried to rewrite it while in prison and after his release, it remained incomplete.

ASSESSMENT OF WILDE'S CAREER

In "The Soul of Man under Socialism" Oscar Wilde teases us with a typical combination of political radicalism and dandyism: "Pleasure is Nature's test, her sign of approval. When man is happy, he is in harmony with himself and his environment. The new Individualism, for whose service Socialism, whether it wills it or not, is working, will be perfect harmony" (*Complete Works,* 1104). The harmony of Wilde's plays, however, is ultimately at least as contrapuntally complex as that of his notorious and ultimately tragic life. It is hard to assess whether his theatrical fame rests more on this witty iconoclasm, which reaches its zenith in his 1895 play *The Importance of Being Earnest,* or on his most notorious and exquisite construction/destruction, his own life. His career lasted only five years after that remarkable year when, having brought together inspiration from dramatists as varied as Goldsmith, Sheridan, Boucicault, Ibsen, Chekhov, and Maeterlinck, he reforged London theater with the premiere of *The Importance of Being Earnest.* Even when his plays originally premiered in London, New York, and Paris, they received a complex and varied response from contemporary critics, and the near century that intervenes between today's critics of Wilde's theater and his original audiences has failed to damp either the variety or intensity of his critical reception.

It is perhaps ill advised to speak of Wilde's plays as a monolithic whole. Broadly speaking, they fall into three categories, although these three formal strains of his dramaturgy develop synchronically rather than diachronically: postmelodrama innovations, variations on the urban comedy convention, and experiments in the symbolist vein. Small's bibliography succinctly described the problem in assessing the plays, for critics then as now, as the result of a tension between "two quite disparate features—the comic elements and the 'problem play' themes" (193). In assessing Wilde's theater, then, a careful distinction must be made between the formal and the thematic, elements between which Wilde delights in creating conflict. While Wilde's earliest formal theatrical experiments, about which he himself had some misgivings, seem to be more intrinsically connected to the theater of the late nineteenth century, especially to the work of Victorien Sardou, Alexandre Dumas *fils,* and Maurice Maeterlinck, even those early plays engage in an ongoing discourse not only with fashionable Continental theatrical conventions but also with their own indigenous thematic heritage in the melodramas of Dion Boucicault and Arthur Wing Pinero and the satirical comedies of Richard Brinsley Sheridan.

Like his childhood emulations of authors he admired, Wilde's mature plays contain much that is derivative from, or at least indebted to, the theater that preceded and surrounded him. His great talent lies in his capacity to write scintillating dialogue, be it tragic or comic, and to dare to place certain sensational topics provocatively on the stage. Whether he is astonishing his audience with a kiss bestowed upon a severed head or lightly alluding to the inner-city problem of abandoned children in handbags, Wilde's final achievement is the fashioning of characters whose power extends beyond their well-educated eloquence. There is a gothic ferocity to Guido Ferranti that rivals Percy Bysshe Shelley's and John Webster's .visions of vengeance, a particular elegance to his idiomatic expression of the predatory Mrs. Cheveley in *An Ideal Husband* that exceeds even Millwood's danger in George Lillo's *The London Merchant,* and a stylish hauteur to Gwendolen that shows greater social expertise than Sheridan's Lady Teazle in *The School for Scandal.* It is particularly in the creation of unorthodoxly compelling female characters that Wilde seems to excel, with their consummation being Salomé herself.

In the century of criticism since ''Bunburyism'' entered the English language, critics have sought to fix and situate Wilde's theater by focusing on a particular derivation or genre question. Much work has been done on Wilde's indebtedness to other dramatists, both precursors and contemporaries. Connections have been made with the experimental theater of the Continent, especially with Goethe (Vortriede) and Ibsen (Powell [3]), and Worth's [2] impressive study traced an elaborate nexus of European influences that range from Maeterlinck and Ibsen to Chekhov and Sardou. Some critics have suggested nondramatic texts as Wilde's inspiration (Bendz, Zagona, D'Astorg, Joost and Court, Nassaar, Rose, and Raby). Modern critics have detected strong affinities between Wilde's plays and the indigenous British theater of Gilbert and Sullivan (al-Hejazi) and Shaw (Andrews, Russell Jackson [1]). Recent critics have even added to this interest in Wilde's ''sources'' a concern to connect his work very specifically to his status as an Irish playwright (Roy, Worth [1]). This debate over the origins of Wilde's theater had its analog in earlier criticism in the concern with genre definition (Bentley, Ganz, and Gregor). Other critics have focused upon particular details of staging, like the approach to the audience (Gagnier [1]). There is also a large group of essays that take up a particular play's text and performance history, among which *The Importance of Being Earnest* is by far the most popular in Britain and *Salomé* receives the greatest treatment by Continental critics. Finally, several critics in the past twenty years have sought to connect Wilde's theater very closely with his own psychology and sexuality (Millet) and have seen in Beardsley's illustrations for *Salomé* rich material to unfold for their arguments (Gilbert, Kravec). So far, only two of Wilde's plays have received detailed discussions of their first productions: *Salomé* (Good, Shewan [1]) and *The Importance of Being Earnest* (Donohue).

Wilde's theater stands at the turning point between two centuries. It invokes the financially rewarding, stable, and familiar structures of the comedy of manners and the melodrama. One might even argue that Wilde's forays into problematic thematics, his concern to comment ironically and tragically on the very real contemporary moral, social, and political crises that haunted the cream of British society as it approached 1900, have their analog in Émile Zola, if not perhaps even earlier in Shakespeare's problem plays. Neither do his appropriations of Maeterlinck's and Villiers' experimental continental staging strategies attest to his originality. Yet, in a manner that would no longer be available to ironizing playwrights in the twentieth century, like Coward and Orton, despite their creative talents, Wilde was able to construct a tense and brilliant theatrical space that depended not only upon ''Oscarisms'' but upon a subtle mockery from within the system. For good or ill, after 1914–18 with the falling bombs in the last seconds of Shaw's *Heartbreak House,* that frame would be shattered forever. It is only now, perhaps, in a similar millennial twilight, that his delicate outrages can be fully critically appreciated.

ARCHIVAL SOURCES

The Oxford English Texts *Complete Works of Oscar Wilde* will, when complete, construct as completely as possible the stemmata for Wilde's dramatic writings and will include previously unpublished manuscripts. There have been many recent individual scholarly studies of Wilde's manuscripts, and all are fraught by the question of which text, from among all of his elaborate revisions, constituted copy text for a performed play. The major collection of Wilde's play manuscripts are in the British Library, the Pierpont Morgan Library, the Clark Library, the New York Public Library, and the Harry Ransom Humanities Research Center at the University of Texas at Austin. The earliest text of *Salomé* is in the Bodmer Library in Geneva.

PRIMARY BIBLIOGRAPHY

Plays

The Duchess of Padua. New York: privately printed, 1883. Reprinted as *The Duchess of Padua: A Play by Oscar Wilde.* Ed. Robert Ross. London: Methuen, 1908.

A Florentine Tragedy. In *Salomé and A Florentine Tragedy.* Introduction by Robert Ross. London: Methuen, 1908.
An Ideal Husband. London: Leonard Smithers and Company, 1899. Also in *Oscar Wilde: Two Society Comedies: A Woman of No Importance and An Ideal Husband,* ed. Ian Small and Russell Jackson. London: A. & C. Black, 1983.
The Importance of Being Earnest: A Trivial Comedy for Serious People. London: Leonard Smithers & Company, 1899; ed. Russell Jackson. London: Benn, 1980.
Lady Windermere's Fan: A Play about a Good Woman. London: Elkin Mathews & John Lane, 1893; New York: Samuel French, n.d. Also in *The First Collected Edition of the Works of Oscar Wilde,* ed. Robert Ross. London: Methuen, 1908; ed. Ian Small. London: Benn, 1979.
La sainte courtisane. In *The First Collected Edition of the Works of Oscar Wilde,* ed. Robert Ross. London: Methuen, 1908.
Salomé. Printed in French as *Salomé: Drame en un acte.* Paris: Librarie de l'Art Indépendant; London: Elkin Mathews & John Lane, 1893. Printed in English as *Salomé: A Tragedy in One Act.* London: Elkin Mathews & John Lane; Boston: Copeland & Day, 1894.
Vera: or, The Nihilists. In *The First Collected Edition of the Works of Oscar Wilde,* ed. Robert Ross. London: Methuen, 1908; ed. John Reed. Lewiston, NJ; Queenston, Ontario, Lampeter, Dyfed: Edwin Mellen Press, 1989.
A Woman of No Importance. London: John Lane, 1894. Also in *Oscar Wilde, Two Society Comedies: A Woman of No Importance and An Ideal Husband,* ed. Ian Small and Russell Jackson. London: A. & C. Black, 1983.

Anthologies

The Annotated Oscar Wilde. Ed. H. Montgomery Hyde. London: Orbis, 1982.
The Complete Works of Oscar Wilde. Oxford University Press [in progress].
Complete Works of Oscar Wilde. Ed. Vyvyan Holland. London: Collins, 1966. Reprint New York: Harper & Row, 1989.
The First Collected Edition of the Works of Oscar Wilde. Ed. Robert Ross. London: Methuen, 1908.
Oscar Wilde. Ed. Isobel Murray. Oxford: Oxford University Press, 1989.
Oscar Wilde: Plays, Prose Writing, and Poems. Introduction by Terry Eagleton. London: David Campbell, 1991.
The Artist as Critic: Critical Writings of Oscar Wilde. Ed. Richard Ellmann. London: W. H. Allen, 1970.
Plays, Prose Writing, and Poems. Ed. Isobel Murray. London: Dent, 1975.
The Portable Oscar Wilde. Ed. Richard Aldington. New York: Viking Press, 1946. Rev. Stanley Weintraub. Harmondsworth: Penguin Books, 1981.
The Works of Oscar Wilde. Ed. G. F. Maine. London: Collins, 1948.

Essays and Articles on Drama and Theater

De Profundis. London: Methuen; New York: G. P. Putnam's Sons, 1905.
Intentions by Oscar Wilde. Includes "The Decay of Lying," "Pen, Pencil, and Poison,"

"The Critic as Artist," "The Truth of Masks." London: James Osgood, McIlvaine & Co.; New York: Dodd, Mead, 1891.

The Letters of Oscar Wilde. Ed. R. Hart-Davis. London: Hart-Davis; New York: Harcourt, Brace & World, 1962.

"The Soul of Man under Socialism." Portland, ME: T. B. Mosher, 1915, 1891. [Mosher's miscellaneous series 28]. Rpt. from *The Fortnightly Review* (Feb. 1891): 292–319.

SECONDARY BIBLIOGRAPHY

Andrews, Alan. "Horrible Flesh and Blood." *Theatre Notebook* 36.1 (1982): 34–35.

Archer, William. [1]. *The Old Drama and the New.* New York: Dodd, Mead, 1926; Benjamin Blom, 1971.

———. [2]. *The Theatrical "World" for 1893–7.* London: W. Scott, 1894–98.

Beerbohm, Max. [1]. *Around Theatres.* London: Rupert Hart-Davis, 1953.

———. [2]. *More Theatres, 1898–1903.* Ed. Rupert Hart-Davis. London: Rupert Hart-Davis, 1969.

Behrendt, Patricia Flanagan. *Oscar Wilde: Eros and Aesthetics.* Basingstoke: Macmillan, 1991.

Bendz, Ernst. "À propos de la *Salomé* d'Oscar Wilde." *Englische Studien* 51.1 (1917): 48–70.

Bentley, Eric. *The Modern Theatre: A Study of Dramatists and the Drama.* London: Hale, 1948.

Bird, Alan. *The Plays of Oscar Wilde.* London: Vision Press, 1977.

Bloom, Harold, ed. *Oscar Wilde.* New York: Chelsea, 1985.

Bradbury, Malcolm, and Ian Fletcher, eds. *Decadence and the 1890s.* London: Edward Arnold, 1979.

Cohen, Ed. *Talk on the Wilde Side: Toward a Genealogy of a Discourse on Male Sexualities.* London and New York: Routledge, 1993.

Craft, Christopher. "Alias Bunbury: Desire and Termination in *The Importance of Being Earnest.*" *Representations* 31 (1990): 19–46.

D'Astorg, Bertrand. "Le Mystère de Salomé." *Revue de Deux Mondes* (April 1971): 93–109.

Davidson, David. "The Importance of Being Earnest: Lubitsch and *Lady Windermere's Fan.*" *Literature/Film Quarterly* 11.2 (1983): 120–31.

Dollimore, Jonathan. [1]. "Different Desires: Subjectivity and Transgression in Wilde and Gide." *Textual Practice* 1.1 (1987): 48–67.

———. [2]. *Sexual Dissidence: Augustine to Wilde, Freud to Foucault.* Oxford: Clarendon Press, 1991.

Donohue, Joseph W., Jr. "The First Production of *The Importance of Being Earnest:* A Proposal for Reconstructive Study." In *Essays on Nineteenth Century British Theatre,* ed. Kenneth Richards and Peter Thomson. London: Methuen, 1971.

Dowling, Linda. *Language and Decadence in the Victorian Fin de Siècle.* Princeton, NJ: Princeton University Press, 1986.

Eagleton, Terry. "Introduction." In *Oscar Wilde: Plays, Prose Writing, and Poems.* London: David Campbell, 1991.

Easthope, Anthony. "Jokes and Ideology: 'The Frogs' and 'Earnest.' " *New Comparison* 3 (1987): 117–32.

Ellmann, Richard. [1]. *Oscar Wilde.* London: Hamish Hamilton, 1987.

———. [2]. *Oscar Wilde: A Collection of Critical Essays.* Englewood Cliffs, NJ: Prentice-Hall, 1969.

Fletcher, Ian, and John Stokes, eds. *The Decadent Consciousness.* New York: Garland, 1979.

Fraser, Hilary. *Beauty and Belief: Aesthetics and Religion in Victorian Literature.* Cambridge: Cambridge University Press, 1986.

Freedman, Jonathan. *Professions of Taste: Henry James, British Aestheticism, and Commodity Culture.* Stanford: Stanford University Press, 1990.

Gagnier, Regenia. [1]. Ed. *Critical Essays on Oscar Wilde.* New York: G.K. Hall, 1991.

———. [2]. ''Stages of Desire: Oscar Wilde's Comedies and the Consumer.'' *Genre* 15 (1982): 315–16.

Ganz, Arthur. ''The Meaning of *The Importance of Being Earnest.''* *Modern Drama* 6.1 (1963): 45–62.

Gilbert, Elliot L. '' 'Tumult of Images': Wilde, Beardsley, and *Salomé.''* *Victorian Studies* 26.2 (1983): 133–59.

Glavin, John. ''Deadly Earnest and Earnest Revised: Oscar Wilde's Four-Act Play.'' *Nineteenth-Century Studies* 1 (1987): 13–24.

Good, Graham. ''Early Productions of Oscar Wilde's Salomé.'' *Nineteenth Century Theatre Research* 11.2 (1983): 77–92.

Gregor, Ian. ''Comedy and Oscar Wilde.'' *Sewanee Review* 74.2 (1966): 501–21.

Guy, Josephine M. *The British Avant-Garde: The Theory and Politics of Tradition.* London: Harvester Wheatsheaf, 1991.

Hardwick, Michael. *The Osprey Guide to Oscar Wilde.* Reading: Osprey, 1973.

al-Hejazi, Ali A. ''Wilde's *The Importance of Being Earnest* and Gilbert's *Engaged:* A Comparative Study.'' *Journal of the College of Arts, King Saud University* 12.1 (1985): 107–14.

Hirst, David L. *Comedy of Manners.* London: Methuen, 1979.

Hyde, H. Montgomery. [1]. *Oscar Wilde: The Aftermath.* London: Methuen, 1963.

———, ed. [2]. *The Trials of Oscar Wilde.* London: Hodge, 1948.

Jackson, John Wyse, ed. *Aristotle at Afternoon Tea: The Rare Oscar Wilde.* London: Fourth Estate, 1991.

Jackson, Russell. [1]. ''A Classic without Danger: The National Theatre's Importance of Being Earnest.'' *Critical Quarterly* 25.2 (1983): 73–80.

———, ed. [2]. *Victorian Theatre.* London: A. & C. Black, 1989.

Johnson, Wendell Stacy. ''Fallen Women, Lost Children: Wilde and the Theatre of the Nineties.'' *Tennessee Studies in Literature* 27 (1984): 196–211.

Joost, Nicholas, and Franklin E. Court. ''*Salomé,* the Moon, and Oscar Wilde's Aesthetics: A Reading of the Play.'' *Papers on Language and Literature* 8 (1972): 96–111.

Jordan, John. ''Shaw, Wilde, Synge, and Yeats: Ideas, Epigrams, Blackberries, and Cassis.'' In *The Irish Mind: Exploring Intellectual Traditions,* ed. Richard Kearney. Dublin: Wolfhound, 1985.

Jullian, Philippe. *Oscar Wilde.* London: Granada Publishing, 1971.

Knox, Melissa. *Oscar Wilde: A Long and Lovely Suicide.* New Haven, CT: Yale University Press, 1994.

Kravec, Maureen T. ''Wilde's *Salomé.''* *Explicator* 42.1 (1983): 30–32.

Review of *Lady Windermere's Fan. Daily Telegraph* (22 Feb. 1892).

Review of *Lady Windermere's Fan. Pall Mall Gazette* (22 Feb. 1892).

Laity, Susan. "The Soul of Man under Victoria: *Iolanthe, The Importance of Being Earnest,* and Bourgeois Drama." In *Oscar Wilde's The Importance of Being Earnest,* ed. Harold Bloom. New York: Chelsea, 1988.

Macqueen-Pope, W. [1]. *Haymarket: Theatre of Perfection.* London: W. H. Allen, 1948.

———. [2]. *St. James's: Theatre of Distinction.* London: W. H. Allen, 1958.

Mason, A.E.W. *Sir George Alexander and the St. James' Theatre.* London: Macmillan, 1935.

Mikhail, E. H. [1]. "The French Influences on Oscar Wilde's Comedies." *Revue de Littérature Comparée* 42.2 (1968): 220–33.

———. [2]. "Oscar Wilde and his First Comedy." *Modern Drama* 10.1 (1968): 394–96.

———. [3]. ed. *Oscar Wilde: Interviews and Recollections.* 2 vols. London: Macmillan, 1979.

———. [4]. "Self-Revelation in An Ideal Husband." *Modern Drama* 11.3 (1968): 180–86.

———. [5]. *The Social and Cultural Setting of the 1890s.* London: Garnstone Press, 1969.

Miller, Robert Keith. *Oscar Wilde.* New York: Ungar, 1982.

Millet, Kate. *Sexual Politics.* Garden City, NY: Doubleday, 1970.

Montague, C. E. *Dramatic Values.* London: Methuen, 1911.

Nassaar, Christopher. *Into the Demon Universe: A Literary Exploration of Oscar Wilde.* New Haven, CT: Yale University Press, 1974.

Nelson, Walter. *Oscar Wilde and the Dramatic Critics: A Study in Victorian Theatre.* Lund: privately printed, 1989.

Page, Norman. *An Oscar Wilde Chronology.* London: Macmillan, 1991.

Parker, David. "Oscar Wilde's Great Farce: *The Importance of Being Earnest." Modern Language Quarterly* 35.2 (1974): 173–86.

Partridge, E. B. "The Importance of Not Being Earnest." *Bucknell Review* 9.2 (1960): 145–58.

Pine, Richard. *Oscar Wilde.* Dublin: Gill & Macmillan, 1983.

Poirier, Richard. *The Performing Self: Compositions and Decompositions in the Languages of Contemporary Life.* New York: Oxford University Press, 1971.

Porter, Laurence E. "Literary Structure and the Concept of Decadence: Huysmans, D'Annunzio, and Wilde." *Centennial Review* 22 (1978): 188–200.

Powell, Kerry. [1]. "Oscar Wilde 'Acting': The Medium as Message in *The Picture of Dorian Gray." Dalhousie Review* 58 (1978): 104–15.

———. [2]. *Oscar Wilde and the Theatre of the 1890s.* Cambridge: Cambridge University Press, 1990.

———. [3]. "Wilde and Ibsen." *English Literature in Transition, 1880–1920* 28.3 (1985): 224–42.

Poznar, Walter. "Life and Play in Wilde's *The Importance of Being Earnest." Midwest Quarterly* 30.4 (1989): 515–28.

Queensberry, [Francis], Marquess of, and Percy Colson. *Oscar Wilde and the Black Douglas.* London: Hutchinson, 1949.

Raafat, Z. "The Literary Indebtedness of Wilde's *Salomé* to Sardou's *Théodora." Revue de Littérature Comparée* 40 (1966): 453–66.

Raby, Peter. *Oscar Wilde.* Cambridge: Cambridge University Press, 1988.

Reed, John R. *Decadent Style.* Athens: Ohio University Press, 1985.

Rose, Marilyn Gaddis. "The Synchronic *Salomé.*" In *The Languages of Theatre: Problems in the Translation and Transposition of Drama,* ed. Ortrun Zuber. Oxford: Pergamon Press, 1980.

Rowell, George. "The Drama of Wilde and Pinero." In *The Cambridge Guide to the Arts in Britain: The Later Victorian Age,* ed. Boris Ford. Cambridge: Cambridge University Press, 1989.

Roy, Emil. *British Drama since Shaw.* Carbondale: Southern Illinois University Press, 1972.

Said, Edward. *The World, the Text, and the Critic.* Cambridge, MA: Harvard University Press, 1983.

Review of *Salomé. The Times* (23 Feb. 1896).

Sammels, Neil. "Earning Liberties: *Travesties* and *The Importance of Being Earnest.*" *Modern Drama* 29.2 (1986): 376–87.

Schwarz, Stanley. "The Influence of Dumas Fils on Oscar Wilde." *French Review* 7.1 (1983): 5–25.

Shewan, Rodney. [1]. "The Artist and the Dancer in Three Symbolist *Salomés.*" Bucknell Review 11.1 (1984): 50–57.

———. [2]. "A Wife's Tragedy: An Unpublished Sketch for a Play by Oscar Wilde." *Theatre Research International* 8.2 (1982): 75–131.

Small, Ian, ed. [1]. *The Aesthetes.* London: Routledge & Kegan Paul, 1979.

———. [2]. *Conditions for Criticism: Authority, Knowledge, and Literature in the Late Nineteenth Century.* Oxford: Clarendon Press, 1991.

Small, Ian, and Russell Jackson. "Some New Drafts of a Wilde Play." *English Literature in Transition, 1880–1920* 30.1 (1987): 7–15.

Stokes, John. [1]. *In the Nineties.* London: Harvester Wheatsheaf, 1990.

———. [2]. *Resistible Theatres.* London: Paul Elek, 1972.

Terry, Ellen. [1]. *The Story of My Life.* London: Hutchinson, 1908.

———. [2]. *Ellen Terry's Memoirs.* London: Victor Gollancz, 1933.

Tydeman, William, ed. *Wilde: Comedies.* London: Macmillan, 1982.

Review of *Vera: or, The Nihilists. New York Daily Tribune* (21 Aug. 1883): 6.

Vortriede, Werner. "A Dramatic Device in *Faust* and *The Importance of Being Earnest.*" *Modern Language Notes* 70.8 (1955): 584–85.

Ware, James. "Algernon's Appetite: Oscar Wilde's Hero as Restoration Dandy." *English Literature in Transition, 1880–1920* 13 (1970): 17–26.

Winter, William. Review of *The Duchess of Padua. New York Tribune* (22 Jan. 1891).

Worth, Katharine. [1]. *The Irish Drama of Europe from Yeats to Beckett.* London: Athlone Press, 1978.

———. [2]. *Oscar Wilde.* London: Macmillan, 1983.

Zagona, Helen Grace. *The Legend of Salomé and the Principle of Art for Art's Sake.* Geneva: Ambilly-Annemasse, 1960.

Zatlin, Linda Gertner. *Aubrey Beardsley and Victorian Sexual Politics.* Oxford: Clarendon Press, 1990.

BIBLIOGRAPHIES

Connolly, L. W., and J. P. Wearing. "Nineteenth Century Theatre Research: A Bibliography." *Nineteenth Century Theatre* 1.2 (1973)–present.

Dowling, Linda. *Aestheticism and Decadence: A Selective Annotated Bibliography.* New York: Garland, 1977.

Finzi, John Charles. *Oscar Wilde and his Literary Circle: A Catalog of Manuscripts and Letters in the William Andrews Clark Memorial Library.* Berkeley and Los Angeles: University of California Press, 1957.

Mason, Stuart [Christopher Millard]. *Bibliography of Oscar Wilde.* London: T. Werner Laurie, 1914.

Mikhail, E. H. *Oscar Wilde: An Annotated Bibliography of Criticism.* London: Macmillan, 1978.

Mikolyzk, Thomas A. *Oscar Wilde: An Annotated Bibliography.* Westport, CT: Greenwood Press, 1993.

Nelson, Walter. *Oscar Wilde: From Ravenna to Salomé: A Survey of Contemporary British Criticism.* Dublin: Dublin University Press, 1987.

Small, Ian. *Oscar Wilde Revalued: An Essay on New Materials and Methods of Research.* Greensboro, NC: ELT Press, 1993.

Selected Bibliography

The following is a selected general bibliography of book-length studies devoted in whole or in part to British drama and theater during the period 1880–1956.

Agate, James. *Those Were the Nights.* London and New York: Hutchinson, 1947.

Archer, William. *The Old Drama and the New: An Essay in Re-valuation.* New York: Dodd, Mead, 1926; Benjamin Blom, 1971.

———. *The Theatrical "World" of 1895.* With a Prefatory Letter by Arthur W. Pinero. 1896. Reprint. New York: Benjamin Blom, 1971.

———. *The Theatrical "World" of 1896.* With an Introduction, "On the Need for an Endowed Theatre." 1897. Reprint. New York: Benjamin Blom, 1971.

———. *The Theatrical "World" of 1897.* 1898. Reprint. New York: Benjamin Blom [1969].

Bentley, Eric. *The Theatre of Commitment.* New York: Atheneum, 1967.

Brandt, George W., ed. *British Television Drama.* Cambridge: Cambridge University Press, 1981.

Bratton, J. S. et al. *Acts of Supremacy: The British Empire and the Stage, 1790–1930.* Manchester: Manchester University Press, 1991.

Brown, John Russell. *A Short Guide to Modern British Drama.* London: Heinemann Educational Books, 1982.

Browne, Terry. *Playwrights' Theatre: The English Stage Company at the Royal Court Theatre.* London: Pitman, 1975.

Brustein, Robert. *The Theatre of Revolt.* Boston: Little, Brown, 1964.

Carlson, Susan. *Women and Comedy: Rewriting the British Theatrical Tradition.* Ann Arbor: University of Michigan Press, 1991.

Clarke, Ian. *Edwardian Drama.* London: Faber & Faber, 1989.

Courtney, Richard. *Outline History of British Drama.* Totowa, NJ: Littlefield, Adams, & Co., 1982.

Craig, Edward Gordon. *On the Art of the Theatre.* London: Heinemann, 1911.

Dietrich, Richard F. *British Drama, 1890 to 1950: A Critical History*. Boston: Twayne, 1989.

Donoghue, Denis. *The Third Voice: Modern British and American Verse Drama*. Princeton, NJ: Princeton University Press, 1959.

Downer, Alan S. *The British Drama: A Handbook and Brief Chronicle*. New York: Appleton-Century-Crofts, 1950.

Dutton, Richard. *Modern Tragicomedy and the British Tradition*. Norman: University of Oklahoma Press, 1986.

Ellis, James, Joseph W. Donohue, Jr., and Louise A. Zak. *English Drama of the Nineteenth Century: An Index and Finding Guide*. New Canaan, CT: Readex Books, 1985.

Elsom, John. *Theatre outside London*. London: Macmillan, 1971.

Evans, Gareth Lloyd. *The Language of Modern Drama*. London: Dent, 1977; Totowa, NJ: Rowman & Littlefield, 1977.

Findlater, Richard. *The Unholy Trade*. London: Gollancz, 1952.

———. *Banned! A Review of Theatrical Censorship in Britain*. London: Panther, 1967.

Gielgud, Val. *British Radio Drama, 1922–1956*. London: Harrap, 1957.

Hartnoll, Phyllis, ed. *The Oxford Companion to the Theatre*. Oxford: Oxford University Press, 4th ed., reprint with corrections 1993.

Hinchliffe, Arnold P. *Modern Verse Drama*. London: Methuen, 1977.

Holledge, Julie. *Innocent Flowers: Women in the Edwardian Theatre*. London: Virago, 1981.

Howe, P. P. *The Repertory Theatre*. London: M. Secker, 1910.

Hunt, Hugh, Kenneth Richards, and John Russell Taylor. *The* Revels *History of Drama in English*. Vol. 7, *1880 to the Present Day*. London: Methuen, 1978.

Innes, Christopher. *Modern British Drama, 1890–1990*. Cambridge: Cambridge University Press, 1992.

Jackson, Holbrook. *The Eighteen Nineties: A Review of Art and Ideas at the Close of the Nineteenth Century*. [New ed., rev. and corr.] London: Grant Richards Ltd., 1922.

James, Henry. *The Scenic Art: Notes on Acting and the Drama, 1872–1901*. Ed. Allan Wade. New Brunswick, NJ: Rutgers University Press, 1948.

Kaplan, Joel, and Sheila Stowell. *Theatre and Fashion: Oscar Wilde to the Suffragettes*. Cambridge: Cambridge University Press, 1994.

Knight, George Wilson. *The Golden Labyrinth: A Study of British Drama*. New York: Norton, 1962.

MacCarthy, Desmond. *Theatre*. London: MacGibbon & Kee, 1954.

McDonald, Jan. *The "New Drama," 1900–1914*. Basingstoke: Macmillan, 1986.

Meisel, Martin. *Realizations: Narrative, Pictorial, and Theatrical Arts in Nineteenth-Century England*. Princeton, NJ: Princeton University Press, 1983.

Nicoll, Allardyce. *English Drama, 1900–1930: The Beginnings of the Modern Period*. Cambridge: Cambridge University Press, 1973.

———. *Late Nineteenth Century Drama, 1850–1900*. Vol. 5 of *A History of English Drama, 1660–1900*. 2nd ed. Cambridge: Cambridge University Press, 1962.

Peacock, D. Keith. *Radical Stages: Alternative History in Modern British Drama*. New York: Greenwood Press, 1991.

Peacock, Ronald. *The Poet in the Theatre*. New York: Harcourt, Brace, 1946.

Postlewait, Thomas, and Bruce A. McConachie. *Interpreting the Theatrical Past.* Iowa City: University of Iowa Press, 1989.

Rabey, David Ian. *British and Irish Political Drama in the Twentieth Century: Implicating the Audience.* New York: St. Martin's Press, 1986.

Rayner, Alice. *Comic Persuasion: Moral Structure in British Comedy from Shakespeare to Stoppard.* Berkeley: University of California Press, 1987.

Roy, Emil. *British Drama since Shaw.* Carbondale: Southern Illinois University Press, 1972.

Salgado, Gamini. *English Drama: A Critical Introduction.* New York: St. Martin's Press, 1980.

Shaw, George Bernard. *Our Theatres in the Nineties.* 3 vols. London: Constable and Co., Ltd., 1932 (reprint 1954).

Simon, Elliott M. *The Problem Play in British Drama, 1890–1914.* Salzburg: Institut für Englische Sprache und Literatur, 1978.

Smith, Leslie. *Modern British Farce: A Selective Study of British Farce from Pinero to the Present Day.* Totowa, NJ: Barnes & Noble, 1989.

Spanos, William V. *The Christian Tradition in Modern British Verse Drama: The Poetics of Sacramental Time.* New Brunswick, NJ: Rutgers University Press, 1967.

Stephens, John Russell. *The Profession of the Playwright: British Theatre, 1800–1900.* Cambridge: Cambridge University Press, 1992.

Taylor, John Russell. *The Rise and Fall of the Well-made Play.* New York: Hill & Wang, 1967.

Trewin, J. C. *The Edwardian Theatre.* Oxford: Basil Blackwell, 1976; Totowa, NJ: Rowman & Littlefield, 1976.

———. *The Gay Twenties: A Decade of the Theatre.* London: Macdonald, 1958.

———. *Shakespeare on the English Stage, 1900–1964.* London: Barrie & Rockliff, 1964.

———. *The Turbulent Thirties: A Further Decade of the Theatre.* London: Macdonald, 1960.

Walkley, A. B. *Drama and Life.* 1908. Reprint. Freeport, NY: Books for Libraries Press, 1967.

Wearing, J. P. *The London Stage, 1890–1959: A Calendar of Plays and Players.* 15 vols. Metuchen, NJ: Scarecrow Press, 1976–93.

Williams, Raymond. *Drama from Ibsen to Eliot.* London: Chatto and Windus, 1952.

Woodfield, James. *English Theatre in Transition, 1889–1914.* London: Croom Helm, 1984; Totowa, NJ: Barnes & Noble, 1984.

Index of Names

Index of Titles

About the Editors and Contributors

TED BAIN completed a doctorate in drama at the University of Toronto in 1992, with a dissertation that included St. John Hankin within the literary tradition of intellectual dandyism. In addition to teaching Edwardian and modern drama at a number of institutions, most recently at Hobart and William Smith colleges, and Cornell University, he has directed and performed in St. John Hankin's *The Burglar Who Failed* and has directed two plays by Stanley Houghton, *Fancy Free* and *Phipps*. His reviews have appeared in *Theatre Journal, New England Theatre Journal, Theatre Survey*, and *Dance Research Journal*.

WILLIAM W. DEMASTES is professor of English at Louisiana State University, Baton Rouge. He is series editor of Greenwood's Research and Production Sourcebooks and is author of that series's *Clifford Odets* (1991), editor of *American Playwrights, 1880–1945* (1995) and *British Playwrights, 1956–1995* (1996), and coeditor (with Bernice Schrank) of *Irish Playwrights, 1880–1995* (1996). In addition to writing numerous articles on theater and drama, he has also authored *Beyond Naturalism: A New Realism in American Theatre* (1988) and *Theatre of Chaos* (forthcoming) and edited *Realism and the American Dramatic Tradition* (1996).

LUE MORGAN DOUTHIT recently received her doctorate from the University of Washington. During the academic year 1994–95 she taught dramaturgy, playwriting, and modern theater history at the University of Arizona. Prior to that, she spent seven months working as a literary intern at the Oregon Shakespeare Festival. Currently, she has returned to Oregon and the festival and will continue her work on new plays in the literary department.

SARAH DUERDEN is an instructor in the Department of English at Arizona State University. She teaches literature, professional writing, and a special section of freshman composition to engineers in a program sponsored by the National Science foundation. Her area of specialization is twentieth-century British literature. Her article on teaching composition in an integrated program was published in the 1995 proceeding papers of *Frontiers in Education,* and a second article will be published in *The Journal of International Engineering Education* (forthcoming).

JAMES FISHER is professor and chair of theater at Wabash College, Crawfordsville, Indiana. He is author of *The Theatre of Yesterday and Tomorrow: Commedia dell'arte on the Modern Stage* (1992), *Al Jolson: A Bio-Bibliography* (Greenwood Press, 1994), *Spencer Tracy: A Bio-Bibliography* (Greenwood Press, 1994), and the forthcoming *Beyond the Theory: The Early Productions of Edward Gordon Craig (1900–1906).* He serves as book review editor of the *Journal of Dramatic Theory and Criticism* and has contributed articles for numerous journals, including *Theatre Journal, Films in Review, Modern Drama, Drama Review, Theater, Shaw: The Annual of Bernard Shaw Studies, Studies in American Drama, 1945–Present, Theatre Research International, Mississippi Quarterly, Comparative Drama, New Theatre Quarterly, Theatre Symposium, Soviet and East European Performance, New England Theatre Journal,* and many others.

ARTHUR GEWIRTZ is associate professor of English at Hofstra University, Hempstead, New York. He is author of *Restoration Adaptations of Early 17th-Century Comedies* (1982), and has written for *Shakespeare Quarterly, New Leader, Newsday,* and *The Mediterranean Review.* He contributed the Sidney Howard entry to *American Playwrights, 1880–1945* (Greenwood Press, 1995). He was codirector of a three-day conference, ''Art, Glitter, and Glitz: The Theatre of the 1920s Celebrates American Diversity,'' which took place at Hofstra University in November 1994, and is coeditor of the book of essays that will derive from that conference.

MARK A. GRAVES is an instructor at Bowling Green State University, where he teaches courses in modern literature, war literature, and rhetoric and writing. He has published articles in *English Language Notes, College Language Association Journal,* and *Theatre Annual.* His interest include war literature, Ellen Glasgow studies, and midwestern writing.

ROBERT F. GROSS is associate professor of English and comparative literature at Hobart and William Smith colleges, where he also serves as director of theater. He is the editor of *Christopher Hampton: A Casebook* (1990) and the author of *Words Heard and Overheard* (1990) and *S. N. Behrman: A Research and Production Sourcebook* (Greenwood Press, 1992).

JANE SEAY HASPEL is a program officer for the National Faculty Southern Region office in New Orleans, Louisiana. She has written articles for *American Playwrights, 1880–1945* (Greenwood Press, 1995), *Literature/Film Quarterly,* and *Texas Books in Review.* Her research interests include interdisciplinary studies in American literature, drama, and film.

LAWRENCE JASPER is associate professor of theater at California State University, Fullerton. He has made numerous contributions to panels and projects for the Association for Theatre in Higher Education and has been active in the leadership of the American College Theatre Festival, Region VIII. His publications include entries in *American Theatre Companies,* edited by Weldon B. Durham (3 volumes, 1986–89); and in *American Playwrights, 1880–1945,* edited by William Demastes (Greenwood Press, 1995).

KATHERINE E. KELLY is associate professor of English at Texas A&M University, College Station. She is the author of *Tom Stoppard and the Craft of Comedy* (1991) and general editor *Modern Drama by Women, 1880s–1930s: An International Anthology* (1996). Her articles on the Actresses' Franchise League, G. B. Shaw's suffrage drama, and the boy actor in Shakespeare's comedies, as well as on the plays of Tom Stoppard, Samuel Beckett, and T. S. Eliot, have appeared in *Theatre Survey, Shaw: An Annual of Bernard Shaw Studies, Theatre Journal, Journal of Beckett Studies,* and *Modern Drama.*

LINCOLN KONKLE is assistant professor of English at Trenton State College in New Jersey, where he teaches courses in modern drama, classical to contemporary drama, American literature, and creative writing. His article on Edward Albee, ''American Jeremiah: Edward Albee as Judgment Day Prophet in *The Lady from Dubuque,*'' is forthcoming in *American Drama,* Fall 1997. He has also published in several small literary magazines.

COLETTE LINDROTH is professor of English at Caldwell College, Caldwell, New Jersey. She has published articles on Jean Rhys, Shelagh Delaney, Milan Kundera, and Susan Glaspell and on film directors Stephen Frears and Spike Lee. She is also coauthor of *Rachel Crothers: A Research and Production Sourcebook* (Greenwood Press, 1995).

MARY LINDROTH is a doctoral candidate at the University of Iowa. She is currently writing her dissertation, entitled '' 'You Will Say Hum and Ha to My Tale': Representations of Audience in English Renaissance Comedies.''

RANDY MALAMUD is associate professor of English at Georgia State University, Atlanta, and senior editor of *South Atlantic Review.* He is author of *The Language of Modernism* (1989), *T. S. Eliot's Drama: A Research and Produc-*

tion Sourcebook (Greenwood Press, 1992), and *Where the Words Are Valid: T. S. Eliot's Communities of Drama* (1994). He has published articles on modern writers including Virginia Woolf, James Joyce, Truman Capote, Alan Paton, and E. L. Doctorow.

PAMELA MONACO recently finished her doctorate at Catholic University of America and currently teaches at Shepherd College in West Virginia. She has published articles on August Wilson and William Saroyan and has presented papers on August Wilson, F. Scott Fitzgerald, and the minority detective.

JANICE OLIVER is assistant professor of English at Southern University, Baton Rouge. She is the author of "Ann Jellicoe" in *British Playwrights, 1956–1995: A Research and Production Sourcebook* (Greenwood Press, 1996).

VINCENT F. PETRONELLA is professor of English at the University of Massachusetts in Boston. He is the author of over thirty articles on Shakespeare and other writers (Ben Jonson, Michael Drayton, Herman Melville) in journals and annuals such as *Shakespeare Studies, Modern Language Review, Journal of English and Germanic Philology, Studies in Philology, Hamlet Studies, Die Neueren Sprachen, Studies in English Literature, American Transcendental Quarterly, Dalhousie Review,* and *Theatre Journal.* In addition to his two essays (on the romantic theater of the Dibdins and on Neoplatonism) in the *Encyclopedia of Romanticism,* he is a contributor to two Modern Language Association volumes: *Approaches to Teaching Shakespeare's "King Lear"* and *Approaches to Teaching Shelley's Poetry,* which features his essay on Shelley's neo-Shakespearean drama, *The Cenci.*

ELIZABETH M. RICHMOND-GARZA is associate professor of English and comparative literature at the University of Texas at Austin. She is the author of *Forgotten Cites/Sights: Interpretation and the Power of Classical Citation in Renaissance English Tragedy* (1994). She has written articles for a number of journals and essay collections on comparative Renaissance drama, narratology, twentieth-century performance theory, film, the studio-theater movement, and decadent and gothic subculture. She is currently writing her second book on European romantic historical tragedy.

VALERIE C. RUDOLPH is associate professor of English at Purdue University. She is the author of "James M. Barrie" in *Modern British Dramatists, 1900–1945* and also of "James M. Barrie" in *Read More about It,* volume 3. She has edited *The Plays of Eliza Haywood* (1983) and also *The Plays of Samuel Johnson of Cheshire* (1980). She has contributed articles to *Critical Survey of Drama, Dictionary of Literary Biography, Educational Theatre Journal, Journal of General Education, Papers on Language and Literature, Restoration and Eighteenth-Century Theatre Research,* and *Theatre Survey.*

RONALD E. SHIELDS is associate professor of theater and chair of the Department of Theatre, Bowling Green State University, Bowling Green, Ohio. He teaches courses in the group performance of literature, performance studies, and directing theory. He currently serves on the editorial board of *Text and Performance Quarterly.*

LIBBY SMIGEL has a doctorate in drama, with Victorian and Edwardian drama as her major field, from the University of Toronto. She has taught drama at York University (Canada) and Hobart and William Smith colleges (New York).

SUE THOMAS is a senior lecturer in English at La Trobe University, Melbourne, and also teaches in its postgraduate Women's Studies program. She has published extensively on twentieth-century women writers, postcolonial writing, and Victorian and Edwardian periodicals. This entry on Cicely Hamilton is based on research for a large project on the iconography of British women's relationship to the state, 1905–18. The project has won generous financial support from the Commonwealth Tertiary Education Commission, Australia; the School of Humanities, La Trobe University; and the Humanities Research Centre, Australian National University.

JACKIE TUCKER is a doctoral student at Louisiana State University. She is currently completing a dissertation on maternal images in early twentieth-century drama.

TRAMBLE T. TURNER is associate professor of English at Penn State University, the Abington-Ogontz Campus. The former mid-Atlantic representative for the American Conference for Irish Studies, he has written articles on Shaw for *Éire-Ireland* and delivered a talk on Shaw and O'Casey's attempts to reinvent communism at the 1990 MLA Conference. Current work includes "James Connolly: A Fit Story for the Playwright of Sergeant Musgrave's Dance," in *John Arden and Margaretta D'Arcy* (1995), and an article on William Kennedy in the Spring 1993 issue of *Melus.*

ROBERT WILCHER is a senior lecturer in English at the University of Birmingham, where he teaches courses in Renaissance literature and modern drama. He is author of *Andrew Marvell* (1985) and *Understanding Arnold Wesker* (1991) and editor of *Andrew Marvell: Selected Poetry and Prose* (1986). He has contributed chapters to *Beckett's Later Fiction and Drama: Texts for Company* (1987) and *British and Irish Drama since 1960* (1993) and has published articles on modern drama, Shakespeare, and seventeenth-century poetry in a number of journals, including *Critical Quarterly, Critical Survey, Journal of Beckett Studies, Modern Drama, Renaissance and Modern Studies, Shakespeare Survey, Southern Review, Theatre Research International,* and *Yearbook of English Studies.*

ISBN 0-313-28758-9

90000>

EAN

9 780313 287589

HARDCOVER BAR CODE